Social Work Ethics

The International Library of Essays in Public and Professional Ethics
Series Editors: Seumas Miller and Tom Campbell

Titles in the Series:

The Ethics of the Environment
Robin Attfield

Academic Ethics
Robin Barrow and Patrick Keeney

The Ethics of Teaching
Michael A. Boylan

Military Ethics
Anthony Coady and Igor Primoratz

Engineering Ethics
Michael Davis

Social Work Ethics
Eileen Gambrill

Development Ethics
Des Gasper and Asuncion Lera St Clair

Correctional Ethics
John Kleinig

Police Ethics
Seumas Miller

Bioethics
Justin Oakley

Research Ethics
Kenneth D. Pimple

Business Ethics and Strategy,
Volumes I and II
Alan E. Singer

Computer Ethics
John Weckert

Social Work Ethics

Edited by

Eileen Gambrill

University of California at Berkeley, USA

ASHGATE

Wherever possible, these reprints are made from a copy of the original printing, but these can themselves be of very variable quality. Whilst the publisher has made every effort to ensure the quality of the reprint, some variability may inevitably remain.

Published by
Ashgate Publishing Limited
Wey Court East
Union Road
Farnham
Surrey
GU9 7PT

Ashgate Publishing Company
Suite 420
101 Cherry Street
Burlington, VT 05401-4405
USA

Ashgate website: http://www.ashgate.com

British Library Cataloguing in Publication Data
Social work ethics. – (The international library of essays in public and professional ethics)
  1. Social service – Moral and ethical aspects
  I. Gambrill, Eileen D., 1934–
  174.9'361

Library of Congress Cataloging-in-Publication Data
Social work ethics / edited by Eileen Gambrill.
    p. cm. – (The international library of essays in public and professional ethics)
  Includes bibliographical references and index.
  1. Social workers–Professional ethics. 2. Social service--Moral and ethical aspects. I. Gambrill, Eileen D., 1934–

  HV 10.5.S62 2009
  174'.93613–dc22

2008027050

ISBN: 978-0-7546-2438-7

Mixed Sources
Product group from well-managed forests and other controlled sources
www.fsc.org Cert no. SGS-COC-2482
© 1996 Forest Stewardship Council

Printed and bound in Great Britain by
TJ International Ltd, Padstow, Cornwall

Contents

PART VII   THE ETHICS OF CLAIMS MAKING

PART VIII   ETHICAL ISSUES REGARDING PROFESSIONAL EDUCATION AND SCHOOLS OF SOCIAL WORK

PART IX   THE OBLIGATION TO ATTEND TO HARMING IN THE NAME OF HELPING

PART X   THE ETHICS OF TECHNOLOGY

PART XI   PROMISING DIRECTIONS FOR THE FUTURE

Acknowledgements

The editor and publishers wish to thank the following for permission to use copyright material.

American Psychological Association for the essay: William O'Donohue, Jane E. Fisher, Joseph J. Plaud and William Link (1989), 'What Is a Good Treatment Decision? The Client's Perspective', *Professional Psychology: Research and Practice*, **20**, pp. 404–07. Copyright © 1989 American Psychological Association.

Copyright Clearance Center for the essays: Helen Harris Perlman (1976), 'Believing and Doing: Values in Social Work Education', *Social Casework*, **57**, pp. 381–90. Copyright © 1976 Alliance for Childine and Families; Sonja Grover (2005), 'Reification of Psychiatric Diagnoses as Defamatory: Implications for Ethical Clinical Practice', *Ethical Human Psychology and Psychiatry*, **7**, pp. 77–86. Copyright © 2005 Springer Publishing Company; Sonja Grover (2004), 'Did I Make the Grade? Ethical Issues in Psychological Screening of Children for Adoption Placement', *Ethical Human Psychology and Psychiatry*, **6**, pp. 125–33. Copyright © 2004 Springer Publishing Company; Martin Leever, Gina DeCiani, Ellen Mulaney and Heather Hasslinger (2002), 'Ethical Decisionmaking', in Martin Leever, Gina DeCiani, Ellen Mulaney, Heather Hasslinger in conjunction with Eileen Gambrill, *Ethical Child Welfare Practice*, Washington, DC: Child Welfare League of America Press, pp. 1–16. Copyright © 2002 Child Welfare League of America Inc.

Elsevier Limited for th essay: Patricia E. O'Hagan (2003), 'Fraudulent Misrepresentation and Eating Disorder', *International Journal of Law and Psychiatry*, **26**, pp. 713–17. Copyright © Elseiver.

Families in Society for the essay: Susan Kiss Sarnoff (1999), '"Sanctified Snake Oil": Ideology, Junk Science, and Social Work Practice', *Families in Society: The Journal of Contemporary Human Services*, **80**, pp. 396–408.

Indiana University School of Social Work for the essay: Elaine P. Congress (2000), 'What Social Workers Should Know About Ethics: Understanding and Resolving Practice Dilemmas', *Advances in Social Work*, **1**, pp. 1–22. Copyright © 2000 Indiana University School of Social Work.

IOS Press for the essayss: David Cohen and David Jacobs (1998), 'A Model Consent Form for Psychiatric Drug Treatment', *International Journal of Risk and Safety in Medicine*, **11**, pp. 161–64. Copyright © 1998 IOS Press.

Journal of Applied Behavior Analysis for the essays: Israel Goldiamond (1978), 'The Professional as a Double-Agent', *Journal of Applied Behavior Analysis*, **11**, pp. 178–84. Copyright © 1978 Journal of Applied Behavior Analysis.

Series Preface

'Ethics' is now a considerable part of all debates about the conduct of public life, in government, economics, law, business, the professions and indeed every area of social and political affairs. The ethical aspects of public life include questions of moral right and wrong in the performance of public and professional roles, the moral justification and critique of public institutions and the choices that confront citizens and professionals as they come to their own moral views about social, economic and political issues.

While there are no moral experts to whom we can delegate the determination of ethical questions, the traditional skills of moral philosophers have been increasingly applied to practical contexts that call for moral assessment. Moreover this is being done with a degree of specialist knowledge of the areas under scrutiny that previously has been lacking from much of the work undertaken by philosophers.

This series brings together essays that exhibit high quality work in philosophy and the social sciences, that is well informed on the relevant subject matter and provides novel insights into the problems that arise in resolving ethical questions in practical contexts.

The volumes are designed to assist those engaged in scholarly research by providing the core essays that all who are involved in research in that area will want to have to hand. Essays are reproduced in full with the original pagination for ease of reference and citation.

The editors are selected for their eminence in the particular area of public and professional ethics. Each volume represents the editor's selection of the most seminal essays of enduring interest in the field.

SEUMAS MILLER AND TOM CAMPBELL
Centre for Applied Philosophy and Public Ethics (CAPPE)
Australian National University
Charles Sturt University
University of Melbourne

Introduction

All professions appeal to ethical obligations and related values to define and forward their profession.[1] All claim the 'high road' regarding their views on moral issues – what is viewed as good and what is viewed as bad. Ethical issues are integral to the question: 'What is a professional?', for example, obligations to clients. Yet we know from harming in the name of helping that the ethical obligations of beneficence, non-maleficence, autonomy and informed consent are often ignored.[2] Ethical issues that arise in social work also arise in other helping professions: for example, clashes between obligations to individuals and concerns regarding equity of distribution of scarce resources among groups.[3] Ethical issues include those related to knowledge – how to get it, is it possible to get it, who is to decide, what is knowledge (evidence) and what is not. Another area concerns the ethics of technology. What technologies should we bring into social work? Who should decide? How should they be evaluated and who is to decide? What are just grounds for excuses offered for inadequate services and what are not? All these topics involve philosophical questions many of which are ignored or are presented in a way that obscures the related context, as is illustrated in essays in this volume.

The profession of social work, in common with other professions, is a highly politicized arena because of the close relationship between practices and policies and related institutions and legislation, and the influence of moral values on all. Perhaps even more than concerns about money, different beliefs about what is moral and what is not, what is right and what is wrong, affect what is done in the helping professions. And perhaps, of all the professions, social work is the most varied and the most influenced by value judgments and their reflection in legislation and policies at all levels of government. Consider, for example, debates regarding welfare (Williams, 1995). Ethical issues regarding professional practice encompass a wide spectrum. This is particularly the case in social work and social welfare which include so many different kinds of 'work' in such a variety of settings.

---

[1]   See, for example, the Code of Ethics of the National Association of Social Workers (1999), available on the Internet. Levy (1973) suggests three dimensions regarding value orientations: preferred conceptions of people, preferred outcomes, and preferred ways of dealing with people. He suggests that, in this value context, how clients and others are to be treated becomes 'Not something that necessarily works better than other things, but rather something that social workers might concede to be right and hence as an obligation or commitment of social workers' (p. 42). Many excellent sources discuss moral thinking (for example, Baron, 2000).

[2]   See, for example, Blenkner, Bloom and Nielson (1971), Petrosino, Turpin-Petrosino and Finckenauer (2000) and Sharpe and Faden (1998).

[3]   Some authors (for example, Pelton, 2001) emphasize ethical issues created by a focus on increasing social justice for groups as this may affect individuals. Issues related to the distribution of scarce resources may not be discussed even though such issues and related decisions involve ethical issues as described in Part IV. Restorative justice has received increasing attention (see, for example, Burford and Adams, 2004).

Differences of opinion about what is a social or personal problem, about what should be funded at what levels, and what is the state's responsibility and what is the individual's, create policies and legislation that may not be faithful to obligations described in professional codes of ethics.[4] As always when conflicting moral judgments are at play, value judgments and related clashes may be distorted or hidden. Flawed arguments may be disguised in a discourse that hides harming in the name of helping. The many books on ethics and social work that focus on informed consent, confidentiality, dual relationships and related boundary problems, and termination often obscure underlying value clashes as well as related research findings regarding what is viewed as a personal or social problem, their causes and interrelationships. For example, although social work and social welfare have a history of attending to environmental factors that influence personal lives and although considerable rhetoric lingers on the environmental level and social justice concerns, attention in everyday practice is often on psychological and biomedical levels.[5]

Beliefs and related decisions about what is bad (sick, unhealthy) and what is not (well, healthy) affect people, and thus are of ethical concern. In the present as in the past, decisions are made about what is moral and what is not, in present times often in the disguise of what is healthy and what is 'mentally ill'. Value judgments about what is good and what is not is reflected in the discourse of psychiatry as well as in the discourse of welfare (see, for example, Conrad, 2007; Moynihan and Cassels, 2005; Williams, 1995). The enormous growth of the health care industry and the medicalization of personal and social problems have had a profound effect, not only on social work but on kindred professions such as psychology, psychiatry and counselling (see, for example, Conrad, 2007; Moynihan and Cassels, 2005). Professional organizations and education programmes as well as accrediting agencies play a role in determining what conceptualizations 'win the day'. If narrow views obscure causes of client miseries, this is an ethical concern. The language of medicalization is encouraged by those who benefit from its consequences, such as pharmaceutical companies which make billions selling medications to treat the 'mentally ill' (see, for example, Brody, 2007). Power differences between professionals and clients engender cause for concern with regard to conflicting preferences and interests, and to influence by misleading discourse, such as value judgments disguised as empirical findings. The powerful have advantages such as the means to employ public relations experts and state mandates to influence the lives of clients (for example, to take away children, lock up people in psychiatric institutions). Disguises include

---

[4]   For examples of the rich literature on the social construction of problems, see Gusfield (2003), Loeske (1999), Conrad (2007) and Conrad and Schneider (1992). Hilgartner and Bosk (1988) illustrate changing views about social problems. How behaviour is viewed, including the value attributed to a given behaviour and presumed causes, influences how those who engage in (or are assumed to engage in) certain behaviours are treated or even noticed. Classification has long affected whether an individual will receive help (or not) for what concerns, and in what form. Michielse and van Krieken (1990) illustrate the longevity of concerns about what to do about the poor. Thus, how deviance (variations in behaviour) is defined is central to questions of ethics. Changing cultural norms and hopes of consumers interact in complex ways with marketing on the part of related industries including the social problems industry.

[5]   Courses on social problems and psychopathology often focus on the psychiatric classification system (American Psychiatric Association, 2000) and give little attention to other perspectives. See LaCasse and Gomory (2003); see also Leonardsen (2007).

bogus empirical findings and pseudoscience masquerading as science.[6] Abstract, fine-sounding terms such as 'social justice', and 'empowerment', may not match related actions (see, for example, Patterson, 2008). Ignoring power differences often results in unethical practices such as not involving clients in decisions as informed participants. Social and economic influences on behaviour are obscured by a focus on individual, psychological characteristics.

Social welfare legislation and related institutions and policies influence the practice of social work but do not determine it, allowing discretion in decision-making on the part of individual social workers. Discretion can work for the benefit of clients or inflict avoidable harm. Ethical issues arise and play out in the intersection of social welfare legislation and policies and the decisions of individual social workers, which in turn are influenced by how social and personal problems/needs are viewed in a society and who controls such views. How they play out is influenced by professional education programmes within which social workers are educated, by the organizations that accredit them (for example, the Council on Social Work Education in the United States), by agency policy, by related laws, by the quality of professional publications, and by the range and quality of theory and research social workers draw on. Ethical codes and related moral obligations provide a guide, but not a rule book for decisions. In the messy everyday world of practice and policy, individuals and groups of professionals must use their discretion in bringing to bear moral principles and ethical obligations in specific contexts. We can draw on codes of ethics to suggest how discretion should be guided. For example the National Association of Social Workers code of ethics calls on social workers to draw on practice- and policy-related research and to involve clients as informed participants. It calls on social workers to think critically about (to reflect on) their work. Thinking critically requires being fair-minded as well as open-minded, a willingness to be our own critic and to candidly acknowledge sources of error and biased views that may influence our decisions about those we are obligated to help.[7] The ethics of discretion requires professionals to make decisions that are most likely to help clients and least likely to harm them. Only if they think critically about their decisions can this be done.

I do not think we can understand the decisions made by individual social workers in relation to ethical concerns unless we understand their context, both past and present. This context includes professional education experiences, agency environments, and published research on which professionals are supposed to draw to inform their decisions. It includes considering the role of the helping professions in a society and how behaviour is defined – for example, what is deviant and what is not, what is revered and what is not, and who has the power to say so. Only in this way can we identify key factors related to ethics and social work, including coercion of clients. The increasing globalization of society may yield new problems and exacerbate old ones. The literature in international social work reflects these changes

---

[6]   Pseudoscience in the guise of science has been of increasing concern, as reflected by Jacobson, Foxx and Mulick (2005) and Lilienfeld, Lynn and Lohr (2003).

[7]   For discussion of critical thinking, see Brown and Keeley (2007) and Paul and Elder (2004). Thinking critically about exercising discretion for the benefit of clients requires knowledge of cognitive ases that can lead us astray, as illustrated by Gambrill (2005) and Trout (2005). It requires detection oral values presented as scientific findings. It requires a willingness to question the 'party line' and wledge of common informal fallacies and how to avoid them. It requires skill in argumentation as ed by Lens (2005). Without this knowledge and the motivation to use it to exercise discretion for t of clients, ethical decisions are unlikely.

and highlights related concerns. To what extent are social workers responsible for addressing problems on a global level that affect clients they see at the local level? Professional codes of ethics purport to provide a guide for action in the intersections between legislation and policies and everyday ethical dilemmas. They are so primal to a profession that discourse concerning related principles and values can obscure what is done to what effect; that is, abstract discourse takes the place of clear descriptions of on-the-job practices and policies. What is welfare – and what is not – is contested, in part because of different views concerning ethical obligations of different players – the state, the federal government, agencies, charities, individual social workers, and clients. In this book I bring together a selection of essays that may help us to clarify and maximize opportunities to honour ethical obligations.

The ethics of transparency is a theme throughout this volume. This focus highlights the importance of being honest brokers of ignorance and knowledge, and encourages remedial actions when this mandate is transgressed. Without transparency of what is done to what effect in all venues related to social work, ethical obligations, especially to clients, cannot be met. Without this, unnecessarily restrictive methods may be imposed. Transparency includes accurate accounts of research projects related to practice and policy decisions. It includes honest acknowledgement of the uncertainties surrounding decisions in a supportive context as illustrated in the essay by Jay Katz (Chapter 20). Honesty regarding uncertainty is a theme in many of the essays included in this volume. Transparency on the part of researchers affects practitioners, administrators, and students. Bogus conclusions in research reports mislead rather than inform. Such misleading accounts are especially pernicious in professions in which practitioners' mission is to help, at least as so stated in mission statements, codes of ethics and accreditation guidelines. The avalanche of inflated claims on the part of industries intertwined with the helping professions – for example,the health care, public relations, and pharmaceutical industries – has resulted in a backlash. This is reflected in books describing propaganda, fraud, and corruption in these industries that affect social work as well as other helping professions (see, for example, Craig and Brooks, 2005). Transparency International was created to decrease corruption in all venues.

Essays in this Volume

Only by taking both a broad look and an in-depth look at factors that influence social work and social welfare can we identify and understand ethical issues that affect clients' welfare and well-being as well as the satisfaction social workers gain in their work. Professional education, professional publications and research related to social work practice and policy, affect the quality of services and therefore are vital ethical venues. So too does the breadth of exploration of published research in other areas as this may help social workers to help their clients. Only if we examine what takes place to what effect can we identify opportunities to enhance ethical practice. Lingering at the level of vague discourse – about empowerment for example which appeals to our emotions – lulls into abeyance our critical appraisal of what services clients receive (or do not), to what effect, and so does not permit opportunities to b faithful to our code of ethics. Thus, ethical issues in a profession include a review of rela discourse. There is an obligation to be clear rather than vague, measured rather than grand and honest rather than dishonest. There is an obligation to accurately describe alter views, especially disliked views (Popper, 1994). I suggest that a number of ethical is avoided in order to protect the status of professional organizations and their members and that these include hiding and minimizing harming in the name of helping, not identifying avoidable mistakes, not clearly describing minimal levels of competencies required to help clients achieve specific valued outcomes, not encouraging meaningful accountability (clear description of services used to what effect) and not candidly confronting the role of social workers as double agents in agencies in which they have coercive power over clients. I have selected topics, and essays within them, that highlight these issues because I think we have an obligation both to acknowledge them and to struggle to responsibly confront them.

Ethical Obligations and Related Values

Part I includes essays that describe values and ethical obligations that pertain to social work. In Chapter 1, Chris Beckett stresses the importance of candidly examining what is done and what can be done under current circumstances. James Leiby (Chapter 4)offers a historical view of the moral foundations of social welfare and social work. Banks McDowell discusses responsibilities of professionals and excuses for breaching obligations in Chapter 5 (see also Pope and Vasquez, 1999). Essays by Elaine Congress (Chapter 2) and Fred Reamer (Chapter 6) describe changes in descriptions of obligations. Chapter 3, my own essay, suggests a client-focused view of social work practice, critiquing Beatrice Barratt's view.

Recurrent Clashes and their Ethical Implications

Part II includes essays that describe recurrent clashes in the history of social work and social welfare including the clash between adjusting individuals to their environment and changing dysfunctional environments. The history of these struggles is illustrated in Chapter 7 by Mimi Abramovitz.[8] Then Donna Franklin's essay (Chapter 8) describes the evolution of social work practice in the writings of Mary Richmond and Jane Addams. The history of social work reflects continuing disagreements regarding the relative importance of environmental variables and individual characteristics in contributing to personal and social problems. Consider the popularity of the psychiatric classification system, the DSM (American Psychiatric Association, 2000), which describes hundreds of alleged 'mental disorders' and the concerns about this classification system.[9] Jerome Wakefield discusses intersections between a mental health focus and a social justice focus in Chapter 9. Given that presumed causes influence selection of services, it is vital to consider both evidentiary and ethical issues regarding classification systems. How behaviour is defined is related to who has (or is given) the authority to define behaviour in given ways and who has authority to decide what should be done. There is a rich literature describing the social construction of problems.[10] A course on deviance was required in the masters curriculum at the University of Michigan in the late 1960s. This is no longer required and is no longer offered. Rather today, we find courses on Psychopathology (see LaCasse and Gomory, 2003).

---

[8]   For other discussions of this topic, see Abramovitz (1985) and Michielse and van Krieken (1990). For a current discussion of related issues, see Handler and Hasenfeld (2007).

[9]   For concerns regarding this system, see, for example, Houts (2002) and Kutchins and Kirk (1997).

[10]   See note 4.

Ethical Dilemmas of being a Double Agent

Part III includes essays that highlight dilemmas that result from being a double agent – a helper to clients and an implementer of agency policy. These two functions often conflict, placing social workers in a position of playing contradictory roles. This dilemma is described by Israel Goldiamond in Chapter 10 and also in the two essays by Yeheskel Hasenfeld (Chapters 11 and 12).[11]

Ethical Issues Regarding the Allocation of Scarce Resources

The two essays in Part IV deal with ethical issues regarding the distribution of scarce resources and related dilemmas. Social workers often confront intractable problems with impoverished resources within a rhetoric of social justice and empowerment. Options include offering minimal services and complaining, ignoring the discrepancy – acting as if it does not exist, proclaiming that the good fight for social justice and empowerment is being fought and won when it is neither being fought nor won, and offering poor services and being content with these. Russell Hardin notes in Chapter 13 that discretion on the part of social workers is limited by decisions concerning the distribution of resources that are made at the city, country, state, and federal levels. Social workers thus cannot function as autonomous agents and, as he argues, nor should they, because, for example, resources may quickly be used up. This explains his title 'The Artificial Duties of Contemporary Professionals'. Disagreements about how to distribute scarce resources abound. Values appealed to in such distribution may not reflect what clients receive. Equity issues may be ignored or dismissed. Many discussions of discrimination and oppression do not candidly confront unsolved (and unsolvable?) issues concerning social justice – how should (or can) different views of social justice be resolved? How should limited resources be distributed?[12] What is the individual's responsibility in relation to life's adversities? In their essay (Chapter 14) Daniel Huff and David Johnson describe federal subsidies to American business to the tune of $150 billion a year. They note that this affects traditional welfare programmes and that this 'phantom welfare state' contributes to the redistribution of wealth. A just distribution of scarce resources is hindered by failing to recognize corporate welfare.

Not recognizing constraints places both social workers and clients in an untenable situation and may be related to 'burnout', lack of advocacy for clients (since the true source of lack of resources is not recognized), moral disengagement (for example, Bandura, 1999), and continuing inequities because candid discussion regarding scarce resources does not occur. There is an alarming acceptance of inadequate services – services being offered at levels far below what is needed, with excuses offered that are often not justifiable (for example,

---

[11]   Different locations of different kinds of professionals in this double agent role may result in misunderstandings as illustrated by Anderson et al. (2007). Proceduralization may compromise quality of services and encourage coercive practices as described by Watson (2002). Being a double agent sets the stage for coerciveness. Coercion in the name of helping has long been of concern to Thomas Szasz (1994). Hasenfeld explores issues related to inequalities between clients and helpers in Chapter 12. Hutchinson (1987) suggests practice principles to guide use of authority with mandated clients. Kultgen (1988) discusses paternalism and client autonomy.

[12]   See for example Center for Evidence Based Purchasing website.

claiming not to know that more effective services were available when this information is readily available). Publications regarding the importance of social justice and alleged progress in increasing social justice abound in the social work literature. Yet, if we examine the gaps between the rhetoric and what is done and what is achieved, what would we find? To what extent is the 'social' in social work reflected in everyday practice? Waterson (1999) raises the question as to whether the focus of community care social work is shifting from addressing needs of clients to reducing risks as a way to ration resources. He notes that risk discourse is increasingly being used as a means of investigating things that go wrong including blaming professionals.

Competence and Accountability as Ethical Issues

Competency and accountability are topics of concern in all professions and are discussed in the essays in Part V.[13] In Chapter 15, Don Baer suggests minimal requisites for evaluation as well as political obstacles. Then Iain Chalmers highlights the vital role of evaluation in trying to do more good than harm in Chapter 16. Judith Favell and James McGimsey's essay (Chapter 17) suggests characteristics of an acceptable treatment environment. Finally, Peter Sturmey discusses clients' rights to competent services in Chapter 18.

Ethical Obligations to Involve Clients as Informed Participants

Part VI describes ethical concerns regarding informed consent. Codes of ethics call on professionals to involve clients as informed participants in making decisions. Typically this does not occur (see, for example, Braddock et al., 1999). Concerns about respect for autonomy are reflected in material by Jay Katz (Chapter 20) and readers are urged to read his entire book (Katz, 2000). Computerized decision aids can facilitate informed decision-making as described by Annette O'Connor and her colleagues in Chapter 21. David Cohen and David Jacobs suggest, in Chapter 19, a model informed-consent form regarding psychotropic medication

---

[13]   Social workers can draw on related research and advances in other professions, such as use of standardized clients and avoiding surrogates of competence that may not be valid as illustrated by Tousignant and DesMarchais (2002). Dawes(1995) raises vital issues regarding standards of practice and discusses the concerning role of professional education in encouraging low standards. Ethical violations that came to the attention of the National Association of Social Workers between 1986 and 1997 are described by Kimberly Strom-Gottfried (2000). Boundary issues such as dual relationships were the most common violation. It is of interest to compare the violations noted in this context with ethical issues reported by 327 third-year medical students described in Caldicott and Faber-Langendoen (2005):

The most common issues were deliberate lies or deceptions (n=68), patients' right to refuse recommended treatment (n=48) and insistence on futile treatment (n=46). Students perceived overt and subtle discrimination toward patients, reflected in substandard or excessive treatment. In 81 cases (12%), students expressed reluctance to speak up about moral conflict for fear of reprisal. This fear was expressed in 18 (45%) of the 40 issues ...

What would be found among a sample of social work students? Should licensing boards devote more attention to lying and deception?

to fully inform clients regarding the risks and benefits of recommended medications as well as of alternatives. In their essay 'What is a good treatment decision?' (Chapter 22), William O'Donohue and his colleagues represent the client's position.

The Ethics of Claims Making

Ethical issues regarding claims making are the topic of Part VII. No profession could acquire its status without millions of claims made, for example about healing. These range from accurate claims that can be readily evaluated to vague claims that can be clarified by no one. Vague and often bogus claims used to establish a profession continue, as described in Chapter 23 by Allen Rubin and Danielle Parrish (see also Pignotti, 2007).[14] The essay by Robert Rosenthal (Chapter 25) describes the close relationship between ethical and evidentiary issues, while those by Patricia O'Hagen and Susan Sarnoff (Chapters 24 and 26, respectively) illustrate the lack of honest brokering of knowledge and ignorance. Dishonest brokering of knowledge and ignorance is illustrated by discourse regarding the process and philosophy of evidence-based practice (EBP). Most of this ignores both the process and philosophy of EBP, and presents a distorted version, or redefines this as use of evidence-based practices (the EBPs approach), without informing readers about this fragmented or distorted presentation (see Gambrill, 2006). Is it true, as Friedson (1994) suggests, that for a view to be considered important other views must be distorted? And, most important, what are the affects of dishonest brokering of knowledge and ignorance on the quality of services clients receive? Karl Popper (Chapter 27) suggests principles for a new professional ethic. He highlights our obligation to learn from our mistakes how to do better in the future. He argues that it is the obligation of the writer to accurately describe alternative views (Popper, 1994). As he notes, unless views are accurately described, we cannot clearly discern their advantages as well as their weaknesses; we cannot accurately critique them because we either do not understand them (perhaps we have not taken the time) or choose to distort them. In either case, there is an ethical lapse in scholarship. Thus Part VII pertains to the ethics of scholarship in a profession.

Ethical Issues Regarding Professional Education and Schools of Social Work

Part VIII includes essays regarding professional education and schools of social work. Ethical obligations regarding those who teach in professional education programs received increased emphasis in the most recent code of ethics as Elaine Congress describes in Chapter 2. The importance of values in social work education is emphasized by Helen Harris Perlman in Chapter 28. Decisions regarding what content to teach in professional schools influences students' views of clients, problems and options. It is during professional education that students are expected to acquire knowledge of ethical obligations as well as knowledge concerning factors such as informal fallacies that may lead them astray. Jay Katz (2002) emphasizes the importance of teaching professionals how to handle uncertainty within a

---

[14]   Inflated claims regarding the accuracy of tests and the effectiveness of interventions thrive in all helping professions including the professional literature. Bogus claims make it difficult for practitioners and clients to sort out the wheat from the chaff. Problems in peer review was one reason for the creation of the process of evidence-based practice and related enterprises such as the Cochrane and Campbell collaborations (see, for example,Gray, 2001).

supportive context characterized by honesty. Without a sound education regarding sources of uncertainty as well as bias and propaganda, both personal and societal, students are unlikely to handle the inevitable discretion involved in making decisions in an informed, ethical manner. Propaganda can be defined as encouraging beliefs and actions with the least thought possible (Ellul, 1965). In Chapter 29, Richard Titmuss notes the vital role of social work education (as distinct from propaganda) in enabling clients to exercise choice, which he viewed as an integral function of social work. He emphasizes the 'broad educational responsibility of social work' in relation to public opinion.

The dual sources of misleading influences – personal (cognitive biases coupled with a lack of fluid knowledge concerning informal fallacies) and societal (propaganda from professional organizations, corporations, governments and agencies) – yield a potent brew working against ethical decision-making in social work and other helping professions. This highlights the vital role of inoculating students against both self- and other propaganda during professional education programmes. So far this is not a reality; for example, few if any schools introduce students to kinds and sources of propaganda. Indeed professional education is often a source of propaganda, as illustrated by LaCasse and Gomory (2003). Some medical schools are taking active steps to inform students about marketing strategies as illustrated in the essay by Michael Wilkes and Jerome Hoffman (Chapter 30). Professional education programmes should address excuses used for poor services, as described by Pope and Vasquez (1999) and McDowell (2000). And they should help students to deal with the inevitable uncertainties in offering services as discussed so movingly by Katz (2002).

The Obligation to Attend to Harming in the Name of Helping

Part IX includes essays related to harming in the name of helping. Unlike the profession of medicine, relatively little attention has been given in the social work literature to harm. Since any intervention may harm as well as help (including assessment measures), such attention is vital so that we can minimize interventions that harm rather than help clients (see, for example, Courtney, Needell and Wulczyn, 2004; Moncrieff and Cohen, 2006; Munro, 1996). Essays by Sonja Grover (Chapter 31), Joan McCord (Chapter 32) and Eileen Munro (Chapter 33) illustrate this. In Chapter 34, William O'Donohue and Jeff Szymanski describe beliefs that may result in offering ineffective or harmful service. Ethical issues regarding nonprofit organizations are both a past (Lewis, 1989) and current concern, as illustrated in recent exposés of fraud in charities.

The Ethics of Technology

Part X includes essays that highlight ethical issues regarding technology. Social work depends on thousands of different kinds of techniques including the case record, diagnoses, hundreds of different kinds of interventions, and scores of evaluation methods.[15] Ethical issues related to technology include what techniques should be used, where, when and with whom; who will offer them; and how or if they will be evaluated. All these questions are vital to social work,

---

[15] Hall et al. (1997) describe how technologies of social work such as the case record are used to construct moral identities such as 'the bad parent'. See also Margolin, (1997) and Tice (1997.

as well as to other helping professions. Ellul (1964) argues that we must understand the term 'technique' in a broad sense. He argues that we live in a technological society that reaches into every aspect of our lives and takes on a life of its own in the service of increased efficiency (ibid.). We are soothed by 'tranquilizing abstractions' that appeal to our emotions and hopes (ibid., p. 397). Specialization is integral to this technological society. He suggests that, since no two techniques have the same dimensions or depth, technique can assert its innocence in terms of control. Ellul argues that the rise of the technological society is facilitated by deeply rooted and widespread myths including the myth of 'man' – not you or I, but an abstract entity. 'The technician intones: "We strive for Man's happiness; we seek to create a Man of excellence" ...' (ibid., p. 390). He suggests that failure to distinguish between individuals and abstractions such as 'man' encourages a lack of curiosity regarding the individual. This point is a vital one in social work where there are so many vague discussions of abstractions such as social justice. Technologies include widely used procedures such as case records, home visits, risk assessment scales, screening instruments, observation of interactions between clients and their significant others, and methods used to evaluate competence (see, for example, Margolin, 1997, and Tice, 1998). Ethical issues concerning technology are related to ethical issues regarding knowledge claims – what is knowledge and how (or if) we can get it. Potential concerns about the use of technology are suggested in the essays by David Cohen and Keith Hoeller (Chapter 35), Gregory Gross and Robert Blundo (Chapter 36), Sonja Grover (Chapter 37) and Nigel Parton (Chapter 38). Gross and Blundo describe how a specific technology encourages a certain construction of identity.

Promising Directions for the Future

Part XI includes essays suggesting promising directions for maximizing attention to ethical issues in the future. Here too (as always), technology plays a vital role: for example, the Internet, systematic reviews such as those in the Cochrane and Campbell Libraries, and decision aids. The essay by Martin Leever and his colleagues (Chapter 39) suggests steps for making ethical decisions. In Chapter 41, Marlee Spafford and colleagues illustrate the importance of transparency regarding what is done (see also Coulter and Ellins, 2007; Hanley et al , 2001; and Holmes-Rovner, 2007).[16] Transparency can be used to illustrate to social workers how they make decisions so they can view these in relation to ethical obligations.

---

[16]   Transparency regarding risk is a vital ethical concern (e. g., see O'Connor, Legare, & Spacey, 2003; Paling (2006). The source of the code of ethics social workers agree to follow is the National Association of Social Workers, a professional organization dedicated to the advance and growth of the social work profession. This key aim conflicts with transparency and open critical discussion concerning what social workers do to what effect as illustrated in the essays in this volume. Lilienfeld (2002) describes the embarrassing actions of staff in the American Psychological Association under pressure from ideologues to censor research findings. Reactions to the NAS (National Association of Scholars) report on social work education by Balch and Wood (2007) show the reluctance of both NASW and CSWE (the Council on Social Work Education – the accrediting body for all social work degree programs) in the United States to candidly and critically discuss examples of flagrant discrimination against students who do not go along with favored views of their instructors. (See related reports on their websites.) Rather, there is a circling of the wagons and attack on the critics. This provides a poor model of how to respond to criticism and results in lost opportunities to critically confront ethical lapses.

That this call for transparency will be a hard fought one is suggested by Ann Florini (2007) in her book *Right to know: Transparency for an open world*. Ann McDonald highlights the potential important role of Human Rights Acts in honouring ethical obligations in Chapter 40.

It is my hope that the essays in this volume will stimulate interest and activity related to enhancing ethical behaviours, especially those that have been ignored such as how to ethically handle the uncertainty involved in making decisions. If rhetoric in social work regarding oppression, discrimination and social justice is to enhance meaningful outcomes for clients, it must be accompanied by a realistic appraisal of options, opportunity costs, constraints and actions. Otherwise, such rhetoric clouds rather than reveals lack of social justice for individuals and lost opportunities for ethical action.

Further Reading

Goodman, K.W. (2005), 'Ethics, Evidence and Public Policy', *Perspectives in Biology and Medicine*, **48**, pp. 548–56.

Gorman, D.M. (1998), 'The Irrelevance of Evidence in the Development of School-based Drug Prevention Policy, 1986–1996', *Evaluation Review*, **222**, pp. 118–19.

Gorman, D.M. (2003), 'Prevention Programs and Scientific Nonsense (Drug Abuse and Violence Prevention Program Evaluation)', *Policy Review*, Feb–March, p. 65(11), Downloaded 31 May 2005.

Handler, J.F., and Hasenfeld, Y. (1991), *The Moral Construction of Poverty: Welfare Reform in America*, Newbury Park, CA: Sage.

Kim, Y.M., Kols, A., Martin, A., Silva, D., Rinehart, W., Prammawat, S., Johnson, S. and Church, K. (2005), 'Promoting Informed Choice: Evaluating a Decision making Tool for Family Planning Clients and Providers in Mexico', *International Family Planning Perspectives*, **31**, at: www.guttmacher.org/pubs/journals. Downloaded 31 December 2007.

Leo, J. and Cohen, D. (2003), 'Broken Brains or Flawed Studies? A Critical Review of ADHD Neuroimagining Research', *Journal of Mind and Behavior*, **24**, pp. 29–56.

Macdonald, G. (1990), 'Allocating Blame in Social Work', *British Journal of Social Work*, **20**, pp. 525–46.

Mattison, M. (2000), 'Ethical Decision Making: The Person in the Process', *Social Work*, **45**, pp. 201–12.

Moynihan, R. (2003), 'The Making of a Disease: Female Sexual Dysfunction', *British Medical Journal*, **326**, pp. 45–47.

Skrabanek, P. and McCormick, J. (1998), *Follies and Fallacies in Medicine* (3rd edn), Whithorn: Tarragon Press.

Wakefield, J.C. (1988), 'Psychotherapy, Distribution of Justice and Social Work', *Social Service Review*, **62**, pp. 187–210 and 353–82.

References

Abramovitz, M. (1985), 'The Family Ethic: The Female Pauper and Public Aid, Pre-1900', *Social Service Review*, 59, pp. 121–35.

American Psychiatric Association (2000), *Diagnostic and statistical manual of mental disorders* (4th edn), Washington, DC: American Psychiatric Association.

Rather than viewing criticism as opportunities to enhance ethical practices, heads are thrust into the sand.

Anderson, A., Barenberg, L. and Tremblay, P.R. (2007), 'Professional Ethics in Interdisciplinary Collaboratives: et al, Paternalism and Mandated Reporting', *Clinical Law Review*, Spring, pp. 659–718.

Balch, S. and Wood, P. W. (2007), *The Scandal of Social Work Education*, National Association of Scholars (NAS), Princeton, NJ: www.nas.org

Bandura, A. (1999), 'Moral Disengagement in the Perpetuation of Inhumanities', *Personality and Social Psychology Review*, **3**, pp. 193–209.

Baron, J. (2000), *Thinking and Deciding* (3rd edn), New York: Cambridge University Press.

Benbenishty, R., Osmo, R. and Gold, N. (2003), 'Rationales Provided for Risk Assessments and for Recommended Interventions in Child Protection: A Comparison between Canadian and Israeli Professionals', *British Journal of Social Work*, **33**, pp. 137–55.

Blenkner, M., Bloom, M. and Nielson, M. (1971), 'A Research and Demonstration Project of Protective Services', *Social Casework*, **52**, pp. 483–99.

Braddock, C. H., Edwards, K. A., Hasenberg, M. N., Laidley, T. L. and Levinson, W. (1999), 'Informed Decision Making in Outpatient Practice. Time to Get Back to Basics', *Journal of the American Medication Association*, **282**, pp. 2313–21.

Brody, H. (2007), *Hooked: Ethics, the Medical Profession and the Pharmaceutical Industry*, New York: Rowman & Littlefield et al.

Brown, N.,and Keeley, J. (2007), *Asking the Right Questions: A Guide to Critical Thinking* (8th edn), Upper Saddle River, NJ: Prentice Hall.

Burford, G. and Adams, P. (2004), 'Restorative Justice, Responsive Regulation and Social Work.', *Journal of Sociology and Social Welfare*, **31**, pp. 7–26.

Caldicott, C. V. and Faber-Langendoen, K. (2005), 'Deception, Discrimination, and Fear of Reprisal: Lessons in Ethics from Third-year Medical Students', *Academic Medicine*, **205**, pp. 866–73.

Conrad, P. (1994), 'Wellness as Virtue: Morality and the Pursuit of Health', *Culture, Medicine and Psychiatry*, **18**, pp. 385–401.

Conrad, P. (2005), 'The Shifting Engines of Medicalization', *Journal of Health and Social Behavior*, **46**, pp. 3–14.

Conrad, P. (2007), *The Medicalization of Society: On the Transformation of Human Conditions into Treatable Disorder*, Baltimore, MD: The Johns Hopkins University Press.

Conrad, P. and Schneider, J. W. (1992), *Deviance and Medicalization: From Badness to Sickness*, Philadelphia: Temple University Press.

Coulter, A. and Ellins, J. (2007), 'Effectiveness of Strategies for Informing, Educating, and Involving Patients', *British Medical Journal*, **335**, pp. 24–27.

Courtney, M. E., Needell, B. and Wulczyn, F. (2004), 'Unintended Consequences of the Push for Accountability: The Case of National Child Welfare Performance Standards', *Children and Youth Services Review*, **26**, pp. 1141–54.

Craig, D. and Brooks, R. (2005), *Plundering the Public Sector: How New Labor Are Letting Consultants Run Off with $20 Billion of Our Money*, London: Constable.

Dawes, R. M. (1995), 'Standards of Practice', in S.C. Hayes, V.M. Follette, R.M. Dawes and K.E. Grady (eds), *Scientific Standards of Psychological Practice: Issues and Recommendations*, Oakland, CA: New Harbinger Publications, pp. 31–43.

Eamon, M. K. and Kopels, S. (2004), '"For Reasons of Poverty": Court Challenges to Child welfare Practices and Mandated Programs', *Children and Youth Services Review*, **26**, pp. 821–36.

Ellul, J. (1965), *Propaganda: The Formation of Men's Attitude*, New York: Vintage.

Ellul, J. (1964), *The Technological Society*, New York: Vintage.

Evans, I., Thornton, H. and Chalmers, I. (2006), *Testing Treatments: Better Research for Better Healthcare*, London: The British Library.

Fawcett, S. B. (1991), 'Some Values Guiding Community Research and Action', *Journal of Applied Behavior Analysis*, **24**, pp. 621–36.

Florini, A. (ed.) (2007), *The Right to Know: Transparency for an Open World*, New York: Columbia University Press.

Friedson, E. (1994), *Professionalism Reborn: Theory, Prophecy and Policy*, Chicago: University of Chicago Press.

Gambrill, E. (2005), *Critical Thinking in Clinical Practice: Improving the Quality of Judgments and Decisions*, Hoboken, NJ: John Wiley & Sons.

Gambrill, E. (2006), 'Evidence Based Practice: Choices Ahead', *Research on Social Work Practice*, **16**, pp. 338–57.

Gray, J.A.M. (2001), 'Evidence-based Medicine for Professionals', in A. Edwards and G. Elwyn (eds), *Evidence-based Patient Choice: Inevitable or Impossible?* New York: Oxford University Press.

Gusfield, J.R. (2003), 'Constructing the Ownership of Social Problems: Fun and Profit in the Welfare State', in J.D. Orcutt and D.R. Rudy (eds), *Drugs, Alcohol, and Social Problems*, New York: Rowman & Littlefield Publishers, pp. 7–18.

Hall, C., Sarangi, S. and Slembrouck, S. (1997), 'Moral Construction in Social Work Discourse', in B.L. Gunnarsson, P. Linell and B. Nordberg (eds), *The Construction of Professional Discourse*, New York: Longman, pp. 265–91.

Handler, J.F. and Hasenfeld, Y. (2007), *Blame Welfare, Ignore Poverty and Inequality*, New York: Cambridge University Press.

Hanley, B., Truesdale, A., King, A., Elbourne, D. and Chalmers, I. (2001), 'Involving Consumers in Designing, Conducting, and Interpreting Randomised Controlled Trials: Questionnaire Survey', *British Medical Journa,*, **322**, pp. 519–23.

Hilgartner, S. and Bosk, C.L. (1988), 'The Rise and Fall of Social Problems: A public Arenas Model', *American Journal of Sociology*, **94**, pp. 53–78.

Holmes-Rovner, M. (2007), 'International Patient Decision Aid Standards (IPDAS): Beyond Decision Aids to Usual Design of Patient Education Materials', *Health Expectations*, **10**, 103–07.

Houts, A.C. (2002), 'Discovery, Invention, and the Expansion of the Modern Diagnostic and Statistical Manuals of Mental Disorders', in L.E. Beutler and M.L. Malik (eds), *Rethinking the DSM: A psychological perspective*, Washington, DC: American Psychological Association, pp. 17–65.

Hutchison, E.D. (1987), 'Use of Authority in Direct Social Work Practice with Mandated Clients', *Social Service Review,* **61**, pp. 581–98.

Jacobson, J.W, Foxx, RM. and Mulick, J.A. (eds) (2005), *Controversial Therapies for Developmental Disabilities: Fad, Fashion and Science in Professional Practice*, Mahwah, NJ: Erlbaum.

Katz, J. (2002), *The Silent World of Doctor and Patient*, Baltimore, MD: Johns Hopkins University Press.

Kultgen, J. (1988), 'Paternalism and Client Autonomy', in *Ethics and Professionalism*, Philadelphia, PA: University of Pennsylvania Press, pp. 274–306.

Kutchins, H. and Kirk, S.A. (1997), *Making Us Crazy: DSM: The Psychiatric Bible and the Creation of Mental Disorders*, New York: Free Press.

LaCasse, J.R. and Gomory, T. (2003), 'Is Graduate School Education Promoting a Critical Approach to Mental Health Practice?', *Journal of Social Work Education,* **39**, pp. 383–408.

Lens, V. (2005), 'Advocacy and Argumentation in the Public Arena: A Guide for Social Workers', *Social Work*, **50**, pp. 231–38.

Leonardsen, D. (2007), 'Empowerment in Social Work: An Individual vs. a Relational Perspective', *International Journal of Social Welfare*, **16**, pp. 3–11.

Levy, C.S. (1973), 'The Value Base of Social Work', *Journal of Education for Social Work*, **9**, pp. 34–42.

Lewis, H. (1989), 'Ethics in the Private Nonprofit Human Service Organization', *Administration in Social Work*, **13**, pp. 1–14.

Lilienfeld, S.O. (2002), 'When Worlds Collide: Social Science, Politics and the Rind et al. (1998), Child Abuse Meta-Analysis', *American Psychologist*, **57**, pp. 177–87.

Lilienfeld, S.O., Lynn, S.J. and Lohr, J.M. (2003), *Science and Pseudoscience in Clinical Psychology*, New York: Guilford.

Loeske, D.R. (1999), *Thinking about Social Problems: An Introduction to Constructionist Perspectives*, New York: Aldine de Gruyter.

Margolin, L. (1997), *Under the Cover of Kindness: The Invention of Social Work*, Charlottesville, VA: University of Virginia Press.

McDowell, B. (2000), *Ethics and Excuses: The Crisis in Professional Responsibility*, Westport, CT: Quorum.

Michielse, H.C.M. and van Krieken, R. (1990), 'Policing the Poor. J.L. Vives and the Sixteenth Century Origins of Modern Social Administration', *Social Service Review*, **64**, pp. 1–21.

Moncrieff, J. and Cohen, D. (2006), 'Do Antidepressants Cure or Create Abnormal Brain States?', *PLoS Medicine*, **3**, p. e240.

Moynihan, R., and Cassels, A. (2005), *Selling Sickness: How the World's Biggest Pharmaceutical Companies Are Turning Us All into Patients*, New York: Norton.

Munro, E. (1996), 'Avoidable and Unavoidable Mistakes in Child Protection Work', *British Journal of Social Work*, **28**, pp. 89–105.

National Association of Social Workers. (1999), *A Code of Ethics*, Washington, DC: National Association of Social Workers.

O'Connor, A., Legare, F. and Spacey, D. (2003), 'Risk Communication in Practice: The Contribution of Decision Aids', *British Medical Journal*, **327**, pp. 736–40.

Paling, J. (2006), *Helping Patients Understand Risks: Simple Strategies for Successful Communication*, Gainesville, FL: Risk Communication Institute.

Patterson, A. (2008), 'Pandora's Boxes: How We Store Our Values', The Tanner Lectures. University of California at Berkeley. April 8, 9, 10.

Paul, R. and Elder, L. (2004), *Critical Thinking: Tools for Taking Charge of Your Professional and Personal Life*, Upper Saddle River, NJ: Prentice Hall.

Pelton, L.H. (2001), 'Social Justice and Social Work', *Journal of Social Work Education*, **37**, pp. 433–39.

Petrosino, A., Turpin-Petrosino, C. and Finckenaurer, J.O. (2000), 'Well-meaning Programs Can Have Harmful Effects! Lessons from Experiments of Programs Such as Scared Straight', *Crime and Delinquency*, **46**, pp. 354–79.

Pignotti, M. (2007), 'Thought Field Therapy: A Former Insider's Experience', *Research on Social Work Practice*, **17**, pp. 392–407.

Pope, K.F. and Vasquez, M.J.T. (1999), *Ethics and Malpractice on Violating the Ethical Standards: Thirty Easy Steps*, at: www.kspope.com/ethics/ethicalstandards.thp.

Popper, K.R. (1994), *The Myth of the Framework: In Defense of Science and Rationality*, ed. M.A. Notturno, New York: Routledge.

Sharpe, V.A. and Faden, A.I. (1998), *Medical Harm: Historical, Conceptual, and Ethical Dimensions of Iatrogenic Illness*, New York: Cambridge University Press.

Strom-Gottfried, K. (2000), 'Ensuring Ethical Practice: An Examination of NASW Code Violations, 1986–97', *Social Work*, **45**, pp. 251–61.

Szasz, T.S. (1994), *Cruel Compassion: Psychiatric Control of Society's Unwanted*, New York: John Wiley.

Tice, K.W. (1998), *Tales of Wayward Girls and Immoral Women*, Urbana: University of Illinois Press.

Tousignant, M. and DesMarchais, J.E. (2002), 'Accuracy of Student Self-assessment Ability Compared to Their Own Performance in a Problem-based Learning Medical Program: A Correlation Study', *Advances in Health Sciences Education*, **7**, pp. 19–27.

Trout, J.D. (2005), 'Paternalism and Cognitive Bias', *Law and Philosophy*, **24**, pp. 393–434.

Waterson, J. (1999), 'Redefining Community Care Social Work: Needs or Risks Led?', *Health and Social Care in the Community*, **7**, pp. 276–79.

Watson, D. (2002), 'A Critical Perspective on Quality within the Personal Social Services: Prospects and Concerns', *British Journal of Social Work*, **32**, pp. 877–91.

Webster, Y.O. (2002), 'A Human-centric Alternative for Diversity and Multicultural Education', *Journal of Social Work Education*, **38**, pp. 17–38.

Weed, D.L. and McKeown, R.E. (1998), 'Epidemiology and Virtue Ethics', *International Journal of Epidemiology*, **27**, pp. 343–49.

Williams, L.A. (1995), 'Race, Rat Bites and Unfit Mothers: How Media Discourse Informs Welfare Legislation Debates', *Fordham Urban Journal*, **22**, pp. 11159–96. Reprinted in L.A. Williams (ed.) (2001), *Welfare Law*. Burlington, VT: Ashgate.

Part I
Ethical Obligations and RelatedValues

[1]

The Reality Principle: Realism as an Ethical Obligation

Chris Beckett

Although a 'realist' stance is sometimes contrasted with a 'principled' one, this article argues that realism is, of itself, an important ethical principle. Acknowledging the problems that exist in defining 'reality', and the fact that the nature of reality is contested, the article nevertheless insists on an 'out there' reality. It asserts that the existence of this external reality is, in practice, generally accepted, and indeed must be accepted if we are to make the important distinction between truth and falsehood. The article proposes that discourse which is not grounded in the concrete reality of the specific situations in which social work is practised is potentially harmful because it results in a decoupling of language from what it is supposed to represent and creates a potential for language to be used to deceive. The article then discusses 'Realism about Outcomes' and 'Realism about Context' as two out of a number of different areas in which realism is important in practice and policy making. It concludes that genuinely ethical social work practice and policy making require that we attempt to engage with the world as it actually is.

Keywords Realism; Reality Principle; Social Work Ethics; Ethical Principles; Pragmatism

Introduction

1. The attitude or practice of accepting a situation as it is and being prepared to deal with it accordingly ...
2. The quality or fact of representing a person, thing, or situation accurately or in a way that is true to life ... (From definition of 'realism', *New Oxford Dictionary of English* (NODE) 2001)

That truth is a good ... is not only a condition of moral discourse, it is a condition of any discourse at all. (Bhaskar, 1989, p. 63)

In life a 'realist' (or 'pragmatic') approach is sometimes contrasted with a 'principled' one, as if they were in some way opposites. However, in this article I

Chris Beckett is a Senior Lecturer in Social Work, Anglia Ruskin University, UK, and Review Editor of *Ethics and Social Welfare*. Correspondence to: Chris Beckett, Anglia Ruskin University, Webb Building, East Road, Cambridge CB1 1PT, UK; E-mail: C.O.Beckett@anglia.ac.uk will suggest that, on the contrary, realism (being prepared to deal with the world as it is) is an important ethical principle in itself, and one which social work practice and discourse quite often fail to meet. (In doing so I will develop an argument previously offered in Beckett & Maynard 2005, pp. 97–100, and Beckett 2006, pp. 27, 171ff.) I will suggest two ways in particular in which realism as an ethical principle should be applied by social workers and policy makers, but is sometimes not. I will call these (1) *Realism about Outcomes* and (2) *Realism about Context*. In both cases what I want to highlight is the fact that talk or actions are likely to be useless or even harmful, whatever the motive behind them, if they do not take into account the known or knowable facts about the specific circumstances to which the talk or action is applied.

Reality and Social Work

'Realism', both in general parlance and in its philosophical sense, refers to a stance which assumes the existence of an external reality and attempts to engage with that reality. The idea of an objective external reality—the novelist Philip Dick once called it 'that which, when you stop believing in it, doesn't cease to exist' (Dick 1991, p. 77)—is not, however, a very fashionable one. Many academic disciplines have for some time been preoccupied with arguing that what we call 'real' is dependent on viewpoint and social context (Michel Foucault spoke of a 'regime of truth' which each society 'makes function as real'; 1980, p. 131) and is a by-product of language and of power. What seems 'real' may be in fact a temporary social construction which does not even represent a consensus view in any sort of democratic sense, but rather reflects what is convenient for the powerful to portray as unchangeable.

It is not my intention in this article to deny these important insights. I do not want to suggest that 'reality' is unproblematic or to claim that any one of us is somehow able to be in direct contact with it. My own position is akin to the 'minimal' or 'subtle' realism (as opposed to 'naïve' realism) described by Parton and O'Byrne (2000, p. 173, drawing on Hammersley 1992), and to Roy Bhaskar's 'critical realism' (1989). Nigel Parton and Patrick O'Byrne offer the following formulation of a subtle realist position which I would endorse: 'The way reality is constructed and reconstructed is an active process and *reality is itself actively involved*' (2000, p. 174; my emphasis). We are word-weaving creatures, we live within nations, communities and systems of social relations that are ultimately 'imagined' (Anderson 1991) in the sense that they only exist because we choose to believe in them. But there is also an 'out there' reality which we cannot afford to ignore. Thus, as David Hume observed 200 years ago, regardless of our philosophical position, we all in practice accept the fact that when we leave a room we must go out through the door:

> Whether your scepticism be as absolute and sincere as you pretend, we shall learn by and by, when the company breaks up: we shall then see, whether you go

out at the door or the window; and whether you really doubt if your body has gravity, or can be injured by its fall; according to popular opinion, derived from our fallacious senses, and more fallacious experience. (Hume 1970 [1779], p. 132)

Just as we exit rooms via doors rather than windows, so in countless other ways we all acknowledge by our actions the existence of the constraints imposed on us by the world 'out there', regardless of our theoretical (or 'pretended') level of scepticism about the existence of objective reality. In particular we all accept in everyday life that there is an important distinction to be made between truth and falsehood, thereby implicitly acknowledging the existence of an external reality against which the truth claims of statements can be judged. It is difficult to see how the distinction between truth and falsehood could be accommodated if it were actually the case that there was no reality at all other than that which 'emerges from the linguistic acts of persons' (Parton & O'Byrne 2000, p. 22). But it is a distinction we need to make, and part of the case for realism as an ethical principle is that to deny reality is to deny the truth.

If we make no distinction at all between discourse and external reality, we are in danger of losing sight not only of the distinction between truth and falsehood but of the difference between aspiration and outcome. It is certainly important to have aspirations and to be alive to the possibility of changing things for the better, but aspirational talk per se is not a valid moral substitute for engagement with practical reality. In social work we are not always good at recognizing this. Our profession, and possibly particularly the academic branch of it, has a weakness for what Mark Doel and Peter Marsh call 'the Grand Statement ... unaccompanied by much in the way of practical advice' (1992, p. 7). But once we decouple our *talk* about what we do from consideration of what we might actually be able to do in specific, concrete situations, then the way is open for language to become a means not of communication but of concealment: a mask with which we deceive others and/or a blindfold with which we deceive ourselves. Leslie Margolin goes so far as to suggest that concealment is in fact the primary purpose served in social work by our elevated aspirations and our emancipatory rhetoric:

> the more intense the belief [on the part of social workers] in social work's essential goodness, the more immune it is to criticism, and the less clients are able to resist its ministrations. That is why social workers are continuously engaged in providing proof for themselves and their clients of the honorableness, sacredness, and utter veracity of their actions. (Margolin 1997, pp. 6–7)

Both the rhetoric of 'helping' and the more radical-sounding rhetoric of 'empowerment' are, according to Margolin, simply smokescreens for social control and the containment of deviancy (rather in the way that the Ministry of Peace, in Orwell's *1984*, was responsible in fact for waging perpetual war). Margolin's is an unnecessarily negative and one-dimensional view—it is not that difficult to find instances where social workers really have helped and empowered the recipients of their services—but I suggest we should take from him the important point that aspirations and noble-sounding rhetoric, unless continuously grounded and re-grounded in reality, can end up concealing something that is more or less opposite to what the aspirational words might seem to represent. Merely to sprinkle our discourse with words and phrases such as 'working in partnership', 'user-led', 'anti-oppressive' and 'empowerment' is in itself meaningless, and may actually make things worse rather than better if we are unable to spell out in concrete terms how such concepts might actually be applied to the specific practice context we are writing or speaking about.

So, for instance, if social work students write in essays that they 'work in partnership with' service users, I suggest that their teachers should challenge them to explain what is added to the meaning of the phrase 'work with' by the insertion of the phrase 'in partnership'. Otherwise two things will tend to happen. Firstly, the word 'partnership', unchallenged, simply becomes decoration, a purely formal addition to the word 'work', rather in the way that the meaningless phrase 'yours sincerely' is a purely formal addition to a polite letter. Secondly, the word 'partnership' becomes a deception, a fig leaf used to conceal something which is actually the opposite of partnership. I have heard social workers say they took family cases to court because the parents were 'unable to work in partnership'. I suggest that, while it is sometimes perfectly appropriate to take cases to court when children are at risk, it is an abuse of the word 'partnership' to apply it to a working relationship in which, if one party does not go along with the wishes of the other, they will be compelled by force to do so. To use the word 'partnership' in this context obscures the reality and degrades the word itself.

Similarly if their teachers make sweeping statements in lectures about the importance of, for instance, always respecting 'service user choice', I suggest that students should challenge them to spell out what this actually means when working, say, in a context of limited resources where demand far exceeds supply, or in a context (such as child protection or youth justice) where most service users are involuntary ones. By establishing the limits of a principle—the caveats, the competing principles, the practical constraints—we do not weaken it (as we might perhaps fear) but rather make it real and robust. (An analogy might be made with the string of a kite, which seems to hold the kite back, but in fact provides it with the necessary rigidity to hold it aloft.)

Realism in Practice

I now want to develop my argument by referring with examples to just two specific ways in which lack of realism, whether on the part of practitioners, policy makers or commentators, may in fact result in harm. Firstly, under the heading of '*Realism about Outcomes*' I will consider the harm that might be done to a child by a practitioner who is overly optimistic about the likely consequences of a course of action and will consider what ethical, realistic practice would entail in this practice context. (Although the example is from practice, it would be perfectly possible to think of examples where lack of realism about outcomes was a problem at the policy-making level.) Secondly, under the heading of *'Realism about Context'*, I will consider the harm that can be done by policy recommendations that take no account of the specific resource context in which the recommendation would be carried out. (This example is not from practice, but lack of realism about context can and does occur at the practice level too.) These are only two ways in which lack of realism can be a problem. I could have referred also to *'Realism about Competence'*, which is actually the one form of realism that is explicitly acknowledged in both British (BASW 2002) and American social work codes of conduct:

> 1.04 (a) Social workers should provide services and represent themselves as competent only within the boundaries of their education, training, license, certification, consultation received, supervised experience, or other relevant professional experience.
> (b) Social workers should provide services in substantive areas or use intervention techniques or approaches that are new to them only after engaging in appropriate study, training, consultation, and supervision from people who are competent in those interventions or techniques ... (NASW 1999)

I could also have discussed *'Realism about Mandate'*, which would involve recognizing that social workers are usually employed and legally mandated to perform certain specific functions, or *'Realism about Complexity'*, which would involve recognizing that real-world situations are messy and normally involve trying to balance different ethical principles which pull in different directions, rather than remorselessly applying one ethical principle without consideration for any other. I hope, however, that my two examples will suffice to illustrate what realism as an ethical principle might mean in a practice and policy context, and how current practice and policy might be described as falling short of it.

Realism about Outcomes

An 11-year-old child, neglected and abused in his family of origin, has been in public care for a year and has experienced several moves between foster-homes. His social worker has identified a new placement with a couple who are interested in offering long-term care. The social worker tells this child that this new home will be his 'forever family'. The social worker doubtless fervently hopes that this will indeed turn out to be true, and that the child will not have to endure further rejection, but my suggestion is that it is dishonest to describe a foster-home under such circumstances as a 'forever family', just as it would be dishonest of a surgeon to describe a procedure as a certain cure if in fact it carried a 50 per cent chance of failure. Research evidence suggests that the risk of breakdown is something in the region of 40 per cent for a child of this age (see PIU 2000, for instance) and a responsible social worker should take account of the likelihood of placement breakdown when choosing how to represent that placement to a child. She needs to think about what harm will be done to the child's capacity to trust adults and believe in what he is told if a placement is confidently presented as being for ever, but then breaks down.

This example illustrates the difficulties involved in talking about external reality as if it was something fixed and static because there is an important complicating factor in this situation: the fact that what the social worker says may well in itself make a difference to what actually transpires. (To use Roy Bhaskar's language (1989), the relationship between social worker and child is a subject–subject relationship, not a subject–object relationship such as exists between physical scientists and the objects of their study.) But the fact remains that, just by saying something, the social worker does not make it true. There exists a body of evidence 'out there' which can and should be used to determine how realistic and indeed how truthful and honest a description 'forever family' is likely to be. The social worker's choice of what to say to a child, and her choice of what to do, should equate to evidence as to likely outcomes and not simply to aspiration. June Thoburn has made this point very well:

> The reader of the statement 'the plan is permanence' at the end of a court report was led to believe that to plan for permanence was to achieve it. Little was said about the risks inherent in placement for adoption, which had to be balanced against the risks involved in children returning home or remaining in long term foster or residential care. (Thoburn 2002, p. 514)

In other words, when deciding whether 'planning for permanence' is a good idea, we should consider not only whether 'permanence' is a desirable objective but also whether 'planning for permanence' is in fact likely to *achieve* permanence, just as, if considering whether or not a particular surgical procedure was ethically justified, we would want to know not only what it was *intended* to achieve but its actual likely consequences. I do not mean by this that the moral worth of each action can be judged on its outcome, for 'even when one can demonstrate that one has chosen the unarguably optimal course of action, some proportion of the time the outcome will be suboptimal' (Macdonald & Macdonald 1999, p. 22). I am suggesting, though, that an action should be considered unethical if no serious consideration has been given to its likely consequences, and am suggesting that it is unethical to speak about the hoped-for outcome as if it were one and the same thing as the outcome that will actually occur.

Realism about Context

We all accept in practice (if not at some of the more rarefied levels of philosophical abstraction) that the laws of arithmetic are a reality. To adapt Hume, whatever our pretended scepticism, few of us would pay for a 40p chocolate bar with a £5 note without insisting on £4.60 in change (please substitute cents, euros, dollars, etc. as required) and few of us would be impressed by a post-modern confectioner who declined to give any change at all on the grounds that the laws of arithmetic were an arbitrary social construct. In the same way we all in practice accept that our physical nature and our location in space and time place certain restrictions upon us. I cannot be in Glasgow at 10 o'clock on Monday morning, if I also intend to be London at 10 that same morning. But these rather dull and mundane kinds of reality are, in my submission, often ignored in social work discourse. Social workers are frequently given guidance, whether by the government or in academic texts, which could in fact only work if they were able to do the logical equivalent of being at both in London and Glasgow at the same time.

The report by Lord Laming into the death of Victoria Climbié (Laming 2003) will provide a convenient illustration for the purposes of this discussion. For international readers I should explain that this was the report of an extensive inquiry into the cruel death in London of a little girl from Cote d'Ivoire, looking into the reasons why the professional system failed to prevent this tragedy. Here is one of the recommendations of the Climbié report:

> **Recommendation 26** Directors of social services must ensure that no case involving a vulnerable child is closed until the child and the child's carer have been seen and spoken to, and a plan for the ongoing promotion and safeguarding of the child's welfare has been agreed. (Laming 2003, p. 374)

On the face of it this recommendation seems ethically irreproachable. Yet closer examination reveals that the recommendation has almost no practical meaning at all. Consider first the word 'vulnerable'. This is a very vague term. It is quite possible to argue, after all, that *all* children are vulnerable. It is certainly possible to argue that all of the children who are referred to social work agencies, whether by their own families, by themselves, or by other agencies, are in some sense vulnerable, since they are all children who have been identified by themselves or others as having unmet needs. Since Recommendation 26 is prompted by the fact that Ealing Social Services, approached by Victoria's aunt for financial assistance and assistance with accommodation, did not see and speak to Victoria herself, we can assume that the recommendation does apply to this second group, that is to all children whose families are identified as having problems of some kind, and not just to children where there is some suspicion of abuse or mistreatment at the outset.

Now let us consider the practicalities of interviewing all children who are 'vulnerable' in those terms. The context in Ealing Social Services at that time was that a substantial proportion of the work of the relevant social work team was carried out with people from abroad presenting as homeless. In the vast majority of such cases the issue would have indeed been homelessness and poverty, not child abuse. I suspect that duty social workers dealt pragmatically with these cases by providing what help they could with accommodation and financial problems on the basis that helping with a family's homelessness problem was a way of helping its children. I suspect too that the agency was probably kept quite busy working in this way. If my surmise is correct, a requirement to interview every child and carer and come up with 'a plan for the ongoing promotion and safeguarding of the child's welfare' before closing each case would create serious problems for the service.

To get down to specifics, which is what the ethical principle of realism requires us to do, how much time would it take to fully implement this recommendation? There is no point in interviewing children unless this is done in a way that would yield useful information, but we know that children do not open up quickly to total strangers. They 'may need time, and more than one opportunity, to develop sufficient trust to communicate any concerns they may have' (DfES 2006, p. 119). In some cases (such as that of Victoria Climbié herself) interpreters would also have to be arranged and in many cases, including those in which parents came into the office without the children, it would be necessary to arrange follow-up home visits, with all the travelling time that that entails, in order to ensure that children were not merely seen but given real, as opposed to purely tokenistic, opportunities to express themselves. And, of course, any interview with children would have to be properly recorded if the information it yielded was to be useful to others.

Putting all this together, I would suggest that to implement in any meaningful sense the 'children being seen and spoken to' element of Recommendation 26 would require not just one but several extra hours of work for every child who would not previously have been interviewed separately. So where would this time come from and what other task should these social workers drop in order to be able to put this recommendation into practice? The Laming report is completely silent on this kind of question, as Eileen Munro has observed:

> The inquiry comments on several things that [a social worker] failed to do but tells us nothing about what she was doing instead. Presumably, they seemed more important to the worker at the time and, without further detail, how can we judge whether she was wrong or not? (Munro 2005, p. 537)

In fact, not only does the report make no comment on tasks that could be dropped to allow this recommendation to be implemented but it in fact makes a number of other recommendations which would also take up additional staff time.

The fact that there are only so many hours in a day is one of those dull everyday realities which those who write inquiry reports, books, newspaper editorials, academic papers and policy documents may if they wish overlook, but which those required to *implement* policy are inevitably up against, just as Hume's philosophers, rising from their learned debate about the nature of reality, were up against the fact that you have to go through a door to exit a room. It is not possible, in fact, to make useful (as opposed to *useful-sounding*) recommendations about risk management without reference to the specific resource context. In one context the introduction of a given procedural requirement might well be a step towards better risk management, but in another context *exactly the same procedural requirement* might make things worse, by diverting resources from some other function which was even more important. For example, suppose a social work agency tried to follow the above recommendation of the Laming report to the letter by requiring that every child referred to it was properly interviewed by a social worker before their case was closed, and suppose that this meant less time available for carrying out investigations of cases of suspected abuse. This might actually result in a net *reduction* in the amount of child maltreatment that the agency was able to prevent. A very high percentage of the interviews carried out to comply with this recommendation would, after all, not unearth any new evidence of child maltreatment. Only a very small proportion of the many hundreds of hours that agencies would spend on this activity would yield information that would result in a child being protected from harm. If time was limited, it might well be better spent on ensuring a proper response to cases where abuse was actually suspected and where thorough investigation was much more likely to result in children being protected from harm.

Usually the most difficult aspect of risk management is not identifying actions which might reduce the likelihood of undesirable outcomes, but deciding *which* of those actions to carry out in a context where you cannot do all of them. But this is something which the Laming report, in the company of much government guidance and a great deal of academic writing about social work, signally fails to get hold of. It criticizes social services departments, for example, for 'devising ways of limiting access to services' (para 1.52), yet also insists that:

> **Recommendation 52** Directors of social services must ensure that no case is allocated to a social worker unless and until his or her manager ensures that he or she has the necessary training, experience and time to deal with it properly.

Actually, in most, if not all, existing resource contexts it simply isn't possible to achieve the latter *without* restricting access to services. Writers on public services have long recognized that some form of rationing—however it might be dressed up—is inevitable in a public agency whose services are 'not actually sold to people at a price which yields a profit and are not withheld from people who cannot afford them' (Flynn 1997, p. 11). I know this from personal experience as a former team manager—I could either allocate every case where there was a recognizable need, or I could protect the workload of workers: *I could not do both*—but it should really be obvious to anyone with a grasp of basic arithmetic.

The sums are not difficult to do. If a social worker has 20 families on her caseload and works a 40-hour week, she has less than two hours per week per family to spend on all the visits, telephone calls, recording, travelling, completing forms and attending meetings that each family case requires. Actual contact time with family members would, of course, be far less than two hours: I understand that one local authority in my area calculated that contact time constituted only about one-eighth of an average social worker's week, in which case two hours per week per family would translate into one hour per month of actual contact with family members. This really is not very much time in which to achieve the hugely ambitious objectives which social workers set themselves and are set by others. One can understand the reluctance of managers, in a situation like this, to give a social work yet more cases to deal with, when her time is already stretched so thinly.

The lack of recognition of these kinds of reality in recommendations of the kind which I have just quoted means that they are in fact no more than 'wishlists' (Beckett 2006, pp. 175–76). They pretend to offer solutions to a problem but in fact they ignore the single aspect of the problem that really is difficult for those on the ground, merely passing this back to them to struggle with, and (in many resource contexts) to fail with. In this light I find such recommendations rather less ethically sound than they appear at first sight.

Eileen Munro and Martin Calder make a similar point, in a scathing critique of the UK policy agenda for children initiated by the Green Paper *Every Child Matters* (DfES 2003):

> They want to shift practitioners' focus *towards* preventative services; this has the logical implication of shifting the focus *away from* its current emphasis on child protection. The consequences of this have not been explicitly addressed, leaving it to agencies and individual practitioners to grapple with the inconsistency of being told to focus on family support without taking attention away from child protection. (Munro & Calder 2005, p. 444 original emphasis)

Conclusion: Counterfeit Money

> ... I suppose he began like other people; took fine words for good, ringing coin and noble ideals for valuable banknotes ... Later he discovered—how am I to explain it to you? Suppose the world were a factory and all mankind workmen in it. Well, he discovered that the wages were not good enough. That they were paid in counterfeit money. (From *Victory* by Joseph Conrad 1973 [1915], p. 166)

Advice that does not take into account the resource context may in fact be not only pointless but actually harmful because it serves to obscure the real issues. Writing not about child protection but about community care, Terry Bamford points out that the idea of user *choice* is 'rarely more than rhetoric' when it comes to the provision of social care services for the elderly, because 'choice requires surplus capacity if it is to be real'. But, as he points out, 'the *rhetoric* of choice *obscures* the unacknowledged conflict between user choice and needs-led assessment' (Bamford 1993, p. 38; my emphasis). In a similar way, Stephen Cowden and Gurnam Singh have argued that rhetoric about 'user involvement' can be a very convenient means for powerful actors 'to *mask the true nature* of the power relations that exist within society and the historical regulatory function of the state' (Cowden & Singh 2007, p. 19; my emphasis). For instance, imagine a situation in which the director of a social work agency employs members of a service users' organization to come and train her staff about the importance of giving choice to service users. Many interests are served. The trainers generate some income for themselves and are made to feel valued; the director is able to demonstrate that she has done her bit for service user involvement; the social workers are given a day out from the office. But, if in fact the lack of choice is the result of budgetary constraints rather than of staff attitudes, the training programme may have served above all the purpose of concealing this dreary and inconvenient fact, and may have resulted in no improvement whatever for the actual users of the service.

We are very easily seduced by aspirational talk and fine-sounding words. Murray Edelman (1985) gives many examples of the ways in which, in the arena of public policy, symbolic gestures may substitute for actual practical change and observes that 'reality can become irrelevant for persons very strongly committed to an emotion-satisfying symbol' (Edelman, 1985, p. 31). In politics, inspirational rhetoric about solving a given problem often serves as a substitute for *actually solving it*, and many interest groups can be satisfied by rhetoric alone, even though 'it is not uncommon to give the rhetoric to one side and the decision to another' (Edelman 1985, p. 39). But academic social work, even though it frequently takes a suspicious and oppositional stance to government policy (complaints about the curtailment of professional autonomy by 'managerialism' being, as Tony Evans & John Harris (2004) point out, particularly common) is often at least as guilty of 'wishlisting' as any government publication. Edelman observes that 'a dramatic symbolic life among abstractions' can become 'a substitute gratification for the pleasure of remolding the concrete environment' (Edelman 1985, p. 9). For a social work academic, writing in bold and radical terms about social work's world-transforming mission can surely sometimes be a rather satisfactory 'substitute gratification' for the much more modest, local and ambivalent changes that he or she was able to make, or would be able to make, as a social worker in practice.

Taken together, a significant amount of what is written and spoken about social work could be said to constitute a kind of pseudo-knowledge. It serves various purposes for those who produce it and for others, but it does not really enlighten or inform us on the questions which it ostensibly addresses. Judged in terms of its compliance with other broadly agreed ethical principles—such as the importance of protecting the vulnerable and standing up for the oppressed—such discourse may *appear* impeccable. But when it is judged against the reality principle it turns out to be something much more questionable: an evasion, a smokescreen, a method of shifting blame. Such discourse has a *symbolic* purpose—it is something to teach and write essays about, something to include in mission statements, something that can be used to reassure or placate various interested parties, something to accuse others of not complying with—but, in terms of *actually bringing about change* for the actual recipients of a social work service, it may achieve nothing at all or even make things worse.

280   BECKETT

In social work we are too ready both to accept and to dispense counterfeit money in place of 'good ringing coin'. I have argued here that a genuinely ethical stance is not about the ability to make aspirational statements but about grappling with practical realities, like the existence of resource constraints, the limits to what can be achieved with a given amount of time and skill and the fact that some things work and some things do not.

References

Anderson, B. (1991) *Imagined Communities*, Verso, London.

Bamford, T. (1993) 'Rationing: A Philosophy of Care', in *Rationing of Health and Social Care*, ed. I. Allen, Policy Services Institute, London, pp. 34–39.

BASW (British Association of Social Workers) (2002) *Code of Ethics for Social Work*, BASW, Birmingham.

Beckett, C. (2006) *Essential Theory for Social Work Practice*, Sage, London.

Beckett, C. & Maynard, A. (2005) *Values and Ethics in Social Work: An Introduction*, Sage, London.

Bhaskar, R. (1989) *The Possibility of Naturalism: A Philosophical Critique of the Contemporary Human Sciences*, 2nd edn, Harvester Press, Hemel Hempstead.

Conrad, J. (1973) *Victory*, Penguin, Harmondsworth.

Cowden, S. & Singh, G. (2007) 'The User: Friend, Foe or Fetish? A Critical Exploration of User Involvement in Health and Social Care', *Critical Social Policy*, Vol. 27, no. 1, pp. 5–23.

DfES (Department for Education and Skills) (2003) *Every Child Matters*, TSO, London.

——. (2006) *Working Together to Safeguard Children*, TSO, London.

Dick, P. (1991) *Valis*, Vintage Books, New York.

Doel, M. & Marsh, P. (1992) *Task-centred Social Work*, Ashgate, Brookfield, VT.

Edelman, M. (1985) *The Symbolic Uses of Politics*, University of Illinois Press, Urbana and Chicago.

Evans, T. & Harris, J. (2004) 'Street-level Bureaucracy, Social Work and the (Exaggerated) Death of Discretion', *British Journal of Social Work*, Vol. 34, no. 6, pp. 871–95.

Flynn, N. (1997) *Public Sector Management*, 3rd edn, Prentice Hall, Hemel Hempstead.

Foucault, M. (1980) 'Truth and Power', in *Michel Foucault: Power/Knowledge*, ed. C. Gordon, Harvester Wheatsheaf, Hemel Hempstead.

Hammersley, M. (1992) *What's Wrong with Ethnography: Methodological Explorations*, Routledge, London.

Hume, D. (1970) *Dialogues Concerning Natural Religion*, Bobbs-Merrill, Indianapolis.

Laming, Lord H. (2003). *The Victoria Climbié Inquiry*, TSO, London.

Macdonald, K. & Macdonald, G. (1999) Perceptions of Risk, in *Risk Assessment in Social Work and Social Care*, ed. P. Parsloe, Jessica Kingsley, London, pp. 17–52.

Margolin, L. (1997) *Under the Cover of Kindness: The Invention of Social Work*, University of Virginia Press, Charlottesville.

Munro, E. (2005) 'A Systems Approach to Investigating Child Abuse Deaths', *British Journal of Social Work*, Vol. 35, no. 4, pp. 531–46.

Munro, E. & Calder, M. (2005) 'Where has Child Protection Gone?', *Political Quarterly*, Vol. 76, no. 3, pp. 439–45.

NASW (National Association of Social Workers) (1999) *Code of Ethics of the National Association of Social Workers*, available at: <http://www.socialworkers.org/pubs/code/code.asp> (accessed July 2007).

Parton, N. & O'Byrne, P. (2000) *Constructive Social Work: Towards a New Practice*, Palgrave, Basingstoke.

PIU (Performance and Innovation Unit) (2000) *Prime Minister's Review on Adoption*, Cabinet Office, London.

Thoburn, J. (2002) 'Out-of-home Care for the Abused or Neglected Child: Research, Policy and Practice', in *The Child Protection Handbook*, 2nd edn, eds K. Wilson & A. James, Bailliere Tindall, Edinburgh, pp. 514–37.

[2]

What Social Workers Should Know About Ethics: Understanding and Resolving Practice Dilemmas

Elaine P. Congress

ABSTRACT: *Recognizing ethical issues and dilemmas that arise in professional practice is crucial for social work practitioners, educators, and students. After a discussion about the limited, although growing, literature on social work ethics, the ten main tenets from the most current NASW Code of Ethics are presented. These topics include limits to confidentiality, confidentiality and technology, confidentiality in family and group work, managed care, cultural competence, dual relationships, sexual relationships, impairment and incompetence of colleagues, application to administrators and relevance to social work educators. In addition to understanding the Code of Ethics, social workers can use the ETHIC model of decision making for resolving ethical dilemmas. This easy to use five step process includes examining personal, agency, client, and professional values, thinking about ethical standards and relevant laws, hypothesizing about consequences, identifying the most vulnerable, and consulting with supervisors and colleagues. A case example involving confidentiality, HIV/AIDS, and family therapy demonstrates how social workers can use the ETHIC model.*

While the social work profession has always been value-based and ethical practice has long been an educational concern (Pumphrey, 1959), within the last twenty years there has been increasing interest in this topic (Reamer, 1995b). Over the years the ethical focus has shifted from a focus on the morality of the client to the ethical behavior of the practitioner (Reamer, 1995b) and most recently to social work educators (NASW, 1996).

The NASW Code of Ethics provides a standard for ethical practice for social work practitioners and educators. This chapter has two objectives 1. a discussion of what is new about the current Code of Ethics and 2. a proposed model for ethical decision making (ETHIC) that is easy to apply to complex ethical dilemmas. The goal is to improve ethical practice and decision making among practitioners and educators.

Elaine Congress, DSW, is professor and director of the Ph.D. Program, Graduate School of Social Service Fordham University.

ETHICS AND PRACTICE

The social work value and ethical base for the profession has been reaffirmed in the centennial year of our profession (Reamer, 1998). In addition to generic texts on social work ethics (Lowenberg & Dolgoff, 1996; Reamer, 1995b; Rhodes, 1991), a review of *Social Work Abstracts* for the last decade lists thirty-one (31) professional journal articles on social work values and ethics. Many of these articles have focused on ethical concerns in health care (Abramson, 1990; Beauchamp & Childress, 1994; Callahan, 1994; Congress and Lyons, 1992; Fandetti and Goldmeier, 1988; Joseph and Conrad, 1989; Proctor, Morrow-Howell & Lott, 1993; Roberts, 1989). Other literature relates to different fields of practice including HIV/AIDS (Abramson, 1990), child welfare (Pine, 1987), and school social work (Berman-Rossi & Rossi, 1990; Congress & Lynn, 1994; Garrett, 1994). With the increase in malpractice litigation, more literature has focused on liability and malpractice issues (Houston-Vega, Nuehring, Dagio, 1997; Reamer, 1994). *Controversial Ethical Issues in Social Work* Practice (Gambrill and Pruger, 1996) considers ethical debates in social work practice, while two of the most recent books on social work ethics have focused on the new Code of Ethics (Congress, 1999a; Reamer, 1998).

CODE OF ETHICS

The first Code of Ethics for the National Association of Social Workers contained fourteen abstract statements listed on one page (NASW, 1960). The Code was revised and expanded in 1967, 1979, 1990, 1993, and 1996. Previous codes had been critiqued as not stressing professional standards (Jayaratne, Croxton, & Mattison, 1997). Although the previous code can be applied to social work educators (Lewis, 1987; Congress, 1992) and administrators (Congress, 1996), there were not specific sections referring to administrators (Congress & Gummer, 1996) and educators (Congress, 1992). Another concern was that the code spoke primarily about individual treatment concerns, rather than group work (Dolgoff and Skolnick, 1992). The current 27-page Code addresses many of these issues. Professional standards are presented, as well as sections on educators, administrators, and group workers (NASW, 1996). Included in the code is a description of core values, as well as ethical standards. While some standards are aspirational, others are enforceable guidelines for professional conduct. The Code of Ethics contains standards for social workers in six main areas: 1. responsibilities to clients, 2. responsibilities to colleagues, 3. responsibilities in practice settings, 4. responsibilities as professionals, 5. responsibilities to the social work profession and 6. responsibilities to society. The new Code was developed by a national committee of social work educators and practitioners appointed by the national NASW Board of Directors. This committee solicited input from professionals around the country before the Code was ratified by the NASW Delegate Assembly in August, 1996.

ETHICS AND SOCIAL WORK EDUCATION

More than forty years ago an early social work educator, Muriel Pumphrey (1959), identified the need to teach students about conflicting values in social work ethics. While ethical dilemmas in supervision have previously been identified (Levy, 1973; Cohen, 1987; Congress, 1992a), ethical challenges for faculty advisors around conflicting duties and responsibilities to school, agency, and student have recently been identified (Congress, 1997). A new area in social work ethics, dual relationships, has been discussed in the context of social work education (Congress, 1996).

The Curriculum Policy statement mandates that social work values and ethics be included in curriculum (CSWE, 1996). How should students learn this content? Should ethics be taught as a discrete course or integrated throughout the curriculum? Research suggests that a discrete course may be more effective in teaching social work students about values and ethics (Joseph, 1991; Joseph and Conrad, 1983; Reamer and Abramson, 1982). A discrete course in ethics can be used to integrate ethics into different areas of required curriculum (Congress, 1993). While in 1989 only 10% of accredited graduate programs offered a separate required or elective course on ethics (Black, Hartley, Whelley, & Kirk-Sharp, 1989), recent research suggests that almost half of graduate programs may offer either a required or elective course on ethics (Congress, 1999).

Students may study social work ethics in a separate course or in many courses. Yet much of ethical behavior is learned through observing their teachers (Congress, 1992b; Congress, 1997; Lewis, 1987). Ethical standards "caught" by students may be more significant than what is taught (Lewis, 1987, p. 3). This speaks to the importance of the social work educator not only knowing the Code of Ethics, but also incorporating ethical standards into educational practice.

NEW PROVISIONS IN CODE OF ETHICS

Preliminary research in this area suggests that even advanced social work practitioners are not that aware of new code provisions (Congress, 1999.) While not exhaustive, the following ten areas focus on new issues in the Code of Ethics:

1. Limits to confidentiality

While the earlier Code of Ethics prevented the disclosure of information only for "compelling professional reasons," the new Code of Ethics spells out what these compelling professional reasons are. (NASW, 1993, p. 4; NASW, 1996, p. 10). Social workers are advised to maintain confidentiality, except when it is necessary to prevent serious, foreseeable, and imminent

4   *Congress*

harm to a client or other identifiable person. Confidentiality can be
breached in reporting child abuse, as the child may be at risk of harm. Also
social workers are able to violate confidentiality when a client is suicidal or
homicidal. The social worker who suspects child abuse or works with a
suicidal client can feel supported by the current Code of Ethics in making a
decision to breach confidentiality.

While the 1996 Code originally contained the phrase "when laws or
regulations require disclosure without a client's consent" the 1999 Delegate
Assembly amended the Code of Ethics to exclude this phrase. There was
concern about the growing number of state laws regarding reporting of
undocumented people or homosexual couples who want to adopt children.
These laws are seen as contrary to our ethical principles that oppose
discrimination against people because of legal status or sexual orientation
(NASW, 1999).

2. Confidentiality in technological age

For the first time, social workers are advised to protect confidentiality in
the use of computers, electronic mail, fax machines and telephone answering
machines. Disclosure of identifying information should be avoided
whenever possible.

While students were previously advised not to leave charts open on their
desks when they went to lunch, they now learn to protect confidentiality by
computer passwords and firewalls (Rock & Congress, 1999).

Fax machines present new confidentiality challenges to social workers.
Often they are not housed in individual offices, but rather in public office
areas where they are accessible to all. Faxed reports are often sent to a fax
number with limited knowledge of where they arrive. One social worker
recently reported that he frequently received hospital discharge summaries as
the number of his home fax machine differed only slightly from that of a
large nursing home. Despite the use of passwords, telephone voice mails
and e-mail do not protect confidentiality, as they can often be accessed by
others.

There are no easy answers. With each new technological advance,
confidentiality as we know it is changed forever. To provide for minimal
standards of confidentiality in an increasingly less private world, social
workers may have to delineate differing degrees of sensitive information
and provide differentially for the securing of confidential information. (Rock
& Congress, 1999).

3. Confidentiality - family and group work

While previous codes focused primarily on individual work in clients
(Dolgoff and Skolnick, 1992; Dolgoff and Skolnick, 1996), the new code

addresses confidentiality issues in group and family work (NASW, 1996). The inclusion of ethical issues about groups and families is especially relevant as many social workers see clients in groups and families rather than only individually (Ginsberg, 1995). In providing services to groups and families, social workers should seek agreement with all parties about the importance of maintaining confidentiality, but also inform participants that it cannot be guaranteed.

Because other group members as well as family members are usually not professional social workers, the social worker cannot have the expectation that they will maintain confidentiality. Yet the social worker can explain the importance of confidentiality and discuss with the client group or family how the worker will handle confidential information.

4. **Managed care**

While managed care is not cited specifically in the new Code, social workers are advised to inform clients of limits to services because of the requirements of third party payers in sections about informed consent (NASW, 1996, 1.03a, p.7-8) and confidentiality (NASW, 1996, 1.07 d, e, and f, p. 10-11). Although social workers debate about whether managed care threatens client and worker autonomy (Munson, 1996) and confidentiality (Davidson and Davidson, 1996), "managing ethics under managed care" has been seen as possible, although challenging for social workers (Reamer, 1997). Social work practitioners must be alert to when managed care conflicts with social work ethics. Challenges to confidentiality with extensive reporting to managed care companies, as well as limits to service for vulnerable populations, are two main areas of ethical concern. Social work practitioners can be active as client advocates in preserving clients rights in a managed care environment.

5. **Cultural competence**

For the first time, the new Code includes a section on cultural competence and social diversity. Social workers are now expected to understand culture and its function in human behavior with an emphasis on the strengths perspective. Social workers are advised to develop a knowledge base of their clients' culture and demonstrate competence in providing services to people from different cultures. Finally, the current Code mandates social workers to "obtain education about and seek to understand the nature of social diversity and oppression with respect to race, ethnicity, national origin, color, sex, sexual orientation, age, marital status, political belief, religious, and mental or physical disability" (NASW, 1996, p.9).

A concern about this code provision is how realistic is the expectation that social workers know about all their client cultures, especially in large urban areas with clients from many countries. One social worker who worked in the emergency room of a large public city hospital reported that in the course of the day she had seen clients from twenty different cultural backgrounds. Asking clients about their cultural backgrounds has been seen as a therapeutic and empowering method to use in learning about clients' cultures (Ortiz-Hendricks, 1997).

Another key question is, does learning about characteristics of specific cultures lead to over generalization and stereotyping about cultural characteristics? Self examination is often an important first step in developing cultural and social sensitivity (Aponte, 1991: Ho, 1992; Ortiz-Hendricks, 1997). Also asking clients about specific aspects of their cultural backgrounds and completing a culturagram (Congress, 1994) have been seen as helpful in this area.

6. Dual relationships

The current Code of Ethics states that social workers should avoid dual relationships in which there is risk of exploitation or potential harm to clients (NASW, 1996). When the primary relationship is therapeutic, social workers should not enter social, business, or educational relationships with clients. If dual relationships cannot be avoided, the responsibility is on social workers to set appropriate culturally sensitive limits. Dual relationships in agency practice may lead to role reversal (Kagle and Giebelson, 1994), while dual relationships in academia may lead to exploitation of students with limited power (Congress, 1996).

After much debate at the Delegate Assembly, the provision about dual relationships appeared for the first time in the 1993 Code of Ethics. Many social workers, especially in rural areas, indicated that avoiding dual relationships with clients was impossible. In small towns often clients' children went to school with social workers' children. Social workers and their clients often attended the same PTA meetings. Because dual relationships at times cannot be avoided, social workers—not clients—should assess if the relationship is potentially exploitative or harmful to the client.

While almost all social workers report that sexual relationships with current clients are unethical, they are much less certain about friendship and employment relationships with former clients (Borys and Pope, 1989). Discussing the appropriateness of dual relationships with other colleagues and applying the ETHIC model of decision making can strengthen their skills in deciding when dual relationships are unethical and should be avoided.

7. Sexual relationships, physical contact, and sexual harassment

The current Code has very extensive prohibitions about sexual relationships with clients.. While the previous code only addressed the avoidance of sexual relationships with current clients, the new Code forbids sexual contact with former clients, future clients, clients relatives, or close friends.

While almost all practitioners believe that sexual contact with current clients is unethical (Borys and Pope, 1989; Gechtman, 1989), there is less consensus about intimate relationships with former clients (Jayartne, Croxton, & Mattison, 1997). Social workers are more likely to condone relationships with former clients if the initial contact has been brief, occurred many years ago, and did not involve psychodynamic therapy. The overwhelming majority (95%) of social work educators believe that sexual contact with current students is unethical, while a much smaller percent (60%) in contrast to practitioners believe that sexual contact with former students (clients) is unethical (Congress, 1999).

The current code prohibits social workers from engaging in physical contact with clients when there is possibility of psychological harm. The responsibility rests with the worker to set appropriate boundaries. While the provision about physical contact with clients arose primarily because of concern about sexual abuse of children, the extent of appropriate physical contact with children is often debated.

A prohibition about sexual harassment with clients and colleagues is also included in the current code. Most agencies, as well as schools, have policies about sexual harassment. Despite institutional policies, however, more than half of the graduate social work programs report one or more incidents of sexual harassment (Singer, 1994). Because cases of sexual harassment often become a school or agency secret, the actual incidence of sexual harassment may be much higher.

8. Impairment and incompetence of colleagues

While in the previous 1993 Code a social worker who believed a colleague's impairment due to personal problems, psychosocial distress, substance abuse, or mental health difficulties interfered with practice effectiveness was advised to consult with that colleague, the new Code extends that responsibility. If the colleague refuses to address the issue and seek help for the problem, the social worker is now advised to take action through employers, agencies, NASW, licensing, and regulatory bodies.

Practitioners must assume responsibility for ensuring that social work colleagues not engage in impaired or incompetent practice. Many professional social workers, as well as students, can report occasions on which professional social workers demonstrated poor practice because of substance abuse, burnout, or mental health problems.

At times, substance abuse becomes an agency secret, similar to a family secret about which all know, but rarely speak. Practitioners quite accurately perceive that they have limited power and fear that if they speak to colleagues about substance abuse problems or report impaired behavior to supervisors, then their own occupational progress might be jeopardized. Often NASW can and does provide support to social workers about how to talk with colleagues about substance abuse problems and how to pursue the problem through other channels (Congress and Fewell, 1994).

9. Application to administrators

While the earlier NASW Code seemed to apply primarily to direct service practitioners, the new Code includes a section specifically on administration. Social work administrators are advised to advocate for resources in and outside of agencies to meet client needs. They should seek to allocate resources in an open and fair manner. When all clients needs cannot be met, they are required to develop an allocation procedure that is nondiscriminatory. The need to provide adequate staff supervision, as well as a working environment consistent with the Code of Ethics, is also enumerated.

Many direct service practitioners believe that administrators are "above" the Code of Ethics. It is important that practitioners learn that the Code of Ethics applies to administrators who often must struggle with making decisions about the equitable distribution of scant resources (Congress, 1996). Practitioners need to become aware of how ethics affect everyone in an agency (Levy, 1983).

10. Education and Training

For the first time the new Code of Ethics specifically addresses issues for educators and trainers. Social work educators are advised to provide instruction only in their areas of competence, and this instruction should be based on the most current knowledge and information. Dual relationships with students should also be avoided when there is a risk of harm or exploitation to the student.. An important new Code provision codified an acknowledged field instruction practice, i.e. that social workers should ensure that clients are informed when students provide services (Feiner and Couch, 1985; NASW, 1996).

In their roles as field instructors, practitioners are required to keep current about social work knowledge and practice skills. This mandate is especially challenging for social work supervisors now with the influx of new knowledge and research in the social sciences. Continuing education for social work supervisors is especially crucial at this time.

ETHICAL DECISION MAKING

Being informed about the current Code of Ethics, however, is only an initial step for social workers, as frequently they encounter ethical dilemmas in which there is a conflict of social work values and/or ethical principles. As Perlman (1975) has written, a social work value has little value unless it can be translated into ethical practice. Only to know about the Code of Ethics does not make one an ethical practitioner.

How social workers resolve ethical dilemmas has been a subject of some concern to the profession. Social workers are often guided by two main principles. The first beneficence (or positive obligations) speaks to providing good, while the second principle nonmalfeasance (or negative obligations) relates to causing no harm (Reamer, 1995b). Both principles affect ethical decision making. Those who favor beneficence would most likely take a proactive stance, while those favoring nonmalfeasance would favor the least intervention. Social workers acting from a nonmalfeasance perspective might decide to take no action and wait for further results.

Although social workers may not be aware of this, they frequently rely on two philosophical models—deontological and teleological—in resolving ethical dilemmas (Reamer, 1995b). Deontological thinkers believe that social work values such as self determination and confidentiality are so absolute and so definitive of the profession that to deny them would lead to distrust of the professional.

Many social workers, however, use a teleological approach that involves examining the consequences of the situation. Deontologists and teleologists, however, do not always find themselves on opposite sides, as two deontological thinkers might argue about the importance of two contradictory absolute principles such as self determination or the protection of society. In a similar way two teleological thinkers might envision two very different consequences of their decisions.

Most social workers use a combination of deontological and teleological thinking. One can argue that the values of the social work profession are deontological in nature, but often social workers use teleological consequential arguments to decide complex ethical dilemmas. Many social workers do not use a philosophical approach at all, but base their decisions on practice wisdom

(Walden, Wolock, Demone, 1990) or the Code of Ethics (Congress, 1992). Although there has been a proliferation of books and articles on ethics over the last twenty years, the number of ethical decision making models are few. Lewis (1984) first developed a model of ethical decision making that incorporates both deontological and teleological thinking but proposes that the deontological approach should prevail. Reamer (1995) proposes a deontological system based on Rawls' theory of justice and Gewirth's rank ordering of conflicting duties. Lowenberg and Dolgoff (1996) use a hierarchical model in which different social work values are ranked to help social workers arrive at the best ethical choice.

Social workers, however, frequently make speedy decisions without much deliberation (Wolock, Walden, Wolock, Demone, 1990). This may be related to limited time in which to make decisions, as well as perceived organizational constraints. Moreover, social work practitioners may approach ethical decision making with dread due to fear of making the wrong decision in a litigious environment. There also is anxiety that the process of ethical decision making will require a consideration of very weighty, abstract principles that may seem very removed from practice realities.

In order to make ethical decision making fast and simple and apply to a variety of ethical dilemmas, the ETHIC model of decision making was developed to help social workers make ethical decisions as quickly and as effectively as possible (Congress, 1999a). The following model includes social work values, the Code of Ethics, and the social work context. Based on an easily remembered acronym, the ETHIC model is presented in Table 1 and described more fully below:

TABLE 1. ETHIC Model of Decision Making

E   **Examine relevant personal, societal, agency, client and professional values.**

T   **Think about what ethical standard of the NASW code of ethics applies, as well as relevant laws and case decisions.**

H   **Hypothesize about possible consequences of different decisions.**

I   **Identify who will benefit and who will be harmed in view of social work's commitment to the most vulnerable**

C   **Consult with supervisor and colleagues about the most ethical choice.**

Examine relevant personal, societal, agency, client and professional values.

Personal, societal, agency, client and professional values all influence ethical decision making. The social worker who relies only on professional values is not likely to have a full understanding of important contextual issues to use in making decisions. An important initial step for social workers is to assess their own personal values if they want to avoid making decisions based on their personal, rather than professional values. Furthermore, an examination of client values is very important, especially with culturally diverse clients whose values may differ from the personal and professional values of many traditional social workers. An example of this occurred when an Anglo social worker became increasingly aware that she was imposing her personal and professional values about self determination on an adolescent client who based his personal educational objectives on family responsibilities.

A discrepancy between agency and professional values can also produce conflict for the social worker. For example, the social worker supported the professional value of confidentiality, yet in an attempt to promote greater efficiency in handling records the agency had introduced a new computer program with inadequate safeguards to protect confidentiality.

Think about what ethical standard of the NASW code of ethics applies, as well as relevant laws and case decisions.

The ethical standards in the NASW Code of Ethics are divided into six sections:

1. Social workers' ethical responsibilities to clients

2. Social workers' ethical responsibilities to colleagues

3. Social workers' ethical responsibilities to practice settings

4. Social workers' ethical responsibilities as professionals

5. Social workers' ethical responsibilities to the profession

6. Social workers' ethical responsibilities to the broader society.

If the ethical dilemma involves an issue about appropriate treatment for clients, the social worker might want to examine the section under responsibilities to clients. Topics in this section include conflicts of interest, self determination, informed consent, confidentiality, access to records, and issues about payment for service and termination of service.   The standards can be viewed as deontological (absolute) principles for the social work profession.

Social workers need to be cognizant of relevant federal, state, and local laws that may affect the ethical dilemmas they encounter.   Social work ethics is different from, but often parallels, legal regulations.   While laws and social work ethics usually coincide, there may be times when they conflict (Thompson, 1990; Dickson, 1995; Dickson, 1998).   The social worker needs to be aware when a law or regulation may be unethical.   Discriminatory laws about reporting of undocumented people or homosexual couples may be current examples.

Hypothesize about possible consequences of different decisions.

This step makes use of teleological reasoning to resolve ethical dilemmas. If protecting confidentiality is a concern, the social worker should think about different scenarios, one in which confidentiality is maintained, and the other in which confidentiality is violated. The social worker can list pros and cons about maintaining confidentiality versus breaking confidentiality. Examining possible results helps the social worker decide which is the preferred alternative for the ethical dilemma.

Identify who will benefit and who will be harmed in view of social work's commitment to the most vulnerable

Often social workers must decide between two bad alternatives, rather than one that is clearly right and clearly wrong (Keith-Lucas, 1977).   This step may elicit very convincing reasons for or against different courses of action, especially when the Code of Ethics seems to support contradictory decisions.

Social work has had a lengthy tradition of concern for the most vulnerable in our society.   The concern for the most vulnerable may distinguish social work from other professions (Lewis, 1972). On a macro level, concern for the most vulnerable has been proposed as a governing principle in regard to downsizing (Reisch & Taylor, 1983).   As the current Code proposes that "social workers should act to expand choice and opportunity for all persons, with special regard for vulnerable, disadvantaged, oppressed, and exploited persons and groups" (NASW, 1996, p 27), this step is most important for social workers in resolving ethical dilemmas.

Consult with supervisor and colleagues about the most ethical choice

Although often ethical decision making occurs alone,   talking to other colleagues who can suggest alternatives or present new information can be very helpful. A social worker who has a supervisor should use this person as a first resource in ethical decision making.   With current cutbacks, more experienced workers and even beginning workers may have minimal supervision. Social workers are encouraged to bring questions about ethical dilemmas to other colleagues for informal consultation. Sometimes, ethical dilemmas can be presented as part of a case conference and social workers can help the agency develop ethics committees.

The formation of ethics committees may be especially useful in a multi-discipline agency in which the social worker works with other professionals who may not share social work values and ethics (Joseph and Conrad, 1989.) Differences between social workers and doctors (Roberts, 1989) and public school educators (Congress and Lynn, 1994) have been noted. When social workers participate in ethics committees, however, their decisions about ethical dilemmas are often respected by other members (Joseph and Conrad, 1989).

APPLYING THE ETHIC MODEL

Since the first identification of HIV/AIDS as a very serious, but greatly stigmatized health problem in the early 1980's, the social work profession has continued to stress the importance of maintaining confidentiality in working with people with AIDS. Preserving confidentiality has been seen as essential to the establishment and continuation of a helping relationship. (Abramson, 1990).

With the spread of AIDS to the heterosexual population and more specifically to those with no known risk behavior, maintaining of confidentiality surrounding AIDS has been questioned. The development of medications that have transformed AIDS from a terminal to chronic illness has also led to the need to know early who is affected even if confidentiality is at risk.

The new Code of Ethics promises confidentiality except when "disclosure is necessary to prevent serious, foreseeable, and imminent harm to a client or other identifiable person" (NASW, 1996, p.10). This principle relates to the Tarasoff Decision in which the courts established a duty to warn an identified victim by stating that "the protective privilege ends when the public peril begins." (Tarasofff 1976: 336-337.) Some have argued that the Tarasoff case is not applicable to the AIDS situation, as often there is not an identifiable victim. Also, violating a client trust may have negative consequences for the client continuing with treatment and/or engaging in safe sexual practices. Others have argued that an HIV-positive individual places an uninformed sexual partner at risk and thus is relevant to the Tarasoff case. The courts as well as ethicists seem to be divided about the correct course of action, but a model of ethical decision making can help the clinician understand more clearly the issues involved and begin to resolve the ethical dilemma of duty to warn with clients who are HIV positive.

The following case example illustrates the application of the ETHIC model in marital therapy when one is HIV-positive.

Marlene, an experienced MSW, was seeing the Smith family for marital therapy. Their conflicts had increased steadily over their four-year marriage. One of their main stressors was financial (Tom had not been able to work steadily, but occasionally found short term construction jobs, while Joan worked full-time as a cashier at a local grocery store). Another involved their futile attempts to start a family. Both came from a large family and wanted many children, but after trying for four years they still did not have any children. Joan's only pregnancy had ended in a miscarriage at three months. Another area of concern was that Tom was increasingly coming home late from construction jobs after stopping off at a local bar to have a few beers with his friends. One afternoon, Marlene received a frantic call from Tom. Recently he had applied and been accepted for a maintenance job at a local hospital and he was completing routine medical tests needed for employment. His test for HIV antibodies had come back positive. He knew there must be some mistake. He was going to have the test repeated, but he had called Marlene because he just needed to talk to someone. Tom felt that he could not tell his wife as she might leave him. She would be sure to blame him for causing his own illness because he had a three-day drinking binge last year when he disappeared from the house and returned not remembering anything that had happened during this period of time. Tom repeatedly asked Marlene not to tell his wife. He reminded Marlene that he had been promised confidentiality when he first began treatment.

In an attempt to resolve this ethical dilemma, Marlene applied the ETHIC model:

Examine relevant personal, social, agency, client and professional values.

Marlene began to look very carefully at her own countertransference reactions to people with AIDS. Many social workers have negative attitudes toward people with AIDS. (Ryan & Rowe, 1988). Marlene realized that although her professional education had taught her otherwise, she felt that a person afflicted with AIDS had almost all the time brought it upon themselves. She thought about homosexuals who were very sexually active, about IV drug users who continued to exchange needles despite the risks. She remembered her family's "black sheep," her second cousin who had been abusing drugs since early adolescence and had died last year of AIDS. She wondered if she blamed

Tom for not pursuing help with his alcohol problem earlier and thus avoiding his three-day binge and infection with the HIV virus.

In terms of her treatment of this couple, Marlene wondered if she was always more supportive of Joan, as trying harder to make the marriage work. She also thought that her identification and greater support of the wife in a marital couple might be related to her interest in feminist issues.

Marlene knew about negative social values regarding people with AIDS. She acknowledged that her own personal values had been in part shaped by societal tendency to blame the victim. Often, people with AIDS are thought to be responsible for their illness because of their behavior either as a member of a stigmatized population of homosexuals or IV drug abusers. Similar to the worthy and unworthy poor concept, Tom would be considered an unworthy AIDS victim as he "brought the illness on himself," while Joan, if she were to contract the disease, would be viewed as a "worthy" AIDS victim as she caught the disease unknowingly as the wife of an infected person.

What were the agency's values about AIDS, about confidentiality? Marlene knew that the mental health agency where she worked did not have any written policies about AIDS, despite a large number of clients who were HIV-positive. She wondered if her agency was similar to many agencies in which not talking about AIDS, maintaining it as a secret, was a way of denying its existence. Her agency did have policies about confidentiality. Most of these policies, however, were written about individual clients, despite the fact that increasingly clients were seen in marital, family or group modalities.

What were the client values? Joan realized that as a marital therapist she must understand the values of both her clients. She knew now that Tom seemed to place a high value on confidentiality, perhaps a lesser value on keeping the relationship together. Marlene was less clear about Joan's values about confidentiality, probably because it had never been challenged. She did know that Joan was very committed to maintaining the marriage, no matter what problems the couple had.

Finally, Marlene examined professional values. She knew that the social work profession believed that people with HIV/AIDS were often stigmatized in society. Maintaining confidentiality was seen as an important way to prevent discrimination. Yet she knew that as a professional, she had a responsibility to both clients. Concerned with ethical issues in regard to working with a couple, she had discussed in the beginning how information should be shared with both people, that she would not maintain "secrets" with one member, yet she never anticipated that the secret would be AIDS, about which there was a strong demand to maintain confidentiality.

Think about which Ethical Standard of the NASW Code of Ethics applies, as well as relevant laws and case decisions.

Marlene looked carefully at the new Code of Ethics in trying to decide what would be the best course of action. She read about clients' "right to privacy (and protecting) the confidentiality of all information obtained in the course of professional service, except for compelling professional reasons" (NASW, 1996, p. 2). She wondered if protection of Joan and a possible child was a "compelling professional reason" for which "disclosure is necessary to prevent serious, foreseeable, and imminent harm to a client or other identifiable person." (NASW, 1996, p. 2) The state she lived in supported maintaining strict confidentiality about HIV status. Marlene knew there had been some attempts to apply the Tarasoff case in terms of duty to warn to HIV/AIDS cases, but that the results had been mixed.

Hypothesize about different courses of action and possible consequences.

Marlene tried to think through various courses of action. If she maintained confidentiality, Tom would be pleased. He would continue to come to see her to work with Joan on their marriage. Furthermore, he could receive her support and help in addressing psychological or physical consequences of his HIV/AIDS diagnosis. He could be encouraged to share his health status with his wife at a later time.

On the other hand, there might be serious consequences of not sharing with Joan information about Tom's HIV status. Joan might not be HIV-positive and every day Marlene delayed informing Joan increased the risk of her also being HIV-positive, especially as they were trying to have children. If Joan learned after the fact that Marlene had known about the risk of exposure to AIDS and did not share this information, she could sue Marlene for exposing her to a "clear and imminent danger." Also, by maintaining Tom's confidentiality, Marlene seemed to be promoting Tom's right to confidentiality as more important than Joan's right to well being. When two clients have conflicting positions, Marlene would appear to be siding with one partner, by entering into a collusion around the AIDS secret.

What would be the consequences of violating confidentiality? The best possible scenario is that Joan will be saved from becoming HIV-positive and will be very supportive of Tom. Tom may secretly thank Marlene for telling Joan the secret he could not share. A more negative consequence is that Tom will leave treatment, break up his marriage, or have increasing binges which might increase the possibility of AIDS infection for others. Also, he could charge Marlene with a violation of confidentiality through the NASW Committee on Inquiry, the State Licensing Board, and/or the state court system.

Identify who will benefit and who will be harmed in view of social work's commitment of the most vulnerable.

If Marlene maintained confidentiality, it would seem that Tom would benefit since his HIV status would remain secret. It can be argued, however, that this would only be time limited. Joan would be harmed in that she would remain uniformed about her exposure to the HIV virus, and furthermore, there is a risk to her anticipated child.

If Marlene decides to tell Joan about Tom's HIV status, Joan will benefit in that she can avoid exposure to HIV virus and also the possibility of giving birth to an HIV infected child. One can anticipate, however, that there may be some harm to Tom in terms of a violation of confidentiality and trust in the therapeutic relationship.

The current Code of Ethics speaks of our professional responsibility to vulnerable people and social work literature has repeatedly addressed the fact that the rights of the most vulnerable should prevail (Lewis, 1972; Reisch and Taylor, 1983). One might argue in the above case example that Joan is the more vulnerable and thus the benefit to her should have greater weight than the benefit to Tom.

Tom and Joan's differing rights are in conflict in this case example. While the principle of confidentiality (Tom's right) is certainly a basic principle in social work practice, the principle of preservation of life (Joan's right) seems more important. While conflicting benefits were in question, a hierarchy of rights such as presented by Lowenberg and Dolgoff (1996) may be helpful.

Consult with supervisor and colleagues about the most ethical choice.

At lunch Marlene discussed the dilemma with two of her colleagues and received conflicting advice. One social worker believed that Marlene definitely should call up Joan, as she (Marlene) had the power to avoid another person being affected with AIDS. Also, Joan was her client, too. What was her responsibility to protect Joan? Her other colleague was concerned about the violation of confidentiality. How could Tom or for that matter Joan ever trust Marlene again? What was the effect on developing a trusting relationship with a client if confidentiality could be so easily violated? Did not Marlene realize why the social work profession had stressed that knowledge about HIV/AIDS must be treated with the utmost confidentiality? By violating confidentiality, did Marlene increase the possibility of stigma and discrimination against Tom as well as Joan?

Unlike many graduates with two years experience, Marlene still had the benefit of a supervisor whom she saw regularly. Her supervisor suggested that Marlene think about what she had discussed about confidentiality with her client. Marlene remembered that at the beginning of therapy she had engaged in an extensive discussion about confidentiality with both Tom and Joan. Ironically, Tom had then raised concerns that Joan would be repeatedly calling Marlene with criticisms about him that Joan would not bring up in the joint sessions. They had then made an agreement that whatever was discussed individually would then have to be brought up in the general session and that Marlene as therapist would support and facilitate the process.

Marlene then used the earlier discussion of confidentiality in terms of this new information. She finally encouraged Tom to share with Joan in a joint session about his HIV status and was there to provide continual support for the couple. Ironically, what seemed to be a major stressor—Tom's HIV-positive diagnosis—brought the couple closer together as both Tom and Joan decided to work jointly on coping with this new problem.

The preceeding discussion illustrates the application of the ETHIC model to an ethical dilemma about AIDS and confidentiality. It also demonstrates the importance of establishing confidentiality guidelines early in work with individuals and couples. One can ask if the situation would have been different if Joan had not been a client. Would Marlene have had any responsibility to share HIV status with a nonclient partner? What about nonclient multiple partners? The duty to warn of the Tarasoff decision has not been applied when there are multiple nonspecific victims (Reamer, 1991).

SUMMARY AND IMPLICATIONS

This paper had two purposes 1. to inform practitioners and educators about the main new provisions in the current Code of Ethics and 2. to present an easily applicable model of ethical decision making. In recent years, the number of charges about unethical practice of social workers has grown (Reamer, 1996). We are also most aware that we live in an increasingly litigious time. Furthermore, there is greater complexity surrounding ethical issues because of greater use of technology, managed care, and medical advances. As social work educators, we must strive to educate future social workers about how to identify and resolve professional dilemmas. How we as educators model ethical practice with students, however, is equally if not more important than what we teach students didactically about ethics (Lewis, 1987; Congress, 1994).

As practitioners, we must struggle with increasingly complex ethical dilemmas. The ETHIC model provides an easy to apply model in a work environment that is increasingly demanding. The last step of the ETHIC model—Consult with supervisors and colleagues—may be especially important when facing thorny dilemmas. Unfortunately, supervision has decreased even

Ethical Practice and Professional Dilemmas *19*

for new graduates in the current environment of diminished social service resources.

When there is minimal supervision, both new and experienced social workers must assume primary responsibility for informal consultation with colleagues within and outside the agency. Continuing education programs and NASW can also be resources for professional social workers struggling with complex ethical dilemmas in the new millennium.

REFERENCES

Abramson, M. (1990). Ethics and technological advances: Contributions of social work practice. *Social Work in Health Care, 15*(2), 5-17.

Abramson, M. (1990). Keeping secrets: Social workers and AIDS. *Social Work, 35*(2), 169-173.

Aponte, H. (1991). Training of the person of the therapist for work with the poor and minorities, *Journal of Independent Social Work 5*(3/4), 23-39.

Beauchamp, T. & Childress, J. (1996). *Principles of biomedical ethics* (4th ed.). New York: Oxford Press.

Berman-Rossi, T. & Rossi, P . (1990). Confidentiality and informed consent in school social work. *Social Work in Education, 12*(3), 195-207.

Black, P.; Hartley, E.; Whelley, J.; & Kirk-Sharp, C. (1989). Ethics curricula: A national survey of graduate schools of social work. *Social Thought XV*(3/4), 141-148.

Borys, D. & Pope, K. (1989). Dual relationships between therapist and client: A national study of psychologists, psychiatrists, and social workers. *Professional Psychology: Research and Practice, 20*(5), 283-293.

Callahan, J. (1994). The ethics of assisted suicide. *Health and Social Work, 19*(4), 237-252.

Cohen, B. (1987). The ethics of social work supervision revisited. *Social Work, 32*(3), 194-196.

Congress, E. (1992a). Ethical decision making of social work supervisors. *The Clinical Supervisor, 10*(1), 157-169.

Congress, E. (1992b). Ethical teaching of multicultural students: Reconsideration of social work values for educators. *Journal of Multicultural Social Work, 2*(2), 11-23.

Congress, E. (1993). Teaching ethical decision making to a diverse community of students: Bringing practice into the classroom. *Journal of Teaching in Social Work, 7*(2), 23-36.

Congress, E. (1994). The use of the culturagram to assess and empower culturally diverse families. *Families in Society, 75*, 531-540.

Congress, E. (1996). Dual relationships in academia: Dilemmas for social work educators. *Journal of Social Work Education, 32*(3), 329-338.

Congress, E. (1997). Value dilemmas of faculty advising: Significant issues in a Code of Ethics for faculty advisors. *Journal of Teaching in Social Work, 14*(2), 89-110.

20   *Congress*

Congress, E. (1999a). *Social work values and ethics: Identifying and resolving professional dilemmas.* Chicago: Nelson Hall.

Congress, E. (1999b). *Dual relationships in academia.* Unpublished research study.

Congress, E. & Fewell, C. (February/March, 1994). Recognizing substance abuse in a colleague: What can I do? What should I do? *Currents.* New York: NASW.

Congress, E. & Gummer, B. (1996). Is the Code of Ethics as applicable to agency administrators as direct service providers. In E. Gambril and R. Pruger, *Controversial issues in social work ethics, values, and obligations* (pp.137-150.) Boston: Allyn Bacon.

Congress, E. & Lynn, M. (1994). Group work programs in public schools: Ethical dilemmas and cultural diversity. *Social Work in Education,* 16(2), 107-114.

Congress, E. & Lynn, M. (1997). Group work practice in the community: Navigating the slippery slope of ethical dilemmas. *Social Work with Groups* 20(3), 61-74.

Congress, E. & Lyons, B. (1992). Cultural differences in health beliefs: Implications for social work practice in health care settings. *Social Work in Health Care,* 17(3), 81-96.

Council of Social Work Education. (1996). *Curriculum Policy Statement.* Alexandria, VA: Author.

Davidson, J. & Davidson, T. (1996). Confidentiality and managed care: Ethical and legal concerns. *Health and Social Work,* 21(3), 208-215.

Dickson, D. (1995). *Law in the health and human services.* New York: The Free Press.

Dickson, D. (1998). *Confidentiality and privacy in social work.* New York: The Free Press.

Dolgoff, R. & Skolnik, L. (1992). Ethical decision making, the NASW Code of Ethics and group work practice: Beginning explorations. *Social Work with Groups,* 15, 99-112.

Dolgoff, R. & Skolnik, L. (1996). Ethical decision making in social work with groups. *Social Work with Groups,* 19,(2), 49-65

Feiner, H. & Couch, E. (1985). I've got a secret: The student in the agency. *Social Casework,* 66(5), 268-274.

Garrett, K. (1994). Caught in a bind: Ethical decision making in schools. *Social Work in Education 16,* 2, 97-106.

Gechtman, L. (1989). Sexual contact between social workers and their clients. In G. Gabbard (ed.), *Sexual exploitation in professional relationships* (pp. 27-38). Washington, DC: American Psychiatric Press.

Ginsberg, L. (1995). *Social work almanac.* Washington, DC: NASW Press.

Ho, M. (1991). The use of the ethnic sensitive inventory (ESI) to enhance practitioner skills with minorities. *Journal of Multicultural Social Work,* (1), 57-68.

Houston-Vega, M., Nuehring, E.; & Daguio, E.(1997). *Prudent practice: A guide for managing malpractice risk.* Washington, DC: NASW Press.

Ethical Practice and Professional Dilemmas *21*

Jayaratne, S; Croxton, T. & Mattison, D. (1997). Social work professional standards: An exploratory study. *Social Work, 42*(2), 187-199.

Joseph, V. (1983). The ethics of organizations: Shifting values and ethical dilemmas. *Administration in Social Work, 7*(3/4), 47-57.

Joseph, V. (1991). Standing for values and ethical action: Teaching social work ethics. *Journal of Social Work Education, 5*(2), 95-109.

Joseph, V. & Conrad, A. (1989). Social work influence on interdisciplinary decision making in health care settings. *Health and Social Work, 14*(1), 22-30.

Kagle, J. & Giebelhausen, P. (1994). Dual relationships and professional boundaries. *Social Work, 31*(2), 213-220.

Kagle, J. & Kopels, S. (1994). Confidentiality after Tarasoff. *Health and Social Work, 19*(3), 217-222.

Keith-Lucas, A. (1977). Ethics in social work . In *Encyclopedia of Social Work* 17th Ed. (pp. 350-355). Washington, DC: NASW.

Levy, C. (1973). The ethics of supervision. *Social Work, 18*(3), 14-21.

Levy, C. (1983). *Guide to ethical decisions and actions for social service administrators: A handbook for managerial personnel.* New York: Haworth Press.

Lewis, H. (1972). Morality and the politics of practice. *Social Casework, 5*(3), 404-417.

Lewis, H. (1984). Ethical assessment. *Social Casework, 65*(4), 203-211.

Lewis, H. (1987). Teaching ethics through ethical teaching. *Journal of Teaching in Social Work, 1*(1), 3-14.

Lowenberg, F. & Dolgoff, R. (1996). *Ethical decisions in social work practice.* Itasca, Ill: Peacock Publishing.

Munson, C. (1996). Autonomy and managed care in clinical social work practice. *Smith College Studies in Social Work, 66*(3), 241-259.

National Association of Social Workers (1960). *Code of ethics.* New York: NASW

National Association of Social Workers (1993). *Code of ethics.* Washington, DC: NASW.

National Association of Social Workers. (1996). *Code of ethics.* Washington, DC: NASW.

National Association of Social Workers. (1999, November 1999). Ethics and Reporting Eyed after Assembly. *NASW NEWS*, p. 5.

Ortiz Hendricks, C. (1997). The child, the family, and the school: A multicultural triangle. In E. Congress, *Multicultural perspectives in working with families.* (pp. 37-60). New York: Springer Publishing.

Perlman, H.(1975). Self determination: Reality or illusion? In. F. McDermott (Ed.), *Self determination in social work.* (pp. 65-89). London: Routledge and Paul Kegan.

Pine, B. (1987). Strategies for more ethical decision making in child welfare practice. *Child Welfare, 66*(4), 315-326.

Proctor, E; Morrow-Howell, N. & Lott, C. (1993). Classification and correlates of ethical dilemmas in hospital social work. *Social Work, 38*(2), 166-177.

Pumphrey, M. (1959). *Teaching of values and ethics in social work education.* New York: Council of Social Work Education.

Reamer, F. (1991). AIDS: The relevance of ethics. In F. Reamer, *AIDS and ethics.* (pp. 1-25). New York: Columbia University Press.

Reamer, F. (1994). *Social work malpractice and liability: Strategies for prevention.* New York: Columbia University Press.

Reamer, F. (1995a). Malpractice claims against social workers: First facts. *Social Work, 40*(5), 595-601.

Reamer, F. (1995b). *Social work values and ethics.* New York: Columbia University Press.

Reamer, F. (1997). Managing ethics under managed care. *Families in Society,* 96 –106.

Reamer, F. (1998). *Ethical standards in social work: A critical review of the NASW Code of Ethics.* Washington D.C.: NASW Press.

Reamer, F. (1998). The evolution of social work ethics. *Social Work, 43*(6), 488-500.

Reamer, F. & Abramson, M. (1982).*The teaching of ethics XI: The teaching of social work ethics.* Hastings on the Hudson, NY: The Hastings Center.

Rhodes, M. (1991). *Ethical dilemmas in social work practice.* Milwaukee, WI: Family Service America.

Reisch, M. & Taylor, C. (1983). Ethical guidelines for cutback management: A preliminary approach. *Administration in Social Work, 7* (3/4),.59-72.

Roberts, C. (1989). Conflicting professional values in social work and medicine. *Health and Social Work, 14*(3), 211-218.

Rock, B. & Congress, E. (1999). The new confidentiality for the 21st century in an managed care environment. *Social Work, 44*(3), 253-262.

Singer, T.(1994). Sexual harassment in graduate schools of social work: Provocative dilemmas. In M. Weil, M. Hughes, and N. Hooyman, *Sexual harassment and schools of social work: Issues, costs, and strategic responses* (pp. 25-37). Alexandria, VA: Council on Social Work Education.

Tarasoff v. Board of Regents of University of California (1976). 17 Cal 3d 425. Thompson, R. (1990). *Ethical dilemmas in psychotherapy.* New York: The Free Press.

Walden, T., Wolock, I. & Demone, H. (1990). Ethical decision making in human services. *Families in Society, 71*(2), 67-75.

Address correspondence to: Elaine Congress, DSW, Professor and Director of the Doctoral Program, Fordham University Graduate School of Social Service, 113 West 60th Street, New York, NY 10021, (212)636-6627, congress@fordham.edu

[3]

A Client-Focused Definition
of Social Work Practice

Eileen Gambrill

University of California, Berkeley

The 1958 working definition of social work practice highlights past and current paradoxes, competing interests, confusions, and mystifications in social work. Outcomes are not mentioned in this definition, reflecting the lack of attention to describing variations in services and their outcomes. This, as well as not clearly distinguishing between objectives selected based on what is good for society and what is valued by individual clients, reveals this definition not to be client focused. The definition downplayed social control functions of social work and controversies concerning how problems are defined. A definition that encourages practitioners to focus on their key responsibility—providing services most likely to help clients attain goals they value while considering others' interests—is needed. Current interest in describing variations in practice and their outcomes, attending to populations and individuals in the distribution of scarce resources, and increased Internet access to practice- and/or policy-related research findings may encourage such a definition.

Keywords: *ethics; client outcomes; professions; evidence-based practice*

Harriet Bartlett (1958) suggested that it is the particular "configuration of value, purpose, sanction, knowledge, and method" (p. 5) that makes social work practice and distinguishes it from the practice of other professions. We were asked to consider whether her definition "works" in view of current realities. Current realities include the nature of social work practice today, what is written about it in professional literature and other sources such as newspapers, and external circumstances including changing demographic, employment, and funding patterns and changing standards of practice in other professions (e.g., evidence-based practice). Realities include the following:

1. Social work practice is varied.

Author's Note: Correspondence concerning this article should be addressed to Eileen Gambrill, School of Social Welfare, Haviland Hall, University of California, Berkeley, CA 94720; e-mail: gambrill@uclink4.berkeley.edu.

2. There is an overlap between the problems social workers address and the knowledge, skills, and values they use with other professions and with nonprofessionals.

3. The problems clients confront are influenced by political, social, and economic factors.

4. The profession of social work claims special expertise to address a broad range of client outcomes.

5. There are large gaps between claims of effectiveness (see Number 4) and evidence for such claims. In fact, there is counterevidence, as illustrated by mandated receivership of child welfare services in many U.S. states. There has been little rigorous critical appraisal of variations in social work practices and their outcomes (e.g., do they do more good than harm?); thus, most services social workers provide are of unknown effectiveness. Good intentions are relied on as indicators of good outcomes.

6. There is no evidence that social workers possess knowledge of unique value in relation to attainment of many outcomes compared with nonprofessionals (e.g., see Christensen & Jacobson, 1994; Dawes, 1994).

7. Purchase of services is not evidence based (e.g., based on demonstrated effectiveness and efficiency of services selected).

8. Exposés of social work practice and policy by journalists are common (e.g., Roche, 2000).

9. Social work is a gendered profession composed mostly of women.

10. Vague outcomes are pursued, such as social justice.

11. There is increasing emphasis on managed care in the helping professions.

12. Licensing and accreditation bodies such as the National Association of Social Workers and the Council on Social Work Education rely on surrogates of competence and high-quality professional education, such as diversity of faculty and size of faculty, degrees, and experiences.

13. There is increasing emphasis on transparency of what is done to what effect in professions such as medicine and on evidence-based practice: "the conscientious, explicit, and judicious use of current best evidence in making decisions about the care of individual [clients]" (Sackett, Rosenberg, Gray, Haynes, & Richardson, 1996, p. 71). It involves "the integration of best research evidence with clinical expertise and client values" (Sackett, Straus, Richardson, Rosenberg, &. Haynes, 2000, p. 1). Involving clients as informed participants is emphasized (e.g., see Edwards & Elwyn, 2001; Entwistle, Sheldon, Sowden, & Watt, 1998).

14. There is increasing access to Internet sources that critically appraise practice- and policy-related research findings (e.g., http://www.cochraneconsumer.com), including sources designed to enhance critical appraisal skills (e.g., http://www.phru.org.uk/-casp/resources/index.htm).

15. Standards are lower today for student admission to social work programs and for student evaluation (grade inflation).

16. There are large gaps between professional rhetoric regarding the importance of attending to environmental factors related to personal problems and what is done in everyday practice; social workers have joined the psychiatric bandwagon in the medicalization of personal and social problems.

17. Clients are typically not informed regarding the evidentiary status of recommended services (e.g., that there is no evidence that these are effective or do

more good than harm) or involved in designing, conducting, and interpreting critical tests of the effectiveness of social work services.
18. There seems to be an inverse correlation between growth of the profession and problems solved.

Does Bartlett's (1958) definition work in view of these realities and, if so, for whom and in what ways—for clients (e.g. to maximize the likelihood of receiving effective, efficient, and ethical services), for social workers (to honor obligations described in our code of ethics), for the public in understanding what social work is all about, for taxpayers (getting value for money), or for the profession (e.g., to maintain and expand turf or to clearly describe goals and values)? Interested parties that may lose or benefit from certain definitions include other professional groups from which we hope to distinguish ourselves, legislators and philanthropic groups from which we hope to gain funds, potential students whom we hope to recruit, and clients whom we hope to entice and help. Different definitions may yield different costs and benefits (e.g., better and more students, more funds, and more status). One reason for defining social work practice is to demark social work from other professions and groups that compete for the same clients (e.g., see Abbott, 1988; Friedson, 1986), allowing it to maintain and expand its turf. The more distinctive (e.g., low cost) and valuable a profession sounds, the more it may guard and expand its turf. The more lofty and praiseworthy a definition sounds, the more others (particularly those with money such as legislators) may be impressed and promote and contribute to the maintenance and expansion of the profession. This is one source of the aspirational nature of social work definitions. The vaguer is the definition and the less transparent is what is done and to what effect, the more flexible are the boundaries of tasks social workers may assume and the easier it is to assert success because no one knows what has been sought or achieved. Given that social work has expanded during the past decade in numbers of social workers employed, programs funded, and professional schools offering degrees, this function has been served. This is true although there is no evidence that services do more good than harm or that educational programs prepare social workers who offer services most likely to achieve outcomes clients value at minimal cost and harm.

Another reason for defining a profession is to help potential users of a profession's services to understand what people in a profession value, do, and achieve and to help both clients and professionals to select efficient, effective, and ethical services. This does not seem to be the key reason here because there is little clear description of variations in services provided and their outcomes. A related reason is to describe a profession's mission and the methods likely to achieve it so that maximum progress can be made in desired directions (i.e., solving problems). Nor does this seem to be the purpose because of the reason previously described and because the mission (e.g., to foster social justice) is vague, hindering description of progress. Indeed, there seems to be a negative correlation between expansion of the profession and problems solved.

VALUE, PURPOSE, AND SANCTION: OBSCURED CLASHES BETWEEN THE INDIVIDUAL AND "SOCIETY"

Bartlett's (1958) definition illustrates two features common to social work throughout its history: the pursuit of vague, idealized purposes (e.g., "to seek out, identify, and strengthen the maximum potential in individuals, groups, and communities," p. 6), and obscuring who (e.g., the individual or representatives of "society") is to decide on what outcomes to pursue (e.g., indicators of maximum potential), how to pursue them, and what criteria to use to make these decisions. (Gordon, 1962, accurately noted that some items included under value in the 1958 statement, such as "There is interdependence between individuals in the society," are matters of empirical investigation, not of value.) Bartlett suggested that "an essential attribute of a democratic society is the realization of the full potential of each individual and the assumption of his social responsibility through active participation in society" (p. 6). Such definitions are aspirational, idealized, religious-like descriptions of deepest hopes. How would one know when full or maximum potential is reached? We could never arrange all environments in which all potentials could flower in a lifetime, even if we had the resources required to do so, and it is not in social work's power to achieve these aims.

Social work has long promised what it cannot deliver in vague terms (e.g., erase poverty). Some may object: "What's the harm?" or "Isn't this a good goal to pursue?" Advantages of idealized definitions include offering hope and inspiration to both clients and professionals. Potential harms include misleading clients, funding bodies, and social workers by encouraging them to believe social workers have powers they do not possess, and distracting them from the pursuit of attainable goals such as decreasing avoidable miseries and arranging a just distribution of scarce resources by fully funding services known to be effective with money saved by not funding services found to be ineffective or harmful. Such definitions distract attention from clearly describing problems of concern to clients and discovering their prospects for resolution. Grandiose promises may yield adverse outcomes such as burnout resulting from the pursuit of unattainable goals and other dysfunctional responses, such as ritualized "services" (those offered although there is little likelihood they will help clients). Idealized, vague definitions create a gap between what is promised and what can be delivered that may undermine social work's credibility in the eyes of social work's many constituencies, and given the trend toward greater transparency of what is done to what effect in the helping professions, this is likely to be an increasing danger. Popper (1994) suggested that we should focus on minimizing avoidable suffering and argued that there is likely to be agreement on what this is. He (as well as others) argued that pursuit of grand social aims such as social justice is ill-advised because what may be justice for some may be injustice for others (i.e., result in imposing unwanted circumstances on some). An idealized view of social work practice is also reflected in the little attention given to errors, mistakes, and accidents that may negatively affect clients, some (or many) of which may be avoidable. Bartlett (1958) suggested that "the individual social worker always makes his own creative contribution in the application of social work methods to any setting or activity" (p. 8). There is no recognition that this creative activity may do more harm than good. Rather, there is a serene assertion (without foundation) of beneficence and good intent with little attention to related evidentiary issues.

An idealized, broad, vague role of "society" is posed in this early statement: "Society has a responsibility to provide ways in which obstacles to this self-realization (i.e., disequilibrium between the individual and his environment) can be overcome or prevented" (Bartlett, 1958, p. 6). (Some would argue that life itself consists of restoring a balance when disequilibriums occur.) How far can this responsibility be exercised against the individual's consent (e.g., consider involuntary commitment)? Who is to say what a disequilibrium is? Who is to say what is "maximal potential" and of what our "social responsibilities" consist (representatives of social institutions or the individual)? The very first statement in Bartlett's (1958) article is, "The central responsibility of a profession is to maintain and promote in all possible ways the effectiveness of its service to society" (p. 3). Notice the appeal to society, not to clients. Social control functions are integral in this appeal (e.g., consider child protective services, efforts to "adjust" how women in settlement houses dressed, such as not to wear "babushkas," and involuntary commitment). Of what does society consist if not the social institutions and related policies and legal regulations for dealing with the dependent, the troubled, and the troubling?

Society is composed of people who make decisions about what is good and what is bad, what to praise and what to punish, what to give and what to deny, and what is healthy and what is not. These decisions are reflected in social welfare institutions. Szasz (1994) argued that the helping professions mainly function to handle problems that arise in all societies regarding the dependent, the troubled, and the troubling. Based on a review of case records from 1859 to 1970, Margolin (1997) suggested that social work has been involved in judging and evaluating clients since its inception and that an ever-changing variety of strategies is used on the part of social workers to kid themselves that they are helping and serving when indeed they are judging and evaluating. Thus, although idealized definitions sound benevolent, they hide a troubling latitude of discretion as well as of unwanted and unacknowledged value judgments and intrusion (coercion and manipulation) into clients' lives. Denial of social control functions and reluctance to acknowledge the lack of evidentiary basis for professional services seems to result in a number of unfortunate effects for clients, such as ignoring informed consent requirements.

Definitions of social work practice based on the institutions in which social workers are employed, such as child welfare departments and public welfare agencies, are more suggestive of the social control functions of social workers. Bartlett's (1958) description of sanctions included "governmental agencies authorized by law, voluntary incorporated agencies and the organized profession." Governmental agencies authorized by law as well as voluntary agencies "have taken responsibility for meeting certain of the needs or providing certain of the services necessary for individual and group welfare" (p. 6). Criteria used to decide what is necessary for individual and group welfare are not described, allowing hidden value judgments that may be imposed on clients. Pursuit of "maximizing potential" may focus on change that fits the values of these authorities. Social control functions in social welfare institutions range from the obvious (involuntary commitment) to subtle manipulation (e.g., encouraging clients to view certain behaviors as dysfunctional when such judgments are arbitrary value judgments; e.g., see Margolin, 1997; McCormick, 1996).

CONFUSION, CONTRADICTIONS, AND MISLEADING DIRECTIONS

Reflective of modern-day practices in Bartlett's (1958) statement are gaps among values promoted, knowledge viewed as valuable, and methods emphasized. Certain values are missing, such as the value of nonmalfeasance—not harming in the name of helping. Although there is an emphasis on the importance of considering interrelationships between individuals and their environments in the section on knowledge, this is not complemented by such an emphasis in the section on methods. Only 1 of the 16 techniques (Number 15) Bartlett listed concerns the environment: "Effecting change in immediate environmental forces operating upon the individual or groups" (p. 7). The relationship between social workers and clients is selected for special attention. Findings that nonprofessionals are as effective as professionals in helping clients achieve a wide range of outcomes suggest that relationship factors are important (e.g., see Christensen & Jacobson, 1994; Dawes, 1994). However, this research also suggests that professional training is not needed to successfully pursue many outcomes of interest to social work clients. Thus, if there is a central core in social work, an argument could be made that much of this core is shared by other helping professions as well as by nonprofessional helpers. (This does not mean that social workers may not possess specialized knowledge in some areas that contributes to success and does not mean that professional education is required to develop such special knowledge and skills.)

There is a contradiction between the emphasis on relationships between individuals and their environments and the emphasis on use of self as a key method social workers employ. This contradiction remains today. In the Purpose section, Bartlett (1958) emphasized helping "individuals and groups to identify or minimize problems arising out of disequilibrium between themselves and their environment" (p. 6). Yet, in the Method section, we find that

the social work method is the responsible, conscious, disciplined use of self in a relationship with an individual or group. Through this relationship the practitioner facilitates interaction between the individual and his social environment with a continuing awareness of the reciprocal effects of one upon the other. (p. 7)

The latter statement also illustrates empirical questions stated as assertions, a common practice today in social work publications. That is, relationships are claimed as established rather than suggested as possible and in need of critical testing.

Because it is the first word in social work, one would think a great deal of attention would be paid to the social; however, the social is often forgotten in everyday practice. Knowledge in environmental psychology and applied behavior analysis is routinely ignored. Social work has allowed psychiatric views to chip away at social work's historic concerns with interrelationships between behavior and the environment. Many social workers have embraced a psychiatric approach to problems in living (e.g., viewing drinking problems as "brain diseases") and given that they are the main providers of mental health services in the United States, this has a significant impact on clients, for example, overlooking options for altering environmental contributors. The social gets little attention in this biomedicalization of personal and social problems (e.g., see Kutchins & Kirk, 1997). Indeed, one could argue that

many social workers fly under a false flag; they call themselves social workers but in large part are psychiatric workers. There are, of course, many
exceptions. Orchestrating many different services to meet the needs of a client, family, group, organization, or community has been a claimed strength of
social work. If social workers are to be effective, efficient, and ethical orches-
trators of resources, they must use a contextual view to understand problems
and their prospects for resolution, drawing on research findings that may
decrease uncertainty about how (or if) a problem can be successfully
addressed.

Empirical and conceptual matters seem to be confused in Bartlett's (1958)
concern with "the inability of the profession to state clearly what knowledge,
skills and values are needed by every social worker for basic competence in
practice" (p. 4). Pursuit of this aim requires empirical investigation of the
relationships of knowledge and skills to attainment of certain outcomes.
Bartlett highlighted "the lag in study of practice" (p. 3). She suggested that
"building of a professional curriculum program . . . should rest upon understanding of the basic knowledge, values, and skills essential for competent
practice" (p. 3). Did she mean identification via empirical research? ("Understanding" may stop at the conceptual or consensual level of analysis, unaccompanied by description of empirical relationships found among certain
values, knowledge, skills, and outcomes sought.) If so, we still do not have
this information after 60 years. Social work has preferred the method of opinion polls (agreement that a given competency is important often stated so
vaguely that what is referred to is unknown). Time and money are spent on
seeking people's opinions about what works and then calling these "empirically derived competencies." We have not described variations in practices
and related outcomes. What information we do have suggests an overlap
between professionals and nonprofessionals in skills used and outcomes
attained.

Bartlett (1958) discussed the role of research in defining social work practice, at many points suggesting its importance in exploring "what has been
accomplished and where gaps exist" (p. 5). She emphasized that "this means
looking at what professionally trained social workers are doing" (p. 8); 1
would add, to what effect? She suggested studying only what "professionally
trained social workers are doing" (p. 8) and recommended postponing study
of the "untrained worker." What we need are comparative studies of these two
groups to identify what may be unique competencies and successes of social
workers. Clients are an absent voice in who should be involved in research
efforts. "To do all this, professional social workers and research experts must
work together" (Bartlett, 1958, p. 9). To see how much things are changing
regarding this, see Hanley, Truesdale, King, Elbourne, and Chalmers (2001).

Bartlett (1958) suggested that one major obstacle to movement in the practice area seems "to have been the lack of any comprehensive scheme by which practice could be analyzed" (p. 3).

> It will be necessary to develop from the working definition of practice a conceptual scheme for classification of conditions (problems) encountered and services rendered in social work practice. Then, and only then, say the research advisors, can adequate research designs for the study of practice be formulated. (p. 9)

(Note again the ignoring of outcomes.) She suggested that "a major obstacle to movement in the practice area seems to have been the lack of any comprehensive scheme by which practice could be analyzed" (Bartlett, 1958, p. 9).

There is a concern with the need for development of research instruments to assess outcome in this early discussion. Clients have real-life problems; we can identify specific subjective and objective indicators of clients' unique goals and track them to determine if hoped-for outcomes are attained and to what degree. We do not need research instruments to evaluate progress, and clear description of problems, related outcomes, and service methods does not have to await the development of a classification scheme. This same kind of distracting argument can be seen today. For example, one objection to the use of client-oriented indicators of high-quality professional education is that we do not know how to measure outcome. Maybe if we involved clients in our deliberations, they could help us out here.

CLIENT-FOCUSED DEFINITIONS

I suggest we use a definition of social work that reflects guidelines in our code of ethics, in which services to clients are emphasized, and that we can be most attentive and faithful to our code if we adopt a client-focused, outcome definition of social work practice. Bartlett's (1958) definition does not work, especially for clients. Little attention is given to key ethical issues of beneficence, nonmalfeasance, and autonomy. Autonomy issues are hidden in appeals to society. Just as we have found harm in other professions such as medicine and dentistry, harm also occurs in social work, perhaps most often by ignoring programs that have been found to help clients and using ineffective services instead. Consider, for example, research by Blenkner, Bloom, and Nielsen (1971) indicating that intensive case management increased mortality of nursing home residents compared with the usual procedures. A number of critical appraisals of social work services show that services we think are effective are really not (e.g., see Meyer, Borgatta, & Jones, 1965; Schuerman, Rzepnicki, & Littell, 1994).

Idealized definitions appealing to society's obligations threaten client interests by their vagueness, impossibility of fulfillment, and hiding of coercive and manipulative aspects of social work practice (e.g., imposing values regarding what is healthy and what is not; e.g., see McCormick, 1996). They discourage careful evaluation of service outcomes, including the possibility of harming in the name of helping, which is also a threat to clients. Vague definitions of social work involving grandiose claims and aims (e.g., we alone cannot attain them) put clients last rather than first in that false promises are made and we are distracted from pursuit of achievable outcomes. Vague, grandiose definitions also harm social workers and the profession by decreasing opportunities for successful problem resolution. Definition by sanction reflected in place of employment (e.g., public agencies authorized by law) ignores client interests if there is no focus on provision of effective, efficient, and ethical services. Bartlett's (1958) statement contains no mention of client outcomes and the importance of discovering what they are. Indeed, an outcome focus in medicine is only recent (e.g., see Sharpe & Faden, 1998). We see in the Knowledge section "the social services, their structure, organization, and methods" (Bartlett, 1958, p. 7); outcomes are not included. A client-oriented outcome definition would go something like this: Social work practice consists of helping clients achieve outcomes they value via provision of effective, efficient, and ethical services. It makes "conscientious, explicit and judicious use of current best evidence in making decisions about clients," involving clients as informed participants (Sackett et al., 1996, 2000).

Client-focused definitions of social work practice encourage us to honor our values and codes of ethics in coercive as well as voluntary settings (e.g., regarding informed consent and competent practice). They highlight obligations to integrate practice- and policy-related research findings when making decisions that affect clients' lives, especially in coercive situations in which clients are reluctant actors. For example, what percentage of parent-training programs provided to parents involved in child protection agencies are those most likely to result in hoped-for outcomes as demonstrated by rigorous research? Even if this is as high as 25% (unlikely), we are not being faithful to our code of ethics (i.e., to offer competent services). Clients have the right to know the evidentiary status of services they are offered. Outcome-oriented definitions suggest how to solve the generalist-specialist problem—by encouraging rigorous research (not opinion polls, as is now the custom) designed to discover the values, knowledge, and skills required to provide effective, efficient, and ethical services in different areas of practice.

Client-oriented definitions encourage us to attend to beneficence, nonmalfeasance, and autonomy. Such definitions should encourage social workers to find out, via rigorous appraisal, (a) if services do more good than harm, (b) if services are efficient in terms of cost and effort, (c) if ethical obligations to clients are honored in deed as well as intention (e.g., informed consent), (d) if avoidable mistakes are minimized within comprehensive risk-management programs (e.g., see Gambrill & Shlonsky, 2001), (e) if judicious use is made of nonprofessionals when such individuals provide as good or better services compared with professionally trained social workers, and (f) if there is a reasoned distribution of scarce resources (e.g., harmful services are not funded, services of unknown effectiveness are not funded unless they are being investigated within a rigorous research design, and programs found to help clients are fully funded, allowing their implementation at a level that maximizes the likelihood of achieving hoped-for outcomes; e.g., see Gray, 2001). The absence of such information reveals definitions of social work to be non–client focused.

Bartlett (1958) noted "the lag in the study of practice" (p. 3). Social work has in large part ignored such study. What is needed is the study of practice and its outcomes in relation to available research findings regarding what services have been found to be effective, efficient, and ethical. Counter to Bartlett's suggestion to postpone studies of the untrained worker, what is needed is to discover the unique competencies of trained social workers (if any) compared with untrained people in relation to outcomes attained. Indeed, it seems that there is a profound scrutiny phobia in social work: an aversion to clearly describing what social workers do and to what effect as well as to clearly describing gaps between what research findings suggest is effective in relation to given hoped-for outcomes and what services are used in everyday practice. Other reasons for avoiding transparency (clearly describing variations in services and their outcomes) might include a basic lack of empathy for clients or caring more about jobs and expansion of services than about discovery whether services do more harm than good and hinder rather than foster a just distribution of scarce resources. Yet another reason may be because professional education programs discourage transparency of what is done and to what effect (e.g., by their absence of critical appraisal of popular definitions of problems and how they may be minimized). For example, we find no courses in social work on social work ignorance.

Client-focused definitions decrease the danger (especially from the client's perspective) of relying on good intentions rather than good outcomes when selecting services and encourage honesty when services and outcomes are imposed on clients. They will hopefully discourage past and current interrelated tendencies to hide the social control functions of social workers employed in social welfare institutions to pursue unattainable goals. These tendencies result in lost opportunities to empower clients by drawing on practice-related research findings to pursue valued outcomes that are attainable. They disempower clients. Service to clients is emphasized in our code of ethics, as is the importance of competent services drawing on practice- and policy-related research findings. Yet, research suggests that social workers rarely draw on practice-related research findings, rarely honor ethical requirements (e.g., to accurately inform clients about the costs and benefits of recommended services as well as of alternatives so that clients are involved in decisions as informed participants), and often ignore client goals.

SUMMARY

Bartlett's (1958) statement almost a half of a century ago is a reflection of the paradoxes, confusions, contradictions, missed opportunities, and mystifications we see in social work today. These include (a) the lack of match between values, knowledge, and skills claimed to be important and actual practice (e.g., claims to focus on client-environment interactions but often neglecting them in everyday decisions); (b) idealized, vague goals that deflect attention from what is or could be done by social workers and to what effect; (c) absence of a client voice; (d) downplaying social control functions; (e) ignoring the possibility of harm in the name of helping; and (f) ignoring unjust distribution of resources while claiming to value social justice (i.e., funding services that are harmful or of unknown effectiveness, limiting opportunities to fully fund programs found to help clients). Bartlett's emphasis on the importance of studying practice (and, I would add, its outcomes) has not been heeded. Bartlett suggested that

> the primary goal [of analyzing social work practice] is not to improve the status of social work (although this will be a side product), but to enable its members to render better service because of their increased competence, clarity, and security in their functions. (p. 8)

Client-focused definitions should contribute to clients', social workers', and the profession's interests. For example, if social workers can demonstrate that they provide services that are more effective, efficient, and ethical compared with those of nonprofessionals and other professionals, they will compete favorably for resources and gain the benefits of satisfaction with a job well done based on real-life findings rather than on wishful thinking. A client-focused definition intertwines ethical, evidentiary, and application issues. It encourages us to attend to discrepancies among what is needed to attain hoped-for goals, what resources are available, and what is drawn on and created.

The future offers opportunities for making "the social" more than a token. Social workers do not have the resources needed to address many of the problems they are asked to tackle. They could take advantage of their everyday practice experiences to gather data that would clearly reveal the gaps between what is needed, what is available, and what is offered. Publication of such data could be routine for each agency, and such data could be collated by professional organizations such as the National Association of Social Workers and the Council on Social Work Education in a yearly "state of the gap" report.

If the definition of social work influences the quality of services clients receive, spending time to craft such a definition would be a worthwhile endeavor. Let us create a definition of social work practice that shows we care about clients in deed as well as word.

REFERENCES

Abbott, A. (1988). *The system of professions: An essay on the division of expert labor.* Chicago: University of Chicago Press.

Barrows, H. W. (1994). *Practice-based learning: Problem-based learning applied to medical education.* Springfield: Southern Illinois University School of Medicine.

Bartlett, H. M. (1958). Toward clarification and improvement of social work practice. *Social Work, 3*(2), 3-9.

Blenkner, M., Bloom, M., & Nielsen, M. (1971). A research and demonstration project of protective service. *Social Casework, 52,* 483-499.

Christensen, A., & Jacobson, N. S. (1994). Who (or what) can do psychotherapy: The status and challenge of nonprofessional therapies. *Psychological Science, 5,* 8-14.

Dawes, R. M. (1994). *House of cards: Psychology and psychotherapy built on myth.* New York: Free Press.

Edwards, A., & Elwyn, G. (Eds.). (2001). *Evidence-based patient choice: Inevitable or impossible.* New York: Oxford University Press.

Entwistle, V. A., Sheldon, T. A., Sowden, A. J., & Watt, I. A. (1998). Evidence-informed patient choice. *International Journal of Technology Assessment in Health Care, 14,* 212-215.

Friedson, E. (1986). *Professional powers: A study of the institutionalization of formal knowledge.* Chicago: University of Chicago Press.

Gambrill, E., & Shlonsky, A. (2001). The need for comprehensive risk management systems in child welfare. *Children and Youth Services Review, 23,* 79-107.

Gordon, W. E. (1962). A critique of the working definition. *Social Work, 7*(4), 3-13.

Gray, J. A. M. (2001). *Evidence-based health care: How to make health policy and management decisions.* New York: Churchill Livingstone.

Hanley, B., Truesdale, A., King, A., Elbourne, D., & Chalmers, I. (2001). Involving consumers in designing, conducting, and interpreting randomized controlled trials: Questionnaire survey. *British Medical Journal, 322,* 519-523.

Kutchins, H., & Kirk, S. A. (1997). *Making us crazy: DSM: The psychiatric bible and the creation of mental disorders.* New York: Free Press.

Margolin, L. (1997). *Under the cover of kindness: The invention of social work.* Charlottesville: University Press of Virginia.

McCormick, J. (1996). Health scares are bad for your health. In D. M. Warburton & N. Sherwood (Eds.), *Pleasure and quality of life.* New York: John Wiley.

Meyer, H. J., Borgatta, E. F., & Jones, W. C. (1965). *Girls at vocational high: An experiment in social work intervention.* New York: Russell Sage.

National Association of Social Workers. (1996). *Code of ethics.* Silver Spring, MD: Author.

Popper, K. R. (1994). *The myth of the framework: In defense of science and rationality.* Boston: Routledge Kegan Paul.

Roche, T. (2000, November 13). The crisis of foster care. *Time, 156,* pp. 74-83.

Sackett, D. L., Rosenberg, W. M. C., Gray, J. A. M., Haynes, R. B., & Richardson, W. S. (1996). Evidence-based medicine: What it is and what it isn't [Editorial]. *British Medical Journal, 312,* 71-21.

Sackett, D. L., Straus, S. E., Richardson, W., Rosenberg, W. S., & Haynes, R. B. (2000). *Evidence-based medicine: How to practice and teach EBM* (2nd ed.). New York: Churchill Livingstone.

Schuerman, J. R., Rzepnicki, T. L., & Littell, J. H. (1994). *Putting families first: An experiment in family preservation.* Hawthorne, NY: Aldine.

Sharpe, V. A., & Faden, A. I. (1998). *Medical harm: Historical, conceptual, and ethical dimensions of iatrogenic illness.* New York: Cambridge University Press.

Szasz, T. (1994). *Cruel compassion: Psychiatric control of society's unwanted.* New York: John Wiley.

[4]

Moral Foundations of Social Welfare and Social Work: A Historical View

James Leiby

Sponsors of social welfare agencies in the United States have historically justified their work on three general grounds: the religious doctrine of charity, especially in its secular form of personal and social responsibility; the constitutional doctrine of police power, or the power of the sovereign to protect or enhance the health, safety, and morals of the community; and the legal doctrine of individual rights. A historical survey of these doctrines and their relationships suggests that social workers should emphasize the first two rather than the third.

BY THE TERM "moral foundation," I want to suggest a distinction between (1) a justification advanced to support or oppose a particular welfare agency or program, and (2) a general rationale offered for any and every sort of social welfare activity. "Foundation" refers to the latter type of argument. Such foundations are part of the religious and political beliefs and attitudes of our culture. They involve profound assumptions about personality and social life, and their scope goes far beyond institutions of social service. If social life were entirely rational, people would understand these fundamentals clearly and develop policies and programs accordingly. In fact, such beliefs are often misunderstood, confusing, and contradictory. This condition of the history of social welfare and social work has weakened our efforts. In the United States, the moral foundations of social welfare and social work may be summed up in three historic doctrines, which overlap but differ significantly, and in our discussion of professional values we emphasize one doctrine too much and ignore the importance and the potential of the others.

When I ask social workers why people should join together to sponsor social agencies and hire social workers (*should* join together, not *do* join together), the answer given most often is that individuals have rights and social agencies should secure or enhance those rights. Such rights are often related to the satisfaction of needs (or "basic" needs): The poor have a right to public assistance, children to proper nurture, the handicapped to appropriate education, pregnant women to abort unwanted pregnancies, and so forth. What is the basis of these rights? It is usual-

ly placed in our Constitution—the Bill of Rights—or the Preamble to the Declaration of Independence, which mentions the rights of "life, liberty, and the pursuit of happiness."

The affirmation of individual rights is indeed one moral foundation of our work, but it appeared recently, and it is not well understood (for example, it now has little to do with the theory of natural law that the signers of the Declaration referred to). The original rationales of social welfare policy, in their historical context, did

not involve individual rights. The oldest rationale for our work was religious and rested on notions of personal and social responsibility that were found in the Bible. The second rationale was the prerogative of the sovereign of a "body politic" to look after the collective interest of the community; in the United States this took the form of a peculiar elaboration of "police power"—the constitutional power to protect the health, safety, and morals of the community. A sketch of these three doctrines —personal and social responsibility, police power, and individual rights— will bring out their difference. My presentation is historical; my question is not "What should the moral foundation be?" but "How did the people who developed our institutions explain the reason for their work?"[1]

PERSONAL AND SOCIAL RESPONSIBILITY

The terms "social welfare" and "social work" came into currency in the United States around 1910. The activities and spirit that they denoted were earlier known as "charity and correction" or "philanthropy," and the activists were "charity workers" or "philanthropists." What activities? "Poor relief" in its many forms; programs for "dependent children"; hospitals (usually a form of charity in the nineteenth century); institutions for the insane, the feebleminded, and others (veterans, for example); and reformatories for promising types of offenders. What was the spirit of such activities? It was to provide help or "service" through an agency that was socially sponsored (hence the later term "social service"). Many people, then and later, were skeptical about whether these efforts were helpful in fact or in spirit, but even the skeptics assumed that they were *supposed* to be helpful. Most of these activities, insofar as they were organized, had at one time been sponsored by the church, and most of the people interested and active in them, even in 1900, believed that there was something religious about their efforts.

> **The terms 'social welfare' and 'social work' came into currency in the United States around 1910.**

It is not necessary to belabor the historical link between religious charity and social welfare, but it is important to be clear about the relationship among the divine commandment of love, the idea of personal and social responsibility, and the basis of public or governmental provision of help. Christians believed that God revealed in the Bible the way to salvation and heaven and that the way involved following certain laws, summarized by Jesus as to "love thy God with all thy heart, with all thy soul, with all thy mind, and with all thy strength" and to "love thy neighbor as thyself" (Mark: 12: 28–31). "Love" was made into "responsibility" because "responsible" meant answerable to or accountable to, and the Bible said that God would at some time judge individuals and communities. In theory, the responsibility was not between persons or between persons and an organized community, but between creatures and their Creator. Although the occasion for charity might arise from a personal or social difficulty, the act was not *in theory* a way of problem solving but a form of worship, a service to God in the form of a service to the person in need: "Inasmuch as ye have done it unto one of the least of these my brethren," Christ said, "ye have done it unto me" (Matt. 25:40).[2]

The early Christian communities described in the Bible were not interested in political organization or the policy of rulers, and the question of how Christian doctrine bore on the policy of rulers was, over the centuries, much disputed.[3] As matters appeared in the United States in the nineteenth century, church and state were separate, and the government should certainly not subsidize or otherwise aid or favor a particular religious denomination. The principle of separation of church and state was clause one of the first amendment to the Constitution—literally the first statement in the Bill of Rights. Most state constitutions had a similar clause. (The last state government to "disestablish" religion was Massachusetts [1833].)[4]

The citizens who separated church and state intended to avoid favoritism among denominations. However, they did not doubt that the government should prevent, punish, or correct sin, or provide for the needy according to the general principles formulated in earlier times when churches had been established and political officials were regarded as under the moral leadership (not necessarily the political power) of religious officials. To be specific about charity, the main public provision for poor relief (or "public charity" as it was called), the Poor Law, had its origin in a system of poor relief offered in the sixteenth century by parishes of the established Church of England. In the United States in the late nineteenth century, public charity was often thought of as a last resort when charitable organizations that had religious sponsors were not available or interested. The spirit of public outdoor relief, or a public almshouse, orphanage, or hospital, was supposed to be less helpful—less dedicated—than that of voluntary and religious agencies.[5]

There was, in the late nineteenth century, a growing criticism of religious-inspired charity and its spirit. The coinage "social welfare" was, in its secular tone, one reflection of this criticism. During the twentieth century, agencies were more and more sponsored by government, without reference to religious doctrine. Today we do not ordinarily think of an agency's help as an act of worship or service to God. But a secular justification of social service as problem solving is not incompatible with the religious idea of helping as a service to God. It was in fact one of the achievements of the charity organization societies and other forerunners

of professional social work to make that point (their original objective was usually to improve the practice of their religious charity). Moreover, many people today believe in the relevance of Biblical revelation, and many are devout and pious in traditional ways. For these people, the general moral foundation of social welfare and social work is plain: It is part of their response to a commandment of God.

NATURAL RIGHTS

The justification of social welfare programs today is ordinarily naturalistic and rationalistic—that is, it rests on observations of social life (rather than the revealed word of God) and on an effort to reach consensus among all reasonable people (not just those committed to a particular divine revelation). This type of thinking about social life and government goes historically by the name "political philosophy." Social sciences, such as economics (first called "political economy"), political science, and sociology, began as specializations in this tradition of philosophical speculation.

In European history, political philosophy appeared long before Christianity. It began in the reflections of students in the philosophic schools of ancient Athens (notably the Academy, the Lyceum, and the Stoa, founded respectively by Plato, Aristotle, and Zeno). The tradition was carried on by teachers in Rome and, after a long lapse, taken up again in the Christian universities of Europe. It did not enter into thinking about charity and correction until the late nineteenth century, because it did not address directly the problems of helping people who needed help. Political philosophers were not interested in the powerless but in the relationships of powerful people and groups; they wanted to understand these relationships so that they could prescribe ways to reduce or eliminate conflict among the powerful. As a practical matter, they were mostly interested in law, especially constitutional law, because law regulated the relationships between powerful people and groups.[6]

The first political philosophers studied relationships within and between the city-states that the Greeks and Romans established around the Mediterranean. Later philosophers studied the relation between the laws of particular city-states and the more general laws of the Roman Empire. After the Christian Church was established in the empire, philosophers studied the relationship between the imperial government and the church. After the barbarian invasions, political philosophy paid attention to the relationship between barbarian kings or dynasties and their vassals. Since the sixteenth century, it has been preoccupied with the nation-states that evolved out of the feudal kingdoms.

So political theory approached charity and correction and later social welfare from the point of view of constitutional relations in the nation-state. Its original implications for social welfare were quite negative. In England, France, and the United States, it took the form of a doctrine called, in the nineteenth century, "liberalism," which was by 1900 identified with a general doctrine called "individualism" and more or less explicitly contrasted with rival doctrines called "socialism" and "collectivism." (Socialism did not at that time refer primarily to Marxist socialism; there were also a "Christian socialism," a variety of utopian socialisms, a "municipal socialism," and a "national socialism," all of which had many supporters.)

The essence of liberalism as a political theory was the notion that individuals had "rights" that were "natural" inasmuch as they were prior to any custom or legislation, that in theory governments were established to clarify and protect such rights, and that the organization of government and its legislation could therefore be judged as good or bad, right or wrong, insofar as they did clarify and protect those rights. The doctrine was important in the United States because it was used to justify the Revolution and it influenced the people who wrote the state and federal constitutions of the new republic.

The theory of natural rights drew on a tradition about a "natural law" or "law or nature." Roman lawyers had envisioned natural law as a consensus or essence that reasonable people might perceive among the variety of systems of municipal law in the city-states of the empire. Later on, Christian scholars had compared this natural law, that ordinary reasoning might define, with the commandments of God in the Bible, and, in time, they discovered a remarkable harmony between them. In any case, natural law was a standard of reason against which particular customs or legislation might be compared and corrected or improved. Its validity as a standard among Christian Europeans depended on the assumption that God the Creator had built such laws into His Creation and had endowed people with the rational ability to make them out. Hence, Thomas Jefferson referred, in our Declaration of Independence, to "the Laws of Nature and of Nature's God" and said that people are "endowed by their Creator with certain inalienable rights." Jefferson and his associates were much influenced by a contemporary theological revision of Christianity called "Deism," whereas the Roman lawyers who had thought about reason and natural law had been influenced by somewhat similar doctrines of the Stoics.[7]

Doctrines about natural rights got the name "liberal" in the nineteenth century because their chief application was to discredit a lot of existing customs and legislation that seemed to limit the freedom of individuals. Some of the existing laws were remnants of feudalism; others were mercantilist legal regulations of economic or social life. Much later, critics would think of this early liberalism as favoring "negative freedom"—freedom from governmental restraint—and contrast it with "positive freedom" or the enhancement of power to act.[8] The right to property, for example, did not give anybody property but protected people who had it in their ability to keep it and use it as they saw fit. The right to life did not guarantee people the means of existence (it was closer to the notion of a right to self-defense). Freedom of contract (a very important right) did not give them anything to make a contract about or with. The rights to freedom of association and speech did not provide individuals with friends or with anything to say.

In fact, when citizens wanted the government to act in a positive way to protect or enhance some community or collective interest, they often encountered the opposition of liberals on the grounds that such government functions were unconstitutional because such functions violated someone's rights. In this way, the liberal emphasis on individual rights and constitutional limits on government played into the hands of people who benefited from the status quo and were reluctant to change it. When it came to "social" or "social welfare" legislation, such "liberal" doctrines gave support to interests that were "conservative," in the sense of unwilling to change.

The emphasis on protecting individual rights and the opposition to legislation that seemed to threaten them increased in the nineteenth century along with the influence of English political economists in the tradition of Adam Smith. Their doctrine became known as "economic liberalism" and gave strong support to the policy that the government should allow leeway to economic enterprise and reduce regulation of economic relations to a minimum (laissez-faire). It reached a high point with the great popular reception of the thought of the English philosopher Herbert Spencer between 1870 and 1890 (social Darwinism).[9]

POLICE POWER

To counter the arguments for laissez-faire and social Darwinism, to assert the interests of the community or the collective against those of the individual, U.S. lawyers elaborated the idea of "police power." The term gained currency in a decision of the Supreme Court in 1837 (New York v. Miln), as a label for the concept that a community had common interests that were distinct from and more important than the rights of particular individuals, and it was the business of a sovereign—a ruling power—to look after such common interests. The word "police" did not refer to the "cops"—a uniformed police force was still in the future—but to a vague general power to regulate for the health, safety, and morals of the community. The term was not really an expansion of government power vis-à-vis the individual; in many circumstances it suggested questions about the limits of such power to those whose interest was to specify or delimit the power. It did not apply primarily to charity and correction but to attempts to pass legislation regulating public health, education, housing, and conditions of labor. It applied ordinarily to state legislation, because under the federal constitution, "local police regulation" was reserved to the states.[10]

Federal (as distinct from state) legislation for social welfare, in the broad sense in which the term is now used to include public health, education, conditions of labor, public assistance, and social services, found various constitutional bases. Early federal laws, such as the Food and Drug Act (1906) and the White Slave Traffic (Mann) Act (1910), rested on the power delegated by the states to the federal government to control interstate commerce, although it was obvious that Congress was not simply interested in transportation. Congress was using this power to promote public health, as state governments did, and this and other legislation was interpreted as defining a federal "police power." But the Social Security Act of 1935 and other welfare legislation of the New Deal and later years rested simply on the "spending power" of Congress. Article 1, Section 8 of the Constitution reads: "Congress shall have the power to lay and collect Taxes. . .to pay the Debts and provide for the common Defence and general Welfare of the United States." In validating the Social Security Act (which was at once challenged as unconstitutional), the majority of the Supreme Court rejected an earlier argument that the words "general welfare" should be interpreted very strictly to add nothing to those powers that the Constitution specifically mentioned.[11]

Actually, with regard to the public assistance titles and most later legislation about social services, the federal legislation did not put the federal government in direct welfare administration. Instead it offered conditional federal grants-in-aid to state agencies, which were established by state laws and justified under state constitutions by the state police power. The federal government did not deal directly with recipients, and it did not force the states to act. It offered the states an incentive to act, which states might (and sometimes did) reject.

In any case, in 1940 as in 1900 the needy did not receive poor relief or other help because they had a "right" to it under the constitution of the federal or state government. Public charity was in fact a heritage of an ancient religious responsibility, which long antedated U.S. constitutional theory. When lawyers had to reinterpret public charity in terms of con-stitutional powers, they included poor relief, along with the prosecution of crime, the protection of health, the education of future citizens, and many other activities as an exercise of power by the community to protect its health, safety, or morals. So poor relief was sometimes justified as a means to prevent the public nuisance of begging, and the vagrancy laws were a means to deal with the nuisance of tramps. Community officials might take action because as Christians they had a responsibility to help or because they were looking out in a prudent way for what they took to be the best interest of the community. The right of a needy person to help was not a consideration.

INDIVIDUAL RIGHTS

The notion of "rights" as a justification for helping that would rival "charity" took form in England, but I have not seen a very plausible historical account of it.[12] There were doubtless a variety of social and intellectual influences at work. For whatever reasons, there was in the nineteenth century a growing sense of the practical futility of traditional charity—it was not meeting the need—and of the indignity or humiliation of receiving it. It is plausible that the sense of personal and social responsibility diminished, or at least changed, as social relations became more impersonal. At the same time helpers and helped became more sensitive to the indignity or humiliation of dependence, especially when the helpers could exhibit a patronizing sort of discretion in whom and how they helped. There were two problems with the perspective of traditional charity: that the fortunate would ignore their responsibility to help those in need and that the unfortunate would ignore their responsibility to help themselves, that is, they would succumb to a temptation to take it easy in dependence rather than strive for self-sufficiency.

There were, it seems, two historic responses to these problems. Some charity reformers, especially those associated with charity organization societies, wanted to rationalize the organization and methods of helpers toward the ends of building social and personal responsibility. In the event they seemed mostly interested in helping dependents become self-sufficient and recognized that the unit of self-sufficiency was not the individual but the family and the neighborhood, they accordingly devised ways to help families and neighborhoods. Other charity reformers emphasized the responsibility of the community to provide help by a formal organization of the government, rather than a revitalized informal network of family and neighbors, and they asserted a "right" of needy people to such public aid. Their argument drew on certain findings and reflections of social scientists: that pauperism (dependence) was like an accident that usually happened to people who lived in poverty, who were likely to suffer from poor food and shelter, and who were especially vulnerable to sickness, unemployment, and personal demoralization (losing their hope, energy, will, and resourcefulness).[13]

In the latter point of view, which steadily gained credence, the problem was not simply or even primarily to relieve and rehabilitate paupers; it was, rather, to improve the conditions of life that made poverty-stricken people so vulnerable to the accident of pauperism. The moral problem was not simply to make individuals, families, and neighborhoods more self-sufficient, but rather to get the organized community, including private associations and especially the government, to improve the social conditions that surrounded pauperism (and also vice and crime). The way to improve conditions was to provide a minimum of well-being to all citizens, and out of deference to the needy person as an individual and a citizen, to provide the help in the form of a "right," a claim that the needy person could make and enforce on a public agency and official. Enter the "welfare state."[14]

This argument, which I have much simplified and compressed, was better developed in Europe than in the United States. A historical narrative would show how it surfaced in fragments—compensation for industrial accidents here, a maternal and child care program there, elaborate forms of compulsory education or school social services elsewhere. In the United States, the general drift of the argument and policy was perceived as collectivist—as socialist by friends and foes of socialism, and later as "totalitarian" or "fascist" by those who thought that Russian socialism was in practice much like Italian and German fascism. In time, however, many liberals came to think that welfare state measures *were* compatible with a relatively free economy—that national policy might combine some national goals and policies ("full employment" and "fair employment," for example) and still leave most economic decisions and initiatives to people pursuing their interest in a market economy. Conservatives continued to criticize the welfare state as a road to serfdom, however, and radicals thought it was an untenable truce in the class war or a sinister plot to preserve privilege.[15] My point is not about the argument over the welfare state but about how people came to think that individual rights were a proper moral foundation for welfare policy and for the practice of professional social work.

1930s–1940s

In the United States, individual rights entered the discussion of charity and correction with regard to the administration of the poor law. After 1900, some states set up programs that separated certain kinds of needy people from ordinary local poor relief, providing a special or "categorical" assistance for the blind, widows with dependent children, and the aged. The new programs were favored as more dignified because they defined more clearly the standards of eligibility and assistance. Often the state shared the cost with local government, so grants were likely to be more generous, and state officials reviewed the process, so it was likely to be more regular and to allow an appeal. These features reduced the discretion of local officials. A needy person could see the legal standard of eligibility and aid and make a claim accordingly. The Social Security Act of 1935 authorized federal subsidies (and supervision) of these state programs.[16]

In 1940, Edith Abbott, Dean of the University of Chicago School of Social Service Administration, published a collection of documents on the subject. Her organizing idea was to contrast the traditional poor ("pauper") laws with modern "public assistance," in which applicants had a more definite claim and a right of appeal. The "right to public assistance" was a claim that, *if and when* the legisla-

ture decided to make help available, administration had to follow well-defined rules. The constitutional basis of state legislation was not the individual's "right to life" but the legislature's belief that such a policy was a good and right way to protect the community's interest.[17]

Social workers like Abbott were interested in the subject because they had from the start been involved in the administration of charity. At first these professionals were likely to be doubtful about public charity, because they observed that, compared with the private agencies in which most of them worked and which aspired to help in a scientific and professional way, public administration of poor relief was bad and not likely to improve. But their skepticism about public charity could change. In time, many of them (notably those around Abbott) argued that public administration might be as "scientific" in spirit as the operation of a charity organization society, family service society, or community chest. In fact many local governments had in the 1920s delegated all or part of their poor relief to private agencies, which applied established principles of casework to ascertain need and promote self-sufficiency and which might also be active in social planning.[18]

After 1935, professional social workers interested in public assistance directed their attention to four points. (1) The administration of public assistance was itself a service, which had important implications for how the applicants would respond to help. (2) The interest of the community was not simply to relieve immediate need, but to help applicants become more self-sufficient and responsible in the long run. (3) Particular applicants might need only money ("income maintenance," as social workers said), but they might also need other services, very likely from other agencies (medical treatment or vocational training, for example). (4) Given that experts themselves did not have a clear scientific or technical understanding of the problems and what to do about them, public opinion in the community was likely to be grossly misinformed or misguided, and consequently policy and administration were likely to be confused and ineffective. (That statement is a euphemism for what was, in the 1930s, an uproar among vari-

ous enthusiasts for social reform and their opponents.[19])

All four considerations helped clarify the community interest in public assistance and other social services. Jane Hoey, the social worker who was chief of the Bureau of Public Assistance in the Social Security Administration (1936–53), had them much in mind when she commissioned Charlotte Towle, professor of social casework at the University of Chicago, to write *Common Human Needs* (1945). This little guide for nonprofessional social workers in public assistance brought enlightenment to everyone and became famous around the world.[20] The considerations also appear in the perspective of a puzzling legal philosophy in *The Right to Life* (1955) by A. Delafield Smith, the legal counsel of the Social Security Administration.[21]

1960s

In the thinking of the 1930s and 1940s, the idea of an individual's right to help appeared as an adjunct to the legislative exercise of the police power. In the 1960s, it became central in the advocacy of many reforms. In a legal sense, these "rights" were claims asserted against unequal or inequitable administration of the law. It was argued that schools should not deny mentally retarded children, or children disadvantaged by race prejudice or poverty, an equal right to education, for example. Delinquents had a right to due process in juvenile court, adults to legal counsel in criminal court, and offenders to a determinate sentence. Newcomers to the community and fetuses in the womb had a right to public assistance just like postnatal residents, and so forth.[22] Whatever the legal technicality, advocates of these various rights drew on the success of the "civil rights" movement of the 1950s, which had won an extension of equal rights in the form of active protection against illegal discrimination, and which encouraged an affirmation of the traditional value of "equality" that had new implications ("affirmative action" for example).

On the international scene, as onetime colonies became independent and joined the United Nations, there was much celebration of "human rights." T. H. Marshall, an English sociologist and historian who was foremost among academic students of the welfare state, discerned an expansion of the concept of rights from civil, to political, to "social," a change which he thought corresponded to the development of "citizenship" in modern society.[23]

In some ways, the excitement of the 1960s confused the discussion of the moral foundations of social welfare institutions and social work. The civil rights movement had drawn a contrast between the ideal and the real in legal rights; in the 1960s, it helped draw a contrast between the poverty of most blacks and general affluence. In the "War on Poverty" of that decade, social welfare agencies and programs were supposed to play an important part. It was then two generations since the Progressives had enacted their welfare measures and a generation since the New Deal had put federal initiative and support behind income maintenance measures; although the condition of the laboring classes had undoubtedly improved, still the persistence of poverty seemed to show that welfare state programs had not succeeded. The question arose, Why? In people's thinking about this question, the terms "equality" and "social control" took on new significance.

Equality. With regard to equality, some people made a distinction between formal legal equality and a more substantial equality of opportunity, or income, or "participation" in society. The expanded notion of equality had been central in the overturn of the segregation laws (which had been based on the principle, "separate but equal"). The distinction corresponded to many other distinctions—between "negative freedom" (absence of restraint) and "positive freedom" (power to act), between a "minimum" and an "optimum" level of support (in English debates about the welfare state), and even between a "residual" and an "institutional" conception of social welfare (coined in the United States in 1957). These distinctions all suggested that welfare programs fell short because they were conceived too narrowly and that a more generous conception of equality would authorize them to function better. In the context of these distinctions, the expansion of individual rights seemed to be a proper rationale for the more generous view. This line of thought generated a formidable opposition, however, from "conserva-

> ## There was, in the late nineteenth century, a growing criticism of religious-inspired charity and its spirit.

tives," "neo-conservatives" (one-time partisans of the welfare state who had become critics), and "libertarians" who upheld the nineteenth-century type of liberalism and believed that efforts to promote equality by bureaucrats and bureaucracies, grants and rules, were likely to frustrate individual liberty, to cost much more than taxpayers were willing to afford, and to fail in any case.[24]

Social Control. With regard to social control, critics argued that welfare-state programs fell short because they were not intended to go very far. Such programs were, in this view, a reluctant concession by privileged classes to those who were disadvantaged in an unequal society; their objective was to preserve the unequal order of society by minimizing agitation and "regulating the poor." Welfare programs were, therefore, a device to control (reduce) protest against injustice rather than to eliminate the injustice—part of the problem rather than part of the solution. Ironically, this 1960s usage of the term "social control" inverted the original sense of the term, which had referred to efforts of the government to protect workers and consumers from antisocial practices of businessmen. (Social legislation to protect child labor and the public health are examples.) In its earlier usage, "social control" was a sociological equivalent of the legal doctrine of police power.[25]

As a catchword of protest in the 1960s, "social control" drew on recent sociological and psychological theories that were much controverted. Its practical effect was to raise doubts about the community interest that the police power was supposed to promote: The so-called community interest was obviously determined by the political factions that happened to dominate lawmakers, executives, and judges, who might ignore or deliberately subordinate the interests of others. The argument also echoed a familiar suspicion among radicals that tinkering with a defective sys-

tem (incremental reform) might only sustain it and postpone the necessary (radical) changes that they advocated.

Controversies over equality and liberty, a central bureaucracy and local control, taxpayers and beneficiaries, and a reluctant or willing welfare state, divisive in themselves as they appeared, were greatly exacerbated in the 1970s by general arguments over national security (foreign and defense policy) and economic growth and inflation.

COMMON INTEREST

It seems obvious in the 1980s that partisans of social welfare programs are on the defensive and that the welfare state may be at a turning point. In any case, legislators and private associations that sponsor and pay for welfare programs have for many years grown increasingly critical in their reviews of social welfare activities and of those who work in them. As a practical matter, these critical reviews seldom refer to fundamental moral values or even polemics about liberty, equality, and social control—they involve analyses of costs, benefits, and cost-effectiveness.

In choosing among various proposals, authorities tend to favor those that are the most cost-effective. In traditional ethical language, their decisions are *utilitarian:* They tend to favor the greatest good for the greatest number, as this judgment is modified by their wish to be reelected and their political ambition. Given the worst (or best) of intentions, authorities face difficult technical problems in determining what is really cost-effective, or the greatest good for the greatest number. Various partisans have different and divergent views. With regard to a utilitarian decision, social workers can contribute by bringing out persuasive facts that will clarify the technical benefit of the programs and support the political position of their beneficiaries.

This technical advice is related to the traditional moral foundation of the police power—determining and realizing a common or collective interest rather than an individual interest. An organized effort to help, in this view, is not simply or even primarily a way to assert individual claims or the interest of a particular group. It is a significant benefit to all those around the troubled individuals or groups.

In European and especially U.S. political thinking, however, there are limits on utilitarian decisions, whether by officials or by professional authorities. There are some concerns that our tradition says authorities should not disregard. In U.S. political thought these reservations took the form of the liberal doctrine of natural law and natural rights, and as our ways of helping became more and more the business of government, it seemed plausible to expand the notion of "rights" from limits on what governments might do to claims for public support. This large expansion of the notion of rights, much agitated in the last 20 years, has not yet won general concurrence.

From one perspective, it is self-defeating for social workers to emphasize individual rights as a moral foundation for social welfare programs, because these arguments play into the hands of those who continue the tradition of nineteenth-century individualism. Furthermore, the emphasis on legal rights overlooks the potential in the argument that the earliest professional social workers made, in the heyday of nineteenth-

century individualism. Those partisans of "scientific charity" rationalized helping in terms not of rights but rather of the responsibilities of people acting as individuals and also as groups in an organized way. In the form of the religious commandment of charity, that old argument still has force with practicing Jews, Christians, and Muslims. But even naturalistic and conservative thinkers may appreciate the insight of these early social workers—that it is a mistake to think of society as primarily a political organization held together by formal legislation and the sanction of force, because society is also an association held together by many kinds of moral expectations, common sentiments, and aspirations, caring, and sharing. The professional methods of casework, group work, and community organization, as they took form, were efforts to realize and encourage that spirit in individuals, the people around them, and society at large. Insofar as these historic professional values, experiences, and methods are well-founded and well presented, they should inform the distinctive contribution of professional social work to the review of the welfare state. They are what professional social workers can see, understand, and support that is different from and better than the reductionism of legal formalism and scientific theorizing.

James Leiby, Ph.D., is Professor, School of Social Welfare, University of California, Berkeley.

Notes and References

1. Some philosophers have recently interested themselves in questions about the proper justification or rationale for social welfare policies, mostly in England, mostly around large public expenditures on social services, and mostly from the point of view of defending or attacking the distributive justice of the market economy. These writers, and I believe most commentators, take "social justice" to mean primarily "distributive justice." Their thinking takes the form of philosophical analysis intended to state concepts and develop arguments clearly, so as to arrive at what the justification or rationale would be if only people thought correctly. A recent summary and analysis of this literature is contained in Raymond Plant, Harry Lesser, and Peter Taylor-Gooby, *Political Philosophy and*

Social Welfare (London, England: Routledge & Kegan Paul, 1980), which has a large bibliography of mostly English publications. (It omits the thoughtful book by Nicholas Rescher, *Welfare: The Issues in Philosophical Perspective* [Pittsburgh, Pa.: University of Pittsburgh Press, 1972].) These philosophical analyses pay little attention to the history of social welfare or to what justifications people have offered for real programs and how the justifications have changed.

2. Jesus thought of himself as a Jew, not a "Christian"; the commandments he referred to were based on Hebrew scriptures.

3. Ernst Troeltsch, *The Social Teaching of the Christian Churches*, 2 Vols. (New York: Harper & Bros., 1960), Vol. 1,

pp. 39–86. This is a reprint of a classic (1911) that summed up much historical and theological writing that was available to the generation that lived through the transition from charity to social welfare in the United States. On Christian doctrine and political theory, see George Sabine, *A History of Political Theory* (4th ed., rev. by Thomas L. Thorsen; Hinsdale, Ill.: Dryden Press, 1973).

4. For a survey of the history of religion in the United States, see Sydney Ahlstrom, *A Religious History of the American People* (New Haven: Yale University Press, 1972). On the question of church and state, see J. R. Pole, *The Pursuit of Equality in American History* (Berkeley and Los Angeles: University of California Press, 1978), pp. 59–111. Pole shows that the movement for separation was an early concrete formulation of the idea of equal rights.

5. On the origin of the Elizabethan Poor Law in the older system of parish charity, see Brian Tierney, *Medieval Poor Law* (Berkeley: University of California Press, 1959), pp. 127–132. On opinions about the relative merits of public and private agencies in the 1890s, see Amos Warner, *American Charities: A Study in Philanthropy and Economics* (New York: Crowell, 1894), pp. 306–309.

6. For a survey of the history of political philosophy, see Sabine, *A History of Political Theory*.

7. On the law of nature and natural rights, three standard works are Otto Gierke, *Natural Law and the Theory of Society* (Boston: Beacon Press, 1957) (first published by Cambridge University Press in 1934; the Beacon edition includes an excellent introduction by Ernest Barker and a lecture on "The Ideas of Natural Law and Humanity" by Ernst Troeltsch); Ernst Cassirer, *The Philosophy of the Enlightenment* (Princeton, N.J.: Princeton University Press, 1968) (first published in 1932), pp. 234–274; and Leo Strauss, *Natural Right and History* (Chicago: University of Chicago Press, 1953), which presents a vigorous defense of the theory. Newer studies include Pole, *The Pursuit of Equality in American History*; and Morton White, *The Philosophy of the American Revolution* (New York: Oxford University Press, 1978).

8. The thought that society or the state should underwrite "positive freedom," as well as "negative freedom" as guaranteed by constitutional law, is relevant to the assertion of "social rights," which are discussed later. See Isaiah Berlin, *Four Essays on Liberty* (New York: Oxford University Press, 1969), pp. 118–172. A penetrating reflection on the history of liberty is in Oscar Handlin and Mary Handlin, *The Dimensions of Liberty* (Cambridge, Mass.: Harvard University Press, 1961).

9. Guido de Ruggiero, *History of European Liberalism* (Oxford, England: Oxford

University Press, 1927), gives a full account of liberalism in the context of the politics and thought of England, France, Germany, and Italy. Stefan Collini, *Liberalism and Sociology: L. T. Hobhouse and Political Argument in England 1880–1914* (Cambridge, England: Cambridge University Press, 1979), is an account of a crucial thinker in historical context.

10. The legislature must decide whether a proposed exercise of police power is good or bad, right or wrong; its standard for that judgment is ordinarily utilitarian (the greatest good for the greatest number). Usually the argument arises over whether that good is great enough to justify overriding individual rights (especially property rights). Consequently, the analysis of police power has been mostly around the question of the regulation of business. There is a history of the idea of police power in W. G. Hastings, "The Development of Law as Illustrated by the [court] Decisions Relating to the Police Power of the State," *Proceedings of the American Philosophical Society*, 39 (September 1900), pp. 359–554. The first comprehensive treatise was Ernst Freund, *The Police Power: Public Policy and Constitutional Rights* (Chicago: University of Chicago Press, 1904), which discusses provision for "dependents" in chaps. 1 and 10. Freund says that this usage of "police" derives from a seventeenth-century distinction between *justice* (the maintenance of private rights) and *policy* (the promotion of the public welfare). p. 6 n.

11. Two standard constitutional histories that put this legislation in context are Carl Brent Swisher, *American Constitutional Development* (2d ed.; Boston: Houghton Mifflin Co., 1954); and Alfred Kelly and Winfred Harbison, *The American Constitution: Its Origins and Development* (5th ed.; New York: W. W. Norton & Co., 1976). Laurence H. Tribe, *American Constitutional Law* (Mineola, N.Y.: Foundation Press, 1978), is a legal textbook that interprets the story to support recent judicial activism.

12. For a history of rights in the English welfare state, see T. H. Marshall, *Social Policy in the Twentieth Century* (London, England: Hutchinson, 1970). It builds on his well-known essay, "Citizenship and Social Class," which is republished with several other articles on the welfare state in Marshall, *Class, Citizenship, and Social Development* (Chicago: University of Chicago Press, 1964). His later thoughts appear in *The Right to Welfare and Other Essays* (New York: The Free Press, 1981), with an introduction on Marshall by Robert Pinker.

13. The chief secondary work on the charity organization societies in England is Charles Loch Mowat, *The Charity Organization Society, 1869–1913* (London, England: Methuen & Co., 1961). Marshall, *Social Policy in the Twentieth Century*, describes the concern with poverty. Insight into the early years is presented in T. S. Simey, Margaret B. Simey, and Charles Booth, *Social Scientist* (London, England: Oxford University Press, 1960).

14. Sidney Web and Beatrice Web, *The Prevention of Destitution* (London, England: Longmans, Green & Co., 1911), an early and influential statement, also reveals the analytical perspective that informed their later definitive history of the English poor law, *English Local Government: English Poor Law History*, I, *The Old Poor Law* [before 1834]; II, *The Last Hundred Years* (New York: Longmans, Green & Co., 1927 and 1929, respectively).

15. James Leiby, *History of Social Welfare and Social Work in the United States* (New York: Columbia University Press, 1978), is a comprehensive account of institutional development. James T. Patterson, *America's Struggle Against Poverty, 1900–1980* (Cambridge, Mass.: Harvard University Press, 1981), reviews ideas about poverty and their influence on policy.

16. Collections of primary sources with well-informed analytical essays are in Edith Abbott, *Public Assistance: American Principles and Practice* (Chicago: University of Chicago Press, 1940); and Sophonisba Breckinridge, *Public Welfare Administration* (rev. ed.; Chicago, University of Chicago Press, 1938).

17. Abbott, *Public Assistance*, pp. vii, 7–12. A succinct and lucid legal analysis is in Hasseltine Taylor, "The Nature of the Right to Public Assistance," *Social Service Review*, 36 (September 1962), pp. 265–267.

18. Abbott, *Public Assistance*, pp. 515–532.

19. The classic statement of these points is the pamphlet by Charlotte Towle, *Common Human Needs* (Washington, D.C.: Social Security Administration, 1945), which has often been reprinted with minor revisions. The bibliography of the original edition is an excellent guide to what social workers were thinking about public assistance at the time.

20. Towle, *Common Human Needs* (rev. ed.; Washington, D.C.: National Association of Social Workers, 1965), pp. iii–iv. There are biographical notices of Hoey and Towle in Barbara Sicherman, ed., *Notable American Women: The Modern Period, A Biographical Dictionary* (Cambridge, Mass.: Harvard University Press, Belknap Press, 1980), pp. 341, 695.

21. A. Delafield Smith, *The Right to Life* (Chapel Hill: University of North Carolina Press, 1955). Smith likens scientific laws describing natural processes to legislative acts; see the scornful review by Bayless Manning, *Yale Law Journal*, 66 (December 1956), pp. 315–318.

22. Donald C. Warner, ed., *Toward New Human Rights* (Austin: Lyndon B. Johnson School of Public Affairs, University of Texas, 1977), includes many papers by leaders of the 1960s. U.S. Commission on Civil Rights, *Accommodating the Spectrum of Individual Abilities* (Washington, D.C.: U.S. Government Printing Office, 1983), includes a full and annotated account of legislation and adjudication of the expansion of civil rights of the handicapped. On the constitutional status and basis of welfare rights, see Samuel Krislov, "The OEO Lawyers Fail to Constitutionalize a Right to Welfare: A Study in the Uses and Limits of the Judicial Process," *Minnesota Law Review*, 58 (December 1973), pp. 211–245; and Frank Michelman, "Welfare Rights in a Constitutional Democracy," pp. 659–693, and Robert Bork, "The Impossibility of Finding Welfare Rights in the Constitution," *Washington University Law Quarterly* (Summer 1979), pp. 695–701. Michael J. Perry, *The Constitution, the Courts, and Human Rights* (New Haven: Yale University Press, 1982), reviews and defends the expansion of constitutional rights.

23. Rex Martin and James Nickel, "A Bibliography on the Nature and Foundation of Rights, 1947–1977," *Political Theory*, 6 (August 1978), pp. 395–413, refers to philosophical discussions of the subject. Jo Bell Whitlatch, "Human Rights," *RQ* [American Library Association, References and Adult Services Division], 18 (Spring 1979), pp. 290–295, is a bibliographical article on government publications, especially of international organizations. Louis Henkin, "Rights: American and Human," *Columbia Law Review*, 79 (April 1979), pp. 405–425, is interesting and clear; Anthony D'Amato, "The Concept of Human Rights in International Law," *Columbia Law Review*, 82 (October 1982), pp. 1110–1159, defends the notion against skeptical critics. D. D. Raphael, ed., *Political Theory and the Rights of Man* (London, England: Macmillan & Co., 1967), is a collection of essays by philosophers. Kathi Friedman, *Legitimation of Social Rights and the Western Welfare State: A Weberian Perspective* (Chapel Hill: University of North Carolina Press, 1981), draws on sociological literature on the theme. See also Marshall, *Social Policy in the Twentieth Century*; Marshall, *Class, Citizenship, and Social Development*; and Marshall, *The Right to Welfare and Other Essays*.

24. The philosophical argument is clearer in England than in the United States. See Plant, Lesser, and Taylor-Gooby, *Political Philosophy and Social Welfare*. A recent discussion is included in Neil Gilbert, *Capitalism and the Welfare State: Dilemmas of Social Benevolence* (New Haven: Yale University Press, 1983), pp. 139–149.

25. See James Leiby, "Social Control and Historical Explanation," in Walter Trattner, ed., *Social Welfare or Social Control? Some Historical Reflections on Regulating the Poor* (Knoxville: University of Tennessee Press, 1983), pp. 90–113.

Accepted April 5, 1984

[5]

Responsibility and Excuses

Banks McDowell

If the problems facing professionals are not ones of learning the expectations of professional ethics, but rather of complying with them, we need to
look closely at the excuses offered and, even more important, those that are
accepted for alleged lapses from ethical standards. As a preliminary matter
before we get to the typical excuses, I want to discuss several central questions. (a) What do we mean by saying that a professional is responsible? (b)
What is the function of excuses? (c) How do we describe successful or unsuccessful excuses? (d) Who decides whether an excuse works?

WHEN CAN WE SAY A PROFESSIONAL IS RESPONSIBLE?

In simple moral analysis, *responsibility* is the consequence of obligation
and the failure to comply, the conclusion of a syllogism in which the major
premise is the duty and the minor premise is the breach. In other words, it is
an inference or conclusion from the presence of other factors.

Responsibility is the major concern of most evaluative judgments of human action. If we think in causal terms about people, we must identify
which actor should be credited for some result we either approve or disapprove of. We then describe that person as the responsible party. Otherwise
we would have to label the occurrence as an accident, act of nature, or act of
God, which are conclusions egocentric human beings are reluctant to draw.
We may need to seriously reexamine the traditional assumption that we
ought to identify a responsible individual for most actions. We will consider that question in Chapter 7.

14   *Ethics and Excuses*

We locate responsibility not only to condemn, but also to praise. One of the most laudatory comments we make about a person is that she is responsible. This means she accepts her duties, carries them out completely and thoroughly, and willingly accepts the consequences of her actions. Just as saying that a person is responsible is great praise, declaring her irresponsible is serious condemnation. It seems almost a character flaw, meaning she is unreliable, untrustworthy, someone who cannot be counted on when difficulties arise.

Responsibility must be accepted before one acts or at the very least while acting and before one knows what the consequences will be. There is always risk of condemnation, but also the possibility of reward or praise. Taking credit after the consequences are known if they are favorable and avoiding it if the consequences are unfavorable is a common human reaction, but one that is the antithesis of taking responsibility.

An important distinction is between responsibility imposed from the outside and that which is voluntarily accepted by the actor. Legal responsibility is imposed by government officials. What might be called social responsibility is imposed by family, friends, and peers. Responsibility that is self-imposed is an important aspect in defining the realm of the ethical.

Responsibility for wrongful actions is difficult for most people to accept. Children instinctively avoid it by denying the reality of wrongdoing, by lying, or by giving excuses, whether persuasive or not. This conduct often continues past childhood. Being held responsible for wrongful or damaging acts leads to unpleasantness, and there is a powerful urge to defend against or to try to evade such consequences. As long as excuses work, one is not held responsible. An important mark of maturity or adulthood is the willingness to accept responsibility. Ethics requires the acceptance of responsibility, particularly when there is no doubt about its appropriateness in the particular context. The signal that one has accepted responsibility is the offering of an apology, rather than the giving of an excuse. In some non-Western cultures, it is very common to offer an apology and that is often accepted as all that is necessary. The more usual response in western culture is to try to avoid responsibility by giving an excuse.

One constantly hears public complaints today that people are no longer responsible. This is often directed toward poor people on welfare, toward some disfavored ethnic or racial groups, or toward young people by parents or teachers. Those who call for acceptance of responsibility mean this criticism for others, not for themselves. Such critics are not noticeably more reticent about using excuses to avoid having to take responsibility themselves.

What does the ascription of responsibility entail in ethics? We know that legal responsibility is almost always followed by some sanction, such as the requirement of paying compensation to victims, payment of a fine, imprisonment, or, in the most extreme cases, capital punishment. In ethics, accepting responsibility means accepting blame for unethical actions and feeling remorse or guilt. Remorse and guilt are powerful forces and can create substantial pain.

For the actor or professional who is accused of acting unethically, we should distinguish conscious and unconscious levels of awareness. If the actor produces an excuse that he finds acceptable at a conscious level, but still feels guilt, he has unconsciously accepted responsibility. The excuse, which appears to work at a conscious level, has not worked at a deeper level of consciousness.

The Ethical Obligation

One never uses the words or claims that we label excuses, justifications, defenses, or alibis unless a putative duty exists that the obligor has not complied with. So the first issue in ascribing responsibility is to determine whether such a duty is present. That has been the primary concern of most ethical analysis and teaching.

There must be a normative *duty* or obligation to act in some way; that is, one ought to do something or refrain from doing something.[1] This creates the ethical obligation. Such a duty can arise from a variety of sources: personal convictions, conscience, the expectations of peers, social conventions about right and wrong actions, and formal statements of moral duties.

From among these sources, formal statements and social conventions will be of continuing importance in this discussion. For professionals, the formal statement is the code of ethics developed by each profession, coupled with whatever glosses are placed on them by the professional association and their ethics committees. There are, in addition to formal codes, social conventions about proper and improper actions, which are more complex, less universal, and tend to operate at a less conscious level. These are the informal moral codes at work in the professions, only imperfectly reflected in the formal codes.

While normative duties are varied and may be legal, ethical, religious, social, or personal, the important qualifier for us is the adjective ethical. Which of the many duties we are subject to should be thought of as ethical and within that subcategory of duties, which should be considered as professional ethical obligations? This question will be considered in Chapter 4 in detail.

We could rest the duty element solely on those obligations created or at least authenticated by the formal professional codes of ethics. I prefer at this stage to keep the sources of ethical obligation broader. Professionals are not just professionals, but human beings, responding not only to professional ethics, but also to all the ethical imperatives placed on individuals. A broader recognition of sources of duty keeps open the theoretical, and often real, possibility of conflicts between professional duties and other obliga-

16   *Ethics and Excuses*

tions. An ongoing conflict for professionals arises because there are informal codes of behavior that are not always consistent with the formal code.
An advantage of looking at professional conduct through the lens of excuses is that these may point to where the formal codes are unrealistic, ignored, or too limited. That critical opportunity would be diminished or
largely lost if we used as a starting basis only the formal professional codes
of ethics themselves.

Lying behind the codes and impinging on professionals as well as ordinary people are cultural notions about right and wrong. Few people deny
that such ethical precepts exist or that they are obligatory. Despite cultural,
ethnic, and religious diversity, there is a surprising agreement about what
in general those obligations are. That agreement is the product of a common human nature and a shared culture.

Those cultural notions of right and wrong we learn as children also contain the notion of special duties in close relationships, such as exist between
family members or close friends. The virtue of loyalty requires us to recognize these special claims unless we were to take the absurd position that we
owe loyalty in equal proportions to every institution and every person.
People understand naturally the concept of fiduciary relationships, such as
guardian and ward, godparent and godchild, mentor and apprentice. The
professional and client relationship on which professional ethics is built is
just another such relationship.

In identifying whether there is an ethical duty in a particular context, the
most reliable guide is not the formal code. Nor is it conduct. It is dangerous
to infer a norm from conduct. We often act in ways we should not. A better
indicator of a real and functioning norm is a feeling of guilt for not complying, manifested by the felt need to give an excuse. Of course, guilt is not a
perfect indicator of improper action, since others may manipulate us into
feeling guilty when we should not.

One excuse always logically possible is that there are no binding ethical
obligations, the analogy in ethics to the anarchist in politics. It is, however,
much more common to deny the existence of the particular norm at issue.
Beyond the broad claim that there are no ethical obligations at all, any other
excuse is a tacit admission of the binding force of the ethical system and
usually of the ethical norm or obligation in question.

Before leaving this introduction to ethical obligation, I want to identify
two analytical distinctions used throughout the book. They were developed by Wesley Hohfeld, a law professor who early in the twentieth century developed a system to help lawyers think clearly.[2] He felt all legal rules
defined relationships, and there were only four fundamental relationships,
out of which more complex relationships were built, much as a molecule is
built of atoms. Much confusion occurred, he thought, because lawyers use
the same term interchangeably to describe quite different relationships, the
best example of this confusing multiple uses being "right." Hohfeld

thought his distinctions made for much clearer thought and analysis in law, and I think they do in ethics as well.

For Hohfeld, "duty" was always the correlative of "right," and unless some identifiable person had a claim or "right," there was no duty. A host of problems and much confused thinking in professional ethics arise from failure to keep this idea clearly in mind. First, one must identify to whom the professional's duty is owed. If she owes competing duties at the same time and place to different people, she must decide which is the overriding or more compelling duty.

A simplistic view of professional ethics says there is no problem because the overriding duty is always owed to the client. This is the product of thinking only in terms of the simple autonomous professional–single client model. The professional has many clients; hence the often unavoidable conflicts of duty. The professional also owes duties to fellow professionals, to family and friends, and often to members of the public with whom he comes into contact in the course of his professional activity.[3] If we think the choice problem is simple and the professional always owes the primary duty to the client, we have defined out of our consciousness some of the most difficult ethical problems professionals face.

Another useful distinction drawn by Hohfeld is the relationship he defined as "privilege–no right." Privilege is the area of freedom where we can act; however, we choose without anyone else having the "right" to complain about what we do. Professional ethics is a continuing battleground about the boundary lines between these two types of relationships. Professionals want their activity to come primarily inside the realm of privilege; that is, they stake out a large claim of professional autonomy. That is a claim with which I have much sympathy. However, when one accepts that a duty is owed to someone else, whether client, fellow professional, or spouse, which is, to say, that person has a right or a claim that we act in a certain way, we are no longer privileged to act as we wish, but only as we must. Even if there are conflicting claims, we are obligated to honor the strongest of the claims. There is no privilege to choose a weaker claim or to ignore all the claims.

Autonomy is important to professionals who believe that they do and should enjoy wide freedom in practicing their profession and utilizing their expertise. Some excuses discussed in the next chapter are based on the notion that in the particular context the professional in fact had no such autonomy and thus should not be ethically responsible.

Autonomy is an important condition not just for professionals, but for all people. The ethical choice has to be a free choice; that is, the actor could have acted in more than one way and the options are not morally indifferent.[4] One way of acting has to be better than the other, or stated in ethical terms, one course of action is good and the other bad. If both courses of action are equally good, there is no problem of ethical choice. And if the actor can act in only one way, it makes no sense to worry about whether that action should be considered ethical or unethical. A major reason for labeling something good or bad is to influence choice.

The Ethical Breach

A *breach* is action that goes against the requirements of the norm. It is action that is regarded as abnormal or wrong. This constitutes the second element in the fixing of ethical responsibility. Breach is a shorthand way of saying that the particular action of the professional does not comply with the appropriate ethical standard. Rule-obeying behavior is generally not noticed or is taken for granted, that is, accepted as normal—as what should occur.[5]

This creates a serious problem of observational bias. Because we take the normal for granted and tend to stress the abnormal, we may exaggerate the degree of criminality or unethical action in our world because we do not clearly notice and consciously record the proportion of human activity that is normal and ethical. This caution needs to be kept in mind when deciding whether to accept the introductory assumption of this book, which is, that we face an ethical crisis.

Small children often deny moral breaches even in the face of overwhelming evidence that they did it. Adults are less likely to deny an obvious breach, but more likely to try to transfer the responsibility to someone else. It is not unknown, of course, for children to use this same technique, claiming, "My brother did it" or "The dog did it." One of the common professional excuses discussed in the next chapter is the claim that someone else actually did the action or was responsible for whatever injury occurred.

Another possible claim about this element that can be made by someone accused of unethical activity is to assert that the action and any resulting damage was insignificant or trivial and so should not be considered an ethical breach by anyone. It is hard to know whether one should treat this as an excuse or as part of the definition of what constitutes a breach. In other words, the definition could require that a breach must be substantial.

Auxiliary Concepts

In addition to the central concepts of duty, breach, and responsibility that are necessary to understand the role of excuses, there are three others that can be relevant. Their importance is not so much in explaining how excuses work, but rather in answering questions that will arise in the rest of the book. First, when is an ethical violation so serious that it calls for an excuse to be made? Second, when there is more than one candidate for the role of responsible party, how do we select the one to be held responsible? Finally, when there has been a serious violation of a norm that is both legal and ethical, how do we assign it to the appropriate realm?

The first auxiliary concept is *damage*. Damage goes to the seriousness of the injury and establishes a threshold. That threshold must be such that a victim is likely to complain and the actor feels a necessity to produce an excuse. Must an unethical act produce some harm to another before it should be considered unethical? As a first-year law student, I was surprised to learn that traditional legal analysis required that an "illegal" act produce harm before it was actionable. For example, a person is often negligent in driving his automobile, either exceeding the speed limit or driving recklessly, but she has not committed a tort, an illegal act, unless somebody is injured by her carelessness. Should the same analysis be used in practical ethics?[6]

The importance of damage as an element in understanding excuses is not so dependent on whether or not one adopts a consequentialist theory, as it is on three practical considerations.

The first reason is essentially administrative. We frequently act in ways that violate prudent, rational, or moral notions, but neither we nor others take such action seriously until it produces harm. The existence of damage is our way of separating trivial from serious matters.

Second, excuses need not be given until someone complains. Excuses are essentially a part of the interpersonal aspect of immoral activity. The other person, usually the victim, would seldom raise the issue of unethical action unless he has been harmed.

Finally, in the practical world, we analyze these issues in reverse form. Responsibility is signaled by the fact we must pay a price, that is, the imposition of some sanction such as physical punishment, monetary fines, or blame. That would normally occur only when we have done some harm to another. We cannot impose the sanction on someone for damage until we are sure he is the one who really caused the injury, so what I have called "auxiliary concepts" are useful to the whole enterprise of determining responsibility, which gives rise to the need for excuses.

Related to this issue of the importance of damage in calling forth the need for excuses and then using excuses as a key to unethical behavior is the question of what kinds of unsatisfactory behavior by professionals should be labeled unethical. When the professional establishes a relationship of trust with a client and then produces an unsatisfactory result, the client will feel he has been mistreated and will make a claim of incompetence or unethical behavior. The explanation given by the professional will be regarded as an excuse and thus falls within the analysis of this book.

There must be *causation*, some connection between the breach of the duty and damage to create legal liability. Should we not say the same of ethical misconduct? It is implicit in the analysis, but often not explicit. Causation becomes an important element only if damage occurs and one is trying to connect that to a responsible actor.

Finally there is the element of *sanction*. When detected, illegal activity is almost invariably followed by the imposition of some unpleasant consequence. Should we say the same of unethical activity? Is blame or the existence of guilt the functional equivalent of a sanction? Certainly blame from others is unpleasant and is a consequence we want to avoid just as we want to avoid the effects of legal sanctions. Guilt is a more interesting puzzle. Like blame, it is also an unpleasant sensation and presumably we wish to avoid pain so the assumption is that we will tend to live our lives in ways that minimize the degree of guilt we feel. It is, however, internal and is not imposed from the outside, so to deal with it as a sanction, we may be forced into the metaphor of the split personality with one part (the superego?) imposing the guilt and another part (the ego?) suffering.

How are these elements related and used in a full-blown analysis of ethical responsibility? We might think we look for an ethical duty, find if there has been a breach, ask if damage was caused by the breach to a victim, and then decide whether there is a connection between the breach and that damage. Responsibility would then be a consequence of finding that all these elements were present. This describes an analytical or theoretical way of talking about responsibility, which is helpful in understanding the elements or concepts involved. Actually this process is almost totally reversed in ordinary human transactions.

What is the trigger for ethical analysis of our daily actions? Most often it is a claim by a victim, an observer, or a supervisor that a person has acted unethically. In an internal analysis, the trigger may be the fear someone might make such a claim. It is only then that excuses are trotted out and one works backward through the chain of elements. A claim of unethical activity is unlikely to be made until there has been harm. The claim comes only after someone has been identified as the causal agent. The excuse raises the question of whether there was a duty and a breach by the actor. This process of evaluating action after the fact is often described as hindsight knowledge or "Monday morning quarterbacking" and often carries a connotation of unfairness about evaluating an activity after the event. Practically, however, that is the only time it is possible to evaluate an actual event, rather than speculate about probabilities or possibilities, which may not even occur.

One way of excusing the breach and thus evading responsibility is to deny the existence of any one of these elements. We might say that there was no duty, that our acts did not breach a duty, that no damage was done, or that our breach did not cause the damage. There are, however, ethical excuses, as we will see in Chapter 3, and legal defenses, as discussed in Chapter 5, which accept that all of these conceptual elements are present and still contend the actor is not responsible.

WHAT ARE THE FUNCTIONS OF EXCUSES?

The excuse intervenes between the breach and the conclusion of responsibility. It is usually a relational act by which a wrongdoer explains himself to another and seeks to avoid the ascription of responsibility. The actor may be excusing himself to himself, engaging in an internal dialogue trying to escape guilt. This could be thought of analytically as a relational act between different parts of the personality. In order to escape responsibility, he must offer some reason why the norm did not apply or that he should not be seen as violating it.

Excuses are Janus-faced. They can be the means by which a "responsible" person avoids the social or personal consequences of improper actions. However, they are also the means by which the rigidity of universal and perfectionist normative systems can be given flexibility and adapted to complex or unusual individual situations. In this latter type of function, excuses are not avoidance of responsibility, but a tool of adaptability and of critical evaluation. In discussing the problem of adapting moral positions and justifications to the incredible variety of contexts in which human beings act, Stuart Hampshire said:

> The parallel with language is useful. It has so far proved impossible to design a translating machine which takes account of the indefinite variety of contexts, linguistic and external, in which a given form of words is used; and normally the contexts affect the sense. However elaborate the programme built into the machine, it is apt to fall short, if only because of the sheer unpredictable variety of contexts encountered. The variety is not only humanly unpredictable but humanly unimaginable. Yet a person translating immediately sees the recurring form of words against the background of a different context and then intuitively makes the required adjustment to the sense. A person is a complex mechanism naturally designed over a long evolutionary period to make such adjustments.[7]

Excuses are often the way an actor accused of acting unethically contends that the context in which the claim is made is different from the set of paradigm cases the rule was intended to cover, so it is inappropriate to hold him morally responsible for violating the rule. Given the abstract and almost universal form of most ethical rules and the way we analyze moral issues, that issue of overinclusiveness cannot be raised directly but must be broached indirectly through the use of an excuse.

This process of excusing questionable behavior may be totally internal; that is, the professional can know she has an ethical duty and that she has probably violated that duty. She then proposes to herself an excuse explaining the way she acted and if the excuse seems persuasive, she does not feel she must assume any responsibility.

22   *Ethics and Excuses*

The process can be totally external. The duty will be imposed by the code of professional ethics or admonitions of other professionals. Some victim, often a client, will claim to have been harmed by the violation of an ethical principle. There might then be a formal hearing by an ethics committee of the professional association where the accused professional will offer an excuse and the committee will decide whether the excuse is persuasive or not and thus find the professional either responsible or not.

Whether the procedure is wholly internal, wholly external, or a mix of the two, excuses function the same way, sometimes as a means of avoiding responsibility, other times as a means of making the ascription of responsibility better adapted to context and complexity.

HOW DO WE DESIGNATE SUCCESSFUL OR UNSUCCESSFUL EXCUSES?

The word "excuse" carries different meanings. One meaning, suggested by the word "alibi," is an attempt to *avoid responsibility* legitimately placed on the actor. Another meaning is a justification,[8] a persuasive reason, for being excepted from an otherwise applicable ethical obligation. "Excuse" may also refer to an *explanation* as to why the unethical conduct occurred. Such explanations are useful if one wants to change conduct.[9]

In order to avoid confusion in the following discussion, I use "excuse" as the generic term. Since an excuse may be either a good or a bad one, the term carries no value connotation. It serves only the function of saying that a claimed duty does not apply to an actor so that his acts are not a breach and therefore he ought not to bear any responsibility for the actions. When discussing a valid excuse, I will call it a "justification," or sometimes, a "persuasive excuse." This means that even if there was a duty and the actor breached that duty, there is some reason why moral responsibility should not be attributed to him.[10]

When describing an unpersuasive or invalid excuse, I will use the term "alibi." The common usage of "alibi" is a claim that the alleged actor was not present at the time and place of the action so he could not be responsible. Since it usually carries a connotation of being unpersuasive, if not untrue, I adopt a wider usage of the term to cover all unpersuasive excuses. In the next chapter, I discuss many common excuses offered by professionals, some of which in the right context are genuine justifications, but in other situations would be alibis.

If I am talking about a reason merely given by the actor to make clear why he acted the way he did, I will call it an "explanation." If the actor decides whether the excuse is persuasive enough to avoid responsibility, the "explanation" will also serve as a justification, but if others make the judgment about the excuse's validity, "explanation" is merely the actor's way of viewing the situation.

Another important linguistic distinction signals the difference between legal and ethical systems. "Excuse" is the appropriate term when discussing ethical obligations. In reference to legal obligations, one speaks of "defenses."

WHO DECIDES WHETHER AN EXCUSE IS SATISFACTORY?

A significant difference between the normative systems of law and of ethics is that the legal system has developed a means by which the validity of an excuse can be determined "objectively." This process is the trial during which a judge and/or jury will hear the reasons given by the actor for not complying with the law and will decide whether they constitute a persuasive defense. Even if no trial is held, the defendant must be prepared for such an eventuality. Thus his defenses must not merely be persuasive to himself, but appear likely to persuade judges and jurors. The decision by the court would, of course, not be merely a personal decision, but constrained by a centuries-long development of rules, standards, and distinctions that the judge and jury are supposed to take account of. No such procedure exists in ethical systems. The closest analog for professionals would be the opinion of peers or possible victims who may indicate whether they find the excuse persuasive or not.

For practical ethics, the actor is the most important judge of whether an excuse is valid. If he feels there is a justification for not obeying an ethical norm, he is free to act in accordance with his perceived self-interest. This makes ethics largely a system of voluntary compliance. Of course, others, such as clients, victims, bystanders, or fellow professionals, may evaluate the excuse and they could well decide that it was not valid. If they do not inform the actor of their feelings, which is a strong possibility in our culture where an important informal moral maxim is "mind your own business," or if the actor does not care about their opinion, there is no constraint on acting in an unethical fashion. As long as an excuse exists that the actor can persuade himself or herself is a valid justification, ethical systems will have little bite in controlling action. This freedom to be indifferent to ethical systems has been exacerbated in modern urban life with the breakup of close communities and tight family structure.

We will return to this problem, which is the primary focus of this book, in Chapter 9.

NOTES

1. For a valuable discussion of the various meanings of "ought" or "obligation" and the dangers of restricting those to rule-based duties, see Joel Feinberg, DOING AND DESERVING: ESSAYS IN THE THEORY OF RESPONSIBILITY (Princeton: Princeton University Press, 1970), pp. 3–9.

2. Wesley N. Hohfeld, FUNDAMENTAL LEGAL CONCEPTIONS (New Haven: Yale University Press, 1919). An abbreviated introduction to Hohfeldian

analysis appears in Arthur L. Corbin, "Legal Analysis and Terminology," 29 YALE LAW JOURNAL (1919): 163–173.

3. An example of this last conflict familiar to lawyers is the question of whether a defendant's attorney in a rape case owes any duties to the victim. This issue is raised by the practice of defense lawyers, who are trying to protect their client, viciously attacking the victim's reputation and veracity, a process so debilitating that many victims refuse to complain rather than face that prospect.

4. Isaiah Berlin in the introduction to his FOUR ESSAYS ON LIBERTY (London, Oxford University Press, 1969), pp. xi–xv, argues persuasively that ethical choices entailing the ascription of responsibility must be free in this sense.

5. There is an interesting question about conduct, which as a matter of politics or rebelliousness violates contemporary norms of customary action. Much creative activity may have this quality. Should one think of this as an excuse or should we define our norms as creating an exception for such activity? A major issue in political theory is how much value should be given to obedient and conforming behavior and what value to iconoclastic and questioning activity against society's norms.

6. For readers trained in moral philosophy, I want to clarify that "damage" is not used in the sense of consequences in utilitarian theory, but the way a lawyer uses the term. The focus is on an identifiable and quantifiable injury done to a person who complains and who insists that justice requires some form of recompense. For the lawyer, this normally means money damages. In ethical systems, it would require acceptance of blame, apologies, or atonement.

7. Stuart Hampshire, "Public and Private Morality," in PUBLIC AND PRIVATE MORALITY, Stuart Hampshire, ed. (Cambridge: Cambridge University Press, 1978), p. 31.

8. The classic analysis of excuses is J. L. Austin, "A Plea for Excuses," PHILOSOPHICAL PAPERS, 3d ed. (New York: Oxford University Press, 1979). Austin gives justification and excuse a different meaning than I do. When an actor admits that she acted in a certain way, but claims it was a good thing is what he means by justification. In contrast, the situation when the actor admits that she acted in a wrong way, but offers an explanation in order to partly or totally escape responsibility is what he means by excuse. I am interested in how one distinguishes between persuasive and unpersuasive excuses. The person to be persuaded may be an objective observer, a professional or legal institution, or the actor herself.

Criminal law theorists also often distinguish justifications from excuses. See George P. Fletcher, RETHINKING CRIMINAL LAW (Boston: Little, Brown and Company, 1978), pp. 759–762. The practical reason for this distinction is that justified conduct would not allow the victim to act in self-defense whereas a mere excuse would. Although that problem can on occasion be a serious one for legal systems, it is not for ethical analysis. The distinction I am concerned with is the difference between those excuses that successfully avoid responsibility by an actor and those which do not.

9. I do not distinguish here between a completely persuasive excuse, a partial excuse, and a totally invalid excuse. These distinctions, which control the degree of responsibility an actor has, fall largely outside the focus and analysis of this chapter.

10. As indicated in Note 8 above, many moral philosophers and legal theorists insist on a difference between justification and excuse, a distinction I will not use. For them, justification is an explanation why the action did not violate a moral duty. An excuse admits there was a violation of moral duty, but is an explanation as to why moral responsibility in part or in full should not fall on the actor. That analysis assumes that the primary issue before the theorist is whether there was a moral duty or not and the decision is being made by an objective observer. My view is that in the practical world, the issue is always whether the actor is responsible or not for a questionable action and that decision is usually being made by the actor or someone affected by the action. "Justification" in ordinary language means a persuasive explanation as to why responsibility is not applicable. Such a broad meaning is given by the *Oxford English Dictionary*: "The action of justifying or showing something to be just, right, or proper; vindication of oneself or another; exculpation . . . b. That which justifies; a justifying circumstance; an apology, a defense" (THE COMPACT EDITION OF THE OXFORD ENGLISH DICTIONARY) [New York: Oxford University Press, 1971], p. 1524). For purposes of my analysis, justification and persuasive excuse are synonymous and I shall so use them.

[6]

The Evolution of Social Work Ethics

Frederic G. Reamer

The recent ratification of a new NASW Code of Ethics—the most ambitious set of ethical guidelines in social work's history—marks an important stage in the profession's development. This article traces the evolution of ethical norms, principles, and standards in social work during four stages in the profession's history: (1) the morality period, (2) the values period, (3) the ethical theory and decision-making period, and (4) the ethical standards and risk management period. In the past 100 years, social work has moved from a preoccupation with clients' morality and values to the formulation of comprehensive ethical guidelines for practice. In recent years social work has also developed rich conceptual frameworks and practical resources to help practitioners identify, assess, and address complex ethical issues. Implications of these developments for the profession are explored, particularly in light of social work's commemoration of its 100th anniversary.

Key words: *ethical decision making; ethical standards; ethics; NASW Code of Ethics; values*

Ethical issues have always been a central feature in social work. Throughout the profession's history social workers have been concerned with matters of right and wrong and matters of duty and obligation. The National Association of Social Workers' (NASW) recent ratification of a new code of ethics (NASW, 1996) signals social workers' remarkable progress in the identification and understanding of ethical issues in the profession. The 1996 code—the first major revision in nearly two decades and only the third code of ethics ratified in NASW's history—reflects the impressive growth in social workers' grasp of complex ethical issues in practice.

The celebration of social work's 100th anniversary provides a particularly auspicious moment to reflect on the evolution of social work

ethics. Social workers' core values and ethical beliefs are the profession's linchpin. Social workers' concern with ethics has matured considerably during the past century, moving from frequently moralistic preoccupation with clients' values to concern about complex ethical dilemmas faced by practitioners and strategies for dealing with these dilemmas. Social work's concern with ethics spans four major, sometimes overlapping, periods: (1) the morality period, (2) the values period, (3) the ethical theory and decision-making period, and (4) the ethical standards and risk management period.

The Morality Period

In the late 20th century, when social work was formally inaugurated as a profession, there was much more concern about the morality of the client than about the morality or ethics of the profession or its practitioners (Leiby, 1978; Lubove, 1965; Reamer, 1995a). Social workers' earliest practitioners focused on organized relief and responding to the "curse of pauperism" (Paine, 1880). Often this preoccupation took the form of paternalistic efforts to bolster poor people's morality and the rectitude of those who had succumbed to "shiftless" or "wayward" habits.

Social workers' focus on the morality of poor people waned significantly during the settlement house movement in the early 20th century, when many social workers turned their attention to structural and environmental causes of individual and social problems, particularly social workers' ethical obligation to promote social justice and social reform. As has been well documented in the profession's literature, many social workers were concerned with "cause" rather than, or in addition to, "case." This was evident in social workers' social reform efforts designed to address the toxic environmental determinants of problems related to poverty, inadequate housing and health care, mental illness, alcoholism, and violence (Brieland, 1995; Lee, 1930).

Emphasis on clients' morality continued to weaken during the next several decades as social workers created and refined various intervention theories and strategies, training programs, and educational models. During this phase, many social workers were more concerned about cultivating perspectives and methods that would be indigenous to social work, partly in an effort to distinguish social work's approach to helping from those of allied professions, such as psychology and psychiatry.

Exploration of Values

Although a critical mass of serious scholarship on social work ethics did not appear until the 1950s, there were several efforts earlier in the 20th century to explore social work values and ethics (Frankel, 1959). As early as 1919 there

> *Nearly a half century after its formal beginning, social work began to develop and publicize ethical standards and guidelines.*

were attempts to draft professional codes of ethics (Elliott, 1931). In 1922 the Family Welfare Association of America appointed an ethics committee in response to questions about ethical problems in social work (Elliott, 1931; Joseph, 1989). In addition, there is evidence that at least some schools of social work were teaching discrete courses on values and ethics in the 1920s (Elliott, 1931; Johnson, 1955). These efforts were consistent with Flexner's (1915) widely respected assertion that a full-fledged profession should have a clearly articulated, values-based ethical foundation.

By the late 1940s and early 1950s, social workers' concern about the moral dimensions of the profession shifted. Instead of the earlier preoccupation with clients' morality, social workers began to focus much more on the morality, values, and ethics of the profession and its practitioners. Nearly a half century after its formal beginning, social work began to develop and publicize ethical standards and guidelines. In 1947, after several years of discussion and debate, the Delegate Conference of the American Association of Social Workers adopted a code of ethics. Several social work journals also published several seminal articles on values and ethics. In 1959 Muriel Pumphrey published her landmark work *The Teaching of Values and Ethics in Social Work Education* for the Council on Social Work Education. Other significant publications during this period included Hall's (1952) "Group Workers and Professional Ethics" and Johnson's (1955) "Educating Professional Social Workers for Ethical Practice" (Pumphrey, 1959).

In the 1960s and early 1970s, social workers directed considerable attention toward matters of social justice, social reform, and civil rights. The social turbulence of this era had enormous influence on the profession. Thousands of new practitioners were attracted to the profession primarily because of social work's abiding concern about values germane to human rights, welfare rights, equality, discrimination, and oppression. This period was marked by a number of important publications, such as Emmet's (1962) "Ethics and the Social Worker," Keith-Lucas's (1963) "A Critique of the Principle of Client Self-Determination," Plant's (1970) *Social and Moral Theory in Casework*, Lewis's (1972) "Morality and the Politics of Practice," Levy's "The Context of Social Work Ethics" (1972) and "The Value Base of Social Work" (1973), Vigilante's (1974) "Between Values and Science," and McDermott's (1975) anthology *Self-Determination in Social Work*. It is significant that NASW adopted its first code of ethics during this period.

Particularly important during this period was the proliferation of commentary on core social work values. These discussions of social work values were of three types (Timms, 1983): (1) broad descriptive overviews of the profession's mission and its core values, such as respect of persons, valuing individuals' capacity for change, client self-determination, client empowerment, individual worth and dignity, commitment to social change and social justice, service to others, professional competence, professional integrity, providing individuals with opportunity to realize their potential, seeking to meet individuals' common human needs, client privacy and confidentiality, nondiscrimination, equal opportunity, respect of diversity, and willingness to transmit professional knowledge and skills to others (see, for example, Arnold, 1970; Bartlett, 1970; Bernstein, 1960; Biestek, 1957; Biestek & Gehrig, 1978; Gordon, 1962, 1965; Hamilton, 1940, 1951; Keith-Lucas, 1977; Levy, 1973, 1976; Lubove, 1965; Perlman, 1965, 1976; Plant, 1970; Pumphrey, 1959; Reynolds, 1976; Stalley, 1975; Teicher, 1967; Towle, 1965; Vigilante, 1974; Working Definition of Social Work Practice, 1958; Younghusband, 1967); (2) critiques of social work values (for example, Keith-Lucas, 1963; McDermott, 1975; Whittington, 1975; Wilson, 1978); and (3) reports of empirical research on values held or embraced by social workers (for example, Costin, 1964; McCleod & Meyer, 1967; Varley, 1968).

A significant segment of the literature during this period focused on the need for social workers to examine and clarify their own personal values (see, for example, Hardman, 1975;

McCleod & Meyer, 1967; Varley, 1968). The premise here was that social workers' personal beliefs and values related, for example, to people living in poverty, race relations, abortion, homosexuality, civil disobedience, and drug use would have a profound effect on their approach to and relationships with clients.

Pumphrey (1959) provided one of the earliest and most influential categorizations of social work's core values, placing them into three groups of value-based objectives. The first group emphasized the relationship between the values of the profession and the values operating in the culture at large. This group was concerned with the compatibility between social work's mission—for example, regarding social justice, social change, and addressing basic human needs—and the broader culture's values. The second category dealt more narrowly with social work's perception of its own values, particularly the ways the profession interpreted and implemented its values and encouraged ethical behavior. The final category emphasized social workers' relationships with specific groups and individuals served by social workers, particularly understanding and responding to clients' values. Of specific importance was the potential for conflict among competing values.

Another key attempt during this period to outline core social work values that guide practice was made by Gordon (1965). Gordon argued that there are six value-based concepts that constitute the foundation of social work practice related to the role of the individual in contemporary society, interdependence among individuals, individuals' social responsibility for one another, individuals' common human needs and uniqueness, the importance of social action and social responsibility, and society's obligation to eliminate obstacles to individual self-realization.

Levy (1973) also provided an important typology of social work's values. The first of Levy's three groups included "preferred conceptions of people," such as the belief in individuals' inherent worth and dignity, capacity and drive toward constructive change, mutual responsibility, need to belong, uniqueness, and common human needs. The second group included "preferred outcomes for people," such as the belief in society's obligation to provide opportunities for individual growth and development; to provide resources and services to help people meet their needs and to avoid such problems as hunger, inadequate housing or education, illness, and discrimination; and to provide equal opportunity to participate in the molding of society. Levy's third group included "preferred instrumentalities for dealing with people," such as the belief that people should be treated with respect and dignity, have the right to self-determination, be encouraged to participate in social change activities, and be recognized as unique individuals. Levy's 1976 publication of *Social Work Ethics* was clearly the most ambitious discussion of the subject at that point in the profession's history.

Emergence of Ethical Theory and Decision Making

Social work entered a new phase in the early 1980s, influenced largely by the invention in the 1970s of a new field known as applied and professional ethics. The principal feature of the applied and professional ethics field, which began especially with developments in medical ethics, or what has become known as bioethics, was the deliberate, disciplined attempt to apply principles, concepts, and theories of moral philosophy, or ethics, to real-life challenges faced by professionals. For decades prior to this development, moral philosophers had been preoccupied with fairly abstract debates about the meaning of ethical terms and the validity of rather abstruse ethical theories and conceptually complex moral arguments, a philosophical specialty known as meta-ethics (Frankena, 1973; Hancock, 1974; Rawls, 1971). Several factors, however, inspired a substantial contingent of moral philosophers to turn their attention to more practical and immediate ethical problems. First, intense social debate in the 1960s concerning such prominent issues as welfare rights, prisoners' rights, patients' rights, human rights, and affirmative action led many moral philosophers to grapple with contemporary issues. Second, a number of technological developments, particularly related to health care issues (for example, reproduction, organ transplantation, abortion, and end-of-life decisions), led many

moral philosophers to explore applied ethical issues. In addition, increasingly widespread media publicity related to moral scandals and ethical misconduct in public and professional life, beginning especially with Watergate in the early 1970s, stirred up interest in professional ethics (Callahan & Bok, 1980). It was during this period that now-prominent ethics organizations got their formal start, most notably the Hastings Center and the Kennedy Institute of Ethics at Georgetown University. (The number of applied and professional ethics organizations has grown so large that there is now a national Association for Practical and Professional Ethics, which includes nearly 100 institutional members.)

Along with most other professions—including nursing, medicine, journalism, engineering, dentistry, law, psychology, counseling, and business—social work's literature on ethics began to change significantly in the early 1980s (Goldstein, 1987). In addition to discussions about the profession's values, a small group of scholars began to write about ethical issues and challenges while drawing on literature, concepts, theories, and principles from the traditional field of moral philosophy and the newer field of applied and professional ethics. Three social work books published during this period were especially noteworthy in this regard: *Ethical Decisions for Social Work Practice* (Loewenberg & Dolgoff, 1982), *Ethical Dilemmas in Social Service* (Reamer, 1982), and *Ethical Dilemmas in Social Work Practice* (Rhodes, 1986). Using somewhat different approaches, each of these books acknowledged explicitly for the first time the relevance of moral philosophy and ethical theory, concepts, and principles in the analysis and resolution of ethical issues in social work. Furthermore, the 1987 edition of the NASW *Encyclopedia of Social Work* included an article directly addressing the relevance of philosophical and ethical concepts to social work ethics (Reamer, 1987a).

Since the early and mid-1980s, literature on social work ethics that draws directly on ethical theory and concepts has burgeoned. Most of this literature explores the relationship between standard ethical theories (known as deontology, teleology, consequentialism, utilitarianism, and virtue theory) and actual or hypothetical ethical dilemmas encountered by social workers. Relevant ethical dilemmas concern direct practice (for example, confidentiality, client self-determination, informed consent, professional paternalism, truth telling), program design and agency administration (for example, adhering to agency policies or regulations and distributing limited resources), and relationships among practitioners (for example, reporting colleagues' unethical behavior or impairment). Examples include social workers who must decide between their duty to respect the client's rights to confidentiality and their obligation to protect third parties from harm; whether to place limits on the client's right to engage in self-destructive behavior; how to allocate scarce or limited resources; and whether to "blow the whistle" and report a professional colleague's ethical misconduct to authorities.

A significant portion of the literature since the mid-1980s has focused on decision-making strategies social workers can engage in when faced with difficult ethical judgments. Typically, these discussions identify a series of steps and considerations social workers can follow as they attempt to resolve difficult ethical dilemmas, focusing on the conflicting values, ethical duties, and obligations; the individuals, groups, and organizations that are likely to be affected; possible courses of action; relevant ethical theories, principles, and guidelines; legal principles and pertinent codes of ethics; social work practice theory and principles; personal values; the need to consult with colleagues and appropriate experts; and the need to monitor, evaluate, and document decisions (Joseph, 1985; Loewenberg & Dolgoff, 1996; Reamer, 1995a).

Maturation of Ethical Standards and Risk Management

The most recent stage reflects the remarkable growth in social workers' understanding of ethical issues in the profession. It is marked primarily by the 1996 ratification of a new NASW code of ethics, which significantly expanded ethical guidelines and standards for social work practice.

As noted, few formal ethical standards existed early in social work's history. The earliest known attempt to formulate a code was an experimental draft code of ethics attributed to Mary Richmond (Pumphrey, 1959). Although several other social work organizations developed draft codes during social work's early years (for example, the American Association for Organizing Family Social Work and several chapters of the American Association of Social Workers), it was not until 1947 that the latter group adopted a formal code (Johnson, 1955). In 1960 NASW adopted its first code of ethics, five years after the association was formed.

The 1960 *NASW Code of Ethics* consisted of only 14 proclamations concerning, for example, every social worker's duty to give precedence to professional responsibility over personal interests; to respect the privacy of clients; to give appropriate professional service in public emergencies; and to contribute knowledge, skills, and support to human welfare programs. A series of brief first-person statements (such as, "I give precedence to my professional responsibility over my personal interests," and, "I respect the privacy of the people I serve," [p. 1]) were preceded by a preamble that set forth social workers' responsibilities to uphold humanitarian ideals, maintain and improve social work service, and develop the philosophy and skills of the profession. In 1967 a 15th principle pledging nondiscrimination was added to the proclamations.

In 1977, based in part on growing concern about this code's level of abstraction and usefulness (McCann & Cutler, 1979), NASW established a task force chaired by Charles Levy to revise the code. In 1979 NASW adopted a new code, which was far more ambitious than the 1960 code. The 1979 code included nearly 80

> *The 1960 NASW Code of Ethics consisted of only 14 proclamations concerning, for example, every social worker's duty to give precedence to professional responsibility over personal interests.*

ethical "principles" divided into six major sections of brief, unannotated statements with a preamble describing the code's general purpose and stating that the code's principles provided guidelines for the enforcement of ethical practices in the profession. The code included major sections concerning social workers' general conduct and comportment and ethical responsibilities to clients, colleagues, employers, employing organizations, the social work profession, and society.

The 1979 code was revised twice (NASW, 1990, 1993) as a result of several important developments. In 1990 several principles related to solicitation of clients and fee splitting were modified following an inquiry, begun in 1986, into NASW policies by the U.S. Federal Trade Commission (FTC). The FTC alleged that the code's prohibition of client solicitation and fee splitting constituted an inappropriate restraint of trade. As a result of the inquiry, principles in the code were revised to remove prohibitions concerning solicitation of clients from colleagues or one's agency and to modify wording related to accepting compensation for making a referral.

In 1992 an NASW task force recommended that five specific new principles addressing two new concepts be added to the code. Three of the principles concerned the problem of social worker impairment, and two concerned the problem of dual or multiple relationships between social workers and clients. Both the problem of social worker impairment (Reamer, 1992a) and dual and multiple relationships between social workers and clients (Kagle & Giebelhausen, 1994) had begun to receive increasing attention in the profession and, the task force argued, needed to be acknowledged in the code. In 1993 the NASW Delegate Assembly voted to add these five new principles.

By the time of the 1993 NASW Delegate Assembly, there was growing awareness among social workers that the *NASW Code of Ethics* required significant revision and that modest changes and "tinkering" would no longer suffice. The vast majority of the scholarly literature on social work ethics—nearly 75 percent—had been published **since** the ratification of the 1979 code, which went into effect as the broader field

of applied and professional ethics was in its infancy. There was widespread recognition that issues explored in the social work literature, not to mention the broader applied and professional ethics literature, since the ratification of the 1979 code needed to be reflected in a new code. Examples included new knowledge and discussions related to ethical misconduct (Berliner, 1989; Bullis, 1995; McCann & Cutler, 1979), ethical decision making (Gambrill & Pruger, 1997; Goldmeier, 1984; Joseph, 1989; Loewenberg & Dolgoff, 1996; McGowan, 1995; Reamer, 1990, 1995a, 1995b, 1998b; Rhodes, 1986), informed consent (Reamer, 1987b; Summers, 1989), dual and multiple relationships and related boundary issues (Jayaratne, Croxton, & Mattison, 1997; Kagle & Giebelhausen, 1994), confidentiality and the protection of third parties (Dickson, 1998; Goldberg, 1989; Kopels & Kagle, 1993; Reamer, 1991; Weil & Sanchez, 1983), privileged communication (Levick, 1981; VandeCreek, Knapp, & Herzog, 1988), ethical issues in social work supervision (Reamer, 1989), ethics consultation (Reamer, 1995c), ethical issues in industrial social work (Kurzman, 1983), the teaching of social work ethics (Black, Hartley, Whelley, & Kirk-Sharp, 1989; Reamer & Abramson, 1982), ethics and unionization (Karger, 1988; Reamer, 1988), ethical issues in organizations (Joseph, 1983; Levy, 1982), impaired social workers (Reamer, 1992a), ethics in social work research and evaluation (Grinnell, 1993; Rubin & Babbie, 1993), professional paternalism (Abramson, 1985; Reamer, 1983), bioethical issues in social work (Reamer, 1985), ethics committees (Conrad, 1989; Reamer, 1987a), professional malpractice (Bernstein, 1981; Besharov, 1985; Besharov & Besharov, 1987; Reamer, 1993, 1994, 1995a), and social work's moral mission (Billups, 1992; Keith-Lucas, 1992; Popple, 1992; Reamer, 1992b; Reid, 1992; Reid & Popple, 1992; Siporin, 1989, 1992).

Because of the exponential growth of ethics-related knowledge—with respect to social work in particular and the professions in general—since the development of the 1979 code, delegates at the 1993 NASW Delegate Assembly recognized the need for an entirely new code. In addition, there was widespread recognition that the profession's code needed to pay more attention to ethical issues facing social workers not involved in direct practice, especially social workers involved in agency administration, supervision, research and evaluation, and education. Thus, the Delegate Assembly passed a resolution to establish a task force to draft a completely new code of ethics for submission to the 1996 Delegate Assembly. The task force was established to produce a new code that would be far more comprehensive and relevant to current practice, taking into consideration the tremendous increase in knowledge since the ratification of the 1979 code.

The Code of Ethics Revision Committee was appointed in 1994 by the president of NASW and spent two years drafting a new code designed to incorporate comprehensive guidelines reflecting the impressive expansion of knowledge in the field (Reamer, 1997, 1998a). The committee included a moral philosopher active in the professional ethics field and social workers from a variety of practice and academic settings (members of the committee included Carol Brill, Jacqueline Glover, Marjorie Hammock, M. Vincentia Joseph, Alfred Murillo, Jr., Frederic Reamer [chair], Barbara Varley, and Drayton Vincent). During the two-year period leading up to the final draft of the new code, the committee reviewed literature on social work ethics and on applied and professional ethics generally to identify key concepts and issues that might be addressed in the new code, reviewed the 1979 code (as revised) to identify content that should be retained or deleted and areas where content might be added, issued formal invitations to all NASW members and to members of various social work organizations (the National Association of Black Social Workers, the Council on Social Work Education, the American Association of State Social Work Boards, and the National Federation of Societies of Clinical Social Work) to suggest issues that might be addressed in the new code, shared rough drafts of the code with a small group of ethics experts in social work and other professions for their comments, and revised the code based on the various sources of feedback. The draft code was published in the January 1996 issue of the *NASW News*, along with an invitation for all NASW members to submit comments to be considered by the committee as it prepared the final draft for submission to the 1996 Delegate Assembly. Committee members also met with each of the NASW Delegate Assembly regional coalitions to discuss the code's development and content and to receive delegates' comments and feedback. The code was then presented to and overwhelmingly ratified by the Delegate Assembly after lengthy discussion that focused primarily on the code's standards on various boundary issues and dual and multiple relationships (especially social workers' relationships with former clients).

The 1996 code, which is clearly the most comprehensive set of ethical standards in social work, reflects the state of the art in social work ethics. The code's preamble signifies a remarkable event in social work's history. For the first time in NASW's history, the code of ethics includes a formally sanctioned mission statement and an explicit summary of the profession's core values. The Code of Ethics Revision Committee felt strongly that the profession's code should include a forceful statement of social work's moral aims, drawing on the profession's time-honored commitments and contemporary concerns. The mission statement emphasizes social work's historic and enduring commitment to enhancing well-being and helping meet the basic needs of all people (Towle, 1965), with particular attention to the needs and empowerment of people who are vulnerable, oppressed, and living in poverty. The mission statement stresses social work's venerated concern about vulnerable populations and the profession's traditional simultaneous focus on individual well-being and the environmental forces that create, contribute to, and address problems in living. The preamble also emphasizes social workers' determination to promote social justice and social change with and on behalf of clients.

A particularly noteworthy feature of the preamble is the inclusion of six core values on which social work's mission is based: service, social justice, dignity and worth of the person, importance of human relationships, integrity, and competence. The Code of Ethics Revision Committee settled on these core values after engaging in a systematic and comprehensive review of literature on the subject.

The code also provides a brief guide for dealing with ethical issues or dilemmas in social work practice. Drawing on recent literature on ethical decision making in social work (Joseph, 1985; Loewenberg & Dolgoff, 1996; Reamer, 1995a), this section highlights various resources social workers should consider when they encounter challenging ethical decisions, including ethical theory, literature on ethical decision-making strategies, social work practice theory and research, relevant laws and regulations, agency policies, and other relevant codes of ethics. Social workers are also encouraged to obtain ethics consultation when appropriate, perhaps from an agency-based or social work organization's ethics committee, regulatory bodies (for example, a state licensing board), knowledgeable colleagues, supervisors, or legal counsel.

The code's most extensive section, "Ethical Standards," greatly expands the number of specific ethical guidelines contained in the code, again reflecting increased knowledge in the profession. The 155 specific ethical standards are designed to guide social workers' conduct, reduce malpractice and liability risks, and provide a basis for adjudication of ethics complaints filed against NASW members (the standards are also used by other bodies that have chosen to adopt the code, such as state licensing and regulatory boards, professional liability insurance providers, courts of law, agency boards of directors, and government agencies). In general, the code's standards concern three kinds of issues (Reamer, 1994): (1) what are usually considered to be "mistakes" social workers might make that have ethical implications (for example, mentioning clients' names in public or semi-public areas, forgetting to renew a client's release of information form before disclosing sensitive documents to a third party, or overlooking an important agency policy concerning

> *The 155 specific ethical standards are designed to guide social workers' conduct, reduce malpractice and liability risks, and provide a basis for adjudication of ethics complaints filed against NASW members.*

termination of services), (2) difficult ethical decisions faced by social workers that have reasonable arguments for and against different courses of action (for example, decisions about whether to disclose confidential information to protect a third party, how to allocate scarce or limited agency resources, whether to honor a picket line at one's employment setting, whether to obey an unjust law or regulation, or whether to interfere with a client who willingly is engaging in self-destructive behavior), and (3) ethical misconduct (for example, sexual exploitation of clients, conflicts of interest, deliberate misrepresentation, or fraudulent activity).

The code's standards fall into six substantive categories concerning social workers' ethical responsibilities to clients, to colleagues, in practice settings, as professionals, to the profession, and to society at large. The first section, ethical responsibilities to clients, is the most detailed and comprehensive, because it addresses a wide range of issues involved in the delivery of services to individuals, families, couples, and small groups of clients. In addition to more detailed standards on topics also addressed in the 1979 code (for example, client self-determination, privacy and confidentiality, client access to records, sexual relationships with clients, payment for services, termination of services), the 1996 code addresses a number of new issues: the provision of services by electronic media (such as computers, telephone, radio, and television); social workers' competence in the areas of cultural and social diversity; use of intervention approaches for which recognized standards do not exist; dual and multiple relationships with former clients, colleagues, and students; confidentiality issues involving families, couples, and group counseling, contact with media representatives, electronic records, and electronic communications (such as the use of electronic mail and facsimile machines), consultation, and deceased clients;

sexual relationships with former clients or clients' relatives or friends; physical contact with clients; sexual harassment; derogatory language; and bartering for services.

The remaining sections of the code also include standards that address new topics. The section on ethical responsibilities to colleagues addresses new issues related to interdisciplinary collaboration; consultation with colleagues; referral of clients for services; sexual relationships with supervisees, trainees, or other colleagues over whom social workers exercise professional authority; sexual harassment of supervisees, students, trainees, or colleagues; and unethical conduct of colleagues. The section on ethical responsibilities in practice settings addresses new issues related to supervision and consultation, education and training, documentation in case records, billing practices, client transfer, administration, continuing education and staff development, challenging unethical practices in employment settings, and labor–management disputes. The section on ethical responsibilities as professionals addresses new issues related to social workers' competence; misrepresentation of qualifications, credentials, education, areas of expertise, affiliations, services provided, and results to be achieved; and solicitation of clients. The section on ethical responsibilities to the social work profession addresses new issues related to dissemination of knowledge, especially evaluation and research. This section includes a greatly expanded set of standards concerning social workers' obligation to evaluate policies, programs, and practice interventions; use evaluation and research evidence in their professional practice; follow guidelines to protect individuals who participate in evaluation and research; and accurately disseminate results. The final section on ethical responsibilities to the broader society addresses new issues related to social workers' involvement in social and political action. The 1996 code includes more explicit and forceful language concerning social workers' obligation to address social justice issues, particularly pertaining to vulnerable, disadvantaged, oppressed, and exploited people and groups.

Conclusion

Changes in social workers' understanding of and approach to ethical issues represent one of the most significant developments in the profession's century-long history. What began as fairly modest and superficial concern about moral issues in the late 19th and early 20th centuries has evolved into an ambitious attempt to grasp and resolve complex ethical issues. Social workers' early preoccupation with their clients' morality is now overshadowed by social workers' efforts to identify and dissect ethical dilemmas, apply thoughtful decision-making tools, manage ethics-related risks that could lead to litigation, and confront ethical misconduct in the profession.

These changes are to be celebrated as social work commemorates its centennial anniversary. The next challenge in social work's development, as it embarks on the 21st century, is twofold. First, the profession must intensify its efforts to educate students and practitioners about ethical issues and standards and ways to address them. Organizations such as NASW, the American Association of State Social Work Boards, the Council on Social Work Education, and social work education programs should implement ambitious agendas to offer in-depth and comprehensive instruction and research on ethical dilemmas and standards, ethical decision-making strategies, risk management, and ethical misconduct. Social workers can no longer afford to have only a vague understanding of prevailing ethical standards (Jayaratne, Croxton, & Mattison, 1997). Second, social workers must be alert to emerging ethical issues as the profession enters its second century. In particular, social workers should be prepared to challenge attempts to undermine the profession's traditional values, especially social work's enduring commitment to vulnerable and oppressed people. In addition, social workers should be prepared to challenge funding policies that limit practitioners' ability to serve people in need (for example, unduly restrictive managed care policies). Finally, social workers must attempt to anticipate the emergence of ethical issues that, while perhaps unimaginable today, are likely to arise in the future as a function of societal and other changes, perhaps as a result of technological developments that have ethical implications (for example, in the health care and computer fields).

As the profession celebrates its 100th anniversary, social workers can be proud of their increasingly mature understanding of the complex ethical issues practitioners face. It is essential that the profession sustain this intellectual growth, because in the final analysis social work values and ethics are the lifeblood of the profession. ■

References

Abramson, M. (1985). The autonomy–paternalism dilemma in social work practice. *Social Casework, 66*, 387–393.

Arnold, S. (1970). Confidential communication and the social worker. *Social Work, 15*(1), 61–67.

Bartlett, H. M. (1970). *The common base of social work practice.* New York: Columbia University Press.

Berliner, A. K. (1989). Misconduct in social work practice. *Social Work, 34*, 69–72.

Bernstein, B. (1981). Malpractice: Future shock of the 1980s. *Social Casework, 62*, 175–181.

Bernstein, S. (1960). Self-determination: King or citizen in the realm of values. *Social Work, 5*(1), 3–8.

Besharov, D. S. (1985). *The vulnerable social worker.* Silver Spring, MD: National Association of Social Workers.

Besharov, D. S., & Besharov, S. H. (1987). Teaching about liability. *Social Work, 32*, 517–522.

Biestek, F. P. (1957). *The casework relationship.* Chicago: Loyola University Press.

Biestek, F. P., & Gehrig, C. C. (1978). *Client self-determination in social work: A fifty-year history.* Chicago: Loyola University Press.

Billups, J. O. (1992). The moral basis for a radical reconstruction of social work. In P. N. Reid & P. R. Popple (Eds.), *The moral purposes of social work* (pp. 100–119). Chicago: Nelson-Hall.

Black, P. N., Hartley, E. K., Whelley, J., & Kirk-Sharp, C. (1989). Ethics curricula: A national survey of graduate schools of social work. *Social Thought, 15*(3/4), 141–148.

Brieland, D. (1995). Social work practice: History and evolution. In R. L. Edwards (Ed.-in-Chief), *Encyclopedia of social work* (19th ed., Vol. 3, pp. 2247–2258). Washington, DC: NASW Press.

Bullis, R. K. (1995). *Clinical social worker misconduct.* Chicago: Nelson-Hall.

Callahan, D., & Bok, S. (Eds.). (1980). *Ethics teaching in higher education.* New York: Plenum Press.

Conrad, A. P. (1989). Developing an ethics review process in a social service agency. *Social Thought, 15*(3/4), 102–115.

Costin, L. B. (1964). Values in social work education: A study. *Social Service Review, 38*, 271–280.

Dickson, D. T. (1998). *Confidentiality and privacy in social work.* New York: Free Press.

Elliott, L. J. (1931). *Social work ethics.* New York: American Association of Social Workers.

Emmet, D. (1962). Ethics and the social worker. *British Journal of Psychiatric Social Work, 6*, 165–172.

Flexner, A. (1915). Is social work a profession? In *Proceedings of the National Conference of Charities and Corrections* (pp. 576–590). Chicago: Hildman.

Frankel, C. (1959). Social philosophy and the professional education of social workers. *Social Service Review, 33*, 345–359.

Frankena, W. K. (1973). *Ethics* (2nd ed.). Englewood Cliffs, NJ: Prentice Hall.

Gambrill, E., & Pruger, R. (Eds.). (1997). *Controversial issues in social work: Ethics, values, and obligations.* Needham Heights, MA: Allyn & Bacon.

Goldberg, J. E. (1989). AIDS: Confidentiality and the social worker. *Social Thought, 15*(3/4), 116–127.

Goldmeier, J. (1984). Ethical styles and ethical decisions in health settings. *Social Work in Health Care, 10*(1), 45–60.

Goldstein, H. (1987). The neglected moral link in social work practice. *Social Work, 32*, 181–186.

Gordon, W. E. (1962). A critique of the working definition. *Social Work, 7*(4), 3–13.

Gordon, W. E. (1965). Knowledge and value: Their distinction and relationship in clarifying social work practice. *Social Work, 10*(3), 32–39.

Grinnell, R. M. (Ed.). (1993). *Social work research and evaluation* (4th ed.). Itasca, IL: F. E. Peacock.

Hall, L. K. (1952). Group workers and professional ethics. *The Group, 15*(1), 3–8.

Hamilton, G. (1940). *Theory and practice of social casework.* New York: Columbia University Press.

Hamilton, G. (1951). *Social casework* (2nd ed.). New York: Columbia University Press.

Hancock, R. N. (1974). *20th-century ethics.* New York: Columbia University Press.

Hardman, D. G. (1975). Not with my daughter you don't! *Social Work, 20*, 278–285.

Jayaratne, S., Croxton, T., & Mattison, D. (1997). Social work professional standards: An exploratory study. *Social Work, 42*, 187–198.

Johnson, A. (1955). Educating professional social workers for ethical practice. *Social Service Review, 29,* 125–136.

Joseph, M. V. (1983). The ethics of organizations: Shifting values and ethical dilemmas. *Administration in Social Work, 7*(3/4), 47–57.

Joseph, M. V. (1985). A model for ethical decision making in clinical practice. In C. B. Germain (Ed.), *Advances in clinical practice* (pp. 207–217). Silver Spring, MD: National Association of Social Workers.

Joseph, M. V. (1989). Social work ethics: Historical and contemporary perspectives. *Social Thought, 15*(3/4), 4–17.

Kagle, J. D., & Giebelhausen, P. N. (1994). Dual relationships and professional boundaries. *Social Work, 39,* 213–220.

Karger, H. J. (Ed.). (1988). *Social workers and labor unions.* Westport, CT: Greenwood Press.

Keith-Lucas, A. (1963). A critique of the principle of client self-determination. *Social Work, 8*(3), 66–71.

Keith-Lucas, A. (1977). Ethics in social work. In J. B. Turner (Ed.-in-Chief), *Encyclopedia of social work* (17th ed., Vol. 1, pp. 350–355). Silver Spring, MD: National Association of Social Workers.

Keith-Lucas, A. (1992). A socially sanctioned profession? In P. N. Reid & P. R. Popple (Eds.), *The moral purposes of social work* (pp. 51–70). Chicago: Nelson-Hall.

Kopels, S., & Kagle, J. D. (1993). Do social workers have a duty to warn? *Social Service Review, 67,* 101–126.

Kurzman, P. A. (1983). Ethical issues in industrial social work practice. *Social Casework, 64,* 105–111.

Lee, P. R. (1930). Cause and function. In *National Conference on Social Work, Proceedings: 1929* (pp. 3–20). Chicago: University of Chicago Press.

Leiby, J. (1978). *A history of social work and social welfare in the United States.* New York: Columbia University Press.

Levick, K. (1981). Privileged communication: Does it really exist? *Social Casework, 62,* 235–239.

Levy, C. S. (1972). The context of social work ethics. *Social Work, 17*(2), 95–101.

Levy, C. S. (1973). The value base of social work. *Journal of Education for Social Work, 9,* 34–42.

Levy, C. S. (1976). *Social work ethics.* New York: Human Sciences Press.

Levy, C. S. (1982). *Guide to ethical decisions and actions for social service administrators.* New York: Haworth Press.

Lewis, H. (1972). Morality and the politics of practice. *Social Casework, 53,* 404–417.

Loewenberg, F., & Dolgoff, R. (1982). *Ethical decisions for social work practice.* Itasca, IL: F. E. Peacock.

Loewenberg, F., & Dolgoff, R. (1996). *Ethical decisions for social work practice* (5th ed.). Itasca, IL: F. E. Peacock.

Lubove, R. (1965). *The professional altruist: The emergence of social work as a career.* Cambridge, MA: Harvard University Press.

McCann, C. W., & Cutler, J. P. (1979). Ethics and the alleged unethical. *Social Work, 24,* 5–8.

McCleod, D., & Meyer, H. (1967). A study of values of social workers. In E. Thomas (Ed.), *Behavioral science for social workers* (pp. 401–416). New York: Free Press.

McDermott, F. E. (Ed.). (1975). *Self-determination in social work.* London: Routledge & Kegan Paul.

McDermott, F. E. (1975). Against the persuasive definition of "self-determination." In F. E. McDermott (Ed.), *Self-determination in social work* (pp. 118–137). London: Routledge & Kegan Paul.

McGowan, B. G. (1995). Values and ethics. In C. H. Meyer & M. A. Mattaini (Eds.), *The foundations of social work practice* (pp. 28–41). Washington, DC: NASW Press.

National Association of Social Workers. (1960). *NASW code of ethics.* New York: Author.

National Association of Social Workers. (1979). *NASW code of ethics.* Silver Spring, MD: Author.

National Association of Social Workers. (1990). *NASW code of ethics.* Washington, DC: Author.

National Association of Social Workers. (1993). *NASW code of ethics.* Washington, DC: Author.

National Association of Social Workers. (1996). *Code of ethics.* Washington, DC: Author.

Paine, R. T. (1880). The work of volunteer visitors of the associated charities among the poor. *Journal of Social Science, 12,* 113.

Perlman, H. H. (1965). Self-determination: Reality or illusion? *Social Service Review, 39,* 410–421.

Perlman, H. H. (1976). Believing and doing: Values in social work education. *Social Casework, 57,* 381–390.

Plant, R. (1970). *Social and moral theory in casework.* London: Routledge & Kegan Paul.

Popple, P. R. (1992). Social work: Social function and moral purpose. In P. N. Reid & P. R. Popple (Eds.), *The moral purposes of social work* (pp. 141–154). Chicago: Nelson-Hall.

Pumphrey, M. W. (1959). *The teaching of values and ethics in social work education.* New York: Council on Social Work Education.

Rawls, J. (1971). *A theory of justice.* Cambridge, MA: Harvard University Press.

Reamer, F. G. (1982). *Ethical dilemmas in social service.* New York: Columbia University Press.

Reamer, F. G. (1983). The concept of paternalism in social work. *Social Service Review, 57,* 254–271.

Reamer, F. G. (1985). The emergence of bioethics in social work. *Health & Social Work, 10,* 271–281.

Reamer, F. G. (1987a). Values and ethics. In A. Minahan (Ed.-in-Chief), *Encyclopedia of social work* (18th ed., Vol. 2, pp. 801–809). Silver Spring, MD: National Association of Social Workers.

Reamer, F. G. (1987b). Informed consent in social work. *Social Work, 32,* 425–429.

Reamer, F. G. (1988). Social workers and unions: Ethical dilemmas. In H. J. Karger (Ed.), *Social workers and labor unions* (pp. 131–143). Westport, CT: Greenwood Press.

Reamer, F. G. (1989). Liability issues in social work supervision. *Social Work, 34,* 445–448.

Reamer, F. G. (1990). *Ethical dilemmas in social service* (2nd ed.). New York: Columbia University Press.

Reamer, F. G. (1991). AIDS, social work, and the duty to protect. *Social Work, 37,* 165–170.

Reamer, F. G. (1992a). The impaired social worker. *Social Work, 37,* 165–170.

Reamer, F. G. (1992b). Social work and the public good: Calling or career? In P. N. Reid & P. R. Popple (Eds.), *The moral purposes of social work* (pp. 11–33). Chicago: Nelson-Hall.

Reamer, F. G. (1993). Liability issues in social work administration. *Administration in Social Work, 17*(4), 11–25.

Reamer, F. G. (1994). *Social work malpractice and liability.* New York: Columbia University Press.

Reamer, F. G. (1995a). *Social work values and ethics.* New York: Columbia University Press.

Reamer, F. G. (1995b). Ethics and values. In R. L. Edwards (Ed.-in-Chief), *Encyclopedia of social work* (19th ed., Vol. 1, pp. 893–902). Washington, DC: NASW Press.

Reamer, F. G. (1995c). Ethics consultation in social work. *Social Thought, 18*(1), 3–16.

Reamer, F. G. (1997). Ethical standards in social work: The NASW *Code of Ethics.* In R. L. Edwards (Ed.-in-Chief), *Encyclopedia of social work* (19th ed., Suppl., pp. 113–123). Washington, DC: NASW Press.

Reamer, F. G. (1998a). *Ethical standards in social work: A critical review of the NASW* Code of Ethics. Washington, DC: NASW Press.

Reamer, F. G. (1998b). Social work. In R. Chadwick (Ed.-in-Chief), *Encyclopedia of applied ethics* (Vol. 4, pp. 169–180). San Diego: Academic Press.

Reamer, F. G., & Abramson, M. (1982). *The teaching of social work ethics.* Hastings-on-Hudson, NY: The Hastings Center.

Reid, P. N. (1992). The social function and social morality of social work: A utilitarian perspective. In P. N. Reid & P. R. Popple (Eds.), *The moral purposes of social work* (pp. 34–50). Chicago: Nelson-Hall.

Reid, P. N., & Popple, P. R. (Eds.). (1992). *The moral purposes of social work.* Chicago: Nelson-Hall.

Reynolds, M. M. (1976). Threats to confidentiality. *Social Work, 21,* 108–113.

Rhodes, M. (1986). *Ethical dilemmas in social work practice.* London: Routledge & Kegan Paul.

Rubin, A., & Babbie, E. (1993). *Research methods for social work* (2nd ed.). Pacific Grove, CA: Brooks/Cole.

Siporin, M. (1989). Moral philosophy in social work today. *Social Service Review, 56,* 516–538.

Siporin, M. (1992). Strengthening the moral mission of social work. In P. N. Reid & P. R. Popple (Eds.), *The moral purposes of social work* (pp. 71–99). Chicago: Nelson-Hall.

Stalley, R. F. (1975). Determinism and the principle of client self-determination. In F. E. McDermott (Ed.), *Self-determination in social work* (pp. 93–117). London: Routledge & Kegan Paul.

Summers, A. B. (1989). The meaning of informed consent in social work. *Social Thought, 15*(3/4), 128–140.

Teicher, M. (1967). *Values in social work: A re-examination.* New York: National Association of Social Workers.

Timms, N. (1983). *Social work values: An enquiry.* London: Routledge & Kegan Paul.

Towle, C. (1965). *Common human needs.* New York: National Association of Social Workers.

VandeCreek, L., Knapp, S., & Herzog, C. (1988). Privileged communication for social workers. *Social Casework, 69,* 28–34.

Varley, B. K. (1968). Social work values: Changes in value commitments from admission to MSW graduation. *Journal of Education for Social Work, 4,* 67–85.

Vigilante, J. (1974). Between values and science. *Journal of Education for Social Work, 10,* 107–115.

Weil, M., & Sanchez, E. (1983). The impact of the Tarasoff decision on clinical social work practice. *Social Service Review, 57,* 112–124.

Whittington, C. (1975). Self-determination re-examined. In F. E. McDermott (Ed.), *Self-determination in social work* (pp. 81–92). London: Routledge & Kegan Paul.

Wilson, S. J. (1978). *Confidentiality in social work.* New York: Free Press.

Working definition of social work practice. (1958). *Social Work, 3*(2), 5–8.

Younghusband, E. (1967). *Social work and social values.* London: Allen & Unwin.

Frederic G. Reamer, PhD, is professor, School of Social Work, Rhode Island College, Providence, RI 02908; e-mail: freamer@grog.ric.edu.

Original manuscript received January 14, 1998
Final revision received May 26, 1998
Accepted July 21, 1998

Part II
Recurrent Clashes and their Ethical Implications

[7]

Social Work and Social Reform: An Arena of Struggle

Mimi Abramovitz

The profession of social work has the potential both to meet individual needs and to engage in social change. However, the profession's position between the individual and society often forces practitioners to choose between adjusting people and programs to circumstances or challenging the status quo. The twin pressures of containment and change have made social work an arena of struggle since its origins in the late 19th century. In honor of social work's centennial, this article examines the sources of the profession's prochange mandate and the structural factors that limit social work's ability to pledge itself to this stance permanently and recommends some steps social workers can take to recommit the profession to greater activism. Special attention is given to documenting the long but largely ignored history of social work activism.

Key words: *activism; history; professionalism; social reform; social work*

The twin pressures of containment and change have plagued social work since its origins in the late 19th century. The profession can boast of a long history of progressive activism directed to individual and social change. At the same time, observers within and outside social work have often accused the profession of serving as a handmaiden of the status quo. This contradiction has made the social work profession a site of ongoing struggle. Although often difficult, the battles the profession has endured have ensured that social work practice with individuals, families, groups, and communities is neither handed down from above nor written in stone. Rather, the design of social work as we know it reflects internal and external political struggles. The presence of this tension becomes critically important, because with it comes opportunity for change.

The centennial gives occasion to celebrations, critical reviews, and future visions for the profession. In this spirit, this article reviews the history of activism in social work in a framework of the relationship between social work and social reform as an arena of struggle. Most histories of social work present the story chronologically. I use the history to bring the activist struggles in social work into bold relief. More specifically, I have developed three parallel narratives centered on social work as an arena of struggle: (1) the largely untold history of activism in the profession during the 20th century, (2) the effect of the process of professionalization on social work activism, and (3) the ways the changing political climate shaped the relationship between the profession of social work and its impulse for social reform.

The Prochange Mandate in Social Work

Social work's commitment to both individual and social change stems from at least three sources: (1) the mandates of our professional organizations, (2) the professional literature, and (3) the long history of activism among social workers themselves.

Professional Mandates

Since the mid-1960s both the Council on Social Work Education (CSWE) and the National Association of Social Workers (NASW) have recognized social work's role in social reform. The 1994 CSWE Curriculum Policy Statement (CSWE, 1994) and the 1996 NASW *Code of Ethics* continue to call for action to improve social conditions as one way for social work to honor its primary obligation to individual and community welfare.

Review of the Literature

Many social worker scholars have articulated social work's commitment to social reform (Galper, 1975; Haynes & Mickelson, 1997; Mahaffey & Hanks, 1982; Withorn, 1984). "Systems," "transactional," "person-in-situation," "empowerment," and other practice theories emphasize the relationship between social conditions and the quality of life for individuals, families, groups, organizations, and communities. The theories assume that individuals grow, change, and develop a sense of mastery best when they can gain self-insight, have real choices, and secure access to the resources and power needed to realize these goals. The theories recognize that communities thrive when governments promote individual and collective responsibility, equal opportunities, and social solidarity. In brief, social work scholarship suggests that, although a focus on individuals is critically important, it may not be enough (Payne, 1991; Simon, 1994).

History of Activism

The third foundation of social work's commitment to social reform stems from the long history of activism among social workers themselves. Social work activism has had many strands. As is the case in any large group of people, the politics of social workers range across the political spectrum. During the past 100 years, the most visible and documented activism of the organized profession has tended toward liberal reform. The goals of the activist members, however, have ranged from liberal to radical, leading to both collaboration and conflict. Given my interest in documenting social work's long history of activism, I define activism to include both liberal and radical efforts, but do not take up the debates between liberalism and radicalism. It is important to note that even during the down times the voices of change within in social work never totally subsided (Ehrenreich, 1985).

Social work activism peaked during three historical periods: the turn of the century, the 1930s, and the 1960s. The initial struggle within social work took place around the issues of individual change and social change. This struggle surfaced around the turn of the century during a period of reform known as the Progressive Era (1896 to 1914). During this time, the social change–oriented Settlement House Movement (SHM) vied for control of the emerging profession with the older and more individually oriented Charity Organization Society (COS) (Day, 1997). This initial conflict between individual change and social change anticipated a century of struggle.

Until the late 19th century, most social work practice followed the dictates of the COS movement, which had arrived in the United States from London in the late 1870s. The COS held that personal failures and the receipt of public relief caused poverty. It also sought to make charitable giving to poor people—the chief social work activity at this time—more efficient. To this end, COS introduced the principles of "scientific charity" to the provision of relief to poor people. The method mirrored the new scientific management theories followed by business at that time. It called for more efficient and rational giving by charities, investigation of and moralistic self-help for people who were destitute, and the abolition of public relief by cities (Axinn & Levin, 1997; Day, 1997).

The COS way of doing social work gradually gained control of the field. Largely uncontested within social work, about 92 private COS agencies were operating in most of the largest U.S. cities by 1892. By 1895 the Conference of Charities and Corrections, previously dominated by the public sector and state agencies, had elected a COS leader from the private sector as its president (Coll, 1971). Influenced by the COS philosophy, among other things, virtually all of the nation's major cities abolished home relief between 1870 and 1900. Meanwhile, the conditions of grinding poverty remained essentially untouched.

The SHM emerged in the late 1880s, largely in reaction to the philosophy of organized charity work. In sharp contrast to the COS perspective, which blamed the victim, the SHM argued that poverty stemmed from adverse social conditions, over which individuals had little or no control. As happened in the English model, the settlement house staff moved into the poorest city neighborhoods. They provided community services, supported unions, and undertook vigorous crusades to remedy the social ills of the day (Axinn & Levin, 1997; Day, 1997).

By the turn of the century the more reform-driven settlement house approach had many adherents. Many social workers who gravitated toward schools, hospitals, neighborhood health centers, and child welfare agencies also favored community service and social justice. Mounting evidence from their own detailed case records even led some COS leaders to recognize the social underpinnings of poverty. The 1910 election of Jane Addams as president of the COS-dominated National Conference of Charities and Corrections signaled that social work had begun to endorse social reform. At its 1912 meeting the conference's Standards of Labor and Living Committee, which included some of the more radical social workers, issued a strong social change agenda. Some items reappeared in the platform of Theodore Roosevelt's Progressive Party, although in watered-down form (Coll, 1971).

Before the end of the Progressive Era, the settlement workers often allied with club women, businessmen, professionals, feminists, university professors, and other reformers. Together they launched a series of movements aimed at improving the quality of urban life on various fronts. They affirmed government intervention and, among other successes, won the passage of worker's compensation, mother's pensions, and protective labor legislation. The leaders of the well-known white settlements— Jane Addams, Julia Lathrop, Florence Kelley, and Lillian Wald—worked within a large women's network. Grounded in the women's club movement, the network had strong political connections and a large popular base. These resources helped the early women reformers—the forebears of social work—play central roles in the modern welfare state (Muncy, 1991). Because of racism and segregation, the settlements and the networks established by African American women never became well known or exercised much influence outside the African American community (Hine, 1994).

The struggle for change in social work and in the nation subsided during World War I and the conservative period that followed it. The silencing of dissent and the indifference to social issues continued into the roaring 20s, yet within the profession the voices of contention persisted. Although she failed to win support, Julia Lathrop, a well-known Settlement House leader and former head of the U.S. Children's Bureau, proposed major resolutions in 1923 on peace, prohibition, child labor, and minimum wages to the National Conference on Social Work (Ehrenreich, 1985). In 1924 Eduard Lindemann, a pioneer of group work, warned that social workers who placed "all the blame for maladjustment upon the individual and none on the social order must in the end become servile to those whose interests are vested in that social order" (Ehrenreich, 1985, p. 82). In 1926 Jane Addams spoke to the "danger" of looking at social work "too steadfastly from the business point of view," subjecting it to "tests which are totally irrelevant to its purposes" (Ehrenreich, 1985, p. 82). Baldwin urged more radically that social workers build "a political class party of producers committed to public control of natural resources, public utilities, money and credit" (Lubove, 1965, p. 136).

The crisis of the 1930s—the longest and deepest economic depression in American history—revived social reform activities nationwide. The collapse of the economy, mounting unemployment, the demands of militant social movements, and fears of more radical change elicited a government response. These conditions, plus the inability of private social agencies to respond adequately to the crisis, renewed the struggles within social work over individual treatment and social change and over the relative merits of private charity and public relief (Ehrenreich, 1985; Trattner, 1994; Woodroofe, 1964).

The profession was not of one voice during this period. The professional leadership regarded public agencies as corrupt, inefficient, and unsuitable settings for social work practice. Indeed, until this time most social workers worked in private agencies, where they gave priority to emotional rather than financial problems. But during the Depression the psychological orientation of the private agencies and their lack of resources left them ill prepared to deal with the demand for help. With growing caseloads and enormous financial needs, many agencies went bankrupt (Ehrenreich, 1985; Trattner, 1994).

Some social workers concluded that the field had no special obligation to become involved in the national emergency created by the Depression. Others began to question the preceding decade's singular pursuit of middle class clients, psychodynamic theory, private agency practice, and professional status. The dire emergency forced social work to reconsider the value of economic assistance, the social underpinnings of poverty, and its own resistance to government programs. The Depression also generated debates about practice theory, such as the meaning of person-in-situation and the merits of the functional compared with the diagnostic schools (Ehrenreich, 1985). Other social workers argued about the place of social action in their profession: Should they consider social action an individual civic responsibility, a specialized function of social work, or an obligation for the entire profession (Wenocur & Reisch, 1989)? Many social workers found themselves calling for reform. The director of

the Department of Social Welfare in Denver concluded: "[The] poor and suffering are not so only by their own fault or peculiar misfortune, but also by the fault of us all.… It is only just that organized society as a whole should struggle with the responsibility and pay the cost" (Woodroofe, 1964, p. 158).

The staunchest social work reformers belonged to the Rank and File Movement. This loose aggregation of insurgent social workers came from the radical wing of social work. Among other things, they increasingly criticized the profession's and the federal government's delayed reactions to the Depression (Fisher, 1936). The movement's discussion clubs, practitioner groups, and protective organizations and its journal *Social Work Today* called for higher standards of practice, comprehensive social welfare programs, and economic democracy. This included fighting against the continued lynching of African Americans and the widespread racial discrimination by relief agencies. The Rank and File Movement also supported the unionization of public and private sector social workers. By 1938 the social work unions claimed about 14,500 members, in contrast to the approximately 10,500 professionally trained social workers who belonged to the American Association of Social Workers, the forerunner of NASW (Ehrenreich, 1985).

The Rank and File Movement numbered 15,000 at its peak. Although it never represented more than a minority of social workers, between 1931 and 1942 its moral and political influence exerted a strong counterforce within the profession (Ehrenreich, 1985). Pressure from the Rank and File Movement helped social workers accept political action as a legitimate professional function. Indeed, by 1933 the economic crisis and the influence of the movement led many of the less radical members of the previously reform-shy social work establishment to become New Deal enthusiasts. Thousands of social workers took jobs in the public sector. Once there, they fought to train caseworkers and otherwise improve public sector services.

Other social workers called for new social policies. In 1934, for the first time since the Progressive Era, the National Conference of Social Work recommended social and economic

Abramovitz / *Social Work and Social Reform: An Arena of Struggle* planning, a federally guaranteed minimum standard of living, and public works programs (Ehrenreich, 1985). Social work leaders also played significant roles in drafting and enacting the Federal Emergency Relief Act of 1933, the Social Security Act of 1935, and other social legislation. They also became deeply involved in the New Deal programs as administrators, consultants, and advocates. For example, Harry Hopkins, a social worker, headed Roosevelt's emergency relief programs, and Jane Hoey, another social worker, directed the public assistance part of the social security program (Popple & Leighninger, 1996). Many social workers favored the more progressive versions of social security and unemployment insurance bills, which were defeated by Southern legislators. These Southern legislators feared the loss of cheap labor—African Americans in the South, Latinos in the Southwest, and poor white people in Appalachia. In the end, most New Deal legislation excluded African Americans and otherwise granted preferential treatment to men, white people, industrial workers, and two-parent families. The legacy still haunts us today (Abramovitz, 1996; Gordon, 1994; Quadragno, 1994).

By the end of the 1930s, vast numbers of social workers and their services had entered the public sector establishment. For better or worse, social work had become a part of the machinery of the state (Trattner, 1994). An improved economy, a liberalized profession, the passage of the New Deal, and the widespread public support for the Democratic party moved the Rank and File Movement closer to the mainstream. Nevertheless, its more radical leaders, such as Mary van Kleeck, continued to warn against being coopted by government reforms. She urged social workers to ally themselves instead with clients and other workers in support of a new economic order (van Kleeck, 1934).

The drive for social change in social work and in the nation subsided again during and after World War II. The risks of speaking out during the "red scare" that followed the war silenced many critics. By the time the red scare had run its course, during the more prosperous 1950s, the general public's interest in social reform waned. Despite these setbacks, social work

activists continued to promote the profession's progressive heritage. They argued that the responsibility of social work included addressing "fundamental needs of human beings" (Pray, 1945, p. 353) and that "social action was a motive force in democracy" (Lurie, 1941, p. 633). Howard said that "social work was not separable from social reform" (Woodroofe, 1964, p. 220). Whitney Young, the African American social worker who later headed the National Urban League, told the National Conference on Social Welfare that "social work was born in an atmosphere of indignation," but that "somewhere along the line the urge to become professional had overcome the initial crusading impulse" (Trattner, 1994, pp. 311–312).

The social work establishment also tried to find ways to honor past commitments to social change during the reform lull by paying somewhat more attention to social policy. The CSWE curriculum standards began to require that social work students learn about social policy and how to participate in policy making. NASW established a paid lobbyist in Washington, DC, appointed a committee to define a method for converting practice data into social policy, and repeatedly stressed its members' responsibility for social action in certain spheres (Woodroofe, 1964).

A coalition of social work organizations, the Committee on Social Issues and Policies of the National Social Welfare Assembly, supported the limited postwar efforts by organized labor and others to expand welfare state programs serving the middle class as well as the poor (Patterson, 1981; Trattner, 1994). Although public assistance came under virulent attacks in the late 1950s, social work helped to draft the 1956 Amendments to the Social Security Act (Trattner, 1994), which added social services to the public assistance program for single mothers. The profession argued that poor people needed psychological assistance along with financial aid to adjust to poverty, parent effectively, and find paid work. The unfunded program reappeared in the more successful 1962 Amendments to the Social Security Act (Trattner, 1994).

It took the massive disorders of the 1960s, however, to rekindle the profession's social action spirit fully. Finding social work far behind the social-change curve, critics from within and outside the field accused it of having its head in the sand (Ehrenreich, 1985; Trattner, 1994). Students charged that organizational maintenance interests overrode addressing clients' needs in agencies. They also lambasted rigid welfare bureaucracies, condemned school curricula as parochial and outdated, reproached social work's view of social problems as rooted in individual development or family dynamics, and protested social work's lack of response to the black revolution. The protest was fueled by a new generation of social workers who either hearkened from or supported the social movements of the day and by the opening of jobs for social workers in VISTA, the War on Poverty, and other Great Society programs (Wagner, 1990).

As the earlier Rank and File Movement did, employed social workers challenged the prevailing premises of professionalism. By the mid-1970s the American Federation of State, County, and Municipal Employees—the largest labor organization representing social workers—claimed some 35,000 professional social work members. Thousands more belonged to smaller labor unions (Ehrenreich, 1985). In response to the profession's failure of inclusion, African Americans formed the Association of Black Social Workers. Likewise, when women realized that their female-populated profession was male dominated, they founded the Association of Women in Social Work and *Affilia: A Journal for Women and Social Work.*

The more radical social workers established still other new organizations such as Radical Alliance of Social Service Workers in New York City (RASSW). Like its counterparts in Boston, Chicago, Philadelphia, New Haven, and Wisconsin (Wagner, 1990), RASSW held that social work's real values and ideals—such as serving people over profits, securing power for the poor, and improving social conditions—made social work practice, if not the requisites of professionalism, compatible with social change. In the mid-1970s activist social workers launched *Catalyst: A Socialist Journal of the Social Services.* The journal was renamed the *Journal of Progressive Human Services* in the 1980s and still traces its heritage to *Social Work Today,* the journal

published by the Rank and File Movement in the 1930s. In the mid-1980s hundreds of social workers joined the newly formed Bertha Capen Reynolds Society (BCRS), a national organization of progressive workers in social welfare. The society was named after a Rank and File Movement leader and is still active, promoting alliances with clients, trade unions, and other progressive groups. It calls for direct practice aimed at individual and social change through advocacy, transformation, and empowerment and emphasizes freedom from racism, sexism, ageism, and heterosexism (BCRS, no date).

The social work profession itself finally responded to the changed political climate. In the early 1960s, sparked by the War on Poverty, community organization returned to its settlement house roots. It redirected its focus from coordinating services to mobilizing clients for community self-determination and the redistribution of resources. In the early 1970s NASW rejected the longstanding separation of professional and political activities. It created Political Action for Candidate Endorsement and Education and Legislative Action Network to support liberal policies and politicians. Likewise, CSWE required the school curricula to pay even more attention to social policy, politics, and diversity. Social workers active in both organizations also became more involved in questions of international peace and justice. They linked social work in the United States to the rest of the world, often around broadly defined issues of human rights.

Obstacles to Social Reform

Given social work's proreform mandates and its long history of activism, why do some social workers and outside observers still accuse the profession of serving as a handmaiden of the status quo? Students of the profession suggest three possible answers: (1) the structural location of the profession in the wider social order, (2) the requisites of professionalization in a market economy, and (3) the effects of the changing political climate during the past 100 years.

Structural Location

Because it is located between individuals and "the system," social work often finds itself in a difficult position. Since its emergence in the late 1800s, social work has helped to mediate between the conflicting needs of individuals and the requirements of the market economy. These conflicts are neither accidental nor short lived. Rather, they flow from the contradictions inherent in the market system that leave many basic needs unmet.

The first contradiction exists between private production and social needs. The market provides the setting for reconciling private production and socially determined needs, but it does not always do the job very well. The market economy depends heavily on the well-being of families for its success. Firms need individuals and families to consume what they produce. Profitable production also depends on the ability of individuals and families to produce, nurture, and socialize the current and future labor force; to care for those who are too old, young, or sick to care for themselves; and to ensure that family members become affiliated with the wider social order. However, the profit-driven market often fails to produce the levels of wages and employment needed by families to fulfill these tasks, which are sometimes collectively referred to as social reproduction (Abramovitz, 1992). Instead, industry's drive for low wages and high productivity may yield substandard levels of health, education, and economic security for many people. The resulting hardships weaken both the capacity of workers as producers and families as caretakers. Because the inequalities resulting from the contradictions between economic production and social reproduction widen the gap between the haves and the have-nots, tensions may provoke social unrest. Similarly, there has also been a discrepancy between the government's historic promise of democratic rights and its failure to sustain policies that ensure equal opportunity for all, not to mention equality of results. The continual reconfiguration of racial, sexual, and other inequalities represents one of the most persistent and serious violations of the nation's democratic pledge.

These contradictions both created and complicated social work's assigned role as mediator of the conflicting needs of individuals and the requirements of the market economy. After all,

to meet the basic needs of individuals and families and to fulfill the democratic vow of equal opportunity for all would undercut profitability. That is, the profit-driven market economy constrains social work's ameliorative agenda for individuals and communities. The effects of the contradictions weaken during liberal and prosperous times when the rising tide lifts all boats. But in periods of conservative reaction or economic decline, social work's ability to reconcile social and corporate needs recedes further. Political and economic developments periodically stretch the tensions between profits and people to a breaking point. When this has happened ordinary citizens have joined forces and called for change. Some ask the state to protect them from the abuses of the market, and others seek more structural changes. They also may insist that the state honor its democratic vows. The resulting social movements and political unrest have periodically forced social work to decide which side it is on (Ehrenreich, 1985; Trattner, 1994).

Professionalization

Early Years. The second force that has constrained social work's commitment to social reform involves the negative imperatives of professionalization. Professionalization typically refers to the ideals, theories, and standards of good practice. But Wenocur and Reisch, in their 1989 book *From Charity to Enterprise: The Development of American Social Work in a Market Economy*, highlighted another meaning. They use the term to refer to a profession's need to build, control, and legitimize an occupational terrain. Wenocur and Reisch argued that the professionalization of social work required the development of an identifiable knowledge base, control of the newly expanding social services market, creation of a commodity that would appeal to a large pool of customers, and the acquisition of support among private donors. In the context of a market economy, they concluded, these requirements pressed social work to narrow its vision and to play it safe.

Social work's pursuit of professional status in the early 1900s paralleled a similar trend in many other areas. Social observers believed that scientifically based professions could find answers to many contemporary social problems (Popple, 1995). About this time the charity organization wing of social work recognized that the professionalization of social work required a specific knowledge base. By 1917 COS leader Mary Richmond had published the profession's first major text, *Social Diagnosis*. It elaborated social work's existing method of detailed investigation into a diagnostic process called casework. Casework quickly became the field's method of choice and its claim to professional status. Written before the Freudian deluge, *Social Diagnosis* emphasized the social environment and financial distress rather than intrapsychic conflict. It considered the "coordination of community services and the creation of new welfare resources indispensable to the helping process" (Lubove, 1965, pp. 107–108).

Early Professionalization. By the 1920s social work had abandoned this more sociological paradigm for a psychological one. With the advent of the psychoanalytic and mental hygiene movements, social work equated professional effectiveness with the application of psychiatric theories. The new knowledge usefully modernized social work practice. It explained facets of behavior and provided a scientific method of treatment that before then had been lacking (Trattner, 1994; Woodroofe, 1964). The tools of psychiatry advanced social work thinking. It allowed the field to replace theories of moral inadequacy with the science of psychology and recommended treatment rather than punishment for troubled individuals. These changes notwithstanding, social work continued its strong emphasis on the individual psyche, which led practitioners to accentuate clients' culpability and downplay their environment. For example, some social workers linked the need for relief to clients' childhood dependency wishes rather than loss of employment. Similarly, the introduction of concepts such as normality and abnormality, maladjusted person, and psychopathic personality created a scientific legitimacy for the notion of deviance. This, in turn, provided new methods, rationales, and opportunities for social control in social work and elsewhere (Ehrenreich, 1985; Woodroofe, 1964). The process of professionalizing caused

social work to shift from "cause" to "function," that is, to move from advocating reform to rendering a technical service efficiently (Lee, 1930). The change won social work greater professional status. But it devalued the profession's historic concern with the community and led it to conclude that social work and social reform did not mix.

Wenocur and Reisch (1989) also argued that professionalization required social work to become a commodity that would appeal to a large group of consumers. By 1929 social work had 25 graduate programs, several professional associations, and three journals (Jansson, 1988). The new psychiatric knowledge also provided social work with a way to escape the stigma attached to the working with poor populations. Emphasis on inner problems gave social work a way to serve middle-class people as well as, if not better than, poor people. By expanding its clientele to include the middle class, the new "psychiatric" social worker could also collect a fee. This practice provided the field with the additional status of having a paying clientele.

The advent of new services furnished social work with opportunities to serve clients above the poverty line. During World War I the American Red Cross provided casework services to uprooted soldiers and their families. About 3,700 Red Cross chapters in 15,000 communities nationwide employed social workers. After the war ended the middle class continued to seek out social work services (Trattner, 1994; Woodroofe, 1964). The rise of the child guidance clinic also exposed the middle class to social work skills. By the 1920s the clinic at the New York Bureau of Children's Guidance reported that 32 percent of its clients were "affluent" or "comfortable" (Ehrenreich, 1985). Toward the end of the 1920s, most social workers identified themselves with these psychiatric clinics rather than with the social reformers whom they now viewed as passé. As early as 1927 some social workers had begun to explore the private practice option (Ehrenreich, 1985; Lubove, 1965; Trattner, 1994).

Finally, professionalization required winning approval from funders. Social work's dependence on funders who benefited from preserving the status quo forced social work to play it safe. Unlike European reformers, who had trade union support, social workers in the United States had to raise money from wealthy Americans—the class that benefited from sustaining the social order (Jansson, 1988). Before World War I social work fundraising relied on individual donors. During the 1920s, however, charitable giving shifted from private contributors to federated community chests with strong ties to the local business community. Federated funding paralleled the consolidation of big business and the period's infatuation with rationalization. Fueled by the growth of the private social welfare system, federated funding streamlined, coordinated, and controlled the financing and management of private giving to social services.

The new funding system favored standardized over individualized philanthropy, organization over innovation, and professional practitioners over volunteers. These preferences disadvantaged both small agencies and programs geared toward social change (Lubove, 1965). The rules of federated funding, for example, forced the settlement houses to redirect their energies from social change to social service. They also led community organization workers to shift their focus from working in neighborhoods to helping social welfare agencies become more efficient (Lubove, 1965; Trattner, 1994). The casework-dominated profession further distanced itself from community organization and group work by refusing to legitimize the professional status of the smaller and more reform-oriented methods.

Crisis in the Field. Social reform gained a new hearing during the Great Depression. But after World War II ended, social work resumed its pursuit of professionalization with renewed vigor. To begin with, the market for private social work services grew, leading social workers to leave public sector jobs for private ones. Social work began to become more firmly entrenched in private social agencies, which paid more and gave social workers the chance to apply their courses in psychiatrically oriented case work (Patterson, 1981). The introduction of fees at private agencies and the continued growth of a middle-class clientele spurned social work's exit from public services. Others

continued the trickle to more lucrative private practice (Trattner, 1994).

Post–World War II Consolidation. During the postwar years the social work establishment essentially justified its abandonment of low-income clientele and the public sector. Along with the wider public, social work assumed that renewed prosperity in the late 1940s and the 1950s basically had eliminated poverty and that those who remained poor would be adequately served by the new public welfare system set up under the New Deal. Instead of addressing the mounting problems that surfaced after World War II, such as drug use, delinquency, and mental illness, social work broadened and deepened its psychotherapeutic skills and knowledge. Still deeply committed to psychoanalysis, social work also began to expand its theoretical repertoire.

The new psychological theories continued to dwell on the personal characteristics of individuals to the exclusion of their surrounding circumstances. Few offered techniques aimed at organizational or social change (Payne, 1991). The continued preference for work with individuals in private agencies reflects the fact that during the 1930s social workers who were not inclined to work with individuals had filled the high demand for social workers by public agencies. The exodus drained both private agencies and social work schools of their more reform-oriented personnel. It left the private agencies and social work schools staffed by the more psychiatrically oriented social workers. As if to mark social work's distance from social reform, *Survey* magazine, the profession's voice of social policy and reform for 50 years, closed down in 1952 (Trattner, 1994).

The postwar pursuit of professionalization led social work to consolidate its gains, which meant securing casework's dominance of the field, merging the profession's numerous specialized associations, and restricting it to practitioners with an MSW degree. During the 1940s and early 1950s, caseworkers continued to resist requests from group workers and community organizers for admittance into the professional club. The opposition to the more change-oriented methods persisted, but in the long run failed. By the mid-1950s the two other methods had become integrated into the field, but not before they had toned down their politics and acquired the accoutrements of professionalism.

Despite the integration of all three methods, the profession continued to marginalize the smaller group work and community organization areas. The division of labor among the three methods isolated them from each other and downplayed social change. To begin with, the division of labor by method implied that caseworkers treated individuals, that group workers worked with groups, and that only community organizers dealt with social change. This interpretation of the methods obscured the reality that any social work method could work for containment or for change. Indeed, the casework paradigm can advocate for adjustment and control or autonomy and liberation of individuals. Likewise, community organization can stress stabilizing existing services or mobilizing communities for change. The failure to recognize this possibility hampered both a critical analysis of social work's contradictory forces and the creation of a profession-wide vision of progressive social work practice in all areas. By assigning social change to community organization—the profession's smallest method numerically—social work effectively took the majority of its practitioners aligned with casework off the social reform hook.

During this period the professional establishment also strengthened its influence within social work and outside by merging its various associations. It formed CSWE in 1952 and NASW in 1955. However, both organizations refused to admit social workers with bachelor's degrees in social work (BSWs), despite the fact that this would have enlarged the profession's base, thereby strengthening its capacity for political and professional influence. At the time more than three-fourths of all social workers lacked graduate training. Many of them worked in the public sector. Fearing that the presence of untrained workers in the field would undermine professional gains, CSWE only accredited graduate schools, and NASW excluded practitioners without MSWs. These restrictions applied until the mid-1970s, when internal pressures led both organizations to open their doors to social workers with bachelor's degrees (Popple, 1995).

The effect of social work's move from charity to enterprise remains to this day. Despite the turbulence of the 1960s, in the mid-1970s many social workers endorsed the separation of professional and political activities and did not include social action as an important professional function. By the mid-1980s only a handful of social work schools offered community organization or social justice specializations. In the early 1990s, the new Motor Voter bill expanded the sites of voter registration to include social agencies as well as motor vehicle bureaus. But many social workers and agencies failed to participate in the efforts (Haynes & Mickelson, 1997). Social workers, along with many others in the liberal community, remained strangely silent while a punitive welfare reform bill worked its way through Congress and the state legislatures. However, the activist wing of social work, which continued to challenge this apolitical stance of many social workers, ensured that the profession remained an arena of political struggle.

Political Climate

Without a doubt social work's structural location and the process of professionalization undercut the profession's commitment to reform. However, the changing political climate also strongly affected its capacity to work for social change. In any particular time the political climate is shaped by the state of the economy, the nature of government intervention, and the strength of social movements. Other influences include changing views about the cause of individual problems, the role of the market, and the role of the state. The mix of these large forces either promotes or discourages political struggle. The political climate also determines if the status quo's response to social unrest leans toward indifference, making concessions, or repressing social critics (Abramovitz, 1996; Ehrenreich, 1985; Piven & Cloward, 1982).

Political and economic conditions became ripe for social reform at the turn of this century. Between 1865 and 1900 the U.S. economy expanded enormously. The nation's productive capacity increased national wealth, raised the standard of living, and sped both urbanization and immigration. The ups and downs of advances in industrial capitalism, however, also destabilized the wider social order. Economic booms and busts created a volatile economy and heightened inequality. Widespread corruption in business and politics and increased working-class support for militant trade unions, populist farmer alliances, and socialist parties yielded considerable social unrest. Fearing that mounting economic instability and increased political turmoil signaled a country in crisis, the nation's more forward-looking industrialists and political leaders became receptive to the need for reform (Kolko, 1963; Weinstein, 1968).

Post–World War I. The stark contrast between splendor and squalor and between concentrated power at the top and powerlessness at the bottom activated the reform impulse. The new middle-class reform movement included social work. The Progressive movement, as it came to be known, hoped to improve social conditions for humanistic reasons. But, along with business and government, the middle-class reformers sought to ease class tensions, stem social unrest, and keep poor people and working-class people affiliated with the mainstream (Ehrenreich, 1985). At the same time the threat of cutthroat competition and militant social movements to profits led the owners of U.S. Steel, Standard Oil, and the large railroad companies to drop their historic preference for laissez-faire policy. They called for government intervention to create better business conditions and to stabilize social order. They wanted the government to regulate the market to stem competition and to pass social legislation to appease workers who were increasingly attracted to trade unions and the Socialist Party. These concessions thwarted more fundamental changes. They also eased the negative effects of the "free" market on the lives of the average people and legitimized the social reformers' call for a more active state (Kolko, 1963; Weinstein, 1968).

The Progressive Era ended with the onset of World War I. Wartime mobilization unified the country and slammed shut the doors to social reform. The outbreak of postwar unrest ended social peace. Feminists continued to agitate for the vote. Workers in various industries participated in a massive strike wave. Outbursts of virulent nativism and racism followed competition for jobs among growing numbers of European immigrants, southern African Americans, and returning white soldiers. Fueled by fears following the success of the 1917 Russian Revolution, the nation's leaders shifted their strategy from ameliorative reforms to harsh repression. The state met labor struggles with troops, deported immigrants, and rolled back Progressive Era reforms as "communistic" (Axinn & Levin, 1997; Ehrenreich, 1985; Trattner, 1994).

The first "red scare" of the 20th century subsided after several years. But the silencing of reform left its mark in and outside of social work. Renewed prosperity took an additional toll on social reform. The 1920s witnessed the rise of mass consumerism, a renewed faith in individualism, heightened praise for private enterprise, and increased hostility toward the state. Social workers turned to professionalization. Along with many other Americans, they convinced themselves that the high standard of living had ended both poverty and the need for any social reform (Axinn & Levin, 1997; Ehrenreich, 1985; Trattner, 1994).

The Depression. The conservative paradigm that governed America during the 1920s came crashing down in the 1930s with the Great Depression. The people did not take the collapse of the economy lying down. The economic disaster and the mass mobilizations by elderly people, employed and jobless people, black and white people, and men and women forced social reform back onto the national and the social work agenda.

The magnitude of events transformed conventional thinking about basic human needs in and outside the profession. The Depression had made it clear that a "free" market could not absorb all those willing and able to work. Nor could it generate adequate levels of education, housing, and health care needed by the average family to support itself and for businesses to make profits. The market placed people at risk of poverty through no fault of their own. During the Progressive Era economic crisis and social unrest had forced state governments to regulate the economy. This time public leaders in business and industry and in the social work profession realized that the federal government had to do even more. It had to step in and actually manage the economy if it was going to bail out business, quiet mounting social unrest, and ward off more radical proposals (Axinn & Levin, 1997).

Post–World War II. The political climate changed dramatically again during and after World War II. Wartime production ended the Depression. Postwar economic growth generated what economist John Kenneth Galbraith (1958) later called "the affluent society." But before this, as in the 1920s, a postwar "red scare" put a lid on dissent and social reform. Senator Joseph McCarthy's witch hunt against individuals deemed "soft on communism" dominated politics in the late 1940s and early 1950s. The Truman Administration's attempt to complete the New Deal by adding to it a National Health Program was defeated as un-American. It became one of many victims of the period's hysteria. The anticommunist repression drove progressives out of the trade unions, forced most reform-oriented groups to shut down or to tow the line, and terrorized individual dissenters. The second "red scare" also crushed the social work unions, left some prominent social work figures such as Bertha Reynolds jobless and shunned, and cost many others their livelihoods. Whereas a small number of social workers resisted McCarthyism, the majority remained quiet.

The second "red scare" ushered in postwar conservatism. World War II had enhanced the power of the military, corporate groups, and the conservative coalition in Congress (Patterson, 1981). These New Deal opponents scuttled many social programs and opposed new ones. The prosperity that followed the "red scare" made it that much easier to ignore poor people, to believe that economic growth alone would end poverty, and to conclude that America had become a classless, consensual society. With few exceptions the social work profession did little to challenge the dominant postwar currents of American life—the Cold War, suburbanization, hostility to public assistance, indifference to the incipient struggle for civil rights, and others (Wenocur & Reisch, 1989). The predominantly white social work profession remained largely unattuned to the needs of the African American community, the work of African American social workers, and other socially excluded groups.

The Vietnam Era. The turbulent 1960s followed the silent 1950s. Ideological shifts, pressure from increasingly militant popular movements, and an expanded welfare state reopened the door to reform. Despite its prosperity, the United States had extreme economic inequality and many social problems. The rediscovery of poverty and new ideas regarding its structural causes revived the call for political activism (Harrington, 1962). The growth of Northern support for the civil rights movement; the rise of the women's, welfare rights, and other popular movements; and the political dictates of the Democratic party provoked a government response. Urban uprisings and the political assassinations of Malcolm X, John F. Kennedy, Robert Kennedy, and Martin Luther King, Jr., intensified the push. The period's radicalism, combined with the new War on Poverty and the Great Society programs, initially placed social work on the defensive. By the late 1960s and early 1970s, however, despite considerable internal resistance to change, the profession once again lifted the banner of reform.

Return to Laissez-Faire. In the mid-1970s amid another major economic crisis, the political climate once again shifted away from reform. Globalization of markets, deindustrialization, and economic stagnation launched a period of conservative "reform" that reversed 60 years of social welfare policy. President Reagan initiated a massive assault on the welfare state in 1981. Presidents Bush and Clinton, along with business and Congress, have continued the attack. They have called for cutbacks, devolution, and privatization to achieve their ends. Although advocacy and activism are far from dead in the United States, both corporations and the state have successfully attacked the trade union and other social movements, leaving them weakened and on the defensive. Without organized social movements to resist, it becomes much easier to dismantle the welfare state that was so painfully built by earlier pressures from below.

Social work now may be better positioned to join those who fight back. It has matured and won the battle for recognition and can devote more resources to social reform. With so many private and public social services and jobs dependent on government dollars, the profession also has a major stake in preventing the dismantling of the welfare state. Unlike in the past, social work also has a large membership base, considerable political expertise, and the organizational infrastructure necessary for a proactive stance.

What Can We Do?

This historical review of social work's relationship to activism suggests several steps the profession can take to strengthen its commitment to social reform. Social workers can reclaim social reform as part of their mission by including the history of social activism and social reform in social work education. The history of social work has virtually disappeared from the curriculum in many schools. My review of some of the major social work text books found that few of them included an extensive history of the profession. The professional journals contain a bit more history, but many practitioners see these journals only on occasion. As a result, except for those historians of the field and others who have a deep interest in social work's history, few, if any, social workers have much awareness of the profession's history, much less its activist tradition.

The relative silence on activism in so many social work publications effectively endorses complacency. Making this largely ignored history more visible would both deepen knowledge and send a proreform message to the next generation of social workers. Social workers also might work to undo the false distinction between micro and macro social work— the division of labor between social workers working with individuals and those working with communities. This split, which now characterizes much of social work practice, obscures the reality that all social work methods have the potential to promote rather than constrain change, be it with individuals, groups, or the wider society.

The drive to silence dissent during previous periods of conservatism suggests that during such times the social work profession has to work even harder to maintain its liberal agenda. History reveals that when conservatives gain control of public opinion and public policy, they push hard for their own goals. Among the use of other tactics, they stymie alternatives by making proposals for progressive social change seem too risky or unfashionable. To fight back, social work and other advocates of the downtrodden have to develop counter tactics. One such tactic involves taking the risk of sticking to the profession's liberal or radical guns. This includes organizing more social workers for change. It also includes making seemingly outrageous proposals that can stimulate public debate and push the social agenda toward more progressive ends.

Finally, social workers can ensure that their profession remains a site of political struggle, especially in down times such as these. Silence and tolerance of actions that violate professional or humane standards only bolster society's more conservative forces and also risks alignment with them. Historically, a small group of social workers consistently kept the voice of change alive. Their ongoing fights against the conflicts stemming from the profession's structural location in society, the narrowing forces of professionalization, and the rise of conservative political climates ensured that social work remained an arena of struggle throughout the 20th century. Without such political struggles neither social work nor society would have changed for the better.

Some people think that when social workers make individual and social change a fundamental part of social work practice, they politicize a previously neutral, objective, and nonpolitical profession. Yet social work has always been political, in that it deals either with human consciousness or the allocation of resources. Arguing for neutrality on professional or public policy issues represents a political stance that favors the status quo by letting it stand unchallenged. Because social workers cannot avoid the political, it is far better to address these issues explicitly than to pretend that they do not exist. The history of the profession suggests that social workers recommit social work to individual growth and social change. These objectives offer a more ethical option than practicing nonpolitical social work. The middle ground, if one ever existed, is quickly receding. Social workers must decide on which side they stand. ∎

References

Abramovitz, M. (1992). Poor women in a bind: Social reproduction without social supports. *Affilia, 7*(2), 23–44.

Abramovitz, M. (1996). *Regulating the lives of women: Social welfare policy from colonial times to the present* (2nd ed.). Boston: South End Press.

Axinn, J., & Levin, H. (1997). *Social welfare: A history of the American response to need* (2nd ed.). New York: Harper & Row.

Bertha Capen Reynolds Society. (n.d.). *Statement of principles.* New York: Author.

Coll, B. D. (1971). *Perspectives in public welfare: A history.* Washington, DC: U.S. Government Printing Office.

Council on Social Work Education. (1994). *Council on Social Work Education Curriculum Policy Statement.* Alexandria, VA: Author.

Day, P. J. (1997). *A new history of social welfare.* Boston: Allyn & Bacon.

Ehrenreich, J. (1985). *The altruistic imagination: A history of social work and social policy in the United States.* Ithaca, NY: Cornell University Press.

Fisher, J. (1936). *The Rank and File Movement in social work: 1931–1936.* New York: New York School of Social Work.

Galper, J. H. (1975). *The politics of social services.* Englewood Cliffs, NJ: Prentice Hall.

Galbraith, J. K. (1958). *The affluent society.* Boston: Houghton Mifflin.

Gordon, L. (1994). *Pitied but not entitled: Single mothers and the history of welfare.* New York: Free Press.

Harrington, M. (1962). *The other America: Poverty in the United States.* New York: Macmillan.

Haynes, K., & Mickelson, J. (1997). *Affecting change: Social workers in the political arena* (3rd ed.). New York: Longman.

Hine, D. C. (1994). We specialize in the wholly impossible: The philanthropic work of black women. In D. C. Hine (Ed.), *Hine sight: Black women and the re-construction of American history* (pp. 109–145). Brooklyn, NY: Carlson Publishing.

Jansson, B. S. (1988). *The reluctant welfare state: A history of American social welfare policies.* Belmont, CA: Wadsworth.

Kolko, G. (1963). *The triumph of conservatism: A reinterpretation of American history, 1900–1916.* Chicago: Quadrangle Books.

Lee, P. (1930). Social work: Cause and function. *Proceedings of the 56th National Conference on Social Work, San Francisco, 1929.* Chicago: University of Chicago Press.

Lubove, R. (1965). *The professional altruist: The emergence of social work as a career.* Cambridge, MA: Harvard University Press.

Lurie, H. (1941). Social action: A motive force in democracy. *Proceedings of the 68th National Conference of Social Work, Atlantic City, 1941.* New York: Columbia University Press.

Mahaffey, M., & Hanks, J. W. (1982). *Practical politics: Social work and political responsibility.* Silver Spring, MD: National Association of Social Workers.

Muncy, R. (1991). *Creating a female dominion in American reform, 1890–1935.* New York: Oxford University Press.

National Association of Social Workers. (1996). *Code of ethics.* Washington, DC: Author.

Patterson, J. T. (1981). *America's struggle against poverty, 1900–1980.* Cambridge, MA: Harvard University Press.

Payne, M. (1991). *Modern social work theory: A critical introduction.* Chicago: Lyceum Books.

Piven, F. F., & Cloward, R. (1982). *The new class war: Reagan's attack on the welfare state and its consequences.* New York: Pantheon.

Popple, P. R. (1995). Social work profession: History. In R. L. Edwards (Ed.-in-Chief), *Encyclopedia of social work* (19th ed., Vol. 3, pp. 2282–2292). Washington, DC: NASW Press.

Popple, P. R., & Leighninger, L. (1996). *Social work, social welfare and American society* (3rd ed.). Needham Heights, MA: Allyn & Bacon.

Pray, K. (1945). Social work and social action. *Proceedings of the 72nd National Conference of Social Work, 1945.* New York: Columbia University Press.

Quadragno, J. (1994). *The color of welfare: How racism undermined the war on poverty.* New York: Oxford University Press.

Simon, B. L. (1994). *The empowerment tradition in American social work: A history.* New York: Columbia University Press.

Trattner, W. (1994). *From poor law to welfare state: A history of social welfare in America* (5th ed.) New York: Free Press.

van Kleeck, M. (1934). Our illusions regarding government. From Proceedings of the National Conference of Social Work reprinted in *Journal of Progressive Human Services, 2*(1), 75–86 (1991).

Wagner, D. (1990). *The quest for a radical profession: Social service careers and political ideology.* New York: University Press of America.

Weinstein, J. (1968). *The corporate ideal in the liberal state, 1900–1918.* Boston: Beacon Press.

Wenocur, S., & Reisch, M. (1989). *From charity to enterprise: The development of American social work in a market economy.* Urbana: University of Illinois Press.

Withorn, A. (1984). *Serving the people: Social service and social change.* New York: Columbia University Press.

Woodroofe, K. (1964). *From charity to social work in England and the United States.* London: Routledge.

Mimi Abramovitz, DSW, PhD, is professor, Hunter College School of Social Work, City University of New York, 129 East 79th Street, New York, NY 10021; e–mail: iabramov@shiva. hunter.cuny.edu.

Original manuscript received July 7, 1998
Final revision received August 19, 1998
Accepted August 24, 1998

[8]

Mary Richmond and Jane Addams: From Moral Certainty to Rational Inquiry in Social Work Practice

Donna L. Franklin
University of Chicago

Mary Richmond and Jane Addams are two of the most influential figures in the history of the social work profession. This paper explores the influence that these women had on the paradigm shift in the profession from moral certainty to rational inquiry. A review of Richmond and Addams's contributions and achievements throws a different light on the historical development of the profession. The impact of their work on ideological tensions that exist within the profession today is also discussed.

Introduction

Thomas Kuhn, in interpreting the history of scientific disciplines, wrote that a crisis derives from the failure of existing rules to solve the problems with which the group deals. Such a crisis requires a discipline to dismantle its existing model of activities and to replace it with another. Kuhn terms this change in models a "paradigm shift."[1] Social work, emerging as a profession, experienced such a shift. Kuhn's interpretation describes what happened in part, however. Although Kuhn's explanation may be sufficient to explain changes in the physical sciences, it does not take into account three major historical developments within the profession of social work. First, such an analysis applied to social work ignores salient differences in substantive ideologies and values. Second, it oversimplifies the consequences of those ideological and value differences in shaping the social purposes of the profession. Third, it fails to consider a set of fortuitous and interrelated causal events that would mark the profession indelibly.

This article examines the roles of Jane Addams and Mary Richmond in the paradigm shift that occurred in social work at the turn of the century. They were the two most influential women in the history of the profession. With barriers to female participation in nineteenth-century American public life, the achievements of these two women were formidable. Addams was one of the chief architects of the Settlement House Movement, and Richmond became the presiding matriarch of the Charity Organization Society philosophy. These were the two movements that interactively shaped the social purposes of the social work profession. This paper explores the major shift in the profession's paradigm from one of moral certainty to one of rational inquiry and delineates the contribution of these women to that paradigm shift.

The Emergence of Social Welfare

Ira Goldenberg speaks of professions as being shaped by the social and political realities of their time and by the societies of which they are a part. He views their orientations and practices as reflections of the prevailing ideologies and values of the greater society in which they are embedded.[2] The emergence of the social work profession lends itself to such an analysis.

Prior to the Civil War in the United States, poverty was not viewed as a major social problem. The society was primarily rural with an abundance of unused fertile land, and the prevailing attitude was that poverty was a personal problem for which society should not take responsibility. "Go West" was the advice to individuals who were unable to make it in the East. However, the transition from an agrarian to an industrial economy brought massive social and economic changes. Violent business fluctuations, depression, and the crisis of the mid-

1880s brought poverty and insecurity to many. There has been no other period in American history in which the needs and demands of industry so dominated the nation's political and social life.

To increase productivity of the factory system and to generate profits, industry needed a large and mobile supply of skilled and unskilled laborers. Because the industrial order was in an incipient stage of development, the labor supply was quite limited. Subsequently, industry began to recruit labor primarily from a pool of newly arrived European immigrants. Poor living conditions made these immigrants vulnerable to disease and poverty, and their vulnerability was increased by the marketplace practice of low wages and unsafe working conditions. As a result, the immigrant slum soon became a common feature in large industrial cities, and as the slums proliferated, their association with delinquency, disease, and poverty became entrenched. Jane Addams described those conditions: "The streets are inexpressibly dirty, the number of schools inadequate, sanitary legislation unenforced, the street lighting bad, the paving miserable and altogether lacking in the alleys and smaller streets and the stables beyond description."[3]

Calvinism, Liberalism, and Pragmatism

The industrialist Andrew Carnegie expressed a then often-stated belief about the unequal distribution of wealth during this period of industrial expansion. "The millionaires who are in active control started as poor boys and were trained in the sternest but most efficient of all schools—poverty."[4] This Horatio Alger perspective was buttressed by the prevailing intellectual and religious ideologies of that time.

Max Weber, in a classical analysis, asserted that the Christian tradition was vital to the development of the expansive capitalist spirit that dominated industrialization.[5] Calvinist and related Protestant creeds were the key components of this tradition. Weber maintains that the overriding issue for devout Christians was whether they could achieve a degree of certainty regarding their salvation by ceaseless ascetic labor that promised material wealth and success. Such success would bring order and rationality to the individual's life so that each person could be numbered among God's few chosen saints.

Secular liberalism was also an influential ideology during this period. Individuals were seen as hedonistic and self-seeking and as avoiding work unless coerced or bribed. This view appealed to those who also supported the Protestant ethic with its emphasis on individual rights, notably, the right to accumulate property. Only possessions could serve as an incentive to work. Thus liberals viewed society as a group of individuals that was pursuing self-interest and that was operating in a free economy.

Darwinian biology and Spencerian philosophy—asserting that life is a fierce competitive struggle in which only the fittest survive—

combined to increase the prestige of liberal individualistic interpretations. Industrial strife, poverty, and insecurity were indicators of the immutable laws of evolution, and evolution was progress not to be restrained. Hence the economic policies of laissez-faire.[6]

Capitalism and liberalism held two beliefs in common: government should not interfere with market forces, and individuals would be best served if the attitudes of personal responsibility and self-reliance were expected. These ideas marked the emergence of a perspective of moral certainty, a perspective that directed attention to the problems of particular individuals and to their failures of personal responsibility.

A third ideological perspective of the nineteenth century that influenced the nascent profession of social work was pragmatism, which supported a commitment to science and the American empirical spirit. John Dewey, reacting to the psychological assumptions of liberalism, argued that people's interests and motives are shaped by their association rather than by flaws inherent in the individuals. One could not speculate about human nature from deductive analyses of a system of social policy as political economists did. According to Dewey, "knowledge is not the sum of some fixed truths but the product of inquiry which itself is a continuing process." As a result, "the attainment of settled belief is a progressive matter. There is no belief so settled as not to be exposed to further inquiry."[7] He further asserted that knowledge of a particular object or event is never complete; hence, the process of rational inquiry, which moves from hypotheses to experimentation to still further hypotheses, becomes all the more important. These pragmatic ideas were translated into a belief that individuals who lived in poverty were not necessarily morally reprehensible but were influenced by a macrosystem that affected social functioning.

These prevailing intellectual and religious ideologies provided conceptual frameworks for two emerging social movements that directed efforts toward alleviating problems associated with poverty. Those who accepted the ideas of liberalism with its emphasis on individual responsibility and action tended to give their support to the Charity Organization Society. Those who embraced the philosophy of pragmatism and who were more concerned with the problems that beset neighborhoods and entire geographical regions worked in the Settlement House Movement.

The Settlements and the Friendly Visitors

Both the Charity Organization Society and the Settlement House Movement emerged from English models and endeavored to address problems of pauperism, crime, and mental and physical disabilities that contributed to dependency. Both organizations also expressed growing enthusiasm for scientific philanthropy, but there the similarities end.

The Charity Organization Society (COS) emerged from a concern for making almsgiving scientific, efficient, and preventative. For the COS, poverty was to be cured not by the distribution of relief but by the personal rehabilitation of the poor. The guiding philosophy was that pauperism could be eliminated through investigating and studying the character of those seeking help and by educating and developing the poor. Case conferences and "friendly visiting" made vivid the problems, the needs for, and the responsibilities of rehabilitation.[8]

Friendly visitors ran into hostility and indifference, however. They came from different neighborhoods in cities that were segregated by social class and ethnicity. The original idea of districting had presupposed local acquaintance and made more sense in communities where the rich and the poor grew up together.[9]

The founders of the Settlement House Movement, in contrast, chose to live and work among the poor as neighbors, seeking to bring their education and goodwill to bear on the problems. They defined problems environmentally and engaged in social melioration. In an attempt to diffuse the tensions that might develop along class lines, Addams refused to call her neighbors clients or cases and could not fully respect younger social workers, for whom service meant an eight-hour day and a home far from the slums.[10] This attitude was consistent with her commitment to learn from her neighbors and to correct workers' mistakes that were caused by their cultural insensitivity and newness to the neighborhood. David Greenstone, analyzing Addams's philosophic perspective, asserts that her method was experimental in Dewey's sense: perform an action, observe its effects, and modify one's response accordingly.[11] The distinctive aspect of the settlement philosophy was its concentration on the totality of problems in a single geographic area. It did not lose sight of economic and social needs of the individual, but the central focus was on the experiences, thinking, and actions of local populations that could effect broad social and economic reforms.[12]

The National Conference of Charities and Corrections
The settlers and visitors differed in ideologies and partisans, but they were closely allied in commitment to scientific philanthropy. This brought them together with other institutions and agencies under the umbrella organization of the National Conference of Charities and Corrections (NCCC), which became the National Conference of Social Welfare. Richmond first attended the NCCC in 1890, when she heard a presentation made by Josephine Shaw Lowell. Lowell discussed her views on pauperism. A social Darwinist organizer of the COS movement,

Lowell believed that poverty had its roots in the character of the poor. Pauperism would be eliminated by educating and rehabilitating the poor. She was convinced that tax-supported relief was not the cure but the cause of pauperism because it undermined self-reliance and the will to work.[13] In Lowell's writings we find the emergence of moral certainty in social work practice. (Lowell later shifted her perspective when she developed an interest in workers as a class and founded the Consumer's League to investigate working conditions, to identify employers with unfair and unsafe labor practices, and to lead consumer boycotts against them.) Some years later, Richmond acknowledged the influence of Lowell's moral approach to poverty in the development of her own ideas.[14]

The depression of 1893 provided the impetus for some changes in American attitudes toward poverty. That event provided clear evidence that all individuals were vulnerable to reversals in the economic arena; thus, causal explanations of the relation between poverty and an individual's moral reprehensibility were weakened. These attitudinal changes served as catalysts for the NCCC to shift its priorities—which had been shaped primarily by the COS's philosophy—from uplifting the poor morally to finding work for the unemployed and food for the starving. Albert O. Wright reflected these changes in his 1896 NCCC presidential address entitled "The New Philanthropy." In this speech he described the new philanthropy as one that "studies causes as well as symptoms and considers classes as well as individuals . . . it tries to improve conditions thus changing the environment of the defective . . . it tries to build up character."[15]

The moral certainty approach was eclipsed further in 1885 when Charles Booth, a conservative Englishman with a liberal individualist perspective, found that illness, accidents, and unemployment were factors related to and possibly caused by poverty. He then introduced the concept of a poverty line and endeavored to establish empirically some reasonable parameters to determine where the line should be drawn.[16] Edward Devine—an economist who was general secretary of the COS of New York and a leader in social work education—later built on Booth's work and recommended in his book, *Principles of Relief,* "the formulation and general acceptance of the idea of a normal standard of living and the rigid adoption of either disciplinary or charitable measures."[17]

Addams made her first appearance before the NCCC in 1897, her ideas shaped by the philosophic perspective of Dewey and buoyed by the effect that the Settlement House Movement was having on the NCCC philosophy. Addams began her presentation by describing the differences between the two philosophies and asserted, "[the visitors] are bound to tell a man he must be thrifty in order to keep his family. . . . You must tell him that he is righteous and a good citizen when he is self supporting, that he is unrighteous and not a good citizen when he receives aid . . . settlements see that a man may perhaps be a bit lazy and be a good man and an interesting person . . . it does not lay so much stress on one set of virtues, but views the man in his social aspects."[18] When Addams finished, Richmond countered her by describing the settlements as being "like old-fashioned missions, doing harm by their cheap, sprinkling sort of charity."[19]

The debate then escalated when Richmond asserted that "[the settlement] can pretend to be scientific when it is nothing of the kind."[20] In this statement she was probably challenging the claims made by Julia Lathrop, a Hull House resident, who later directed research at the Chicago School of Civics and Philanthropy. In the 1896 NCCC proceedings, Lathrop had stated that "the scientific information gathered by their (settlement) residents can nowhere be duplicated."[21] This statement was consistent with Addams's philosophy that social workers not only help people but also study the conditions under which they lived. Social work, according to Addams, was a form of sociology.[22]

Sources of Ideological Differences

One can conclude from Richmond's remarks that she either misunderstood or possibly devalued science that fell beyond the boundaries of biological science. She had been heavily influenced by the medical profession while working at the Baltimore COS. Her writings carried many quotations from William Osler, the famous Johns Hopkins surgeon, and two of her closest advisers in Baltimore were prominent physicians at Johns Hopkins. In addition, medical students were friendly visitors throughout Richmond's tenure at the Baltimore COS.[23] Thus Richmond was clearly more favorably disposed to the biological rather than the social sciences, which may explain her rather narrow view of science.

While Addams was one of the first generation of college women, Richmond was not. The dialogue between the two women is probably an indication of their divergent social origins and backgrounds. Richmond, an orphan, was reared by her grandmother and an aunt with meager financial resources. Addams, on the other hand, was from a family with some wealth and influence (her father was an Illinois state senator). Addams attended college and traveled internationally, meeting Tolstoy when she visited Russia and visiting Toynbee Hall in London, where she developed her plans for Hull House in Chicago.[24] Richmond was a high school graduate who had joined the ranks of the COS as a clerk and had then been promoted to general secretary, the highest position in that agency.[25] Richmond was sensitive about her lack of formal education and often noted to friends that their minds had been trained while hers had not.[26] Addams has been described as having unusual intellectual and literary talents.[27] These differences may explain the personal rivalry between these two women.

Mary Richmond and Jane Addams   511

What may provide even more insight into the mutual antagonism that developed between these two women is the social context of their struggle. During this era, single, independent women were viewed as misfits in a society that perceived women's primary roles as those of mother and wife. These women did not reject the Victorian notion that women should exude self-sacrifice, purity, and spiritual superiority; rather, they moved these qualities out of the home and into the public world of professional work.[28] The social pressures on these women must have been tremendous as they endeavored to carve out roles for themselves that were both socially acceptable and personally meaningful. Both of these women emerged as commanding and inspiring figures—a formidable accomplishment during this time period.

The divergence of these two women's perspectives is further illuminated in a paper written by Richmond in 1899 entitled "The Settlement and Friendly Visiting." At that time she wrote, "If I could choose a friend for a family fallen into misfortune and asking for relief . . . I would rather choose for them one who had this practical resourcefulness than one who had a perfect equipment of advanced social theories. . . . The former would find the most natural and effective way out . . . the other would say that the whole social order was wrong and must pay a ransom for its wrongness by generous material help to its victims."[29] Richmond's perspective is also reflected in her view of environmental reform as an unwelcome distraction from the task of perfecting the techniques of casework.[30] Muriel Pumphrey has noted that, during that period, Richmond remained antagonistic to such ideas as a minimum wage, a limited work day, and improved working conditions.[31]

Richmond's bias against a liberal arts education was apparent in her proposals for social work education. When she joined the editorial staff of *Charities and the Commons* in 1905 (which was the first professional journal in social work and which would later become a part of the Russell Sage Foundation), she used the journal as a base to argue for an emphasis on the practical preparation of social workers, using case records as teaching materials. She argued against making social work programs academic units of universities with too much emphasis on "theory and academic requirements."[32] On the basis of these recommendations, the Russell Sage Foundation withdrew a promised grant to the Chicago School of Civics and Philanthropy that would have supported a plan to make the school a part of the University of Chicago.[33] The Chicago School, founded by leaders of the settlement movement, did not adhere to Richmond's curricular recommendations and instead developed an academic curriculum based on social theory with an analytic and reform orientation and a focus on social policy and social philosophy.[34] Richmond's emphasis on practical experience over academic training is further reflected in her decision not to hire Jessie Taft in the early 1920s for a job at the Russell Sage Foundation. She admonished Taft, who had just received a Ph.D. from the University of Chicago, to get some experience first.[35]

Two fortuituous events occurred in 1909 that gave Richmond a major victory for her educational views, perhaps unwittingly. First, the old Social Science Association (later to become the American Sociological Association) would finally dissolve, and the dissolution pointed to the difficulty of fitting social science theoretical formulations to the practicalities of welfare policy and administration.[36] Second, Richmond's influence was further enhanced when she was persuaded to leave the editorial staff of *Charities and the Commons* to head the Russell Sage Foundation's new Charity Organization Department. The Russell Sage Foundation gave out nearly $5.8 million in grants to social work organizations, publications, and professional social work associations from 1907 to 1931.[37]

While Richmond's leadership buoyed the profession's commitment to dealing with the practical tasks and issues of poverty and dependency, a consequence of the emphasis has been the social work profession's legacy of vulnerability to criticisms from other social scientists for either lacking or having too fragmentary conceptual frameworks to be taken seriously as an academic discipline.[38] It should be noted, however, that in spite of the ascendency of Richmond's influence, by 1909 Addams would become the first woman president of the NCCC. But due to a set of fortuitous occurrences, her influence would be short-lived.

Addams, the Progressive Party, and Pacifism

Addams, more than any other woman in her times, symbolized the new woman who took her place in the world of work. In this role she applied her intelligence and education to advocating improved working and living conditions in industrial cities. She also asserted the values of social cooperation against the satisfactions of the individual, spoke out against laissez-faire policies that justified industrial capitalism, endorsed woman suffrage, and supported welfare-state programs—programs that Samuel Gompers's American Federation of Labor (AFL) found unacceptable.[39] At Hull House she helped to organize various worker organizations, regularly siding with the workers in the great Chicago labor strikes.[40]

In 1912, a presidential election year, the Occupational Standards Committee of the NCCC decided that it should draft a minimum platform to "direct public thought and secure official action." The committee had been appointed in 1909, the year that Addams was elected president of the organization. The Social Standards for Industry, as the committee called its platform, included demands for an eight-hour day in continuous twenty-four-hour industries, a six-day week for all, abolition of tenement manufacture, the improvement of housing conditions, prohibition of child labor for those under age sixteen, and careful regulation of employment for women. The platform also called for a federal system of accident, old-age, and unemployment insurance. The committee insisted that these minimum standards were require-ments for any community "interested in self-preservation."[41]

A group of social workers presented their platform of industrial minimums to the platform committee of the Republican National Convention but found no interest. Addams also appeared briefly before the platform committee to plea for reform proposals but was virtually ignored.[42] A few days later, however, Theodore Roosevelt walked out of the convention to form a new party. The NCCC committee then presented its program to the new Progressive party, and most of the specific proposals were included in the Progressive party platform.[43] The importance of this event was that it represented a merger of philanthropy and social policy, two interests that formerly had been addressed only separately.

The year 1912 was an exciting time for social reformers. After years of struggling to prohibit child labor and to promote better housing, they now had a national leader who took their social justice programs seriously. The Progressive party campaign attracted enthusiastic support from many social workers. Addams seconded Roosevelt's nomination and compared the convention with sessions of the NCCC, characterizing the exuberance and enthusiasm as religious-like.[44] When Addams rose to speak, having been introduced by Senator Albert Beveridge, "the cheers, applause, and feet-stamping rivaled that which greeted Roosevelt himself." There were other nominating speeches for Roosevelt, but the newspapers gave hers the most attention.[45]

This single appearance catapulted Addams into high national visibility. She was a member of the Cook County Progressive Committee, the Illinois State Progressive Committee, and the National Progressive Committee. She prepared articles for magazines and syndicated news-papers across the country to attract attention to the platform of the new party. What Addams did not anticipate, however, was that her entry into partisan politics would make her vulnerable to criticism from those who felt that someone of her stature should not permit her name to be used in support of a political party.

Mabel Boardman—who had taken over the leadership of the Red Cross in 1905 after initiating a congressional investigation into Clara Barton's misuse of funds and who herself had played an important role in the Republican party as president of the Women's Advisory Committee—was the first to criticize Addams for supporting the Progressives.[46] She argued that Addams "should not be handicapped by the limitations of party affiliations nor trammeled by becoming involved in the bitterness of controversies over candidates and utterly irrelevant policies."[47]

It was criticism by Edward T. Devine of the New York COS, however, that Addams interpreted as a personal attack. As published in *Survey* magazine (whose editor, Paul Kellogg, had served on the NCCC platform committee with Addams), Devine's comments asserted that "it was the first political duty of social workers to be persistently and aggressively non-partisan, to maintain such relation with men of social goodwill in all parties as well as insure their cooperation in specific measures for the promotion of the common good."[48] These remarks were an early omen of the impending decline of Addams's influence in the emerging social work profession. Devine, a founder of the New York School of Philanthropy, would emerge as a leader in professional education.

Addams reached the peak of her popularity between the years 1909 and 1915. She not only was the first woman to be elected president of NCCC but, in that same year, was also the first woman awarded an honorary degree by Yale University. She published six books and more than 150 essays from 1907 to 1916. In the period just before the war, there was no other American woman who was so venerated.[49]

When the war broke out in Europe in 1914, Addams was again swept into a position of leadership, this time in the peace movement. However, her opposition to the war and her later support for the Deb's Socialist ticket made her a major target of the Red scare. She received the Nobel Peace Prize in 1930 for her efforts, but it would be some time before her prewar reputation would be restored.

Richmond and the Quest for Professionalism

The outbreak of World War I was perceived by most social workers as a threat to the social initiatives that the NCCC had been able to bring to the attention of the public; that is, the international crisis would only be a distraction from domestic issues. While social workers as a group did not favor the war, once war was declared social workers took one of two positions: (1) that, once in the war, we had an obligation to win or (2) that we should end our participation in the war. When *Survey* published a neutralist editorial, the mail response was about equally pro and con.[50]

Again Richmond and Addams were on opposing sides. Richmond represented the position that supported the war and was eager for social work to rise to the occasion by developing skills to care for the families of soldiers and sailors. This commitment eventually led to her involvement with the Home Service Bureau of the Red Cross. Addams, on the other hand, was strongly opposed to the war and was actively involved in the peace movement.

Richmond's influence had been gaining momentum in the social work profession prior to the outbreak of the war. Between 1907 and 1912, Richmond made presentations every year at the NCCC. (The only exception, 1909, was the year of Addams's election as president.)

In 1912 Richmond's paper, entitled "Medical and Social Cooperation," addressed the similarities between the professions of social work and medicine. This address keenly influenced the new profession of social work. Richmond did not appear on the program for the next two years, but when she reappeared in 1915, her influence was clearly felt. An example of her stature in the profession was evidenced by an invitation to give the prestigious Kennedy lecture in 1914 at the New York School of Philanthropy, an endowed course delivered each year by an eminent scholar. Her lecture was so well received that two additional sessions were offered.[51]

It was evident in the presentations to the 1915 NCCC conference that social work education was receiving major attention among conference leaders. Two of the major speakers were associates of Richmond, namely, Edward Devine and Abraham Flexner. The theme of the conference was the status of social work as a profession.

Edward Devine, a critic of Addams's partisan political participation, presented a paper focused on the curriculum of the professional school of social work while reflecting on the developments at the New York School of Philanthropy. He had hired Richmond as one of the first instructors, and she taught from time to time, serving on the Committee on Instruction while he was the school's director.[52] Devine recommended that the first priority among curriculum subjects should be a course "which deals with individuals and families and the complicated disabilities of intervention."[53] This statement reflected the influence of the rehabilitative philosophy of COS, a philosophy that placed an emphasis on the individual and that did not directly address environmental or structural constraints. He did add, however, that the next important element after the study of the family rehabilitation was "the history and nature of social movements," an effort to address social change and reform.[54] Devine's mentor had been Simon Patten, also an economist, who had delivered a Kennedy lecture at the New York School of Philanthropy and had argued that social work should focus on fundamental social policy issues.[55] It seems clear that Devine's thinking by 1915 had been strongly influenced by Richmond.

The program committee had also invited Abraham Flexner to address the 1915 meeting on the topic "Is Social Work a Profession?" At that time, Flexner was one of the more influential individuals in the United

516   Social Service Review

States in the area of medical education. Flexner had studied at Johns Hopkins as an undergraduate and influenced several of Richmond's writings. Since many medical students worked as friendly visitors at the Baltimore COS, he had some familiarity with social work.

The main thrust of Flexner's 1915 remarks was that social workers were not experts but rather mediators who summoned the experts. Flexner's pronouncements, documented in social work annals, are seen by some historians as the most significant event in the development of the intellectual rationalization for social work as an organized profession.[56] There was no report on the audience's reaction to Flexner's authoritative pronouncement that social work was not a profession. However, it appears that his arguments were not challenged, even though some conference speakers did not agree with his analysis.[57]

With the decline of Addams's influence in the NCCC, Richmond had more of an opportunity to assert her ideas regarding the social work profession. In her 1915 presentation to the conference she pointed to the differences between social casework and social reform. The proceedings of the NCCC that year quote her argument that "social casework does different things for and with different people—it specializes and differentiates; social reform generalizes and simplifies by discovering ways of doing the same thing for everybody. . . . The only kind of social casework in which I believe, therefore, and the only kind to which I shall refer today may be defined as the art of doing different things for and with different people by cooperating with them to achieve at one and the same time their own and society's betterment."[58]

It took two years for Richmond, again speaking to the conference, to counter Flexner's assertions by arguing that "social work did have skills and techniques of its own rather than being primarily a mediating agency."[59] And, with the publication of her canonical book, *Social Diagnosis,* she had proof that social work was a certifiable profession. Produced and marketed under the auspices of the Russell Sage Foundation, reviews of Richmond's book appeared in such prestigious journals as *Political Science Quarterly, Dial, Journal of Political Economy,* and *American Sociological Review."*[60]

Richmond's credibility was further confirmed by her influence in enabling social workers to provide services to families of soldiers serving their country in the war. After World War I was officially declared in 1917, President Wilson established a war council of bankers and businessmen to enlist contributors to the Red Cross. They raised over $400 million that was targeted for four areas, one of which included "home service." Richmond coined the terminology and was retained to plan the training institutes for the volunteers. The institutes included six weeks of full-time training in a family agency and focused on

Mary Richmond and Jane Addams   517

teaching volunteers how to approach families and aid them in identifying and solving problems.[61]

With the publication of her book *Social Diagnosis* and her work with the Red Cross Home Service, Richmond emerged as the leader of the profession. Her book not only facilitated an easier transition to the helping processes as a technical service analogous to that of a doctor or lawyer, but, more importantly, it defined social diagnosis as "the attempt to make as exact a definition as possible in relation to the other human beings upon whom he (the person) in any way depends or who depends upon him, and in relation to the social institutions in his community."[62]

In her second book, *What Is Social Casework?*, she provided even more clarity on the objective of diagnosis when she stated, "Social casework consists of those processes which develop personality through adjustments consciously effected, individual by individual, between men and their social environment."[63] In Richmond's view, the most critical element in work with individuals was the home and family; there, the first lessons in "individuality and sociality" were learned.[64] These definitions indicate the importance she placed on the relationship between the client and his or her social environment. However, although she acknowledged the person's relation to the social institutions in his or her community in her first book, by the publication of her second she had added the word "personality," which set the profession on a different course.

Richmond is generally credited with getting social workers involved with the Red Cross, but what is discussed less frequently is the demise of this alliance. Mabel Boardman, the earlier critic of Addams's involvement in partisan politics, was still hostile to social workers as a group when she was appointed chairperson of the Bureau of Volunteers of the Red Cross in 1922. She expressed fear that the continued use of social workers would change the American Red Cross from a voluntary aid society into an "amorphous welfare organization."[65] Boardman's position encouraged the Red Cross to use volunteers instead of paid social workers—a major setback for the fledgling profession. This policy decision made social workers further aware of the need to focus their attention on professional identity, recognition, and increased compensation for their labor.

It is an irony of history that Hull House became a training ground for the first generation of professional women. Florence Kelley, Julia Lathrop, Grace Abbott, Sophonisba Breckinridge, and Edith Abbott all went from there into professional social work careers. Addams, however, refused to become professionalized and never took a salary.[66] During that era, the sentiments of social workers regarding professionalization were reflected in the following statement of goals for the profession: "Skilled service in place of or in addition to good intentions and sympathy; making knowledge and skill available to persons who wish to use them rather than setting out to reform people . . . and expectation of reasonable compensation rather than a spirit of self-sacrifice."[67]

Addams's popularity among social workers further eroded when she took a stand against the professionalization of social workers, a position at variance with her stand on women's issues. (To ask why she took this position, however, misunderstands her ethical opposition to self-interested materialism.)[68] While addressing the national conference in 1926, Addams stated that "the danger involved [for social workers] is to look at social work too steadily from the business point of view, to transfer it into the psychology of the business world."[69] And, while Addams's views extended far beyond the Settlement House Movement, her philosophical views were not aligned with those that prevailed in the profession, hence eroding her popularity among social workers. It was Richmond's views that would have the most enduring effect.

In 1921, Addams's diminished authority became apparent when Smith College overlooked her and granted Richmond an honorary master's degree for "establishing the scientific basis of a new profession."[70] This had to be especially disappointing to Addams for two reasons. First, she was one of the first generation of college-educated American women, and Smith was one of the first universities that made college education a reality for women. Second, she had applied to Smith and had planned to attend until she suffered from an undefined illness with severe physical symptoms, which forced her to cancel her plans. And, although the University of Chicago would grant her an honorary L.L.D. degree and Northwestern University, Swarthmore, Rollins, Knox, the University of California, and Mt. Holyoke awarded her honorary degrees, not one school of social work conferred that honor on her.

Addams's declining influence within the profession was further confirmed in 1922 when social workers gathered for the fiftieth anniversary of the NCCC, which by then was the National Conference of Social Work. A few of her friends—Edith Abbott, Julia Lathrop, Alice Hamilton (first woman professor at Harvard), and Graham Taylor—had organized a campaign for her election as president of the conference. They did not anticipate the amount of opposition from individuals who had disagreed with Addams's pacifist stand during the war. The leaders of the opposition campaign were identified as Richmond as well as Homer Folks of the New York Charities Aid Association.[71] Addams's candidacy was subsequently withdrawn, and the conference chose Homer Folks, who was much more conservative.

By the 1920s even the weakening belief in moral certainty could not mute the profession's escalating interest in mental health and psychiatry, the hallmarks of the mental hygiene movement. Roy Lubove observed that social workers could identify with psychiatry and disassociate themselves from charity and relief-giving functions; hence, a new form of therapy emerged.[72] He further asserted that, with this shift, social workers became preoccupied with the person and all but forgot the person's situational context.[73]

Richmond's and Addams's Influence on Social Work Practice Today

Richmond's achievement was the promotion of the professional spirit among social workers and her emphasis on technical competence in the provision of social services. She was keenly interested in the component parts of the interventive process, and she organized these parts into a systematic procedure. Her interest in the social environment developed into an interest in the family as a social unit and contributed to the profession's pioneer work in the field of family therapy.

While her limitations did not diminish the effect of her contributions, they should be noted nonetheless. On the issue of client confidentiality, she was influenced by John Glenn's idea of the ideal agent as a detective. Hence she never saw the contradiction of proceeding with an investigation without the client's awareness or "informed consent" of the steps being taken.[74] This has contributed to the public's perception of social workers as being agents of social control. More specifically, social workers have been accused of having "hidden agendas" or of being outright unethical in their pursuit of the "facts" about the client's situation. Another limitation was her failure to connect epistemology to ideology and, subsequently, to link the methods or techniques she proposed to a theory of practice. This failure on her part has contributed to the profession's vulnerability to Freud's theory of personality. Lela Costin argues that this theory moved social workers away from a form of treatment based on rational assumptions, information, and environmental manipulation. Psychoanalysis, in her view, became the "scientific method for understanding the individual."[75]

There were theoretical formulations extant during that era that were more compatible with the principles set forth in Richmond's writings (e.g., the writings of George Herbert Mead, a pragmatist and social psychologist). As a result, the psychiatric influence dominated the profession for four decades and would not be seriously challenged until the 1960s.[76]

Addams never regained her popularity with social workers, but she generally is credited with enhancing the profession's role as "the conscience of society" by promoting social democracy and the palliation of social injustice. What is too often overlooked, however, is her contribution to scientific research in social work practice. Addams's utilization of Dewey's techniques of rational inquiry and experimentation introduced the concept of research and accountability into social work practice, a concept that was overlooked by four generations of social workers. Such an approach depends on defining a problem by moving from hypothesis through experiment and confirmation to still a further hypothesis, a process that is critically important to practitioners. This process ensures that the practitioner will think critically about the assumptions made concerning the nature of the client's problem(s) and will actively test the logic of these assumptions. The process provides some safeguard against the practitioner making reductionistic and premature classification of the client's behavior, thereby increasing exponentially the possibilities for intervening into the various systems that effect the client's social functioning.

Addams's approach had its limitations as well. Lasch has observed that, while Addams stressed the importance of addressing social and economic changes, she had no real method for dealing with powerful structural and institutional barriers, "interests which could not be simply educated into a more altruistic . . . view."[77] And, while she expressed in her writings a concern with the social problems of the slum, Addams mainly thought and wrote not about the poor or workers as a class but about the problems and potential of particular persons.[78]

Although these two perspectives coalesced into one of rational inquiry, the divergence in these two perspectives subsequently created a cause-function debate within the profession. In his 1929 presidential address to the NCCC, Porter Lee (who had succeeded Edward Devine as the director of the New York School of Philanthropy in 1917), was one of the first to discuss these ideological tensions within the profession. He expressed concern at that time that social work was becoming preoccupied with techniques, methods, and efficiency, which had accompanied the rational organization of services. He then noted that the achievement of a cause, such as a new way of meeting human need, depends on methodical function to implement it and that, while social work must develop and administer its service as an efficient, science-based activity, it must also retain its capacity to inspire enthusiasm for a cause.[79]

For over fifty years these ideological tensions have persisted within the profession, and members of the profession continue to debate methodological, theoretical, and ideological issues. Charlotte Towle addressed this issue in a classic paper entitled "Social Work: Cause and Function," which was published in 1961. In this paper, Towle quoted from Richmond and Addams and noted that "consideration of broad social implications in specific case situations could well produce beneficial effects on casework performance."[80] She also wrote that the adequate meeting of needs through the close interrelations of social movements were problems "that had defied solution and must all become causes in a near tomorrow."[81]

In the current social and political climate we again see the resurgence of the moral certainty perspective, and the social work profession clearly faces serious challenges to its commitment to social justice and social responsibility.[82] And, while the profession now has a theoretical framework that is consistent with the rational inquiry perspective, the challenge that lies ahead is to ensure congruence between belief systems and action systems in the principles that we set forth in our interventions with clients.

The profession can bring the union of cause and function together that Towle envisaged by bringing its coalition-building potential together, by collectively addressing social issues that emerge, and by reflecting these in the range of interventive strategies employed. More than a decade ago, Carel Germain wrote that "the humanization of our superurban life becomes the cause and the range of casework roles and tasks and the flexibility of agency arrangements becomes the function."[83]

Notes

The author wishes to thank Laura Epstein, Bernece Simon, Margaret Rosenheim, and Elizabeth Kutza for their comments on an earlier draft of this paper.

1. Thomas S. Kuhn, *The Structure of Scientific Revolutions* (Chicago: University of Chicago Press, 1961).

2. See Ira Goldenberg, *Build Me a Mountain: Youth, Poverty and Creation of New Settings* (Cambridge, Mass.: MIT Press, 1971).

3. Jane Addams, *Twenty Years at Hull House* (New York: Macmillan Publishing Co., 1910), pp. 97–100.

4. Richard Hofstadter, *The American Political Tradition* (New York: Vintage Books, 1954), p. 166.

5. Max Weber, *The Protestant Ethic and the Spirit of Capitalism*, trans. T. Parsons (New York: Charles Scribner's Sons, 1958).

6. For an excellent discussion of the relation between laissez-faire economic policies and social Darwinian theories, see Max Lerner, *America as a Civilization: Life and Thought in the United States Today* (New York: Simon & Schuster, 1957); and James Leiby, *History of Social Welfare and Social Work in the United States* (New York: Columbia University Press, 1978).

7. John Dewey, "The Logic of Judgments of Practice," in *Pragmatic Philosophy*, ed. Amelie Rorty (Garden City, N.Y.: Anchor Books, 1966), p. 246, and "The Functions of Logic," in ibid., p. 254.

522   Social Service Review

8. Ralph E. Pumphrey and Muriel W. Pumphrey, *The Heritage of American Social Work* (New York: Columbia University Press, 1961), pp. 168–91.

9. See Pumphrey and Pumphrey, p. 173; and Joanna Colcord and Ruth Z. S. Mann, *The Long View: Papers and Addresses by Mary E. Richmond* (New York: Russell Sage Foundation, 1930), p. 137.

10. Daniel Levine, *Jane Addams and the Liberal Tradition* (Madison: State Historical Society of Wisconsin, 1971), p. 43.

11. David Greenstone, "Dorothea Dix and Jane Addams: From Transcendentalism to Pragmatism in American Social Reform," *Social Service Review* 53, no. 4 (December 1979): 527–59.

12. See Robert A. Woods and Albert J. Kennedy, *The Settlement Horizon: A National Estimate* (New York: Russell Sage Foundation, 1922); and Pumphrey and Pumphrey.

13. See the paper by Josephine Shaw Lowell in *Proceedings of the National Conference of Charities and Corrections* 17 (1890): 81–91.

14. Muriel W. Pumphrey, "Mary Richmond and the Rise of Professional Social Work in Baltimore" (D.S.W. diss., Columbia University, School of Social Work, 1956), p. 168 (University Microfilms no. 17,076); and Colcord and Mann, p. 35.

15. Albert O. Wright, "The New Philanthropy," *Proceedings of the National Conference of Charities and Corrections* 23 (1896): 4–5.

16. T. S. Simey and M. B. Simey, *Charles Booth, Social Scientist* (London: Oxford University Press, 1960), pp. 184, 275–79; and Charles Booth et al., *Life and Labor of the People of London*, 1st ser. (1902–4; reprint, New York: AMS Press, 1970).

17. Edward T. Devine, *Principles of Relief* (New York: Macmillan Publishing Co., 1904), p. 19.

18. Jane Addams, "Social Settlements," *Proceedings of the National Conference of Charities and Corrections* 24 (1897): 339.

19. Richmond's comments can be found in ibid., p. 473. Addams herself observed the marked similarities between Hull House and the "actual activities of a missionary school"; see Addams, *Twenty Years at Hull House* (n. 3 above).

20. Addams, "Social Settlements," pp. 472–76.

21. Julia Lathrop, "What the Settlement Work Stands for," *Proceedings of the National Conference of Charities and Corrections* 23 (1896): 106.

22. Christopher Lasch, ed., *Social Thought of Jane Addams* (Indianapolis: Bobbs-Merrill Co., 1965), p. xiv.

23. Pumphrey, "Mary Richmond and the Rise of Professional Social Work in Baltimore," pp. 232, 313–15.

24. When Addams visited Tolstoy, who had renounced his wealth for the life of a Russian peasant, he questioned her devotion to the people. He pointed out that the sleeves of her dress were so full "that there was enough stuff on one arm to make a frock for a little girl." He also asked her if she was an absentee landlord when he found that she lived on the unearned increment from her land in northern Illinois. Addams returned to Chicago determined to spend two hours a day in the Hull House bakery laboring with her own hands. When she realized how time consuming this was, she remarked that Tolstoy was "more logical than life warrants." See Addams, *Twenty Years at Hull House* (n. 3 above), pp. 268–77.

25. In 1891, in spite of Richmond's "comparative youth, her sex, and her lack of academic training" (the two preceding secretaries had been Johns Hopkins men with doctoral degrees in economics), she was elected general secretary. Colcord and Mann (n. 9 above), p. 35.

26. Ibid., p. 427.

27. Lasch, ed., p. xv.

28. Martha Vicinus, *Independent Women: Work and Community for Single Women, 1850–1920* (Chicago: University of Chicago Press, 1985); Carroll Smith-Rosenberg, *Disorderly Conduct: Visions of Gender in Victorian America* (New York: Alfred A. Knopf, Inc., 1985).

29. Colcord and Mann (n. 9 above), p. 122.

30. Pumphrey, "Mary Richmond and the Rise of Professional Social Work in Baltimore" (n. 14 above), p. 285.

31. Ibid., p. 243.

Mary Richmond and Jane Addams   **523**

32. Mary Richmond, "The Need of a Training School in Applied Philanthropy," *Proceedings of the National Conference of Charities and Corrections* 24 (1897): 181–88.

33. Lela B. Costin, "Edith Abbott and the Chicago Influence on Social Work Education," *Social Service Review* 57, no. 1 (March 1983): 94–111.

34. Ibid., pp. 105–6.

35. Carel B. Germain and Ann Hartman, "People and Ideas in the History of Social Work Practice," *Social Casework* 61 (1980): 323–31.

36. See Luther L. Bernard and Jessie Bernard, *The Origins of American Sociology* (New York: Cromwell, 1943), pp. 591–607; and Frank J. Bruno, *Trends in Social Work, 1874–1956: A History Based on the Proceedings of the National Conference of Social Work* (New York: Columbia University Press, 1957), pp. 133–34.

37. John Glenn, Lillian Brandt, and F. E. Andrews, *The Russell Sage Foundation: 1907–1946* (New York: Russell Sage Foundation, 1947); Horace Coon, *Money to Burn: What the Great American Foundations Do with Their Money* (New York: Longmans, Green & Co., 1938).

38. C. Wright Mills, in a paper entitled "The Professional Ideology of Social Pathologists," was one of many social scientists to levy this criticism against social workers, and the profession has reacted to such attacks in recent years. See Council on Social Work Education, "Curriculum Policy for the Master's Degree and Baccaulaurate Degree Programs in Social Work Education," *Social Work Education Reporter* 30, no. 3 (1982): 5–12; see also "Special Issue: Conceptual Frameworks," *Social Work* 22, no. 5 (September 1977); and "Special Issue: Conceptual Frameworks," *Social Work* 26, no. 1 (January 1981).

39. The programs that Addams supported included workmen's compensation; social insurance benefits for the aged; child labor, wages, and hours; programs to protect women in industry; and health and safety laws; see Jane Addams, *Second Twenty Years at Hull House* (New York: Macmillan Publishing Co., 1930), chap. 2, *The Spirit of Youth and the City Streets* (New York: Macmillan Publishing Co., 1912), p. 96, and *Twenty Years at Hull House* (n. 3 above), p. 76. See also Allen F. Davis, *Spearheads of Reform* (New York: Oxford University Press, 1967), p. 112; Levine (n. 10 above), pp. 162–63; and Lasch, ed. (n. 22 above), p. xxx.

40. As Levine points out, Addams actually supported neither workers nor employers. For Addams the real sin of capitalism was not the economic fact that capitalists made profits but rather the social consequence that the poor had no genuine opportunity for cultural expression and self-development. For an excellent discussion, see Levine (n. 10 above), pp. 160–65.

41. Owen R. Lovejoy, "Standards of Living and Labor," *Proceedings of the National Conference of Charities and Corrections* 39 (1912): 388–94.

42. Levine (n. 10 above), p. 189.

43. Ibid.

44. Addams, *Twenty Years at Hull House* (n. 3 above), pp. 28–32.

45. Allen F. Davis, *American Heroine: The Life and Legend of Jane Addams* (New York: Oxford University Press, 1973), pp. 188–89; Levine (n. 10 above), pp. 188–90.

46. Boardman's initiation of a congressional investigation into Clara Barton is reported in Phyliss Atwood Watts, "Casework above the Poverty Line," *Social Service Review* 38 (1964): 303–15.

47. Davis, *American Heroine* (n. 45 above), p. 193.

48. Ibid.

49. Jill Conway, "Jane Addams: An American Heroine," in *The Women in America*, ed. Robert Jay Lifton (Boston: Beacon Press, 1967), pp. 247–66; Davis, *American Heroine* (n. 45 above), pp. 204–5.

50. Clarke A. Chambers, *Paul U. Kellogg and the Survey* (Minneapolis: University of Minnesota Press, 1971), p. 59.

51. Elizabeth Meier, *A History of the New York School of Social Work* (New York: Columbia University Press, 1954).

52. Ibid.

53. Edward T. Devine, "Education for Social Work," *Proceedings of the National Conference of Charities and Corrections* 42 (1915): 609.

54. Ibid.

55. For further discussion on Patten and Devine's relationship, see Daniel Fox, *Discovery of Abundance: Simon H. Patten and the Transformation of Social Theory* (Ithaca, N.Y.:

524   Social Service Review

Cornell University Press, 1976); and Simon Patten, *The New Basis of Civilization* (New York: Macmillan Publishing Co., 1921).

56. David M. Austin, "The Flexner Myth and the History of Social Work," *Social Service Review* 57, no. 3 (September 1983): 357–77.

57. For example, the presentations that followed Flexner on the program (i.e., those of Felix Frankfurther, Porter Lee, and Edward Devine) did not reflect doubts about social work's status as a profession but recommended university affiliation, provided conceptions of social work that distinguished it from other professions, and provided curricular guidelines. See *Proceedings of the National Conference of Charities and Corrections* 42 (1915): 591–611.

58. Mary Richmond, "The Social Caseworker in a Changing World," *Proceedings of the National Conference of Charities and Corrections* 42 (1915): 43.

59. Meier, p. 46.

60. Michael Reisch and Stanley Wenocur, "The Future of Community Organization in Social Work: Social Activism and the Politics of Profession Building, *Social Service Review* 60, no. 1 (March 1986): 70–93.

61. Watts (n. 46 above), pp. 306–7.

62. Mary Richmond, *Social Diagnosis* (New York: Russell Sage Foundation, 1917), p. 357; see also ibid., pp. 51, 62.

63. Mary Richmond, *What is Social Casework?* (New York: Russell Sage Foundation, 1922), p. 98.

64. Ibid., p. 188.

65. See Watts (n. 46 above), p. 312.

66. Florence Kelley went on to become the head of the National Consumers' League; Julia Lathrop was a member of the Illinois Board of Charities before becoming the director of the Children's Bureau; Grace Abbott was the director of the Immigrants' Protective League before becoming director of the Child Labor Division of the Children's Bureau and then replaced Julia Lathrop as the head of the bureau in 1921; Alice Hamilton became the first woman professor at Harvard Medical School and an expert on industrial medicine; and Sophonisba Breckinridge and Edith Abbott were professors at the Chicago School of Civics and Philanthropy. For further discussion, see Davis, *American Heroine* (n. 45 above), pp. 80–81.

67. Amos Warner, Stuart A. Queen, and Ernest B. Harper, *American Charities and Social Work*, 4th ed. (New York: Thomas Y. Crowell Co., 1930), p. 25.

68. Addams had an ethical opposition to what she termed self-interested materialism. Her views are expressed in *Twenty Years at Hull House* (n. 3 above), p. 247, and in *The Spirit of Youth and the City Streets* (n. 39 above), pp. 42, 49. For Levine's excellent discussion, see Levine (n. 10 above), pp. 160–65.

69. Jane Addams, "How Much Social Work Can A Community Afford: From the Ethical Point of View?" *Proceedings of the National Conference of Charities and Corrections* 53 (1926): 108.

70. Colcord and Mann (n. 9 above), p. 427.

71. Davis, *American Heroine* (n. 45 above), p. 270.

72. Roy Lubove, *The Professional Altruist* (Cambridge, Mass. Harvard University Press, 1965), p. 89.

73. Ibid.

74. Muriel W. Pumphrey, "Mary E. Richmond—the Practitioner," *Social Casework* 42 (1961): 375–85.

75. Costin (n. 33 above), p. 104.

76. Gordon A. Hearn, ed., *The General Systems Approach: Contributions toward a Holistic Conception of Social Work* (New York: Council on Social Work Education, 1968); Werner A. Lutz, *Concepts and Principles Underlying Social Work Practice*, monograph 3 (New York: National Association of Social Workers, 1958); Mary Paul Janchill, "Systems Concepts in Casework Theory and Practice," *Social Casework* 50 (1969): 74–82; Carel B. Germain, "Social Study: Past and Future," *Social Casework* 49 (1968); Donald E. Lathrope, "Use of Social Science in Social Work Practice: Social Systems," in *Trends in Social Work Practice and Knowledge* (New York: National Association of Social Workers, 1966).

77. See Lasch (n. 22 above), pp. 200–201.

78. Levine (n. 10 above), p. 127; cf. Addams, *The Spirit of Youth and the City Streets* (n. 39 above), p. 8; Lasch, pp. 34–35.

79. Porter R. Lee, "Social Work: Cause and Function," *Proceedings of the National Conference of Charities and Corrections* 56 (1929): 3–20.

80. Charlotte Towle, "Social Work: Cause and Function, 1961," *Social Casework* 42 (1961): 385–97.

81. Ibid.

82. Leonard Schneiderman of the Council on Social Work Education in a keynote address in 1985 summarized this perspective of others when describing the prevailing societal perspective concerning the poor: "poverty and deprivation are best explained by the idleness, dissipation and self-indulgence of the poor." The ascendancy of the neoconservative argument is best represented in Charles Murray, *Losing Ground: American Social Policy, 1950–80* (New York: Basic Books, 1984). Murray's book asserts that liberal welfare policies are contributing to the increase in female-headed families, a thesis that serves to strengthen Schneiderman's argument.

83. Carel B. Germain, "Casework and Science: A Historical Encounter," in *Theories of Social Casework*, ed. Robert W. Roberts and Robert Nee (Chicago: University of Chicago Press, 1970), p. 28.

[9]

Putting Humpty Together Again: Treatment of Mental Disorder and Pursuit of Justice as Parts of Social Work's Mission

Jerome C. Wakefield

As the social work profession enters its second century, it remains divided and confused about how to define its essential mission and especially about the relation of its psychotherapeutic activities to its more traditional responsibilities. One common view is that social work is primarily concerned with social justice, particularly with providing for the deprived and oppressed. Another view, reinforced by social work's immense role in mental health care and by state licensing of social workers as mental health clinicians, holds that social work is primarily a mental health profession aimed at treating mental disorders, perhaps distinguished from other mental health professions by a more person-in-environment emphasis. These conflicting views have led to an intellectual fragmentation of the profession about its own foundations. A profession that lacks a clear, consensual understanding of its mission is likely to function less effectively and to have trouble presenting its case to the public. Therefore, attaining an intellectually defensible resolution of the question of how each of these conceptions is in fact related to the profession's mission should be among the profession's highest priorities.

This chapter contains a revised version of material that appeared in J. C. Wakefield, "Psychotherapy, Distributive Justice, and Social Work Revisited," *Smith College Studies in Social Work* 69 (1998): 25–57.

Minimal Distributive Justice as the Essential Mission of Social Work

There is a straightforward sense in which psychiatry, clinical psychology, and psychiatric nursing are mental health professions; the basic mission that they exist to pursue, or what I have called their *organizing value* (Wakefield 1988a), is mental health, in the specific medical sense of treating (including preventing) mental disorder. Just as medicine aims at health, law at legal justice, and teaching at transmission of knowledge as their essential defining goals, so the mental health professions aim to treat mental disorder.

When we say that social work is a mental health profession (or even that clinical social work is a mental health profession—I will return to the sub-specialty of clinical social work below), we mean something much more complex than we do in these other cases (Wakefield 1988a, 1988b). It is not that social work is not concerned with mental disorder; of course it is. But the conceptual relationship between the profession and its treatment of mental disorder is different from what it is in the other mental health professions. Unlike the other mental health professions, social work did not originate as and has never primarily been a mental health profession but has rather been concerned with a broad range of interventions addressing human need and deprivation, including economic aid to relieve the effects of poverty, provision of housing for the homeless, child protection and placement, helping broken families to meet their basic needs, guiding wayward youth, helping medical patients to gain access to medical care and to get their nonmedical needs met, guiding immigrants in coping with their new life, helping children to take advantage of the opportunity for schooling, ensuring that the needs of the elderly are met, and many other interventions aimed at problems that are not inherently mental disorders.

While not specifically concerned with mental disorders, all of these interventions potentially involve a psychological component, and thus from the beginning social workers became competent in the methods for encouraging psychological growth and change that evolved into what we now call psychotherapy. These psychological methods are an essential part of our profession's skill base. Clinical social workers may specialize in the application of such methods, but throughout the profession's history these clinical methods have been applied to a broad range of problems. Given the social need for such interventions to treat mental disorder and the lack of adequate personnel trained in them, however, society licenses social workers to perform psychotherapeutic services for those who have mental disorders.

I have argued elsewhere that social work's essential organizing value—the mission that defines it as a profession and encompasses all of its traditional tasks—is not mental health but rather ensuring that all members of society possess at least a minimally acceptable level of a variety of basic economic, social, and psychological goods necessary to live a decent life and participate in social institutions (Wakefield 1988a, 1988b). In putting forward this account of social work's mission as "minimal distributive justice," I rely on John Rawls's (1971) theory of justice, and especially his concept of the "social minimum," a certain level of possession of socially produced economic, social, and psychological goods below which it would be unfair to allow any member of society to fall. Distributive justice demands that no member of society be allowed to fall below the social minimum of such goods. Note that the notion of a social minimum or "safety net" is widely accepted and is not really dependent on Rawls's theory, although Rawls tried to present a systematic theoretical rationale for this wide agreement.

We might think of social work, then, as a "safety net" institution, where the safety net is interpreted broadly to encompass protection against unjust deprivation of needed economic (e.g., money, housing), social (e.g., fair occupational opportunity, fair opportunity for social participation), and psychological (e.g., self-respect) goods. The inclusion of psychological goods is a relatively novel aspect of Rawls's theory that I use to explain certain strands of clinical social work, as I detail below.

The goods subject to considerations of justice are those Rawls calls "primary social goods," that is, goods (in the broad sense of "good things") that are necessary for the effective pursuit of virtually any life plan (i.e., they are "primary" goods that everyone needs) and that are created through social cooperation or distributed in accordance with social rules and structures (i.e., they are "social" goods). Note that this latter sense of "social," referring to the fact that certain primary goods are socially created, shaped, and/or distributed (unlike other goods that are not mainly socially distributed, like beauty or height or health) and thus are subject to considerations of justice, is to be distinguished from the sense of "social" noted above in which certain goods are social as opposed to economic or psychological (e.g., educational opportunity as opposed to money or self-respect) in their content. All these kinds of goods can be "social" in the creation/distribution sense, and if they are social goods in this sense, they are subject to considerations of just distribution.

When people fall below a contextually defined "social minimum" of any one of such goods so that they cannot pursue a life plan at even a minimally effective level, that constitutes deprivation and injustice, according to Rawls. Social work, I argued, is ultimately concerned with ensuring that each individual possesses at least the minimal acceptable level of each of the primary social goods, a goal I labeled *minimal distributive justice.*

The analysis of the essential mission of social work as the pursuit of minimal distributive justice allows for both the profession's involvement in social reform and its concern for individual change in the quest for distributive justice for deprived individuals. At first glance, however, the redistribution of primary social goods to deprived individuals does not seem to involve psychotherapy. The analysis thus leaves us with the question "What is the relation of clinical social work to social work?" That is, why should a justice-oriented profession use psychotherapeutic methods?

Two Questions About Clinical Social Work

The identification of clinical social work with the use of psychotherapy depends on some rough distinctions among categories of social work. First, there is traditional casework, which encompasses all direct social work intervention with individuals and families, whether the intervention is psychotherapeutic (e.g., intervention to alleviate demoralization or to impart new coping skills) or nonpsychotherapeutic (e.g., cash relief, child placement, provision of housing, concrete advice, etc.) in nature. One area of casework is *psychiatric social work,* a form of medical social work, in which the mental patient's basic needs, such as needs for housing, for family support, or for case management in the community, are pursued using nonpsychotherapeutic interventions. However, psychotherapeutic-style interventions may also be used in psychiatric social work to build social skills, reduce symptoms, and accomplish other intervention goals, which may in effect involve treating the mental disorder in the course of trying to help the client to meet basic needs. So, both casework and psychiatric social work can include psychotherapeutic as well as nonpsychotherapeutic methods. *Clinical social work* refers to those aspects or forms of casework intervention that are specifically psychotherapeutic in nature.

However, the above clarifications still leave the term "clinical social work" ambiguous in an important way. Analogously to clinical psychology, clinical social work is often construed as that branch of the social work profession that treats mental disorders. But psychotherapy as a set of methods can be used to change internal mental states and processes even when no disorder exists, and sometimes "clinical" intervention is construed as any intervention that uses such psychological change methods, whether the target is mental disorder or some other kind of psychological problem. It is important here to remember that current diagnostic criteria in *DSM-IV* (APA 1994) are overly inclusive and incorrectly classify many social problems as mental disorders (Wakefield 1993b, 1996, 1997). Many social work problems do not involve a mental disorder, even when they do involve problematic psychological states. Reflecting this distinction between mental disorders and non-disordered problematic psychological states, *clinical social work* sometimes refers to casework in which psychotherapeutic methods are used to change any kind of disordered or non-disordered problematic psychological state. One must distinguish psychotherapy in the sense of psychotherapeutic techniques themselves—which were developed to treat mental disorder but which can be used for other purposes—from psychotherapy aimed specifically at treatment of mental disorder. Each sense of *psychotherapy* gives rise to a corresponding sense of *clinical social work*.

Thus, there are really two different conceptual questions that one can ask about clinical social work: (1) Does psychotherapy have a role in social work's pursuit of justice? (2) Is the treatment of mental disorder part of the profession's essential justice-related defining mission?

Regarding the first question, caseworkers commonly use psychotherapeutic-style methods to help remove the client's internal psychological impediments to better social functioning or to provide the client with basic psychological needs and thus to pursue social work's goal of justice. The fact that justice rather than mental health is the ultimate goal is important because it makes a great difference to which cases one thinks are most appropriate for treatment, to the focus of one's intervention, and to one's criteria for success.

Regarding the second question, although there is a great overlap between psychological problems related to justice and mental disorder, still mental disorder is not, as such, part of social work's essential mission because mental disorder is not generally intrinsically unjust (except perhaps in those cases where unjust social circumstances are directly responsible for the existence and maintenance of the disorder). Mental disorder may make it impossible to effectively pursue a life plan, but in itself it is not generally an injustice committed by society in maldistributing its goods. Thus, alleviating mental disorder is not an essential part of providing minimal distributive justice, although helping people to obtain fair access to mental health treatment is a matter of justice. Moreover, mental disorder will often be treated incidentally as social workers attempt to help people develop the capacity to meet their basic needs. Analogously, physical disorder can deprive a person of primary goods necessary to pursue a life plan and warrant action to make sure that the person has those primary goods that can be redistributed (e.g., food, housing, social support), but physical disorder is not generally an injustice in itself in the literal sense that society is responsible and owes the person a cure (except in some cases where society has failed to provide fair distribution of environments or other conditions necessary for maintaining health). Feelings of benevolence and caring and a desire to alleviate suffering, not a perception of injustice, generally motivate us to try to cure the mentally and physically disordered.

Of course, social work is also ultimately motivated by feelings of benevolence and caring and the desire to alleviate suffering. The difference between social work and other professions lies not in this shared motivation but in the specific causes of suffering that are addressed by each profession. Just as medicine attempts to address suffering resulting from physical disorder, law attempts to address suffering resulting from legal injustice, the clergy attempts to address suffering resulting from spiritual challenges, and educators attempt to prevent suffering resulting from ignorance, so social work as its specific mission attempts to alleviate suffering resulting from deprivation of basic needs, that is, from minimal distributive injustice. Physical disorders in themselves (as opposed to the distributive problems they entail), although they cause suffering that social workers, like all empathic human beings, would like to alleviate, are not generally injustices. The same considerations apply to mental disorders.

Treatment of Mental Disorder as a Derived Task of Social Work

In addition to my denial that treatment of mental disorder is encompassed by social work's traditional organizing value of minimal distributive justice, I also hold that the treatment of mental disorder does have a place in the social work profession's mission as what I called a *derived task*. That is, it is a task that is not part of social work's essential defining mission or organizing value, but because social workers have the appropriate skills, it is a task that society has nonetheless mandated the profession to add to its other, more traditional responsibilities. Thus, social work is indeed a mental health profession, but only in the same conceptually incidental way that, for example, medicine is a profession concerned with beauty by virtue of its performance of cosmetic surgery. Physicians have been socially sanctioned and licensed to relieve suffering by providing cosmetic surgery because they have the necessary skills, but that is not an essential task of medicine, since it does not aim at health. People who are trained as social workers and then practice psychotherapy with the purpose of treating mental disorders just like other mental health professionals are social workers in the legal sense, but they are not doing social work in the essential conceptual sense, any more than doctors who specialize in cosmetic surgery are doing medicine in the strict conceptual sense.

The analogy between social workers treating mental disorders and physicians performing cosmetic surgery is misleading in one important respect. Cosmetic surgery—even though it often relieves considerable suffering—is generally considered less important than essential medical goals. However, treatment of mental disorder is not in my view less important than relief of distributive injustice. As a general principle, there is nothing necessarily more superficial or less important about a derived versus an essential task; it all depends on the particular tasks.

It must be admitted that most psychotherapeutic practices include not only disordered patients but also many people who, partly because of internal psychological impediments that are not disorders, are having difficulty functioning adequately in their social roles (as noted earlier, *DSM* criteria are overinclusive and cannot be used as a guide to mental disorder). So, in day-to-day practice there is only a fuzzy distinction between psychotherapists who treat mental disorders and clinical social workers who use psychotherapeutic methods to pursue social work's goals. But there is an important conceptual distinction nonetheless.

The failure of society to create a separate profession of psychotherapy to treat mental disorders has meant that practitioners from several existing professions, including social work, have been pressed into service in this important area, where their skills are urgently needed. It is hypocritical for the social work profession to ignore this expanded mandate, to continue to pretend that it is inappropriate for students to enter the profession expecting to be psychotherapists, and to resist providing adequate educational opportunities for them to be trained for this option, while accepting the social benefits that come with the profession's involvement in the mental health field. Of course, it is equally undesirable for the profession to become so enamored of these possibilities that its traditional mission becomes obscured. One needs a balance here between respect for the essential mission and acceptance of the derived task.

Note that treatment of mental disorder is not the only possible derived task of clinical social workers using psychotherapy. As Specht (1990) emphasizes, there are many people looking for meaning in their lives who have all the primary goods. Their problem is neither mental disorder nor deprivation but rather that life is intrinsically painful and puzzling as to its meaning. I agree with Specht that treatment of such problems has nothing to do with social work's traditional mission. If clinical social workers are mandated to use their expertise to help such people, this is a derived task, like treatment of mental disorder.

Psychotherapy and the Pursuit of Minimal Distributive Justice

A critical challenge arising out of the above account is to identify some instances where the use of psychotherapeutic methods serves the essential mission of the profession, and thus to show that the justice account can explain the profession's traditional use of psychological change methods. Psychotherapy's place in pursuing social work's essential mission is often

300 • *Psychotherapy and Social Work*

questioned because the goods traditionally associated with justice are economic and social goods, not psychological change. However, an adequate understanding of the demands of justice, including Rawls's (1971) point that there are psychological as well as economic and social primary goods, helps to explain why psychotherapy has long been an integral part of social work's interventive approaches. Rawls persuasively argues that the possession of at least a minimal level of certain socially imparted psychological properties is as basic to the pursuit and enjoyment of any life plan as are economic and social goods. Because psychotherapeutic methods can influence such justice-related psychological properties, such methods are directly relevant to a profession pursuing minimal distributive justice.

To the question of exactly how psychotherapy can be used to pursue justice, there are three basic answers. First, there is the traditional answer that internal psychological states are often impediments to acquisition of basic justice-related goods and can curtail adequate social functioning. The classic cases include lack of adequate coping skills to deal either with challenging environments or with transitions to new environments or roles; demoralization or low self-esteem caused by chronic deprivation and failure; reaction to frustration by diversion into substance abuse; and use of antisocial strategies for survival in threatening or opportunity-deprived environments. But the potential forms are endless. Such psychological states usually are not mental disorders but rather problematic but normal responses to difficult environmental conditions. It is normal to be sad over loss, anxious about threat, and to survive as best one can even if that entails breaking the rules. For example, it is not a mental disorder for an adolescent who comes to America after growing up in a war-torn country where he or she is used to violence as a routine way of dealing with conflict to continue to engage in such learned behavior in the new environment (even *DSM-IV* acknowledges this possibility of environmental, non-disordered causation of adolescent antisocial behavior). Working with such an adolescent, perhaps using psychotherapeutic techniques, is a legitimate task of social work as it attempts to enable the youth to function in our society and to meet basic needs in this new environment. Many clinical social work interventions are of this nature; they are interventions aimed not at alleviating mental disorder but at changing psychological properties that do not qualify as disorders but are blocking adequate social functioning or the meeting of basic needs.

In addition to the role of psychological traits in enabling people to meet basic economic and social needs, there is a further sense in which psychological traits can be justice-related. Here I rely heavily on Rawls's theory to make my point. Contrary to the traditional focus exclusively on economic and social goods in theories of justice, Rawls argues that the psychological property of self-respect—or at least the social experiences that are the basis for development of self-respect—is a central social good. That is, self-respect is essential in effectively pursuing almost any life plan, yet the bases for self-respect are largely determined by social rules and opportunities and thus in effect are "distributed" by society. Each individual should thus, as a matter of justice, have at least a minimally adequate opportunity to partake of those activities that form the basis for self-respect.

In earlier publications (Wakefield 1988a, 1988b), I built on Rawls's argument regarding self-respect to suggest that the social bases for other psychological traits as well—such as the experiences that build self-esteem, self-confidence, and self-knowledge—must be an integral part of a theory of minimal distributive justice. These traits are like self-respect in that they are largely socially based (i.e., developed and "distributed" via social rules and interactions) and are as integral to effectively pursuing any life plan as economic relief and social opportunity. Thus these psychological goods are in themselves justice-related, and lack of them, or lack of the social conditions for developing them, is a form of unjust deprivation. Psychotherapy, when aimed at providing the conditions for the development of these justice-related psychological traits, is justice-related psychotherapy and thus an essential task of social work.

There is a third sense in which psychotherapy can be justice-related. The lack of justice-related psychological goods often occurs partly because of deprivation in the family or broader social environment during the individual's maturation and socialization. Thus there is a sense in which clinical social work is often an after-the-fact attempt to redistribute the opportunity to develop justice-related psychological properties when the social system of distribution of environments has failed to give a person a fair allocation of such early facilitating environmental conditions. Clinical intervention cannot of course guarantee that the individual will change for the better, but it can provide some compensating opportunities in response to earlier deprivation.

In sum, aside from the use of psychotherapy to perform the derived task of treating mental disorder, social workers who pursue the traditional professional mission of minimal distributive justice may use psychotherapy in at least three conceptually overlapping ways: (1) to change psychological attributes that are obstacles to the individual's capacity to obtain basic economic or social goods or to function socially; (2) to provide psychologically deprived individuals with missing psychological primary social goods (i.e., psychological attributes that are necessary for the effective pursuit of any life plan and depend for their development on social experiences), such as self-respect, self-esteem, self-confidence, and self-knowledge; and (3) to provide individuals who were deprived of the psychosocial environment where psychological primary goods generally develop with a therapeutic environment that gives the individual a second opportunity to experience the conditions that encourage the development of such psychological goods.

Two Confusions About the Minimal Distributive Justice View

The complexity of my position—specifically, the fact that I reject treatment of mental disorder as part of the traditional essential mission of the profession but accept psychotherapeutic methods as part of the set of techniques useful for pursuing that mission and accept treatment of mental disorder as a derived part of the mission—has made my view a target for both sides in the broader debate between clinically oriented and justice-oriented thinkers. Neither side tends to distinguish the goal of curing mental disorder from the use of psychotherapeutic techniques, or essential (primary) from derived (secondary) tasks. Thus, failing to acknowledge the distinctions on which my analysis is based, both sides see my view as problematic. Those who, like Specht (1990) and Specht and Courtney (1994), want to defend the traditional mission of the profession attack my view because they mistakenly see my defense of the use of psychotherapy in social work as a rejection of social work's traditional mission. Those who, like Dean (1998), want to defend clinical social work attack my view because they mistakenly see my exclusion of mental health from the essential organizing value of social work as a rejection of the use of psychotherapeutic methods by social workers or as a rejection of the treatment of mental disorders by social workers.

In a critique of my views, Harvey Dean (1998) characterizes my position as follows: "Wakefield (1988) defines social justice as the primary mission of social work and thereby relegates mental health as outside of social work's mission" (12). He argues, in opposition to what he thinks I say, that social work's mission does encompass psychotherapy. However, Dean's statement of my views is potentially misleading in several ways. First, note a gap in the logic of his statement; the fact that I define justice as social work's primary mission does not "thereby" relegate mental health to being outside of social work's mission altogether, because the primary mission need not be all of the mission. Nor does it even relegate outside of social work's primary mission those aspects of mental health that are themselves interpretable as aspects of justice. A correct inference would be that my identification of social work's primary mission as justice relegates those aspects of mental health treatment not directly related to justice to at best a secondary or derived role in the mission. And in fact, this is exactly what my view does; it identifies a variety of mental health–related tasks that are aspects of justice, places them squarely within the traditional primary mission of the profession, and holds that treatment of mental disorder per se, to the degree that it is not an aspect of the striving for justice but rather strictly aimed at curing mental disorder, is a secondary (or "derived") part of social work's overall mission. This may not be enough for those who want to feel that the mental health focus is conceptually primary in social work, but it is a lot more than critics like Dean acknowledge in my view.

There are other misleading elements of Dean's statement. In approaching the nature of social work, I do not arbitrarily *define* social work as aimed at social justice but rather *analyze* the concept of social work implicit in common intuitions, trying to explain the judgments we make about what is and what is not social work. I conclude not that the mission is social justice but that it is minimal distributive justice, a narrower and more precise idea than social justice (see below). And, as elaborated above, my view of the relationship of mental disorder, psychotherapy, and social work is much more complex and multifaceted than Dean's summary suggests. My view implies a wide range of essential and derived reasons for social workers to intervene with individuals who have mental disorders.

However, it remains true that I claim that treatment of mental disorders in itself is not an essential function of the social work profession. This is the contention that Dean and many other clinically minded social workers find unacceptable. Yet it seems plainly true. Consider the following thought experiment: Imagine that social workers stopped doing any psychotherapy aimed at cure of mental disorder and pursued strictly minimal distributive justice goals (for which, as noted, psychotherapeutic intervention is sometimes appropriate). In such an eventuality, there would be no doubt that the social work profession would continue. But now imagine that all the justice-related activities of the profession ceased and that social workers strictly treated mental disorder aiming at cure of disorder. In such an eventuality, it seems plain that the social work profession would have ceased to exist in any other than an institutional sense and that social work would in fact have become part of a generic psychotherapy profession. If the reader's intuitions agree here with mine, then the reader implicitly agrees that, although treatment of mental disorder might be part of the mission of social work, it is not part of the essential mission that makes the profession what it is and distinguishes it conceptually from other professions.

A second and opposite kind of confusion appears in Specht and Courtney's (1994) book, *Unfaithful Angels: How Social Work Has Abandoned Its Mission*, in which they critique the psychotherapeutic turn in social work. They assert that my view that psychotherapy can be part of social work's justice-related mission simply comes down to the claim that social workers have the aim of bringing psychotherapy to the deprived who would not otherwise be able to afford it. This is a misreading of my view. Of course social workers should be concerned about fair access to mental health services for the deprived. But that alone would not imply that they should do the treatment themselves. The justice element in the use of psychotherapy that makes psychotherapy a legitimate part of social work is not related to the goal, however noble, of fairly distributing access to psychotherapy. To understand why, just consider that the same argument would justify social workers' actually performing medical services like surgery, legal services such as defending clients in court, and other professional services that are unfairly distributed and that are not as available to the deprived as to the affluent. But no one thinks that social workers should actually provide such services, although they do have the mission of assuring adequate access to such services compatible with the requirements of a just distribution of social resources. My view explains why, in the case of psychotherapy, society mandates that social workers not only help the deprived to gain access to the mental health services they need but also provide the actual services themselves. The answer lies, first, in justice-related non-mental-health goals of the application of psychotherapy as elaborated above, and second, in the derived assignment to use the skills that social workers obtain in their training that can also be used for treatment of mental disorder. Neither rationale applies to the skills of other professions.

The Overinclusiveness and Underinclusiveness Fallacies

There are two fallacies that are very common in conceptual analyses of social work's mission. The first fallacy is to define the profession in terms of a mission that is too broad and overinclusive. Definitions of social work's mission in terms of self-realization, well-being, improvement of social functioning, improvement of the fit between individual and environment, and many other such goals are just too broad to identify social work as distinct from other professions. Even distributive justice is too broad a concept for social work's mission, because many aspects of justice (e.g., should executives earn so much more than the workers they supervise?) concern relative distributive fairness and not issues of minimally acceptable levels of primary goods, and accordingly are not seen as within social work's essential domain. This is why I suggested minimal distributive justice as social work's mission; the focus on deprivation of basic goods seems to be unique to social work.

For example, Harvey Dean (1998; see Wakefield 1998) commits the overinclusiveness fallacy by arguing that the goal of clinical social work is to provide meaningful narratives to people. Narratives, as Dean uses the concept, encompass just about all meaning, and both individual minds and cultures are essentially meaning systems, so basically he is assigning to social work a task that is common to every profession and social institution. Doctors, lawyers, teachers, priests, and journalists all are mandated to create certain interpretations and meanings and to impart those "narratives" to their clients. A narrativist account of clinical social work must begin by defending a view of exactly what kinds of narrative problems are the special domain of social work, and Dean does not adequately confront this problem.

The second fallacy is to define social work in terms of a mission that is preferred by the theoretician but is manifestly too narrow to encompass the essential core activities of the profession. The most common strategy here is to try to define the profession in terms of non-clinical practice—such as social action or case management or interfacing between individuals and institutions—and to conclude that clinical practice is not part of the profession. An example is Specht's (1990; see Wakefield 1992) rejection of the legitimacy of using psychotherapeutic methods in social work, based on his definition of the profession in terms of community development goals, which arbitrarily ignores the strong clinical social work tradition dating from Mary Richmond. These overly narrow, partisan accounts are not really conceptual analyses but rather what philosophers call "stipulative definitions" (i.e., decisions to use a word in a new way) or "persuasive definitions" (i.e., attempts to get others to accept a new definition). Such definitions are attempts to transform the profession to be in one's desired image rather than to analyze the profession's actual nature.

Does my definition of social work in terms of minimal distributive justice also fall prey to the same problem of excessive narrowness because of promoting one segment of the profession's activities? Rather than arguing that social work ideally ought to be about justice, I conclude on the basis of an analysis of social work's varied activities that the profession is in fact aimed at justice. I argue that the history of the field makes it clear that the use of psychotherapeutic methods is integral to the profession and must somehow fit into any acceptable definition, and I use Rawls's theory of justice to explain how the use of psychotherapy can indeed be an essential part of a justice-oriented profession. Rather than being stipulative or persuasive, my analysis is primarily an attempt to provide a "lexical" definition of the profession—that is, a definition that explains how social workers and others actually think about social work and how they judge whether an activity is or is not social work. I mainly attempt to explain people's judgments, not to legislate or change them. Whether my view is adequate or inadequate, it is at least an attempt to directly address the real complexity of the profession's goals.

What about the objection that Rawls's theory provides not an account of overall benevolence but only of justice and that social work is concerned with benevolence generally? The sense of justice and feelings of benevolence are two different things. Benevolence often goes beyond justice (e.g., helping a friend at considerable personal cost), and justice is often not a matter of benevolence (e.g., refusing to give someone something he or she wants but has no right to). On the basis of such examples, I would argue that it is minimal distributive justice, not benevolence more generally, that social work pursues.

306   •   *Psychotherapy and Social Work*

Indeed, minimal distributive justice requires impartiality and thus some judgments that may go against what clients or others want, and therefore may at moments seem less than benevolent to some. Does this aspect of the justice account conflict with the traditional nonjudgmental approach of social workers?

The suggestion that social workers traditionally take a nonjudgmental approach is quite true in relation specifically to clinical social work, for that attitude is at the heart of clinical intervention. However, clinical intervention takes place after it has been established that there is a psychological need for such intervention, so such nonjudgmentalness is not in conflict with the justice account. But social work is not just clinical intervention, and with regard to other areas of intervention, it is quite untrue that social workers are entirely nonjudgmental. For example, from the profession's inception in friendly visiting, social workers have been seriously concerned about the legitimacy of clients' claims for material assistance. The reason for such judgments is obvious; in the material domain, to give more to a client than is warranted by minimal justice considerations would be unjust both to others who really need (not just desire) the limited resources and to those who give the resources because they think justice demands it. To take another example, social workers involved in child placement make judgments all the time about the suitability of parents or of proposed foster parents, and these judgments may at times go against the desires of the involved individuals. The issue that provokes such judgments is obvious; each child deserves as a matter of justice at least a minimally adequate psychosocial environment in which to grow. So, looking at the ways that social workers have been judgmental in some areas of their endeavors, it appears that these judgments are entirely consistent with the justice view. It is no doubt true that benevolence (or what I elsewhere consider as "altruism" [Wakefield 1993a]) does play at least a motivating role in social work; as noted earlier, a concern about minimal distributive justice is generally motivated by benevolence. But from a conceptual point of view, justice is the essential concept, and benevolence is overinclusive. Medicine and nursing, for example, are equally motivated by benevolence. Social work has always been concerned with those who are deprived of basic needs, and this suggests a concern specifically with justice.

Again, it is sometimes suggested by psychodynamically oriented practitioners that self-knowledge of the kind imparted in psychotherapy is the general mission of social work. Beyond a certain minimal amount required to pursue most life plans, self-knowledge is not a primary good but rather part of an individual's distinctive vision of the good. Some people believe in a life of action and are determinedly non-psychologically minded, perhaps even averse to looking inward; contrary to the fantasies of mental health professionals, not all such people fall ill, and many lead fulfilling lives. Others, from Socrates to Woody Allen, enshrine the pursuit of self-knowledge as a central part of what makes life worth living, although the precise form that this self-knowledge takes may vary dramatically, reminding us that even fervently held beliefs about the self may not always constitute true "knowledge." It is not a matter of justice, and certainly not social work's concern, whether everyone pursues a life devoted to such concerns. Beyond its limited role in minimal distributive justice, self-knowledge in general is not by any historical or conceptual criterion the distinctive mission or mandate of social work (Socratic philosophy and psychoanalysis might have better claims).

In defending a broad psychotherapeutic mission of social work and specifically a mission of treating mental disorder, the point is often made that clinical social workers are confronted daily with the reality of the relationship between clients' inner psychological realities and the failures of their interpersonal and social worlds. I agree that we are confronted with such manifest links between the psychological and the social. However, this argument is based on a confusion between psychological problems that may form obstacles to social functioning versus mental disorders. Most inner psychological obstacles to social functioning (e.g., demoralization, lack of coping skills) are not disorders. Nor do all mental disorders lead to failed social functioning; certain kinds of depressive or anxiety disorders, for example, may be terribly painful to the individual but may not significantly affect social functioning or access to basic needs. This argument that social work specifically and essentially aims to cure mental disorder is based on a spurious equation between psychological obstacles to social functioning and mental disorders.

Of course, mental disorders would be a form of injustice if they were socially imposed psychological injustices. But mental disorders are not generally just the result of social rules and decisions about the distribution of meanings. There is no evidence for anything like such a thoroughly social account of mental disorder; indeed, there is much evidence against it. Like physical illness, mental disorder transcends the system of social distribution on which the principles of distributive justice are based. And even in those cases where mental disorders do lead to deprivation, it is not the mental disorder itself but its effects on acquisition of other goods that are a matter of injustice. It is clearly the case that deprivation sometimes is a factor in causing mental disorder, but by no means is this a regular feature. For all these reasons, mental disorders do not in themselves generally constitute minimal distributive injustice.

Conclusion

Many social workers insist that mental health must be included within the essential mission of the social work profession by definition, much as thinkers

308 • *Psychotherapy and Social Work*

of an earlier generation, reacting against what they saw as social workers' excessive zeal for psychoanalysis, attempted to exclude therapeutic intervention from the profession by definition. The strategy by which treatment of mental disorder is encompassed within the essential mission of social work generally is to inflate the essential mission until it is large enough to encompass mental health as well as justice. The typical result is a portrayal of the profession as having such a vast and nebulous domain that the profession loses its authority as a repository of specialized skills and knowledge aimed at performing a specific, mandated social function.

By contrast, the "minimal distributive justice" account, which conceives of social work as a "safety net" profession concerned with ensuring that no one falls below some acceptable minimum in the possession of basic economic, social, and psychological goods necessary to pursue life plans and participate socially, offers a relatively delimited domain that corresponds to the realities of the profession's historical mandate. Psychotherapy can be seen to have a secure place in the techniques that are useful to such a profession because of the intimate relationship of psychological states to social functioning and, as illuminated by Rawls's theory, to distributive justice. The cost of this understanding of the profession is that we must confront the fact that treatment of mental disorder, while a legitimate function mandated by the public, is not part of the essential mission of social work and has a more indirect, derived conceptual status within the profession's set of responsibilities.

References

American Psychiatric Association (APA). 1994. *Diagnostic and Statistical Manual of Mental Disorders (DSM-IV)*. 4th ed. Washington, D.C.: APA.

Dean, H. E. 1998. The primacy of the ethical aim in clinical social work: Its relationship to social justice and mental health. *Smith College Studies in Social Work* 69:9–25.

Rawls, J. 1971. *A Theory of Justice*. Cambridge, Mass.: Harvard University Press.

Specht, H. 1990. Social work and the popular psychotherapies. *Social Service Review* 64:345–357.

Specht, H. and M. E. Courtney. 1994. *Unfaithful Angels: How Social Work Has Abandoned Its Mission*. New York: Free Press.

Wakefield, J. C. 1988a. Psychotherapy, distributive justice, and social work: I. Distributive justice as a conceptual framework for social work. *Social Service Review* 62:187–210.

———. 1988b. Psychotherapy, distributive justice, and social work: II. Psychotherapy and the pursuit of justice. *Social Service Review* 62:353–382.

————. 1992. Why psychotherapeutic social work don't get no re-Specht. *Social Service Review* 66:141–151.

————. 1993a. Is altruism part of human nature? Toward a theoretical foundation for the helping professions. *Social Service Review* 67:406–458.

————. 1993b. Limits of operationalization: A critique of Spitzer and Endicott's (1978) proposed operational criteria for mental disorder. *Journal of Abnormal Psychology* 102:160–172.

————. 1996. DSM-IV: Are we making diagnostic progress? *Contemporary Psychology* 41:646–652.

————. 1997. Diagnosing DSM-IV, Part 1: DSM-IV and the concept of mental disorder. *Behavior Research and Therapy* 35:633–650.

————. 1998. Psychotherapy, distributive justice, and social work revisited. *Smith College Studies in Social Work* 69:25–57.

Part III
Ethical Dilemmas of Being
a Double Agent

[10]

THE PROFESSIONAL AS A DOUBLE-AGENT

ISRAEL GOLDIAMOND

THE UNIVERSITY OF CHICAGO

The joke about the Martian who lands on Earth in a bed of mushrooms and says, "Take me to your leader", reflects a fact well-known to many Earthlings and, apparently, to Martians as well: in every social system there are those who wield disproportionate control over the resources of that system. By making the availability of these resources contingent on behaviors they require, under conditions and in manners they also specify, they exert considerable influence over behaviors and conditions in the system. In a complex society such as ours, much of the control is filtered through subsidiary systems in direct line from their source. A complex society such as ours also contains professional systems. These generally function in circumscribed areas necessary for the functioning of the larger social system. Accordingly, the larger system will allocate resources, and use its powers in other ways (for example, state grants of monopoly through licences) in support of these subsystems. It will thereby enmesh much of the subsystem in its contingencies. It will set requirements for the maintenance of social support. The subsystem will set related requirements for its professionals. To the extent that this is the case, professional behaviors may be said to be a function of a function, that is, to be ultimately explainable by resort to the larger social contingencies. At different times, the requirements noted may vary in the degree of their explicitness, in the time periods in which the requirements are to be met, in the immediacy of evaluation, and so on.

Social and professional relations have been systematically studied for some time in fields such as economics, planning, political science, social thought and sociology, among others, and by nonacademic commentators and activists. Ideologies and patterns of systematized social analysis (including those just noted) have themselves been subjected to social contingency analysis. For example, in the sociology of knowledge (cf. Wirth, 1936), such systematization has been analyzed as derivative to and interacting with the regnant economic, political, and social contingencies.

Consider the case of programmed instruction (p.i.), a major scientific and technological contribution by radical behaviorists. The publication of Skinner's article in *Science* (1958) brought teaching machines to the attention of a wide and important audience. The article was one of a cluster of major articles on teaching, and especially on teaching of science. That year, the National Defense Education Act (NDEA) was enacted. Was this act in response to the intellectual activities mentioned, and in response to concern over education? Or did the articles, the discussions, and the concern reflect societal contingencies that became salient at that time?

In 1957, space was penetrated dramatically— by the Russians. Sputnik I went up. It was followed by Sputnik II. Mastery of space and of the relevant technology by our system thereby became a major goal. American behaviors in this direction included the founding of the National Aeronautic Space Administration (NASA), the NDEA, concern with and support of scientific manpower and training, and of education in gen-

[1]Professor of Psychology in the Department of Psychiatry, the Department of Behavioral Sciences (Biopsychology), and in the College. Mailing address for reprints: Department of Psychiatry (Box 411), the University of Chicago, 950 East 59th Street, Chicago, Illinois 60637. This article was written under a grant from the State of Illinois, Department of Mental Health and Developmental Disabilities.

eral. The support of p.i. is clearly relatable to social contingencies.

Did these contingencies elicit or produce the behavioral technology of p.i. and the analytic system ("system of thought", "ideology") common to p.i. and radical behaviorism? Clearly not. Skinner and those around him had been engaged in p.i. for some time, and operant research and systematization even longer. The social system made available financial support and other resources for such research, and contingent upon it. It thereby increased the probability of this hitherto low-probability educational behavior. As noted elsewhere: "The statement, 'There is nothing as powerful as an idea whose time has come' translates into the power of an 'idea which rationalizes contingencies whose time has come' or increases their probability" (Goldiamond, 1974, pp. 11f).[2]

Social contingencies do not necessarily produce or elicit ideologies or specific components of social behavior. Rather, they may affect the probability of these available components, when they are emitted. They may thereby shape and alter them into completely novel patterns. The fact that a parallel can be drawn between, on the one hand, individual behavior components and their contingencies and, on the other hand, social behavior components and their social contingencies, suggests that analytic procedures of either area may be profitably extended to the analysis of the other (*cf.* Goldiamond, 1976*a*). "What is needed is a marriage of social analysis and behavior analysis" (Goldiamond, 1976*b*).

In this issue, Jim Holland (1978) applies one of the systematized methods of social analysis to the professional behaviors that behavior modifiers regard as helping, and to the professional role ideology that rationalizes their behaviors. Thereby, he consigns behavior modifiers to being part of the problem. He suggests that we apply our own area of expertise, behavior analysis, to problems on the social scene. He suggests that we shift the control of our behavior to other social contingencies. Thereby, behaviorism becomes part of his solution.

Currently, authors of an increasing number of books and studies have been applying social contingency analysis to health care.[3] In this context, they have been analyzing professional and patient roles and, indeed the very prevalence of the problems that the clients present, and which occasion professional treatment. In addition to setting up programs that produce beneficial change, "[s]ocial contingencies can also deteriorate the behaviors [of patients and of their physiological conditions so that] . . . deterioration is being programmed" (Goldiamond, 1976*b*, 129-130). In such cases, the long-term answer to the alleviation and attenuation of individual suffering obviously lies in attention to the regnant social contingencies. Indeed, even the *short-term* answer may then lie in attention to social contingencies, since attention to individual contingencies (those immediately governing individual behavior), no matter how skilled, may be ineffective. Individuals whose behavior does not yield to professional attention (because it is governed by other social contingencies, *e.g.,* an impending disability claim whose magnitude is contingent on magnitude of disability) may then be "described as 'unmotivated' or 'impossible to reach' or, in less charitable moments, 'goof-offs' " (p. 104), hostile, or resistant. The professionals involved may then lament the state of their art, or may instead "blame the victim" (Holland, 1978), rather than blame their own insensitivity to regnant societal variables. And the professionals and arts so involved are not confined to behavior modification, of course. It has been my experience that compared to other professionals dealing with similar problems, applied behavior

---

[2]The government of Argentina, concerned that population increase of its neighbors, accompanied by its own low birthrate, will become, in time, a temptation for invasion of Argentina, is conducting a campaign to get women into their homes. This includes support of appropriate social actions and of an ideology stressing sex differences.

---

[3]The social contingencies governing such increased intellectual effort are the same ones governing impending federal support of health insurance or its facsimiles.

analysts have been among the *more sensitive* to regnant societal variables. And there is very little blaming of the victims, or assignment of characterological deficit or flaw in the literature of behavior modification. On the contrary, the laboratory dictum that "the pigeon is always right" had tended to what is often a naively-accepted corollary that "the system is always wrong" in its training procedures, aims, *etc*. It would appear from Jim Holland's article that behavior analysts consider the pigeon wrong, and the system right. Other issues are raised.

1. With regard to alcoholism, he chastises behavior analysts by means of lengthy quotations and references to an investigator who is *not a behaviorist*. As is evident from designations in the published report (Mello and Mendelson, 1971, ix, 730), Gallant is a psychiatrist at Tulane. His interests have included placebo response by schizophrenics, dexedrine and sulphates with hyperactive children, alcoholic treatment services, among others. The views Jim Holland cites are not those of a behaviorist psychiatrist, but of one of a different persuasion. It is instructive to note how the presentation turns these views into an example of behaviorist formulations. 1. Gallant used antabuse, among other procedures, with alcoholics. 2. "Antabuse is a drug that induces severe nausea when alcohol is ingested. Hence, it is a form of aversion therapy" (p. 165). 3. Gallant is thereby a behaviorist: "*Other* behavior analysts" (p. 166, emphasis mine—I.G.) are then cited. Behaviorism is held accountable for his views. There is an interesting syllogistic fallacy here. 1. A psychoanalyst hands out M&M's to a child (or otherwise approves). 2. M&M's (or approval) have been used as reinforcers; this is a reinforcement procedure used by behavior analysts. 3. Therefore, behaviorists believe in Id, Ego, and Superego. Or, Texas ranchers use barbed wire; barbed wire hurts cattle that rub against it, they shun it, hence it is a form of aversion therapy; therefore behaviorists use alfalfa, vote for Reagan . . .[4]

Possibly, to return to alcoholics, skidrow alcoholics drink themselves blotto to escape a miserable world they never made, and which a commercial culture did. However, alcoholism is a problem in the Soviet Union, and excessive use of hashish is a problem in certain feudal Muslim states, where alcohol is taboo. Contingencies of *positive* reinforcement often operate. Keehn, whose applied operant research is as insightful as his experimental and theoretical work, *observed* skidrow alcoholics. He noted that they had been cast out by their families and other social referent groups. Social acceptance seemed available only on skidrow, and the *required operant* for membership was drinking and getting blotto. The system that Keehn helped set up provided such a social referent group. Membership in it was contingent on other behaviors (Keehn, *et al.*, 1973; Collier and Somfay, 1974).

2. With regard to criminals, it was Anatole France who noted over 70 years ago (1903) that the law "in its majestic equality forbids the rich as well as the poor to sleep on the bridges, to beg on the streets, and to steal bread."[5] And we have also known for some time that the alternatives available to people, what alternatives are called criminal, what criminal acts are pursued, which violator gets incarcerated, and what sentences are meted out, are relatable to social class and influence. For those of us who have not kept up with such issues, Jim Holland's sketch brings us up to date. The problem has been with us for some time. It antedates behaviorism.

---

[4]Space considerations preclude discussion of other issues raised regarding use and nonuse of aversive procedures (page 165), but see another explanation for differential use offered in Rachman and Teasdale (1969, p. 172), namely, between "surplus disorders, and . . . deficit disorders". Yet other systematizations are possible which seek constructional alternatives to aversive and other eliminative procedures (Goldiamond, 1974), since behavior patterns of either type are then not systemized as pathologies or disorders. Even so, Rachman and Teasdale's conclusion is instructive: "Aversion therapy should only be offered if other treatment methods are inapplicable or unsuccessful *and* if the patient gives his permission after a consideration of all the information which his therapist can honestly supply" (p. 174, italics in original).

[5]Anatole France, *Le lys rouge*, 1903, Ch. VII, statement by M. Choulette.

It has been fashionable to apply behaviorist terminology to legitimize classical penal procedures. There is nothing new about "behavior treatment units" other than the name. Enforced isolation has been so designated. At one time it was called "solitary confinement", and at others "the hole". It may now be called "behavior control" or "timeout". And token economies in prisons are often as relevant to applied behavior analysis as dream analyses at cocktail parties are to psychoanalysis. A graded tier system at Patuxent was, *subsequent* to the establishment and implementation of the system, rationalized as behavioral, and attacked as such (Holland, 1975, p. 86). The gross violations, which occasioned court action, were also rationalized in terms of mental illness, and the director (not a behaviorist), in one interview, reported that *love* was the critical issue. If those engaged in "tinkering with . . . fictional mental causes" of crime are to "stop" (Holland, 1978, p. 00), I venture that few behaviorists will be found in the halted legion. But Jim Holland's article specifically enjoins "the behaviorist" from mental fictionalizing!

One more point will be made. Charles Manson spent over half his life behind institutional walls. He charged, and rightly, that his antisocial behaviors were the product of such socialization. He is a "victim" of the system and a casualty of it. It might therefore be said that punishing him constitutes punishing the victim. However, the reader need not be reminded of *his* victims, Sharon Tate, and the others. The issue is not punishment nor blaming of Manson, nor his "correction" nor "rehabilitation". Rather, it is that others in society are better served by his removal from their social scene.[6] Perhaps Manson is one of the prisoners whom Holland cites as being looked down on by the rest. But what is

one to say regarding the assailants of the graduate student who was held up *for economic reasons* (money), and the teenager who was mugged? The assailant of the latter is in prison, is being "rehabilitated", and "will probably get time off for good behavior". The one beaten (I hesitate to use the term "victim") "too, wants to rehabilitate himself."[7] He is in a rehabilitation hospital, and the brain-damage produced by the beating may confine him to a wheelchair for the rest of his life. No parole for him. The graduate student is a quadraplegic. No release from confinement here. If violent crimes and white-collar crimes are class-related, and greater social concern about the former places an inequity in sentencing upon the poor, I submit that outcomes of the kind noted contribute to the social concern. And the fact that "we have all been victimized by small consumer frauds that leave us defenseless, because the cost of recovering the loss is larger than the loss itself" should not be surprising. It finds legal expression in *de minimus non curat lex*—the law is not concerned with trivialities. Ethics, in contrast, may be. An ethicist might regard cheating a child of a nickel as being as unethical as a million-dollar swindle, but the law will attend to the latter and ignore the former on *de minimus* grounds. If the consumer frauds are widespread so the sum of small recoveries by legal action exceeds response cost of recovery, victimization of the consumer may be halted—*de minimus* no longer applies.

3. We come to the third victim, behavior analysts themselves. Jim Holland's analysis, like others within its frame of reference, raises questions with regard to *all* professionals, not just behavior analysts. Consider the civil engineer who designs a highway from town to seashore. He may thereby make surf and sunshine available to urban dwellers, an outcome of service to them. However, the same highway may improve access to a plant that makes weapons of destruction. Even if it does not do so, maintaining the health

---

[6]Judged by the deathly silence of downtown areas in many cities and by the security measures in dwellings, the others in society are removing *themselves* from the social scene and are incarcerating *themselves* behind locked doors. For another reason for social concern over violent crime, see text.

[7]Quoted from *Chicago Tribune*, "Victims of crime ask: 'What about our rights?'," February 1, 1977, Page 1, Section 1, at 2-6; Page 16, Section 1, at 1-6.

of urban dwellers and thereby of a steady source of skilled labor may also be an outcome of service to the social system. Or consider the orthopedic surgeon who sets a fractured leg. The medical outcome is of service both to patient and social system, and both may contribute payment. And the behavior analyst who develops an effective reading program may be of service to the child. But he is also regarded in some quarters as a fink who thereby makes children's minds more receptive to the brain-washing techniques of an exploitative society.

In essence, professionals are double agents.[8] One client is the patient or student (p-s). The other client is the social system. To the extent that professionals fulfill p-s obligations, they can and do take personal and professional pride in so doing. In such cases, the *occasion* for p-s *application* is a situation whose *reversal* (or tranformation) is the professionally-produced outcome, *e.g.,* illness to health, ignorance to knowledge. Professional *behavior* (treatment, training of p-s) is also reinforced by *reversal* of the presenting *occasion*. And system *behavior* (support of professional roles and opportunities, support of p-s roles and opportunities) is also reinforced by the same *reversal* (or a probability of such reversal) of the presenting *occasion*. In all three contingencies depicted (governing p-s, professional, and system behavior), the occasion-outcomes that govern the behaviors are congruent (see Goldiamond, 1976a, for more extensive analysis). The professional is thereby the agent of both p-s and social system. The law, as it does elsewhere, tries to be most explicit about double-agency. The defense lawyer is not only an agent of the defendant, he is also simultaneously *an officer of the court*. Where there is congruence in occasion-outcomes for all three behaviors (p-s,

professional, system), the fact that the professional is a double-agent should not be cause for concern, on its own. And, I submit, *a large proportion of behavioral studies belong in this category.*

It is where such congruence does not exist that related problems arise. For instance, the p-s agenda may be congruent with the social agenda, but the professional behaviors are inadequate to the task. Children may want to read, society may want them to, but the professional programs are not doing the job. Generally, behavior modifiers see themselves as *correcting this lack of congruence.* On the other hand, the p-s agenda may not be congruent with the social agenda. The regnant outcomes differ. In such cases, professionals should know where they stand. It is this issue to which, I believe, *much of Jim Holland's analysis is directed.* Depending on their orientation, professionals may or may not agree with the resolutions Jim Holland suggests. And there are consequences, and probabilities of consequences, both long and short term, involved. Jim Holland's analysis is useful in bringing this possibility to the attention of those practitioners who have not been attentive to it. It is unfortunate that it is presented in a context which at times deprecates behavioral contributions when the occasions-outcomes are congruent, or noncongruent in certain ways. It would seem that before one accuses a field of being part of the problem, one might collect evidence to indicate how prevalent and how serious this is (Goldiamond, 1975).

Regardless of whether we consider the three sets of occasions-outcomes to be congruent, their existence should enter into any analysis. Professionals are double-agents. The fact that they can blithely continue in their activities when the occasions-outcomes are congruent, and there seems to be no problem, should not blind them to the fact that there are always at least three different contingencies involved. Occasionally, contingencies may involve noncongruent occasions-outcomes. An analysis is then not only helpful, but necessary.

---

[8]Since the acceptance of this article for publication, an article with a similar title has appeared, namely, "The therapist as double agent" (Powledge, 1977). Its thrust is given by the caption below the title: "should patients be warned that anything they reveal in therapy may be disclosed to a third party?" Who was it who wrote of the "power of an 'idea which rationalizes contingencies whose time has come' "?

4. As somewhat of an anticlimax, I turn to the question of whether behaviorism is part of the solution. As just indicated, it can be quite helpful. But it should be noted that it is helpful when it makes contact with our repertoires. Certainly, we have professional-qua-professional repertoires. A problem arises when behaviorism does not make contact with our repertoires, or makes superficial contact.

Consider the experimental analysis of behavior. Its originating domain was the learning-conditioning laboratory of experimental psychology. And that field was then rife with learning theories, *i.e.,* systematizations. Some of the terms were derived from physiology (inhibition, latency), others from physics (oscillation), others elsewhere. Among Skinner's major contributions were the clear statements that the systematizations had outrun the data, and that the data should be subjected to fine-grain analysis; relevant categories might then be assayed and a different kind of theory might emerge (1950, 1969). Therefore, such theory must rest on immersion in the data of the area about which one theorizes. There are, of course, other contributions.

The success of this enterprise has now reached the point where the system developed is being extended to other areas. Where the analysts have not been immersed in a fine-grain analysis of the other area, the following question is raised: how different are the analysts' extensions of their theory to the new area different from the earlier extensions and theories of the learning theorists? Are the analysts, spurred by their successes, ignoring the lessons that helped them become successful?

Anyone familiar with my writings will know that I am not saying that behaviorism is meaningless in areas other than its origin. What I am questioning is its effectiveness and the effects upon it of its summary extension to areas whose fine-grain analysis is not in the repertoires of the extenders. I believe one of our tasks is to try to develop procedures for such fine-grained analysis. When we do so, we shall discover that there

are many sensible investigators in those areas who have something to say. They have been immersed in their fields for some time. They are often in contact with exceedingly fine-grained data. They will welcome our contributions—when we have something to contribute. But we can best contribute when we bring our own skills to the area. Like all behavior analytic formulations, being part of the solution is possible only under certain conditions.

Jim Holland cites the Twin Oaks community. As it so happens, I have been a steady subscriber to the *Leaves of Twin Oaks,* their quarterly publication.[9] It is a disarmingly honest document. One of the incidents that they report is the failure of a particular crop. They were applying their own system. A neighboring farmer then told them what they should be doing and what other farmers did who had been there for some time. They then decided that there was a lesson here: it made sense to take into account the experience of others who had been in the field for some time.

REFERENCE NOTE

[1]Powledge, F. The therapist as double agent. *Psychology Today,* July 1977, pp. 44-47.

REFERENCES

Collier, D. F. and Somfay, S. A. *Ascent from Skid Row: the Bon Accord Community 1967-1973.* Toronto: Addictive Research Foundation, 1974.

Goldiamond, I. Toward a constructional approach to social problems: Ethical and Constitutional issues raised by applied behavior analysis. *Behaviorism,* 1974, **2,** 1-84.

Goldiamond, I. Singling out behavior modification for legal regulation: Some effects on patient care, psychotherapy, and research in general. *Arizona Law Review,* 1975, **17,** 105-126.

Goldiamond, I. Protection of human subjects and patients: A social contingency analysis of distinctions between research and practice and its implications. *Behaviorism,* 1976, **4,** 1-41. (*a*)

[9]*Leaves of Twin Oaks,* Twin Oaks Community, Merion Branch, Route 4, Box 17, Louisa, Virginia 23093. Subscription, $3.00 a year.

Goldiamond, I. Coping and adaptive behaviors of the disabled. In Gary E. Albrecht (Ed), *The sociology of physical disability and rehabilitation.* Pittsburgh: University of Pittsburgh, 1976. Pp. 97-138. (*b*)

Holland, J. Behavior modification for prisoners, patients, and other people as a prescription for the planned society. *Mexican Journal of Behavior Analysis,* 1975, 1, 81-95.

Holland, J. Behaviorism: part of the problem or part of the solution? *Journal of Applied Behavior Analysis,* 1978, 11, 163-174.

Keehn, J. D., Kuechler, H. A., Oki, G., Collier, D., and Walsh, R. Interpersonal behaviorism and community treatment of alcoholics. In M. Chafetz (Ed), *Research on alcoholism: I. Clinical problems and special populations.* Washington: U.S. Public Health Service, 1973. Pp. 153-176.

Mello, N. K. and Mendelson, J. H. (Eds), *Recent advances in studies of alcoholism: An interdisciplinary symposium.* Rockville, Maryland: National Institute on Alcohol Abuse and Alcoholism, 1971.

Rachman, S. and Teasdale, J. *Aversion therapy and behavior disorders: an analysis.* Coral Gables, Florida: University of Miami, 1969.

Skinner, B. F. Are theories of learning necessary? *Psychological Review,* 1950, 57, 193-216.

Skinner, B. F. Teaching machines. *Science,* 1958, 128, 969-977.

Skinner, B. F. *Contingencies of reinforcement: A theoretical analysis.* New York: Appleton-Century-Crofts, 1969.

Wirth, L. Preface. In Karl Mannheim, *Ideology and Utopia* (L. Wirth and E. Shils, Eds and Trans). New York: Harcourt, Brace, 1936, xiii-xxxi.

[11]

Organizational Forms as Moral Practices: The Case of Welfare Departments

Yeheskel Hasenfeld
University of California, Los Angeles

Human service organizations that aim to change behavior inevitably do moral work. As institutionalized organizations, they enact in their structure and practices dominant moral systems. Moral systems and rules within them emanate from several sources, including nationally powerful interest groups and organizations, local constituencies, and organizational and street-level moral entrepreneurs. By studying the historical transformation of welfare departments, I show how changes in the moral assumptions about poor single mothers have transformed the organizational forms and practices of these offices. In doing so, these forms and practices enact and enforce these moral rules on the clients.

Human Service Organizations and Moral Work

I have proposed elsewhere (Hasenfeld 1992) that human service organizations, especially those that aim to change human behavior, engage in moral work. That is, every action taken on behalf of clients not only represents some form of concrete service, such as counseling a family or determining eligibility for welfare, but also confers a moral judgment about their social worth, the causation of their predicament, and the desired outcome. This is because work on people who are themselves imbued with values cannot be value neutral. Andrew Abbott (1988) points out that the typifications of clients via diagnoses, treatments, and inferences of causality are socially constructed categories reflecting the jurisdictional claims of the particular helping profession. Yet, these categories are inherently moral because, as technically neutral as they may seem, they publicly confer a moral status to clients, they provide moral justifications for the actions caregivers take, and clients internalize them as a reflection of their own self-identity and valuation. Moreover, as I will suggest later, these typification schemes reflect and represent broader moral conceptions sanctioned by the state, by the professions, and by other authoritative bodies that give rise to these organizations and legitimate their practices. For example, the decision of whether a single poor mother qualifies for public assistance is not merely a technical question of assessing her needs in relation to the resources available to her. It is also a moral assessment of her "deservingness," including a judgment about her commitment to the work ethic and to family values (Handler and Hasenfeld 1991).

There is another sense in which working on people is inherently moral. Fundamental to such work are decisions about the allocation of resources to the clients. These may include money, time, and expertise. Inevitably, the demand for these resources outstrips their supply, resulting in a system of rationing (e.g., first come first served, clients with greatest perceived need, younger over older patients). Rationing resources to clients involves a moral categorization of deservingness. Whatever may be the rationale and merit of the allocation rule, fundamentally it conveys an evaluation of social worth, since some clients become more deserving than others (Roth 1972; Prottas 1979; Lipsky 1980). As a result, evaluations of social worth locate and reaffirm the place of clients in a moral stratification system that determines their rights and claims to scarce resources. As I show later, these systems of moral evaluations determine and rationalize the activities of the workers.

The New Institutional Perspective

Organizations that engage in moral work are institutionalized organizations par excellence. They obtain their legitimacy by affirming and reinforcing institutionalized moral systems in their environment. Following W. R. Scott (1995), these systems consist of normative, regulative, and cognitive components. They uphold dominant values about desired behavior; they enforce these values through laws, rules, and regulations; and they provide typification schemes to categorize and classify people. For example, moral assumptions about welfare recipients are echoed in welfare laws and regulations, such as the Temporary Aid for Needy Families, and a complex classification system has been developed to differentiate between recipients who are required to participate in work activities and recipients who are exempt (Handler and Hasenfeld 1997). These institutionalized moral systems, in turn, become embedded in organizational forms, often expressed in myths and ceremonies (Meyer and Rowan 1977). Institutionalized organizations are valued less for their technical efficiency or their specific products than for the moral symbols that they uphold. Put differently, the survival of these organizations depends on the extent to which they become isomorphic with these moral systems.

By shifting the emphasis from technical rationality to institutionalized rules as the engine that drives organizational forms, the new institutional perspective has provided a powerful framework for understanding human services organizations. It has sensitized us to the importance of organizational structure as a manifestation of institutional rules rather than technology. C. R. Hinings and C. Greenwood (1988, p. 8) express the relationship between institutional values and structure in the concept of "archetype," which they define as "a particular composition of ideas, beliefs and values connected to structures and systems." Moreover, the emphasis on conformity with the institutional environment points to processes of structural isomorphism; organizations in the same sector acquire similar structures that the institutional environment imposes on them through coercive, mimetic, and normative processes (DiMaggio and Powell 1983).

While we recognize that human service organizations are embedded in institutionalized moral systems, it is important to emphasize that these systems may lack consensus or internal consistency (D'Aunno, Sutton, and Price 1991). Moreover, as I will point out, moral work is highly contextualized, reflecting the particular cultural, political, and economic exigencies of the local community in which such work takes place. As a result, these organizations have to make choices among contending moral systems or conflicting rules within them that, in turn, will be reflected in the elements that constitute their organizational forms. The moral choices are not only reflected in the structure but also in the service technologies themselves. S. R. Barley and P. S. Tolbert (1997) use the concept of "scripts" to denote the mechanism by which institutional rules are enacted in the technology. They define scripts as "observable, recurrent activities and patterns of interactions characteristic of a particular setting" and propose that institutions are enacted through them (Barley and Tolbert 1997, p. 5). In his study of two hospital radiology departments, Barley (1986) showed how the scripts that CT scanner technicians used embodied the institution of medical dominance. Finally, the new institutional perspective has also shown how both the organization and its workers can be active agents in deciding which moral rules to enact or ignore. C. Oliver (1991), for example, proposes that organizations can engage in a variety of tactics in response to institutional pressures, ranging from avoidance to manipulation, especially when there is a lack of institutional consensus. Thus, the organizations themselves can undertake moral entrepreneurship—mobilizing constituencies and developing network relations that reinforce and institutionalize their own moral beliefs (Zucker 1988). This is exemplified by the feminist health centers C. Hyde has studied (1992). Moreover, workers in organizations doing moral work are active interpreters and promoters of moral rules, not the least of which are their own. For example, welfare workers often evoke their personal moral standards in deciding to sanction recipients for noncompliance (Hasenfeld and Weaver 1996).

Moral Work and Organizational Forms

As indicated earlier, work on people involves a series of moral assumptions about them. These include moral assumptions concerning (*a*) the social worth of the person, (*b*) attribution of responsibility, (*c*) amenability to change, (*d*) desired end results, and (*e*) the view of the person as an object or a subject. These assumptions are clearly not mutually exclusive and affect each other.

When a client is accorded high social worth, the staff are motivated to mobilize all the necessary organizational resources to affirm such a status. In contrast, when a client is viewed as morally deficient she becomes "undeserving" and is subject to a moral test before gaining access to organizational resources. Mothers who become single parents because of the death of a working spouse are morally deserving of universal benefits (i.e., Survivor's Benefits). Mothers who become single parents because their spouse deserted them are morally undeserving and can only apply for means-tested public assistance (Fraser 1989). Attribution of responsibility signifies whether the clients themselves are morally responsible for their predicament or whether they are victims of circumstances beyond their control. This assumption, in turn, affects the degree to which the organization puts the onus on the clients to justify their claim for services. In the first instance, clients must often undergo "repentance" or publicly profess their moral deficiencies to qualify for services. For example, applicants for general assistance are assumed to be responsible for their predicaments because of lack of a work ethic and must undergo a work test (i.e., participate in work activities) to obtain relief. In contrast, persons eligible for unemployment compensation are assumed to be victims of economic circumstances. Assumptions about amenability to change influence the degree to which the organization commits itself to bringing about change in the client's circumstances. Students tracked into vocational versus academic tracks are assumed to lack the capacity to excel intellectually, and the school is less likely to invest in them because they are socially devalued (Oakes 1995). Similarly, assumptions about the desired end results influence the service goals and objectives of the organization. Schools that truly believe that developmentally disabled children can be educated to function in the "normal society" commit themselves to finding effective educational technologies that can integrate the children into regular classrooms (Handler 1986). Other schools that only give lip services to the idea of mainstreaming are more likely to find reasons to segregate these children (Weatherley and Lipsky 1977). Finally, whether the organization treats its clients as objects or subjects determines the extent to which clients will have a voice in what is done to them. Organizations that treat their clients as subjects encourage them to become active participants and to have a voice in the decisions about their course of service. In contrast, when clients are treated as objects, they are worked *on* rather than worked *with*.

Following the new institutional perspective, I propose that these moral assumptions find expression in organizational forms and practices. By organizational forms and practices I mean especially (*a*) the organizational output goals, (*b*) the interorganizational network or task environment, (*c*) the service technology, (*d*) the organization of work, and (*e*) client-worker relations (see also Hannan and Freeman 1989). Specifically, the output goals will reflect the assumptions the organization makes about the social worth of the clients and the desired end results. The interorganizational network will manifest the commitment of the organization to mobilize the necessary resources to achieve the desired end results and to legitimate its moral assumptions. The service technology is also influenced by assumptions about the clients' social worth, attribution of responsibility, and amenability to change. The organization of work reflects the value placed on the needs of the client in contrast to the needs of the workers. Client-worker relations reflect, in addition, assumptions about the clients as objects or as subjects.

Organizations that ascribe high social worth to their clients—seeing them as victims of circumstances beyond their control and viewing them as amenable to change and entitled to an active voice in the decisions about their service trajectories—are more likely to be structured as "client-centered" organizations. By this I mean that organizational ideologies will place a high degree of commitment on the clients; the interorganizational network will focus on mobilizing needed resources and services for them; the service technology will be highly individualized and tailored to the specific attributes and needs of the clients; the formal structure will be debureaucratized; and staff-client relations will be extensive and characterized by a high degree of mutual trust. Examples of such organizations are the feminist health centers Hyde (1992) studied, especially during their formative years, or the response of the Madison (Wis.) School District to the needs of developmentally disabled children (Handler 1986). In contrast, organizations that ascribe to their clients low social worth—attributing responsibility to innate deficiencies in the clients themselves, not seeing them as amenable to change, and treating them as objects—are more likely to develop organizational forms that will demean them. In such organizations ideologies toward the clients tend to be punitive, interorganizational relations are formed mostly with other social control agencies to affirm the moral inferiority of the clients, the service technology is highly routinized and bureaucratized, and client-staff relations are limited and based on suspicion and mistrust.

Contemporary welfare departments exemplify such forms (Prottas 1979; Bane and Ellwood 1994).

Organizations that encounter multiple and conflicting moral systems are likely to give them expression within the organization through service units that are decoupled from each other. It is not uncommon for such organizations to have, for example, multiple service technologies that are guided by different if not conflicting moral assumptions (Strauss et al. 1985). Examples of such organizations are mental health agencies that have added drug abuse treatment units, or what T. D'Aunno and R. H. Price call "hybrid organizations" (1985). By decoupling the different service units and their respective technologies from each other, conflict is avoided and legitimacy is maintained.

Organizations cannot always institutionalize all of their moral assumptions, that is, give them an expression in their organizational forms. The institutionalization process requires adequate resources, knowledge and expertise, and cooperative external network relations. Yet, the organization may experience obstacles in attaining them. This is particularly the case when interest groups controlling key resources that the organization needs do not accept its moral assumptions. As I show later, the failure of welfare departments to implement a "rehabilitation" ideology was due, in part, to a lack of adequate external and internal resources. Moreover, organizations may change their moral assumptions in order to rationalize organizational forms that arise from the need to adapt to changing environmental exigencies. In other words, when the needs of the organization to survive and adapt no longer support its original moral assumptions, these assumptions, in turn, are likely to be changed to fit the new reality (Scott 1969). Thus, the moral assumptions both constitute and are constituted by organizational forms and practices.

The Origins and Transformation of Institutional Moral Rules

There are at least four sources for institutional moral rules ranging from macro- to micro-origins. At the first source, the broader macrolevel, such rules emanate from politically powerful interest groups that advance and enforce such rules through social policies sanctioned by the state. They pursue the institutionalization of their moral agendas to legitimate their ideological, political, and economic positions. In the case of welfare policies, these groups may include political and religious elites who want to push their moral agendas about the work ethic, gender, family values, and ethnicity. They also include business organizations and labor unions concerned with the regulation of labor and state agencies that want to strengthen their organizational domain (see, e.g., Weir, Orloff, and Skocpol 1988; Handler and Hasenfeld 1991). The resulting social policies contain explicit or implicit moral assumptions that welfare departments are expected to pursue. A good example is the recently enacted Personal Responsibility and Work Opportunity Reconciliation Act of 1996 (PRWORA). It contains such explicit moral rules as "Marriage is the foundation of a successful society. Marriage is an essential institution of a successful society that promotes the interests of children. Promotion of responsible fatherhood and motherhood is integral to successful child rearing and the well-being of children" (U.S. Public Law 104-193). These rules change in response to transformations in national political, economic, and cultural conditions. As we will see, the rapid entry of women into the labor force changed the moral conception of a "good" mother from the mother who stays home to care for her children to the mother who is gainfully employed.

Yet, these broad moral edicts get their own particular spin in the local community, the second source for institutional moral rules. When moral work is conflictual and ambiguous, especially regarding the control and management of deviance, upper-level politicians delegate considerable discretion to the local level. In doing so, they buffer themselves from the controversies that surround the symbols they espouse, and they need not be concerned with the difficult issues of implementing the programs that must do the moral work. Local officials, in turn, design the programs in response to the local political economies and the moral assumptions that justify them. Welfare programs are a prime example. Each local welfare office is distinctive and reflective of the dominant moral assumptions in the local community in which it is embedded. Indeed, when local conditions change so do the moral assumptions guiding the program. When Massachusetts experienced an economic boom and a consequent decline in its welfare rolls, it instituted a welfare-to-work program, the Employment and Training Choices Program, that viewed welfare recipients in favorable moral terms. The program was in effect voluntary, it provided welfare recipients with many services as incentives to participate, and it aggressively developed job opportunities for the recipients. However, with a declining economy, rising welfare rolls, and a shift to a politically conservative government, welfare recipients were redefined as the "enemy." The program was transformed to become mandatory and punitive, setting strict time limits on receipt of aid and putting the onus on the recipients to find jobs (Handler and Hasenfeld 1997).

The organization itself is a third source of moral rules through its own entrepreneurship. The feminist health centers Hyde (1992) studied pursued and instituted new moral rules in their services and internal structure based on a feminist ideology. The ideology was expressed in service goals that aimed to give women control over their own health through self-help and participation in social action, and in an internal structure that was based on collective governance. The Madison School District, in contrast to other schools, assumed that disabled children were morally worthy, amenable to change, and could be effectively mainstreamed. It developed an organizational ideology that saw parents as part of the solution and sought actively to involve them in curricular decisions about their children. It gave parents knowledge, promoted their active participation, and assigned them advocates who negotiated on their behalf with school officials (Handler 1986).

When organizations can form coalitions and join other interest groups that share their moral rules, they may be able to influence social legislation in order to institutionalize these rules. When they are successful, their organizational forms and practices also gain prominence through normative and mimetic processes. For example, the National Alliance for the Mentally Ill, through an effective coalition of parent groups, has been very successful in changing dominant conceptions about schizophrenia, resulting in significant changes in treatment practices (Hatfield 1991).

Organizations also change their own moral rules when they need to rationalize their adaptive strategies in the face of a changing environment. R. Scott's (1969) classic study of agencies for the blind shows how sheltered workshops changed their moral assumptions from the position that the blind ought to be integrated into the regular labor market to a position that they ought to be protected from such a market. The change was a result of pressures on the workshops to maintain their fiscal viability and, thus, to keep the more productive and able blind persons. In other words, moral assumptions not only underlie new organizational forms and practices but are also used to justify forms and practices that arise out of the need to adapt to external political and economic forces.

Organizational forms and practices produce moral consequences by the way in which clients are treated and services are delivered. Although these forms might be justified based on technical rationality or efficiency, they implicitly generate and reinforce moral conceptions about their clients. These conceptions may, of course, be incompatible with publicly espoused belief systems. Yet, these implicit conceptions have greater currency in guiding the behavior of the staff and are, therefore, institutionalized in the organizational form and organizational practice. Being mutually reinforcing, forms and assumptions reproduce themselves over time.

Finally, at the microlevel, workers are a fourth source of moral rules. Workers engage in moral entrepreneurship through their own actions. Inevitably, in organizations that do moral work, staff members exercise considerable discretion. The organization is dependent on them to interpret the rules and apply them to specific cases. No matter how many rules the organization promulgates, it is left to the line staff to gather and interpret the information about their clients (Lipsky 1980). They can always manipulate the information and find rules or organizationally sanctioned rationales to justify their actions. Clients, especially when they lack power, become dependent on the workers to construct their cases in moral terms, and they have little recourse to redress such constructions (Handler 1986). Therefore, the personal belief systems of the workers play a significant role in operationalizing the service technologies and, particularly, in shaping client-staff relations (Hasenfeld and Weaver 1996). Moreover, workers develop practices that enable them to cope with and manage the particular exigencies they encounter, such as the amount of time and resources available to them and the size of their caseloads. They typify their clients and make service decisions that take into account these factors. Furthermore, they rationalize their actions by morally constructing their clients. That is, they engage in moral entrepreneurship. These personal belief systems and moral rationalizations are shared among groups of staff members because they have similar backgrounds, training, and experiences; they face the same work exigencies; and they communicate with each other about their work situation. It is through this process of sharing that personal moral entrepreneurship becomes institutionalized in organizational practices. In effect, they represent social policies enacted from below (Lipsky 1984; Sandfort 1999).

The "Iron Cage" Revisited?

Within the new institutional perspective, P. D. DiMaggio and W. W. Powell (1983, p. 728) propose, "once disparate organizations in the same line of business are structured into an actual field . . . powerful forces emerge that lead them to become more similar to one another." DiMaggio and Powell go on to identify three such forces—coercive forces stemming from political influence, mimetic forces resulting from standard responses to uncertainty, and normative forces arising from professionalization. My discussion of the sources of institutionalized moral rules suggests that in the case of organizations doing moral work, the level of institutional isomorphism may not be as pervasive as DiMaggio and Powell suggest. To be sure, welfare offices, mental health centers, and child protection programs, on the surface, look alike. They also seem to interact with similar organizational networks that further constrain their actions. Yet, when closer attention is paid to the organizational forms and practices they enact, especially regarding the delivery of services and their interaction patterns with clients, considerable diversity is found. One is likely to expect diversity rather than uniformity of organizational practices when one recognizes that organizations doing moral work must contend with abstract, conflictual, and ambiguous moral rules; that their work is highly contextualized at the local level; and that discretion prevails both at the organizational and the street levels. For example, all welfare departments must separate the deserving from the undeserving poor. However, beyond these abstract symbols, who is defined as deviant

338   Social Service Review

and what organizational forms are enacted to sort the poor into the appropriate categories vary considerably both across states and within states across counties. As I will show, this has always been the story of welfare, no matter what reform was legislated. To test the usefulness of the perspective developed here, I use it to analyze the organizational transformations of welfare departments, examining the extent to which these transformations were driven by changing moral assumptions about poor single mothers.

The Organization of Welfare Departments as Moral Practices

I focus on four historical transformations of welfare departments. I begin with the early years of the Aid to Families with Dependent Children (AFDC), the 1930s through the 1950s, when the "suitable home" policy dominated. I then look at the attempts to institute a "rehabilitation" model in the early 1960s. The 1970s brought about the "bureaucratization" of welfare, and finally the 1980s ushered in "welfare-to-work" programs (Banc and Ellwood 1994). I should preface this discussion by pointing out that, throughout this history, certain underlying moral assumptions have remained fairly constant no matter what particular twists they got in each era (Handler and Hasenfeld 1997). First, welfare mothers have always been viewed as "outsiders." Being poor is always considered an individual moral fault. Therefore, the question of deservingness pervades much of the administration of welfare. Second, the giving of public aid is always seen as a threat to the work ethic. Therefore, the conditions and amount of aid have always forced recipients to work. Third, welfare is always about upholding the dominant moral code regarding family relations, gender, and ethnicity. This is done through coercive intrusion into the lives of the recipients, whether through "home investigations" or restrictions in how the grant can be used. Fourth, the giving of aid always involves the stereotyping and moral degradation of the recipients. Today, the stereotype is young inner-city African Americans or illegal Latino immigrants. Fifth, because it is locally administered, welfare is always a reflection of the community's sentiments and values, as well as its political and economic conditions. Within this overarching moral system, each era offered its own distinct emphasis or interpretation resulting in appreciably different moral practices. Put differently, these underlying assumptions provide the grammar of welfare, while the enacted practices represent the speech of welfare, thus allowing for a variety of expressions (Barley and Tolbert 1997).

The "Suitable Home" Ideology (1935–50)[1]

The early years of the federal Aid to Dependent Children were heavily influenced by the Mothers' Pension philosophy and, specifically, by the ambiguous moral concept of a "suitable home." It was driven by the domestic code of the mother as a homemaker responsible for maintaining a good home life and providing for the proper moral, physical, and mental development of her children. Single mothers who did not conform to the moral code were viewed as having low social worth and as a danger to the community. Because of their moral flaw, they were not perceived as amenable to change. Thus, to qualify for aid the mother had to prove that she was morally "fit." Not surprisingly, in many states coverage was limited to what became known as the "gilt-edged widows." While Aid to Dependent Children legislation did not require that children live in "suitable homes," the concept nonetheless was widely practiced and endorsed by the professional community, including the American Public Welfare Association and officials of the Children's Bureau (Bell 1965, p. 29).

Local welfare departments were left to interpret the concept of the "suitable home" according to prevailing community standards. Thus, local offices and individual workers engaged in their own moral entrepreneurship in defining what was meant by suitable homes, particularly since the workers exercised enormous discretion. As W. Bell (1965, p. 41) put it, "Emphasis was placed according to the importance attached to certain subjective standards by the community, the agency and the individual worker." Typically, it meant that mothers with illegitimate children and women of color were excluded from aid. Southern states were particularly blatant in their moral degradation of African Americans. Louisiana was the first to adopt the "employable mother" rule "requiring all AFDC families with children seven years old or older to be refused assistance as long as the mother was presumed to be employable in the fields" (Piven and Cloward 1971, p. 134).

There were also considerable local variations in the organization of welfare offices and the aid eligibility practices that they instituted. Political appointees with strong local ties and values staffed local offices (quoted in Bell 1965, p. 37). Only in 1939 did federal legislation require that a merit system be used to select workers. Still, most workers were not trained professionals in social work doctrine and practice (Bell 1965, p. 134).

Over time, a service technology evolved that placed considerable emphasis on surveillance and the imposition of coercive standards of conduct. During the 1950s and early 1960s, with the increased migration of African Americans to the large urban centers and the advent of the civil rights movement, many local communities felt morally threatened by the rise of families of color (including those with illegitimate children) seeking aid and by the increasing costs of aid. Many communities reacted by instituting more punitive practices. In the infamous case of Newburgh, New York, which instituted highly restrictive welfare policies, one of the councilmen stated, "this is not a racial issue, but there's hardly an incentive to a naturally lazy people to work if they can exist without working"

(Bell 1965, p. 65). Workers made sure that the mothers did not maintain a liaison with any man ("man-in-the-house" rule) and made eligibility for aid contingent on establishing paternity. Midnight raids in search of the elusive man were not uncommon. Fear of fraud resulted in extensive use of "collateral contacts" with relatives, neighbors, friends, landlords, merchants, employers, schools, police departments, health agencies, public agencies administering unemployment compensation and old age and survivors' insurance, banks, and credit bureaus to uncover hidden family resources (Bell 1965, p. 87). Welfare offices developed specialized investigation and fraud detection units. Workers used their authority and considerable discretion to invade homes at will and to demand that their norms of conduct regarding child rearing and child care, money management, and work be followed. The relationship between the welfare workers and their clients was based on mistrust, suspicion, and the presumption of client immorality. Welfare applicants and recipients had few if any rights.

The "Rehabilitation" Approach (1956–67)

The "rediscovery" of poverty in America (i.e., Michael Harrington's 1962 book) and the ascendancy to power of liberal advocacy groups, including professional social workers, coupled with the continued rise in the welfare caseloads and costs prompted a reexamination of welfare strategies at the federal level. A moral shift took place that viewed welfare recipients less as outcasts and more as persons suffering from social and personal pathologies who needed rehabilitation. The desired outcome was independence and self-sufficiency, and it was assumed that most recipients were amenable to change through the provision of casework. These beliefs were expressed in the 1956 amendment to the Social Security Act that provided for a federal match of 50 percent of the administrative costs for social services and in the 1962 amendment that increased federal matching to 75 percent of the administrative costs (Derthick 1970, pp. 129–38).

However, the triumph of the social casework ideology proved elusive to institutionalize in organizational practices. First, the goal of rehabilitation had to compete with the goal of eligibility determination and redetermination. Second, both at the federal and state levels, insufficient resources were allocated for rehabilitation. In states such as Massachusetts, caseworkers were overwhelmed by large caseloads, and most had no professional social work training.[2] Moreover, there were no resources to forge effective interorganizational relations with other service organizations in order to provide needed services such as job training, day care, and rehabilitative services. Fourth, the service technology—social casework—was highly indeterminate. It was expressed in the professional rhetoric of "producing change in the lives of welfare recipients through the techniques of counseling, advice and guidance" (Handler and Hollingsworth 1971, p. 55). Or, as M. Derthick put it, "Casework, in short, is what the caseworker does" (1970, p. 136). The new mandate did not increase the actual services that welfare recipients obtained but greatly expanded the paperwork for the workers, who had to document how each contact with the client constituted a "unit of service" so that the department would qualify for the federal match.

Still, one should not lose sight of the fact that the changes in the moral assumptions had important effects on organizational practices. They transformed the welfare office to what may be best described as a "benign bureaucracy." J. F. Handler and E. J. Hollingsworth's (1971, p. 127) study of six welfare offices in Wisconsin showed that "for the vast majority of AFDC families, social service means a caseworker's visit a little more than once every three months for a little less than forty minutes per visit, with an occasional client's call to her caseworker." The visit itself could be best described as a "friendly chat." Clients reported that workers mostly discussed issues about children, health, and general plans for future education and employment. The caseworkers avoided topics that could generate complaints or requests or make it difficult to deliver services. The clients themselves reported a high degree of trust in their caseworkers and were quite satisfied with the advice and counsel they received. Handler and Hollingsworth (1971) argued that because the workers did so little, especially in providing concrete services, they did not bother their clients, and the clients approved of the arrangement. That is, the clients were not morally degraded, but, equally, no expectations for change were demanded of them. The desired outcome of independence and self-sufficiency was a myth.

Again, it is important to recognize that considerable local variations existed in organizational practices. Bell (1965, p. 161) reported that departments that had more restrictive eligibility requirements were less likely to provide social services (i.e., casework). Moreover, each state and county provided its own operative definition of what "social services" meant.

Over time, the recognition that eligibility determination and social casework expressed incompatible moral assumptions and service technologies resulted in the two functions being decoupled. Indeed, the social work profession strongly advocated for the separation because it did not want to be associated with the morally problematic function of aid determination. In her famous editorial in *Social Work*, Gordon Hamilton strongly advocated for the separation, writing that "the money function disables or overwhelms the social services" (1962, p. 128). According to M. J. Bane and D. T. Ellwood (1994, p. 15), "Social Workers argued that the dual role of counselor and investigator was impossible to achieve. Such perceptions of coercion, accurate or not, poisoned the 'therapeutic' value of the counselor/client relationship." The federal government

342   Social Service Review

urged the separation on welfare departments in 1967 and mandated it in 1972 (Simon 1983, p. 1215).

The Bureaucratization of Welfare (1972–88)

The continued explosion in the welfare rolls by 36 percent between 1962 and 1967 served as proof that the rehabilitation model was not working (Bane and Ellwood 1994, p. 11). Many factors may have contributed to the continued growth (Handler and Hasenfeld 1991, pp. 117–19). Undoubtedly, a major cause was demographic—the rapid increase in single-parent families. However, it was also a period of expansion and extension of citizenship rights to previously disfranchised social groups, particularly ethnic minorities and women. It was a period of active political liberalism that resulted in the passage of the Civil Rights Act in 1964 and the Voting Rights Act in 1965. Several antipoverty measures were passed, some in response to the breakout of civil disorders in many urban centers (Piven and Cloward 1971). There were major changes in the legal culture. The rights of welfare recipients were greatly expanded by declaring many exclusionary practices illegal, including residency requirements, man-in-the-house rules, and employable-mother rules. Due process hearings were required to check arbitrary case closures, and highly discretionary grants for "special needs" were consolidated into uniform grant allocations. Liberal federal administrative regulations, combined with aggressive legal representation of the poor and the grassroots activities of the National Welfare Rights Organization, instituted a climate of entitlement.

Thus, the period from 1967 to 1972 witnessed a moral tilt toward defining welfare as an entitlement (Sosin 1986). Welfare departments came to accept the new moral assumptions that welfare recipients had a qualified entitlement to aid, that eligibility and the amount of aid could no longer be made contingent on the moral fitness or rehabilitative needs of the applicant, and that the poor were not necessarily in need of being "reformed." In turn, caseworkers eased eligibility determination and were less likely to use their discretion to withhold benefits (Sosin 1986, p. 271).

However, the continued rise in welfare costs and the number of recipients coupled with slow economic growth reinforced the sense that the program was out of control and that it was undermining dominant moral values. With implicit racial overtones, attention focused on "the large number of African-Americans, out-of-wedlock births, the moral consequences of marital disruption, single parenthood, and generational dependency" (Handler and Hasenfeld 1991, p. 120). Indeed, the passage of the 1967 Social Security Amendment reaffirmed these moral assumptions by making welfare receipt contingent on participation in a work incentive program (WIN). One of the administrative responses to the rising welfare costs was the reassertion of quality control to weed out "fraud, abuse and errors" (Brodkin and Lipsky 1983). In other words, welfare recipients were again recast as morally suspect and prone to abuse their entitlements.

Beginning in 1972, sanctions were imposed on states that exceeded a certain error rate, and both supervisors and workers in local welfare offices were subject to penalties because of errors in determining eligibility and grant amounts. Welfare departments developed a set of highly complex and detailed administrative rules and regulations. The test of deservingness now meant being able to meet seemingly endless administrative requirements in a Kafkaesque bureaucracy.

W. H. Simon (1983, p. 1199) suggested that welfare departments acquired a new organizational form characterized by formalization of entitlement, bureaucratization of administration, and proletarianization of the workforce. Not unlike the Internal Revenue Service, the goals of the welfare department were now to verify eligibility, write checks, and reduce errors (Bane and Ellwood 1994, p. 16). The interorganizational relations of the departments became highly circumscribed to those public agencies that could provide documentary verification of eligibility claims, such as family status, income and assets, unemployment and work history, health, birth of children, school enrollment, and living arrangements. In an attempt to purge discretion, rules and regulations were promulgated to govern every possible contingency, resulting in volumes of instructions being updated and changed, often before workers had a chance even to absorb the instructions that they had replaced. If prior norms allowed workers to exempt a car from an applicant's assets when it was judged to be "needed," now the car could be exempted only if its value was less than $1,500 (Simon 1983, p. 1202). The technology of eligibility determination became highly mechanistic and impersonal, focusing on the verification of every statement required for eligibility. Simon (1983, p. 1205) reported that "the Massachusetts welfare department gives applicants a list of thirty documents that they may be asked to supply . . . [and] many of the documents must meet stringent technical requirements."

The organization of work was divided into several discrete work units. Applicants began at "intake," which consisted of staff specializing in eligibility determinations. Once eligibility was established, clients were typically assigned an "eligibility technician" responsible for periodic eligibility redetermination. These workers had large caseloads of about 200 cases. If the client was required to participate in a work program, she would be referred to a separate "human resources" unit (Simon 1983, p. 1216; Bane and Ellwood 1994, pp. 4–5).

To ensure reduction in errors, quality control units were established. They used statistical methods to select a sample of cases to review for possible overpayment errors. The review was very detailed, as states were subject to penalties if the error rates exceeded a certain acceptable level.[3] There were two characteristics to these reviews. First, they were concerned with overpayments rather than underpayments (Brodkin and Lipsky 1983), reflecting the moral assumption that many welfare recipients were undeserving and prone to cheating. Second, most of the errors could be classified as "paper errors" unrelated to substantive eligibility determination (Simon 1983, p. 1211).

The new organization of work also led to further de-skilling of the workers to lower-level clerical positions. Indeed, in many welfare departments, the eligibility workers were not appreciably different from the applicants they processed and came to resent the recipients for getting an undeserved entitlement denied to them. The effects of the new organizational practices on worker-client relations were quite apparent. The division of labor and high staff turnover prevented the formation of any continuous relationships. The relations became far less trusting and more adversarial. Problem clients became a problem because they required more paperwork and more time to process the case, and they caused a greater probability of error. Discretion was exercised through the workers' control over information and when and how to invoke various regulations. The onus of responsibility fell on clients to prove and maintain their eligibility. Most case closures were due to administrative reasons—the failure of the clients to submit proper forms in a timely fashion. In short, paperwork replaced people work, resulting in what M. Lipsky (1984) termed "bureaucratic disentitlement." Benefits to recipients were curtailed and terminated under the guise of obscure and hidden bureaucratic rules.

The "New" Welfare-to-Work Ideology

The ascendancy of the neoconservatives to power signaled another shift in the moral assumptions about welfare recipients, culminating in a liberal and conservative "consensus" expressed in the Family Support Act of 1988 (Handler and Hasenfeld 1991, pp. 209–30) and more recently in the PRWORA. First, welfare benefits are no longer an entitlement. The social rights of welfare recipients are made contingent on meeting obligations to the state. As expressed by L. M. Mead (1986), accepting public aid signals a failure in citizenship that justifies the right of the state, in return for public assistance, to exercise paternal authority—requiring the recipients to work and demanding that they lead a moral life and raise their children to become law-abiding citizens. Second, welfare recipients are obligated to work for their relief. If in the past the model welfare recipient was the "gilt-edged widow," now it is the mother who works full-time while raising her children with proper care. Since the majority of mothers are now in the labor force, why not welfare mothers? Again, welfare is viewed as corroding the work ethic. Third, laying the specter of the "underclass" squarely at their doorsteps has reaffirmed the moral condemnation of never-married mothers, especially African Americans and Latinos. Marriage, paternity, and child support have to be strengthened. Fourth, educational failure leads to welfare dependency. Therefore, poor teenaged mothers should be obligated to graduate from high school. Finally, local discretion is seen as the most effective way to respond to the problems of welfare dependency.

Once again welfare departments are being transformed in order to institutionalize these moral conceptions. Welfare departments have developed new organizational forms whose overall goal is to place recipients in the labor market and to ensure that teenaged parents remain in school. In most states, these new forms are add-ons to the current welfare departments and are decoupled from the income maintenance functions, although some have experimented in integrating both (Brock and Harknett 1997). The ambiguities inherent in these moral conceptions, combined with local discretion, have resulted in the proliferation of diverse organizational forms and practices, each echoing the moral imprint of the particular state and local community (Hagen and Lurie 1994). Communities may opt to emphasize one of two competing moral conceptions. The first views welfare recipients as morally deficient, especially in lacking a work ethic. The second views recipients as suffering from human capital and environmental deficits, such as lack of education and training. Departments that emphasize moral deficiency are more likely to blame the recipients for their predicament and to accord them low social worth. Therefore, they are more likely to institute mandatory participation, immediate job placement, and the threat of sanctions to elicit compliance. Departments that emphasize human capital deficits are more likely to view their clients as victims of circumstances and attribute to them higher social worth. They encourage voluntary participation, remedial education, and training, and they use persuasion to elicit compliance (Hasenfeld and Weaver 1996).

Still, the emerging dominant organizational form is modeled after Riverside, California, because it has been shown to be effective in moving a larger proportion of recipients into the labor market at low program costs (Riccio, Friedlander, and Freedman 1994). Led by a charismatic director, Riverside engaged in its own moral entrepreneurship and developed a program that was widely different from most other county programs in California. It did so by assuming that welfare recipients lacked in work ethic rather than in human capital and by adopting the philosophy that a low-paying, entry-level job was better than no job and could lead to a better job. So, it emphasized a strong employment message, inexpensive job search, and quick entry into the labor market. The message was addressed to the staff and the recipients. The program developed extensive relations with local employers by hiring job developers. The county was able to promise local employers job applicants "that afternoon." The staff were specially recruited for commitment to the mission of the agency and were tightly organized and monitored. Staff performance was rated, in large part, on job development and placement. The staff engaged in close monitoring of attendance and recipient job performance. The threat of sanctions was used frequently. The success of Riverside in reaching its goal of pushing recipients into the labor market at low service costs has led California and other states to institutionalize this service model in their recent welfare legislation (see, e.g., Holcomb et al. 1998; U.S. General Accounting Office 1998).

At the other end of the moral spectrum is Utah (Pavetti 1995; Pavetti and Duke 1995). Welfare officials there assume that recipients experience many employment barriers that can be removed through the provision of individually tailored services. Therefore, participation is broadly defined. For example, participation includes education, training, part-time employment, mental health counseling, parenting education, and substance abuse treatment. Eligibility workers have been replaced by "self-sufficiency" workers who develop a self-sufficiency plan for families applying for welfare for the first time. The staff is encouraged to develop strategies to engage recipients with multiple employment barriers. The assumption is that with appropriate help, multiple problem families can eventually become self-sufficient. The Utah program has a system of incentives and sanctions ranging from a bonus for participation to a loss of the grant for continued refusal to participate. If a family loses welfare for nonparticipation, it can requalify only after participating in a structured program "designed to overcome recipient's fears of change" (Pavetti 1995, p. 3).

The service technology for working with long-term, multiple-barrier families reflects the moral assumptions and goals of the program. Specially trained workers have been hired and assigned small caseloads (30–35 cases). They provide home visits and one-on-one counseling and conduct regular reviews. Still, the staff felt that they were in "uncharted territory, often having to rely on trial and error to identify the best strategy for helping a family overcome their barriers to employment" (Pavetti 1995, p. 12). One can see why this organizational form may not last. The program is expensive, treatment is time-consuming, and results, measured by self-sufficiency, are not easily attained.

In her study of the work program in Chicago, E. Z. Brodkin (1997) showed how fiscal considerations led officials to modify their moral assumptions and the resulting treatment of welfare recipients. In trying to reduce costs while maximizing federal reimbursement, Illinois shifted the work program from a voluntary program emphasizing education and training to a mandatory program emphasizing job search. In doing so, the state simply redefined its moral assumptions about welfare recipients and their service needs. Other constraints added to the reduced social service approach to welfare recipients. Because the department deprofessionalized its casework staff, it was unable to staff the work program with trained workers. Moreover, because of union rules, most workers were recruited from the income eligibility and grant determination units that emphasize highly bureaucratic routines. The pressure to meet caseload quotas further eroded giving attention to the specific service needs of the recipients. As a result, the caseworkers undertook their own moral entrepreneurship to cope with a difficult situation: "Caseworkers tended to define client needs to fit available slots, avoid eliciting service claims, and pressure clients to accept the bureaucratic construction of welfare rights and obligations" (Brodkin 1997, p. 15).

As noted above, PRWORA encouraged states to shift to a "work first" ideology, resulting in the adoption of new organizational forms that emulate the Riverside model by trying to become employment placement agencies. Connecticut's Jobs First program is a good example (Bloom, Andes, and Nicholson 1998). The state's welfare-to-work program shifted from an emphasis on education and training to rapid job placement. The program limits cash assistance to 21 months, and recipients are required to participate in employment services such as job search and job club whose aims are quick job placement. Education and training are available only to recipients who fail to get a job after substantial and lengthy tries. In comparison to previous organizational practices, the eligibility workers are more likely to emphasize the new employment regulations and time limit. The employment service workers are more likely to urge the participants to work and to take jobs that do not pay enough. The workers rely on sanctions to achieve compliance. Structurally, the employment service has become more bureaucratic (i.e., there is more paperwork), with a correspondent increase in caseloads (often exceeding 500 clients per worker).

In addition, PRWORA permits states to privatize the delivery of their welfare services, and several states and counties are taking up the option (see, e.g., Bernstein 1996; Hughes 1996; U.S. General Accounting Office 1997). Such efforts are rationalized in the name of efficiency. Still, the firms being hired to administer welfare do moral work. Whatever practices these firms institutionalize to optimize their profits inevitably produce moral consequences for their clients. First and foremost, recipients become commodified—their value to the firm is contingent on the revenues they generate. Hence, there is a potential that recipients with "problems" who require more attention and resources are likely to be defined as "unprofitable." Second, if profits depend on reductions in the welfare rolls, the firms will have an incentive to terminate cases as expeditiously as possible. Therefore, greater emphasis will be placed on rapid job placements, and most likely sanctions will be the preferred mode to enforce compliance and to close cases. More ominously, as commodities welfare recipients are in danger of being stripped of whatever minimal social rights they have left. The firms will serve as buffers between the recipients and the public officials responsible for their welfare, and the officials will have greater incentives to side with the firms rather than with the recipients.

Conclusion

Since a distinct feature of human service organizations is their moral work, we need to understand how these organizations select the moral rules that guide their work and how these rules become enacted in their organizational forms and practices. The new institutional perspective on organizations is particularly useful in drawing attention to the ways in which institutionalized moral rules become embedded in organizational forms. It also recognizes that the organization itself and its workers actively participate in shaping and enacting moral rules in organizational practices. The dynamic interrelations between moral rules and organizational forms and practices suggests that organizational forms and practices both constitute and are constituted by the moral rules these organizations adopt.

Within this perspective, I give particular attention to the multiplicity of moral rules these organizations encounter both externally and internally. As the analysis of welfare departments shows, organizational and personal moral entrepreneurship play a significant role in shaping organizational forms and practices. My analysis of the historical changes in the organizational forms and practices of welfare departments shows that while these changes reflect the transformations in moral assumptions about welfare recipients, they are also highly contextualized. There are wide variations in local practices in response to both locally defined moral ideologies and political economies. Therefore, contrary to the "iron cage" argument, human service organizations tend to display greater variations in organizational forms.

Future research on human service organizations needs to identify more explicitly the dynamic forces that produce variations in organizational practices and in the moral rules they enact. Recent attempts to integrate institutional, political economy, and structuration perspectives (e.g., Oliver 1992; Orlikowski 1992; Barley and Tolbert 1997; Sandfort 1999) may be a promising direction.

In one sense, the historical analysis also lends support to the emphasis of the new institutionalism on broad cultural influences that are powerful rationalizing agents of organizational practices. Despite the changes that welfare departments have undergone, certain central features have remained the same, echoing broad dominant and fairly stable moral conceptions about the able-bodied poor. These include viewing the poor as deviants and "others"; ensuring that the giving of aid will not corrode the work ethic; and upholding the moral code about family values, gender, and ethnicity by degrading the poor. No matter what specific organizational forms welfare departments institutionalize over time, these basic moral values have remained their guides.

References

Abbott, A. D. 1988. *The System of Professions.* Chicago: University of Chicago Press.
Bane, M. J., and D. T. Ellwood. 1994. *Welfare Realities: From Rhetoric to Reform.* Cambridge, Mass.: Harvard University Press.
Barley, S. R. 1986. "Technology as an Occasion for Structuring: Evidence from Observations of CT Scanners and the Social Order of Radiology Departments." *Administrative Science Quarterly* 31:78–108.
Barley, S. R., and P. S. Tolbert. 1997. "Institutionalization and Structuration: Studying the Links between Action and Institution." *Organization Studies* 18:93–117.
Bell, W. 1965. *Aid to Dependent Children.* New York: Columbia University Press.
Bernstein, N. 1996. "Giant Companies Entering Race to Run State Welfare Programs." *New York Times,* September 15.
Bloom, D., M. Andes, and C. Nicholson. 1998. *Jobs First: Early Implementation of Connecticut's Welfare Reform Initiative.* New York: Manpower Demonstration Research.
Brock, T., and K. Harknett. 1997. *Separation versus Integration of Income Maintenance and Employment Services: Which Model Is Best?* New York: Manpower Demonstration Research.
Brodkin, E. Z. 1997. "Inside the Welfare Contract: Discretion and Accountability in State Welfare Administration." *Social Service Review* 71:1–33.
Brodkin, E. Z., and M. Lipsky. 1983. "Quality Control in AFDC as an Administrative Strategy." *Social Service Review* 57:1–34.
D'Aunno, T., and R. Price. 1985. "Organizational Adaptation to Changing Environment: Community Mental Health and Drug Abuse Services." *American Behavioral Scientist* 26: 669–84.
D'Aunno, T., R. I. Sutton, and R. H. Price. 1991. "Isomorphism and External Support in Conflicting Institutional Environments: A Study of Drug Abuse Treatment Units." *Academy of Management Journal* 34:636–61.
Derthick, M. 1970. *The Influence of Federal Grants: Public Assistance in Massachusetts.* Cambridge, Mass.: Harvard University Press.
DiMaggio, P. D., and W. W. Powell. 1983. "The Iron Cage Revisited: Institutional Isomorphism and Collective Rationality in Organizational Fields." *American Sociological Review* 48:147–60.
Fraser, N. 1989. *Unruly Practices: Power, Discourse and Gender in Contemporary Social Theory.* Minneapolis: University of Minnesota Press.
Hagen, J. L., and I. V. Lurie. 1994. *Implementing JOBS: Progress and Promise.* Albany, N.Y.: SUNY, Nelson A. Rockefeller Institute of Government.
Hamilton, G. 1962. "Editorial." *Social Work* 7:2, 128.
Handler, J. 1986. *The Conditions of Discretion.* New York: Russell Sage.
Handler, J. F., and Y. Hasenfeld. 1991. *The Moral Construction of Poverty.* Newbury Park, Calif.: Sage.
———. 1997. *We the Poor People: Work, Poverty, and Welfare.* New Haven, Conn.: Yale University Press.
Handler, J. F., and E. J. Hollingsworth. 1971. *The "Deserving Poor": A Study of Welfare Administration.* Chicago: Markham.
Hannan, M. T., and J. Freeman. 1989. *Organizational Ecology.* Cambridge, Mass.: Harvard University Press.
Harrington, M. 1962. *The Other America: Poverty in the United States.* New York: Macmillan.
Hasenfeld, Y. 1992. "The Nature of Human Service Organizations." In *Human Services as Formal Organizations,* edited by Y. Hasenfeld. Newbury Park, Calif.: Sage.
Hasenfeld, Y., and D. Weaver. 1996. "Enforcement, Compliance, and Disputes in Welfare-to-Work Programs." *Social Service Review* 70:235–56.
Hatfield, A. B. 1991. "The National Alliance for the Mentally Ill: A Decade Later." *Community Mental Health Journal* 27 (2): 95–104.
Hinings, C. R., and R. Greenwood. 1988. *The Dynamics of Strategic Change.* Oxford: Blackwell.
Holcomb, P. A., L. Pavetti, C. Ratcliffe, and S. Riedinger. 1998. *Building an Employment Fo-*

350   **Social Service Review**

cused *Welfare System: Work First and Other Work-Oriented Strategies in Five States.* Washington,
    D.C.: Urban Institute.
Hughes, P. R. 1996. "Texas Blazing Welfare Trail." *Houston Chronicle*, October 29.
Hyde, C. 1992. "The Ideational System of Social Movement Agencies: An Examination
    of Feminist Health Centers." In *Human Services as Formal Organizations*, edited by
    Y. Hasenfeld. Newbury Park, Calif.: Sage.
Lipsky, M. 1980. *Street-Level Bureaucracy.* New York: Russell Sage.
————. 1984. "Bureaucratic Disentitlement in Social Welfare Programs." *Social Service
    Review* 58:3–27.
Mead, L. M. 1986. *Beyond Entitlement: The Social Obligations of Citizenship.* New York: Free
    Press.
Meyer, J. W., and B. Rowan. 1977. "Institutionalized Organizations: Formal Structure as
    Myth and Ceremony." *American Journal of Sociology* 83:340–63.
Oakes, J. 1995. "Matchmaking: The Dynamics of High School Tracking Decisions." *Ameri-
    can Educational Research Journal* 32:3–33.
Oliver, C. 1991. "Strategic Responses to Institutional Processes." *Academy of Management
    Review* 16:145–79.
————. 1992. "The Antecedents of Deinstitutionalization." *Organizational Studies* 13:
    563–88.
Orlikowski, W. J. 1992. "The Duality of Technology: Rethinking the Concept of Technology
    in Organizations." *Organization Science* 3:398–427.
Pavetti, L. 1995. "And Employment for All: Lessons from Utah's Single Parent Employment
    Demonstration Project." Paper presented at the seventeenth annual research confer-
    ence of the Association for Public Policy and Management, Washington, D.C., No-
    vember 2–4.
Pavetti, L., and A. E. Duke. 1995. *Increasing Participation in Work and Work-Related Activities:
    Lessons from Five State Welfare Demonstration Projects.* Washington, D.C.: Urban Institute.
Piven, F. F., and R. Cloward. 1971. *Regulating the Poor: The Functions of Public Welfare.* New
    York: Random House.
Prottas, J. M. 1979. *People Processing.* Lexington, Mass.: Heath.
Riccio, J., D. Friedlander, and S. Freedman. 1994. *GAIN: Benefits, Costs, and Three-Year Impacts
    on a Welfare-to-Work Program.* New York: Manpower Demonstration Research.
Roth, J. A. 1972. "Some Contingencies of the Moral Evaluation and Control of Clientele:
    The Case of the Hospital Emergency Service." *American Journal of Sociology* 77 (5):
    839–56.
Sandfort, J. 1999. "The Structural Impediments to Human Service Collaboration: Examin-
    ing Welfare Reform at the Front Lines." *Social Service Review* 73:314–39.
Scott. R. 1969. *The Making of Blind Men.* New York: Russell Sage.
Scott, W. R. 1995. *Institutions and Organizations.* Thousand Oaks, Calif.: Sage.
Simon, W. H. 1983. "Legality, Bureaucracy, and Class in the Welfare System." *Yale Law
    Journal* 92:1198–1269.
Sosin, M. R. 1986. "Legal Rights and Welfare Change, 1960–1980." In *Fighting Poverty*,
    edited by S. H. Danziger and D. H. Weinberg. Cambridge, Mass.: Harvard University
    Press.
Strauss, A., S. Fargerhaugh, B. Suczek, and C. Wiener. 1985. *Social Organization of Medical
    Work.* Chicago: University of Chicago Press.
U.S. General Accounting Office. 1997. *Social Service Privatization: Expansion Poses Challenges
    in Ensuring Accountability for Program Results.* Washington, D.C.: General Accounting
    Office.
————. 1998. *Welfare Reform: States Are Restructuring Programs to Reduce Welfare Dependence.*
    Washington, D.C.: General Accounting Office.
U.S. Public Law 104-193. Cong. 104th sess., August 22, 1996. *Personal Responsibility and Work
    Opportunity Reconciliation Act of 1996.* Title I Block Grants for Temporary Assistance for
    Needy Families. Sec. 101, p. 110, Stat. 2105.
Weatherley, R., and M. Lipsky. 1977. "Street-Level Bureaucrats and Institutional Inno-
    vation: Implementing Special-Education Reform." *Harvard Educational Review* 47:
    171–97.
Weir, M., A. S. Orloff, and T. Skocpol, eds. 1988. *The Politics of Social Policy in the United States.*
    Princeton, N.J.: Princeton University Press.

Organizational Forms as Moral Practices 351

Zucker, L. 1988. "Where Do Institutional Patterns Come From? Organizations as Actors in Social Systems." In *Institutional Patterns and Organizations,* edited by L. Zucker. Cambridge, Mass.: Ballinger.

Notes

I want to thank Mayer Zald for his insightful guidance and the three anonymous reviewers for their thoughtful comments. Throughout this article the term "welfare department" denotes the state or county administrative unit that administers AFDC or Temporary Aid for Needy Families.

1. Much of the following discussion is based on Bell (1965).

2. Welfare departments were also reluctant to hire professionally trained workers for fear that they would be left with an expensive workforce once federal funds dried up.

3. No state, however, was ever actually penalized despite findings of unacceptable error rates.

Power in Social Work Practice **471**

whom. The roots of the power of social workers are not only in expertise and interpersonal skills but also in the fact that they are members of an organization that controls critical resources needed by the client. The power of the agency is reinforced by the fact that clients must yield some control over their own fate to the agency when seeking help from it.[8]

The Power of the Service Agency

Practice theory generally does not address the power of the agency over the role performance of the workers. There is an implicit assumption that the professionalism and expertise of the workers will provide them with sufficient autonomy to guard against organizational intrusion into the helping process. Nonetheless, as pointed out by various researchers, the performance of social workers is significantly determined by the organizational context in which they work.[9] Much of the power of the organization over its workers is invisible and operates through its standard operating procedures. The agency, in effect, controls the decision-making processes of its workers by constraining the type of information they will process, by limiting the range of alternatives available to them, and by specifying the decision rules for choosing among the alternatives.

By constraining the decision-making processes of its workers the agency makes sure that its core activity—the delivery of services—maintains, strengthens, and reinforces its operative goals. These goals, in turn, represent the interests of those who control the key resources of the agency.[10] Such interests may, and often do, represent the professional values and norms of the social workers and may also incorporate the interests of the clients. Nonetheless, the values and interests of any individual worker or client are subordinated to and shaped by organizational policies that take precedence and are enforced by a collective power generally greater than the power of either the individual worker or the client. Public welfare workers, for example, quickly realize that they lack sufficient agency resources to meet the needs of their clients. Recognizing that as individual workers they have little power to change the situation, they develop personal coping mechanisms such as capitulation, withdrawal, specialization, or self-victimization.[11]

It is important to emphasize that the power of the agency is influenced by the environment in which it is located. Political, economic, and cultural factors greatly affect how the resources of the agency will be used. A "humane" agency, in which the needs of the clients are integrated in its operative goals, can exist only when key groups in its environment endorse and support such values.

Recognizing that social work practice is agency based, Weissman, Epstein, and Savage have proposed to augment traditional therapeutic skills with organizational skills, which they see as equally important in helping people in an agency context.[12] They conceptualize these additional skills in the form of roles that are "framed by an organizational perspective [that] provides the clinical social worker with access to the array of problem-solving resources agencies provide."[13] Among the roles they identify are (*a*) the diagnostician, who utilizes in the assessment process not only personality or ecological theory but also an organizational theory to identify the barriers to effective functioning; (*b*) the expediter, who can get things done for the client, particularly in the organization, mostly through bargaining; (*c*) the case manager, who plans, coordinates, and monitors client services; (*d*) the advocate, who tries, on behalf of the client, to break down organizational barriers to access to services; (*e*) the program developer, who uses feedback from clients to initiate, plan, and implement new programs to improve service effectiveness; and (*f*) the organizational reformer, who attempts to change organizational structure and the processes that impede service effectiveness. In articulating these roles, the authors attempt to demonstrate the close interrelation between clinical and therapeutic skills and the organizational skills associated with these roles. In contrast to other theorists, they accord the agency its rightful place in the practice process and try to derive practice principles that fully acknowledge the ubiquity of the agency in the worker-client relationship.

The difficulty with this approach is that it does not fully account for the role of power, that is, the power of the agency, of the worker, and of the client in shaping the practice process. While they clearly attempt to formulate practice principles that reduce the power gap between agencies and clients, the lack of a systematic theory about the role of power in worker-client relations renders their approach too limited and somewhat simplistic. Therefore I propose a model of worker-client relations in which power assumes a central role.

A Power-Dependence Perspective

What motivates the worker and client to interact? This seemingly obvious question becomes less trivial if we reject the often implicit professional assumption that there is a mutuality of interests between the worker and the client. It is commonly assumed that, since clients want help and agencies wish to provide help, they share a common goal. In fact, however, the interests of the worker and the client are determined by their respective systems. Like all living systems, the agency and the client want to maximize their own resources while minimizing the costs of attaining them. Therefore a person becomes a client in order to get needed services and tries to do so with minimal personal costs. The agency, via the worker, engages the client in order to obtain resources controlled by him or her while minimizing organizational costs. It is this exchange of resources that makes both systems interdependent. For example, a person needing financial assistance will initiate an encounter with the welfare department in order to get maximum aid with as little harassment as possible. The workers representing the department need the client to justify the agency's mandate, and thus their own position, but try to conserve personal and agency resources in processing the client.

What governs this relationship, and particularly the ability of each party to optimize its interests, is the power each brings to the exchange. We say that A has power over B when A has the potential to obtain favorable outcomes at B's expense.[14] Moreover, the power of A over B indicates the dependence of B on A. The amount of power A has over B is a direct function of the resources A controls and B needs and an inverse function of the ability of B to obtain these resources elsewhere. Thus, the amount of power the welfare worker has over the client is a direct function of the client's need for financial aid and an inverse function of the client's ability to obtain the aid elsewhere. Similarly, the amount of power the client has over the agency is a direct function of how much the agency needs the resources controlled by the client and an inverse function of the agency's ability to obtain these resources elsewhere. It is quite obvious from this definition that agencies having a monopoly over services wield considerable power over clients. In this instance we say that the agency has the power advantage over the client because the client needs the agency more than it needs him or her. In contrast, potential clients having extensive personal resources (e.g., income and education) or highly desirable attributes (e.g., youth, verbal skills, and intelligence) wield significant power, particularly if the agency needs their resources. Clients with extensive resources have greater choices in selecting the agency, the worker, and the mode of intervention. They may, therefore, have a power advantage over the agency.

A power advantage does not imply that it will always be used to obtain favorable outcomes at the expense of the other party. There are values and norms that govern the use of power. The welfare worker, for example, is bound by departmental rules and regulations that define how the worker can use his or her power. Moreover, the worker is also socialized to a set of professional norms and ethics that ensure such power will not be abused. In general, the institutionalization of professional values and ethics emphasizing the rights of clients comes in recognition of the potentially exploitable power advantage professionals have over clients.

From this perspective, social work practice is actually an exchange of resources in which the power-dependence relationships between the worker and the client are being played out. The social work contract reflects the terms of the exchange—what is being exchanged and how—as determined by the power-dependence relationships.

The ideal model of social work practice, while acknowledging the power gap between the worker and the client, assumes that the mutuality of interests and the contractual relationship between the worker and the client will reduce the gap and result in a power balance. To quote Loewenberg, "The power gap may be unavoidable, but most social workers, just as most of their colleagues in other helping professions, think that it is undesirable and that it should be reduced as much as possible."[15] However, it can be argued that it is precisely such a power differential that enables workers to engage in social intervention. Yet social work practice tends to understate the importance of power in shaping worker-client relations because of the assumption that the interests of the client and the worker are compatible.

The power-dependence perspective also recognizes that the exchange relationship may be either voluntary or involuntary for each party. The degree of choice available to each party, as noted earlier, is a key determinant of the power-dependence relationships between the client and the worker. For example, when the client is coerced to interact with the agency, as in the case of involuntary commitment to a mental hospital, the client is at a significant power disadvantage. Even when the patient may formally consent to treatment, the extreme power disadvantage does not give him or her a real choice. Patients, of course, can band together in informal groups to counteract some of the consequences of the power imbalances they experience, but they cannot eliminate them.

Social work practice tends to ignore involuntary interaction since most social work techniques assume that the client has the right of self-determination. In reality, in many social services, particularly those for vulnerable groups such as children, the poor, or the chronically ill, worker-client relationships are involuntary. Again, in social work practice theory we encounter reluctance to admit and often denial that many worker-client relationships are involuntary. To illustrate, Garvin and Seabury state, "In a sense, there is no such thing as an involuntary client as we defined a client as a person or persons who accept a contract for social work services."[16] They reach such a conclusion because they, like others, assume that a contract is based on mutuality of interests and equality of power between the worker and the client. They fail to recognize that the client may accept the contract for lack of other alternatives or may pretend to accept the contract with no intention of adhering to it. Indeed, what the contract does is confirm the power-dependence relationships between the worker and the client. Therefore what is normally taken for granted in social work practice theory, namely, mutuality of interest and symmetry of power, is made problematic in this perspective.

In this framework, social work intervention techniques, such as enhancing the client's awareness through confrontation and interpretation or modifying the client's behavior through reinforcement and modeling, are actually utilizations of power by the worker to elicit desired outcomes from the client. In a broader sense, the worker uses power resources as means of influence to bring about desired changes in the client in accordance with the agency's interests.

Gaining and Using Power Advantage in Social Work Practice

There is generally an asymmetry of power between the agency and the client, and therefore between the worker and the client, that is maintained through the structure of social services. First, most agencies are not directly dependent on their clients for procurement of resources. Typically, funds are obtained from third parties who are not the direct recipients of the services. Second, the demands for services often outstrip their supply. Third, many agencies have a quasimonopoly over their services. Within the agency, the asymmetry is reinforced by the worker's monopoly of knowledge and by limiting the client's access to other workers, making the continuation of services contingent on the client's compliance, and limiting the client's options for alternative services. The same organizational power that shapes the decision-making processes of the worker also influences the decision-making processes of the client while in the agency.

The power advantage of the agency and worker shapes the social work process in several distinct ways. As noted earlier, the agency uses its power to set the parameters of the social work process in a manner that maintains and strengthens the interests of the organization. It does so primarily through its control over the intake, processing, and termination of clients. First, the agency will prefer clients who reflect positively on the evaluative criteria used by the key external legitimizing and funding bodies. Scott found that agencies for the blind prefer young over old blind clients because the former evoke greater sympathy among donors.[17] Similarly, the agency may prefer clients who are covered by insurance. Second, the agency will prefer clients who conform to its moral assumptions about human behavior. Roth noted that emergency room staff delay treatment of patients who appear to be morally inferior, such as welfare recipients, the homeless, and alcoholics.[18] Third, the agency will select clients whose attributes affirm and fit its dominant service technologies. Link and Milcarek found that patients selected to individual and group therapies in New York State psychiatric hospitals were the youngest, most competent, most communicative, and most motivated.[19] Finally, the agency will send clients into different service routes as a way to maintain the efficiency of its operations.

Social workers may also use their power advantage to enhance their work values and interests. Heller argues that power is used by psychotherapists in every aspect of their work, including controlling the environment in which they see their patients, defining the agenda of

476   Social Service Review

the psychotherapeutic session, determining interaction patterns with
the patient, and controlling the onset and termination of the psychotherapeutic process.[20] By using power to control most aspects of the
helping process, social workers aim to substantiate their personal and
professional moral and practice ideologies.[21] They do so to protect,
in effect, the enormous investment and commitment they have made
in their moral and professional socialization. Social workers obviously
rely on scientific knowledge to justify their activities and modify their
tactics when they fail to achieve the desired outcomes. Nonetheless,
they rarely step out of the boundaries of their basic moral and professional ideologies, and they use their power to protect such boundaries.

The power of the worker is a critical element of the social work
process and a determinant of its successful outcome. Heller suggests
that power enables therapists to initiate the intervention process, to
enhance the therapeutic relationship, to become an indentificatory
figure for the client, to foster confidence and hope, and to manage
the interaction process effectively.[22] Power resources are indispensable
when the aim of the clinical intervention is to achieve attitudinal and
behavioral changes in the client.[23]

Clients are not without power resources that they can use to negotiate
favorable outcomes. Clients may possess resources that are sought
after by the agency (i.e., they may possess "desirable" attributes); they
may have a broad range of alternative service providers to choose
from; they may have knowledge and expertise regarding the services
they seek; and they may have support of larger collectivities with which
they are affiliated whose power resources can be mobilized on their
behalf, such as kin and friendship networks, trade unions, or civic and
business associations. Clearly, clients with power resources, particularly
income and education, are better able to obtain the services they want
and are more likely to influence the social work process to suit their
needs and interests. This is manifested, first and foremost, in the
choices they have in selecting agencies and workers. The ability to
choose and, particularly, the range of available choices are the core
of power.

For both the agency and the worker, access to power resources
means having a greater potential to provide superior services. Actualizing
such potential depends on the extent to which the interests of those
controlling these power resources are compatible with the interests
and needs of clients. I propose that such compatibility is more likely
to occur when there is a power balance between workers and clients.

The Inequality of Practice and the Practice of Inequality

In a society such as ours, characterized by considerable social inequality,
the distribution of power among agencies and clients is inherently

Power in Social Work Practice   477

unequal. Agencies are differentiated by the amount of resources they possess and the control they have over their environment. Urban hospitals, for example, are stratified according to the resources at their disposal, including the quantity and quality of medical personnel and facilities, and their ability to select their patients. These factors result in an unequal distribution of medical services, and as Milner has shown, high-quality hospitals are able to maintain their superior position by relying on low-quality hospitals where they can "dump" their undesirable patients.[24] Thus more powerful social service agencies are able to use their advantage to buttress their own power, partly through their ability to invest in and maintain superior practice, and partly by selecting desirable clients who ensure service effectiveness. Hence the dynamics of power are such that they perpetuate an unequal distribution of quality practice, unless checked and controlled by countervailing powers, such as government intervention.

Within the agency, an analogous process occurs. Workers with more power are better able to control the conditions of their work. They too can use their power advantage to improve the quality of their practice by having, for example, control over the type and number of clients they serve and by having greater access to sources of knowledge and expertise. Being able to provide superior practice in turn strengthens their power. Hence even within the agency there are forces that, unless checked, accentuate the inequality of practice.

The unequal distribution of power resources among clients, a reflection of social class differences, also results in unequal access to quality services. It is not surprising, therefore, that poor clients tend to receive poor services. One of the most striking consequences of the inequality of practice is that clients from low socioeconomic groups are more likely to interact with social service agencies whose primary function is social control and surveillance rather than prevention and rehabilitation. Nowhere is this pattern more apparent than in services for children and youths. Children from low socioeconomic groups and oppressed minorities are much more likely to be placed in out-of-home facilities, to be routed to the juvenile justice system, and to be cared for in social control institutions.[25] This pattern repeats itself in diverse sectors of the social welfare systems, such as in services to low-income female heads of households or in treatment of the mentally disabled.[26]

The use of power advantages by agencies, workers, and clients results not only in the inequality of practice but, what is more important, in the practice of inequality as well. Access to power resources enables both clients and workers to maintain and reinforce their power advantage by controlling the nature of the practice itself. The differential ability to control the process and content of social work practice in turn perpetuates the practice of social inequality.

478   Social Service Review

Empowerment as the Cornerstone of Social Work Practice

Because power is such a central element in social work practice and yet is largely neglected in the formulation of practice principles, a major shift is necessary in current theory and practice. If we view social work practice as an exchange of resources, social work effectiveness, then, is predicated on the reduction of the power imbalance between workers and clients—specifically on increasing the client's power resources. What is needed, therefore, is to place client empowerment at the center of social work practice. The perspective I advocate calls for a revision of social work practice theory in a way that defines the major function of social work as empowering people to be able to make choices and gain control over their environment. The distinctiveness of social work and its practice theory and principles can be achieved only if it embraces empowerment as its domain rather than emulating other helping professions.

Social work practice that focuses on increasing the power resources of the client requires a shift in orientation from person- to environment-centered practice. Kagle and Cowger point out that in a person-centered practice there is a much greater tendency to blame the clients for their problems.[27] In contrast, Gambrill proposes that, "if you believe that the problems result from the transactions between people and their environments and that the individual himself is a rich source of resources, then you will attend to personal assets and will examine the social context within which the person exists to determine the extent to which it could be altered to achieve outcomes."[28] The structural approach to social work practice proposed by Middleman and Goldberg offers the beginnings of an empowerment-based practice because it presupposes that "large segments of the population—the poor, the aged, the minority groups—are neither the cause of, nor the appropriate locus for, change efforts aimed at lessening the problems they are facing." It follows that the main function of social workers is to "help people to connect with needed resources, negotiate problematic situations, and change existing social structures where these limit human functioning and exacerbate human suffering."[29]

A theory of empowerment is based on the assumption that the capacity of people to improve their lives is determined by their ability to control their environment, namely, by having power.[30] Being powerless results in both loss of control and negative self-valuation. Focusing on the latter, Solomon defines empowerment as a "process whereby the social worker engages in a set of activities with the client or client system that aim [sic] to reduce the powerlessness that has been created by negative valuations based on membership in a stigmatized group."[31] My conception is at once broader and more fundamental: empowerment

Power in Social Work Practice   479

is a process through which clients obtain resources—personal, organizational, and community—that enable them to gain greater control
over their environment and to attain their aspirations.

There are four principal ways in which clients can gain power over
the social services environment: (*a*) by reducing their need for specific
resources and services; (*b*) by increasing the range of alternatives
through which they can meet their needs; (*c*) by increasing their value
to those elements in the environment whose services and resources
they need; and (*d*) by reducing the alternatives available to the elements
in the environment whose services and resources they need. These
four principles are the building blocks of a theory of empowerment.
It is important to recognize that empowerment must occur on at least
three levels. First, it must be undertaken at the worker-client level and
be directed at improving the client's power resources. Second, it must
also occur at the organizational level, aiming generally at harnessing
the agency's power advantage to increasingly serve the needs of the
client. Third, it must occur at the policy level so that the formulation
and enactment of policy decisions are influenced by those directly
affected by them.

At the worker-client level, some of the strategies to increase the
clients' power resources directly might include (*a*) providing clients
with greater information about the agency and its resources, and particularly about the clients' entitlements; (*b*) training clients to assert
and claim their legitimate rights in the agency; (*c*) increasing clients'
knowledge and expertise in handling their needs; (*d*) enhancing the
personal skills of the clients to manipulate their environment effectively
to achieve desired outcomes; (*e*) increasing the clients' resources through
coalescence with significant others;[32] (*f*) teaching clients when threats
or disruptions may be effective tactics in obtaining needed resources;
(*g*) linking clients to a supportive social network that can lend them
resources, reduce their dependence on the agency, or that can help
the clients to negotiate better their environment; and (*h*) using the
workers' own power resources, such as information, expertise, and
legitimacy, to obtain needed benefits or services.

Harnessing organizational resources on behalf of clients requires
that clients become a key interest group affecting organizational policies.
Clearly, in the current structure of social services this is not the case.
Nonetheless, social workers can play a significant role in affecting these
policies if they subordinate their own interests to those of their clients
and represent them effectively. One of the avenues available to social
workers for influencing organizational policies and procedures is the
selection of practice technologies. The agency is generally dependent
on the knowledge and expertise of social workers in choosing such
technologies. The workers can therefore use their professional power
to endorse adoption of empowerment-based practice technologies.[33]

480   Social Service Review

Second, social workers can use their professional power to influence the agency to adopt accountability measures that are based on empowerment principles. In contrast to accountability measures based on social control, these measures evaluate the extent to which staff activities successfully increase the client's power resources rather than the client's conformity to prescribed behaviors. Such measures may include the degree of fairness and equity in the provision of services, the freedom of clients to determine their service needs and objectives, and the extent to which intervention technologies focus on mobilizing resources for the client and on environmental changes. The incorporation of evaluations by clients is also an important element of empowerment-based accountability.

An effective implementation of such a system of accountability invariably circumscribes the discretion of workers by limiting their activities so that the empowerment of clients is ensured. As noted by Handler, professional discretion may actually disempower clients when its exercise results in discriminatory, unequal, and unfair practice.[34] Therefore limiting worker's discretion to conform to the principles of client empowerment is an important step in attaining these principles.

Finally, social workers can organize within the agency as an interest group advocating on behalf of their clients. Through such organization, social workers can provide mutual support to colleagues and reinforce shared values. More important, they can more effectively mobilize power resources to influence agency policies and procedures.

Making social service agencies more responsive to their clients necessitates, ultimately, changes at the social policy level. The point of such policy changes is to increase the clients' control over resources needed by the agency and to increase the availability of alternative sources for the services controlled by the agency. The transfer of power from the agency to the clients will require some drastic changes in the policies and the resultant structure of social service agencies. Such a transfer may require several approaches. (*a*) Give the clients greater control over the fiscal resources of the agency. Currently, clients have little say about the allocation of such resources to the agencies that serve them. By giving them control over such resources (e.g., through vouchers) they are transformed into an important interest group. (*b*) Organize clients into an advocacy group so that the agency will be required to interact with the clients as a collectivity rather than only as individuals. As a collectivity, clients can articulate common goals and be more effective in expressing their views and in negotiating with the agency. (*c*) Break up, when appropriate, the monopoly of the agency over services by creating alternative programs.

These strategies require social workers to engage in political activities that transcend the boundaries of their own agencies and professional specializations. The leadership role that social workers have taken in voter registration drives in the human services and in organizing clients to lobby for better services is a pertinent example. That leadership represents the commitment of the social work profession to social action. Such a commitment, often neglected in the rush of the profession to adopt the latest developments in clinical practice, must be reintegrated in social work practice because it is only through these political activities that the tension between agency goals, client needs, and professional values can be reduced.[35]

Conclusion

I have argued that social work practice theory tends to understate the importance of power as a key factor shaping the process and outcome of the client-worker relationship. Such a theoretical bias arises because of the underlying assumption that there is a compatibility of interests between the client and the worker. I have shown, however, that, once this assumption is removed, power emerges as an inherent element in social work practice. To understand and analyze its function I have proposed a power-dependence perspective that views social work practice as an exchange of resources between clients and workers; the terms of the exchange are determined by the respective power resources of the client and the worker. I have further proposed that social work practice theory must shift its emphasis from a person-centered practice to one that takes as its core activity the formulation of strategies to empower clients. The essence of these strategies is to create a balance of power between social service agencies and clients. These strategies call for redefining the role of the social worker, harnessing agency resources on behalf of clients, and, most important, reorganizing social service agencies. Bertha Reynolds, one of the great pioneers in social work practice, advocated client-controlled agencies as the means for achieving such a power balance. On the basis of her experience in the United Seamen's Service, she wrote:

> If this membership control seems shocking to some social workers who believe that they are responsible to nobody but their own conscience before God, it is useful to be reminded, as were the personal service workers at the National Maritime Union Hall, that in a social agency there is interposed between the caseworker and God a Board of Directors whose interests are more remote from those of the clients than are the interests of officials elected by their fellow members. . . . Responsibility of a caseworker to an organized group which is at once her board of directors and her clientele is, in part, a responsibility of knowing what the members want in the way of help. Being close to their daily lives, in an association with their own organization so that they feel free to say what they think, is an immense advantage.[36]

Social workers should follow the tradition of Bertha Reynolds by taking a leadership role in planning, mobilizing resources, and or-

482   Social Service Review

ganizing alternative social service agencies that are increasingly based
on the sharing of power between workers and clients. It is through
such a partnership that the profession will be able to retain its distinctive
identity and mobilize its constituencies to counter the attacks on the
welfare state.

Notes

1. Siebolt H. Freiswyk, Jon G. Allen, Donald B. Colson, Lola Faye Coyne, Glen
O. Gobbard, Leonard Horowitz, and Gavin Newsom, "Therapeutic Alliance: Its Place
as a Process and Outcome Variable in Dynamic Psychotherapy Research," *Journal of
Consulting and Clinical Psychology* 54 (February 1986): 32–38; David E. Orlinsky and
Kenneth I. Howard, "The Relation of Process to Outcome in Psychotherapy," in *Handbook
of Psychotherapy and Behavior Change*, ed. Sol Garfield and Allen Bergin, 2d ed. (New
York: John Wiley & Sons, 1978).
2. Carel B. Germain and Alex Gitterman, *The Life Model of Social Work Practice* (New
York: Free Press, 1980), p. 15.
3. Charles Garvin and Brett Seabury, *Interpersonal Practice in Social Work* (Englewood
Cliffs, N.J.: Prentice-Hall, Inc., 1984), p. 82.
4. Elliot Studt, "Worker-Client Authority Relationship in Social Work," *Social Work*
4 (January 1959): 18–28.
5. Sally E. Palmer, "Authority: An Essential Part of Practice," *Social Work* 28
(March–April 1983): 120–25.
6. David Heller, *Power in Therapeutic Practice* (New York: Human Sciences Press,
1985), p. 17.
7. Alan Pincus and Anne Minahan, *Social Work Practice: Mode and Method* (Itasca,
Ill.: F. E. Peacock, 1973); Sheila Feld and Norma Radin, *Social Psychology for Social
Work and the Mental Health Profession* (New York: Columbia University Press, 1982),
pp. 194–200.
8. James Coleman, *Power and the Structure of Society* (New York: W. W. Norton & Co.,
1974).
9. Nina Toren, "The Structure of Social Casework and Behavioral Change," *Journal
of Social Policy* 3 (1973): 341–52; Irwin Epstein and Kayla Conrad, "The Empirical
Limits of Social Work Professionalism," in *The Management of Human Services*, ed. Rosemary
C. Sarri and Yeheskel Hasenfeld (New York: Columbia University Press, 1978).
10. Yeheskel Hasenfeld, *Human Service Organizations* (Englewood Cliffs, N.J.: Prentice-
Hall, Inc., 1983).
11. Wendy R. Sherman and Stanley Wenocur, "Empowering Public Welfare Workers
through Mutual Support," *Social Work* 28 (September–October 1983): 375–79.
12. Harold Weissman, Irwin Epstein, and Andrea Savage, *Agency-based Social Work*
(Philadelphia: Temple University Press, 1983).
13. Ibid., p. 7.
14. Robert Emerson, "Power-Dependence Relations," *American Sociological Review* 27
(1962): 31–41.
15. Frank M. Loewenberg, *Fundamentals of Social Intervention*, 2d ed. (New York:
Columbia University Press, 1983), p. 138.
16. Garvin and Seabury (n. 3 above), p. 84.
17. Robert A. Scott, "The Selection of Clients by Social Welfare Agencies: The Case
of the Blind," *Social Problems* 14 (Winter 1967): 248–57.
18. Julius A. Roth, "Some Contingencies of the Moral Evaluation and Control of
Clientele: The Case of the Hospital Emergency Service," *American Journal of Sociology*
77 (March 1972): 839–56.
19. Bruce Link and B. Milcarek, "Selection Factors in the Dispensation of Therapy,"
Journal of Health and Social Behavior 21 (September 1980): 279–90.
20. Heller (n. 6 above), pp. 109–22.
21. By practice ideology I mean "formal systems of ideas that are held in great tenacity
and emotional investment, that have self-confirming features, and that are resistant to

change from objective rational reappraisal." See Robert Rapoport, *Community as a Doctor* (London: Tavistock Publications Ltd., 1960), p. 269.

22. Heller, pp. 151–57.

23. Herbert C. Kelman, "Compliance, Identification, and Internalization: Three Processes of Attitude Change," in *Basic Studies in Social Psychology*, ed. H. Proshansky and B. Seidenberg (New York: Holt, Rinehart & Winston, 1965).

24. Murray Milner, Jr., *Unequal Care* (New York: Columbia University Press, 1980).

25. Barry Kriesberg, Ira Schwartz, Gideon Fishman, Zvi Eisikovitz, Edna Guttman, and Karen Joe, *The Incarceration of Minority Youth* (Minneapolis: University of Minnesota, Hubert Humphrey Institute, 1986).

26. Rosemary C. Sarri, ed., *The Impact of Federal Policy Change on Working AFDC Women and Their Children* (Ann Arbor: University of Michigan, Institute for Social Research, 1984).

27. Jill D. Kagle and Charles D. Cowger, "Blaming the Victim: Implicit Agenda in Practice Research?" *Social Work* 29 (July–August 1984): 347–52.

28. Eileen Gambrill, *Casework: A Competency-based Approach* (Englewood Cliffs, N.J.: Prentice-Hall, Inc., 1983), pp. 205–6.

29. Ruth Middleman and Gale Goldberg, *Social Service Delivery: A Structural Approach* (New York: Columbia University Press, 1974), pp. 26–27.

30. Elaine B. Pinderhughes, "Empowerment for Our Clients and for Ourselves," *Social Casework* 64 (June 1983): 331–46.

31. Barbara B. Solomon, *Black Empowerment* (New York: Columbia University Press, 1976), p. 19.

32. John F. Longress and Eileen McLeod, "Consciousness Raising and Social Work Practice," *Social Casework* 61 (May 1980): 276.

33. See, e.g., Stephen M. Rose and Bruce L. Black, *Advocacy and Empowerment: Mental Health Care in the Community* (Boston: Routlege & Kegan Paul, 1985).

34. Joel F. Handler, *Protecting the Social Service Client: Legal and Structural Controls on Official Discretion* (New York: Academic Press, 1979).

35. Ann Withorn, *Serving the People: Social Services and Social Change* (New York: Columbia University Press, 1984).

36. Bertha C. Reynolds, *Social Work and Social Living* (New York: Citadel Press, 1951), pp. 59–60.

Part IV
Ethical Issues Regarding the
Allocation of Scarce Resources

[13]

The Artificial Duties of Contemporary Professionals

The *Social Service Review* Lecture

Russell Hardin
University of Chicago

Professional ethics in the era of the mass production of welfare has become increasingly the ethics of role holders in institutions. It is not a collection of natural duties as it has traditionally been conceived and as it typically still is framed in contemporary professional codes of ethics. Such codes often include injunctions to the individual professional to do more than he or she could do under the constraints of public policies on, for example, welfare delivery or health care. Indeed, what the individual ought to do, under these policies, may conflict with what current professional ethics codes seem to require.

In "The Adventure of the Abbey Grange," Sherlock Holmes explains to Dr. Watson why he does not share his clues with Inspector Stanley Hopkins: "You must look at it this way: what I know is unofficial, what he knows is official. I have the right to private judgment, but he has none. He must disclose all, or he is a traitor to his service. In a doubtful case I would not put him in so painful a position, and so I reserve my information until my own mind is clear upon the matter."[1] Holmes identifies a difference between what one can reasonably call the ethics of Holmes and the ethics of Hopkins in their very different institutional roles. Despite our perhaps sentimental attachment to Holmes, contemporary professionals should have greater sympathy for Hopkins.

They may like the romantic Holmes, but their lives are more like that of the professional Hopkins.

The difference that Holmes grasps underlies a strong view of professional ethics in an era of mass production of welfare, a view that I wish to articulate. I will not be concerned with what specific ethical principles should govern the practice of social work, law, medicine, or whatever. Instead, I will be concerned with how to ground such principles in actual practice. As a utilitarian, I believe the chief justification of ethical principles is their contribution to human welfare. But even if one is not a utilitarian, one must be concerned with the way in which professional ethics depends on what is possible. As moral theorists of almost all stripes would say, ought implies can. If it is impossible for you to do something, it cannot be true that you ought to do it. I will return to this concern with possibility.

There are two rough ways we may conceive of society. (1) We are just a lot of individuals interacting with each other. Government and other institutions may intervene to make things go better by enabling us to interact productively. Still, it is individuals who are responsible for their lives and their interactions with others. Morality, then, might be seen as strictly an individual problem. If there is a set of requirements on how you ought to behave, that same set also says how I ought to behave. The only differences between us are in what we can do. Professionals have more demanding duties than others only because they have greater abilities of various kinds. (2) Society is a joint enterprise in which roles and interactions are created, both unintentionally and deliberately. Individuals enter these roles, which partly determine the content and the value of their interactions with others. Morality might be seen as partly, even largely, a matter of institutional determination. That is not to say that institutions can simply determine what is moral and what is not, but rather that what is moral action by a particular individual may depend on the nature of that individual's role.

Much of traditional ethics in general and much, even most, of what is called professional ethics seems to be fitted to the first view. I will show how professional ethics differs if we hold the second view. I also wish to argue that, for contemporary practice in many professions, we must essentially hold the second view.

Duties: Natural and Artificial

Much of the individual moral life in social contexts has traditionally been governed by what are called natural duties. I have a natural duty to help you out of the pond in which you seem to be drowning if I can. That the duty is natural is seen partly in the condition "if I can," partly in the easy stipulation of what I must do to bring about a good result. One need not have a very complicated understanding of one's relationships in the world to know one's natural duties. One can simply consider the direct effects of one's own actions on the welfare of relevant others.

There are many duties that are not natural in this sense. One of the striking facts of modern life is that the weight of natural duties seems to be much less than in earlier times. Increasingly, our duties are structured by contingent institutional arrangements, by social expectations and organizations. Institutions can take an overview of our interactions and regulate our behaviors in ways that benefit us, in a sense, only indirectly. We depend overwhelmingly on institutional arrangements for large areas of our lives, whether they be in the background or at the very center of our daily lives. We may complain about that fact and about many of the ways in which our states intrude in our lives, but most of us could not consistently claim that we would prefer to depend on individual commitments without mediating institutions.

Consider these changes from another perspective, the perspective of what they mean for our own individual lives as actors rather than as beneficiaries of the state and its institutions. Most of us still have duties within families that may fit the rubric of natural duties. But much time in our lives is spent in organizations or is governed by organizations. For example, many of the duties that I have are duties that derive from the peculiar form that universities have taken and even from the specific form of my own university. Those duties have been changing in content since I entered my first university appointment less than 20 years ago. In the past few years my university has considered the adoption of new policies on conflict of interest and sexual harassment. In both cases, the policies make explicit certain duties that faculty members have that they might reasonably have claimed not to have had previously.

The Scottish philosopher David Hume calls these contingent, institutionally derived duties artificial.[2] They are not inherent in the nature of human beings. They are created by us. Many of the codes adopted by various organizations to govern their members are artificial. To say they are artificial in Hume's sense is not to say that they are not good. But it does suggest that they could have been other than what they are. For example, the American legal code is different from the Mexican, Swedish, and Indian legal codes. Yet all of these might be quite good codes in that they all produce good results and make social life congenial and rewarding.

Until recent times, legal codes were often defended as derived from natural principles. Indeed, they have often been religious codes, as are the legal codes of Iran and Saudi Arabia in large part today. The separation has been a long and sometimes hard-fought process. The urge to justify principles for behavior with claims of their natural rightness is seemingly powerful.

Perhaps the oldest secular code of ethics is a professional code. The Hippocratic oath, which dates from about the end of the fifth century B.C., was supposed to govern the relations of doctors and their patients.[3] Although it has been modernized, that oath is still recognized as the professional code of medical doctors today. It is not unlike many other professional codes of more modern vintage, such as codes for social workers and lawyers. Codes for professionals commonly include many principles whose purpose is to uphold the prerogatives of the profession itself. For example, after a general promise to keep the oath, the Hippocratic oath opens with a promise to respect one's master—it's clear who wrote the oath. The codes go on, of course, to include constraints on the professional's dealings with clients, with, for example, proscriptions on sexual misconduct in the professional-client relationship.

Apart from their concern with intraprofessional issues, these codes often read as though the professional's duties toward clients were natural duties. The Hippocratic oath is a list of such duties that supposedly apply to all doctors in their one-on-one relationships to their patients. Yet the biggest issues in medical ethics today do not concern such relationships. Many of these issues have to do with policies on, for example, abortion, care for severely compromised newborns, euthanasia, and other difficult problems. Many have to do with allocation of resources. Almost all are new issues that involve other than one-on-one doctor-patient relationships.

Contemporary Practice

What has changed since Hippocrates? Obviously, the possibilities of medicine have changed dramatically. Medical intervention now takes place on a scale that would stymie the imagination of people living only a century ago. Similar claims apply to many other professions, including some that did not exist much before this century. Against this view, one might suppose that many professions, such as social welfare and law, are very different from medicine, that changes in professional roles in social welfare and law do not mimic those of medicine. But consider the similarities.

Medical care has become high tech, with extraordinarily expensive possibilities for intervention. But the changes in medicine are institutional as well as scientific and technological. Many of the possibilities for medical intervention require vast institutional structures for their application. They require teamwork and coordination of many specialists and organizations. Moreover, it is primarily the use of large hospitals that drives up the cost of contemporary medical care. It is not simply that we have the medical know-how to spend far more on health care than ever before; we also have the institutional capacity necessary to make use of our know-how. Indeed, even that know-how is, as never before, inherently institutional. There is no individual who knows enough to take care of one's complex disease. It is only vast teams of specialists and auxiliary technical personnel who collectively have sufficient knowledge. Without organization much of the know-how would not exist, and it would be impossible to put most of what did exist to effective use.

In a related but functionally quite different way, social welfare programs depend on the growth of modern organizational capacities. They often require massive organization merely for the delivery of services. They also require substantial organization to acquire relevant information about target populations. Finally, they require substantial expenditures of public funds. The required funds come from general tax collections.

Even the function of individual charity has been transformed into state welfare programs. Two centuries ago the notion of charity was central to moral theory and moral debate. Today it is more a matter for tax law than for moral theory. This happened only because the state became better able to organize what one might call the wholesale delivery of charity. There have, of course, also been debates over the proper scale of such charity. Opponents typically argue against extensive aid on the ground that it induces dependence rather than self-reliance. They also note that there are other ways to spend the money, ways that they prefer.

What difference do such changes make for professional ethics? The purpose of various professions is to serve a relevant clientele, chiefly to improve their health, well-being, or welfare. Much of the ethical code of a profession is directed at insuring that the client's welfare is served, in part by prohibiting actions or practices that would harm the client and in part by requiring actions or practices that would benefit the client. In the jargon of moral theory, such codes are consequentialist. That is, they are directed at the consequences of actions rather than at the actions per se. What makes an action prohibited is that it harms a client. What makes an action required is that it benefits a client in a way that the professional is especially qualified to accomplish.

What a doctor ought to do is what that doctor can do to restore my health. No doctor can do much, if anything, about my cancer or my congestive heart failure except in organized concert with many others working directly or indirectly on my problem. If my problem is to be addressed successfully, there must be coordinated teams of professionals. They will, of course, also be coordinated to take up your problems and those of many others. Oddly, they would not likely be any good for me if they were not organized for many others. But this means that they are inherently burdened with a conflict. They cannot serve all comers if demand exceeds their capacity.

In one way or another, we pay for the efforts of professionals, we determine the scale of those efforts, and, in consequence, we determine the conflict among ourselves in our demands for their services. We determine the structure of their organization and, therefore, what kinds of positions there ought to be for them to fill. We may not determine these things directly. Rather,the roles of the relevant professionals are functionally determined by what achieves the purpose we want, the purpose of health care up to some level. The individual professional in this scheme no longer has merely natural duties. A doctor in a hospital has institutional duties that are, in Hume's sense, artificially created.

There are still important aspects of the doctor-patient relationship that carry over from the past and that involve individual moral norms or natural duties. For example, doctors should not use their role to take advantage of patients in various ways. This norm is straightforwardly based in direct effects of what a doctor might do that would cause harm without offsetting benefits. A doctor's duty under the original Hippocratic oath not to assault a patient sexually is no different from my duty not to assault anyone sexually. It is merely a more urgent concern because the doctor may more often be in a peculiarly opportune position to assault people. Professional codes may, however, go even further than to impose this natural duty. Contemporary doctors and social workers are altogether prohibited from engaging in sexual relations with their patients or clients.

Surely, however, concern with professional ethics today goes beyond such matters as sexual assault or seduction by those in professionally privileged positions. Such matters may be of no concern in the vast majority of professional-client relationships. The more common ethical problems are essentially ramifications of public and institutional policies. They are allocation decisions. How much care should this client or patient receive? Once, the answer to that question was almost purely the technical question of what care would be beneficial. Now it is necessarily in part a question of how limited resources are going to be used. We may take some of those decisions out of the hands of individual professionals by making public or institutional policies. For example, we may simply deny any organ transplant for patients suffering from certain complications or over a set age. No individual doctor may be able to override that policy. Or we may restrict the level of support that an impoverished mother may receive for each of her children and stipulate that no case-specific considerations can override that policy.

But many of these allocation decisions are left to professional discretion. Hence, a major role of doctors today is to mediate the conflict between society and the patient. This conflict of interest is defined by the patient's needs for care in a given moment and cost and other constraints imposed by the larger society, often in the form of explicit public policies or in the form of perceived social norms concerning, for example, who is deserving.[4]

Professionals may cope with such constraints, but they cannot ignore them. For example, doctors may bond with their patients, becoming advocates for the patients in getting hospitals, insurers, and other health care organizations to permit the extension of greater care, or they may identify with their institutional employers to defend them against the demands of patients. In either case, the doctor cannot simply do what the Hippocratic oath requires: "I will use my power to help the sick to the best of my ability and judgement."[5] The doctor's judgment is insufficient authority to determine the course of treatment. Various institutions often override that determination.

A young resident commented: "We are social agents. Nobody told me that. What I really resent is that in the face of these constraints we are still told we have to follow the Hippocratic oath." Of his own allocational decisions, he says, "You'd feel guilty as though it were your fault."[6] Without intending to, the physician has become a gatekeeper. As one doctor puts it: "There are many situations where resources are sufficiently short so that there must be decisions made as to who is treated. Given that circumstance, the physician, in order to live with himself and to sleep well at night, has to look at the arguments for not treating a patient. And there are always some—social, medical, whatever. In many instances he heightens, sharpens or brings into focus the negative component in order to make himself and the patient comfortable about not going forward."[7] Social workers must often share this doctor's experience.

In health care, there is little doubt that we have reached the possibility of demand exceeding even potential capacity. The cost of medical care in the United States has surpassed 11 percent of gross domestic product (GDP). If doctors did everything that could be expected to be beneficial in every case, costs of medical care might soon exceed the entire GDP. That will surely not be our choice, nor should it be. We would have to sacrifice living well for staying alive. If the point of the system is to make us better off, we can wonder whether spending less would make us even better off. Social welfare costs could not, even in principle, exceed the GDP in reasonably good economic times in market economies. Hence, social welfare programs need not be limited by massive fiscal constraints. But they have arguably come up against political constraints that tie the hands of social welfare professionals.

Artificial Duties   535

There may be no welfare profession that has more clearly faced the problem of massive social constraints than has the American social work profession. The profession grew out of private charitable efforts and the commitment of a few universities to educate professional social workers. But despite the growth of private practice, the role of many social workers has been to work within institutions under institutional policies and constraints. This is especially true over the past 2 or 3 decades. More generally, much of the program of social work is to change behaviors in ways that are socially, not merely medically, beneficial. This naturally raises value issues in determining what is good for clients. Doctors have been able to frame their task as much more nearly univocal, as the improvement of health. Lawyers look to a relatively single concern for their clients. There is inherently much more in dispute when a social worker decides what is best for a client, even without concern for the trade-offs of using resources for one client and not for another. Every social worker involved in public welfare programs must often face the dilemma of serving as an agent of the state as well as of the client.[8] This is a burden that doctors have only recently come to bear.

Does this mean the professional is a cost-benefit analyst, judging each case by quasi-economic criteria? No. It is not for the professional to draw the conclusion on what to do in a given case from an analysis of costs and benefits per se. Rather, the professional often merely follows a hospital, insurance company, or government policy in deciding where to draw the line on some treatment or service. But the professional is then genuinely a social agent, not the patient's agent. Many doctors have heatedly rejected this claim. They insist the doctor is still the patient's agent.

The codes of ethics of doctors and of social workers seemingly represent these doctors' views. "The Principles of Medical Ethics" of the American Medical Association (AMA) is a very long document, including eight sections of "opinions" on various aspects of medical practice. The longest section of opinions is section 2, on "Social Policy Issues." All that this long section has to say about the doctor's role in allocation decisions is essentially negative, that the doctor has no role:

A physician has a duty to do all that he can for the benefit of his individual patient. To expect a physician when treating a patient to make rationing decisions based on governmental or other external priorities in the allocation of scarce health resources creates an undesirable conflict with the primary responsibility of the physician to his patient. [Sec. 2.03, "Allocation of Health Resources"]

While physicians should be conscious of costs and not provide or prescribe unnecessary services or ancillary facilities, social policy expects that concern

536   Social Service Review

for the care the patient receives will be the physician's first consideration. [Sec. 2.09, "Costs"]

In the section on "Hospital Relations," there is this further negative constraint:

In a situation where the economic interests of the hospital are in conflict with patient welfare, patient welfare takes priority. [Sec. 4.04, "Economic Incentives and Levels of Care"][9]

The "Code of Ethics" of the National Association of Social Workers, which is much shorter but is still several pages long, includes no mention of allocational responsibilities except by implication from its positive charges, which are framed as though they were natural duties:

The social worker should serve clients with devotion, loyalty, determination, and the maximum application of professional skill and competence. [II.F.1]

The social worker should act to ensure that all persons have access to the resources, services, and opportunities which they require. [VI.P.2][10]

These ethical restrictions on doctors and social workers are entirely in the form of positive duties toward individual patients or clients, in keeping with the tradition of the Hippocratic oath. They reject consideration of larger social concerns that might justify restriction of services to individuals. We know that doctors commonly practice triage when demand outruns the supply of medical care. Most of us would approve that policy. But it is a wholly consequentialist policy that does not fit with the strictly hortatory charges of the AMA's code of ethics. Yet, situations that call for triage or some variant may be the norm. Social workers in government agencies also practice something like triage when their limited resources are stretched by demands, as they often are.[11] This is not surprising. In everything we do that involves substantial resources and talent, we make trade-offs between various objectives.

When we must decide on trade-offs, our choices cannot be dictated by natural duties of the kinds found in codes of professional ethics. It can be obvious what to do, as it must be for action under the command of a natural duty, only if there are no complex trade-offs. It is a dogma of modern economics that there are always complex trade-offs.

Cost-benefit analysis suggests that one can compare the costs and benefits of an action and then conclude for or against it. Among the most important costs are the opportunity costs of actions. If I go to a lecture this afternoon, I do not get other things done. Should I go to the lecture? It depends partly on what other things I might do instead.

There is no reason to suppose that a professional is especially able to weigh all the relevant opportunity costs of professional interventions. Professional expertise is limited to the professional domain. For example, a social worker or doctor may be able to say that some expenditure on care for me will likely be less beneficial than an equal expenditure on care for you—perhaps because I am not in need of much care or perhaps because no care would do me much good. But the choices we have to make are about opportunity costs of other kinds as well, such as spending our resources on education, leisure, and consumption as well as social welfare and medicine.[12] The social worker or doctor may be no more qualified to judge these trade-offs than is the typical citizen.

If we want to make policy choices about the larger range of opportunity costs associated with the work of the caring professions, we may have to enlist relevant professionals to share their partial expertise in the task. And, of course, they may participate as citizens. But their more direct role will be as agents of the larger society in carrying out various policies. A code of professional ethics that does not seriously address that role is increasingly derelict. Unfortunately, the role of professionals as social agents and not merely agents for their clients may be a hard political issue for a professional body. The intern who discovered that he was a social agent was willing to accept that role because he understood the conditions of medical practice in our time. He merely resented being indoctrinated beforehand in the contrary principle of the Hippocratic oath. His professional body is apparently not yet willing to recognize that the Hippocratic principle cannot apply.

Ought, Can, and the Individual Professional

Let us return to the perspective of individual professionals, which is the perspective of the overwhelming body of official doctrine on professional ethics. Individual practitioners may feel that the contemporary demands—to be agents of the larger society—are a painful distortion of their commitments to their professions. For many professionals, the act of professing is grounded in a moral commitment. This sense of commitment is surely valuable to their clients. Can we make this commitment consistent with social constraints of various opportunity costs?

Recall the moral theorist's principle: Ought implies can. If it is impossible for me to do x, it cannot be true that I ought to do x, or that I do wrong if I do not do x. For example, if someone is drowning 100 yards from shore and I cannot swim, it cannot be true that I ought to swim out to rescue the person. Perhaps you ought to because you can swim very well and are strong enough to bring the person back without great risk to yourself. Or perhaps you ought to because you are a lifeguard and you have signed on for this duty.

Professional social workers and doctors are not like an idle passerby who happens to see someone floundering in the lake. As committed professionals, what can they do? They probably cannot do anything even vaguely like what the grandiose rule of the social work profession requires with its injunction to "act to ensure that all persons have access to the resources, services, and opportunities which they require." It is not even clear what this could mean without reading a lot into it, including much of the foregoing discussion of opportunity costs. No one professional could do much toward ensuring that all persons have access to what they require. Nor is there any simple sense in the notion of what people require. Similarly, the physician's "duty to do all that he can for the benefit of his individual patient" is glib and uninformative.

These injunctions can finally be seen as little more than exaggerated exhortations, not ethical requirements. What one can do as a professional is to provide care within reasonable limits. Some of those are limits of personal energy, ability, and time. But some of the limits are social constraints. The resident who became angry while talking about the misfit between Hippocratic injunctions of natural duties and the actual practice of medicine in a large hospital called his profession's code of ethics "the hypocritic oath."

The fundamental issue for individual professionals is that they are mediators between their clients' or patients' needs and social constraints imposed by policy. This conflict of interests is one between each client and the larger society, not between the professional and the client. But it is mediated through the professional. It is the social worker or the doctor who faces the burden of saying no when a needed service or procedure is contrary to policy. It may be contrary because we simply refuse to supply that kind of service, because we prefer to concentrate on prevention rather than later remedy, or because we choose to restrict overall costs.

Perhaps we will all be better served if professionals bond with their clients in this conflict while nevertheless submitting to policy. Part of what we are doing when we set limits on expenditures for various kinds of care is setting limits on what individual professionals may do at our expense. We cannot set our limits in general the way a professional might set limits in a particular case. We cannot craft the limits to the case. We can only crudely fit them. We replace the tailor with mass production. But because there are genuine opportunities for decisions on particular cases, we may expect individual professionals with their specific knowledge in given cases to act with some discretion, to bond with the client and buck the system. Alas, this is not the kind of autonomy that many professionals have aspired to and valued. They have typically thought of their roles as autonomous, constrained only by the science they bring to bear on the singular value they seek to promote.

Professional Ethics in a Political Society

So far I have described contemporary professional practice. Can it be justified? I think it can, at least in principle. Because health care and social welfare delivery without big institutions would be woefully inadequate, we should want such institutional arrangements if we want health care and social welfare delivery. But if we are to provide care with big institutions and if we are to provide it according to politically accepted principles, we will want the agents within those institutions to work according to what makes the institutions work best. This provides a justification for assigning individual duties within the institution.[13] That is, of course, why we call their duties artificial rather than natural. But those duties are no less morally justified than are duties that we may still think of as natural. Indeed, the artificial duties of contemporary welfare institutions override the former natural duties of traditional professions to the extent that the new institutional ways of delivering welfare should displace the old one-on-one ways of delivering much of it.

If our ethical requirements are largely determined by our roles in relevant institutions, then they are largely determined by political decisions about what those institutions should be and do. In principle, most of us would not argue with that fact. We would generally agree that policies on welfare should be determined by the polity. For one thing, a system in which individual professionals determined how much public money should be spent on each case might be bankrupt immediately, unable to deliver any services over the longer run. Moreover, it would be a highly inegalitarian and self-contradictory system.

The burden for much of what we want to achieve must be placed on the larger society rather than on each of us as individuals. I may have the resources to help someone in dire need, and perhaps I ought to do so. Our society has the resources to help many people in dire need. Should it do so? Unfortunately, this is not an easy question to answer. A society or a group is not like an individual in all relevant respects. It is a fallacy—the fallacy of composition—to suppose that a society can act on its resources the way an individual can.

What if the polity is mean and selfishly opposed to any but a minimal welfare program? What then are the ethics of the professional? Those parts of the profession's ethics that can sensibly be seen as natural duties, such as prohibitions on taking sexual advantage of clients, still apply fully. But those parts that derive from particularities of the professional's role may change. An individual professional is left with

540 Social Service Review

the usual, more-or-less natural duty to work for better policies, a duty shared by all, although the professional may have special knowledge that strengthens the demands of the duty. But the bottom line may simply be that individual professionals cannot make much difference in what the policies are. That may sound like pessimism, but one should be reluctant to conclude too quickly that it is. There is one sense in which it is a matter of great optimism. None of us would wish to live in a society in which large numbers of people could make the kinds of differences they would make if they could.

Note that the argument for the dependence of professional ethics on political decisions about levels and kinds of service depends on the justifiability of creating the institutions in the first place. If we create harmful institutions, or even irrelevant institutions, there can be no indirect inference to the morality of following the requirements of the roles within them. Those who think welfare delivery and good health care are morally justified in our era must conclude that professional duties are to be inferred from relevant institutional structures and their purposes. To a large extent, what social welfare workers and doctors ought to do as professionals has become a matter of policy, of law, not of individual morality. Actual practice seems to have adapted to this change from the way things were in the time of Hippocrates. The ethics codes of the professions and the articulate ethical views of many professionals, however, are still given to hortatory exaggeration and to the neglect of actual institutional roles and constraints.

There are real costs to new professionals from a code that so neglects the greatest range of actual cases of difficult moral choices they will face on the job. They may often be angry at their position, and they may often, like the young resident I quoted earlier, feel guilty for their inability to do what they had once conceived as their moral commitment. Not only will they be unable to fulfill the grandiose principles of their ethics codes, but they will typically have no categories to apply to the difficult moral choices they have to make. Social workers may have advantages over other welfare professionals in that their profession did not long precede the rise of state welfare programs. Hence, social welfare workers have often debated to what extent their role is one of agents of the state or of its policies. Still, oddly, that debate seems not to have entered the profession's code of ethics.

In addition to their direct concern with welfare, the welfare professions must be concerned with the fairness of their services and with making reasonable trade-offs between competing, honorable ends. Fairness requires regularization. It requires a profession with institutionally defined as well as scientifically determined roles. There was a time when professionals were like Sherlock Holmes: They were entitled to keep their own judgments because they were not part of a larger social organization or purpose. Increasingly they have become like Inspector

Hopkins: If they keep their own judgments, they may be traitors to their professions.

Notes

This is the fourteenth *Social Service Review* lecture delivered at the School of Social Service Administration, the University of Chicago, April 26, 1990.

1. Arthur Conan Doyle, "The Adventure of the Abbey Grange," in *The Annotated Sherlock Holmes,* ed. William S. Baring-Gould (New York: Clarkson N. Potter, 1967), 2:491–507, quote on 504.

2. David Hume, *A Treatise of Human Nature* (any edition; first published, London: John Noon & Thomas Longman, 1739–40), bk. 3, esp. pts. 1 and 2.

3. The Babylonian Code of Hammurabi, set down during the eighteenth century B.C., gave extensive, detailed rules for the practice of medicine. But this was a legal, not an ethical, code that prescribed sometimes harsh penalties for medical failures.

4. See, e.g., Laura A. Schmidt, "Problem Drinkers and the Welfare Bureaucracy," *Social Service Review* 64 (September 1990): 390–406.

5. From the Hippocratic oath, in *Hippocratic Writings,* ed. G. E. R. Lloyd (1950; reprint, Harmondsworth: Penguin, 1983), p. 67.

6. In conversation, November 2, 1989, at the University of Chicago.

7. Quoted in Henry Aaron and William B. Schwartz, "Rationing Health Care: The Choice before Us," *Science* 247 (January 26, 1990): 418–22.

8. See, e.g., Joel F. Handler, *The Coercive Social Worker: British Lessons for American Social Services* (Chicago: Rand McNally, 1973).

9. "Principles of Medical Ethics and Current Opinions of the Council on Ethical and Judicial Affairs—1989," in *Codes of Professional Responsibility,* 2d ed., ed. Rena A. Gorlin (Washington, D.C.: Bureau of National Affairs, 1990), pp. 189–221, quotes on pp. 193, 196, 204. Gorlin's volume is a valuable collection of 43 current professional codes of ethics.

10. "Code of Ethics" of the National Association of Social Workers, in Gorlin, ed. (n. 9 above), pp. 269–75, quotes on pp. 271, 274.

11. See Handler (n. 8 above), pp. 139–41.

12. Moreover, we may discover or decide that preventive devices are more beneficial to us than are later interventions. Then, in order to secure the success of a policy of prevention, we may have to enforce the incentive for individuals and professionals to use preventive measures by prohibiting later interventions. This is an old argument against certain welfare programs: If we give food or money to street beggars, we encourage them to continue as beggars rather than to seek work. In child welfare cases, the problem of preventive incentives is often compounded by the fact that the chief person to be strategically motivated is a parent rather than the child who is actually at risk.

13. Russell Hardin, *Morality within the Limits of Reason* (Chicago: University of Chicago Press, 1988), pp. 100–105.

[14]

Phantom Welfare: Public Relief for Corporate America

Daniel D. Huff and David A. Johnson

This article describes and quantifies the major types of federal subsidies to American businesses. These subsidies, although they do not strictly conform to conventional definitions of welfare, are important policies that directly affect more traditional welfare programs. Representing a federal expenditure in excess of $150 billion a year, the policies responsible for this "phantom welfare state" represent a major redistribution of wealth that partially accounts for the growing gap between the rich and the poor. Additionally, these programs also compete with more traditional welfare programs for scarce federal dollars. The implications of these "phantom welfare" programs for the traditional welfare state are discussed.

British sociologist Richard Titmus (1965) exhorted students of welfare policy to broaden their definition of social welfare to include more than programs designed for the poor population. Some policy analysts in social work have advocated for a broad definition of social welfare, one that includes redistributive schemes such as business subsidies (Abramovitz, 1983; Rein, 1977). In spite of this urging, few attempts have been made to describe and quantify the profusion of programs, subsidies, and other devices used to redistribute income to the U.S. business community.

Although the "phantom welfare state" for business may not neatly fit into conventional definitions of social welfare, knowledge of these programs is important to social workers for a number of reasons. First, continued avoidance of nonpoverty welfare programs puts social work in a poor position from which to advocate for fundamental reform of current budget priorities. The dollars shunted into corporate welfare schemes have diverted billions of dollars that might have been more reasonably spent on programs that benefit the poor. Tullock (1983) estimated that if corporate welfare dollars were distributed to the poorest 10 percent of U.S. families, each family would receive an additional yearly income of $47,000.

Second, the corporate welfare system is at least partly responsible for the growing economic imbalance between the poor and rich populations that accelerated during the 1980s. The poorest segments of the United States now receive a smaller share of national income than at any time since the late 1940s (Levy, 1987). This imbalance trend helps explain why in the past decade the United States is losing the battle against poverty even with large social welfare budgets.

Third, the nation cannot continue to ignore this fiscal colossus, which is estimated by some analysts as totalling more than $500 billion a year (Anton, 1989). The phantom welfare state represents a vast redistribution of U.S. national wealth and is simply too large to ignore during a period when traditional welfare programs for the poor population are under constant attack.

Corporate Welfare

Five major vehicles are used to distribute benefits from various federal sources to U.S. businesses: (1) direct expenditures, (2) credit subsidies, (3) tax expenditures, (4) subsidized services, and (5) trade restrictions (Table 1).

Direct Expenditures

The simplest and most straightforward of all corporate welfare vehicles are those that send money. Businesses from airlines to gold mines receive direct expenditures. The largest single recipient of this type of aid is the agriculture industry, which receives subsidies from the

Table 1

Government Spending for Corporate Welfare in the 1980s

Type	Amount ($ billions)
Direct expenditures[a]	17
Credit subsidies[b]	15
Tax expenditures[c]	79
Subsidized services[a,d]	10
Trade restrictions[e]	60
Total	181

[a]SOURCE: Congressional Budget Office. (1984). *Federal support of U.S. business*. Washington, DC: U.S. Government Printing Office.

[b]SOURCE: Congressional Budget Office. (1989). *Special analysis of the 1990 budget*. Washington, DC: U.S. Government Printing Office.

[c]SOURCE: Peachman, J. (1987). *Federal tax policy*. Washington, DC: Brookings Institution.

[d]SOURCE: Culhane, P. (1981). *Public land politics*. Baltimore: Johns Hopkins University Press.

[e]SOURCE: Consumers for World Trade. (1989). *The economic effects of significant import restraints* (statement before the International Trade Commission investigation). Washington, DC: Author.

Commodity Credit Corporation (CCC). The CCC provides farmers with a guaranteed minimum income, paying the difference between the market price and the target price, or guaranteed price, of selected commodities. These payments totaled more than $11 billion in 1988 (Office of Management and Budget, 1989).

Another major recipient group for direct expenditures are local industrial interests that receive funds through Community Development Block Grants and Economic Development Assistance, programs that provide funds to stimulate local economies. Although not all the funds funneled through these programs go to private interests, the Congressional Budget Office (1984) estimated that almost $2 billion a year goes to local industries.

Many businesses receive federal support through research and development activities. The energy industry accepts about $2 billion annually for such purposes, agricultural interests receive $1 billion, and airlines receive $1 billion (Congressional Budget Office, 1984). The maritime industry receives direct subsidies that average $60,000 per sea-going billet, totaling about $350 million a year. These funds are used to maintain the merchant marine fleet in the face of cheaper foreign competition (Reischauer, 1982).

The total direct expenditures devoted to support U.S. businesses amount to $7 billion a year (Congressional Budget Office, 1984).

Credit Subsidies

A more complex set of programs extend myriad federal credit subsidies to many commercial pursuits. In 1985 all federally sponsored credit totaled more than $1 trillion (Bosworth, Curron, & Rhyne, 1987). The world of government-subsidized credit is an intricate maze of programs, each with its own methods and subsidy levels. In some instances the government supplies the total loan at below-market interest rates. In other instances the government relies on the traditional capital markets, providing a subsidy through guaranteeing the loan. Individual programs also differ in the amount of subsidy they provide, with some extending loans at near-market rates and others providing loans at less than half the market value (Office of Management and Budget, 1989). The loan guarantee programs dispense multiple subsidies that provide investors with a source of credit and that guarantee a profit to the banks while the government assumes all the risks.

About one-half of all federal credit subsidies funnel through the Rural Electrification Administration and are used to finance electrical power plants, chiefly nuclear plants (Congressional Budget Office, 1984). Two billion dollars in credit subsidies are earmarked for agricultural interests through a system that provides loans to farmers on which they then default if crop prices fall below the loan value (Congressional Budget Office, 1984).

U.S. manufacturers receive substantial subsidies through the credit programs of the Export-Import (EXIM) Bank, which extends low-interest loans to foreign governments that wish to purchase U.S. equipment and goods but that lack the economic or political stability to qualify for conventional loans. The experts differ on just how much subsidy is in these arrangements. Critics have charged the EXIM Bank with using creative accounting methods and claim the bank is losing about $2 billion a year (Gannon, 1989).

The Bush administration has estimated that the subsidies inherent in overall federal credit activities total more than $15 billion a year (Office of Management and Budget, 1989).

Tax Expenditures

The Internal Revenue Service provides subsidies to businesses through tax exemptions and deductions. The 1990 budget listed them under the nomenclature of "tax expenditures." Although one goal for the Tax Reform Act of 1986 was the elimination of tax breaks, they continue to provide liberal subsidies to U.S. businesses. The accelerated depreciation allowance, which allows the depreciation of buildings, machinery, and other equipment at rates greater than their actual deterioration, provided more than $23 billion in subsidies in fiscal year 1988. Investment credits, often criticized for encouraging U.S. corporations to invest in machines that displace workers, were worth another $11 billion the same year (Peachman, 1987).

One of the advantages enjoyed by businesses that receive government subsidies via the tax system is that the subsidy is obscure and public scrutiny, such an important aspect of traditional welfare, is difficult. Industrial Development Bonds (IDBs) are a good example of this. Since the 1930s, states have been able to issue bonds that are exempt from federal taxes and as a consequence entice lenders to charge lower interest rates (Congressional Budget Office, 1984). These IDBs are a subsidy for everyone involved. The borrower can obtain lower than normal interest rates, the lender receives lower tax rates on his profits, and the financial institutions receive participation fees (Congressional Budget Office, 1984).

Although many IDBs have financed worthwhile projects, many others have underwritten more controversial activities. The Congressional Budget Office found IDBs were used to finance private golf courses, restaurants, and even a topless nightclub (Richardson, 1981). The Tax Reform Act of 1986 restricted the size of IDB transactions, but the cost of this subsidy was still more than $3 billion in fiscal year 1990 (Office of Management and Budget, 1989).

The largest single tax loophole for U.S. businesses is the accelerated depreciation allowance, worth $26 billion a year, followed by the investment credit deduction, worth another $11 billion per year. Tax expenditures for corporate America totaled more than $79 billion in fiscal year 1988 (Peachman, 1988).

Federal tax expenditures are only part of the total tax subsidy picture. State and local authorities offer an array of tax breaks to businesses located within their borders. Although their diversity and jurisdictional intricacies make it difficult to calculate their value, it is known that those subsidies are worth billions of dollars (Vaughan, 1979). What makes many state and local tax expenditures so curious is that although their purpose is to encourage the relocation of new industries, no evidence exists that they do in fact cause such desirable migration. Furthermore, because virtually every state now offers what amounts to similar tax packages, it has become a zero sum game, with no single state or area enjoying any real advantage (Leonard, 1988).

Subsidized Services

The federal government provides a mixture of services to a diverse collection of businesses at rates below true costs (Congressional Budget Office, 1984). The water transportation industry receives major assistance in the maintenance and administration of coastal harbors and inland waterways. Typical fees for these services are less than half the actual costs, representing an annual subsidy of about $500 million (Congressional Budget Office, 1984).

Another water-associated subsidy is extended to western irrigators. Benefits from federal water projects include not only larger profits from the additional production of crops but also enhanced land values resulting from the transformation of dry acreage into more prolific irrigated farms. In spite of legislation demanding that the recipients of federal water projects pay their own way, most are supported by a 90 percent subsidy: For every dollar spent by the government to provide irrigation water, the farmer pays 10 cents (U.S. General Accounting Office, 1981). Federal irrigation projects constitute a $1 billion a year subsidy to select western growers (Fitzgerald, 1988).

Many western ranchers benefit also from access to government grazing lands. Access to these lands is so much a part of western custom that "grazing rights" are usually considered a part of a ranch's assets (Culhane, 1981). The actual amount of subsidy fluctuates from region to region, but typical grazing rights leased from the government cost one-third of what is charged for similar private land (Ferguson & Ferguson, 1983). The estimated value of the subsidies inherent in land-leasing policies is more than $300 million a year (Lash, 1984).

Oil and coal mining companies also use public lands for commercial purposes. Oil and coal companies must bid for access rights to develop mines and wells. Bids are usually not competitive, and once a mine or well develops, royalties paid to the government are well below rates paid to private landowners (Culhane, 1981). For example, federal onshore oil leases engender royalties of 12 percent to 16 percent, whereas royalties paid to private landowners are usually 33 percent (Friends of the Earth, 1982). The U.S. General Accounting Office has estimated that a modest royalty increase up to a more reasonable 20 percent would generate additional annual revenue of $2 billion (Culhane, 1981).

No industry enjoys as much benefit from national lands as hard rock mines, which have free access to public lands and never pay royalties. Phasing in a royalty charge of 12 to 15 percent would generate an annual revenue of $2 billion a year (Culhane, 1981).

The Congressional Budget Office (1984) puts the amount of subsidies involved in providing access and services at more than $6 billion a year. That figure does not include subsidized access to public lands granted to the lumber, coal, oil, and mining industries. Adding those subsidies to the Congressional Budget Office's estimate brings the total amount up to $10 billion a year (Culhane, 1981; Friends of the Earth, 1982).

Trade Restrictions

Government-sponsored trade restrictions provide a unique type of relief to U.S. businesses. Trade restrictions, which include not only tariffs but the more effective voluntary import quotas, protect specific industries from foreign competition. The cost of those activities is reflected in higher consumer prices. Import restrictions are not only a hidden tax, but are also regressive, hitting hardest the pocketbooks of low-income consumers.

In spite of a political atmosphere that seems to favor free trade, current U.S. trade policies impose some form of restriction on virtually all imports and set tariffs on 66 percent of all imported items (Weidenbaum, 1988). Although the bulk of those policies protect manufactured goods, farm products, particularly dairy items, also benefit (Hufbauer, Berliner, & Elliott, 1986).

The costs of trade restrictions are spread throughout the economy and hidden in slightly higher prices of thousands of items purchased by millions of consumers. The total subsidy dispensed through restricting the import of foreign goods is more than $60 billion a year (Consumers for World Trade, 1989; Navarro, 1984).

Secondary Mechanisms

Besides the major mechanisms used to distribute subsidies, there are other arrangements that are more oblique. Because accurate cost estimates are difficult to extract, they have not been included in the overall figures. They are supplied here only to give the reader a notion of their significance and to provide a frame of reference.

Regulations

Government regulations administered through a host of regulatory agencies furnish subsidies to favored business interests by restricting the entry of competition into the marketplace and by mandating artificially high rates (Tolchin & Tolchin, 1983). Regulated industries have been ingenious at using regulatory authority for their own benefit. Even the apparently neutral Environmental Protection Agency has protected segments of the power industry from new competition. The Clean Air Act Amendments of 1977 required all new electric plants to include expensive sulphur-scrubbing equipment. The regulation, promoted by eastern coal interests, virtually eliminated competition from western low-sulphur coal (Bardach, 1989).

How much are these hidden subsidies worth? It has been estimated that the cost of regulation is as high as $26 billion a year (Parenti, 1980). Ironically, the consequences of deregulation will cost much more. When Congress passed deregulation legislation for the savings

and loan industry in the early 1980s, a part of the package increased deposit insurance from $40,000 to $100,000. Another deleted regulation permitted the savings and loans to expand their loans from secure home loans to more speculative ventures, thus setting the stage for the current financial debacle that is predicted to exceed $250 billion in costs to the taxpayer (Congressional Budget Office, 1989).

Purchase Arrangements

Congress has passed a number of laws that restrict government purchases and thereby eliminate competition from cheaper foreign products (Congressional Budget Office, 1984). Such prohibitions force the U.S. Department of Defense to exclusively purchase U.S.-made clothing and requires the navy to purchase only vessels made in the United States.

Only about 6 percent of all weapons contracts are put out for bids (Stubbing & Mindel, 1986). The result is that almost half of the U.S. Department of Defense's budget, $150 billion a year, is available to the defense industry on a cost-plus basis, ensuring contractors of substantial profits at little or no risk (Gansler, 1988). Authorities have estimated that reforming current purchasing policies would save between $20 billion and $30 billion a year (Kaufman, 1972; Lambro, 1984; National Economic Commission, 1989).

Upside-Down Means Test

Not only do the corporate welfare programs constitute a drain on public resources, making the adequate funding of programs for poor people more difficult, but they contribute further to the disparate allotment of wealth that became a growing problem during the 1980s. Furthermore, distributive policy not only favors the corporate community over the poor population, but favors wealthy businesses over smaller enterprises. In almost every instance, corporate welfare programs heavily favor the affluent and powerful. Nowhere is this more apparent than in subsidies designated for agriculture, subsidies that are commonly sold to Congress as important aids to struggling family farmers.

In absolute terms, agriculture is one of the largest recipients of corporate welfare schemes and annually costs more than $25 billion (Luttrell, 1989). Two-thirds of the payments went to only 3,000 farmers who had sales exceeding $100,000 a year. Half of the nation's poorest farmers received no subsidy at all (Pearlberg, 1988). Irrigation provided by the U.S. Bureau of Reclamation was originally planned as a subsidy for small-farm families, and today's project policy limits recipient farmers to owning no more than 160 acres. A 1981 study by the California Institute of Rural Studies found that in five water districts, two-thirds of the land was owned by only eight companies. These agribusinesses are a far cry from the striving family farmer so colorfully depicted during debates in Congress over farm subsidies (Keisner, 1986).

The EXIM Bank distributes its largess disproportionately to the larger wealthier manufacturers, with only 18 companies receiving 60 percent of all subsidized credit (Lambro, 1984). The federal government has spent $40 billion over the past 30 years to promote and subsidize the nuclear power industry, an enterprise reserved for a few megacorporations (Munson, 1985). Smaller businesses are at a disadvantage when competing with corporations that not only have millions of dollars at their disposal but also receive additional help from government subsidy programs. The billions of federal dollars available to large businesses greatly exceeds the relatively small amount—some $334 million—earmarked for the Small Business Administration (Office of Management and Budget, 1989).

Discussion and Conclusions

How much are corporate welfare programs worth? Planned obfuscation makes accurate estimates difficult. Taking a conservative view, eliminating indirect benefits and schemes that are so complex they foil projections, we arrive at an annual projection of over $170 billion for the phantom welfare state. The magnitude of this amount is more easily grasped by comparing phantom welfare expenditures with government expenditures on other significant programs.

In 1990 the federal government spent $4.7 billion on all forms of international aid (Congressional Budget Office, 1989). Pollution control programs received $4.8 billion of federal assistance, and secondary and elementary education together were allotted only $8.4 billion (Congressional Budget Office, 1989). More to the point, whereas more than $170 billion is expended on assorted varieties of corporate welfare, the federal government spends $11 billion dollars on Aid to Families with Dependent Children. The most expensive means-tested welfare program, Medicaid, costs the federal government $30 billion a year, or about half of the amount corporations receive each year through assorted tax breaks (Congressional Budget Office, 1989). Supplemental Security Income, the federal program for disabled people, receives $13 billion, whereas U.S. businesses are given $17 billion in direct federal aid (Congressional Budget Office, 1989).

The injustice of spending priorities is apparent when it is pondered what could be done with these dollars. Economist Alicia Munnell (1986) estimated that every person in the United States could be guaranteed an income above the poverty line for about $80 billion more than is now spent on means-tested poverty programs. A less-ambitious program that provided a minimum income for low-income families that equals 65 percent of the federal poverty standard and ensures that all children receive necessary nutritional and developmental support would cost $21 billion (Smeeding, 1991), about one-eighth of what is now spent on current federal subsidies to U.S. businesses.

Over the past several decades, policymakers and politicians have created a multitiered welfare state. In the past decade, one segment of this system, programs for poor people, has been slashed, and stringent means tests are required before meager benefits are doled out by a parsimonious government. But another segment of the welfare state is reserved for the upper classes, distributing lavish allowances neither contained by a means test nor subject to the moralizing that often accompanies poverty programs. The distributive elements described in this article help explain why the 1980s were kind to the very wealthy. In the past 10 years, more than $2 trillion has been redistributed to U.S. businesses, and many of those dollars were directed into the pockets of shareholders. Phillips (1991) recently estimated that the richest 1 percent of Americans own 60 percent of all privately held corporate stock.

In her article, "Everyone Is on Welfare," Abramovitz (1983) noted that a constricted image of social welfare "perpetuates a narrow and compartmentalized view of the welfare state. In this view, only the poor receive aid, making them especially vulnerable to cuts when the government's economic policies go awry" (p. 442). Social work must expand the traditional boundaries of social welfare to encompass the programs that direct scarce funds to the more affluent segments of our society. This will lead to the profession's developing more expertise on nonpoverty welfare programs and will prepare social workers for leadership in the crusade to reform current budget priorities. The current budget crisis may be an opportunity for helping turn the country in a more compassionate direction.

Since its birth, social work has been in the vanguard of many national reforms, often speaking on behalf of populations who are too beleaguered to forcefully represent themselves. Of late, too many social workers have abandoned the traditional mission as advocates for social justice. In this age of tight money, bank failures, and low taxes, social work priorities should be reordered. Social workers must rededicate themselves to leading a new reform movement dedicated to a more equitable redistribution of America's wealth. ■

References

Abramovitz, M. (1983). Everyone is on welfare. *Social Work, 28,* 440–445.

Anton, T. J. (1989). *American federalism and public policy.* Philadelphia: Temple University Press.

Bardach, E. (1989). Social regulation as a generic policy instrument. In L. Solomon (Ed)., *Beyond privatization: The tools of government action* (pp. 192–212). Washington, DC: Urban Institute.

Bosworth, B., Carron, A., & Rhyne, E. (Eds.). (1987). *Economics of federal credit programs.* Washington DC: Brookings Institution.

Congressional Budget Office. (1984). *Federal support of U.S. business.* Washington, DC: U.S. Government Printing Office.

Congressional Budget Office. (1989). *Special analysis of the 1990 budget.* Washington, DC: U.S. Government Printing Office.

Consumers for World Trade. (1989). *The economic effects of significant import restraints* (statement before the International Trade Commission investigation). Washington, DC: Author.

Culhane, P. (1981). *Public land politics.* Baltimore: Johns Hopkins University Press.

Ferguson, D., & Ferguson, N. (1983). *Sacred cows at the public trough.* Bend, OR: Maverick.

Fitzgerald, R. (1988). *When government goes private.* New York: Universe Books.

Friends of the Earth. (1982). *Ronald Reagan and the environment.* San Francisco: Pantheon Books.

Gannon, J. (1989, May 21). Lawmakers view Export-Import Bank as red-ink gusher. *Idaho Statesman,* p. 5f.

Gansler, J. (1988). *The defense industry.* Boston: MIT Press.

Hufbauer, G. C., Berliner, D. T., & Elliott, K. A. (Eds.). (1986). *Trade protection in the United States: 31 case studies.* Washington DC: Institute for International Economics.

Kaufman, R. (1972). *The war profiteers.* Princeton, NJ: Doubleday.

Keisner, M. (1986). *Cadillac dessert.* San Francisco: Viking.

Lambro, D. (1984). *Washington D.C.: City of scandals.* New York: Little, Brown.

Lash, J. (1984). *A season of spoils.* New York: Pantheon Books.

Leonard, H. (1988). *Checks unbalanced.* New York: Basic Books.

Levy, F. (1987). *Dollars and dreams: The changing American income distribution.* New York: Russell Sage Foundation.

Luttrell, C. (1989). *The high cost of farm welfare.* Washington, DC: Cato Institute.

Munnell, A. (1986). Lessons from the income maintenance experience: An overview. In A. Munnell (Ed.), *Lessons from the income maintenance experiment* (pp. 1–12). Washington, DC: Federal Reserve Board and Brookings Institution.

Munson, R. (1985). *The power makers.* Los Angeles: Rodale Press.

National Economic Commission. (1989). *Report on the deficit.* Washington, DC: U.S. Government Printing Office.

Navarro, P. (1984). *The policy game.* New York: John Wiley & Sons.

Office of Management and Budget. (1989). *Special analysis of the budget, fiscal 1989.* Washington, DC: U.S. Government Printing Office.

Parenti, M. (1980). *Democracy for the few.* New York: St. Martins Press.

Peachman, J. (1988). *Federal tax policy.* Washington DC: Brookings Institution.

Pearlberg, R. (1988). *Fixing farm trade.* New York: Ballantine Books.

Phillips, K. (1991, February 7). Capital gains tax—A worse idea than ever. *Wall Street Journal,* p. A15.

Rein, M. (1977). Equality and social policy. *Social Service Review, 51,* 586.

Reischauer, R. (1982). The federal budget: Subsidies for the rich. In A. Wildavsky & M. Boskin (Eds.), *The federal budget, economics and politics* (pp. 238–243). San Francisco: Institute for Contemporary Studies.

Richardson, P. (1981). *Small-issue industrial revenue bonds.* Washington, DC: Congressional Budget Office.

Smeeding, T. (1991). The debt, the deficit, and disadvantaged children: Generational impacts and age, period and cohort effects. In J. Rock (Ed.), *Debt and the twin deficits debate* (pp. 31–54). Mountain View, CA: Mayfield.

Stubbing, R., & Mindel, R. (1986). *The defense game.* New York: Harper & Row.

Tax Reform Act of 1986, P.L. 99–514, 100 Stat. 2085.

Titmus, R. (1965). The role of redistribution in social policy. *Social Security Bulletin, 39,* 188–199.

Tolchin, S., & Tolchin, M. (1983). *Dismantling America: The rush to deregulate.* Boston: Houghton Mifflin.

Tullock, G. (1983). *Economics of income redistribution.* New York: Kluwer.

U.S. General Accounting Office. (1981). *Federal charges for irrigation.* Washington, DC: U.S. Government Printing Office.

Vaughan, R. (1979). *State taxation and economic development.* Washington, DC: Council of State Planning Agencies.

Weidenbaum, M. (1988). *Rendezvous with reality.* New York: Basic Books.

Daniel D. Huff, MSW, is professor, and David A. Johnson, ACSW, is chairman/professor, Department of Social Work, Boise State University, 1910 University Drive, Boise, ID 83725.

Accepted December 20, 1991

Part V
Competence and Accountability as Ethical Issues

[15]

PROGRAM EVALUATION: ARDUOUS, IMPOSSIBLE, AND POLITICAL

Donald M. Baer

People's problems often seem to require a program; programs require evaluation. However, the analysis of program evaluation first requires a definition of *program*, which in turn requires a definition of *problem*.

In most behavioral contexts, the word *problem* means only an absence of the right behaviors and an abundance of the wrong behaviors, or a lack of the stimulus controls for the right behaviors and an abundance of the stimulus controls for the wrong behaviors. The only thing that is "right" about right behaviors is that they help people have the future they want or the one that others want for them. The only thing that is "wrong" about wrong behaviors is that they bar people from the future they want or the one that others want for them.

Not everything is known about behavior or about the behavior changes that are problematic with social work clients, but it is known that environmental contingencies are powerful in changing behavior and thereafter maintaining it, and that individual differences do not alter that behavior. So, if a problem is an absence of the right behaviors and an abundance of the wrong behaviors, or of their stimulus controls, the cause might be an absence of the right contingencies and an abundance of the wrong ones. If the contingencies are changed, the right behaviors and their controls might appear, and the wrong behaviors and their controls might disappear.

The contingencies are changed to determine how often doing so is correct, but sometimes there are many of them to change, and sometimes they need to be changed in just the right order. This calls for a lot of carefully planned work over a long time.

So, a program is a large recipe for solving a large problem. It explains how to decide who receives the program, who applies the program, and what they should do, and in what order they should do it.

Usually, social workers can imagine many different programs that might solve the same problem. So it becomes crucial to ask how well any particular program solves the problem. If a program does not do well, an alternative can be tried, which should occur because programs are expensive. To pursue a bad program is to waste a lot of time and resources. Thus, program evaluation is required. This chapter will sketch the general form of behavioral program evaluation to determine how it should be performed, how it is performed, and when it cannot be performed.

Modern Program Evaluation

Modern program evaluation has six steps, or at least it should. Not one of them is simple.

Step 1: Measure the Program's Effect.   A program is intended to solve a problem. If the problem can be measured, then it should be measured at least once just before the program is applied and at least once after the program is completed. The difference between the two measures is the first evaluation of the program. The difference shows what the program has done and what type of difference the program has made. The postprogram measure, no matter how impressively different from the preprogram measure, reveals something else: Is the problem solved now? If the answer is "yes," then celebrate; if it is "no," then more of the program, and perhaps some additional program, is required; all that extra work needs to be evaluated too.

Incidentally, if the answer is "yes," before you celebrate, remember that whoever funded the problem solving will now stop funding. It is always prudent to have a second, even more urgent problem with a priority that becomes clear when the first problem has been solved—a problem that another program can probably solve.

Step 2: Evaluate Program Fidelity.   How much of the prescribed program was actually performed? Was anything else done, anything not prescribed? If the program did not do well, it would seem to be a bad program, but if not much of it was actually done, or done correctly, it may not be a bad program. It might be a good program if it were done correctly and thoroughly. However, this cannot be determined until the program is done correctly and thoroughly, which brings about an additional problem: How can the program be properly carried out?

Step 3: Show Cause and Effect.   It is essential to determine that a program was carried out correctly, and it is good when it is determined that the problem has been solved. It is also essential to be sure that the problem was solved as a result of the program being run correctly. It is necessary to know whether something else solved the problem, because programs are expensive.

Step 4: Check Generalization.   If the appropriate and desired generalization has not occurred, a program is needed that makes it happen. Many programs change their target behaviors at the time and place of the program. However, programs often are run when and where it is convenient; and when and where it is convenient is not always when and where behavior changes are most useful. Behaviors changed at one time and place do not always change at other times and places. A successful program makes its behavior changes appear when and where they are most needed and are most valuable. This is usually in the social mainstream, which is also where generalized changes last longest. The social mainstream is also one of the most difficult places in which to perform measurement.

Step 5: Measure the Costs and Benefits of the Program and Its Outcome. Do the programs benefits justify its cost? There are many audiences. Some of them believe that the solution to a problem must cost less than the problem costs. Otherwise, they believe that the solution is a bigger problem than the problem itself. To answer to this audience, the program's costs and benefits need to be measured in the same units. The audience usually wants the measurement units to be dollars.

Step 6: Assess the Social Validity of the Program. Determine who has power over the future of this program. Ask them how much they like its goals, procedures, costs, benefits, and personnel. It is easy to like some of those things and dislike others, and any dislike can be fatal to program survival. The people with power over a program can be the program's consumers and their families and advocates. Sometimes the professionals who design and use the program have some power over its future. The people who maintain the program's setting and who pay for it certainly have some power over the future of any programs done there, but so do a lot of other people, if they wish (Schwartz & Baer, 1991). The most difficult part about social validity is the brute fact of sociology: The people who can maintain or end a program can do so whether the program is effective or ineffective, whether it was performed faithfully or not, whether it caused its apparent outcomes, and whether it was cheap or expensive. The evaluation of a program's effectiveness depends on its measures, its generalization, the fidelity of its execution, the proof that it was the cause of what happened, and its cost-benefit ratio. In contrast, the evaluation of a program's future hinges only on its social validity. There is a need for effective programs that are also liked by the people who can determine their future. If those people do not like the programs, they need to at least dislike them less than any of the alternatives. In other words, if you like a program or dislike a program, you had better be sure you have enough power over its future.

Difficulties in Implementing Program Evaluation

None of the previous six steps is easy; each has its problems and requires discussion. To begin, these days, many agencies, especially public agencies, claim to evaluate their programs. On close examination it is clear that all they do is create paper-and-pencil forms for their employees to fill out. The forms ask the employees whether they carried out the program's procedures. Sometimes, the real point of the forms is to allow the employees to say that they could not carry out the program because of a lack of sufficient funding. Sometimes, the program receives more funding, but when funding is sufficient, the forms have a different purpose. At this point, the agencies allow the employees to say that they *did* carry out the program. The employees know that it is customary to say so. Thus, many programs fail until they are well funded; until they are well funded their forms are full of responses about program failures. After funding improves, many programs succeed because their forms are filled with stories about success. That is often referred to as accountability, but responses about success mean only that the employees claim that the program was carried out. Responses that claim success do not mean that the program succeeded. So many agencies cannot imagine that their programs could fail or do poorly if they are executed; thus, accountability becomes any documentation that the programs were executed.

For objective program evaluation, it is necessary to know much more than that the personnel say that the program was performed. To begin, how faithfully was the program performed, and what happened as a result of it? There is no point in criticizing agencies for solving their survival problems, but there remains some point in understanding the evaluation of their programs, apart from a program's role in an agency's survival. Evaluation explores how well the programs solve the problems to which they are applied. If the only problem the programs are meant to solve is the survival of the agency, then the length of that survival is the program evaluation. If the programs are also meant to solve some problems of the agency's clients, then it is necessary to know whether the programs induce more of the right behaviors and stimulus controls and fewer of the wrong ones in those clients.

Views of the Problem.   The problems that the program is meant to solve must be measurable. If a problem can be measured, then one can ask how much of a program's changes are measured. Immediately, two different professional views about measuring problems emerge.

First, the traditional view posits that most problems are too large and complex to be measured directly. The problem can only be represented by many various measures, and each measure only "reflects" the problem. People of the traditional view often have favorite measures. Sometimes those measures are so favored that they are used to measure all the programs that their users ever evaluate, no matter how strained their relation is to the problem at hand. In this context, naming a measure becomes crucial. Increase a measure named "prediction of personal outcomes," and very few people will know if the program is a good one or a bad one. Name that same measure "self esteem," and everyone will know that the program is good.

The assumption that measures only reflect a problem immediately generates a difficult question: How do you *know* whether a measure reflects the problem well? Answering that question leads easily to political program evaluation, sometimes consciously and sometimes not. There are two paths that lead to this program evaluation. One way is to assume that the program is good and ask whether it improves the current measure. If it does, then the measure is good, and the assumption that the program is good is proved. If the program does not improve the measure, then the measure is bad and should be replaced by another measure, until some measure is found that shows that the program is good. The found measure is a good measure. The second way is to assume that the program is bad and then ask whether the program worsens the current measure. If it does, then the measure is good and proves the assumption that the program is bad. If the program does not worsen the measure, then the measure is bad and should be replaced by another measure, until some measure is found that shows the program is bad. That found measure is a good measure. People who use this approach do not actually evaluate programs; they evaluate measures until they find one that yields the desired evaluation of their program. Then they announce that their program has been evaluated.

The second view is that of behaviorists, who, of course, hold to a nontraditional view. Behaviorists assume that a measure "reflects" only itself and nothing else. From the behaviorist's perspective, a measure does not represent a problem, either well or badly. The problem *is* its measure. There is no way to know whether there is a problem unless it is measured. If the measure is problematic, then the measure is the problem. Anyone who claims multiple measures of a problem is a person of multiple problems to solve.

Thus, behaviorists do not screen measures; they evaluate programs by asking whether the program changes the measure in the desired direction. If many behaviors are changed in order to program the solution to a problem, the program should be evaluated by just as many measures. Each behavior to change receives its own subprogram, and the subprogram is evaluated by how well it changes its measure. The program is evaluated by how well all its subprograms change their measures.

It follows that if a problem cannot be measured, a program aimed at solving it cannot be evaluated. Politically, that is the best kind of problem to solve. It is necessary, then, only to find out whether the relevant people like the program and if they do not, to find ways to make them like it. However, that is not an evaluation of the program's effectiveness; it is an evaluation of its social validity. It predicts the program's future, not its effectiveness, generality, fidelity, or cost-benefit ratio. There are quite a few ineffective, low-fidelity, ungeneralized, expensive programs that people seem to like. Perhaps that is because many people say that they like some program not because they like it, but because they like it better than no program. Often, the most important evaluation of a politically inspired program is simply that it exists.

Apart from its social validity, there is still a truth about the effectiveness of a program to consider. Suppose that the problem is aging, which is often accompanied by the diminution of many valuable behaviors and the emergence of new challenging behaviors. Sometimes society's methods of addressing aging lead to six classes of behavior change: (1) the recovery and maintenance of communication, (2) social skills, (3) problem-solving skills, (4) self-care, (5) the diminution of self-injury, and (6) the diminution of self-stimulation. Each class has many members; members are measurable, and thus program evaluation is possible.

When a program's subprograms are running, it is possible to determine how much better any participant is at, for example, the three specific language skills, the two particular problem solutions, the one social skill, and the two self-care skills that he or she is learning that month. It is possible to know just how much the one form of self-injury and the two types of self-stimulation that emerged last month have been eliminated. It is possible to know all these things if they are measured every week, every month, for as long as the program exists. If the program is effective, all or most of those measures will improve. The ones that do not improve instantly reveal that more effective subprograms are needed.

Program fidelity.   Next, consider the problems that arise when program fidelity is questioned. Suppose that the program is running, and the measured changes are good and occur just when and where they should. It is still necessary to know *which* program caused them, to know whether the prescribed program is the program that was actually carried out. In modern terms, program fidelity needs to be evaluated. Evaluation of program fidelity requires a program that is written in a wonderfully special way: (1) planning exactly what would be done by whom to whom and when that would happen, where it would happen, and how often it would happen; (2) measuring how often the plan was carried out; and (3) measuring whether anything else was done that was not prescribed.

If an evaluation of program fidelity finds that only a fraction of the prescribed program was actually carried out, and some unprescribed things were done as well, then program evaluation becomes impossible. If the program achieves its goals, then it could mean that the program is so good that even a fraction of it can solve the problem, or it could mean that the program is bad and that the problem was solved by some of the unprescribed things that happened. If the program does not achieve its goals, then it could mean the program is bad. It could also mean that the program really is good; it just looks bad because it was not done thoroughly or because of the nonprescribed things that were done that were bad. So, lacking program fidelity, the program is either good, bad, or a nonevent, and it is not possible to determine among these. In other words, the program has not been evaluated, and program infidelity means that it cannot be evaluated.

Thus, a small program should always be part of the large program to ensure that the program staff perform the large program as exactly as possible. Ideally, it should not be necessary to evaluate program fidelity because it is programmed. If we are programming program fidelity, that is a program that also needs to be evaluated.

A gloomy rule of thumb follows: Do not bother to evaluate programs unless you know the program staff carried out almost all the program and almost nothing but the program. Next, consider the problem of proving that the apparent results of a program were in fact caused by the program. A problem may improve because of the program applied to it, but sometimes a problem improves without a program being applied to it. Improvements in the program should be separated from improvements the program did not make.

Consider a case in point: Suppose that a program aims to recover and maintain the skills that elderly participants need to continue living independently in their own housing. The necessary program has to recover and maintain certain language, social, problem-solving, and self-care skills and to diminish any problematic challenging behaviors. Suppose that the maintenance and changes are observed. How do you evaluate whether that was because of the program?

There are two grand evaluation strategies. The first is quite traditional. In this case, many elderly participants must be found, and they and their families and caretakers must consent to the evaluation. Then half of them must be assigned at random to the program and the other half to something different. The chosen group participates in the program, and the other group participates in something different. As time passes, it is possible to measure how long each participant of each group maintains independent living. The question is whether, on average, the program maintains independent living longer than occurs in its absence. But this is clearly very expensive.

The second evaluation strategy is the single-subject alternative, or allowing single-subject designs to show cause and effect. That is not traditional, but it can work if one assumption is made. This strategy requires only one participant to agree, but it can always be used with each participant who agrees, and if generality is valued in program evaluation, then it should. Set up steady, ongoing measurement of each skill being recovered or maintained and each challenge being decreased as well as steady, ongoing measurement of the prescribed program procedures. This measurement never stops. Suppose that at some moment in this program, three specific skills are being recovered and two particular challenges are being reduced. The most basic skill is recovered; a few days after it is mastered one challenge is reduced if it is still ongoing; a few days after that the next most basic skill is recovered; after it is mastered the second challenge is reduced if it is still ongoing; and a few days after that the third skill is recovered. It is very nearly what would have been done without formal evaluation of cause and effect.

There is steady, ongoing measurement of the skills and challenges and of the program's procedures. Then the evaluation of program effectiveness, fidelity, and cause and effect will emerge; if measurements are graphed and examined every day, it will become clear how perfectly the program personnel proceeded, and if each of the participant's skills emerged and became dependable promptly after it was recovered, but not before. It will become clear whether each of the participant's challenges decreased promptly after the reduction procedures were applied, but not before. The degree of change in each skill and challenge will become clear, repeatedly, and the size and durability of these changes can be evaluated. If size and durability are lacking, program longer, and perhaps better, until they are satisfactory. Many changes occurring just when they should means they are not coincidental; they match too perfectly the recovery, maintenance, or reduction procedures aimed at them. Any one of them might be a coincidental change, but not all five, especially not when those meant to increase actually increase and those meant to decrease actually decrease.

That is program evaluation only—only if one assumption is made. If you know science—that is, if you know that these *are* the changes that, made thoroughly and dependably, will maintain the kind of independent living desired—*then* this program is evaluating itself as it unfolds.

The traditional strategy of group comparison, at great cost and over a long period of time, evaluates the length of independent living that the program typically achieves compared with that achieved in its absence. The nontraditional single-subject design economically and quickly evaluates how well the program makes the behavior changes believed to be crucial to independent living. The single-subject evaluation is only as good as the knowledge that these *are* the crucial behaviors to increase and decrease.

The next problem is to check generalization, which usually seems straightforward. If it is known how to measure program effects when and where the program is running, it is probable that they can be measured at other times and in other places by pretty much the same techniques. The problem is only the remarkable expense of doing so. It is difficult enough to receive program funding; receiving funding for the evaluation of its generalization is even more difficult, especially if the funders do no know that generalization is always problematic.

The evaluation of costs and benefits usually happens late, if at all. The question is whether the benefits are worth the costs. This is an easy question to ask, but not to answer. It is often a matter of political debate to decide whether a cost is a cost rather than a benefit or if a benefit is a benefit rather than a cost. It is often a matter of accountancy debate of whether to include costs that will be paid whether the program proceeds or not.

In some cases, the question is irrelevant. Perhaps the maintenance of independent living by the elderly is a good example. The cost of institutionalizing elderly dependent people in a humane manner for the remainder of their lifetime is extremely high. It would be a rare program aimed at extending their independent living that would come close to those costs. Thus, almost any program that achieves some extension of that independent life will be worth its costs. That is true, even if the only cost calculated is the maintenance costs if independent living is not extended. When the benefits of the program are considered in terms of human joy and the costs of the nonprogram in human anguish, the bargain becomes hugely better, even if incalculable.

Finally, effective programs need social validity. The people with the power to continue or to end any program must want to continue the program. The usual advice is to educate these people in the effectiveness of the program, which I have just described as a six-step process. A program evaluation centering on proven effectiveness confidently attributable to the program is the first ingredient in such education. It allows for a presentation of the various cost-benefit ratios that can be applied: estimates of the money saved or political credits gained by effectiveness compared with the losses of the commodities that come with failure.

All this is fine with a totally rational audience of critical thinkers. With any other audience, show business may be more relevant; it often can obtain good social validity.

Next, note that the social validity of the program should be checked with everyone who has any power over its future. In a free and wealthy society, it is difficult to predict who has or can acquire power over the future of a social program. A mere bystander, if sufficiently distressed simply by the spectacle of a program, can organize a protest against it. That kind of protest sometimes can end the program, especially if the program is publicly funded, no matter its effectiveness, ease of faithful performance, social validity with its direct consumers, generalization costs, or benefits. The biggest problem with social validity is the need to know how power over a program's future is distributed in society. That is not easy knowledge to acquire.

SUMMARY

This discussion makes behavioral program evaluation seem formidable, tedious, prone to lengthy detours, and very expensive, yet possible, if program fidelity can be achieved. But there is another view of behavior that makes program evaluation impossible.

To establish the appropriate context for this other view, remember the usual assumption that interventions will change the targeted behaviors and not others. The intent to change any other behaviors requires special programming. If that assumption were always true, program evaluation would be the simply expensive, tedious, and frequently frustrating but nonetheless possible process just described.

In 1974, Willems argued the contrary. His thesis was based on a collection of facts and an "ecological" logic. It might also have been labeled "systems theory" (see Huse, 1975; Nichols & Everett, 1986; Weinberg, 1975). The basic idea of systems theory is that most of the events in physical and behavioral domains systematically interact, such that changing any one of them always changes others, and sometimes many others. Conversely, changing any one event often requires changing many others. Willem's thesis was and still is arguable, but the facts alone were sufficient to provoke ongoing debate (e.g., Evans, Meyers, Kurkjian, & Kishi, 1988) and a certain prudence among program appliers (see Rogers-Warren & Warren, 1977).

The facts that Willem cited were many examples of programs that had achieved their intended effects but had also achieved unintended effects, some of them intensely undesirable. Not all these cases can be dismissed as poor initial planning; some showed that even sophisticated planners did not always know enough about the problem and the program to predict all the outcomes, no matter how careful their initial analysis. Thus, ecological prudence suggests that programs should be applied only when the programmer can predict and measure all likely consequences. But how can programmers ever learn to predict all of what will happen, if not from experiments done in ignorance?

Even so, ecological prudence is increasing. Programmers have begun to measure more outcomes than the targeted ones. They also have begun to use global subjective measures such as social validity. They do so to predict program survival, of course, and because they assume that any unexpected, unmeasured bad outcomes of a program may escape programmers' attention but are not lost on the consumers: Unexpected, unmeasured bad outcomes should lower consumer satisfaction. Only uniformly high social-desirability ratings should imply no unexpected, unmeasured bad outcomes.

The imprecision of this logic is obvious: global, subjective ratings of events such as satisfaction certainly can reflect unexpected bad outcomes, but they may not always do so. They can reflect many other processes as well. So, they have no systematic relation to unpredicted consequences, good or bad.

Ecological and systems-analytical logics make program construction problematic and program evaluation impossible. If a program typically can have many costs and many benefits, they all must be measured to evaluate the program. That necessity is fatal: if some outcomes of any program are unpredictable and can be bad, then program evaluation requires measurement of every possible outcome, not just the targeted outcome. But that is obviously an impossible prescription: People do not know enough, they are not rich enough, and they do not live long enough to measure every side effect that a program could have. To measure some possible outcomes but not others is arbitrary, often yields an incorrect program evaluation, and is dangerous. If evaluation programs are insisted on nonetheless, it seems that it is necessary to proceed as if ecological, systems-analytical logic did not exist, existed but had no merit, had merit but in contexts other than program evaluation, or had merit for some programs' evaluations but not the particular program's evaluation.

Before agreeing that only close-minded program evaluation is possible, since unselectively open-minded program evaluation is impossible, perhaps the usual case should be considered, not the scientific ones. I begin with an anecdote from an educational psychologist in a certain developing country. She had spent her professional life urging her government to provide a free, public education to the children of the countryside, just as it did to the children of the cities. Her government always refused on grounds of inadequate public funds. Then, a turn in world markets made the government suddenly much richer than ever before. The government commissioned her to develop its new rural-education program. Overjoyed, she designed the program of her dreams. It included a very thorough program evaluation. The government agreed to fund every part of her expensive proposal—except the relatively cheap program evaluation. Astounded, she asked why. A patient politician undertook her education: the government would receive great credit for spending so much money to educate rural children. If an evaluation showed that the program was good, the government would gain no additional credit; in political logic, expensive programs are supposed to do well. If the evaluation showed the program was bad, then the government would lose all the credit it had just gained. In the next election, it would be accused accurately of having wasted a great deal of money. Surely, the politician suggested, even a Ph.D. could understand when there is no more to gain and everything to lose?

This anecdote suggests that program evaluation can be intensely political, and everyday experience suggests that it often is. Allow the decision to be made politically and, quite rationally, little program evaluation will get done. When it is done, it very rarely will include the six components that modern behavioral science prescribes. Instead, it probably will emphasize whatever worked and ignore whatever failed. An alternative political strategy, as in the ongoing governmentally funded evaluation of day care, is to use a measurement system so complex that no outsider will understand it. That enables the evaluators to put good labels on what increases and bad labels on what decreases, with fear of rational contradiction.

There is one form of political program evaluation that often seems appealing to people who would like an objective program evaluation. It is the concurrent schedule of operant psychology. It asks the organism under study to demonstrate which of two environments, and thereby which of two programs, it prefers. Applied to humans, this is a form of social validity applied to the program's target participants. It does not ask them to talk about the programs; instead, it watches them to determine whether they would rather leave Program A to enter Program B or leave Program B to enter Program A. Laboratory versions of the concurrent schedule can be quite complex (Catania, 1985, pp. 182–187), but its applied, human versions are simple enough to state, though tedious and expensive to do. The process involves five basic steps:

1. Create two concurrent environments, one of them characterized by the program and its outcomes and the other similar in all respects but those. In other words, the difference between these two environments is Program A versus no program or Program A versus Program B.

2. Ensure that the participant has extensive, repetitively alternating experience in both environments.

3. Create a very-easy-entry response to each environment, and teach these entry responses to the participant.

4. Create a very-easy-exit response from each environment, and teach these exit responses to the participant.

5. Allow the participant to enter and exit from either environment at any time, and watch that for a long enough time to determine the participant's preferences for the two environments.

This leads, very expensively, to the participant's evaluation of the program or programs. It may be a different evaluation from that which the participant would give verbally; for participants who cannot or do not speak well, it may be the only evaluation of the programs that can be obtained from them.

In some politics, the participant's evaluation may be the only truly relevant evaluation. This is sometimes the case for professionals who believe that their only politics are their participants' politics; they want for their participants as much as possible of what their participants want for themselves. Their problem is to know what their participants want for themselves (Evans et al.; 1988; *Journal of the Association for Persons with Severe Handicaps*, 1998). In that case, effectiveness, program fidelity, generalization, proof of cause and effect, cost-benefit ratios, and other people's ideas of social validity are far less relevant to program evaluation.

The concurrent schedule can be a heartbreaking event for nearly selfless professionals, because it can show them that sometimes their participants want distressingly different things for themselves than the relevant professional wants for them. However, those times can also be the occasion for a complex, good-hearted negotiation among all concerned parties (cf. Bannerman, Sheldon, Sherman, & Harchik, 1990). That negotiation should be at least better informed by the results of a concurrent-schedule evaluation.

Thus, from a political point of view, program evaluation is always the outcome of an often unspoken debate and an art. It is the four skills of (1) knowing what to measure for a program to look good, (2) knowing what to measure for a program to look bad, (3) knowing what to measure for no one to know clearly what the program did, and (4) knowing how to avoid measuring anything while still drawing the desired conclusion.

From a basic-science point of view, of course, program evaluation is simply knowing as much of the truth about what a program accomplishes as is possible. That is a constantly fruitful yet never-ending venture. From an applied-science point of view, program evaluation is simply knowing as much of the truth about what a program accomplishes as is justified by the relevant costs and benefits. The end of that venture presumably depends on the resultant cost-benefit ratio. However, because calculation of cost-benefit ratios is such an uncertain process, it too may be a never-ending venture.

REFERENCES

Bannerman, D. J., Sheldon, J. B., Sherman, J. A., & Harchik, A. E. (1990). Balancing the right to habilitation with the right to personal liberties: The rights of people with developmental disabilities to eat too many doughnuts and take a nap. *Journal of Applied Behavior Analysis, 23,* 79–89.

Catania, A. C. (1985). *Learning.* Englewood Cliffs, NJ: Prentice Hall.

Evans, I. M., Meyer, L. H., Kurkjian, J., & Kishi, G. S. (1988). An evaluation of behavioral interrelationships in child behavior therapy. In J. C. Wit, S. N. Elliot, & F. N. Gresham (Eds.), *Handbook of behavior therapy in education* (pp. 189–215). New York: Plenum Press.

322 Using Evidence in Social Work Practice

Huse, E. F. (1975). *Organization, development, and change.* St. Paul: West.

Journal of the Association for Persons with Severe Handicaps. (1998). Special series on participatory action research, *23*(3).

Nichols, W. C., & Everett, C. A. (1986). *Systematic family therapy.* New York: Guilford Press.

Rogers-Warren, A., & Warren, S. F. (Eds.). (1977). *Ecological perspectives in behavior analysis.* Baltimore: University Park Press.

Schwartz, I. S., & Baer, D. M. (1991). Social validity. *Journal of Applied Behavior Analysis, 24,* 189–204.

Weinberg, G. (1975). *Introduction to general systems thinking.* New York: John Wiley & Sons.

Willems, E. P. (1974). Behavioral technology and behavioral ecology. *Journal of Applied Behavior Analysis, 7,* 151–165.

[16]

Trying to Do More Good than Harm in Policy and Practice: The Role of Rigorous, Transparent, Up-to-Date Evaluations

By
IAIN CHALMERS

Because professionals sometimes do more harm than good when they intervene in the lives of other people, their policies and practices should be informed by rigorous, transparent, up-to-date evaluations. Surveys often reveal wide variations in the type and frequency of practice and policy interventions, and this evidence of collective uncertainty should prompt the humility that is a precondition for rigorous evaluation. Evaluation should begin with systematic assessment of as high a proportion as possible of existing relevant, reliable research, and then, if appropriate, additional research. Systematic, up-to-date reviews of research—such as those that the Cochrane and Campbell Collaborations endeavor to prepare and maintain—are designed to minimize the likelihood that the effects of interventions will be confused with the effects of biases and chance. Policy makers and practitioners can choose whether, and if so how, they wish their policies and practices to be informed by research. They should be clear, however, that the lives of other people will often be affected by the validity of their judgments.

Keywords: evaluation; research synthesis; research methodology; ethics

Why Do We Need Rigorous, Transparent, Up-to-Date Evaluations of Policy and Practice?

It is the business of policy makers and practitioners to intervene in other people's lives. Although they usually act with the best of intentions, however, their policies and practices sometimes have unintended, unwanted effects, and they occasionally do more harm than good.

Iain Chalmers qualified in medicine in the mid-1960s and practiced as a clinician for seven years in the United Kingdom and the Gaza Strip. In the mid-1970s, after further training at the London School of Hygiene and Tropical Medicine and the London School of Economics and Political Science, he became a full-time health services researcher with a particular interest in assessing the effects of health care. He directed the National Perinatal Epidemiology Unit between 1978 and 1992 and the U.K. Cochrane Centre between 1992 and 2002.

This reality should be their main motivation for ensuring that their prescriptions and proscriptions for others are informed by reliable research evidence.

In her address at the opening of the Nordic Campbell Center, Merete Konnerup, the director, gave three examples showing how the road to hell can be paved with the best of intentions (Konnerup 2002). An analysis of more than fifty studies suggests that effective reading instruction requires phonics and that promotion of the whole-language approach by educational theorists during the 1970s and 1980s seems likely to have compromised children's learning (National Institute of Child Health and Human Development 2000). A review of controlled assessments of driver education programs in schools suggests that these programs may increase road deaths involving teenagers: they prompt young people to start driving at an earlier age but provide no evidence that they affect crash rates (Achara et al. 2001). A review of controlled studies of "scared straight" programs for teenage delinquents shows that, far from reducing offending, they actually increase it (Petrosino, Turpin-Petrosino, and Finchenauer 2000; Petrosino, Turpin-Petrosino, and Buehler 2003).

One example of several that I could use to illustrate how my good intentions as a medical practitioner turned out to be lethal is the advice I promulgated after reading Benjamin Spock's (1966) record-breaking bestseller, *Baby and Child Care*. I bought the book when I was a recent medical graduate in the mid-1960s and marked the following passage:

> There are two disadvantages to a baby's sleeping on his back. If he vomits, he's more likely to choke on the vomitus. Also he tends to keep his head turned towards the same side. . . . this may flatten the side of his head. . . . I think it is preferable to accustom a baby to sleeping on his stomach from the start. (Pp. 163-64)

No doubt like millions of Spock's other readers, I passed on this apparently rational and authoritative advice. We now know that it led to thousands, if not tens of thousands, of avoidable sudden infant deaths (Chalmers 2001).

Uncertainty and Humility:
Preconditions for Unbiased Evaluations

Individual policy makers and practitioners are often certain about things that are a matter of opinion. But surveys of practice reveal that these individual certain-

He is the editor of The James Lind Library, *and his main current interest is the history of the development of methods to test the effects of medical treatments (see www.jameslindlibrary.org).*

NOTE: This article is based on a presentation on 6 June 2002 at a symposium on "Randomised Controlled Trials in the Social Sciences," Nuffield College, Oxford, United Kingdom; and on preparations for the Jerry Lee Lecture at the third annual Campbell Colloquium, 27 February 2003, Stockholm, Sweden. I am grateful to Phil Alderson, Mike Clarke, Diana Elbourne, David Farrington, Judith Gueron, Tim Newburn, and Jan Vandenbroucke for comments on an earlier draft of this article and to Ann Oakley for providing unpublished information.

ties are often manifested in a very wide range of practices, not infrequently providing indirect evidence of mutually incompatible opinions. This evidence of collective uncertainty about the effects of policies and practices should prompt professionals and the public to find out which opinions are likely to be correct. A lack of empirical evidence supporting opinions does not mean that all the opinions are wrong or that, for the time being, policy and practice should not be based on people's best guesses. On matters of public importance, however, it should prompt efforts to obtain relevant evidence through evaluative research to help adjudicate among conflicting opinions.

Because professionals sometimes do more harm than good when they intervene in the lives of other people, their policies and practices should be informed by rigorous, transparent, up-to-date evaluations.

If advice as apparently innocuous and "theoretically sound" as recommending a baby's sleeping position can be lethal, there is clearly no room for complacency among professionals about their potential for harming those whom they purport to help. Evidence of collective uncertainty about the effects of their policies and practices should prompt the humility that is a precondition for rigorous evaluation. In a moving account, Judith Gueron (2002, 27-28) has reported how professionals delivering an education and training program for high school dropouts agreed to a randomized trial to assess its effects, in spite of their concern that this might fail to find any beneficial effects of their work. (In fact, the results of the trial were positive and led to a fifteen-site expansion serving hundreds of disadvantaged youth.)

A recent example from medical research illustrates the importance of remaining uncertain about the effects of an intervention until reliable evidence is available showing that it has at least some beneficial effects that outweigh negative effects (Freed et al. 2001). There have been reasons to hope that transplantation of fetal tissue into the brains of people with Parkinson's disease can improve the symptoms of that distressing condition. Accordingly, a randomized trial comparing fetal implants with placebo surgery was done to assess whether these hopes were borne out by experience. Not only did the study fail to detect any beneficial effects of the implants; it eventually showed that they seemed to cause a serious deterioration in symptoms in some patients.

Those patients who had been randomly assigned to placebo surgery were initially protected from these unanticipated adverse effects. But because they had been desperate to receive this new treatment, the clinical investigators had promised at the time they were randomized to placebo that they, too, would receive fetal implants after one year of follow-up. Unfortunately, the full extent of the adverse effects had not become clear within this time period, so the controls, too, were exposed to an intervention for which only adverse effects, and no benefits, have so far been shown in controlled trials (Freed et al. 2001).

One of the factors preventing a wider appreciation of the need for professional uncertainty and humility about the effects of interventions is that disappointing results tend to get hidden and forgotten. Studies that have yielded "disappointing" or "negative" results are less likely to be presented at scientific meetings; less likely to be reported in print; less likely to be published promptly, in full, in journals that are widely read, in English, and more than once; and less likely to be cited in reports of subsequent studies (Sterne, Egger, and Davey Smith 2001). An analysis of "successful case studies" in situational crime prevention (Clarke 1997), for example, is likely to be less informative than a systematic review of all relevant case studies—successful and unsuccessful.

How Should Uncertainties about the Effects of Policy and Practice Be Addressed?

Systematic reviews of existing research evidence:
A scientific and ethical imperative

Whatever the study designs considered appropriate for reliable detection of the effects of policies and practices, individual studies should not be considered in isolation but interpreted in the context of systematic reviews incorporating any other, similar studies. Application of this principle in practice is no more or less than an acknowledgement that science is a cumulative activity. Yet the principle is widely ignored within academia, not only in "stand alone" reviews but also in the Discussion sections of reports of new studies (Clarke, Alderson, and Chalmers 2002).

The science of research synthesis—as in any other scientific research—implies that those who practice it will take steps to avoid misleading themselves and others by ignoring biases and the effects of chance. A systematic review thus has the same basic components as any other scientific investigation, and so involves

- stating the objectives of the research;
- defining eligibility criteria for studies to be included;
- identifying (all) potentially eligible studies;
- applying eligibility criteria;
- assembling the most complete data set feasible;
- analyzing this data set, using statistical synthesis and sensitivity analyses, if appropriate and possible; and
- preparing a structured report of the research.

It is not easy to conceptualize any justification for ignoring these principles, regardless of the sphere of scientific activity or the study designs and type of data available. Social scientists in the United States and their statistician colleagues have played a key role in the evolution of research synthesis, particularly since the late 1970s (Chalmers, Hedges, and Cooper 2002). Significant interest emerged in the medical field only in the late 1980s.

Some academics question the very notion of a systematic review (see, for example, Learmonth and Watson 1999; Webb 2001). The British educational researcher Martyn Hammersley (2001), for example, criticized the concept because the positivist model is committed to "procedural objectivity"; and he rejects the notion that bias "can and must be minimised," because this is "assumed to maximise the chances of producing valid conclusions" (p. 545). Hammersley's unfamiliarity with the field of research synthesis is revealed most clearly in the following:

> To be even more provocative, we could ask whether some of these forms of synthesis actually constitute reviewing the literature at all. A few seem to be closer to actually *doing* research, rather than reviewing it. (Hammersley 2002, 4)

This is a remarkably tardy insight, coming as it does two decades after a fellow educational researcher published a seminal paper pointing out that "integrative research reviews" are research projects in their own right (Cooper 1982).

Ignorance about the field of research synthesis and cavalier lack of concern about bias in reviews may simply reflect views about the purposes of research. Towards the end of his critique, Hammersley (2001) suggested,

> It is not proven that providing solutions to practical problems, or evaluating them, is the most important contribution which research can make to policy making and practice. (P. 550)

Views such as this may have prompted the U.K. secretary of state for education and employment, David Blunkett, to question the relevance of social science to government. The decision by Blunkett's department to establish a Centre for Evidence-Informed Policy and Practice at London's Institute of Education appears to have been driven partly by concerns about "ideology parading as intellectual inquiry and about the relevance and timeliness of research and the intelligibility of its results" (Boruch and Mosteller 2002, 2).

What kind of studies should be included in research syntheses to reduce biases in estimating intervention effects?

Study designs must be "fit for purpose"

Failure to distinguish research designs intended to lead to reliable causal inferences about the effects of interventions from other research designs, appropriate

Social Work Ethics

for other purposes, is not uncommon (see, for example, Webb 2001). Researchers need to draw on a variety of research designs (Oakley 1999, 2000; Macintyre and Petticrew 2000), for example, to develop defining criteria for attention-deficit hyperactivity disorder, to survey the frequency of mental illness in prison populations, to investigate the validity of methods used to assess school performance, and to explore and record the subjective experiences of asylum seekers.

Surveys often reveal wide variations in the type and frequency of practice and policy interventions, and this evidence of collective uncertainty should prompt the humility that is a precondition for rigorous evaluation.

Indeed, a variety of study designs are required to assess the effects of specific factors on some health or social characteristic, life course, or putative "outcome." As the British sociologist John Goldthorpe (2001) has noted, a fundamental issue is whether the researchers can manipulate the factors concerned. Often this will not be possible, for example, in efforts to understand the effects on child development of genetic characteristics or of divorce. Studies of the relationship between child development and these factors may help to develop theory about the nature of the relationship and lead to ideas about how to intervene in an effort to protect or improve child development.

It is at this point—when interventions have been conceptualized on the basis of theory derived from observed associations—that it is important to ensure rigorous evaluation of the effects of these interventions, for example, gene therapy, marriage guidance, or child counseling. All such interventions can, in principle, be manipulated, and empirical evaluation in controlled experiments can assess whether they have the effects predicted by theory.

Sometimes the results of controlled experiments will be consistent with theory and can inform the development of policy and practices. On other occasions, controlled experiments will not yield evidence of the intervention effects predicted by theory. This does not necessarily mean that the theory is wrong; but it does mean that the possible reasons for the discrepancy between the predicted and observed effects should be explored, possibly leading to a refinement or rejection of the theory; and it should certainly be a warning that deploying the intervention in practice may do more harm than good.

Estimates of intervention effects vary with study design

Reliable studies of the effects of interventions are those in which the effects of policies or practices are unlikely to be confused with the effects of biases or chance. Rarely, estimates of the effects of interventions are so large that they are very unlikely to reflect the effects of insufficiently controlled biases or chance. Returning to an earlier example, once the adverse effects of placing babies to sleep on their tummies had been recognized, the effect of promulgating the opposite advice to the public in "Back to Sleep" campaigns was dramatic—a reduction in death rates to between a half and a quarter of their previous levels—and unlikely to be explained by biases or regression to the mean (Gilbert 1994; Wennergren et al. 1997).

Usually, however, plausible effects of policies are modest but worth knowing about. In these circumstances, research syntheses must be designed in ways that minimize the effects of biases and chance. For example, we would probably still not have learned that very low doses of aspirin offer the potential for an important reduction in the risk of suffering cardiovascular morbidity and mortality had investigators not prepared scientifically robust syntheses of scientifically robust studies (Antiplatelet Trialists' Collaboration 1988).

Reliable detection of moderate but important real intervention effects requires adequate control of the biases that may distort estimates of effects and of the effects of chance. The effects of biases and chance can mislead people into believing that useless or harmful interventions are worthwhile (as has been the case with long-standing claims that postmenopausal hormone therapy reduces the risk of cardiovascular disease) or that interventions are useless when, in truth, they have beneficial effects (see explanation of Cochrane Collaboration logo, below).

People considering which studies should be included in systematic reviews of research assessing the effects of interventions must take into account that studies with different research designs tend to yield different estimates of the effects of interventions (Kunz and Oxman 1998; Britton et al. 1998; MacLehose et al. 2000; Kunz, Vist, and Oxman 2003). For example, in a comparison of the results of studies to assess the effects of crime reduction strategies, Weisburd, Lum, and Petrosino (2001) found that estimates of effect sizes were larger in studies in which there had been fewer precautions to minimize biases. Even in studies that purport to have used random allocation or alternation to create comparison groups, those in which the allocation schedule has not been concealed from the people making decisions about the eligibility and assignment of participants yield larger estimates of treatment effects (Juni, Altman, and Egger 2001; Kunz and Oxman 1998; Kunz, Vist, and Oxman 2003).

There is no easy escape from the dilemma posed by these differences. Although observational data yield estimates of effects that are larger, *on average*, than those using data from randomized trials, in any particular instance it is not possible to predict whether different estimates will emerge using the two different approaches. One cannot even predict with confidence the direction of any differences that are found (Kunz, Vist, and Oxman 2003).

*Random allocation is the only defining
characteristic of randomized trials*

Just as social scientists in the United States have pioneered research synthesis, so also have they pioneered the use of randomized trials to assess the effects of social and educational interventions (Boruch 1997; Petrosino et al. 2000). Some commentators reject the use of randomized trials to test social and educational interventions (see, for example, Dobash and Dobash 2000; Prideaux 2002; Kippax 2003). These comments sometimes reveal a failure to understand that the *one and only* defining feature of randomized trials is random allocation to comparison groups to abolish selection bias and, thus, to ensure that unmeasured as well as measured factors of prognostic importance in the comparison groups differ only by chance (Kleijnen et al. 1997).

A professor of education writing in the *British Medical Journal*, for example, stated,

> Randomisation relies on the maintenance of blind allocation. Maintaining blinding is rarely possible in research on educational interventions. (Prideaux 2002)

And a reviewer consulted by the Economic and Social Research Council about a proposal to prepare systematic reviews of randomized trials and studies with other designs stated (Ann Oakley, personal communication 2002),

> With double bind [sic] and other safeguards generally impossible in social science research, and typically with biases due to differential attrition, it is not evident that randomised control trials are invariably preferable.

A comment from another, anonymous, reviewer of the proposal is illustrative of the genre of vague statements, unsupported by any reference to empirical evidence, that often characterize comments about randomized trials:

> The straightforward extrapolation of judgements about rigour and generalisability from medical to behavioural evaluation by randomised comparison can, of course, be subjected to a quite serious empirical and theoretical critique. Such a critique would argue that randomised comparisons can yield biased assessments of true effects of interventions.

Sometimes comments on randomized trials are little more than polemic and the erection of straw men:

> Randomized designs have, like all designs, important limitations. (Dobash and Dobash 2000, 257)

> It is not the case, even in abstract terms, that some research designs have all the advantages and others have none. (Hammersley 2001, 547).

> The orthodoxy of experimental manipulation and RCTs is dangerous when applied unthinkingly to health promotion. (Kippax 2003, 30)

Those who reject randomization are implying they are sufficiently knowledgeable about the complexities of influences in the social world that they know how to take account of all potentially confounding factors of prognostic importance, including those they have not measured, when comparing groups to estimate intervention effects.

Double standards on the ethics of experimentation

Additional misconceptions result from unacknowledged double standards on the ethics of evaluative studies. As Donald Campbell (1969) noted many years ago, selectively designating some interventions as "experiments"—a term loaded with negative associations—ignores the reality that policy makers and practitioners are experimenting on other people most of the time. The problem is that their experiments are usually poorly controlled. Dr Spock's ill-founded advice would

---

Evaluation should begin with systematic assessment of as high a proportion as possible of existing relevant, reliable research, and then, if appropriate, additional research.

---

probably not be conceptualized by many people as a poorly controlled experiment, yet that is just what it was. Had he proposed testing the effect of his advice on infant mortality in a well-controlled evaluation, however, many people would have had no hesitation in characterizing that as "an experiment," invoking all the "guinea pig" images conjured up by that term in the public's mind.

As noted in a *Lancet* editorial published more than a decade ago, "The clinician who is convinced that a certain treatment works will almost never find an ethicist in his path, whereas his colleague who wonders and doubts and wants to learn will stumble over piles of them" (Medical ethics 1990, 846). Or, as put more bluntly by the pediatrician Richard Smithells (1975, 41), "I need permission to give a drug to half of my patients, but not to give it to them all."

This double standard (Chalmers and Lindley 2000) results in some bizarre ethical analyses (see, for example, Graebsch 2000). Professionals who are uncertain about whether a particular intervention (a policy or practice) will do more good than harm, and so wish to offer it only within the context of a controlled trial so that they protect people in the face of current uncertainty and learn about its effects, are expected to observe elaborate informed consent rituals. If exactly the same intervention is offered by other professionals—because it was recommended during their professional training three decades previously, or because there is a plausible theory that suggests it will be helpful, or because it is an accepted routine, or because they or the institutions for which they work have a vested financial or political interest in promulgating it (Oxman, Chalmers, and Sackett 2001)—the standard of consent is relaxed.

People not infrequently raise questions about the ethics of well-controlled, randomized experiments designed to address uncertainties about the effects of inadequately evaluated policies and practices. They would do well to consider the ethics of acquiescing in professional promulgation of the same policies and practices among recipients who have not been made aware either of the lack of reliable evidence of their effects or of the real reasons that they are being recommended to accept these interventions.

What can be done to reduce the effects of chance?

As with the methods to reduce biases in systematic reviews, social scientists and statisticians in the United States were prominent among those developing methods to reduce the effects of chance using quantitative synthesis of the results of separate but similar studies (Chalmers, Hedges, and Cooper 2002). Indeed, it was an American social scientist who coined the term "meta-analysis" to describe this process (Glass 1967).

Sometimes meta-analysis is impossible with the data available, and even when it is possible it may not be appropriate. When it is both possible and judged appropriate, however, meta-analysis can reveal "reconcilable differences" among studies. The Cochrane Collaboration logo (Figure 1), for example, is based on a meta-analysis of data from seven randomized trials. Each horizontal line represents the results of one trial (the shorter the line, the more certain the result), and the diamond represents their combined results. The vertical line indicates the position around which the horizontal lines would cluster if the two treatments compared in the trials had similar effects; if a horizontal line touches the vertical line, it means that that particular trial found no statistically significant difference between the treatments. The position of the diamond to the left of the vertical line indicates that the treatment studied is beneficial.

This diagram shows the results of a systematic review of randomized trials of a short, inexpensive course of a corticosteroid given to women expected to give birth prematurely. The first of these randomized trials was reported in 1972. The diagram summarizes the evidence that would have been revealed had the available randomized trials been reviewed systematically a decade later: it indicates strongly that corticosteroids reduce the risk of babies dying from the complications of immaturity. By 1991, seven more trials had been reported, and the picture in the logo had become still stronger. This treatment reduces the odds of the babies of these women dying from the complications of immaturity by 30 to 50 percent. Because no systematic review of these trials had been published until 1989, however, most obstetricians had not realized that the treatment was so effective. As a

FIGURE 1
THE COCHRANE COLLABORATION®

result, tens of thousands of premature babies have probably suffered and died unnecessarily (and cost the health services more than was necessary). This is just one of many examples of the human costs resulting from failure to perform systematic, up-to-date reviews of randomized trials of health care.

One of the reasons that the Cochrane logo conveys the message it does is that estimates of the effects of the treatment have been shown as 95 percent confidence intervals. Emphasis on point estimates of effects and reliance on p values derived from statistical tests can result in failure to detect possible effects of interventions that may be important. This danger is illustrated in a paper by two British criminologists titled "The Controlled Trial in Institutional Research—Paradigm or Pitfall for Penal Evaluators?" (Clarke and Cornish 1972). This drew on the authors' experience of a randomized trial of a therapeutic community for young offenders. Because similar numbers of boys in the experimental and control groups went on to reoffend, the authors concluded that therapeutic communities were ineffective and that randomized trials are inappropriate for assessing the effects of institutional interventions.

Had they taken account of the confidence interval surrounding the point estimate of the difference between experimental and control groups, as well as the results of other, similar studies, they might have come to a more cautious conclusion (Table 1). An overall estimate of the effects of therapeutic communities based on a systematic review of eight randomized trials suggests that this category of intervention may halve the odds of adverse outcomes, an effect of great public

TABLE 1

**SYSTEMATIC REVIEW OF EIGHT RANDOMIZED CONTROLLED
TRIALS ASSESSING THE EFFECTS OF THERAPEUTIC
COMMUNITIES ON ADVERSE OUTCOMES**

	Odds Ratio	95 Percent Confidence Interval
All ($N = 8$)	0.46	0.39 to 0.54
Secure democratic		
Cornish and Clarke (1975)	1.04	0.76 to 2.79
Auerbach (1978)	0.52	0.28 to 0.98

SOURCE: NHS Centre (1999).

importance if true. An analysis restricted to the two trials of the "secure democratic" model studied by Clarke and Cornish (1972) suggests that although the beneficial effect may be somewhat less in these, the evidence is still suggestive of a potentially very important benefit. As a consequence of a failure to take proper account of the effects of chance, a useful methodology and a useful intervention may both have been jettisoned prematurely.

Systematic Reviews Need to Be
Rigorous, Transparent, and Up to Date

Whatever decisions are made about which studies are eligible for inclusion in systematic reviews, and whether or not meta-analysis is used to analyze them, reviews should be published in sufficient detail to enable readers to judge their reliability. The advent of electronic publishing has transformed the potential for providing the detail required and allows systematic reviews to be updated when additional data become available and improved in other ways when ways of doing this are identified, for example, to incorporate relevant qualitative data (see, for example, Burns et al. 2001). Electronic publication also facilitates prompt publication of comments and criticisms.

The advantages of electronic publication are particularly welcome when the matter at issue is very contentious. A very extensive systematic review of the effects of water fluoridation (www.york.ac.uk/inst/crd/fluorid.htm) shows how electronic media enable research synthesis to be done transparently, accountably, and democratically. For many years, there have been two opposing lobbies on this issue in the United Kingdom. Following a debate in the House of Lords, the government commissioned the NHS Centre for Reviews and Dissemination in York to review the relevant evidence. An advisory group, on which the two main warring parties were both represented, was established to agree a protocol for the review before the data collection started. The list of studies to be assessed for eligibility was posted on a public Web site, and people were invited to suggest additional studies for consideration. As the review progressed, the Web site showed the results of applying the agreed inclusion and exclusion criteria and displayed the data abstracted from eligible studies and eventually the draft data tables. As it happens, the investigators were unable to identify any randomized experiments of water fluoridation, and they were disappointed with the quality of most of the observational data (McDonagh et al. 2000). (These suggested a modest reduction in caries and an increase in disfiguring dental fluorosis.)

This transparent process is relevant to a point made by the president of the Royal Statistical Society in 1996. After referring approvingly to the Cochrane Collaboration—which prepares, maintains, and disseminates systematic reviews of the effects of healthcare interventions (Chalmers 1993)—he wrote,

> But what's so special about medicine? We are, through the media, as ordinary citizens, confronted daily with controversy and debate across a whole spectrum of public policy issues. But typically, we have no access to any form of systematic "evidence base"—and therefore no means of participating in the debate in a mature and informed manner. Obvious topical examples include education—what does work in the classroom?—and penal policy—what is effective in preventing reoffending? (Smith 1996)

It was after reading this presidential address and Robert Boruch's excellent book, *Randomized Experiments for Planning and Evaluation* (1997), that I decided to beat a path to the latter's door in October 1998. I wanted to try to persuade him to take up the challenge of leading an effort to establish an analogue to the Cochrane Collaboration to prepare systematic reviews of social and educational interventions. For reasons that should now be clear, although I felt it was essential that such collaboration should be international, I believed that it would fail without the leadership and active involvement of social scientists in the United States, and I suggested that it might be named after one of them—Donald Campbell.

The Cochrane Collaboration and the Campbell Collaboration are both exploiting the advantages of electronic media. Electronic publication means that protocols (containing the introduction to and materials and methods planned for each review) as well as complete reports of systematic reviews can be made publicly available in considerably more detail and promptly after submission than is usually possible with print journals, and that they can be modified in the light of new data or comments.

As far as I am aware, these two collaborations currently provide the only international infrastructure for preparing *and maintaining* systematic reviews in the fields of health and social care and education. Estimates suggest that more than ten thousand people are now contributing to the Cochrane Collaboration (which was inaugurated in 1993), most of them through one or more of fifty Collaborative Review Groups (all international), which have collectively published nearly two thousand systematic reviews in *The Cochrane Database of Systematic Reviews*. Members of these groups are supported by ten Cochrane Methods Groups (all international) and twelve Cochrane Centres, which are geographically based, and share collective responsibility for global coverage (www.cochrane.org).

The Campbell Collaboration (which was inaugurated in 2000) currently consists of Coordinating Groups in Crime and Justice, Education, and Social Welfare, with more than fifty registered titles of reviews in preparation. These groups preparing reviews are supported by a Methods Group, as well as by the Collaboration's Secretariat and staff at the Nordic Campbell Centre (www.sfi.dk/sw1270.asp). There is growing recognition of the need for international collaboration in preparing systematic reviews. For example, a review of British educational research conducted in 2002 by the Organization of Economic Cooperation and Development (2002) commended the work on systematic reviews being coordinated by the Evidence for Policy and Practice Information and Co-ordinating Centre (the EPPI-Centre) but noted,

> Making the EPPI Centre activities broadly international in scope (perhaps by increasing collaboration with the Campbell Collaborative [*sic*]) could further increase the gain policy makers and the research community may expect from the EPPI Centre. If similar centres could be created in other countries and similar reviews conducted, the gain in knowledge would be greater and some economies of scale could be expected in terms of methodology. (Para. 66)

There are encouraging examples of Campbell and Cochrane groups working collaboratively, especially to tackle methodological challenges, for example, to explore how best to incorporate qualitative and economic data within systematic reviews assessing the effects of policies and practices.

The Role of Systematic Reviews of Research Evidence in the Development of Policy and Practice

Conclusions about the effects of policies and practices will always remain a matter of judgement. As Xenophanes put it in the sixth century B.C., "Through seeking we may learn and know things better. But as for certain truth, no man hath known it, for all is but a woven web of guesses." Or, in Mervyn Susser's words twenty-five centuries later,

> Our many errors show that the practice of causal inference . . . remains an art. Although to assist us, we have acquired analytic techniques, statistical methods and conventions and logical criteria, ultimately the conclusions we reach are a matter of judgement. (1984, 846)

Our judgments can affect other people's lives, however. After comparing the results of systematic reviews with the recommendations of experts writing textbooks and narrative review articles, Antman and his colleagues (1992) concluded that because reviewers have not used scientific methods, advice on some life-saving therapies has been delayed for more than a decade, while other treatments have been recommended long after controlled research has shown them to be harmful.

One needs to bear in mind Xenophanes' words and empirical evidence of this kind when assessing nonspecific questions about the validity of systematic reviews. Hammersley (2001, 547) is not the only person to have asked the question, "Where is the evidence that systematic reviews produce more valid conclusions than narrative reviews?"

Not only do those who pose such questions ignore the existing evidence, they almost never confront the reality that different methods of reviewing tend to lead to different conclusions or explore the reasons for and consequences of this. For policy makers, practitioners, and others wishing to use research evidence to inform

---

[Policy makers and practitioners] should be clear, however, that the lives of other people will often be affected by the validity of their judgments.

---

their choices about interventions, these discrepancies obviously have practical implications: which reviews should they believe? As I have made clear elsewhere, evidence of the discrepant conclusions of systematic and narrative reviews in the health field leave me in no doubt about which type of review I wish to be taken into account when I am a patient (Chalmers 1995, 2000, 2001). And if I had a delinquent teenage son, I would be in no doubt that I would not wish him to be exposed to a "Scared Straight" program, however many uncontrolled before-and-after observational studies suggested that this would divert him from a criminal career (Petrosino, Turpin-Petrosino, and Buehler 2003). Put bluntly, it is time that those academics who offer general—often polemic—criticisms of efforts to reduce the effects of bias and chance in reviews begin to face up to the reality that different materials and methods used for reviews usually result in different conclusions, and show which conclusions they would prefer, and why.

None of the foregoing is meant to suggest that systematic reviews of research evidence speak for themselves. They do not, as has been stated repeatedly by those involved in this work. But up-to-date, reliable, systematic reviews of research evidence, or a demonstration that no relevant research exists, should be regarded as desirable and often essential for informing policy and practice. Judgments will always be needed about how to use the evidence derived from evaluative research. As well as the research evidence, these judgments need to take account of needs, resources, priorities and preferences, and other factors.

I can illustrate how evidence does not speak for itself by drawing on a personal experience. Many years ago, I worked for two years as a United Nations medical officer in a Palestinian refugee camp in the Gaza Strip. Some of my child patients who developed measles, who were often malnourished, died from the complications of the disease. During my medical training, it had been impressed on me that I should not prescribe antibiotics routinely to children with measles. Had I had access then to the Cochrane review of controlled trials of prophylactic antibiotics in measles (Shann, D'Souza, and D'Souza 2002), the authority of the research evidence would have trumped the authority of my teachers at medical school, and I would have used antibiotic prophylaxis. I believe that this would have prevented some of my child patients from suffering and dying. Although that would have been my response to the research evidence, however, this is not to suggest that everyone would have responded similarly (Chalmers 2002). Factors that might weigh more heavily in the judgments of others in different circumstances include the moderate quality of the available relevant studies, the likely magnitude of the beneficial effects, costs, and concerns about the development of antibiotic resistance.

This brings me back to the rationale for evaluations of policy and practice that are rigorous, transparent, and up to date, namely, that policy makers and practitioners who intervene in other people's lives should acknowledge that although they act with best of intentions, they may sometimes do more harm than good. That possibility should be sufficient motivation for them to ensure that their prescriptions and proscriptions are informed—even if not dictated—by reliable research evidence.

Concluding Observations

I have tried to make clear and to justify in this article how I conceptualize reliable research evidence. This entails the preparation of systematic reviews designed to minimize bias, drawing on research studies designed to minimize bias. I have deliberately concentrated on bias because the other important issue, taking account of the effects of chance, is a more straightforward matter (by using meta-analysis and doing larger studies). I believe that the principle of minimizing bias applies across all of science, and certainly in applied fields like the health and social sciences, because of the impact research may have on policies and practices.

In conclusion, my interest in research to assess the effects of interventions arises from a long-standing concern that, acting with the best of intentions, policy makers and practitioners have sometimes done more harm than good when interfering in the lives of others. I believe that the empirical evidence showing associations between study design and study results—whether among reviews or among individual studies—is likely to be explained by differential success in controlling biases. If only as a patient, therefore, I want decisions about my care to take account of the results of systematic reviews and studies that have taken measures to reduce the effects of biases and chance. As a citizen, too, I want these principles to be respected more generally—by policy makers, practitioners, and the public—

than they are currently. However, to return to my starting point, uncertainty and humility among policy makers, practitioners, and researchers are the preconditions for wider endorsement of the approaches I have outlined. Sadly, these qualities are too often in short supply.

References

Achara, S., B. Adeyemi, E. Dosekun, S. Kelleher, M. Lansley, I. Male, N. Muhialdin, L. Reynolds, I. Roberts, M. Smailbegovic, and N. van der Spek. 2001. Evidence based road safety: The Driving Standards Agency's schools programme. *Lancet* 358:230-32.

Antiplatelet Trialists' Collaboration. 1988. Secondary prevention of vascular disease by prolonged antiplatelet treatment. *BMJ* 296:320-31.

Antman, E. M., J. Lau, B. Kupelnick, F. Mosteller, and T. C. Chalmers. 1992. A comparison of results of meta-analyses of randomized control trials and recommendations of clinical experts. *Journal of the American Medical Association* 268:240-48.

Auerbach, A. W. 1978. The role of the therapeutic community "Street Prison" in the rehabilitation of youthful offenders. University Microfilms no. 78-01086. Doctoral diss., George Washington University, Washington, DC.

Boruch, R. 1997. *Randomized experiments for planning and evaluation: A practical guide*. Thousand Oaks, CA: Sage.

Boruch, R., and F. Mosteller. 2002. Overview and new directions. In *Evidence matters: Randomised trials in education research*, edited by F. Mosteller and R. Boruch, 1-14. Washington, DC: Brookings Institution.

Britton, A., M. McKee, N. Black, K. McPherson, C. Sanderson, and C. Bain. 1998. Choosing between randomised and non-randomised studies: A systematic review. *Health Technology Assessment* 2 (13): 1-124.

Burns, T., M. Knapp, J. Catty, A. Healey, J. Henderson, H. Watt, and C. Wright. 2001. Home treatment for mental health problems: A systematic review. *Health Technology Assessment* 5 (15): 1-139.

Campbell, D. T. 1969. Reforms as experiments. *American Psychologist* 24:409-29.

Chalmers, I. 1993. The Cochrane Collaboration: Preparing, maintaining and disseminating systematic reviews of the effects of health care. In "Doing more good than harm: The evaluation of health care interventions," edited by K. S. Warren and F. Mosteller. *Annals of the New York Academy of Sciences* 703 (special iss.): 156-63.

————. 1995. What do I want from health research and researchers when I am a patient? *BMJ* 310:1315-18.

————. 2000. A patient's attitude to the use of research evidence to guide individual choices and decisions in health care. *Clinical Risk* 6:227-30.

————. 2001. Invalid health information is potentially lethal. *BMJ* 322:998.

————. 2002. Why we need to know whether prophylactic antibiotics can reduce measles-related morbidity. *Pediatrics* 109:312-15.

Chalmers, I., L. V. Hedges, and H. Cooper. 2002. A brief history of research synthesis. *Evaluation and the Health Professions* 25:12-37.

Chalmers, I., and R. Lindley. 2000. Double standards on informed consent to treatment. In *Informed consent in medical research*, edited by L. Doyal and J. S. Tobias, 266-75. London: BMJ Publications.

Clarke, M., P. Alderson, and I. Chalmers. 2002. Discussion sections in reports of controlled trials published in general medical journals. *Journal of the American Medical Association* 287:2799-801.

Clarke, R. V. 1997. *Situational crime prevention: successful case studies*. 2d ed. New York: Harrow and Heston.

Clarke, R. V. G., and D. B. Cornish. 1972. *The controlled trial in institutional research—Paradigm or pitfall for penal evaluators?* Home Office Research Study no. 15. London: Her Majesty's Stationery Office.

Cooper, H. M. 1982. Scientific principles for conducting integrative research reviews. *Review of Educational Research* 52:291-302.

Cornish, D. B., and R. V. G. Clarke. 1975. *Residential treatment and its effects on delinquency*. Home Office Research Study no. 32. London: Her Majesty's Stationery Office.

Dobash, R. E., and R. P. Dobash. 2000. Evaluating criminal justice interventions for domestic violence. *Crime & Delinquency* 46:252-70.

Freed, C. R., P. E. Greene, R. E. Breeze, W. Y. Tsai, W. DuMouchel, R. Kao, S. Dillon, H. Winfield, S. Culver, J. Q. Trojanowski, D. Eidelberg, and S. Fahn. 2001. Transplantation of embryonic dopamine neurons for severe Parkinson's disease. *New England Journal of Medicine* 344:710-19.

Gilbert, R. 1994. The changing epidemiology of SIDS. *Archives of Disease in Childhood* 70:445-49.

Glass, G. V. 1967. Primary, secondary and meta-analysis of research. *Educational Researcher* 10:3-8.

Goldthorpe, J. H. 2001. Causation, statistics, and sociology. *European Sociological Review* 17:1-20.

Graebsch, C. 2000. Legal issues of randomized experiments on sanctioning. *Crime & Delinquency* 46:271-82.

Gueron, J. 2002. The politics of random assignment: Implementing studies and affecting policy. In *Evidence matters: Randomised trials in education research*, edited by F. Mosteller and R. Boruch, 15-49. Washington, DC: Brookings Institution.

Hammersley, M. 2001. On "systematic" reviews of research literatures: A "narrative" response to Evans & Benefield. *British Educational Research Journal* 27:543-54.

———. 2002. Systematic or unsystematic, is that the question? Some reflections on the science, art, and politics of reviewing research evidence. Text of a talk given to the Public Health Evidence Steering Group of the Health Development Agency, October, in London.

Juni, P., D. G. Altman, and M. Egger. 2001. Systematic reviews in health care: Assessing the quality of controlled clinical trials. *BMJ* 323:42-46.

Kippax, S. 2003. Sexual health interventions are unsuitable for experimental evaluation. In *Effective sexual health interventions: Issues in experimental evaluation*, edited by J. Stephenson, J. Imrie, and C. Bonell, 17-34. Oxford: Oxford University Press.

Kleijnen, J., P. Gøtzsche, R. H. Kunz, A. D. Oxman, and I. Chalmers. 1997. So what's so special about randomisation? In *Non-random reflections on health services research: On the 25 anniversary of Archie Cochrane's* Effectiveness and efficiency, edited by A. Maynard and I. Chalmers, 93-106. London: BMJ Books.

Konnerup, M. 2002. The three main pillars of the Campbell Collaboration. Presented at Nordic Campbell Center Inauguration Seminar, 12 November, in Copenhagen, Denmark. Retrieved 18 January 2003 from from http://www.nordic-campbell.dk/MereteKonnerupsforedrag4/index.htm.

Kunz, R., and A. D. Oxman. 1998. The unpredictability paradox: Review of empirical comparisons of randomised and non-randomised clinical trials. *BMJ* 317:1185-90.

Kunz, R., G. Vist, and A. D. Oxman. 2003. Randomisation to protect against selection bias in healthcare trials (Cochrane methodology review). In *The Cochrane Library*, iss. 1. Oxford: Update Software.

Learmonth, A. M., and N. J. Watson. 1999. Construing evidence-based health promotion: perspectives from the field. *Critical Public Health* 9:317-33.

Macintyre, S., and M. Petticrew. 2000. Good intentions and received wisdom are not enough. *Journal of Epidemiology and Community Health* 54:802-3.

MacLehose, R. R., B. C. Reeves, I. M. Harvey, T. A. Sheldon, I. T. Russell, and A. M. Black. 2000. A systematic review of comparisons of effect sizes derived from randomised and non-randomised studies. *Health Technology Assessment* 4 (34): 1-154.

McDonagh, M. S., P. F. Whiting, P. M. Wilson, A. J. Sutton, I. Chestnutt, J. Cooper, K. Misso, M. Bradley, E. Treasure, and J. Kleijnen. 2000. Systematic review of water fluoridation. *BMJ* 321:855-59.

Medical ethics—Should medicine turn the other cheek? 1990. *Lancet* 336:846-47.

National Institute of Child Health and Human Development. 2000. *Report of the National Reading Panel. Teaching children to read: An evidence-based assessment of the scientific research literature on reading and its implications for reading instruction.* NIH Publication no. 00-4769. Washington, DC: Government Printing Office.

NHS Centre for Reviews and Dissemination, York and School of Sociology & Social Policy, Nottingham. 1999. *Therapeutic community effectiveness.* CRD Report 17. Retrieved 18 January 2003 from www.york.ac.uk/inst/crd/.

Oakley, A. 1999. Paradigm wars. *International Journal of Social Research Methodology* 2:247-54.

———. 2000. *Experiments in knowing.* Oxford: Polity Press.

Organization of Economic Cooperation and Development. 2002. *Educational research and development in England. Examiners' report.* CERI/CD10, September, p. 21.

Oxman, A. D., I. Chalmers, and D. L. Sackett. 2001. A practical guide to informed consent to treatment. *BMJ* 323:1464-66.

Petrosino, A., R. F. Boruch, C. Rounding, S. McDonald, and I. Chalmers. 2000. *The Campbell Collaboration Social, Psychological, Educational & Criminological Trials Register (C2-SPECTR). Evaluation and Research in Education* 14:206-19.

Petrosino, A., C. Turpin-Petrosino, and J. Buehler. 2003. "Scared Straight" and other juvenile awareness programs for preventing juvenile delinquency (Cochrane Review). In *The Cochrane Library*, iss. 1. Oxford: Update Software.

Petrosino, A., C. Turpin-Petrosino, and J. O. Finchenauer. 2000. Well-meaning programs can have harmful effects! Lessons from experiments such as Scared Straight. *Crime & Delinquency* 46:354-79.

Prideaux, D. 2002. Researching the outcomes of educational interventions: A matter of design *BMJ* 324:126-27.

Shann, F., R. M. D'Souza, and R. D'Souza. 2002. Antibiotics for preventing pneumonia in children with measles (Cochrane Review). In *The Cochrane Library*, iss. 2. Oxford: Update Software.

Smith, A. 1996. Mad cows and ecstasy. *Journal of the Royal Statistical Society* 159:367-83.

Smithells, R. W. 1975. Iatrogenic hazards and their effects. *Postgraduate Medical Journal* 15:39-52.

Spock, B. 1966. *Baby and child care*. 165th printing. New York: Pocket Books.

Sterne, J. A. C., M. Egger, and G. Davey Smith. 2001. Investigating and dealing with publication and other biases. In *Systematic reviews in health care: Meta-analysis in context*, 2d ed. of Systematic Reviews, edited by M. Egger, G. Davey Smith, and D. Altman, 189-208. London: BMJ Books.

Susser, M. 1984. Causal thinking in practice: Strengths and weaknesses of the clinical vantage point. *Pediatrics* 74:842-49.

Webb, S. A. 2001. Some considerations of the validity of evidence-based practice in social work. *British Journal of Social Work* 31:57-79.

Weisburd, D., C. M. Lum, and A. Petrosino. 2001. Does research design affect study outcomes in criminal justice? *Annals of the American Academy of Political and Social Science* 578:50-70.

Wennergren, G., B. Alm, N. Oyen, K. Helweg-Larsen, J. Milerad, R. Skjaerven, S. G. Norvenius, H. Lagercrantz, M. Wennborg, A. K. Daltveit, T. Markestad, and L. M. Irgens. 1997. The decline in the incidence of SIDS in Scandinavia and its relation to risk-intervention campaigns. Nordic Epidemiological SIDS Study. *Acta Paediatr* 86:963-68.

[17]

Defining an Acceptable Treatment Environment

JUDITH E. FAVELL AND JAMES F. MCGIMSEY

"Our knowledge of the characteristics of effective treatment environments for severely and profoundly retarded people is only in an emergent state of development" (Bruinicks, Rotegard, Lakin, & Hill, 1987, p. 37).

This statement is both true and remarkable. Services for people with developmental disabilities have steadily evolved over the last decades. The methods of habilitation and treatment have advanced, as have the overall service delivery systems of which they are a part. The primitive methods of teaching skills and treating behavioral problems applied within custodial, institutional environments have been steadily replaced by more finesseful, systematic, and sophisticated strategies of active treatment provided in more humane and therapeutic living environments. Despite the unarguable progress seen, the definition of the precise elements that constitute an acceptable treatment environment remain very much an issue of discussion and debate.

Such a perspective may seem uninformed and untrue in light of the vast array of standards that have been promulgated to define and regulate quality in service delivery settings (Holburn, 1990). These standards, including those from the Title XIX Medicaid Reimbursement Program for Intermediate Care Facilities for the Mentally Retarded (ICF/MR), the Accreditation Council for Developmental Disabilities (ACDD), and those developed by individual states and agencies, specify a comprehensive array of dimensions that are deemed necessary in providing adequate services and judged to be reflective of their quality. Such standards have been developed and revised through a

JUDITH E. FAVELL AND JAMES F. MCGIMSEY • Au Clair Program, Mount Dora, Florida 32757.

process that reflects both competence and experience in provision of active treatment, and they have been of undeniable benefit in increasing the level of services to people with developmental disabilities (Sparr & Smith, 1990). Most agree, however, that much more needs to be done to validate empirically the characteristics of an effective and acceptable therapeutic environment.

Empirical tests of current standards and definitions of an acceptable treatment environment are likely to result in improvements in the efficiency and effectiveness of many dimensions of services. For example, when evaluating the acceptability of an environment, an issue commonly raised relates to the age appropriateness of the materials available in that environment. This quite legitimate issue should not, however, eclipse an equally vital question of whether leisure and habilitative materials are actually used and whether they actually teach functional skills. Regardless of their apparent social appropriateness and instructional potential, materials should not be considered acceptable unless they are actually engaging to clients. Thus, appearance alone cannot define appropriate materials; their functional use must be empirically assessed.

As a further example, adequate staff training constitutes another ingredient of services considered essential in defining an acceptable program. Too often, however, the adequacy of staff training is judged on such dimensions as the number of hours spent in didactic instruction or the written material read. Most agree that these indirect barometers of quality must be replaced by a focus on validating staff training methods against their effectiveness and efficiency in changing client behavior (Christian & Hannah, 1983). Though the point has been made repeatedly, staff training efforts continue to feature methods and content that do not optimally teach caregivers skills that affect clients.

For example, research has shown the power and efficiency of teaching staff through the use of checklists that define tasks such as how to complete client health care routines (Lattimore, Stephens, Favell, & Risley, 1984). Despite convincing effects, in common practice most of these caregiver skills continue to be taught in workshop or didactic formats, often with lengthy verbal and written presentations. These methods are often not effective in ensuring correct staff performance and thus are of dubious benefit. Further, their inefficiency often constitutes a direct interference with client services, as staff spend hours in training and away from their clients. The reluctance to change to more efficient and effective methods of training staff is caused by many factors. Among these is the continued premium placed on documented amount of staff training as a valued barometer of the adequacy of a treatment environment. As standards of staff training are subjected to an empirical analysis of their actual impact on client care, a variety of practices are likely to be changed, and standards redefined.

In a similar fashion, every structural or procedural component currently used to define an acceptable treatment environment can be improved through empirical evaluation. Regardless of their face validity, all dimensions of a program's adequacy must be analyzed for effectiveness and efficiency in benefiting clients. The habilitation planning process, the number and credentials of staff, the due process system whereby treatment plans are reviewed, the monitoring and documentation of services—each element of a treatment environment warrants analysis.

In short, the definition of an effective treatment environment must be *functional*, specifying how its individual aspects and composite milieu actually affect the behavior of individuals within it. Thus, the question of what defines an acceptable treatment environment may be productively addressed by defining a process of analyzing the functional impact of an environment in an individual case and, where effects are found wanting, examining and reordering the means. The examples that follow focus on how an emphasis on functional effects alters the way an acceptable treatment environment is defined, and how it changes the practices in that environment that are designed to promote acceptable and effective treatment.

AN ACCEPTABLE ENVIRONMENT IS AN ENGAGING ENVIRONMENT

Of the literally hundreds of elements and indicators that might constitute a definition of an acceptable and effective treatment environment, *client engagement* may be the most fundamental measure of whether an environment is responsive to individual needs. Engagement means the active participation of clients in the activities provided in the living environment. Active interaction with the environment, including using materials and interacting with others, may arguably be the least common denominator in defining the adequacy of a therapeutic setting. High levels of engagement denote high levels of reinforcement. Indeed, the "Premack principle" defines high-frequency behavior (i.e., engagement) as reinforcement (Premack, 1959). Thus, frequent engagement with an environment reflects and even defines the extent of reinforcement in that environment.

Dr. Todd Risley (1990), who has articulated and advanced this concept, has discussed the important benefits of engagement in six pivotal areas. First, many studies have shown a negative correlation between engagement and occurrences of problem behavior (Horner, 1980). In short, people who are actively occupied in activities are less likely to exhibit behavior problems. Second, behavior problems are less likely to develop in highly engaging environments. In nonreinforcing environments, behavior problems may emerge as the only reliable means of producing reinforcement of any sort (Steege, Wacker, Berg, Cigrand, & Cooper, 1989). In contrast, in environments in which reinforcement is abundantly available for many behaviors, occasional reinforcement for problems will be less salient and potent, and thus less likely to differentially shape problems relative to other appropriate behavior.

Third, successful management of behavior problems typically depends directly on high levels of reinforcement for appropriate behavior and reduced levels of reinforcement for undesirable behavior. In highly engaging environments, even brief and benign methods of reducing reinforcement contingent upon behavior problems can be expected to have substantial effects, because the period in "time-out" will contrast markedly with higher relative rates of reinforcement in the ongoing "time-in" environment. Conversely, in environments in which engagement in reinforcing activities is low, methods of further reducing reinforcement as a time-out consequence for problem behavior will have to be very depriving and restrictive, if effective at all.

Further, engagement sets the occasion for natural teaching and exploratory play and practice. The best time to teach skills is in the context of activities in which an individual has demonstrated an interest. For example, communication training can effectively be focused on words and signs pertaining to a leisure material the individual has selected and is engaged with (Hart & Risley, 1974; Koegel, O'Dell, & Koegel, 1987). Using engagement as an opportunity for incidental teaching stands in contrast to attempting training with arbitrarily selected and imposed tasks that may have no inherent reinforcing properties.

Aside from the benefits of formal incidental teaching strategies, engagement per se may teach and elaborate skills through exploration and practice. One learns from interacting with the environment, and with sustained engagement one is likely to become more fluent in skills through practice. Though for people with handicaps this process may not be as sure and swift as with normally developing children, at the very least it is clear that unless some level of engagement is ongoing, the environment cannot shape and elaborate skills.

Finally, engagement fundamentally reflects whether an environment is humane. People have a right to live in an environment that is interesting and appropriate for them. Engagement reflects just that; it directly denotes that the environment offers activities and interactions that the individual finds reinforcing. One of the clearest and most basic indicators of an impoverished, unresponsive environment is the lack of activity by its inhabitants. people sitting passively with nothing to do, slouched or sprawled on furnishings and floors, idly milling about and engaged only in persistent stereotypies and periodic episodes of behavior problems—this is perhaps the ultimate image of an inhumane environment. These visions of early institutional environments can still be seen today. Though physical facilities may be attractive, habilitation plans well conceived, staff elaborately trained, and all other foundations of active treatment in place, a program cannot purport to be humane, educative, or acceptable if it does not promote active engagement in its clients. Though levels of engagement may vary across clients with differing characteristics, it is incumbent upon programs to investigate strategies that maximize engagement in each individual.

The benefits and importance of engagement articulated by Todd Risley and his Living Environment colleagues have served as a basis for reforming and reorganizing services for a wide variety of populations with special needs, ranging from infant, toddler, and preschool day care (O'Brien, Porterfield, Herbert-Jackson, & Risley, 1979; Twardosz, Cataldo, & Risley, 1974) to programs serving individuals with developmental disabilities (Risley & Favell, 1979). Measurements of engagement have been developed to track its variations across differing activities. The PLA Check, or planned activity check method (Risley & Cataldo, 1973), for example, consists of repeated instantaneous time samples in which the number of people present in an activity area is divided into the number of people engaged with that activity. The resulting percentage can reveal activities in which individuals are actually occupied and the time spent, as well as those services that are not having a functional effect because individuals are not engaged with them.

Such a measure, which may be used for a group or an individual, can then serve as a basis for reorganizing activities that have been found to have little or no engagement value. For instance, it is not uncommon to find low engagement during transitional periods from one activity to the next. As students move from classroom tasks to lunch, for example, some wait as others finish schoolwork, all wait while individual students wash their hands, and so on. These low-engagement periods, which reflect functional wastes of time, may be constructively filled by orchestrating routines such that children move individually from one activity to the next, rather than moving as a group and thus principally waiting for all to complete each step. This "activity zone" method of scheduling activities is one of many tactics utilized in the Living Environment programs by Risley and his colleagues to increase engagement and realize its attendant benefits (LeLaurin & Risley, 1972). This and many other strategies can similarly be employed in the design of services that optimize engagement and thus improve the educative, therapeutic, and humanitarian properties of environments (Favell, Favell, Riddle, & Risley, 1984).

In summary, measures of engagement are central to the definition of an acceptable treatment environment, for they directly reflect the functional impact of services through the behavior of individuals served. Engagement is the foundation on which functional habilitation, effective treatment, and humane living rests.

AN ACCEPTABLE TREATMENT ENVIRONMENT TEACHES AND MAINTAINS FUNCTIONAL SKILLS

There is virtually universal agreement that the acceptability of a setting or program must rest in large part on whether individuals learn skills that functionally improve their independence, enjoyment, and overall quality of life. Though there is agreement that the teaching of functional skills is central to the definition of an acceptable treatment environment, a number of points bear directly on how this dimension is measured, implemented, and interpreted.

When seeking to determine whether an environment has the mechanisms to teach each client functional skills, a variety of indicators are commonly reviewed. For example, a comprehensive written plan and evidence of an interdisciplinary planning process are typically considered essential elements in the delivery of habilitation services. Likewise, adequate documentation of progress in graphic and/or narrative form is a commonly accepted standard of quality. Although these are of clear value in developing and monitoring training programs, the means employed deserve careful analysis. It is commonly understood that written plans and progress notes do not assure that habilitative services are provided in a reliable fashion. Research and experience support the reality of inconsistent delivery of habilitative programs, despite the existence of written reports dictating and documenting their conduct (Repp & Barton, 1980). For example, the pattern of increased compliance to training and treatment prescriptions during monitoring surveys by funding agencies such as ICF-MR has been documented in a number of studies (Bible & Sneed, 1976; Reid, Parsons, Green, & Schepis, 1991).

Of equal concern is the inefficiency of these planning and monitoring processes (Jacobson, 1987). The many hours consumed in the development and documentation of training may actually result in a net reduction in actual training for clients as program staff invest substantial portions of their time to these efforts. A number of years ago, it was estimated that staff in one residential facility devoted 30% of their time to planning and paperwork. A given interdisciplinary team meeting typically included 20 staff members and consumed 2 hours (J. I. Riddle, 1978, personal communication). It was not known whether the cost of these processes was justified by benefits to clients.

Was the quality and consistency of programming and the client gains achieved worth the time and money invested? There was no formula to apply to the question or latitude to ask it. The standards and surveying practices that prevailed at the time focused heavily on the process of how plans were developed and documented; deviations in that process risked negative survey results and serious funding consequences. As the functional effects of these systems were increasingly questioned, standards and regulations were revised correspondingly. Currently, standards such as ICF-MR have deemphasized the paper and planning process, focusing instead on observed evidence of training and demonstrable client progress.

Such a reorientation affords an opportunity to analyze experimentally alternative methods of planning, implementing, and monitoring training (Greene, Willis, Levy, & Bailey, 1978). These systems are as amenable to and worthy of empirical test as any other clinical or educational intervention. Measures of the functional impact of such processes as client evaluations, habilitation planning, and documentation and orchestration of training activities should include the cost of the process (i.e., the time invested in it) weighed against the tangible benefits to clients. Does a standardized client evaluation functionally alter the training goals and daily activities of that client? If so, what is the cost relative to the outcome achieved? Are there more efficient alternatives to the usual habilitative planning process? It should be possible to analyze the contribution of components of that process to assess their contribution to a quality product.

Similarly, it should be reasonably straightforward to investigate alternative means of devising the plan, in pursuit of methods that minimize time spent without compromising quality. Is a 2-hour interdisciplinary meeting necessary to devise a meaningful and manageable habilitation plan? Are there more time-efficient methods that can produce similar results? Such questions sound either obvious or heretical, but they must be asked if we are to find optimal means of service. Experimental analyses can be expected to shift the focus of definitions of acceptable treatment environments from untested processes and practices to those that have demonstrated efficacy in functionally benefiting clients.

An example of this empirically based evolution may be seen in the methods of training used to teach functional skills. In the past, the most common model of training involved specialized sessions in which a skill was taught in a controlled and contrived setting, often by a specialist in the domain being addressed. Thus, clients' programming days tended to be characterized by a series of discrete training sessions, often deliberately removed from ongoing activities. Although this model enabled documentation of training and was effective in teaching many skills, it had serious limitations. In particular, the skills taught under these conditions in some cases did not generalize or maintain well in the natural environment. Skills taught under sequestered circumstances were often not in evidence in the normal course of activities in which the skill would ordinarily be functional.

Though it is certainly possible to program for generalization and maintenance, it also became apparent that some skills were most efficiently and effectively taught in situ—that is, under natural conditions in which the skill should be appropriately displayed. Thus, incidental teaching strategies were developed to teach communication, self-care, and other adaptive skills in the context of individuals' everyday environments (Halle, 1987; Hart & Risley, 1974, 1975). This training is conducted within the setting that should naturally set the occasion for and reinforce the behavior and is focused on client-initiated engagement and interactions during which brief but frequent teaching interactions occur (McGee, Krantz, Mason, & McClannahan, 1983). This incidental approach to the training of skills is changing the standards and definition of appropriate education and habilitation. Documentation of discrete training sessions is increasingly not considered adequate evidence that training is being conducted. Greater emphasis is now placed on the demon-

Social Work Ethics

stration of training in functional settings, times, and activities (Reid, Parsons, McCarn, et al., 1985; Schepis et al., 1982).

The shift in the definition of active treatment has altered the focus of methods used to evaluate its adequacy. The focus is now on evidence of frequent, positive interactions that include appropriate prompting and reinforcement procedures aimed toward increasing independence and use of skills in normal routines. The nature of the activities and materials is now examined more closely to ascertain whether they are functional and reinforcing, rather than arbitrarily selected and imposed on the individual (Favell & Cannon, 1977; Williams, Koegel, & Egel, 1981). This evolution in the methods of teaching skills serves as an important example of how the definition of acceptable treatment changes as the functional impact of practices is empirically tested.

Although certain methods of instruction are increasingly used to define an acceptable treatment environment, debate remains. For example, some contend that acceptable treatment consists solely of normalized methods. In this view, instructional strategies used with persons with developmental disabilities should match or closely resemble training methods used with nonhandicapped individuals. Normalized methods are associated with many advantages; they are less stigmatizing and may effectively teach skills and increase the probability of maintaining those skills in naturalized environments. For example, social praise may be a potent reinforcer in teaching adaptive behavior, and the fact that it is a socially normative reinforcer may greatly enhance the chances that skills will continue to be reinforced and thus maintained. Chapter 6, by Ron Van Houten and Ahmos Rolider, describes a variety of means by which natural conditions and contingencies may be used to promote behavior change effectively.

When normalized and natural consequences and educational methods are effective, they should of course be used in preference to more contrived and artificial procedures. In cases in which they are systematically sampled but found not to be sufficient, however, alternative means should be utilized. If edibles, tokens, and other contrived events are the only functional reinforcers identified for an individual, their use should not be prohibited for other reasons. In such situations, systematic efforts should be undertaken to establish more natural events as functional stimuli. Training efforts should be applied, for example, to pairing natural reinforcers (e.g., social approval) with the more contrived reinforcers that are currently functional. In a similar fashion, teacher prompts and other forms of externally imposed structure should be systematically replaced through familiar processes of fading and thinning, in which controlling conditions and contingencies are gradually changed.

The point is not to assume and remain content with contrived training procedures that may be unnecessary and may in fact impede a client's future progress. Instead, the point is to maintain a clear empirical and pragmatic referent for selecting and utilizing instructional strategies. A client's ongoing progress should not be sacrificed to others' values. As scientists and practitioners, we should assume neither that contrived procedures are the only vehicle for change nor that clients must respond to practices used with typical individuals. The challenge is to identify and analyze means of systematically teaching clients to learn with naturalized methods while not denying them effective education in the process.

Just as initial teaching efforts may require departures from wholly normalized practices, it may be necessary to maintain some level or type of specially designed therapeutic support in order to sustain improvement. Although it is desirable to aim training efforts toward environments and procedures that are as natural and normalized as possible, all such arrangements can only be justified if they are effective in maintaining improvement. For example, fading from highly structured caregiver-controlled conditions and contingencies to honor systems and other types of self-control and peer support programs may successfully maintain skills. In cases where progress deteriorates under less structured conditions, however, return to greater structure and external control is justified. Once again, the definition of an acceptable maintenance regime must rest on its functional properties in sustaining improvement, not on its normalized appearance or adherence to philosophical values. Though the degree of normalization should be extended as far as possible in the lives of each person with a handicap, all changes must be referenced against the habilitative and clinical rights of individuals served.

In summary, acceptable treatment environments are ones that teach and maintain functional skills. They are not defined solely by evidence of habilitation plans or other processes of planning, delivering, and monitoring training. The benefits of each dimension must be empirically tested and verified, validated by their functional effects in the acquisition and maintenance of skills in the natural environment.

AN ACCEPTABLE ENVIRONMENT AMELIORATES BEHAVIOR PROBLEMS

As with the development of functional skills, a defining dimension of an acceptable environment consists of its effectiveness in treating problem behavior. Problems such as self-injury and aggression are associated with substantial risks and often interfere with habilitative efforts and opportunities to live in less restrictive settings. For this reason, a primary focus is often placed on the methods and outcomes of treatment for such problems.

The acceptability of various methods of clinical intervention has been heavily debated in recent years (Harris & Handleman, 1990; Repp & Singh, 1990). One contingent advocates the sole use of positive treatment strategies, including reinforcement for alternative appropriate behavior, environmental alterations that set the occasion for desirable behavior, and benign behavioral consequences (e.g., verbal reprimands, brief interruption, or prompted redirection for problems). Proponents argue that such nonintrusive methods constitute the only ethical and acceptable means of treating these problems. Others contend that in addition to the procedures described above, severe cases of behavior problems may justify and require the use of behavioral consequences such as "room time out" or even contingent shock (see Chapter 14).

Resolution to the debate over acceptable methods will be aided by changes in both language and practice. First, the acceptability of a method is often based on a priori judgments of its restrictiveness, aversiveness, potential for harm and abuse, and conformance with social norms. Most standards and guidelines used in regulating treatment programs rank order techniques on these bases, allowing those considered most benign to be used routinely while requiring increased levels of due process, expertise, and monitoring for those considered most invasive. Some guidelines prohibit more invasive procedures altogether. The difficulty with these systems of defining acceptability lies in their use of categorical labels assigned to procedures without functional assessments of their actual properties in individual cases.

A procedure is typically labeled restrictive or nonrestrictive without defining the functional nature or extent of restriction that the technique actually imposes for an individual. Similarly, values of aversiveness, potential for harm and abuse, and social acceptability are assigned to techniques without reference to the realities of their application and effect. For example, verbal reprimanding is typically considered quite benign on most dimensions, and thus is viewed as an acceptable nonaversive consequence. In reality, whether or not a reprimand is aversive depends upon its definition and actual effects in an individual case.

The use of the term *aversive* often implies that it is synonymous with punishment. For an event to be functionally defined as a punisher, however, its presentation contingent upon a response must decrease the future probability of that response. Contingent reprimands may have that effect in an individual case (i.e., it may decrease behavior that it follows). Reprimands may have quite different functions, however, with other individuals or in other situations; it may be a neutral consequence (have no effect on behavior) or indeed be an effective reinforcer (increase behavior that it follows). If aversiveness is equated with the emotional reaction that a procedure evokes, reprimanding may have similar variable effects as a result of the individual's learning history. Reprimands may produce dismay, disinterest, or delight, depending upon whether they have been paired with punishment, neutral events, or positive reinforcement, respectively. In short, the effects of a procedure such as reprimanding are a function of its conditioning history and the parameters used in its application. It is not possible to determine this function on the basis of the appearance of the procedure; it must be demonstrated empirically (Van Houten, 1980).

Just as it is not possible to assign an arbitrary label of nonaversive to the procedure of verbal reprimanding, it is similarly not reasonable to assume that reprimands are benign on other dimensions. The procedure can clearly become abusive, drifting into denigrating and offensive diatribes. It can certainly be harmful. Many behavior problems (e.g., self-injury) are developed and maintained by the attention they produce; verbal reprimands constitute one form of attention and thus may similarly serve to reinforce harmful behavior. In these cases, a procedure that is "benign" in appearance may have extremely deleterious effects. Finally, social reprimanding is often viewed as socially acceptable in that it is widely employed in our culture. Many socially normalized practices including ridicule, ostracism, and reprimanding, however, must be questioned from both a humanitarian and a functional perspective.

A similar analysis of such categorical labels should be made of virtually every procedure. The acceptability of a procedure must be judged on the parameters of its application and on its functional properties in individual cases. For example, physical restraint can be punishing to some (Hamilton, Stephens, & Allen, 1967), but it can also be reinforcing, actually increasing the behavior upon which it is contingently applied (Favell, McGimsey, & Jones, 1978, 1981). Similarly, virtually any intervention can restrict freedom and access to opportunities to participate and develop. Such seemingly benign forms of time out as holding an individual's hands down or seating him or her a short distance from the group, if applied repeatedly and/or vigorously, can actually restrict access to activities for longer cumulative durations and to greater extents than versions of time out that are presently labeled more restrictive.

Just as any intervention can be aversive or restrictive; similarly, any procedure can be abusive or harmful. Virtually any procedure can be misapplied with unfortunate or even tragic results. Further, this potential for harm and abuse associated with any intervention must always be referenced against the harm and abuse that can result from lack of effective treatment. Behavior problems such as aggression and self-injury are themselves associated with stress, physical and psychological harm to oneself, and abuse from others and are equally associated with restrictions derived from practices (e.g., physical and chemical restraint) that are used to protect the individual.

In general, categorical and arbitrary labels do not contribute to functional definitions of acceptable treatment environments. These labels must be replaced by individually analyzed and defined procedures. Such a step is fundamental to holding programs and professionals accountable for using procedures that are functionally the least restrictive, and at the same time functionally the most effective, in individual cases (Van Houten et al., 1988).

Aside from labels placed on methods used to treat problems, a second issue bears on the definition of an acceptable treatment environment, in this case relating to measures of effective outcome. Though most would agree that a program must demonstrate successful amelioration of behavior problems, the demonstration of effects is now being critically analyzed. Research and practice in treatment of behavior problems has been appropriately criticized for its narrow focus on single targeted inappropriate behaviors. The reduction of a small number of inappropriate behaviors has traditionally defined a successful intervention. In current thought and practice, however, it is recognized that more expansive measures are required to assess the full benefits and limitations of treatment efforts. For example, in addition to measuring the rate of problem behavior, measures of main effects must be expanded to include methods of assessing changes in the severity and intensity of these problems. Without refined scales of measuring the severity of behavioral episodes, important clinical effects may be overlooked (Iwata, Pace, Kissel, Nan, & Farber, 1990).

Furthermore, the side effects of all interventions must be monitored as well. Though restrictive interventions are sometimes identified as uniquely causing negative side effects, in reality the use of these procedures has been associated with beneficial side effects as well (Newsom, Favell, & Rincover, 1983). At the same time, both positive and negative side effects have been correlated with positive interventions (Epstein, 1985). In short, the high likelihood of collateral changes in behavior associated with virtually any treatment strategy requires that methods of monitoring side effects be routinely incorporated into the evaluation of all treatments.

Third, the generality and durability of behavior change should be carefully monitored. Both the research literature and clinical practice have been characterized by relatively circumscribed and short-term evaluation of effects. In contrast, the goal of all treatment must be pervasive and durable improvement, that is, reductions in the rate and intensity of problems in all life settings and over extended periods. To that end, measurement systems capable of tracking behavioral improvement over extensive periods of time must be developed. This may require the use of different recording methods (e.g., reliable and valid rating scales) that are at once cost-efficient to employ and accurate in reflecting true behavioral change.

Finally, effectiveness of treatment must be measured and judged by the outcomes it produces in terms of functional changes in individuals' lives. The efficacy of treatment approaches and entire therapeutic environments must ultimately rest on whether behavioral improvements result in greater freedom, increased development, and enhanced quality of life (see Chapter 3). Such outcomes provide the most meaningful and legitimate method of evaluating whether means used are justified in terms of ends achieved. The use of invasive interventions can only be justified to the extent that they result in sufficiently improved outcomes (Lovaas & Favell, 1987). At the same time, positive interventions must be held to the same standard.

In short, acceptable treatments and environments of which they are a part must be defined ultimately by whether they positively affect a comprehensive array of measures of behavior change reflecting pervasive, durable improvement and whether these changes in turn result in measurable, meaningful life-style changes. The process of analyzing the adequacy with which an environment provides these means and achieves these ends is not served well by convenient (though unfounded) assumptions about methods, nor by narrow or shortsighted measures of success. Instead, the functional properties of a treatment approach must be analyzed in an individual case and its acceptability ultimately validated on the basis of not only the means employed, but also the outcomes it achieves for that individual.

An Acceptable Environment Is the Least Restrictive Alternative

A major tenet appearing in many definitions of an acceptable environment refers to living in the least restrictive setting possible. In applying this doctrine, a placement continuum has evolved, with large segregated institutions and their associated practices typically considered the most restrictive, and community living with fully integrated work and educational opportunities typically viewed as the least restrictive. Along this continuum, varying residential, vocational, and educational arrangements are placed according to such variables as proximity to typical homes and individuals, location and nature of employment, and access to leisure activities commonly used by other members of the community.

It is relatively easy to define restrictiveness in physical terms, such as proximity to typical individuals or access to normalized activities. The true test, however, is whether a placement results in functionally fewer restrictions and functionally increased participation in these activities. Access and proximity do not define a least restrictive setting; that designation must be based on the actual behavior of the individual in that situation (e.g., whether the setting enables demonstrable increases in freedom of movement and engagement in reinforcing activities). In practice, restrictions typically attributed to institutional settings can be and are replicated in community arrangements. Lack of free access to the outdoors may be imposed by institutional inflexibility, but the prohibition has the same functional effect when imposed for reasons of neighborhood intolerance or proximity to a busy street. Similarly, access to community experiences is not enough; measurable differences in actual and successful participation in these activities must validate the claim of reduced restrictiveness. In short, the definition of restrictiveness must be based upon objective measures of each individual's behavior. Actual measures of restrictiveness must be substituted for those based upon assumptions and ideals (Van Houten et al., 1988).

AN ACCEPTABLE ENVIRONMENT IS A STABLE ENVIRONMENT

Of the many dimensions typically cited in the definition of an acceptable treatment environment, one of the most basic is often not explicitly addressed—its stability, that is, the degree to which its services and personnel provide clients with predictability and continuity in their lives. Like all human beings, people with challenging behaviors require and deserve consistency in their interactions and activities, a sense of stability in their daily routines, and order in their lives. Frequent changes in schedules, programs, caregivers, and peers are clear precipitators of problem behavior in many individuals with developmental disabilities. For some, even slight alterations in meal schedules or other expected events may provoke major outbursts. In addition to causing problems, constant change directly interferes with efforts to treat these clients. Effective treatment requires extraordinary degrees of consistency. If environmental arrangements, interactions, and contingencies are provided unreliably and unsystematically, little progress can be expected (Favell & Reid, 1988).

Despite the acknowledged importance of stability to the quality of a therapeutic environment, many programs evidence serious problems in this area. Staff absenteeism and turnover (withdrawal), perhaps the single most disruptive factor in providing stable services, is a chronic and widespread problem in most settings. What was thought to be an institutional problem was found to be equally troublesome in community programs (Zaharia & Baumeister, 1978). Though virtually everyone understands and acknowledges that caregiver withdrawal is an endemic and insidious problem, it continues unabated, viewed as an evil but immutable reality in our field. Although some research has been done with absenteeism, very little can be found in the area of turnover in human service settings. In actual experience, the most reliable variable affecting turnover appears to be the level of unemployment. When unemployment increases, turnover decreases; when the economy improves, human service staff leave to higher-paying and less demanding jobs.

Though staff withdrawal is a potent and pervasive problem, instability in therapeutic environments also occurs for other reasons. Chief among these is the premium placed on change itself. In habilitation plans, for example, emphasis is placed on teaching new skills and adding new dimensions of service. Though this is of unquestionable value, an equal emphasis should be placed on ensuring that previously acquired skills are maintained and that stable routines which clients have adjusted to and enjoy are not excessively disrupted. An opportunity to perform and practice a previously learned skill should be given as high a priority as learning a new one. The opportunity to relax to preferred music in the evening should similarly be honored, even as efforts are under way to teach new leisure skills.

The intent of this discussion is not to discourage efforts to improve services and skills. Instead, it is aimed toward highlighting the importance of stability in therapeutic environments. From that perspective, each factor that influences the continuity and predictability of clients' lives and programs should be critically scrutinized. We can no longer accept such "necessary" evils as staff turnover. Though advocating improved salary scales may seem naive and futile, there is no more important issue that can be addressed. Salaries aside, there are also many other ways of improving the quality of the work environment that can have important benefits for staff morale and performance, and thus for withdrawal. For example, ensuring that staff receive regular, positive feedback has been shown to be a powerful motivator, yet too often this is neglected by supervisors, who themselves too rarely receive positive support. Reorienting such practices can have effects on what is otherwise the most crippling intrusion on the quality of therapeutic environments. In a similar spirit, other factors, even those intended to improve services and skills, deserve careful analysis.

In assessing the adequacy of an environment or program, professional and funding credit should be placed on doing a manageable number of things well and unfailingly. "New and improved" practices and programs should remain the goal, but must be effected in such a way as not to influence negatively those aspects that are essential and in place.

AN ACCEPTABLE TREATMENT ENVIRONMENT IS A SAFE ENVIRONMENT

The acceptability of an environment very basically rests on whether individuals are safe within it. Individuals must be protected from physical and psychological harm, from injury resulting from behavior problems such as self-injury and aggression, from inappropriate access to activities and materials, and from treatments that improperly restrict freedoms or impose unnecessary stress, intrusion, and discomfort (Hannah, Christian, & Clark, 1981). The importance of safety transcends all other dimensions of program quality; without it, no other barometer of acceptability can be justified.

As clear as the mandate for safety may be, the issues surrounding it are complex. Safety from physical harm resulting from behavior problems can only be assured by the effective treatment of those problems. In attempts to remediate these problems, however, practitioners are constrained by a number of disparate forces. First, the clinical procedures available for use in treatment are not of guaranteed effectiveness. Even in the most competent hands and under the best of conditions, results of treatment are not predictable and rarely result in absolute amelioration of a problem. To this clinical imprecision is added strong ethical pressure to employ the least restrictive means of treating a problem. By this tenet, the more positive and benign methods of treatment should be attempted before resorting to more invasive and restrictive means.

The use of protective restraint (e.g., helmets to protect against head banging, and arm splints to reduce the likelihood of aggression against self or others) have been tightly restricted by current regulations, with pressure applied to discontinue their use quickly and permanently. These principles are reasonable and have properly challenged professionals to avoid unnecessary and excessive use of restrictive practices. Clinicians, however, are now faced with a double bind: attempting to treat problems with methods that may have less decisive clinical effects and that do not assure safety through means such as protective restraint, while being required to guarantee the safety of individuals against the harmful effects of problems.

Once again, this dilemma cannot be resolved by broadly framed policies or philosophies. Instead, practices to assure an individual's right to safety must be devised and analyzed in individual cases, with pragmatics taking precedence over philosophy. As the facts of an individual case are examined, realistic and imaginative solutions may be found. For example, when designing services around an individual, it often becomes apparent that changes in the design of the physical environment are required to assure safety and facilitate treatment. Collaboration between architects, designers, and behavior analysts can be expected to result in innovations in materials, furnishings, and other aspects of the physical environments in which people with challenging behaviors live. Far from the tile-and-terrazzo interiors of the past, living environments can be made both attractive and safe.

Just as new approaches to environmental design may be brought to bear in assuring safety, other practices within the environment must be evaluated as to their impact on safety. For example, shift staffing (which involves scheduling different staff for day, evening, and night duties) has been criticized as an institutionalized and nonnormative arrangement, and thus it is not allowed in some community programs. Certain behavior problems, however, require the constant vigilance of awake staff at all times. In such cases, the use of shift staffing seems a small compromise indeed if it allows an individual to live safely in a more integrated setting. If individuals instead are denied this opportunity because of their unique needs, our advocacy for full integration of people with challenging behaviors takes on a hallow and hypocritical tone.

In a similar spirit, other methods of protecting individuals must be individually analyzed. Protective devices such as helmets (to protect against head banging and to prevent pica) have in some cases been used for very prolonged periods as an alternative to treatment. This practice is now recognized as improper, and pressure is increasingly applied to eliminate chronic protective strategies. The appropriate emphasis on treating problems instead of preventing their occurrence through restraints and other restrictive means is well-founded. For example, many individuals who engage in pica respond well to treatment and thus can be freed from the helmets and other restraints that had been used to control the problem artificially (Mace & Knight, 1986). At the same time, it must be acknowledged that our therapeutic technology is imperfect, and clinicians cannot guarantee that even successful treatment will totally eliminate the risk of harm from this dangerous behavior.

To disallow the use of protective devices under all conditions places improper trust in the power of our technology and thus places individuals at risk. As an alternative to categorical prohibitions, a thorough analysis in an individual case may insist on sound treatment for problems such as pica while still allowing judicious use of protection. Methods of protection may be faded over time, but only to the extent that an individual's safety can be assured.

The protection of individuals extends beyond the realm of safety from physical harm. Acceptable treatment environments must provide safeguards to ensure that individuals' rights are protected. Human rights and peer review committees have been established to review and monitor programs for their adherence to legal and ethical standards, and for the appropriateness of the therapies that are employed. These mechanisms have been widely credited with controlling improper use of behavioral technology and holding professionals accountable for providing effective and acceptable treatment. Though in general these plaudits are deserved, it cannot be assumed that these systems work well in all cases. For example, in some instances the review process itself is so lengthy and cumbersome that it functionally becomes an impediment to providing treatment in a timely and efficacious manner. In other instances, these committees have improperly assumed the role of clinician, dictating practices and usurping professional judgement without assuming the responsibility and liability of the practitioner who is in fact responsible for treating the client (see Chapter 8).

A fine line is sometimes crossed between appropriately questioning the rationale and method of treatment and inappropriately requiring that a procedure be used or not used. Such drifts from the original intent and function of human rights and peer review committees may be relatively rare, but they highlight once again the need to analyze empirically the functional impact of all practices, in this case those of due process. At present, most standards and regulations require only that due process mechanisms be in place; the benefits of these procedures are assumed. In order to assure that these methods in fact promote acceptable and effective treatment, however, further analysis of these practices and decisions is needed.

An Acceptable Environment Is One in Which a Client Chooses to Live

Shifting the focus away from procedural definitions and toward measures of client behavior as the most fundamental and valid barometer of an acceptable treatment environment raises a final issue, notably that of client choice. In a very basic sense, an acceptable treatment environment may best be defined as one in which the client chooses to live. Expressed preference may be the ultimate index of the social validity of a setting and the practices within it. A number of issues are attendant, however, with the use of client choice as a basis for placement or as a means of defining the social acceptability of an environment.

First, methods of measuring preference are quite limited, especially for individuals who cannot verbalize their choices (Guess, Benson, & Siegel-Causey, 1985). On one hand, the task of measuring choice of foods and activities is relatively straightforward. In these cases, several items can be presented concurrently, and the percentage of times each is selected can be recorded. Such methods can be used in evaluating other aspects of a therapeutic setting, including preference for habilitative activities and reinforcement systems (Mithaug & Hanawalt, 1978; Parsons, Reid, Reynolds, & Bumgarner, 1990).

The challenge is more formidable when attempting to assess preference for one placement or environment relative to another. Though the logistics and measurement systems necessary to access choice between global variables such as living environments are difficult and at present limited, it is essential that such means be developed. Reliable and valid methods of enabling individuals to sample options and then to assess their preferences may provide important information in developing therapeutic services. The choice of particular caregivers, activities, and even living environments denotes that these are associated with some reinforcing valence that may be beneficial in teaching skills and treating problems. A task that is inherently nonreinforcing may both be more difficult to acquire and provoke behavior problems when presented. Changing that task to one that affords higher levels of reinforcement may increase its educative value and reduce the probability of problematic escape behavior. In the same fashion, assessing the reinforcing value of other aspects of the therapeutic environment (e.g., people, activities, and settings) may provide vital information in teaching skills and treating problems. Thus, asking a client's preference may enhance functional habilitation.

Aside from its therapeutic potential, client choice should clearly be included in any definition of an acceptable treatment environment. At present, social validation of procedures and settings is often based on broadly framed cultural norms and values that may be rigidly applied in treatment and placement decisions for persons with developmental disabilities. If we work for money, then people with developmental disabilities should only work for that version of "a token economy"; if many citizens live in neighborhoods, so should people with handicaps. Such pronouncements too often ignore the unique characteristics of an individual whose preferences and needs do not conform to a narrowly defined concept of social acceptability. Some of us elect to live in rural, sparsely populated settings, others in large cities. Living in an apartment is desirable to some, but isolating and demoralizing to others. We select our friends, our hobbies, our work, and the therapeutic treatments we receive. As with other citizens, the preferences of persons with developmental disabilities should be assessed and weighed seriously in decisions ranging from the selection of treatment techniques to living arrangements. Our own values cannot substitute for the development of means to access and act on their preferences.

Categorical assumptions regarding the need and desirability of institutional placement are wrong; assumptions regarding the need and desirability of neighborhood living are equally presumptuous. In the quest for an acceptable treatment environment, we too frequently substitute one set of imposed values for another. Instead, services should be developed around the individual, incorporating the unique preferences and needs of that person. The value of those services must be validated by demonstrable changes in the behavior of the individual, measured by his or her development of skills, reduction in aberrant behavior, and increased participation in reinforcing experiences. Analyzing the functional impact of an environment in individual cases may avoid arbitrary decisions about what is acceptable, decisions which may result in nonfunctional, even deleterious therapeutic efforts and environmental arrangements.

In summary, the acceptability of a treatment environment ultimately rests on the behavior of the individual within it. Explicit assessment of client behavior—including preferences, progress in development, and participation in reinforcing activities—needs to replace assumptions and arbitrary designations regarding what constitutes an acceptable treatment environment.

REFERENCES

Bible, G. H., & Sneed, T. J. (1976). Some effects of an accreditation survey on program completion at a state institution. *Mental Retardation, 14,* 14–15.

Bruinicks, R. H., Rotegard, L. L., Lakin, K. C., & Hill, B. K. (1987). Epidemiology of mental retardation and trends in residential services in the United States. In S. Landesman & P. Vietze (Eds.), *Living environments and mental retardation* (pp. 17–42). Washington, DC: American Association on Mental Retardation.

Christian, W. P., & Hannah, G. T. (1983). *Effective Management in Human Services.* Englewood Cliffs, NJ: Prentice-Hall.

Epstein, R. (1985). The positive side effects of reinforcement: A commentary on Balsam and Bondy (1983). *Journal of Applied Behavior Analysis, 18,* 71–78.

Favell, J. E., & Cannon, P. R. (1977). Evaluation of entertainment materials for severely retarded persons. *American Journal of Mental Deficiency, 81*(4), 367–361.

Favell, J. E., Favell, J. E., Riddle, J. I., & Risley, T. R. (1984). Promoting change in mental retardation facilities: Getting services from the paper to the people. In W. P. Christian, G. T. Hannah, & T. J. Glahn (Eds.), *Programming effective human services: Strategies for institutional change and client transition.* New York: Plenum.

Favell, J. E., McGimsey, J. F., & Jones, M. L. (1978). The use of physical restraint in the treatment of self-injury and as positive reinforcement. *Journal of Applied Behavior Analysis, 11,* 225–241.

Favell, J. E., McGimsey, J. F., & Jones, M. L. (1981). Physical restraint as positive reinforcement. *American Journal of Mental Deficiency, 85*(4), 425–432.

Favell, J. E., & Reid, D. H. (1988). Generalizing and maintaining improvement in problem behavior. In R. H. Horner, G. Dunlap, & R. L. Koegel (Eds.), *Generalization and maintenance: Lifestyle changes in applied settings.* Baltimore: Paul H. Brookes.

Greene, B. F., Willis, B. S., Levy, R., & Bailey, J. S. (1978). Measuring client gains from staff implemented programs. *Journal of Applied Behavior Analysis, 11,* 395–412.

Guess, D., Benson, H. A., & Siegel-Causey, E. (1985). Concepts and issues related to choice-making and autonomy among persons with severe disabilities. *Journal of the Association for Persons With Severe Handicaps, 10,* 79–86.

Halle, J. W. (1987). Teaching language in the natural environment: An analysis of spontaneity. *Journal of the Association for Persons With Severe Handicaps, 12,* 28–37.

Hamilton, J., Stephens, L., & Allen, P. (1967). Controlling aggressive and destructive behavior in severely retarded institutionalized residents. *American Journal of Mental Deficiency, 71,* 852–856.

Hannah, G. T., Christian, W. P., & Clark, H. B. (Eds.). (1981). *Preservation of client rights: A handbook for practitioners providing therapeutic, educational, and rehabilitative services.* New York: Free Press.

Harris, S. L., & Handleman, J. S. (Eds.). (1990). *Aversive and nonaversive interventions: Controlling life-threatening behavior by the developmentally disabled.* New York: Springer.

Hart, B., & Risley, T. R. (1974). Using preschool materials to modify the language of disadvantaged children. *Journal of Applied Behavior Analysis, 14,* 95–107.

Hart, B., & Risley, T. R. (1975). Incidental teaching of language in the preschool. *Journal of Applied Behavior Analysis, 8,* 411–420.

Holburn, C. S. (1990). Symposium overview: Our residential rules—have we gone too far? *Mental Retardation, 28,* 65–66.

Horner, R. D. (1980). The effects of an environmental "enrichment" program on the behavior of institutionalized profoundly retarded children. *Journal of Applied Behavior Analysis, 13,* 473–491.

Iwata, B. A., Pace, G. M., Kissel, R. C., Nan, P. A., & Farber, J. M. (1990). The Self-Injury Trauma (SIT) Scale: A method for quantifying surface tissue damage caused by self-injurious behavior. *Journal of Applied Behavior Analysis, 23,* 99–110.

Jacobson, J. W. (1987). Individual program plan goal content in developmental disabilities programs. *Mental Retardation, 25,* 157–164.

Koegel, R. C., O'Dell, M. C., & Koegel, L. K. (1987). A natural language teaching paradigm for non-verbal autistic children. *Journal of Autism and Developmental Disorders, 17,* 187–200.

Lattimore, J., Stephens, T. E., Favell, J. E., & Risley, T. R. (1984). Increasing direct care staff compliance to individualized physical therapy body positioning prescriptions: Prescriptive checklists. *Mental Retardation, 22,* 79–84.

LeLaurin, K., & Risley, T. R. (1972). The organization of day-care environments: "Zone" versus "man-to-man" staff assignments. *Journal of Applied Behavior Analysis, 5,* 225–232.

Lovaas, O. I., & Favell, J. E. (1987). Protection for clients undergoing aversive/restrictive interventions. *Education and Treatment of Children, 10*(4), 311–325.

Mace, F. C., & Knight, D. (1986). Functional analysis and treatment of severe pica. *Journal of Applied Behavior Analysis, 19,* 411–416.

McGee, G. G., Krantz, P. J., Mason, D., & McClannahan, L. E. (1983). A modified incidental-teaching procedure for autistic youth: Acquisition and generalization of receptive object labels. *Journal of Applied Behavior Analysis, 16*, 329–338.

Mithaug, D. E., & Hanawalt, D. A. (1978). The validation of procedures to assess prevocational task preferences in retarded adults. *Journal of Applied Behavior Analysis, 11*, 153– 162.

Newsom, C., Favell, J. E., & Rincover, A. (1983). The side effects of punishment. In S. Axelrod & J. Apsche (Eds.), *The effects of punishment on human behavior* (pp. 285–316). New York: Academic Press.

O'Brien, M., Porterfield, J., Herbert-Jackson, E., & Risley, T. R. (1979). *The Toddler Center: A practical guide to day care for one- and two-year olds*. Baltimore: University Park Press.

Parsons, M. B., Reid, D. H., Reynolds, J., & Bumgarner, M. (1990). Effects of chosen versus assigned jobs on the work performance of persons with severe handicaps. *Journal of Applied Behavior Analysis, 23*, 253–258.

Premack, D. (1959). Toward empirical behavior laws: I. Positive reinforcement. *Psychological Review, 66*, 219–233.

Reid, D. H., Parsons, M. B., Green, C. W., & Schepis, M. M. (1991). Evaluation of components of residential treatment by Medicaid ICI/MR surveys: A validity assessment. *Journal of Applied Behavior Analysis, 24*, 293–304.

Reid, D. H., Parsons, M. B., McCarn, J. M., Green, C. W., Phillips, J. F., & Schepis, M. M. (1985). Providing a more appropriate education for severely handicapped persons: Increasing and validating functional classroom tasks. *Journal of Applied Behavior Analysis, 18*, 289–301.

Repp, A. C., & Barton, L. E. (1980). Naturalistic observations of institutionalized retarded persons: A comparison of licensure decisions and behavioral observations. *Journal of Applied Behavior Analysis, 13*, 333–341.

Repp, A. C., & Singh, N. N. (Eds.), (1990). *Perspectives on the use of nonaversive and aversive interventions for persons with developmental disabilities*. Sycamore, IL: Sycamore.

Risley, T. R. (1990). *Treatment of severe behavior problems in persons with developmental disabilities*. Workshop presented at the annual convention of the Association for Advancement of Behavior Therapy.

Risley, T. R., & Cataldo, M. I. (1973). *Planned activity check: Materials for training observers*. Lawrence, KS: Center for Applied Behavior Analysis.

Risley, T. R., & Favell, J. E. (1979). Constructing a living environment in an institution. In L. A. Hamerlynck (Ed.), *Behavioral systems for the developmentally disabled: II. Institutional, clinic, and community environments*. (pp. 3–24). New York: Brunner/Mazel.

Schepis, M. M., Reid, D. H., Fitzgerald, J. R., Faw, G. D., van den Pol, R. A., & Welty, P. A. (1982). A program for increasing manual signing by autistic and profoundly retarded youth within the daily environment. *Journal of Applied Behavior Analysis, 15*, 363–379.

Sparr, M. P., & Smith, W. (1990). Regulating professional services in ICF's/MR: Remembering the past and looking to the future. *Mental Retardation, 28*, 95–99.

Steege, M. W., Wacker, D. P., Berg, W. K., Cigrand, K. K., & Cooper, L. J. (1989). The use of behavioral assessment to prescribe and evaluate treatments for severely handicapped children. *Journal of Applied Behavior Analysis, 22*, 23–33.

Twardosz, S., Cataldo, M. F., & Risley, T. R. (1974). Open environment design for infant and toddler day care. *Journal of Applied Behavior Analysis, 7*, 529–546.

Van Houten, R. (1980). Social validation: The evaluation of standards of competency for target behaviors. *Journal of Applied Behavior Analysis, 12*, 581–591.

Van Houten, R., Axelrod, S., Bailey, J. S., Favell, J. E., Foxx, R. M., Iwata, B. A., & Lovaas, I. (1988). The right to effective behavioral treatment. *Journal of Applied Behavior Analysis, 1988, 21*, 381–384.

Williams, J. A., Koegel, R. C., & Egel, A. L. (1981). Response-reinforcer relationships and improved learning in autistic children. *Journal of Applied Behavior Analysis, 14*, 53–60.

Zaharia, E. S., & Baumeister, A. A. (1978). Technician turnover and absenteeism in public residential facilities. *American Journal of Mental Deficiency, 82*, 580–593.

[18]

Ethical Dilemmas and the Most Effective Therapies

Peter Sturmey
Queens College and The Graduate Center
City University of New York

Ethics is a term that is bandied about with a sense of near abandon in the field of developmental disabilities. Broadly, in this context, the term *ethics* or *ethical* is generally used to refer to a position, or rule, stated in the form of a moral imperative, with the implication that if one's conduct is guided by this rule, one will be acting in an ethical manner. Over the past 150 (or so) years of organized developmental disabilities services, these moral imperatives, and therefore the nature of ethical conduct, have changed dramatically, and at an increasing pace during the past 15 years. In some cases and over the short term, changing moral imperatives have consisted of a subtle re-cloaking of past imperatives; on the other hand, some of the more aspirational imperatives of the 1970s that developed as providers and clinicians sought to develop alternatives to then prevalent institutional care have not been completely realized today. Nonetheless, while there are some aspects of ethical conduct that have changed dramatically over time, for example, the conduct of workers within services as the nature of those services progressively changes, there are some aspects, of professional conduct, as a contrasting example, that endure and have not changed to the same degree. This chapter will focus on the contrast between ethical positions set forth in publications within the field, and more typical perspectives in society and among ethicists with respect to how and on what basis conduct is judged to be ethical or unethical.

A SIMPLE ETHICAL ISSUE

Green (1999) published a chapter, "Science and Ethics in Early Intervention for Autism," which I want to present as a point of departure for this discussion and analysis of ethics. In her chapter, she cites "The Right to Effective Behavioral Treatment" (Van Houten et al., 1988) as a basis for ethical practice in applied behavior analysis (ABA). She notes that this document states that recipients of ABA services "... have the right to: (1) a therapeutic environment, (2) services whose overriding goal is personal welfare, (3) treatment by a competent behavior analyst, (4) programs that teach functional skills, (5) behavioral assessment and ongoing evaluation, and (6) *the most effective treatment procedures available"* (Van Houten, et al., 1988, abstract; italics added). Green contrasts science with pseudoscience. Science is based on publicly observable phenomena, controlled replicable experiments, and clear distinction between facts, opinions, and conclusions; whereas pseudoscience uses some of the vocabulary of science, but appeals to the new and innovative, and does not conduct science itself to back up its claims. She uses the research on facilitated communication as a good example of pseudoscience that led to ineffective treatment, harm to clients by denying them effective treatment, and harm to family members who were falsely accused of abuse. She appeals to the reader: "I hope most behavior analysts would agree that pseudoscientific practices are unethical" (p. 17). (Who has proposed that pseudoscientific practices and ineffective or harmful therapies *are* ethical? The debate is not whether or not pseudoscientific, unethical, and ineffective therapies are ethical, but rather which therapies are effective and what constitutes evidence for effective therapies. Yet, there may be some who *believe* that the therapies they provide are efficacious, despite scant evidence aside from that stemming from such faith.) She goes on to note that there are many certification programs for many therapies, including ineffective and harmful therapies that give the appearance of an aura of effectiveness. Finally, she notes the variable quality of many programs that claim to be based on ABA.

Green ends her chapter with a call for action. The actions she calls for include urging readers to get more data on different forms of ABA, child characteristics, treatment integrity, and complete cost–benefit analyses of ABA. She also calls for reduction of polarization within the behavior analytic community, basing practice more closely on science and certifying practitioners. Finally, she called for behavior analysts to speak out against pseudoscience and ineffective therapies.

A similar appeal is made in Van Houten's (1999) revisitation of the right to effective treatment issue, but his appeal is based on a claim that clients have specific rights related to behavioral treatment.

Where did these rights come from? They did not come from an ethical treatise or from the Constitution of the United States of America. These "rights" are not "rights" in a legal sense; the Constitution of the United States of America does not explicitly guarantee these rights. Rather, these so-called rights are espoused in the work of a committee, admittedly a committee of some of the most influential and well-published ABA researchers in the world, but nevertheless, still, a committee.

Green and Van Houten appeal to the reader for the adoption of the most effective forms of treatment as an ethical thing to do. Their call for ethical action in ABA is an interesting one, but one which I argue actually contains no analysis of ethical issues. Rather, these sources appeal to authority, specifically Van Houten et al.'s position paper, and the right stated therein to the most effective treatment. In this chapter, I argue that this position does not include a systematic and broader analysis of what ethics are, and how they might apply to treatment of children or adults with autism or other developmental disabilities or other members of society. Such documents are rhetorical devices that serve a variety of purposes, but do not contain an analysis of ethical issues. Can we not do better than an appeal to authority in our analysis of ethics? We should consider the manner in which an ethics code is characteristic of a profession. We should differentiate professional ethics from foundational ethics, with the former perhaps derivative of the latter. Consensus on professional ethics does not necessarily mirror an appeal to authority; rather, it reflects a social contract with society, in which professionals are granted certain prerogatives in exchange for accountability in a variety of forms, including ethics as principles or guidelines for conduct. So, what are ethics?

CONVENTIONAL ETHICS

Ethics

Webster's dictionary defines ethics as a branch of philosophy that is concerned with morals and the science of moral duty. Ethics includes a variety of approaches, including ethics based on the greatest good, the search for perfection, and absolute moral standards. Thus, Webster's definition of ethics identifies at least three different ideas about what ethics are. Society enshrines a version of ethics in professional standards, position papers, laws, and regulations. However, it is easy to point out that many things that are or have been legal are not ethical. It has been legal to sterilize, kill, and starve people with disabilities; it remains legal to abort fetuses because they have developmental disabilities. Not everyone would argue that all of these legal acts are ethical. One might also point out that psychological, medical, and other scientists have engaged in many egregious unethical practices, including infecting people with diseases without their informed consent, committing fraud, lying about data and lying about procedures, participating in the murder of people with developmental disabilities, and coercing their scientific colleagues in various ways. Scientists and professionals have no special status or claim to innocence when it come to ethics, and society attempts to protect its citizens from the unethical behavior of scientists, as it does from the unethical behavior of other groups. Similarly, therapists and therapy, including psychological therapies and therapists, may not merely be ineffective and neutral, but may be dangerous and harmful in their practices or behavior as private citizens. Thus, the FDA attempts to protect the public from harmful drugs, such as thalidomide. Likewise, psychological therapies can cause positive harm: Witness the recent case where a client was killed, apparently by her two therapists, during rebirthing (*Colorado*, 2001). Thus, society moves to protect citizens from unethical and harmful therapies and therapists.

Professional Ethical Standards

One source of ethical behavior is professional standards developed and revised by committees that have been set up for this purpose. The American Psychological Association (APA, 1992) promulgates ethical standards for its members. These ethical standards include competence, integrity, professional and scientific responsibility, concern for others' welfare, and social responsibility. In addition to broad and aspirational ethical standards, the APA also promulgates specific ethical standards that prohibit or require certain specific actions from psychologists. Many professional organizations (including those of counselors, occupational therapists, physicians, and behavior analysts) also have similar kinds of ethical standards (Sturmey & Gaubatz, 2003, chap. 2). Indeed, Van Houten et al.'s position paper is one example of such a cultural practice. For some of these ethical principles and specific standards of conduct, there are no corresponding laws or regulations (although in some cases there are; e.g., National Commission, 1979). In addition, many states have practice acts, or regulatory boards that can take actions, that have the force of law. These practice acts or regulatory boards often refer back to professional codes of conduct or ethical codes in order to identify responsibilities and prerogatives. Federal law may also apply to the provision of therapies to people with developmental disabilities. For example, the Individuals with Disabilities Education Act (IDEA) requires that students must receive a Free and Appropriate Public Education (FAPE). Exactly what each of these four words means and how they apply to individual students continues to evolve. Exactly what constitutes an "appropriate" education is not simple. Debate continues over whether anyone, including students with or without disabilities, is entitled to a good, or the best, education. So far, American courts have ruled that students in regular or special education do not have a right to the best education, or even a good education. Thus, it may be legally sufficient to demonstrate any change in functioning as the minimum progress required by law. Where a child makes absolutely no progress, regresses, or is harmed by education, then school districts may have a harder time demonstrating that a legally sufficient education has taken place. Perhaps a carefully documented program of good faith efforts to teach the child might be a defense, but hearing officers and juries may be influenced a great deal by the outcome for the child, even if extensive good faith efforts were made. Similarly, what constitutes "education" is clear neither to lawyers nor educators, and minimal progress seems to be legally sufficient (Driscoll, 2001), even if parents and professionals want more for the children.

Another set of standards for ethical conduct is practice guidelines. For example, the New York State Department of Health issued a series of practice guidelines for both the assessment and selection of therapies in services for young children with autism spectrum disorders (New York State Department of Health, 1999a, 1999b, 1999c). These practice guidelines are not binding on anyone, as they do not regulate any licensed profession or members of any specific profession or have the force of law. However, they create a precedent for professional ethical conduct that might be applied in a judicial context or considered to be precedent-setting. For example, when a specific type of therapy is described as useless or harmful and a practitioner nevertheless proceeds to use the therapy *and* that action results in some harm to the child or someone else, then a case could be made that the therapist did or should have known not to engage in that form of therapy. Further, applying the principles of tort, one could easily argue that the actions of the therapist caused the harm when they had a relationship to the client and a duty of care, and hence, he or she is liable for the harm caused. Of course, if a therapist knowingly engaged in a contraindicated therapy, but obtained informed consent from the parents and guardian, including an explanation of all the risks and benefits of the treatment, then even if harm ensued, they *might* be on safer ground. After all, many of us choose to engage in experimental treatments with uncertain outcomes and negative side effects under certain circumstances; many of us value the freedom to make that choice if we so wish.

Indeed, although people generally disapprove of restrictive or coercive treatments, they may approve of them if they are effective, at least under some circumstances, especially if they are lifesaving, other treatments have been attempted or ineffective, or if a focal behavior involves social taboos (e.g., Sturmey, Thomsett, Sundaram, & Newton, 2003). Many would argue that the central ethical question is not the use of ineffective or harmful treatment, but rather the lack of informed consent and deceptive practices on the part of charlatans or incompetent therapists.

Consider a case of a therapy that practice guidelines had deemed to be contraindicated, and it was unclear if the child benefited or was actually harmed by the treatment. Perhaps the best defense that a therapist might have would be accurate, reliable, and valid data on that child's response to treatment to demonstrate that there was "benefit", or at least a lack of harm to the child. Clinical impressions, narrative notes, and therapist verbal behavior would probably not suffice for this purpose.

Practitioners and researchers are also subject to common law such as malpractice. Malpractice is a *tort*, or wrongdoing, in which (a) a professional relationship exists between two parties, (b) there is a demonstrable standard of care, (c) harm or injury occurs to the client, and (d) the legal proximate cause of harm or injury was the action of the therapist (Bennett, Bryant, VandenBos, & Greenwood, 1990). Thus, practitioners in the field of autism using any kind of therapy may be sued for malpractice if all four criteria for malpractice are met.

PHILOSOPHICAL APPROACHES TO ETHICS

Not only are ethics a code of professional conduct enshrined in law and codes of conduct, but ethics is also a branch of philosophy. Thiroux (2001) distinguishes two broad approaches to ethics. Consequentialist, or teleological, ethics are approaches in which behavior is judged on the basis of its consequences. An action might be deemed ethical because it leads to the greatest good, happiness, or money for oneself, others, or society. Robin Hood might have been adopting a consequentialist ethic when he robbed a few rich people to make many poor people happy. Nonconsequentialist or deontological ethics are those based on some absolute standard; here it would be unethical to consider the consequences of one's actions: One must do what is right. For example, a physician might truthfully tell their patient they are going to die and that chemotherapy is hopeless. They might do so even though they knew it was going to cause terrible distress to the patient and their family. However, the physician might do this from an ethical standpoint that people should be respected and told the truth, irrespective of the consequences.

BEHAVIOR ANALYTIC VIEWS OF ETHICAL BEHAVIOR

Skinner's (1953) model of behavior identified three sources of behavior: (a) behavior that has evolved with the species, (b) behavior that evolved during the course of the organism's lifetime, and (c) behavior that evolves as part of cultural evolution; he termed this last source "group control" of behavior. Skinner discussed how group control took place through controlling agencies such as the government, law, religion, psychotherapy, economic control, education, and through the deliberate design of cultural practices. Skinner argued that group control of an individual's behavior occurred when the group defines behavior as "good" or "bad," "right" or "wrong," and the group applies reinforcement or punishment—often punishment—accordingly. Such classifications of behavior may not be formally codified and may be consequated imperfectly and only by some members of the group. Such contingencies generate secondary punishers, such as emotional behavior called shame. Thus, Skinner considered ethics to be the controlling practices of the group on the individual.

For example, a government may control the behavior of individuals by specifying contingencies of punishment, by taking away a person's property or restricting a person's access to reinforcers, through house arrest. A government achieves this by codifying laws, and assigning tasks of behavior control to different government agencies and parts of agencies. Governments also periodically use punishment with certain citizen behaviors, such as use of the police or armed forces to suppress rioting or to detain potentially harmful citizens. Thus, the law and ethics are examples of one kind of cultural control of the behavior of therapists.

So how do such cultural practices evolve? Skinner (1953, pp. 430–436) hypothesized that cultural practices evolve by contributing to the survival value of the culture. Hence, cultural practices that avoid famine or extinction of too many members of the culture or other aversive states are likely to be selected and maintained within the culture. Diamond (1991, 1998) provided multiple examples of cultural selection and extinction of a wide variety of cultural practices during human history. Thus, ethical behavior may be seen as the product of cultural evolution that contributes to the survival of the culture.

Hayes, Adams, and Rydeen (1994) took this functional analytic perspective on the cultural evolution of ethical behavior and offered a behavior analytic view of ethics, choice, and value based on Kantor's analysis of cultural behavior (Kantor, 1982; Kantor & Smith, 1975). Although Kantor's view of cultural evolution includes many common elements with Skinner's view, there are some differences between these two (Lahten, 1999). Kantor and Smith (1975) distinguished three kinds of behavior based on their origin. Universal actions are those that are shared across members of a species, such as salivation to lemon juice in the mouth. Idiosyncratic actions are those that individuals acquire over the course of their lifespan. These vary from person to person because their learning histories are different. Finally, there are cultural actions that are conventional, limited to the culture in which the person lives and are relatively stable over time. These three kinds of behavior roughly correspond to reactions to unconditional stimuli, the products of individual histories, and cultural or conventional behaviors (Lahten, 1999).

Cultural behavior is limited in distribution over time, geography, and people. It is conventional in that cultural behavior is not based on any other kind of reason. Laws and ethical standards too are cultural artifacts that are often the product of verbal behavior and the special form of verbal behavior called logic. Further, it is arbitrary in that it there are no fixed or absolute standards of the behavior imposed from outside. Hence, Hayes et al. (1994) argued that ethical behavior is conventional, culturally specific and relatively enduring over time—that it is an example of a cultural action. Using this framework, Hayes et al. argued that values are not absolute, but rather, relative, and fairly specific to each society, time, and place. Skinner took a different position from this, arguing that that which is ethical contributes to the survival of the individual and culture. Survival of the culture may not be immediately evident. Cultures change, and some fade away. Thus, both concur that values are not absolute or idealized, but rather exist in the natural world (Lahten, 1999).

IMPLICATIONS OF CONVENTIONAL ETHICS

One might ask a number of ethical questions relating to choosing data-based, effective treatments or fads. Some of these questions are listed in Table 26.1. What do conventional ethics tell us about such choices? Green (1999) *inter alia* and Van Houten et al. (1988) argued that clients have a right to the *most* effective treatment. This standard is not shared with ethical standards. Professional ethical standards may require the professional to do no harm; the law of tort may require a professional not to harm their client; IDEA may require educators to provide a FAPE; however, none explicitly require that clients receive the most effective treatment or education. Indeed, in contrast to Green and Van Houten et al., some elements of society are completely up front that people are *not* entitled legally or constitutionally to the most effective treatment.

When writing about a class action lawsuit in Texas for a mental patient, the Federal Judge could plainly write that the case was about protection of constitutional rights and nothing more: the constitution did not guarantee a high quality program (Pharis, 1999). Articles during 2001 in the *New York Times* reported that state courts have affirmed that typical students have no right to a good education or one that prepares them for a good job (Dewan, 2002). Rather, the state constitution perhaps guarantees them sufficient education to know how to vote, participate in a jury, and get an unskilled manual job, but no more—this differs from state to state. Society is of course free to do more; it may vote in a government that raises taxes and expands the education budget; so far the behavior of the American electorate has spoken clearly on this issue.

If we apply a Skinnerean-like definition to ethical behavior, there does appear to be a society-wide consensus that people with disabilities, as with the rest of us, should be protected from positive acts of harm. However, there does not appear to

TABLE 26.1

Ethical Dilemmas Created by the Use of Nonvalidated or Fringe Therapies

Should clinicians be held accountable for nonhabilitative impacts of nonempirically validated or fringe therapies and how should they be held accountable?
Should professional organizations be held accountable for the nonhabilitative impacts of nonempirically validated or fringe therapies if these therapies have been promoted at their conferences or endorsed by the organization?
Should an organization develop an ethical code of conduct regarding the promulgation of therapies by it or its members?
How should a member of an organization deal with the organization's promotion of nonempirically validated or fringe therapies?
Should an human services agency or school district be held accountable for the nonhabilitative impacts or effects of nonempirically validated or fringe therapies if these therapies have been delivered by employees or endorsed by the agency?
Do professionals have a duty to warn consumers and parents of the nonhabilitative effects of nonempirically validated or fringe therapies?
Should the assessment of whether or not a therapy has empirical validation become one of the responsibilities of an organization's peer review and human rights committees?
Should universities or colleges be held accountable for the nonhabilitative impacts of nonempirically validated or fringe therapies that were part of the curriculum developed and taught by faculty members?
Do developmental disabilities professionals or human services professionals need a Hippocratic oath?

be such a consensus over lack of effective treatment, even when more effective alternatives exist. Likewise, there appears to be a broad, but incomplete consensus within American society that people, including people with autism or other developmental disabilities, do not have a right to the *most* effective treatment or education available (see Table 26.1 for some examples of common ethical questions raised by ineffective treatments).

Thus, position statements, such as those by Green (1999) and Van Houten et al. (1988), should not be regarded as an analysis of the ethical issues, but rather as an aspirational call by advocates for better services for people with disabilities. On the other hand, there are provisions that are more affirmative; for example, the remaining aspects of the Americans with Disabilities Act, the Olmstead decisions, and Good Samaritan laws that prohibit prosecution of health care professionals who provide aid in emergencies in order to encourage such aid. The FDA has banned the purchase of the audiokinetron for auditory integration therapy due to the absence of scientific evidence for its use. Federal rules of evidence stress that expert testimony in fields where scientific methods are relevant must meet demonstrable standards of science, that is, have a scientific foundation.

There seems to be greater consensus within society over other ethical issues related to fads and data-based therapy as opposed to those relating to effectiveness of treatment per se. Professional ethical standards and laws do agree on ethical principles such as honesty and competency. When a therapist misrepresents treatment cost, effectiveness, and outcome, and some harm occurs to the client or others, then society is more likely to agree that this is unethical and that sanctions should be applied against the therapist. Inasmuch as professional societies and large universities have deep pockets and hefty insurance policies, it is possible that they might be held accountable for their actions as well if there is some link between their behavior and negative impact on the client, although universities cannot be held directly accountable under contemporary law for teaching or encouraging the use of ineffective or damaging therapies by therapists who later use these methods in their practices.

Lawyers have no problem rounding up groups of clients who may have been harmed by corporate pollution or drugs that were harmful. Responding to the contingencies of legal work done on contingency fee basis, they have even been successful in leveraging hefty payments from industry for alleged damage to clients when the scientific community concurs that there is no evidence of a causal relationship between the product and the harm that may have occurred, as in the case of silicon breast implants (see Huber, 1993).

As ABA services entered the realm of routine professional practice, the dangers of program dilution and therapist competency immediately became apparent (Green, 1999). Individual behavior analysts—motivated by profit, gratification from family members, professional reputations for Prospero-like powers, and the notoriety, controversy, adulation and shrimp of the conference circuit—are increasingly vulnerable to making excessive claims, shorting the families out of hours, and engaging in hours of billable but ineffective service. In a marketplace where demand far exceeds supply, they may carefully select only the pliant, intelligent families with values and vocabularies most congruent to their own. For-profit companies are motivated by profit. For them, the largest number of families they can sign up and the number of hours they can bill for with the cheapest available labor will enhance their profits most efficiently. Parents or school districts may still pay for less than optimal or even ineffective behavior analytic services, if there are no alternatives if no positive harm is done, or if no one complains. A fad of ineffective, but billable behavioral services could easily evolve in some local cultures. Even not-for-profit agencies have to pay the bills, including the sometimes generous salaries and benefits of their directors and supervisors.

Conventional ethics already has answers to these problems. Individual therapists can be held personally liable for any fraud or bill padding through the law. If they fail to act in the best interest of their client, then they can be held accountable for the harm that they have done in the court of professional ethics.

Implications of Effective Therapies

Previous appeals for ethical behavior by implementing the most effective treatment available (Green, 1999; Van Houten, 1999; Van Houten et al., 1988) focused on the outcome for the client, that is, the avoidance of client harm from ineffective or harmful therapies. By focusing on the most obvious examples of unethical behavior, these analyses have avoided other, equally important ethical questions raised by the presence of effective therapies. For example, such analyses have focused on the child with developmental disabilities, but have not acknowledged other interested parties, such as family members, therapists, impact on services, and impact on society more generally. What does the right to the most effective treatment mean? Does it mean that the most effective treatment must be implemented at any cost? *Should* parents sell their house and cash in their retirement and their parents' retirement to fund the most effective treatment? *Should* other children with disabilities and typically developing children forego a better education, let alone their own most effective treatment, in order to fund the most effective treatment for children with disabilities? *Should* family members undergo extraordinary distress, depression, divorce, or unemployment to facilitate the most effective treatment for a child with a disability? *Should* the development and education of siblings be held back in order to facilitate the development of a child with developmental disabilities? *Should* members of the general taxpayer community work harder and pay more taxes to fund the most effective treatment for all children with autism, which can not be funded out of current budgets (Jacobson, Mulick, & Green, 1998). *Should* resources be diverted from other programs, such as drug programs for seniors or mainstream education, to fund the most effective treatment? These ethical questions have been greatly underplayed in current discussions of ethical of treatment by behavior analysts. This is because current ethical analyses focus on the client and emphasize the contrast between data-based behavioral interventions and other treatments, many of which typically lack empirical evaluation or have been evaluated and found wanting (New York State Department of Health, 1999a, 1999b, 1999c).

One strand in ethical thinking that does address greater societal considerations is that which analyzes the costs and benefits of an intervention. Jacobson et al. (1998) present a cost–benefit model of early intensive behavioral intervention (EIBI), which appears to show massive savings in terms of avoidance of costs of human services associated with reduced use of special education and reduced consumption of adult services. This model has been contested because of possibly making overly optimistic assumptions about the proportions of children who make substantial benefit, for failing to consider the costs and benefits of alternate programs, and for using cost–benefit analysis methodology, as opposed to other costing methods (Marcus, Rubin, & Rubin, 2000). However, the use of cost–benefits analysis as an ethical justification for effective therapies raises some interesting ethical questions. Clearly, this is a consequentialist argument of some sort. The ethical stance here may be that by saving society the costs of services that are not used, society will benefit in terms of increased happiness that results from investing the saved money in other public programs or through reduced suffering for taxpayers who pay fewer taxes and perhaps have to work less.

If better financial efficiency for tax-funded programs is truly the ethical imperative for EIBI, this places EIBI on a very slippery slope. If there were children who did not contribute to society's cost benefit, would we deny them services on the basic of this ethical principle? If new programs were developed that saved society more money, would we advocate for the wholesale shutting down of EIBI, and transfer of the funds to those programs that saved society more money? Probably not! Why? Because, concerns over cost savings are unlikely to be the ethical imperative behind EIBI. Rather, cost savings are another rhetorical device to advance these services, which we believe to be ethical for *other* reasons; if not a rhetorical device, then at the least cost savings are a secondary consideration, except as it may weigh heavily in governmental policymaking.

The underlying consequentionalist ethical arguments for EIBI are various. They include reducing human suffering and increasing happiness, and autonomy in children with autism, their families, and staff. Even if some of these outcomes are very modest for some of the children—those who learn useful skills, but who will continue to have severe intellectual, social, language, and behavioral disabilities—many behavior analysts, other professionals, and staff value these goals alone as worthy ones. Behavior analysts should also recognize other personal consequences of disseminating effective interventions. We gain paychecks, status, and other personal benefits. Reducing one's own suffering and increasing one's own happiness are worthy, ethical goals in many circumstances; (Thiroux, 2001), and we should at least recognize that these are important consequences for ourselves. Another ethical imperative for the dissemination of EIBI is that behavior analysts believe that behaviorism is not merely the basis for effective therapy, but is a coherent and true worldview. In this sense, EIBI is a vehicle for disseminating behaviorism, a vehicle for disseminating a truth, which is a kind of philosophy, the love of truth.

Equity of Access to Effective Treatments.   A final ethical question concerning the existence of effective treatments is that of equity of access and nondiscrimination on grounds of class, race, gender, ethnicity, skin color, religion, age, sexual orientation, language, immigrant status, or other irrelevant personal qualities. If behavior analysis has the most effective treatments, does behavior analysis have a responsibility to ensure that they are delivered without discriminatory practices? Society (in general) and professional codes of conduct and many American laws (specifically) would indicate that they should. And yet, education and health services are pervasively distributed in an inequitable manner, as any sociology textbook shows (e.g., Bilton et al., 1981).

These issues show up directly in the literature on people with developmental disabilities. For example, the mean lifespan of African Americans with Down syndrome in the 1990s was a mere 25 years, compared to an average of 50 years for whites with Down syndrome (Friedman, 2001). No biological basis for this difference in mortality is known to account for this difference. It is much more likely that this difference in mortality is due to inequitable access to health care in general and cardiac care specifically for African Americans (Editor's note, 2001). A similar issue related to ethnicity and childhood disability comes from Sharma, Nicholson, Briderick, and Poyser (2002), who reported higher rates of severe mental retardation, sensory disability, and slight increases in cerebral palsy and autism in children from Pakistani families compared to Continental Indian and White families. They also observed a 10-fold increased risk of genetic disorders. Sharma et al. speculated that these findings may reflect higher rates of consanguineous marriages within the Pakistani families. To date, we have no data on access to behavior analytic treatments and race. Recent scale immigration into Europe, the United States, and Canada has changed the ethnic and cultural mix of these societies. We can not assume that service models that were developed 10 or 20 years ago are uniformly appropriate for our present culture. Similarly, we can not unquestioningly generalize the results of outcome research done in the past with different populations to current populations.

Social class may also an important variable accounting for access to services for people with autism and other developmental disabilities. For example, there is general convergence of findings from several empirical studies that the prevalence of autism, unlike mild and moderate mental retardation of unknown etiology, is not related to social class (Fombonne, 1999). However, there is both direct and indirect evidence that social class affects the likelihood that families of children with autism will obtain access services. Wing (1980) found that fathers from upper socioeconomic backgrounds were much more likely than fathers of working-class background to self-refer to an outpatient clinic and to the National Society for Autistic Children. Schopler, Andrews, and Strupp (1979) compared families with an autistic child and found that those from a higher socioeconomic background were more likely to report an early age of onset, give a more detailed child history, travel further for services, and have greater access to services. In contrast, DeGiacomo and Fombonne (1998) found that social class was not related to age of recognition of onset of autism.

Although not directly addressing social class, there is considerable evidence that parental stress and related family characteristics might be related to social class and access to the most effective treatment. Johnson and Hastings (2002) surveyed 141 families who were receiving intensive early behavioral intervention services for their children with autism. The parents were asked to name common facilitative factors for, and barriers to, the services they were receiving. Commonly named barriers included recruitment and retention of therapists and lack of time and personal energy. Henderson and Vandenberg (1992) found that maternal social support and perceived efficacy correlated with family adjustment to having a child with autism. Inasmuch as the factors identified in these two studies might be related to social class, the two studies also suggest that social class might be important in determining access to the most effective interventions.

An important ethical question that has not been addressed rigorously by the current literature on the most effective treatment is equity of access to the most effective treatment by all families with a child with autism. There is some limited evidence that social class and ethnicity mediate access to treatment for children with autism. To date, research has not yet directly explored this issue. In order to ensure that the most effective services are delivered in an equitable and nonbiased manner, future research should address this question.

Cultural Design and Promotion of Ethical Behavior

Some aspects of this analysis might give the reader cause for pessimism: The values of society generally do not coincide with those of behavior analysts advocating for a better situation for people with disabilities. However, behaviorism is not passive with regard to cultural evolution. Skinner's *Science and Human Behavior* (1953) devotes an entire chapter to cultural design, and his *Walden Two* (Skinner, 1948) was an attempt to outline how to design an Utopian community as well as a statement about what behaviors we should find prevalent in a Utopian community. Some, such as the Los Horcones community in Mexico, have taken up Skinner's challenge and continue to work on the design and evolution of their own culture.

Skinner (1953) argued that the deliberate design of cultures is an activity in which many cultures engage. We place alarms to deter violence. We fine people for double parking. We tax to minimize consumption or remove taxes to stimulate consumption in our own neighborhood. Skinner suggested that much of this deliberate cultural design is operant behavior. We emit such cultural practices to avoid negative consequences such as famine or inflation; cultures that do not have such a cultural repertoire are generally no longer around. Skinner also noted that these cultural practices are emitted not because of the possibility of future or even distant consequences, but because of the culture's learning history and experience of consequences in the *past*. Thus, we might infer that society's general avoidance of implementing the most effective treatment is a practice that has been reinforced. Why does society continue to engage in such practices, even when there might be long-term benefits (Jacobson et al., 1998)? First, it may be that society has not yet come into contact with the benefits of such practices (e.g., the practices may rely on developing technologies). Second, it seems likely that avoidance of such practices has been negatively reinforced through loss of resources and increased effort. The situation seems analogous to self-control problems in which an individual's behavior that is harmful in the long run is reinforced by immediate consequences. Practices do change; for many years, early intervention was funded as a haphazard and almost exclusively state-initiative service. When IDEA was implemented, it required that early intervention be put in place in each state, in order to receive other education funds. The resistance to this new cultural practice is evident in that nearly a decade later, after the enactment of IDEA, many states had only just begun to implement early intervention. It remains a service seldom funded in the manner and to the degree that either preschool services or primary and secondary educational services are funded. Perhaps aversive contingencies for states are an essential component of maintaining this new cultural practice, at least initially. A model of cultural evolution must account for changes as well as resistance to changes.

Implementation of EIBI nationally might be viewed as a nascent indicator of a growing right to treatment. Perhaps in time this might be transformed to a right to effective treatment. It may be useful to distinguish a right to treatment from a right to effective treatment. Prior to IDEA, hundreds of thousands of American children with disabilities were excluded from any form of education. Similar practices existed in the United Kingdom and elsewhere. The precursor to IDEA guaranteed *some* form of education; it did not guarantee the *most* effective form of education. Over time, some children now have gained what their families and advocates believe to be the most effective form of intervention. Likewise, some children have gained access to preventative forms of intervention, some of which are highly effective, such as PKU (phenylketonuria) diets.

Several authors have noted that the behavior of many parents, therapists, policymakers, and legislators is not greatly under the control of data, or least behavioral outcome data from individual clients or programs (Howard, 1999). Yet, I suggest that their behavior is under the control of other data: data on costs, outcomes of regulatory surveys, budgets, and profits. We may regard such behavior as unethical, but it may be a description of the natural world as it is. If this is the case, the gauntlet is thrown down to advocates for the most effective treatments to establish their data as more reinforcing than these other data. How can we do that? Currently we do so by adding punitive contingencies to these other data through due process hearings and court cases. By demonstrating that all a school district or other service provider cares about is the bottom line, but not client outcomes, we shame, coerce effortful responses, and then take away the callous providers' reinforcers. By taking such action, we set up contingencies of negative reinforcement. Unfortunately, the escape behavior of providers associated teaches them to make the minimum responses required to avoid the contingency—to meet the letter of the law—but does not teach the provider to love the most effective treatments and repeatedly approach them because such approach responses are positively reinforced. Can advocates for the most effective treatments design contingencies for providers under which they approach these effective treatments?

A LAST WORD ON ETHICS

Behavior analysts have been very active in advocating for effective behavioral treatments. We cite endorsements from the New York State Department of Health (1999a, 1999b, 1999c) and the Surgeon General of the United States (Satcher, 2002) and readily point to the shortcomings of many other treatments that generally have little empirical basis to support their use. Some may find these endorsements a little too shrill. We should be aware that the evidence in favor of behavior analysis is strong, but imperfect. Further, we know treatment efficacy is important, but not a sufficient criterion for society to adopt an intervention (Howard, 1999). So, appeal to treatment efficacy may help or hinder the evolution of evidence-based treatments; as yet, we do not have the data to see how our culture will evolve.

Let me give Skinner the last word on ethics. Skinner (1953, p. 434) noted that cultural evolution parallels evolution of organisms and the operant. Some mutation or variation in behavior must occur for selection to occur. Some forms of behavior or cultural practice will be extinguished, and others selected, according to Skinner, if they promote the survival of that culture. We can promote such variation in order to design new cultures. Obviously some forms of cultural practices—slavery, aggression, some forms of fertility control—may promote the survival of cultures, but would today in our culture be considered ethically odious. (Who says we will survive, anyway?)

What can we say about these new cultural mutations, the fads *du jour*? Most fads, by definition, are passing and do not endure: They are weeds on the margins of cultural evolution, which grow too tall only to die away when the host culture no longer selects such practices, through punishment or extinction. But what of these other cultural mutations, the newly developed effective forms of treatment? We know that many effective forms of cultural practice arise and rapidly extinguish (Howard, 1999). Diamond's (1998) book is replete with examples of new cultural practices that arose and rapidly extinguished, for example, the possible development of printing in ancient Greece and the arrival of bows and arrows in New Zealand hundreds of years before the arrival of Europeans. Are data-based effective treatments to follow the way of bows and arrows in New Zealand? Skinner (1953) answers this question as follows:

> We have no reason to suppose that any cultural practice is always right or wrong according to some principle or values regardless of the circumstances or that anyone can at any given time make an absolute evaluation of its survival value. So long as this is recognized, we are less likely to seize upon the hard and fast answer as an escape from indecision, and we are more likely to continue to modify cultural design in order to test the consequences. (p. 436)

REFERENCES

American Psychological Association. (1992). *Ethical principles for psychologists and code of conduct.* Washington, DC: Author.

Bennett, B. E., Bryant, B. K., VandenBos, G. R., & Greenwood, A. (1990). *Professional liability and risk management.* Washington, DC: American Psychological Association.

Bilton, T., Bonnett, K., Jones, P., Stanworth, M., Sheard, K., & Webster, A. (1981). *Introductory sociology.* London: MacMillan.

Colorado Governor signs 'rebirthing' ban. (2001). CNN.com/law center. Downloaded January, 23, 2003, from http://www/cnn.com2001/LAW/04/17/rebirthing.ban/index.html

De Giacomo, A., & Fombonne, E. (1998). Parental recognition of developmental abnormalities in autism. *European Journal of Child and Adolescent Psychiatry, 7,* 131–136.

Dewan, S. K. (2002, September 13). Pataki attacks June ruling that 8th-grade education is enough. *New York Times,* Final, p. B6.

Diamond, J. (1991). *The rise and fall of the third chimpanzee. How our animal heritage affects the way we live.* London: Vintage.

Diamond, J. (1998). *Guns, germs and steel: The fates of human societies.* New York: Norton.

Driscoll, D. P. (2001, November 20). *Administrative advisory SPED 2002-1: Requirement to review refusals to evaluate for special education eligibility—Guidance on the change in the special education standard of service from "maximum possible development" to "free appropriate public education" ("FAPE").* Boston: Department of Education, Commonwealth of Massachusetts.

Editor's Note. (2001). [No title]. *Morbidity and Mortality Weekly Report, 50,* 464–465.

Fombonne, E. (1999). The epidemiology of autism: A review. *Psychological Medicine, 29,* 769–789.

Friedman, J. M. (2001). Racial disparities in median age at death of persons with Down syndrome–United States, 1968–1997. *Morbidity and Mortality Weekly Report, 50,* 463–465.

Green, G. (1999). Science and ethics in early intervention for autism. In P. M. Ghezzi, W. L. Williams, & J. E. Carr (Eds.), *Autism: Behavior analytic perspectives* (pp. 11–28). Reno, NV: Context.

Hayes, L. J., Adams, M. A., & Rydeen, K. L. (1994). Ethics, choice and value. In L. J. Hayes, G. J. Hayes, S. C. Moore, & P. M. Ghezzi (Eds.), *Ethical issues in developmental disabilities* (pp. 1–39). Reno, NV: Context.

Henderson, D., & Vandenberg, B. (1992). Factors influencing adjustment in the families of autistic children. *Psychological Reports, 71*, 167–171.

Howard, J. (1999). Data are not enough. In P. M. Ghezzi, W. L. Williams, & J. E. Carr (Eds.), *Autism: Behavior analytic perspectives* (pp. 29–32). Reno, NV: Context.

Huber, P. (1993). *Galileo's revenge: Junk science in the courtroom.* New York: Basic Books.

Jacobson, J. W., Mulick, J. A., & Green, G. (1998). Cost-benefit estimates for early intensive behavioral intervention for young children with autism: General model and single state case. *Behavioral Interventions, 13*, 202–226.

Johnson, E., & Hastings, R. P. (2002). Facilitating factors and barriers to the implementation of intensive home-based behavioural intervention for young children with autism. *Child: Care, Health & Development, 28*, 123–129.

Kantor, J. R. (1982). *Cultural psychology.* Chicago: Principia.

Kantor, J. R., & Smith, N. M. (1975). *The science of psychology.* Chicago: Principia.

Lahten, B. (1999). Ethical behavior. In L. J. Hayes, G. J. Hayes, S. C. Moore, & P. M. Ghezzi (Eds.), *Ethical issues in developmental disabilities* (pp. 40–43). Reno, NV: Context.

Marcus, L. M., Rubin, J. S., & Rubin, M. A. (2000). Benefit–cost analysis and autism services: A response to Jacobson and Mulick. *Journal of Autism and Developmental Disorders, 30*, 595–598.

National Commission for the Protection of Human Subjects of Biomedical and Behavioral Research. (1979). *The Belmont report: Ethical principles and guidelines for the protection of human subjects of research.* Washington, DC: Department of Health, Education, and Welfare.

New York State Department of Health. (1999a). *Clinical practice guidelines: Report of the recommendations. Autism / Pervasive Developmental Disorders. Assessment and intervention for young children (age 0–3 years)* (Publication No. 4215). Albany, NY: Author.

New York State Department of Health. (1999b). *Clinical practice guidelines: Quick reference guide. Autism / Pervasive Developmental Disorders. Assessment and intervention for young children (age 0 –3 years)* (Publication No. 4216). Albany, NY: Author.

New York State Department of Health. (1999c). *Clinical practice guidelines: The guideline technical report. Autism / Pervasive Developmental Disorders. Assessment and intervention for young children (age 0–3 years)* (Publication No. 4217). Albany, NY: Author.

Pharis, D. (1999). *State hospital reform. Why was it so hard to achieve?* Durham, NC: Carolina Academic Press.

Satcher, D. (2002). *Report of the Surgeon General's conference on children's mental health: A national action agenda.* Washington, DC: Office of the Surgeon General of the United States, Public Health Service, Department of Health and Human Services.

Schopler, E., Andrews, E., & Strupp, K. (1979). Do children with autism come from upper-middle-class parents? *Journal of Autism and Developmental Disorders, 9*, 139–152.

Sharma, M. R., Nicholson, J., Briderick, M., & Poyser, J. (2002). Disability in children from different ethnic groups. *Child, Health Care and Development, 28*, 87–93.

Skinner, B. F. (1948). *Walden two.* London: MacMillan.

Skinner, B. F. (1953). *Science and human behavior.* New York: Collier-MacMillan.

Sturmey, P., & Gaubatz, M. D. (2003). *Clinical and counseling practice. A case-guided approach.* Boston: Allyn & Bacon.

Sturmey, P., Thomsett, M., Sundaram, G., & Newton, J. T. (2003). The effects of method of behavior management, client characteristics, and outcome on public perception of intervention in pediatric dentistry. *Behavioural and Cognitive Psychotherapy, 31*, 169–176.

Thiroux, J. (2001). *Ethics: Theory and practice.* Upper Saddle River, NJ: Prentice-Hall.

Van Houten, R. (1999). The right to effective behavioral treatment. In P. M. Ghezzi, W. L. Williams, & J. E. Carr (Eds.), *Autism: Behavior analytic perspectives* (pp. 103–119). Reno, NV: Context.

Van Houten, R., Axelrod, S., Bailey, J. S., Favell, J. E., Foxx, R. M., Iwata, B. A., et al. (1988). The right to effective behavioral treatment. *Journal of Applied Behavior Analysis, 21*, 381–384.

Wing, L. (1980). Childhood autism and social class: A question of selection? *British Journal of Psychiatry, 137*, 410–417.

Part VI
Ethical Obligations to Involve
Clients as Informed Participants

[19]

A model consent form for psychiatric drug treatment *

David Cohen [a],[**] and David Jacobs [b]

[a] School of Social Work and Research Group on Social Aspects of Health and Prevention, Université de Montréal, Canada
[b] Center for the Study of Psychiatry and Psychology – West, USA

1. Introduction

The model consent form which appears below was first developed in 1991. It was included in a package of information and advocacy material that David Cohen prepared for a group of current and ex-psychiatric patients attending his workshops on psychiatric drugs. The purpose of the form was to summarize, from a critical perspective, some information about psychiatric drugs and the context of their prescription which might make prospective consumers more knowledgeable. Most of the patients and ex-patients who read it said that not a single point mentioned on the form was ever discussed with them by their prescribing doctor.

The original version was written in an ironic tone, to make it an entertaining read while trying to impart scientifically validated information. Over the years, as it included recent evidence, as colleagues asked to use it in their own practice, and as others suggested ways to modify it, the tone became more factual. Traces of irony probably remain but do not intend any belittling of drug prescribers or drug users.

Typically, consent forms used in many helping interventions (medical or otherwise) serve to protect professionals, not inform and empower clients to make intelligent decisions about their own fate and well-being. If it seeks to achieve the latter goal, we believe that informed consent for psychiatric drug treatment should contain the following elements:

- a statement to the effect that the biomedical status of what is to be treated is uncertain, even speculative;
- unbiased, up to date information concerning treatment options, including of course strictly psychological forms of treatment;
- realistic and comprehensible information concerning the somatic and psychological effects of drug use and drug withdrawal, both in the short run and in the long run.

We are inclined to think that no one who was so informed would consent. Of course, this is an exceedingly complex question. It would be greatly simplified if psychiatry and clinical psychopharmacology rested on rigorous research and valid findings, showed genuine concern for the patient's or subject's bests

*This paper appears simultaneously in this journal and the *Journal of Humanistic Psychology*, by agreement with the Editors of that Journal and with the approval of the authors.

**Correspondence: David Cohen, Ph.D., School of Social Work, Université de Montréal, C.P. 6128 (Stn Centre-ville), Montréal, QC, Canada H3C 3J7.

interests, and operated in a mental health system designed to meet patients' or clients' needs. We have argued elsewhere in detail that this is not the case [1–3]. If our analysis has any validity, no consent form will do. Nevertheless, therapists, clinicians, or researchers must obviously make a sincere effort to convey the risks, the drawbacks, the unknowns of psychiatric drug treament – even if many prospective patients might understandably recoil.

2. A model consent form for psychiatric drug treatment

I, the undersigned, understand that I am about to be prescribed one or more drugs by Dr. _____ . The drug(s) I am to be prescribed is (are) the following: _____ .

I understand that a DSM-IV diagnostic label has been assigned to me, based on my doctor's (and perhaps also on other people's) subjective judgment of my speech, manner, and behavior during our meeting, which lasted approximately _____ minutes. I am aware that I will never be able to remove this diagnosis, or any other that will be added in the future, from my medical record.

I understand that although my doctor says that I am sick or that I have a treatable illness or disease, he or she is just using a figure of speech and cannot establish, with any test or procedure known to medical science that I in fact "have" the "illness" implied by the diagnostic label. Indeed, I realize that although medical opinion may now hold that a "chemical imbalance" or a "brain abnormality" or some physical problem "underlies" or "produces" my distress or suffering, I am aware that no objective information (through lab tests, scans, etc.) concerning the state of my body has been obtained in order to arrive at a DSM-IV diagnosis. If by chance such information has been obtained for that purpose, I understand that it played no role whatsoever in fulfilling any criteria for the DSM-IV diagnosis or diagnoses that I have been given by my physician – except perhaps for diagnoses related to drug-induced disorders such as tardive dyskinesia.

I have been informed that the drug or drugs which my doctor is prescribing cannot cure whatever "illness" or "chemical imbalance" medical opinion might believe I have, but only affect symptoms of my distress or suffering.

I understand that the drug I am about to take cannot restore any of my physical or psychological functions "back to normal". Rather, the drug is expected to produce many new mental and physical symptoms, which might help make my original complaints seem less disturbing for a while.

I understand that it is exceedingly difficult to determine what is brought about (both desired and un-wanted) by a psychoactive drug which has wide and diverse effects on the brain and other organ systems. I further understand that the problem of how to accomplish this adequately is a controversial issue within psychiatry and the Food and Drug Administration (FDA).

I realize that FDA approval of the drug I am about to take is based upon very short-term studies (usually 6 to 8 weeks) which are designed, paid for, and supervised by the drug's manufacturer. I further realize that the FDA does not require or expect that all of a drug's adverse effects will be known prior to marketing and prior to lengthy exposure of ordinary patients to that drug. I am also aware that the FDA's knowledge about the drug's adverse effects after marketing comes mostly from spontaneous physician reports, even though the FDA itself recognizes that these reports are just "the tip of the iceberg" of the probable true frequency of adverse effects. I know that wording in the package insert and in the *Physician's Desk Reference* is the outcome of a complex negotiation between the manufacturer and the FDA. I also realize that it sometimes occurs that the FDA belatedly learns that the manufacturer did not fully disclose what it actually knows about a drugs' adverse effects. Finally, I understand that despite FDA approval for psychiatric drugs being granted on the basis of short-term studies, the long-term effects of continuing drug use is not systematically studied by any responsible organization or government agency.

If I am consenting to take the drug as part of a research study, I understand that the researcher's primary interest and loyalty is not to me as a patient, not to my personal interests or welfare.

I understand that the "needs of the research project" come before and have priority over my own personal needs. I understand that the drug will have a wide range of effects on my brain, body, consciousness, emotions, and actions. My sleep, my memory, my judgment, my coordination, my stamina, my sexuality are likely to be affected. I understand in particular that the effects of a psychoactive drug may undermine my ability to monitor and report upon just how the drug has affected me, even impaired me, perhaps in a dangerous direction (judgment, social perception, impulse control, etc.). I further understand that what to do to protect me, as a patient or subject, against this possibility is a basically unanswered problem in psychiatric drug treatment and research.

I understand that effects that have a 1 in a 100 chance of occurring are actually considered "frequent" effects that should be mentioned to an adult, competent, prospective patient like myself. My doctor (or the researcher) has specifically advised me that the following toxic or adverse reactions may occur, and has provided these estimates of the frequency of their occurrence in patients like myself: _____.
I understand that I may experience an adverse effect which might then abate after a few days or weeks. This will usually mean that my body has developed a tolerance to the drug's presence, not that the effect will never bother me again in the future.

I understand that if I inform my doctor of the occurrence of adverse effects, he or she will have five basic options: (1) cease the drug, (2) decrease the dose, (3) increase the dose, (4) switch to another drug, (5) add another drug. I understand that no rules exist to determine which option is best to follow in individual cases, and it is likely that several options will be followed simultaneously. I also understand that most doctors are not likely to report to the FDA any adverse effect they suspect or have observed, contributing to the generally inadequate picture of a drug's true impact on patients like myself.

I have been informed, if I am prescribed a neuroleptic drug such as Haldol or Risperdal[1] and if I take it regularly for a few years, that I have at least a 30% chance over the next 5 years of developing tardive dyskinesia, a possibly irreversible disorder characterized by abnormal involuntary movements of my face or other body parts. I have been informed that I may also suffer from other acute or chronic movement problems, such as parkinsonism, akathisia, and dystonia, and their associated unpleasant mental states.

I have been informed, if I am prescribed a tranquillizer like Xanax or Klonopin and I take it regularly for more than three or four weeks, that I run the risk of becoming physically dependent on it. I will then have a good chance of experiencing "rebound" insomnia and anxiety, and many other unpleasant sensations, when I try stopping the drug, or even while I continue to take it. I understand that these drugs are not effective anti-anxiety or sleep-inducing agents after a few weeks of use. I realize that some people are unable to withdraw and must therefore permanently endure the consequences of daily use.

I have been informed, if I am prescribed lithium, that I do not have a "lack" of lithium in my body, nor can such a "lack" be demonstrated by any existing test. I understand that the blood tests that I will undergo regularly will be for the sole purpose of determining just how much lithium has been introduced in my bloodstream and whether this could produce toxic symptoms, since, as a result of the mental dullness that lithium is expected to produce, I will be in no position to recognize some of these toxic symptoms.

---

[1] Editorial note: The trade names included here are used by the authors as examples of names likely to be familiar to patients; they are not presented as indicative of any particular risk attaching to these drugs.

I understand that the drug is likely to provoke various unpleasant effects when I stop taking it, especially if I stop too suddenly. I understand that although withdrawal reactions are systematically ignored in psychiatric drug treatment or research, they might represent the worst part of my whole drug-taking episode. I understand further that these reactions will often closely resemble the original symptoms for which the drug was first prescribed to me, and are likely to be taken for a return of these symptoms (a "relapse"), rather than for withdrawal effects. I realize that my doctor, or the researcher, is likely to interpret these reactions as a sign that my "illness" is chronic and that my drug is "effective".

I also understand that once I have been taking drugs for months or years, I will have much difficulty finding a health professional to assist me in withdrawing prudently and safely from the drugs, if I so wish.

Having understood the above, I realize that the drug treatment may cause severe pain or discomfort, worsen my existing problem significantly, or even damage me permanently. However, most doctors or experts will never formally or informally acknowledge that the drug harmed to me in this manner. I will have practically no chance of proving that the drug caused my damage and obtaining compensation for me.

I understand that no body of research clearly shows that the problems indicated by my diagnosis or diagnoses require or respond more favorably to drug treatment than to one or more forms of non-drug treatment. It is obvious to me that non-drug treatment would enable me to completely avoid whatever dangers or risks are associated with taking the drug or drugs I am agreeing to take. My doctor (or the researcher) has made it clear to me that existing evidence does not indicate that it is in my best interest to choose drug treatment as a first recourse. I am choosing to be treated with *[write in the name of the drug or drugs]* for the following reasons *[provide ample space; this section must be filled in by the patient or subject]*:

_____.

Signed: _____.

References

[1] D. Cohen, A critique of the use of neuroleptic drugs in psychiatry, in: *From Placebo to Panacea: Putting Psychiatric Drugs to the Test*, S. Fisher and S. Greenberg, eds, John Wiley, New York, 1997, pp. 173–228.
[2] D.H. Jacobs, Psychiatric drugging: forty years of pseudo-science, self-interest, and indifference to harm, *Journal of Mind and Behavior* **16** (1995), 421–470.
[3] M. McCubbin and D. Cohen, Extremely unbalanced: interest divergence and power disparity between clients and psychiatry, *International Journal of Law and Psychiatry* **19** (1996), 1–25.

[20]

Respecting Autonomy: The Struggle over Rights and Capacities

Jay Katz

IN RECENT CENTURIES, the belief that persons have a right to individual self-determination has captured the imagination of the Western world. This right has been asserted on many grounds—political, philosophical, religious, moral, and legal. It also rests on the notion that human beings have the capacity to chart their own course of action in accordance with a plan they themselves have chosen.

The idea that a similar right should be accorded to patients has surfaced largely, and surely more insistently, during the last few decades. That the call for patients' right to self-determination has engendered a bitter controversy is not surprising once one appreciates that patient self-determination is an idea alien to medicine. Since physicians have generally maintained that patients do not have the *capacity* to participate in decision making, patients' "autonomy" was not a concept inscribed in medicine's vocabulary. Thus the contemporary debate over patient self-determination has been fought out over two issues that require separate consideration: rights and capacities. The proponents of patient participation in decision making have marshalled various theories of autonomy—moral autonomy, civil autonomy, and autonomy of the will—in order to assert their claims. Their opponents have argued that the demand for patient choice ignores the reality of the human incapacity to make decisions when persons become patients.

The proponents' assertions have suffered from a lack of integration of abstract notions of rights with a psychological view of human beings' capacities for autonomous choice. Any claim that individuals possess certain rights, however, presupposes an inherent capacity for the exercise of such rights. Opponents of patient self-determination, on the other hand, have not developed a systematic theory of the psychology of the physician-patient relationship. They have largely based their claims on scattered clinical observations. Even their observations have suffered from not inquiring, for example, whether the observed incapacities of patients to make decisions are fundamental to and inherent in patienthood, or engendered and reinforced by extraneous factors such as physicians' conduct. If doctors' conduct makes an essential contribution to the perceived incapacities of patients as choice makers, then such incapacities may be significantly moderated by doctors' becoming more sensitive to, and nurturing of, patients' adult capacities.

In developing a foundation for patients' rights to decision making, I shall pursue three objectives: to distinguish between rights to and capacities for decision making; to develop a more systematic view of patients' psychological capacities to chart their own course of action; and to examine the implications of my view of capacities for a right to self-determination.

Definition of Terms

Let me begin with a few broad definitions that I shall refine as I go along. The right to self-determination is defined here as the right of individuals to make their own decisions without interference from others. Autonomy has often been used interchangeably with self-determination but I shall employ the concept of autonomy, or "psychological autonomy" as I shall call it, to denote solely the capacities of persons to exercise the right to self-determination. In my scheme, psychological autonomy speaks to persons' capacities to reflect about contemplated choices and to make choices. The extent and limits of such capacities of course vary from individual to individual, but I am not concerned here about such individual variations. I wish to focus instead on those capacities for self-determination that depend on one's views of the psychological nature of human beings. In essense psychological autonomy is a concept that "informs" the right to self-determination by explaining, refining, and pointing up human capacities and incapacities for the exercise of such a right.

I have given autonomy's root meaning—*autos* and *nomos* = self law—an unaccustomed construction, for traditionally it has emphasized different areas of rights, be they political, legal, or moral rights. I wish to emphasize, however, the psychological capacities that underlie rights, including the right to self-determination. Indeed, underlying, although generally unidentified, assumptions about human psychology have shaped decisively the views on all political, legal, and moral rights to which persons are supposedly entitled. I retain the term autonomy to call attention to the fact that traditional definitions of autonomy, and of rights as well, contain a great many psychological assumptions that have been given insufficient consideration in understanding the complexities of decision making between physicians and patients.

The pervasive psychological assumptions that underlie autonomy and the many senses in which it has been employed, emerge in Tom Beauchamp's and James Childress' definition of autonomy:

> Autonomy is a form of *personal liberty* of action where the individual determines his or her own course of *action* in accordance with a plan chosen by himself or herself. The autonomous person is one who not only *deliberates* about and *chooses* such plans but who is *capable* of acting on the basis of such deliberations. . . . A person's autonomy is his or her independence, self-reliance, and self-contained *ability* to decide. A person of diminished autonomy, by contrast, is highly dependent on others and in at least some respect *incapable* of deliberating or acting on the basis of such deliberations. . . . The most general idea of autonomy is that of being one's own person, without constraints either by another's action or by a *psychological* or *physical* limitation. The term "autonomy" is thus quite broad, for it can refer to both *the will* and *action in society*; and both internal and external constraints on action can limit autonomy.[1]

Beauchamp and Childress appreciate that the term autonomy can be used quite broadly. It speaks in the language of rights—''autonomy is a form of personal liberty''—and in the language of capacities—''the autonomous person is one . . . who is capable of acting. . . .'' To encompass both notions under the same term can lead to confusion unless great care is taken. The confusion begins to creep in, for example, when Beauchamp and Childress observe that autonomy ''is his or her independence, self-reliance, and self-contained ability to decide.'' Do these terms address rights, capacities, or both? Moreover, striking about their definition is the emphasis on psychological criteria rather than on rights.

Similarly, Robert Veatch uses autonomy as a principle defining rights when he speaks of ''inalienable rights,'' and as a concept defining capacities when he introduces distinctions between ''autonomous'' persons and those who ''are substantially nonautonomous, whose actions are essentially nonvoluntary.''[2] I intend to make clear distinctions between rights and capacities. I also depart from Veatch and others by not drawing distinctions between persons who are either ''autonomous'' or whose actions are ''nonvoluntary.'' Instead, I start from the assumption that *all* human beings' ''autonomous'' functioning is affected by their capacities *and* incapacities to act ''voluntarily.''

Principles and Human Psychology

Abstract principles tend to express generalizations about conduct that are ill-suited for application to actual cases in which human psychological capacities to exercise rights must be considered. Abstract principles, to resolve problems posed in specific clinical situations, require mediating principles. Such mediating principles do not exist. Instead, in the fields of medical ethics and bioethics, the theoretical views of Kant, Mill, and others are often invoked to give answers to clinical problems that the principles' abstract formulations cannot provide. Such principles at best can provide a ''Weltanschauung'' which in the course of translation to practical cases tend to become wittingly and unwittingly infiltrated by idiosyncratic personal and professional preferences and unanalyzed assumptions about human capacities.

The conclusions drawn from these principles say more about the commentators—their orientation and assumptions—than about the principles or the problems before them. If commentators, on the other hand, try to avoid that trap by relying solely on abstract principles to guide their recommendations, their answers are too general to even come close to answering the practical questions posed by specific cases.

Yet, the problem with abstract principles is not that they are devoid of psychological assumptions, but that principles are frequently formulated without making the underlying psychological assumptions explicit. A careful scrutiny of many philosophical, moral, political or legal principles reveals all kinds of hidden, albeit woefully mutilated, assumptions about human nature. Principles, therefore, can sound foreign and strange to the heart, if not to the mind.

Immanuel Kant, in restricting his conception of autonomy to capacities to reason, without reference to human beings' emotional life and their dependence on the external world, projected a vision of human nature that estranged his principle from human beings and the world in which they must live. That Kant did so deliberately and with full awareness, because he wished to isolate and abstract a single aspect of human psychology, i.e., rationality, into its pure form, is a separate matter. What matters here is that the Kantian principle of free will, since it is based on this single aspect of human psychology, makes, if applied to actual situations, demands for human conduct that human beings cannot fulfill.

Since Kant looms large in the literature on bioethics, let me say a bit more about his views. In *Groundwork of the Metaphysic of Morals*[3], he emphasized human beings' capacity for reason. He commanded man to aspire to exercising his rational will, "to [choosing] *only that* which reason independently of inclination recognizes to be practically necessary, that is, to be good." Kant's reference to "inclination," i.e., passion, indicates that he was aware that in the real world human beings are ruled by emotions as well as reason. But Kant counselled human beings not only to resist and exercise control over inclination, but he also expected them to go a long way toward obeying only those laws that they rationally found in their uncoerced self.

Listen to his categorical imperative: "Act only on that maxim through which you can at the same time will that it should become universal law.'' Kant was aware of the ''subjective imperfections of the will.'' He observed that a ''perfectly good [human] will'' would collapse the distinction between human and divine (holy) will. But he slighted this human, empiric fact in his theorizing. At a minimum he thought it possible to narrow the gap decisively by exhorting each person to live by his or her categorical imperative. In doing so, Kant substituted a conception of the rational will for the divine will—the notion that through the exercise of reason human beings would ultimately stand, if not closer to God, at least, as expressed in Judeo-Christian liturgy, ''just somewhat lower than the angels.''

The theoretical and aspirational nature of Kant's views of human beings must be clearly kept in mind. Kant did observe that ''the principle of humanity is not borrowed from experience . . . it is admittedly an Ideal.'' Equally kept in mind must be Kant's awareness that the power of ''inclination'' is buried deeply in the human psyche. Kant only hoped that ''it must be the universal *wish* of every rational being to be wholly free from them.'' Instead, some commentators have intimated, claiming Kant as authority, not that human beings *ought* to be possessed of reason alone, but that they *can* be possessed of reason alone. Such statements have made it easier to entertain the possibility of basing disclosure and consent upon notions of ''pure'' free will.

Such interpreters of Kant not only have failed to subject Kant's views on human nature to a critical examination, but also have obliterated his distinctions between theoretical man and living man. Yet Kant contributed to this misunderstanding by projecting a view of human nature that endows human beings with greater capacities for living a life of reason than is in fact the case. Kant's view of *theoretical* man is hopelessly estranged from *real* man. He created the impression, perhaps unintended, that human beings can, and therefore must, employ solely their innate and developed capacities to reason in contemplating their choices.

When he wrote that ''in the case of men . . . the will is not in itself completely in accord with reason,'' he did not find it necessary to ask whether ''the law of his own needs'' must be given equal status with ''reason'' to account for the lawfulness of human nature. Instead, he proceeded to define only one facet of human behavior, the capacity for reason, and to leave unconsidered its polar opposite, man's capacity for unreason as well as the dy-

namic interrelations between reason and unreason. I believe that
even in theory, autonomy must take both polar opposites into account, for human beings are not totally possessed of either alone.
Human beings are subject to the influence of reason and unreason, with the relative strength of either being affected by many
innate, developmental, and situational factors. Moreover, capacities for reason are impaired whenever human beings are in pain,
in love, in mourning, or in the throes of biological, environmental, or social crises. Kant's theoretical conception of the nature of
human beings is too neglectful of the complex interrelations between reason, emotions, and the external world; it is therefore of
little relevance to practical situations. The debate over the relevance of principles to the resolution of human problems needs to
encompass a new dimension and pose new questions: To what
extent should principles comport with the biological, psychological, and social nature of human beings? To the extent that they
do not, what is the relevance of such principles as guides to human conduct?

Self-Determination and Psychological Autonomy

I have already suggested that psychological autonomy and self-
determination, although interrelated, need to be clearly distinguished. I shall use self-determination to refer only to the rights
of individuals to make decisions without interference by others.
At its extreme, it is an ideal construct, unattainable in human affairs, as the need for civil, criminal, and moral laws restricting
certain conduct clearly indicates. Paternalism, one of self-determination's contrary siblings, is a principle on the same level of
abstraction. At its extreme, it implies total surrender of decision
making to the will of others. The debate about patient self-rule in
physician-patient interactions has sought to pinpoint the location
of the right to make decisions on the continuum between self-determination and paternalism.

   Self-determination contains, as my discussion on psychological autonomy will soon make clearer, two intertwined, though
separable ideas. One looks at conduct in relation to the external
world, at conduct in relation to action. I call this external component of self-determination *choice*. It has also been spoken of as
freedom of action. The other looks at conduct in relation to the

internal world, at conduct in relation to thinking about choices
by oneself and with others prior to action. I call this internal
component of self-determination *reflection* or *thinking about choices*.
Traditionally, discussions of self-determination have emphasized
the external component. I shall argue instead that both the external and internal components deserve equal and separate consideration.

Psychological autonomy refers to the extent and limits of a
person's capacities to reflect and to make choices inherent in the
psychological nature of human beings. As an ideal construct,
psychological autonomy refers to the capacity of persons to reflect, choose, and act with an awareness of the internal and external influences and reasons that they would wish to accept. It
must be clearly kept in mind that this is an ideal definition.
Choice on the basis of a complete awareness of the influences and
reasons that impinge on it is never attainable, but awareness can
be significantly improved through self-reflection and conversation with others.

Internal Reflection and External Choice

A number of considerations have led me to introduce distinctions
between internal reflection and external choice, as well as to
highlight the importance of psychological autonomy. The external-internal distinction permits the posing of two sets of fundamentally different questions about persons' capacities for psychological autonomy. One external question is: "To what extent
should an individual's *choices* be respected?" Two internal questions are: "To what extent should an individual's *thinking about
choices* be respected?" and "Can and should a person's capacity
for reflection be enhanced through conversation?" The last question is important if I am correct in assuming that human psychological capacities for autonomy are limited, yet subject to enhancement by conversation.

In all human encounters the respect accorded to self-determination is influenced by assumptions about human beings' psychological capacities to think and to act. The only psychological
assumption that the medical profession has acknowledged and
endorsed is that patients under the stress of illness and as a result
of ignorance about medical matters are incapable of making deci-

sions on their own behalf. The external-internal distinction draws attention to a crucial question that challenges this assumption: If physicians were to provide patients with a meaningful opportunity for conversation, could whatever incapacities to reasoning illness engenders be moderated sufficiently for patients' choices to be treated with greater respect? It is likely that the answer would be affirmative for a significant number of patients, particularly those who do not suffer from acute illnesses. If physicians were to pay greater attention to conversation—to patients' capacities to reflect about choices—it could change their traditional attitudes toward patients' capacities to make their own decisions and, in turn, could radically transform the current state of physician-patient decision making.

The respect one wishes to accord to the internal and external components of self-determination, however, also depends upon how one weighs political, legal, and moral value preferences such as privacy, beneficence, loyalty and freedom. Looked at from this perspective, the external component also encompasses the choices individuals must be allowed to exercise to uphold these values (e.g., respect for liberty and freedom of action) and the internal component encompasses the extent of reflection and conversation that individuals should be obligated to engage in prior to acting, to respect these values. For example, respect for the great importance physicians place on beneficence and loyalty to their patients may suggest that physicians have a right and need to be informed why their patients do not choose to follow a proposed course of action so that doctors can be reasonably certain that their patients have understood their recommendations.

The internal-external distinction also permits separate consideration of the relevance of assumptions about human psychological functioning to reflection, on the one hand, and to choice, on the other. Whenever patients' right to self-determination has been discussed, the focus of discussion about psychological capacities has been on choice. The proponents of self-determination have argued that the choices of all but incompetent individuals must be honored and that the introduction of any psychological assumptions is irrelevant or even treacherous. For the most part, I share these views. Even though choices are influenced by psychological considerations, it is one thing to appreciate that fact and quite another to interfere with choice on the basis of speculations, or even evidence, about underlying psychological reasons that seemingly led a patient to make the "wrong" choice. Such psychological explanations can be found too readily and exploited too easily for purposes of over-reaching and coercion. Thus the dangers of interfering with patients' choices on psychological grounds are too great and too difficult to control. Short of substantial evidence of incompetence, choices deserve to be honored.

Reflection, however, deserves to be treated differently. Here psychological assumptions suggest that physicians and patients are under an obligation to reflect and to converse. Ignorance, misconceptions, exaggerated fears, and magical hopes about matters such as diagnostic tests and therapeutic interventions, as well as about what physicians and patients want and are able to do for one another, can decisively influence choice. The danger is great that patients' and doctors' choices will be distorted by such internally and externally engendered mistaken ideas. Thus, conversation will have to be more extensive and more searching if one believes that such distortions affect choice and that they can and must be sorted out. On the other hand, such conversation can be more limited if one holds to the belief that thought and action are based largely on a reasoned awareness by both parties of the motivations and reality factors that influence their conduct.

Finally, the separation of the internal from the external aspects of self-determination helps to focus attention on the largest, yet least examined, problem in physician-patient decision making: physicians' unquestioning acceptance of patients' affirmative responses to a proposed intervention. The right to self-determination has most extensively been discussed in relation to refusals of diagnostic and therapeutic procedures, that is, in relation to honoring "negative" choices. However important an issue, outright refusals are rare events in physician-patient encounters.

Affirmative responses deserve study in their own right. Doctors' acceptance of a mere "yes" response is often meaningless because they have no idea what it means to the patient. In addition, an all too ready acceptance of a "yes" response can constitute what Edmond Cahn has called an "engineering of consent by exploiting the condition of necessitous men."[4] Cahn identified a most troublesome flaw in physician-patient conversation: the witting and unwitting manipulation of disclosure and, in turn, of choice by trading on the ignorance and fears of scared patients. For example, this can happen in instances of "unnecessary surgery," when an elective procedure, such as a hysterectomy for fibroid tumors, is represented without qualifications as the one medically indicated to "avoid cancer." If I am correct that the process of thinking about choices can be improved, then subsequent problems of disagreement between physicians and patients over choice, or patients' outright refusals, may prove to be less disturbing than they now are. Attention to thinking about choices may either reconcile physicians' and patients' differences in expectations or clarify the differences sufficiently for both to feel more comfortable in going their separate ways.

Psychoanalytic Considerations

My views on self-determination have been shaped by psychoanalysis, particularly by the concepts of conscious-unconscious, rationality-irrationality, and primary and secondary process. A brief presentation of these concepts is offered to clarify the subsequent discussion of my views on psychological autonomy and their implications for decision making between physicians and patients. Of course, psychoanalysis is only one of many theories about human psychology and my views must be evaluated from the vantage point of my specific theoretical commitment. Whether one adheres to psychoanalytic theory or not, however, one must commit oneself to some psychological theory, for assumptions about human nature loom large in whatever views one entertains about self-determination and decision making between physicians and patients.

The pervasive influence of the unconscious on the lives of human beings has been one of psychoanalysis' most significant discoveries. After amassing extensive data on his own and his patients' symptoms, dreams, and ordinary mistakes, Sigmund Freud concluded that:

> [M]ental processes are in themselves unconscious and . . . of all mental life it is only certain individual acts and portions that are conscious. [P]sychoanalysis . . . cannot accept the identity of the conscious and the mental. It defines what is mental as processes, such as feeling, thinking, and willing, and it is obliged to maintain

that there is unconscious thinking and unapprehended willing. . . . [T]he hypothesis of there being unconscious mental processes paves the way to a decisive new orientation in the world of
science.[5]

The proposition that "there are purposes in people which can become operative without their knowing about them" raises challenging problems for traditional notions of individual autonomy,
as well as for legal, moral, philosophical, and political views
about human nature. Such views on autonomy generally seem to
assume either that human beings can readily become aware of
the significant intentions that shape their conduct or that unconscious intentions can or should be disregarded.

Psychoanalysis, on the other hand, asserts that any conception of psychological autonomy must take the unconscious into
account. If both conscious and unconscious forces affect behavior—or, as Stuart Hampshire has put it, if "the occasions on
which we have, to a greater or lesser degree, misrepresented to
ourselves what we are trying to do is much more common than
we had previously believed"[6]—then human beings are not totally
free, in the sense of being fully conscious about why they act in
certain ways. The importance psychoanalysis attributes to the
unconscious also suggests that we can become "freer" only if we
acknowledge that unconscious motivations influence the decisions we make and then explore the sources of these motivations,
or at least appreciate the influence of such hidden forces on
thought and action.

A functional definition of psychological autonomy, therefore,
must encompass unconscious purposes. It must take into account
that an ideational system can exercise motivational force without
being introspectively accessible. Yet the presence of unconscious
forces, and their impact on thought and action, are not the only
factors that must be considered in arriving at a more appropriate
concept of psychological autonomy. Attention must also be paid
to the existence of conflict between conscious and unconscious
motivations. Such conflicts generally lead to compromise formations that, once they reach consciousness, can express, for example, motivations that have less to do with one's current situation
and more with unresolved problems from earlier years. Thus
one's conscious thought or action may distort one's current
needs and desires.

A second psychoanalytic concept important for an understanding of psychological autonomy is primary and secondary process. In his biography of Freud, Ernest Jones observed that "Freud's revolutionary contribution to psychology was not so much his demonstrating the existence of an unconscious, and perhaps not even his exploration of its content, as his proposition that there are two fundamentally different kinds of mental processes, which he termed primary and secondary respectively, together with his description of them.''[7] The existence of two different kinds of mental processes, each following its own laws, has profound implications for the conceptualization of psychological autonomy. I shall refer to these processes as irrationality and rationality respectively. (The two sets of terms are roughly equivalent, except that rationality-irrationality is not weighted down with the same specific meanings as primary and secondary processes, important to psychoanalysis but not to the present discussion.)

Thought and action are influenced by the simultaneous operation not only of conscious and unconscious forces but also of rational and irrational determinants. Thought and action are rarely, if ever, under the domination of either rationality or irrationality alone, and the admixture of the two differs from person to person, and for the same person under the impact of different external conditions. The mixture is also affected by the quality of the conversation between persons.

Rationality refers to the impact on thought and action of consciousness, reality needs, time perspectives, varied and subtly blended emotions, realistic expectations, necessary postponements of gratification, reflective thought prior to action, and regard for facts. Irrationality refers to the impact on thought and action of unconscious impulses and ideation, fantasies, timelessness, concreteness, unmodulated emotions, confusions of past and present realities, unattainable and infantile conceptions, and disregard of facts. Roy Schafer has made the important point that the contrasts drawn between rationality and irrationality "present ideal polar positions. Any specific behavior must be assessed . . . in terms of the particular admixture of [rationality and irrationality] in it. There are all degrees of transition.''[8]

Conscious-unconscious and rational-irrational are often erroneously used interchangeably. They need to be distinguished. When I use "conscious-unconscious" I wish to convey that thought and action are simultaneously influenced by determinants of which the individual is both aware and unaware. The degree of awareness-unawareness will vary, but complete awareness is never possible: "Conscious-unconscious" refers to internal mental states, to the constant interplay of consciousness and unconsciousness on thoughts and feelings.

The terms "rational-irrational" highlight capacities for adaptation to the external world, that is, persons' conscious and unconscious efforts to reconcile their internal mental processes with the external possibilities and limitations of the world in which they live. They denote persons' abilities to take reality into account and to give some account of the conflicts between their inner and outer worlds to themselves and others. An observer's evaluation of a subject's rationality and irrationality must encompass information on how the subject perceives the external world. Since persons may perceive the world in different ways, observer and subject can differ radically on what they consider rational and irrational. This fact makes the evaluation of rational-irrational more a matter of interpersonal dynamics than is true for conscious-unconscious which depends more on how individuals react *qua* themselves. Thus, any evaluation of perceived "irrational" conduct must take into account that such a judgment may be based on differences in values, life style, and other personal matters between the two interacting parties.

Take Iphigenia as an example. It is one thing to say that her choice of radiation therapy was influenced by unconscious factors and another to say that it was, as some physicians believed, an irrational choice. Whether it was "rational," however, depends on how one balances the competing values of longevity and physical appearance. Iphigenia decided to adapt to the world in which she wished to live by opting for radiation therapy and she gave a reasonably good account of her choice. It was an irrational choice only if one assumes that she should have adapted to her world differently. Some doctors believed that she should have made a different choice, but this only proves that her and their value preferences diverged. The irrational ones were those doctors who could not entertain the idea that they and she might differ on what is rational.

Therefore an assessment of rationality-irrationality in medical decision making demands a new inquiry based not only on an understanding of patients' views in relation to their perceptions of the world but also on a scrutiny by both physicians and patients of the significance to be assigned to their respective views of the other's "irrationality" and their own "rationality." It often will turn out that positions must be reversed. For example, it may turn out that what a physician first perceived to be an expression of a patient's "irrational" behavior was based on different value preferences about the importance of longevity, quality of life, bodily invasions, or the risks a patient is willing to take for purposes of greater well-being. Neglect of such influences has often led doctors to label a patient's judgment irrational prematurely, without a sustained effort to sort out their own and their patients' reasons for choices recommended or made.

Efforts at clarification need to be conducted in the spirit of a better understanding of the context in which the "irrationalities" have arisen. Premature struggles to convince the other of his or her "irrationality" are counterproductive; they only preclude the possibility of mutual understanding.

Irrationality may be conscious or unconscious. Consciousness of a thought or action does not determine its rationality. "The rational plan," as Heinz Hartmann put it, "must [always] include the irrational as a fact."[9] Optimal ego functioning employs rational regulations and simultaneously takes into account the irrationality of other mental achievements.

Therefore, irrational thought must not be equated with pathology. It is an essential ingredient of life, as it is of the life of dreams, artistic creations, and scientific achievements. Hans Loewald has expressed all this well:

> . . . Not only do irrational forces overtake us again and again; in trying to lose them we would be lost. The id, the unconscious modes and contents of human experience, should remain available. If they are in danger of being unavailable—no matter what state of perfection our "intellect" may have reached—or if there is danger of no longer responding to them, it is our task as historical beings to resume our history making by finding a way back to them so that they may be transformed, and away from a frozen ego. . . .

*   *   *

Freud called the dynamic unconscious indestructible in comparison with the ephemeral and fragile, but infinitely precious, formations of consciousness. Where id was, there ego shall come into being. Too easily and too often ego is equated with rigid, unmodulated, and unyielding rationality. So today we are moved to add: where ego is, there id shall come into being again to renew the life of the ego and of reason.[10]

Indeed, paradoxical as it may sound, exclusion of all irrationality leads to pathology. Obsessive-compulsive personalities are living examples of this point.

Thus, in conceptualizing autonomy in terms of the simultaneous operation of rationality and irrationality, it is important to recognize that one does not necessarily speak to the healthy, and the other to the pathological, aspects of human behavior. Both activities can define normal and abnormal human psychological functioning. They work hand in hand. If either is impaired, human conduct is impaired. One is not an expression of man's "lower nature" and the other of man's "higher nature." I do not believe that these observations blunt my argument that through conversation and self-reflection the impact of the unconscious and of irrationality on thought and action can be reduced and that doing so is to the good. My observations only emphasize that before the unconscious and irrational influences on thought and action can be evaluated, they need to be identified and compared with one's views of oneself and of one's world.

The two sets of distinctions—conscious-unconscious and rational-irrational—have different implications for psychological autonomy. If I am correct in assuming that greater consciousness of the determinants that influence thought and action can enhance decision making, then attempts to achieve such an awareness through self-reflection and reflection with others become necessary for optimal decision making. On the other hand, given human beings' limited capacities for greater consciousness and the fact that unconscious thoughts may express integrated, essential, and significant wishes, beliefs, and values of the individual, unawareness does not suggest that a person has not made a "good" decision. If these statements sound paradoxical, they only attest to the fact that human psychology contains many paradoxes. Yet the paradox can be placed in better perspective: It is more of a paradox if one expects reflection to lead to total consciousness and rationality. The paradox becomes significantly reduced, however, if one only expects reflection to make it more certain that persons do not fall victims to those irrational and unconscious influences that they wish to avoid *and*, with reasonable care, can recognize.

My concerns about assuming that unconscious and irrational motivations are always inherently inferior also have practical implications. For example, unawareness cannot be taken as a justification for substituting professional judgments for those of a patient in the belief that it is in the latter's "best interest" or that a patient would have followed doctors' orders if he had only been more rational. In his lectures on *Two Concepts of Liberty*, Isaiah Berlin eloquently spoke to the danger of ignoring persons' wishes based on the notion that "they are actually aiming at what in their benighted state they consciously resist, because there exists within them an occult entity—their latent rational will, or their 'true' purpose." He continued:

> This monstrous impersonation, which consists in equating what X would choose if he were something he is not, or at least not yet, with what X actually seeks and chooses, is at the heart of all political theories of self-realization. It is one thing to say that I may be coerced for my own good which I am too blind to see; and another that if it is for my good, I am not being coerced, for I have willed it, whether I know this or not, and am free even while my poor earthly body and foolish mind bitterly reject it, and struggle against those who seek however benevolently to impose it, with the greatest desperation.[11]

These dangers to which Berlin alerted the world of rulers and citizens have been insufficiently heeded in the world of physicians and patients as well. Since Hippocratic days, physicians have asserted that their rational individual and professional commitment to the pursuit of health can be distinguished from the common irrationality of patients who, by virtue of ignorance and/or illness, may not pursue their own enlightened self-interests. Such views of patients have also led doctors to argue that patients would have agreed to the choices made for them if their real self had been in better control. Thus when doctors control choices by silence and evasions, they do not deem it to be a form of coercion. Instead, doctors believe that such conduct is guided only by their considerations of patients' own good at a moment in time when patients are too blind to see it for themselves.

Berlin despaired of the likelihood of controlling such abuses. Perhaps he gave up too easily. In time, the conflicted nature of human beings—the inevitable presence of internal and interpersonal disharmony and tension as well as the constant interplay of consciousness and unconsciousness, of rationality and irrationality—may be more fully accepted, and its influence on both rulers and the ruled, physicians and patients, acknowledged. If that were to happen, perhaps the abuses of such concern to Berlin will be better contained. If I am correct, then individual freedom should be equated neither with simply permitting patients to do what they initially desire nor with requiring them simply to make complete sense to their physicians. Instead, and above all, respect for freedom would demand respectful conversation. True freedom entails constant struggle and anguish with oneself and with others. This is the lesson of psychoanalysis and its theories about human conduct and interactions.

Implications for Physician-Patient Decision Making

In contrast to other definitions of psychological autonomy, mine is not solely "linked . . . to those higher forms of consciousness that are distinctive of human potential."[12] I reject such artificial restrictions to conduct regulated primarily by reason. Since reason and unreason always act in concert, both are facets of psychological autonomy. I now turn to the implications of my views on psychological autonomy for decision making between physicians and patients.

First, thought and action can never be brought fully under the domination of consciousness and rationality. Physicians and patients, however, can become more aware of the ever-present and pervasive impact of the unconscious and of irrationality on thought and action. An appreciation of the limits of rationality would sensitize physicians and patients to the need for subjecting their thoughts and contemplated actions to prior reflection, both alone and with one another. It would also sensitize them to the inevitable persistence, even after conversation, of lingering, nagging, and quite healthy doubts about the continuing influence of unconscious and irrational determinants on their conduct. Such an awareness, which unites physicians and patients in common vulnerabilities, can only make them more careful about apodictic judgments and more respectful of conflicting wishes and expectations.

For example, physicians would have to pay greater attention to reflection if they believed that their conduct was influenced by the same underlying unconscious and irrational determinants as that of their patients. The contrary assumption, that doctors', but not patients', contributions to any conversation are influenced largely by rational (personal and professional) considerations, has made self-reflection by physicians and even searching conversation between physicians and patients—from which *both* can learn—largely irrelevant. If physicians and patients recognized that physicians' communications are also affected by unconscious and irrational determinants, the parties' perceptions of one another and conversations between them would be decisively affected. Awareness of the irrationalities that physicians bring to decision making has been impeded by the idea that medical decision making involves largely technical-scientific issues that physicians can evaluate more rationally than patients can. Technical issues, however, as Iphigenia's story illustrates, are only one of the determinants that impinge on thinking about choices.

Second, the simultaneous domination of thought and action by rational and irrational, conscious and unconscious, determinants can be shifted in the direction of greater rationality and consciousness. At a minimum ill-considered and mistaken ideas can be clarified, uncertainties specified, fears dispelled, and the confusions of past experiences that have no relevance to the present situation untangled. Self-reflection and reflection with others can aid this process immeasurably. Thus, physicians and patients need to engage in conversation to clarify their mutual expectations to the extent possible. Most importantly, physicians must assume the primary obligation of facilitating such conversation.

Indeed, I take a further step and postulate a duty to reflection that cannot easily be waived. Asserting such a duty sounds strange. We are accustomed to recognizing a right to choice as an aspect of the right to self-determination, but a duty to reflection as a component part of the concept of autonomy is quite another matter. Yet, if my views on psychological autonomy have merit, then respect for the right to self-determination requires respect for human beings' proclivities to exercise this right in both rational and irrational ways. Doctors are obligated to facilitate patients' opportunities for reflection to prevent ill-considered rational and irrational influences on choice.

Patients, in turn, are obligated to participate in the process of thinking about choices. In arguing that both parties make every effort to facilitate reflection in order to sort out the rational and irrational expectations that eventually can converge on choice, I express a value preference for the enhancement of individual psychological autonomy. John Stuart Mill, the most celebrated and uncompromising champion of "liberty of action,"[13] anticipated my views on the need for conversation. He eloquently argued that his "principle"—that "the sole end for which mankind are warranted, individually or collectively, in interfering with the liberty of action of any of their number, is self-protection"—is misunderstood if it is interpreted to require "selfish indifference, which pretends that human beings have no business with each other's conduct in life." He most insistently asserted instead that "[c]onsiderations to aid his judgment, exhortations to strengthen his will, may be offered to him, even obtruded on him, by others." Only after such an enforced conversation must individual men and women be allowed to be "the final judge," since "they have means of knowledge [about their feelings and circumstances] immeasurably surpassing those that can be possessed by anyone else."

Thus, Mill, whose concern over human "fallibility" had a significant impact on his insistence for liberty of action, may also have instinctively appreciated that human beings' psychological functioning is fragile and can readily be compromised. Therefore he advocated invasions of privacy through exhortations and obtrusions. He may have recognized that human beings' psychological functioning needed nurture and support in the service of "freedom of action." That amount of intrusion, that degree of paternalism, he tolerated, indeed advocated. He hoped that such intrusions would be carried on with a clear recognition by both parties that the choice ultimately made, no matter how foolish or idiosyncratic, must be honored. Mill viewed this imposition of dialogue as a necessary corrective to the uncompromising demand for liberty of action. It also foreshadowed the distinctions I have introduced between internal reflection and external choice.

Mill fervently believed in man's rational nature. He observed that "on the whole [there is] a preponderance among mankind of rational opinions and rational conduct." Yet he was aware of at least one facet of man's propensity to irrationality—the pervasive need to deny fallibility. "Unfortunately for the good sense of mankind," he wrote, "the fact of their fallibility is far from carrying the weight in their practical judgment which is always allowed to it in theory; for while everyone well knows himself to be fallible, few think it necessary to take any precautions against their own fallibility." The existence and denial of fallibility became a crucial argument in support of conversation. "Human beings owe to each other help to distinguish the better from the worse, and encouragement to choose the former and avoid the latter. But neither one person, nor any number of persons, is warranted in saying to another human creature of ripe years, that he shall not do with his life for his own benefit what he chooses to do with it."

His awareness of man's irrationality, as evidenced by man's denial of fallibility alone, was sufficient reason for Mill to assert the necessity of both freedom of action and conversation. "[Man's] errors," he wrote, "are corrigible. He is capable of rectifying his mistakes, by discussion and experience. Not by experience alone. There must be discussion, to show how experience is to be interpreted."

In my view, the right to self-determination about ultimate choices cannot be properly exercised without first attending to the processes of self-reflection and reflection with others. This holds true for patients as well as for physicians. Contrary views have paid insufficient respect not only to human proclivities for unconscious and irrational decision making but also, and more importantly, to the possibilities of bringing some of these determinants to greater awareness. Such views on autonomy and self-determination do not pay respect to "self-defined" individuals; instead, such views inhibit opportunities for women and men to become clearer about how they may wish to define themselves, abandoning them instead to a malignant fate. In the context of physician-patient decision making, it must be recognized that illness—including the fears and hopes it engenders, the ignorance in which it is embedded, the realistic and unrealistic expectations it mobilizes—can contribute to tilting the balance in patients and physicians further toward irrationality and choices that, on reflection, both might wish to reconsider. In short, I seek to justify the duty to reflection on the grounds of human beings' capacities to take their unconscious and irrationality more fully into account.

I am not suggesting, however, that the conversations between physicians and patients be converted into an exploration of the psychological roots of patients' and physicians' motivations and expectations. This is neither warranted nor possible. I have in

mind only a bona fide attempt by physicians and patients to explain what they wish from one another and what they can do for
and with one another, and to clarify, to the extent possible, any
misconceptions they may have of each others' wishes and expectations. In the end, irreconcilable differences may persist. If they
then realize that they must part company, at least they will do so
with a greater appreciation of their respective positions.

The third implication of my views on psychological autonomy
is that the limitations inherent in fully knowing oneself or others,
and their potential tragic implications for choice making and
choice, demand thoughtful consideration of whether and when to
interfere with patients' choices. One must determine when such
limitations justify interference with choice or thinking about
choice and whether such interferences comport with fidelity to
other values, such as respect for dignity, integrity, equality, loyalty, health, and beneficence. For example, mere acceptance of
patients' "yes" or "no" response to a proposed intervention
may not express respect for their self-determination, dignity, or
integrity. Indeed, blindly accepting either response may violate
their integrity and constitute an act of disloyalty to the person.
Either response, if accepted without question, is disrespectful of
patients' capacities for reflective thought, which might have led
to a different choice more consonant with their own wishes and
expectations. This is particularly true for a "yes" response to a
doctor's recommendations accompanied by a patient's disclaimer
of a need for information. At least for some time to come, the traditional medical climate in which patients are expected and expect to follow doctors' orders will continue to force patients to ab-
dicate decision-making responsibility for reasons that doctors
should question and put to rest. For example, on inquiry, patients may reveal their concerns about imposing on physicians'
time, their fears about annoying doctors with their questions, or
their embarrassment about not being able to ask the right questions without assistance from their doctors. These and other fears
and misconceptions need to be dispelled. A patient's waiver of
the physician's obligation to disclose and obtain the patient's
consent should be accepted only after a committed effort has
been made to explore the underlying reasons for the patient's abdication of decision-making responsibility.

In opposition to such suggestions, doctors have frequently asserted that most patients wish physicians to decide for them with-

out much prior conversation, and that doctors only support the wisdom of such desires. If this assertion is true, then the demand for conversation is disrespectful of physicians' and patients' wishes. This problem deserves careful study. In a recent interview the author-surgeon Richard Selzer was asked whether he had developed a philosophy about how much a patient has a right to know. He responded:

> The patient has a right to know everything. The patient may not wish to know everything. Ever since the 1960's, we've been told that the patient must be the colleague of his doctor and that the decision-making must be shared equally by the two of them. Intellectually and philosophically I certainly do agree. Unfortunately, it doesn't quite work out that way. When I try to call the patient in on a consultation and say, "Which alternative would you prefer?" *invariably* the patient says, "What do you mean, which alternative? I want you to tell me what to do. You're the doctor." The only unspoken word is daddy; tell me what to do, daddy. When a person is desperately ill or frightened, there is a certain kind of regression that makes you want to place yourself in someone's loving care. It is the responsibility of the doctor to have the courage to make decisions for the patient, in as kind and wise a way as he can. To be a father or mother and comfort. There are, of course, strong people who want to know everything and decide everything but they are a distinct minority.[14]

It is unclear from the interview whether Selzer tries to explore patients' statements, "I want you to tell me what to do. You're the doctor," before submitting to their request. A surgeon might very well say to a patient, in response to "I want you to tell me": "Of course I shall eventually give you my recommendation, but I prefer not to do so yet. Since there are a number of alternatives available, each with its risks and benefits, I would like to hear first what your preferences are. After all it is *your* body that I intend to treat and I can do so in a variety of ways. Since you will have to live with your body for a long time to come, you must have some opinions about which consequences would be easier or more difficult for you to tolerate. Once I have a better idea of your preferences and needs, I can make a recommendation that reconciles the best that surgery has to offer with the best that you envision for yourself after I have discharged you from my care."

Surely many physicians "hear" the "unspoken word . . . daddy" too readily in patients' voices. They then proceed to take

care of their patients without further inquiry, much as Dostoy-
evsky's Grand Inquisitor suggested human beings wish to be
dealt with:

> There are three forces, the only three forces that are able to conquer
> and hold captive the conscience of these weak rebels for their own
> happiness—these forces are: miracle, mystery and authority. . . .
> Is the nature of man such that he can reject a miracle and at the
> most fearful moments of life, the moments of his most fearful, fun-
> damental, and agonizing . . . problems, stick to the free decision of
> the heart? [S]ince man is unable to carry on without a miracle, he
> will create new miracles for himself, miracles of his own, and will
> worship the miracles of the witch-doctor and the sorcery of the wise
> woman. . . . And men rejoiced that they were once more led like
> sheep and that the terrible gift [of freedom] which had brought
> them so much suffering had at last been lifted from their
> hearts. . . . Tell me. Did we not love mankind when we admitted
> so humbly its impotence and lovingly lightened its burden . . .?[15]

The Grand Inquisitor's views of human nature, shared by many
physicians, have shaped the conversations between persons in
powerful and self-fulfilling ways. There may be other unspoken
messages in patients' voices, however, that ask at least for a father who appreciates that his children are not only children but
also adults who wish and deserve to be heard. If doctors were to
listen more to these adult voices, they might learn that more patients prefer to participate in decision making than physicians
commonly believe. The task of distinguishing between patients
who wish to be treated as adults or as children still needs to be
undertaken.

The fourth implication of my views on psychological autonomy is that the requirement for conversation creates inevitable
conflicts with the right to privacy—the right to keep one's
thoughts and feelings to oneself. Thus, the imposition of an obligation to converse is disrespectful of the right to have one's initial
choice, including the right not to converse, honored. Refusals to
converse, however, totally obscure both patients' and doctors'
understanding of how they arrived at their decision. This is particularly true when patients either decline a needed medical intervention or accept it unquestioningly. Respect for psychological autonomy becomes severely compromised when refusals or
acceptances are heeded without question. Here the principle of

privacy must bend to psychological autonomy. (This may turn out to be a rare Hobson's choice, for I expect that most patients, if invited by their physicians, will welcome conversation.)

Fifth, the posited obligation to converse introduces an element of paternalism into my prescription. Yet, it must also be recognized that my views about psychological autonomy and its accompanying obligations to reflect and converse seek to avoid paternalism and to strengthen patient self-determination. The obligations that I advocate are imposed on *both* parties; they do not ask for one party to submit to the other; they are grounded in mutuality; and they are dictated by a respect for human psychological functioning in the specific context of physician-patient decision making: patients' wishes to be an adult *and* a child, and doctors' wishes to treat patients more as children than as adults.

Respect for psychological autonomy requires that both parties pay caring attention to their capacities and incapacities for self-determination by supporting and enhancing their real, though precarious, endowment for reflective thought. In conversation with one another, patients may uncover mistaken notions about their diseases and their treatment that they have held for a long time or have recently acquired through misunderstanding the import of their doctors' recommendations. Physicians may uncover the fact that their unconscious preferences and biases compelled patients to yield to their recommendations even though consciously they had intended otherwise. Without conversation, individual self-determination can become compromised by condemning physicians and patients to the isolation of solitary decision making, which can only contribute to abandoning patients prematurely to an ill-considered fate.

It has been said that remonstrances against paternalism, while logically not inconsistent with concern for others, may nevertheless diminish one's concerns for others. Karl Marx said it more strongly: "the right of man to liberty is based not on the association of man with man, but on the separation of man from man. It is . . . the right of the restricted individual, withdrawn into himself."[16] While there is some truth in these statements, it must be remembered that except in the rarest of circumstances, the ultimate decision belongs to the patient who has to live with the decision. One can only try to help a patient to make *his* or *her* best choice. Both of these considerations loom large in my distinction between reflection and choice.

Summing up

This chapter highlighted the crucial significance of the concept of psychological autonomy to a better understanding of the principle of self-determination. The respect accorded to self-determination and, in turn, to disclosure and consent is affected by assumptions about human capacities for reflection and choice. If I am correct that a comprehensive definition of individual autonomy must take into account the conscious and unconscious, rational and irrational forces that shape all thoughts and actions, then the simultaneous operation of these forces imposes new obligations on physicians and patients as they attempt to arrive at mutually satisfactory decisions. This chapter addressed some of these obligations from the vantage point of theory. I now move from theory to practice in order to explore the relevance of theory to interactions between physicians and patients at the bedside.

[21]

Toward The 'Tipping Point': Decision Aids And Informed Patient Choice

Access to high-quality patient decision aids is accelerating, but not at the point of clinical care.

by Annette M. O'Connor, John E. Wennberg, France Legare, Hilary A. Llewellyn-Thomas, Benjamin W. Moulton, Karen R. Sepucha, Andrea G. Sodano, and Jaime S. King

ABSTRACT: Preference-sensitive treatment decisions involve making value trade-offs between benefits and harms that should depend on informed patient choice. There is strong evidence that patient decision aids not only improve decision quality but also prevent the overuse of options that informed patients do not value. This paper discusses progress in implementing decision aids and the policy prospects for reaching a "tipping point" in the adoption of "informed patient choice" as a standard of practice. [Health Affairs 26, no. 3 (2007): 716–725; 10.1377/hlthaff.26.3.716]

T REATMENTS WITH ADEQUATE SCIENTIFIC EVIDENCE about outcomes can be classified as "effective" or "preference-sensitive."[1] For "effective" treatments, the benefits far outweigh the possible harms, and the goal is to promote their uptake, using professional and patient education, organizational changes, and funding incentives. The best choice for "preference-sensitive" treatments, in contrast, depends on how patients value benefits versus harms. Although it is more difficult to judge the appropriate rate of uptake, Karen Sepucha and colleagues propose a benchmark of "decision quality"—that is, the consistency between eligible patients' treatment uptake rates and the underlying distributions of patients' informed values.[2]

Annette O'Connor (aoconnor@ohri.ca) is a professor in the School of Nursing and Department of Epidemiology and Community Medicine and a Tier 1 Canada Research Chair at the University of Ottawa. John Wennberg is director of the Center for the Evaluative Clinical Sciences (CECS) at Dartmouth Medical School in Hanover, New Hampshire. France Legare is a Tier 2 Canada Research Chair and an associate professor, Department of Family Medicine, at Laval University in Quebec City, Quebec. Hilary Llewellyn-Thomas is a professor in the Department of Community and Family Medicine and the CECS. Benjamin Moulton is executive director of the American Society of Law, Medicine, and Ethics in Boston, Massachusetts. Karen Sepucha is a senior scientist with the Health Decision Research Unit at Massachusetts General Hospital and an instructor in medicine at Harvard Medical School in Boston. Andrea Sodano is a consultant to the CECS and an adjunct faculty in the Dartmouth Medical School. Jaime King is a fellow in the Law and Biosciences Program at Stanford Law School in California.

We know that decision quality resulting from standard counseling is inadequate.[3] Patients have unrealistic expectations of treatment benefits and harms,
clinicians are poor judges of patients' values, and, as a consequence, there is overuse of treatment options that informed patients do not value. Indeed, the use of
"preference-sensitive" surgical options (for example, hip replacement, prostatec-
tomy, hysterectomy, mastectomy, discectomy, and coronary bypass) can vary two-
to fivefold.[4] Patient decision aids (informational documents designed to help
patients make decisions about treatment options), when used as adjuncts to counseling, improve decision quality and reduce the overuse of surgical treatments by
25 percent.[5] Decision aids differ from conventional educational materials by presenting balanced personalized information about "options" in sufficient detail for
patients to arrive at informed judgments about the personal value of those options. The aim of a decision aid is to improve decision quality and to reduce related
unwarranted practice variations by (1) providing facts about the condition, options, outcomes, and probabilities; (2) clarifying patients' evaluations of the outcomes that matter most to them; and (3) guiding patients in the steps of deliberation and communication so that a choice can be made that matches their informed
values. Decision aids are delivered as self- or practitioner-administered tools in
one-to-one or group sessions. The media for delivery vary (for example, print,
video, computer disk, and Web).

This paper summarizes progress in implementing an infrastructure to support
informed patient choice, as well as the policy initiatives required to reach the "tipping point" that assures widespread adoption of decision aids as the standard of
practice for preference-sensitive care.

Infrastructure To Support Informed Patient Choice

Over the past decade or so, major progress has been made in developing the infrastructure needed to support a change in the standard of practice from delegated
decision making to clinical decision making based on shared decisions. The efficacy of good-quality decision aids in improving the quality of clinical decision
making has been established. The infrastructure for building and maintaining libraries of effective decision aids is growing and improving. International consensus standards for designing and testing these supports have been developed, as
have several models for implementing decision support services. National certification standards are being developed to certify that health care organizations
meet the requirements for informed patient choice. Measures of decision quality
are under development to monitor performance and provide clinical feedback on
the quality of clinical decision making for preference-sensitive treatment choices.
And new methods for conducting the clinical evaluation of preference-sensitive
treatments are under way. The following briefly summarizes the progress that has
been made in each of these domains.

■ **Efficacy.** The Cochrane Collaboration has systematically reviewed more than fifty randomized clinical trials (RCTs) of decision aids for preference-sensitive options.[6] The review confirms that decision aids help patients participate in decision making, leading to informed choices that are consistent with their values. Specifically, superior effects were shown in the form of (1) increased knowledge scores; (2) improvements in patients' realistic perceptions of the chances of benefits and harms; (3) lowered scores for decisional conflict; (4) smaller numbers of patients who are passive in decision making; (5) smaller numbers of patients who remain undecided after counseling; and (6) improved agreement between a patient's values and the option that is actually chosen. Moreover, several trials focused on decision aids about accepting or rejecting major elective surgery have demonstrated reductions in the more invasive surgical options by 25 percent, with no adverse effects on patient satisfaction or health outcomes.

■ **Cost-effectiveness.** Three trials have measured the economic impact of using patient decision aids. One U.K. trial evaluated the cost-effectiveness of aids to reduce hysterectomy rates in cases of heavy menstrual bleeding.[7] The mean total costs and quality-adjusted life-years (QALYs) were superior for groups exposed to decision aids or the combination of aids with nurse coaching as follows: (1) standard care: U.S.$2,751 per patient, 1.572 QALY; (2) aid video alone: U.S.$2,026, 1.567 QALY; and (3) aid video plus nurse coaching (involving eliciting values for outcomes): U.S.$1,566, 1.582 QALY. Two other cost-minimization trials of decision aids for prostate enlargement treatment and menopausal hormones reported that the aid would have been cost-neutral if less costly delivery methods were used (for example, the Internet rather than supplying equipment for interactive videodisks).[8]

■ **Libraries of decision aids.** The Cochrane Collaboration has catalogued and evaluated the quality of a growing number of decision aids, created by a wide range of developers (Exhibit 1).[9] Examples of developers include the Foundation for Informed Medical Decision Making and its commercial partner, Health Dialog; Healthwise; the Mayo Clinic; and the Ottawa Health Research Institute. U.S. organizations that have compiled and are managing clearinghouses of decision aids include the National Cancer Institute and the Centers for Disease Control and Prevention.

■ **International standards.** The International Patient Decision Aid Standards (IPDAS) Collaboration is a network of more than 100 researchers, practitioners, patients, and policymakers from fourteen countries.[10] These collaborators have developed quality criteria in the domains of essential content (providing information, presenting probabilities, clarifying values, and guiding deliberation and communication); development (systematic development process, balance, evidence base, plain language, and disclosure); and evaluation (decision quality). The endorsed criteria are summarized in a checklist for users, to guide payers, practitioners, patients, developers, and researchers.

■ **Models for implementing decision-support services.** Models include call-center models at the health plan level (for example, Health Dialog in the United States; BC Healthguide in Canada; and Australia Cancer Call Centers) as well as

EXHIBIT 1
Growth In Number Of Patient Decision Ald Trials And Number Of Patient Decision Aids Registered In The Cochrane Collection Library, Selected Years 1999–2006

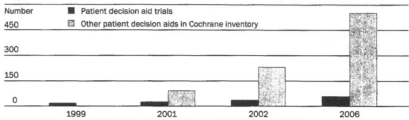

SOURCE: A.M. O'Connor et al., "Decision Aids for People Facing Health Treatment or Screening Decisions," *Cochrane Database of Systematic Reviews* no. 2 (2003): CD001431.

models that integrate decision aids into clinical practice. The use of decision aids in call centers and public or health plan portals has expanded rapidly. For example, high-volume decision-aid producers estimate that decision aids were accessed about nine million times in 2006, mostly via the Internet.[11]

Barriers and facilitators. The use of decision aids as part of clinical care has had a much slower rollout. A recent systematic review identified health professionals' most commonly perceived barriers to implementing shared decision making: lack of applicability because of patient characteristics; time constraints; lack of applicability due to the clinical situation (for example, emergency situations); and perceived patient preferences for a model of decision making that did not fit a shared decision-making model.

Identified factors that facilitated shared decision making included the perception that it would lead to a positive impact on patient outcomes or the clinical process, or both; patients' preferences for decision-making roles fit a shared approach; health professionals were motivated to use the aids; and the perception that shared decision making is useful or practical.[12]

Successful uptake of decision aids will also depend on the development of electronic infrastructures to support triggering of the aids, plus secure messaging and patient health records to deliver them to patients. The Center for Information Therapy is working with electronic medical record (EMR) developers and health information producers and health care providers to define electronic "moments of care" and provide just-in-time information before, during, and after clinical encounters.[13]

Care sites using decision aids. Despite the aforementioned barriers to uptake, several sites of care are developing models for delivering decision aids. For example, more than twenty Massachusetts cancer centers are using decision aids to help patients make treatment decisions; Massachusetts General Hospital has started an "ePrescribe" effort, where primary care physicians can prescribe decision aids through the hospital's EMR system; Dartmouth-Hitchcock Medical Center

(DHMC) and White River Junction Veterans Affairs Medical Center are using decision aids as part of a larger reengineering initiative in primary care; ten community-based primary care practices at the University of California, Los Angeles (UCLA), are using patient decision aids; and UC San Francisco and Allegheny General Hospital are incorporating aids into routine breast cancer care, and the University of North Carolina is incorporating them into colorectal cancer screening.

Key role of IT systems. An important element of these practice models is the key supportive role played by specially designed IT systems. For example, the DHMC breast cancer program is attempting to improve clinical care quality by incorporating IT to screen patients, inform physicians, cue the decision aid, assess naïve and informed preferences, flag emotional distress, and monitor decision quality. Typically, the delivery of decision support involves some combination of clinical consultation and counseling, decision aids, and coaching. The sequence, combination, and professionals involved depend on the type of decision, patient population, and service context in which care is provided; these are being spelled out in clinical and care pathways.[14]

International examples. Examples of implementing decision support also exist outside the United States. Several urology centers in the U.K. National Health Service (NHS) have care pathways for benign prostatic hyperplasia and early-stage prostate cancer treatments. These involve a medical consultation with the urologist to confirm the diagnosis and to clarify the options and roles in decision making; referral to the urology nurse specialist, who provides a decision aid about relevant treatments and a personal decision form that elicits decision quality (knowledge, values, and preferred treatment) and unresolved decisional conflict; and a follow-up coaching visit with the nurse specialist to discuss the patient's decisional needs and next steps.[15]

In Canada, Ottawa Hospital is beginning to embed decision support for cancer and obstetrical services into its care pathways as part of the informed-consent process. In Quebec City, the implementation process of shared decision making is being evaluated in five large family medicine sites. This program is closely associated with a residency program in family medicine. Training workshops on shared decision making take place in each teaching site. Simple clinical tools eliciting patients' decisional needs are disseminated through small-group learning sessions occurring throughout the residency, and an annual three-hour training session for clinical teachers is offered.

Developing National Certification Standards

The practice models described above can also be used as examples for developing two kinds of national standards—one for health professionals and the other for health care organizations.

Certification for professionals would involve strategies such as the credentialing of professional skills through completion of training programs. For example, the Ottawa Health Research Institute has evaluated strategies that include auto-tutorial and skill-building workshops in decision support and the use of decision aids; structured decision-support protocols; and performance feedback with real or simulated patients. Dawn Stacey and colleagues demonstrated that when this strategy was used in a general nurse call center and in a cancer call center, practitioners' knowledge and skills in decision support improved, particularly in assessing decisional needs, clarifying values, and addressing support needs.[16]

France Legare and colleagues have monitored the implementation of shared decision making in the practices of 122 primary care providers. The exposure to a training workshop, feedback, and reminder at the point of care explained a major proportion of the behavioral intention of interest in a dose-response manner.[17]

In one U.K. study, primary care physicians were able to acquire the skills of shared decision making and use risk communication aids after two sets of two three-hour training sessions.[18] The U.K. Urology Service has adapted the Ottawa training program with its service teams; the program also includes performance feedback on decision quality and addresses barriers to implementing decision aids in clinical care pathways.

These training initiatives can be adapted for national roll-out. There would need to be capacity building in training clinical teachers in shared decision making. Integration of shared decision making would need to occur in the certification processes of faculties of health sciences, including medicine and residency programs, and continuing medical education (CME) activities.

An example of certification for health care organizations is the convening of a panel of experts by the National Committee for Quality Assurance (NCQA) to work on credentialing for cancer care. The panel's work is still in its early stages and will focus on using available data to devise its first set of standards. The main work to date has been developing measures to indicate the level at which an institution has implemented decision support, assessing the reliability or validity of those measures, and piloting their inclusion in a certification process.

■ **Measures of "decision quality."** Measures of patients' decision quality are also under development.[19] *Decision quality* refers to the extent to which patients arrive at choices that are informed and preference-based. The Foundation for Informed Medical Decision Making (FIMDM) is supporting research into the development of decision-specific instruments to measure decision quality across multiple domains. The instruments focus on assessing the extent to which patients understand the key facts about the decision and the extent to which their choices are consistent with their reported preferences for the good and bad outcomes of the options.

Work is under way to supplement these decision-specific measures with generic items to assess the quality of the process; both types of measures reflect the consensus recommendations of the IPDAS collaboration. These measures will serve as important outcome criteria for evaluating the effectiveness of providers' and organizations' decision-support interventions. An NCQA expert panel is developing and piloting these kinds of measures, to demonstrate that they are valid and reliable and can be considered for inclusion in evaluative work.

In addition, several programs have been using the measures as a screen to reveal knowledge deficits and patients' values before a consultation. The programs testing and using both generic and decision-specific decision-quality measures include the breast cancer program and the Spine Center at the DHMC, as well as the NHS urology services. The breast cancer centers at UCSF and at the Allegheny General Hospital are also starting to use decision-quality measures, along with video-based decision aids.

■ **Clinical evaluation of preference-sensitive treatments.** This refers to the use of decision aids and patient registries in "everyday practice" for long-term follow-up studies that compare the outcomes of different treatment options when the treatment choice has been based on patients' preferences. The Spine Patient Outcomes Research Trial (SPORT) of back surgery is an example that includes both an RCT and preference-based observational arms based on informed patient choice. This work rests on the ethical principle that trial entry for preference-sensitive treatments should be based on informed patient choice. The rich database generated by SPORT is providing Dartmouth investigators with the opportunity to assess outcome probabilities under active choice versus randomization.[20]

Toward The 'Tipping Point': Emerging Opportunities For Accelerated Change

Although progress has been made in building the infrastructure to support shared decision making, cultural, regulatory, legal, and economic barriers must be overcome to make informed patient choice the standard of practice for preference-sensitive treatments. Cultural resistance resides primarily in the change required in the doctor-patient relationship—that is, replacing the traditional reliance on the physician's opinion to define *medical necessity* with the shared decision-making model, which defines new roles for both patient and physician. The good news is that the research and development agenda described above has established that patients and physicians who participate in shared decision making make better decisions and are comfortable in their new roles. The bad news is that shared decision making remains the exception, not the rule.

To take the next steps to the "tipping point," the health policy community needs to develop new standards for defining the medical necessity of preference-sensitive treatment options. Health plans and employers need to develop new payment strategies that encourage both patients and providers to participate in shared decision making. The legal profession needs to recognize the limitations of traditional informed consent in assuring shared decision making and adopt a new standard based on the requirements for achieving informed patients through shared decision making. Each of these changes is amplified below.

■ **New standards for medical necessity.** The standard for review of medical necessity now commonly exercised by the Centers for Medicare and Medicaid Services (CMS) and private health plans is based on the physician as the determinant of medical necessity. We envision a different standard based on the assertion that the informed patient is the final arbiter of the necessity of preference-sensitive treatment. Under our recommendation, the medical profession would continue to determine which options are reasonable, and health plans would determine which options are covered. The process of informed patient choice should be well defined, transparent, and subject to review (along the lines discussed above). Decision aids should be assessed by external standards to ensure that they provide evidence-based, up-to-date, balanced information on all relevant treatment options and that they promote the clarification of values. Quality should be evaluated and reported using appropriate patient decision-quality measures. This process would also be certified or accredited.[21]

■ **New payment strategies.** The economic incentives embedded in traditional Medicare and most other payers reward providers for utilization, not for informed patient choice. Pay-for-performance (P4P) models that reward providers who implement shared decision making need to be designed and tested through demonstrations.[22] The effectiveness of health savings accounts (HSAs) and other "consumer-choice" strategies for involving patients in choice of discretionary treatments should increase patients' demand for shared decision making, but these models need to be tested. We believe that the existence of certification processes and decision-quality measures would provide the basis for qualifying providers for reimbursement and for monitoring the outcomes of the decision process.

■ **Informed patient choice as the legal standard.** We concur with several legal commentators who have suggested that the states should rethink current informed-consent requirements and adopt shared medical decision making as a prerequisite to valid, informed patient choice. The states are largely divided between two categories of informed-consent standards: physician-based and patient-based. In physician-based states, physicians must provide patients with the same information that a reasonable physician would under similar circumstances.[23] In patient-based states, physicians must provide patients with all of the information that an objective, reasonable patient would want under similar circumstances.[24]

Both standards prove insufficient, but for different reasons. The physician-based standard does not acknowledge that often no true objective standard for physicians exists.[25] In fact, reasonable physicians exhibit wide variations in practice patterns even within the same region. Likewise, the objective patient standard used in nearly all patient-based states does not go far enough to protect a patient's right to make medical decisions.[26] It fails to acknowledge that patients' values and preferences vary widely. In many cases, a patient's lifestyle, values, and preferences should dictate what course of treatment to follow. Under the objective patient standard, to the extent that the person's preferences do not correspond

I N D I V I D U A L   L E V E L

with those of a "reasonable" patient, however defined, that person may be denied information that he or she would deem relevant to making the treatment decision.[27] Shared medical decision making offers a promising alternative to our current informed-consent system. It allows both physicians and patients to honor the values and preferences of the patient, while also permitting the physician to provide medical expertise to promote the patient's health. In fact, evidence suggests that shared medical decision making strengthens the therapeutic alliance between the physician and patient and improves patient satisfaction.

Critics of the shared decision-making approach have questioned the feasibility of proving that a true shared process had occurred, but the certification processes of care and decision quality measures discussed previously should provide transparent ways of measuring whether the standard of informed choice has been met.

T O   R E A C H   T H E   T I P P I N G   P O I N T, we need to make the use of high-quality decision aids unavoidable and a part of the informed-consent process. The best way to accomplish the ease of prescription is to embed high-quality decision aids within EMR systems. At the national policy level, we need to design and introduce model legislation about informed patient choice, as well as to convene payer groups under the leadership of the CMS to redefine the patient's role in determining medical necessity and claims review. National policies focused on informed consent, a redefinition of *medical necessity*, and new payment strategies should accelerate adoption of informed patient choice as the standard for practice, with resulting benefits to patients, physicians, and the health care community.

Annette O'Connor, Hilary Llewellyn-Thomas, and Karen Sepucha receive research funds from the Foundation for Informed Medical Decision Making (FIMDM). The FIMDM, a nonprofit, has a licensing agreement with Health Dialog, a commercial company that promotes the use of patient decision aids. John Wennberg is a consultant for the FIMDM and has a financial interest in Health Dialog.

NOTES

1. J.E. Wennberg, "Unwarranted Variations in Healthcare Delivery: Implications for Academic Medical Centres," *British Medical Journal* 325, no. 7370 (2002): 961–964; and R.P. Harris et al., "Current Methods of the U.S. Preventive Services Task Force: A Review of the Process," *American Journal of Preventive Medicine* 20, no. 3 Supp. (2001): 21–35.

2. K.R. Sepucha, F.J. Fowler Jr., and A.G. Mulley Jr., "Policy Support for Patient-Centered Care: The Need for Measurable Improvements in Decision Quality," *Health Affairs* 23 (2004): VAR-54–VAR-62 (published online 7 October 2004; 10.1377/hlthaff.var.54).

3. A.M. O'Connor et al., "Decision Aids for People Facing Health Treatment or Screening Decisions," *Cochrane Database of Systematic Reviews* no. 2 (2003): CD001431.

4. J.E. Wennberg and M.M. Cooper, "The Surgical Treatment of Common Diseases," in *The Dartmouth Atlas of Health Care, 1998* (Chicago: American Hospital Publishing, 1998), 108–111.

5. O'Connor et al., "Decision Aids."

6. Ibid.

7. A.D. Kennedy et al., "A Multicentre Randomised Controlled Trial Assessing the Costs and Benefits of Using Structured Information and Analysis of Women's Preferences in the Management of Menorrhagia," *Health Technology Assessment* 7, no. 8 (2003): 1–76.

8. E. Murray et al., "Randomised Controlled Trial of an Interactive Multimedia Decision Aid on Benign Prostatic Hypertrophy in Primary Care," *British Medical Journal* 323, no. 7311 (2001): 493–496; and E. Murray et al., "Randomised Controlled Trial of an Interactive Multimedia Decision Aid on Hormone Replacement Therapy in Primary Care," *British Medical Journal* 323, no. 7311 (2001): 490–493.

9. For an inventory of decision aids and the Cochrane Review, see Ottawa Health Research Institute, "A–Z Inventory of Decision Aids," http://decisionaid.ohri.ca/AZinvent.php (accessed 24 October 2006); a Web search on 30 October 2006 for "decision aid" produced 960 hits at the NIH site, http://www.cancer.gov, and 29,789 hits at the CDC site, http://www.cdc.gov.

10. G. Elwyn et al., "Developing a Quality Criteria Framework for Patient Decision Aids: Online International Delphi Consensus Process," *British Medical Journal* 333, no. 7565 (2006): 417; and International Patient Decision Aids (IPDAS) Collaboration, "IPDAS 2005: Criteria for Judging the Quality of Patient Decision Aids," Table 3, http://ipdas.ohri.ca/IPDAS_checklist.pdf (accessed 9 February 2007).

11. Don Kemper, chief executive officer, Healthwise, personal communication, January 2007; David Wennberg, president and chief operating officer, Health Dialog Analytic Solutions, personal communication, January 2007; and Anton Saaramaki, computer systems analyst, Ottawa Health Research Institute, personal communication, January 2007.

12. K. Gravel, F. Legare, and I.D. Graham, "Barriers and Facilitators to Implementing Shared Decision-Making in Clinical Practice: A Systematic Review of Health Professionals' Perceptions," *Implementation Science* no. 1 (2006): 16.

13. For more information, see the Center for Information Therapy home page, http://www.information therapy.org.

14. For more-in-depth discussion of pathways, see J.N. Weinstein, K. Clay, and T.S. Morgan, "Informed Patient Choice: Patient-Centered Valuing of Surgical Risks and Benefits," *Health Affairs* 26, no. 3 (2007): 726–730.

15. National Steering Group for Decision Support Aids in Urology, *Implementing Patient Decision Aids in Urology—Final Report*, October 2005, http://www.pickereurope.org/Filestore/Research/Urology_steering_group_report.pdf (accessed 26 October 2006). See also E. Wirrmann and J. Askham, *Implementing Patient Decision Aids in Urology*, September 2006, http://www.pickereurope.org/Filestore/Downloads/UrologyFINAL-REPORTSep06.pdf (accessed 12 February 2007).

16. D. Stacey et al., "Barriers and Facilitators Influencing Call Center Nurses' Decision Support for Callers Facing Values-Sensitive Decisions: A Mixed Methods Study," *Worldviews on Evidence-Based Nursing* 2, no. 4 (2005): 184–195; and D. Stacey et al., "Addressing Barriers Influencing the Provision of Telephone-Based Patient Decision Support by Cancer Helpline Professionals" (Presentation at the Fourteenth International Conference on Cancer Nursing, Toronto, Ontario, 27 September–1 October 2006).

17. F. Legare, "Implementation of the Ottawa Decision Support Framework in Five Family Practice Teaching Units: An Exploratory Trial" (Doctoral dissertation, University of Ottawa, 2005).

18. G. Elwyn et al., "Achieving Involvement: Process Outcomes from a Cluster Randomized Trial of Shared Decision Making Skill Development and Use of Risk Communication Aids in General Practice," *Family Practice* 21, no. 4 (2004): 337–346.

19. Sepucha et al., "Policy Support for Patient-Centered Care"; and K. Sepucha et al., "An Approach to Measuring the Quality of Breast Cancer Decisions," *Patient Education and Counseling* 65, no. 2 (2007): 261–269.

20. N.J. Birkmeyer et al., "Design of the Spine Patient Outcomes Research Trial (SPORT)," *Spine* 27, no. 12 (2002): 1361–1372.

21. J.E. Wennberg and P.G. Peters Jr., "Unwarranted Variations in the Quality of Health Care: Can the Law Help Medicine Provide a Remedy/Remedies?" *Wake Forest Law Review* no. 37 (2002): 925–941.

22. J.E. Wennberg, E.S. Fisher, and J.S. Skinner, "Geography and the Debate over Medicare Reform," *Health Affairs* 21 (2002): w96–w114 (published online 13 February 2002; 10.1377/hlthaff.w2.96).

23. *Tashman v. Gibbs*, 556 S.E.2d 772, 777 (VA 2002).

24. *Canterbury v. Spence*, 446 F.2d 772, 784 (DC 1972).

25. J.S. King and B. Moulton, "Rethinking Informed Consent: The Case for Shared Medical Decision-Making," *American Journal of Law and Medicine* 32, no. 4 (2006): 429–501.

26. Ibid.

27. Ibid.

[22]

What Is a Good Treatment Decision? The Client's Perspective

William O'Donohue, Jane E. Fisher, and Joseph J. Plaud
University of Maine

William Link
Quinco Consulting Center
Columbus, Indiana

63 adult outpatient clients of a community mental health center evaluated five methods of clinical decision making: intuition, research, therapist's informal successful experience, professional recommendation to therapist, and no rationale. Clients rated their therapists' informal successful experience and the use of research as favorable decision methods. Clients thought that their therapists would also rate these methods as favorable. We conclude that clients want their therapists to make clinical decisions on the basis of informal or formal experience in which the efficacy of the recommendations is demonstrated.

The ethical codes and the training strategies of the mental health professions dictate that practitioners should know and use research in their clinical practice (American Medical Association, 1972; American Nurses Association, 1968; American Psychological Association, 1947; National Association of Social Workers, 1985). One obvious rationale for this position is that many critical decisions in the course of psychotherapy are essentially empirical questions, such as "By what method can the presence or magnitude of some entity (depressive affect, intelligence, marital discord, etc.) be reliably and validly measured?" or "Under what conditions will the level of a variable of interest (selective attention, manic behavior, suicidal intent, etc.) change?" As empirical questions, these can be best addressed in clinical practice only by reference to prior observations of similar situations structured so that antecedently plausible hypotheses can be tested and either corroborated or falsified.

Investigations of the influence of research on clinical practice, however, have consistently revealed that clinicians rarely know or use clinically relevant research (see the special issues of the *American Psychologist*, 1986, and the *Journal of Consult-*

WILLIAM O'DONOHUE is an assistant professor of psychology at the University of Maine. He received a PhD from the State University of New York at Stony Brook in 1986. He also received a master's degree in philosophy from Indiana University in 1988.
JANE E. FISHER is an assistant professor of psychology at the University of Maine. She received a PhD from Indiana University in 1987.
JOSEPH J. PLAUD is a doctoral graduate student in clinical psychology at the University of Maine. He received a BA in psychology from Clark University in 1987.
WILLIAM LINK received a BA in psychology from Indiana University in 1986 and his MSW from Indiana University in 1989. He is currently a clinical social worker at the Quinco Consulting Center in Columbus, Indiana.
THE AUTHORS ACKNOWLEDGE the kind assistance of Michael Bramel.
CORRESPONDENCE CONCERNING THIS ARTICLE should be addressed to William O'Donohue, Department of Psychology, University of Maine, 301 Clarence Cook Little Hall, Orono, Maine 04469-0140.

ing and Clinical Psychology, 1981, for reviews and discussions of this issue). For example, Cohen, Sargent, and Sechrest (1986) reported that of 30 psychologists who were primarily service providers and who had an average of nine years of practice, 27% (8) stated that no empirical study had ever affected their work, 37% (11) stated that not even the general literature had affected their work, and no psychologist was able to identify a specific study that had affected his or her practice. Generalization of these data must be made with caution because of the small sample size and because of the limited representativeness of the sample (e.g., no psychologists identified their orientation as behavioral or cognitive–behavioral). O'Donohue, Curtis, and Fisher (1985) analyzed 416 intake evaluations from a community mental health center that required a "rationale/justification for preliminary mode and type of therapy" and found that only one treatment rationale was based on an appeal to research.

The apparent lack of consumption and use of research in clinical practice has led some to conclude that psychotherapy is "crystal-ball gazing" or "trial-and-error eclecticism." This state of affairs potentially has wide-ranging significance. For example, O'Donohue, Fisher, Plaud, and Curtis (1988) suggested that the lack of effectiveness of psychotherapy in studies such as Eysenck's (1952) might be due, in part, to this practice. They suggested that although meta-analytic reviews attest to the general efficacy of psychotherapy, future reviews should distinguish between data-based therapy and therapy that is not data based; that is, in studies of the general efficacy of psychotherapy, a case in which the therapist reviews research literature and treats an individual with an animal phobia by participant modeling should be distinguished from a case in which the client is rolfed.

At present there is information relevant to the questions of what mental health professions believe is a good clinical decision and whether actual treatment decisions conform to this model. However, there is little or no information regarding what clients believe is good clinical decision making and no information regarding clients' beliefs about how their therapists actually make these decisions. This information is important for several reasons. First, it is useful to understand the client's views regarding the clinical decision-making process, as previous studies have suggested that the client's views and expectations regarding psychotherapy can influence the outcome of therapy (Ullmann & Krasner, 1975). Second, answers to these questions may provide information regarding the seriousness of the apparent nonuse of research in clinical practice. One can potentially discover whether much clinical practice not only fails to meet professional standards but also fails to meet the standards of our clients. Last, it allows further explication of the degree of consistency between what the client assumes is happening and what actually is happening. This gives us a further indication regarding the extent to which the client typically has given proper informed consent in psychotherapy; that is, there currently is little information concerning whether clients are acting under accurate or inaccurate assumptions about how their therapists make clinical decisions.

In this study we addressed the questions of what clients believe are good treatment decisions and what clients believe about how their therapists make clinical decisions. Five methods of clinical decision making were evaluated: intuitive decisions, decisions entirely lacking justification, research-based decisions, decisions made from the therapist's past experience, and decisions based on past informal professional contacts. Furthermore, we assessed the extent to which clients believed their therapists used each of these methods.

Method

Subjects

Sixty-three current outpatient clients of a Midwestern community mental health center participated in this study. The ages of the subjects ranged from 18 to 71 ($M = 38.1, SD = 11.4$). Twelve (19%) were men. The number of years of education completed by subjects ranged from 4 to 17 ($M = 11.6, SD = 2.2$). Clients who were 18 years old or older, who were not obviously psychotic or mentally retarded, and who had seen their therapist at least one time were eligible for participation in the study. All clients of five geographically distinct clinics who met these criteria were asked by the outpatient secretaries if they would consent to participate in a research project investigating clinical decision making.

Procedure

The clients who volunteered were presented with the following written scenario:

> Imagine that you go to a psychotherapist to seek help for a certain problem that has been troubling you. After you explain your problem to the therapist, the psychotherapist recommends a certain method for treating your problem. You then ask your therapist, "Why did you decide to use this particular method to treat my problem?" Suppose your therapist says....

The clients were then presented with five methods of treatment decision making. To minimize the influence of possible order effects, we counterbalanced the order of presentation of these treatment methods by using the Latin square design.

The decision methods were presented in the following manner: Method A, in which the decision was based on past informal experience ("I'm not sure if other therapists have used this treatment method in the past, but I have used this method in the past with success, and for that reason I think it will work again"); Method B, in which the decision

was intuitive ("I just have a gut feeling—an intuition—that this treatment method will work"); Method C, in which the decision was made from past informal professional contacts ("I have heard from other therapists at this agency that they have used this treatment method with success, and for that reason I think this treatment method will work"); Method D, in which the decision lacked justification entirely ("I have no reason or rationale. I just decided, based on no real reason, that this treatment method will work"); and Method E, a research-based decision ("Because I have looked at scientific research regarding this problem. The research data indicate that the method I'm recommending will work").

After each presentation of a treatment decision method, subjects were asked to "Rate how good you think this approach to making a treatment decision is" and to respond on a 5-point Likert scale (1 = *this is a terrible way to make a treatment decision; 2 = this is a bad way to make a treatment decision; 3 = this is neither a bad nor a good way to make a treatment decision; 4 = this is a good way to make a treatment decision; 5 = this is an excellent way to make a treatment decision*). Subjects were then asked to indicate how they thought their therapist would rate the approach to decision making. The same response options were given. Subjects were then debriefed.

Results

The number of sessions reported between therapists and subjects before completion of the questionnaire ranged from 1 to 650 ($M = 33.2, SD = 101.4$).

To investigate whether there was a relation between the clients' ratings of their own opinions and their estimates of how their therapists would rate the five treatment decision methods presented, we performed Pearson product–moment correlations between both questions for each of the five treatment decision methods. The results (see Table 1) indicate significant correlations ($p < .01$ in all cases) for each treatment decision method between clients' self-ratings and their ratings of how they thought their therapists would respond.

Means and standard deviations for the subjects' self-ratings for each of the five treatment decision methods are presented in Table 1. To determine whether there were differences between clients' evaluations of the different treatment decisions, we performed dependent sample t tests between each possible pair of treatment methods (see Table 1). The ratings of Methods A and E did not differ significantly, and those methods were judged best. These were followed in rating by Methods C, B, and D. The ratings of treatment decisions B and D were not significantly different.

Means and standard deviations for the subjects' ratings of their therapists' opinions of each of the five treatment decision methods are presented in Table 1. As in the case of the subjects' self-ratings, dependent sample t tests were performed on subjects' estimations of how their therapists would rate the different treatment methods between each possible pair of treatment methods (see Table 1). Again, judgments of Methods A and E did not differ significantly, and those methods were judged best. These were followed in rating by Methods C, B, and D, and each difference was significant.

We performed Pearson product–moment correlations for both the subjects' self- and therapist ratings for each treatment method with demographic variables: subject's age, number of years in school, and number of sessions in therapy. No significant correlations were found between these demographic vari-

Table 1

Subjects' Self- and Therapist Ratings for Five Treatment Decision Methods

Treatment decision method	Subjects' self-rating		Subjects' therapist rating		Pearson product–moment correlation coefficient
	M	*SD*	*M*	*SD*	
Therapist's experience	3.92_{abc}	0.77	3.83_{ijk}	0.97	.70*
Intuitive	2.46_{ade}	1.06	2.67_{limn}	1.11	.65*
Professional contacts	3.17_{bdfg}	1.06	3.39_{jloz}	1.00	.62*
No justification	2.05_{cih}	1.22	1.97_{kmoq}	1.18	.82*
Research	3.78_{egh}	0.87	3.74_{nzq}	0.93	.72*

Note. For dependent sample *t* tests, all numbers that share common subscripts are significant at $p < .01$ (except z, which is significant at $p < .05$). Each $n = 63$.
* $p < .01$.

ables and either self- or therapist ratings on any of the treatment methods presented. Furthermore, a dependent sample *t* test between male and female subjects revealed no significant differences.

Discussion

Clients rated most favorably those treatment decisions that were based on their therapists' experiences of success and on a consideration of research findings. These were rated significantly more favorably than were decisions that were based on the recommendations of other professionals, on intuition, or on no apparent rationale. Decisions based on the recommendations of other professionals, although rated significantly less favorably than the two most favored methods, were rated significantly more favorably than decisions based on intuition or on no apparent rationale.

There were significant positive correlations between clients' ratings of their therapists' evaluations of these decision methods and the clients' own ratings of the decision methods. Thus similar results were found with the exception that clients' beliefs about therapists' decisions based on intuition were rated significantly higher than decisions based on no apparent rationale. Thus it appears that if therapists have not previously had success in implementing the therapy that they are recommending (perhaps because this is the first time that they have attempted this form of therapy or because the therapy has not been effective) and if their recommendations of this therapy are not data based, then therapists are making decisions in what clients perceive as a suboptimal manner.

The finding that clients positively rate decisions made on the basis of their therapists' past successful experience is interesting. This decision strategy was presented in such a way that it was obvious that the therapist was ignorant of any research regarding the general efficacy of this treatment. It appears that clients rate decisions based on the informal, personal experience of their therapists as favorably as decisions made on more formal grounds.

In future research, it would be interesting to assess whether there are additive effects or interactions. It might be the case that clients would rate a decision that is made on the basis of both a consideration of the research literature and positive personal experience significantly higher than any of these considerations alone. Another direction for future research is to assess the effects on the outcome of therapy of clients' expectations of how treatment decisions should be made, their estimation of how their therapists are making decisions, and how the therapists actually make decisions. A limitation of our study is the representativeness of the sample. Future studies in which stratified random sampling of clients is used to improve representativeness would also be worthwhile.

An implication of our results is that the extent to which clients are giving informed consent to participate in psychotherapy is unclear, given the previous findings that therapists tend not to use research in their decision making. It appears that clients may be making inaccurate assumptions about how their therapists make decisions. Clients rated appeals to the therapists' past personal successful experience as a desirable way for the therapist to make decisions. Given findings from earlier research (e.g., O'Donohue et al., 1988), it is likely that therapists would provide exactly this kind of rationale for much of their decision making. It is obvious that such experience is important because even therapies that are in principle effective can become ineffective when incompetently delivered. However, it seems that this rationale misses the main point. Professionally trained therapists should realize that informal, instructioned experience is essentially ambiguous, and conclusions about the "success" and "effectiveness" cannot be properly drawn from such experience. The therapist cannot validly conclude that the improvements were not due to spontaneous remission or placebo effects or that some other therapy would have been more effective.

Our results argue for an important modification of the informed consent procedure. We suggest that all therapists explain to the client the procedure that they used to arrive at their treatment decision. Therapists should put in writing whether research was reviewed and, if so, which specific studies were considered; they should also write down the extent to which the therapist has had personal experience with delivery of this type of therapy or should explicate another decision method so that it is clear whether the therapist's decision method meets the standards of the client, as well as the standards of the professional community.

In sum, our results are consistent with the hypothesis that

clients are critical empiricists in that they favor treatment decisions that are based on a review of the research literature or on their therapist's past positive experience. They also believe that their therapists hold similar views.

References

American Medical Association (1972). *Principles of medical ethics.* Washington, DC: Author.

American Nurses Association (1968). *Code for nurses with interpretive statements.* Washington, DC: Author.

American Psychological Association (1947). Recommended graduate training programs in clinical psychology. *American Psychologist, 2,* 539–558.

Cohen, L. H., Sargent, M. M., & Sechrest, L. B. (1986). Use of psychotherapy research by professional psychologists. *American Psychologist, 41,* 198–206.

Eysenck, H. J. (1952). The effects of psychotherapy: An evaluation. *Journal of Consulting Psychology, 16,* 319–324.

National Association of Social Workers (1985). *Code of ethics* (D. Watson, Ed.). London: Routledge, Chapman & Hall.

O'Donohue, W. T., Curtis, S. D., & Fisher, J. E. (1985). Use of research in the practice of community mental health: A case study. *Professional Psychology: Research and Practice, 16,* 710–718.

O'Donohue, W. T., Fisher, J. E., Plaud, J. J., & Curtis, S. D. (1988). *Treatment decisions: Their nature and their justification.* Manuscript submitted for publication.

Ullmann, L. P., & Krasner, L. (1975). *A psychological approach to abnormal behavior.* Englewood Cliffs, NJ: Prentice-Hall.

Received December 22, 1988
Revision received March 28, 1989
Accepted June 30, 1989 ■

Part VII
The Ethics of Claims Making

[23]

Problematic Phrases in the Conclusions of Published Outcome Studies: Implications for Evidence-Based Practice

Allen Rubin
Danielle Parrish
University of Texas at Austin

Objective: This study examined the extent to which conclusions of published outcome studies contain phrases that could be misconstrued as implying more empirical support than is warranted. Methods: All articles (N = 138) reporting outcome studies from 2000 to 2005 in two social work research journals and two topical database searches were assessed regarding research design, findings, and wording of conclusions. Substantial interrater agreement was indicated by kappa values of .95 for research design, 1.00 for nature of findings, and .70 for wording of conclusions. Results: Of the articles, 70% used designs that do not warrant making conclusive causal inferences, and 60% of articles with those designs contained phrases that could be misconstrued or exploited as implying an inflated evidence-based status. Conclusion: To prevent evidence-based practice from becoming a meaningless shibboleth, authors, reviewers, and editors should become vigilant in avoiding wording that could be misconstrued as implying more empirical support than is warranted.

Keywords: evidence-based practice; research; practice; implementation

Advocates for an increased emphasis on evidence-based practice (EBP) in social work and allied fields are recognizing various challenges to the success of the EBP movement (Chwalisz, 2003; Gibbs & Gambrill, 2002; Jenson, 2005; Mullen & Streiner, 2004; Rosen, 2003; Thyer, 2004). Among these challenges is disagreement regarding the value of some sources of evidence in judging whether an intervention should be deemed empirically supported or evidence based. Although randomized clinical trials (RCTs)—along with systematic reviews and meta-analyses of RCTs—have long been considered the gold standard in the EBP research hierarchy, the definition of EBP leaves room for taking other sources of evidence into account in making practice decisions. The most widely cited definition of EBP, for example, emphasizes "the integration of best research evidence with clinical expertise and patient values" (Sackett, Straus, Richardson, Rosenberg, & Haynes, 2000, p. 1).

Although the importance of clinical expertise and unique client factors is generally recognized, controversy exists regarding the relative importance of various types of evidence and how much emphasis to put on clinical expertise versus whatever one deems best research evidence (Norcross, Beutler, & Levant, 2005). Reasons for a greater emphasis on clinical expertise in the EBP process—and a broadening of the types of evidence to consider—commonly focus on perceived limitations of RCTs, such as the following: (a) RCTs are scarce for many areas of social work practice; (b) RCTs tend to have dubious generalizability because of their narrow eligibility requirements regarding diagnosis and comorbidity that make their participants unlike clients typically seen in actual everyday practice; (c) RCTs are biased toward treatments that can be manualized; (d) research has supported the importance of the therapeutic alliance and of therapist experience and expertise in maximizing therapeutic outcomes; and (e) it follows that rigid adherence to treatment manuals can harm the therapeutic alliance and result in poorer treatment outcomes. In light of the above concerns, various scholars are advocating less reliance on RCTs as the basis for deeming practice to be evidence-based and for increased recognition in the EBP process of the value of less well-controlled studies (Messer, 2006; Mullen & Streiner, 2004; Reed, 2006; Westen, 2006; Zlotnik & Galambos, 2004).

For example, Norcross et al. (2005) include case studies and qualitative studies among the types of research that can qualify for judging what interventions are effective in EBP in the mental health field. Zlotnik and Galambos (2004) propose that the evidence base for social work practice should include nonexperimental, clinical, and descriptive studies. Thyer (2004), a prolific advocate of EBP, reviewed the types of evidence that can be considered in the EBP process. Although clearly endorsing a research hierarchy with RCTs and systematic reviews and meta-analyses of RCTs at the top, he included anecdotal case reports, correlational studies, and uncontrolled pretest-posttest trials among the types of evidence that can be considered as offering provisional empirical support for an intervention. Thyer clarifies that the foregoing three types of studies should not be valued as much as well-controlled studies. However, he argues that in the EBP process one should be guided by the best evidence available, and if such limited studies are the best available, then it is acceptable to be guided by them in a provisional manner.

Yet Thyer (2004) also warns that the EBP concept "is subject to considerable misinterpretations, as those invested in the status quo attempt to distort this new and growing movement into existing practices" (p. 167). Likewise, and particularly germane to the softening of standards as to what evidence can qualify in the EBP process for judging what interventions are effective, Shlonsky and Gibbs (2004) warn that EBP "is in danger of becoming a catchphrase for anything that is done with clients that can somehow be linked to an empirical study, regardless of the study's quality, competing evidence, or consideration of clients' needs" (p. 137).

Has the softening of evidentiary standards and the increased emphasis on clinical judgment in the EBP process enabled those invested in a particular form of intervention to claim to have gone through the EBP process and still be strongly influenced by their predilections in reaching a conclusion about how to intervene? Will they interpret the EBP process as permitting them to disregard an intervention supported by strong studies in favor of one that is supported by weaker studies primarily on the basis of their practice wisdom? Will practitioners who have limited time and/or minimal research expertise latch on to whatever type of evidence happens to be handy as a basis for deeming interventions that they prefer as evidence based?

Shlonsky and Gibbs (2004) argue that those who seek or use evidence in the above ways are distorting the EBP process. Some may know they are distorting the process but conceivably may do so anyway so as to promote a treatment modality in which they have a vested interest as an evidence-based intervention. Others, however, may not be aware of how their biases are influencing them to distort the process. They may truly believe that they are doing the best they can in light of their limited time to implement the process properly, especially in light of the emphasis on the clinical judgment component in the EBP process. Moreover, it may be much easier and quicker for busy practitioners to find relatively weak studies that seem to support an intervention of interest than to find randomized experiments or well-controlled quasi-experiments. Past reviews of the literature have documented the scarcity of well-controlled experimental and quasiexperimental outcome studies, as compared to the much more prevalent works based on anecdotal case reports, correlational studies, case studies, qualitative studies, and uncontrolled pretest-posttest evaluations (Austin, 1999; Glisson, 1995; Kirk & Reid, 2002; Rosen, Proctor, Marrow-Howell, & Staudt, 1995; Task Force on Social Work Research, 1991).

The abundance of outcome studies utilizing limited designs underscores the need for their authors to avoid wording inferences in ways that might lead some readers to inappropriately deem the evaluated intervention as effective, or evidence based. This study examines several sources of literature utilized by social workers to determine the extent to which the authors of outcome studies are wording some of their conclusions in ways that could be misconstrued as implying more empirical support for the evaluated intervention than the authors intended.

THE CURRENT STUDY

The current study surveyed a purposive three-pronged sample of published articles reporting evaluations of the effectiveness of interventions, programs, or policies. For each article, we recorded the following information: (a) What was the type of design? (b) Was there a significant finding for any outcome measure? and (c) Did the authors conclude that the intervention, program, or policy was effective? Of particular interest was the extent to which the conclusions of weakly controlled studies contained any wording in any part of the text that could be misconstrued as implying more empirical support for the evaluated intervention than the authors intended. We reasoned that the greater the prevalence of such wording, the greater the risk of the EBP process being distorted.

Our reasoning was not based on the notion that the authors necessarily did anything wrong in the way they worded their conclusions. Rather, we reasoned that readers might misconstrue or selectively perceive the conclusions if they think that weakly controlled studies with positive results are sufficient grounds for calling an intervention evidence based. That is, given various levels of familiarity with research methods and/or investment in one particular treatment method, such readers might not appropriately interpret the author's stated design-related caveats or put enough stock in them if they do not think that such design limitations should prevent them from calling an intervention evidence based. Moreover, if some readers with vested interests in the evaluated intervention think this way or if they selectively read only the conclusive statements in the abstract or discussion, then this would be all the more reason to fear Thyer's (2004) warning that the EBP concept "is subject to considerable misinterpretations, as those invested in the status quo attempt to distort this new and growing movement into existing practices" (p. 167).

For example, one of the articles included in our sample was coauthored by the lead author of the current study (Rubin). Various design limitations rendered its results inconclusive. Its discussion section contained the following conclusion, "The statistical findings of this study provide inconclusive evidence of the effectiveness of [the intervention], but the various indices of effect size and treatment success ratios indicate that *the treatment is in the ballpark of effective interventions* [italics added]" (Gordon-Garofalo & Rubin, 2004, p. 23). At the time the article was written, Rubin saw nothing wrong with the italicized part of that statement in light of the study's extremely low statistical power and consequential huge risk of a Type II error. In light of his current concern about the potential distortion of EBP, however, he would not use that wording. His current concern is based on recent articles warning of the potential distortion of the EBP process and on the results of a recent national survey—conducted by the current authors—of faculty in MSW programs. In those results, 41.5% of faculty members indicated that positive findings from pretest-posttest studies without control groups would be sufficient grounds to tell students that the intervention is evidence based. Likewise, approximately half of the faculty members indicated that qualitative studies that describe positive client outcomes would be sufficient grounds to teach an intervention as evidence based (Rubin & Parrish, 2007). Thus, the current study—rather than implying criticism of the way in which some conclusions have been worded—is merely based on the notion that we may need new ground rules regarding the way authors word things in light of the potential for readers to disregard the caveats we express.

METHOD

We selected our sample of articles in three ways. First, we examined every issue over 6 years (2000-2005) of two research journals in social work: *Research on Social Work Practice* and *Social Work Research*. We chose those two journals for several reasons. One was that the prime focus of our study was on the social work profession. Another was their prominence as research journals in social work. A third reason was our expectation that they would contain many articles reporting evaluations of the effectiveness of an intervention, program, or policy. We read only those articles that evaluated the effectiveness of an intervention, program, or policy.

Although the articles found in those two journals would represent some of the best research in social work, just limiting our sample to them would not represent the range of outcome studies that social work practitioners would find in conducting an Internet search for studies in the EBP process. Consequently, two additional sampling approaches were employed. In both, we conducted searches of PsycINFO, an electronic database that we deemed likely to yield studies that practitioners would find if they employed the EBP process. In one search, we used the search phrase "child maltreatment" in combination with "children" and "treatment" to search for articles related to child abuse and maltreatment. In the other search, we utilized the search phrase "domestic violence" in combination with "treatment" to search for articles that address the treatment of domestic violence. All articles reporting an evaluation of an intervention, program, or policy during the past 6 years (2000-2005) were included in both searches. To obtain a large enough sample for each search, treatment approaches with all potential target treatment populations (parents, children, batterers, and survivors of domestic violence) were included. Despite the vast array of topics that relate to and have relevance to social work practice, we selected child abuse and domestic violence as search topics given their historical relevance to and interest within social work practice and the consequent likelihood that social work practitioners would attempt to access these articles.

All of the articles that composed the study sample are cited in the Appendix. If a study employed more than one type of design, we counted only the one that had the strongest controls with regard to internal validity. Thus, if a mixed-methods study combined a randomized experiment with a qualitative investigation, we recorded it as a randomized experiment. We did this not to imply that quantitative inquiry is more valuable than qualitative inquiry, but rather because the focus of our study is on internal validity and the basis for making causal inferences. The types of design categories are listed in Tables 1 and 2 and were identified a priori to ensure consistency between raters in labeling the designs. More specific designs, such as various kinds of pre-experimental, correlational, or single-case designs, were recorded by the researchers but were categorized into the general design categories listed in Table 1. We used two categories for quasi-experimental designs involving comparison groups—one category for designs that seemed to employ good controls for potential selectivity biases and another category for designs that seemed more vulnerable to possible selectivity biases. We made

TABLE 1:   Frequency of Articles by Type of Design and Type of Outcome

Type of Design	Social Work Research Journal Articles		PsycINFO Search Articles		Total	
	At Least One Significant Outcome	Null Findings Only	At Least One Significant Outcome	Null Findings Only	n	%
Randomized experiment	16	3	8	1	28	20
Quasi-experiment with good controls for selectivity bias	8	1	4 (−1)	1	13	9
Quasi-experiment with potential vulnerability to a selectivity bias	20	5	6	1 (−1)	31	22
Pre-experimental (one group pretest/posttest)	21	2	10 (−2)	1	32	23
Single-case design	9[a]	0	2	0	11	8
Correlational	11	0	6	0	17	12
Qualitative	1	0	1	0	2	1
Case study	0	0	4	0	4	3
Total	86	11	41 (−3)	4 (−1)	138	100

NOTE: (−1) = removed one article from this cell when calculating the total sample because of duplication of the same article in both samples; (−2) = removed two articles from this cell when calculating the total sample because of duplication of the same article in both samples; (−3) = removed three articles from this cell when calculating the total sample because of duplication of the same article in both samples.
a. One of the articles reporting a single-case design deemed its results as uneven, yet recommended implementing the evaluated intervention.

this judgment on the basis of whether the article supplied a persuasive argument as to the comparability of the groups and/or multivariate statistical analyses that controlled for salient extraneous group differences that could account for differences in outcome.

We found 97 relevant studies published in the two social work research journals and 45 from the PsycINFO search. Because 4 of the studies appeared in both subsamples, we found a total of 138 relevant studies overall. To assess interrater reliability, the two authors of this article independently (blind to each other's data) recorded the desired information for 46 (33%) of the articles that were randomly selected from the 138. Both authors agreed on all but 2 (95.7%) of the 46 articles as to type of design ($\kappa = .95, p < .001$). The first and second authors differed on their assessment of the potential for selectivity bias for 2 of the quasi-experimental designs, with each author finding potential concern for selectivity bias in one study that the other did not. The authors agreed on the nature of the findings for all (100%) of the 46 articles, yielding a kappa statistic of 1.00 ($p < .001$). Finally, the authors agreed on 39 (85%) of the 46 articles with regard to whether any conclusions contained any wording that could be misconstrued as implying more empirical support for the evaluated intervention than is warranted in light of the design ($\kappa = .70, p < .001$). This rating was given if such wording was present in any part of the text, even if the overall quality of reportage in the article was exemplary and even if other parts of the article appropriately alerted readers to methodological limitations and caveats about causal inferences. Our rationale for this rating method was that consumers of research might only scan the abstract and/or

discussion sections when seeking to identify evidence-based interventions and thus not be privy to other, more appropriate statements regarding the intervention's effectiveness. Also, some consumers might have predilections or vested interests that influence them to disregard caveats and selectively put more stock in certain conclusions than is warranted. As the senior investigator, the first author's ratings of the data were used in this study when the ratings differed. (The second author agreed to this based on a discussion of each discrepancy.) Had the second author's ratings been used, the results would have indicated a greater proportion of studies containing conclusions worded in ways that could be misconstrued.

RESULTS

Table 1 displays the frequency of each type of design used in the 138 published studies we reviewed. More than half (52%) of the studies used experimental or quasi-experimental designs that—on the basis of the design label alone—reside high on the EBP research hierarchy. These included 20% using experimental designs, 9% using quasi-experimental designs with good controls for potential selectivity biases, and 22% that seemed to be more vulnerable to a selectivity bias that would call into question the comparability of the groups being compared. If we aggregate the 31 quasi-experiments with a greater vulnerability to a selectivity bias with those using designs that are lower on the EBP research hierarchy, we see that the majority of studies (70%) used designs that do not warrant making conclusive causal inferences about intervention outcomes.

Only 10% of the studies had exclusively null findings. Of the 41 well-controlled studies (in the first two rows of Table 1), 6 (15%) had null findings. Only 8 (8%) of the remaining 97 studies had exclusively null findings, whereas 89 (92%) of them reported at least one statistically significant outcome. As shown in Table 2, 56 (63%) of those 89 studies contained some wording that could be misconstrued by some readers as implying more empirical support for the effectiveness of the evaluated intervention than is warranted in light of the design (and more support than most of the authors apparently meant to imply, in light of the caveats they expressed elsewhere in the articles). These phrases are available for review in Table 3 by design type and journal citation.

In all—counting studies with and without null results—70% ($n = 97$) of the articles used designs that do not warrant making conclusive causal inferences, and 60% ($n = 58$) of the articles with those designs contained some wording that could be misconstrued by some readers as implying at least partial evidence-based status for the evaluated intervention, program, or policy. A chi-square analysis found that the differences between the articles in the two subsamples (the social work research journal articles and the PsycINFO search articles) were not statistically significant with regard to the proportions of studies that contained any wording that could be misconstrued as implying more support than is warranted regarding the effectiveness of the evaluated intervention, program, or policy ($\chi^2 = 3.405$, $df = 2$, $p = .182$).

DISCUSSION AND APPLICATIONS TO RESEARCH

Consistent with past reviews of the literature (Austin, 1999; Glisson, 1995; Kirk & Reid, 2002; Rosen et al., 1995; Task Force on Social Work Research, 1991), most of the studies in our sample employed methodologically limited designs that do not warrant conclusive causal inferences. Nevertheless, most of the reports of these limited studies contain at least one phrase that could be misinterpreted or misused by readers as a basis for labeling the intervention, program, or policy to be at least somewhat evidence based. Had we appraised the potential threats of measurement bias and experimental demand, we might have identified a larger proportion of studies with problematic phrases.

As mentioned earlier, we do not intend to imply that the phrases in Table 3 represent inappropriate scientific reportage. Virtually every article that contained these phrases included comments that described the methodological limitations of the research and signaled the

tentative nature of the findings in light of those limitations. In fact, as mentioned earlier, the lead author of this article coauthored one of the phrases appearing in Table 3! Rather than implying criticism of the authors of those articles, we are merely suggesting that the advent of the EBP movement—and its potential distortion—calls for more vigilance by authors of outcome studies in wording the practice implications of studies whose limited designs do not warrant conclusive causal inferences. Our premise, based on our review of the EBP literature and the potential softening of its evidentiary standards, is that many readers of such studies might be inclined to misconstrue or exploit statements as implying more of a basis for deeming an intervention to be evidence based than the authors intended to imply.

One limitation of our study was its use of a purposive sampling strategy that did not yield a probability sample. Although purposive sampling is less ideal than probability sampling, it tends to be preferable to availability sampling and when reasonably employed can offer useful findings (Rubin & Babbie, 2005). We feel that this is the case with our findings. For example, we believe that it is reasonable to suppose that the research articles in the two prominent social work research journals that we purposively selected are more likely to be of high quality in design and reportage than are research articles in most other social work journals. Thus, although they perhaps are not representative of all published social work research articles, the prevalence in those journals of phrases that could be misinterpreted conceivably underestimates the prevalence of such phrases in the social work research literature overall.

We also believe that our purposive strategy of augmenting those two journals with broad searches of the PsycINFO database in two problem areas (child maltreatment and domestic violence) that are highly relevant to social work practice offers a reasonable way to approximate the kinds of EBP-relevant studies that social work practitioners would likely find if they were to search a database for the best available evidence to guide their selection of an intervention. PsycINFO includes 27 reputable social work journals in various areas of social work practice and research and access to interdisciplinary articles in areas of the psychological, social, behavioral, and health sciences (American Psychological Association, 2006).

We were impressed by the consistently careful and appropriate delineation of design limitations in most articles (including all those in the two social work research journals), suggesting exemplary review processes. Moreover, the publication of weakly controlled outcome studies is consistent with the notion that when RCTs are not available for a particular type of problem or client, then the

TABLE 2: Frequency of Articles by Type of Design and Inclusion of Phrases That Can be Misconstrued as Implying More Support Than Warranted Regarding Effectiveness

	Social Work Journals		PsycINFO Search Journals		
Type of Design	No Problematic Phrases	At Least One Problematic Phrase[a]	No Problematic Phrases	At Least One Problematic Phrase[a]	Total
Randomized experiment	19	0	8[b]	1[c]	28
Quasi-experiment with good controls for selectivity bias	9[b]	0	5[b] (−1)	0	13
Quasi-experiment with potential vulnerability to a selectivity bias	11[d]	14[e]	4[b] (−1)	3	31
Pre-experimental (one group pretest/posttest)	5[e]	18	5[b] (−1)	6 (−1)	32
Single-case design	2	7	2	0	11
Correlational	5	6	5	1	17
Qualitative	0	1	0	1	2
Case study	0	0	2	2	4
Total	51	46	31 (−3)	14 (−1)	138

NOTE: (−1) = removed one article from this cell when calculating the total sample because of duplication of the same article in both samples; (−3) = removed three articles from this cell when calculating the total sample because of duplication of the same article in both samples.
a. As illustrated in Table 3.
b. One of these had null results.
c. Experimental design comparing interventions without a control group.
d. Three of these had null results.
e. Two of these had null results.

EBP process recommends being guided in a provisional manner by evidence emanating from lesser designs (Thyer, 2004). Furthermore, phrases such as those appearing in Table 3 technically can be justified on the grounds that the authors acknowledged their study's limitations, that the authors noted that their inferences were tentative and provisional, and that the studies met one or two of the three conditions for making causal inferences regarding establishing correlation and time order. Thus, we imply no criticism whatsoever regarding the editorial policy or processes of the journals included in this study.

Nevertheless, we wonder whether some changes might be in order in light of the emerging challenges confronting the EBP movement, especially regarding the danger of the EBP process "becoming a catchphrase for anything that is done with clients that can somehow be linked to an empirical study, regardless of the study's quality" (Shlonsky & Gibbs, 2004, p. 137). Mullen and Streiner (2004) suggest that it is very difficult to teach students and staff critical appraisal skills that will enable them to "differentiate between limitations and fatal flaws; that is, to judge whether the problems are serious enough to jeopardize the results or should simply be interpreted with a modicum of caution" (p. 118).

Things might be fine if we can safely assume that journal readers will be unbiased, have sufficient research expertise to know where to draw the line regarding which design flaws are too serious and how much caution should be required in interpretations, and follow all the steps of the EBP process appropriately. However, this assumes that practitioners, even if they have research expertise, will have time to carefully critique each article they read rather than scan the abstract and discussion sections for conclusive statements of the intervention's effectiveness (which in much of our sample could be misinterpreted). In addition, this assumption seems even more dubious in light of studies showing that social work practitioners tend to reject or ignore findings that question the effectiveness of their cherished interventions and findings that suggest that alternative interventions are more effective (Casselman, 1972; Kirk & Fischer, 1976; Kirk & Reid, 2002; Rosenblatt, 1968). It also seems dubious in light of the many studies showing that despite the emphasis in social work education on using single-case designs to evaluate practice, practitioners trained in these designs rarely use them as part of their practice (Kirk & Reid, 2002).

Using single-case designs as part of practice is only one of the five steps of the EBP process (the other four include formulating an answerable question, tracking down the best evidence to answer that question, critically appraising the evidence, and integrating the appraisal with one's clinical expertise and client values and circumstances; Thyer, 2004). It seems far fetched, therefore, to suppose that busy practitioners or those with vested interests in certain interventions will now appropriately implement the full EBP process and not be inappropriately influenced by—or inappropriately exploit—weakly controlled studies that word some of their inferences or conclusions in ways that

340   RESEARCH ON SOCIAL WORK PRACTICE

TABLE 3:   Phrases With Potential for Misinterpretation by Source and Type of Design

Journal, Volume, Issue, and Starting Page Number	Type of Design	Phrase
RSWP, 10, 1, 15	Pre-experimental	"Preliminary results support the conclusion that the . . . program had positive effects on the three variables of concern" (p. 15).
RSWP, 10, 1, 98	Single case (no baseline)	". . . interventions are potentially effective . . ." (p. 98). ". . . there is some evidence for the effectiveness of the intervention" (p. 107).
RSWP, 10, 4, 428	Pre-experimental	"Findings from this study . . . indicate that . . . is an effective means of providing training in knowledge and skills required for social work practice" (p. 436).
RSWP, 10, 4, 438	Correlational	"The data seem to support the notion that distance education . . . provided community intervention through enhancing service delivery resources" (p. 453).
RSWP, 10, 4, 467	Pre-experimental	". . . proved to be an effective and well-like tool" (p. 483).
RSWP, 10, 4, 589	Quasi-experiment with potential vulnerability to a selectivity bias	"The findings from this study suggest that the . . . may be effective in . . ." (p. 602).
RSWP, 10, 6, 749	Single case	"The social work intervention was effective . . ." (p. 749).
RSWP, 10, 6, 759	Single case	"A . . . program . . . is an effective treatment method . . ." (p. 761).
RSWP, 11, 1, 53	Quasi-experiment with potential vulnerability to a selectivity bias	"The . . . model . . . is an effective treatment for depression . . ." (p. 53).
RSWP, 11, 3, 277	Quasi-experiment with potential vulnerability to a selectivity bias	"However, the results suggest that combining an intervention with . . . techniques may positively affect client outcomes beyond the effect of the intervention alone" (p. 277).
RSWP, 11, 3, 300	Quasi-experiment with potential vulnerability to a selectivity bias	"Out of the five psychosocial measures of distress, four . . . were found to be significantly altered by type of treatment provided . . ." (p. 300).
RSWP, 11, 3, 321	Correlational	"The current findings have several implications for social work practice [follows with several recommendations for effective programs]" (p. 335).
RSWP, 11, 3, 338	Single case with self-report data only	"The case study demonstrates how . . . can promote children's independent functioning . . ." (p. 338).
RSWP, 11, 4, 411	Single case	"This work would undoubtedly increase teacher effectiveness" (p. 432).
RSWP, 11, 5, 531	Pre-experimental	"The results suggest that the intervention was successful . . ." (p. 542).
RSWP, 11, 6, 645	Pre-experimental	"The evidence from this study suggests that if men can complete the . . . treatment . . . they are likely to experience a number of positive changes . . ." (p. 666).
RSWP, 12, 1, 143	Quasi-experiment with potential vulnerability to a selectivity bias	"These results demonstrate program effectiveness . . ." (p. 154).
RSWP, 12, 1, 159	Correlational	"Overall, the program appeared to have an impact on participants' lives and behaviors . . ." (p. 159).
RSWP, 12, 2, 205	Quasi-experiment with potential vulnerability to a selectivity bias	". . . the model shows promise of providing services that will decrease time in out-of-home care" (p. 205).
RSWP, 12, 4, 534	Pre-experimental	"The results suggest the effectiveness of a cognitive-behavioral group . . ." (p. 534).
RSWP, 12, 4, 546	Pre-experimental	"The present study provides some evidence to support the effectiveness of . . . intervention for social work practice" (p. 546).
RSWP, 12, 4, 558	Pre-experimental	"The effectiveness of the empowerment group . . . was supported by the findings" (p. 558).

(continued)

TABLE 3: (continued)

Journal, Volume, Issue, and Starting Page Number	Type of Design	Phrase
RSWP, 12, 5, 589	Quasi-experiment with potential vulnerability to a selectivity bias	"Despite limitations, the research provides evidence for the short-term effectiveness of . . . services . . ." (p. 589).
RSWP, 13, 4, 432	Pre-experimental	"Results provided preliminary evidence of the effectiveness of . . . the . . . program" (p. 432).
RSWP, 13, 5, 588	Pre-experimental	"Findings suggest that . . . may be critical components" (p. 602). "Our findings suggest that . . . is a key element to reducing . . . problems among delinquents" (p. 604).
RSWP, 13, 5, 608	Pre-experimental	"The utility and efficacy of the . . . is suggested by study findings" (p. 608).
RSWP, 13, 6, 675	Pre-experimental	"Nevertheless, the treatment program appears to be having the desired effect . . ." (p. 688).
RSWP, 14, 1, 14	Quasi-experiment with inconclusive results and low statistical power	"Despite these results, treatment effect and power analyses support the viability of this treatment method" (p. 14). "The statistical findings of this study provide inconclusive evidence of the effectiveness of [the intervention], but the various indices of effect size and treatment success ratios indicate that the treatment is in the ballpark of effective interventions" (p. 23).
RSWP, 14, 2, 112	Single case	"Findings support the effectiveness of cognitive-behavioral interventions in schizophrenia" (p. 112).
RSWP, 14, 3, 163	Pre-experimental	"Overall, the group intervention was effective in . . ." (p. 163).
RSWP, 14, 4, 240	Quasi-experiment with potential vulnerability to a selectivity bias	"The findings from this study indicate that . . . can provide . . . with an opportunity to [lists goals that were met]" (p. 246).
RSWP, 14, 4, 259	Qualitative	"Survivors' narratives indicate that . . . produces greater trauma resolution" (p. 259). "The data indicate that [clients receiving one intervention] experience a deeper sense of trauma resolution with . . . than is found among those who receive . . ." (p. 270).
RSWP, 14, 5, 344	Pre-experimental	"In summary, the current study demonstrated that a . . . resulted in a clinically significant improvement . . ." (p. 349).
RSWP, 14, 6, 397	Pre-experimental	"Our results indicate that administration of . . . produced relatively high rates of treatment adherence and patient satisfaction" (p. 405).
RSWP, 15, 3, 154	Correlational	". . . underpin an effective home care program" (p. 154).
RSWP, 15, 3, 165	Pre-experimental	"The . . . intervention was found effective in reducing children's . . ." (p. 165).
RSWP, 15, 4, 246	Quasi-experiment with potential vulnerability to a selectivity bias	". . . this research on . . . shows that a . . . can affect recidivism rates for those families who complete the program" (p. 255).
RSWP, 15, 5, 323	Pre-experimental	". . . the current study results are promising. They guide us in our effort to use evidence-based practice principles to identify efficacious interventions in the development of healthy families" (p. 336).
RSWP, 15, 6, 431	Single case	". . . is an effective strategy for teaching parents with deficient parenting skills" (p. 431).
RSWP, 15, 6, 470	Quasi-experiment with potential vulnerability to a selectivity bias	"The program appears to be successful" (p. 470).
RSWP, 15, 6, 481	Quasi-experiment with potential vulnerability to a selectivity bias	"Our findings suggest that the administration should continue funding . . ." (p. 489).
RSWP, 15, 6, 501	Pre-experimental	"These . . . results also reinforce the findings of a few other studies that parents . . . may benefit from . . . parent education" (p. 513).

(continued)

342 RESEARCH ON SOCIAL WORK PRACTICE

TABLE 3: (continued)

Journal, Volume, Issue, and Starting Page Number	Type of Design	Phrase
SWR, 25, 2, 71	Quasi-experiment with potential vulnerability to a selectivity bias	"The intervention had a significant effect on the treatment group's knowledge about, . . . attitudes towards prevention, and coping with . . . high-risk situations" (p. 71).
SWR, 25, 2, 89	Quasi-experiment with potential vulnerability to a selectivity bias	". . . the findings suggest that the program was effective in increasing . . ." (p. 98).
SWR, 27, 3, 163	Correlational	"The study found that these programs would greatly increase the . . ." (p. 163).
SWR, 28, 1, 5	Correlational	". . . significantly reduced placement rates or delayed placements . . . is shown to be effective in reducing out-of-home placements . . ." (p. 5).
Child Abuse and Neglect, 29, 7, 825	Pre-experimental	"This study describes the effectiveness of . . ." (p. 825). "This study showed that it was possible to show significant improvements in . . . using . . . procedure . . ." (p. 838).
Psychiatric Annals, 35, 5, 443	Pre-experimental	"These findings indicate that . . . may be a particularly effective treatment for . . ." (p. 447).
Clinical Social Work Journal, 32, 2, 141	Case study	". . . evidence of program engagement and short-term behavioral change, such as that reported here, is promising" (p. 155).
Child Maltreatment, 8, 3, 204	Quasi-experiment with potential vulnerability to a selectivity bias	". . . the study does suggest that . . . increases information to the courts while likely decreasing involvement of the GAL" (p. 208).
Public Health Nursing, 19, 5, 377	Quasi-experiment with potential vulnerability to a selectivity bias	". . . evaluation . . . showed significant effects of the program on . . ." (p. 386).
Families in Society, 85, 4, 463	Pre-experimental	"Findings of this study provided initial empirical evidence of the effectiveness of . . . for treating domestic violence offenders" (p. 472).
Journal of Community Psychology, 32, 5, 593	Correlational	". . . the results of the education and collaboration showed increased . . . and greater success in early referrals for intervention and treatment" (p. 593).
Child Care in Practice, 10, 2, 193	Case study	". . . the . . . .appears to enhance the child's ability to attend to the difficult circumstances . . ." (p. 203).
Journal of Family Violence, 19, 1, 1	Pre-experimental	". . . training increased participants' self-efficacy and . . ." (p. 10).
Journal of Interpersonal Violence, 18, 11, 1311	Experimental (compared two randomly assigned treatment conditions but without a control group)	". . . the results of this study are promising and provide preliminary evidence for the effectiveness of . . ." (p. 1321).
Journal of Interpersonal Violence, 18, 7, 717	Pre-experimental	". . . the findings provide further evidence that . . . counseling services benefit battered women" (p. 728).
Violence Against Women, 8, 2, 206	Qualitative	". . . the program has had some positive long-term effects . . ." (p. 228).
Journal of Substance Abuse Treatment, 19, 1, 1	Quasi-experiment with potential vulnerability to a selectivity bias (report only pre-post findings because of problematic attrition)	"In sum, the results indicate that . . . is feasible and effective in increasing . . ." (p. 4).

NOTE: *RSWP = Research on Social Work Practice; SWR = Social Work Research.*

such practitioners might misinterpret as meaning that their favored interventions can be called evidence based. Moreover, given the wiggle room implied by suggestions that clinical judgment can sometimes outweigh the best research evidence (Reed, 2006), it would seem that such practitioners can claim to be employing at least part of the EBP process in selectively finding evidence that supports their predilections. (We are not implying that this problem applies only to practitioners and not to other research consumers, such as students, professors, and researchers. We are focusing on practitioners because a major controversy in EBP pertains to whether and how practitioners will carry out the EBP process. As noted earlier, our recent survey of social work faculty members suggests that this problem applies to many of them as well.)

Whenever a concept gets broadened to the point that it includes everything, it becomes indistinct and thus really means nothing. We suggest that this may happen to EBP if it becomes softened to the point that virtually any published study purporting to evaluate practice can qualify in considering whether an intervention is evidence based. What can be done to reduce the risk that EBP will be misused as a meaningless, anything-goes shibboleth that includes virtually any published study, regardless of the study's quality or the risk that EBP will be exploited by those invested in the status quo who "attempt to distort this new and growing movement into existing practices" (Thyer, 2004, p. 167)? One possibility is for journal editors to require that articles reporting pre-experimental designs or other designs that have significant limitations regarding causal inferences not use any wording (in the abstract or elsewhere) either that conclusively implies that the evaluated intervention, program, or policy was effective or that resembles the phrases in Table 3—phrases that can be misinterpreted or exploited.

We recognize that editorial implementation of the foregoing recommendation may seem difficult. But we believe that guidelines for authors could be developed regarding how best to word the implications or conclusions of weakly controlled studies with positive outcomes. For example, authors of such studies could be instructed to eschew words that might depict the evaluated intervention as "effective" or "evidence based"—even in a tentative sense. Thus, instead of saying, "Preliminary results support the conclusion that the program had positive effects," authors might say, "Although the methodological limitations of our study keep us from drawing causal inferences about program effects, our results provide a basis for further evaluation of the program with more rigorous designs."

In conclusion, we acknowledge that our study does not warrant definitive generalizations about the prevalence in the social work literature of uncontrolled or weakly controlled outcome studies that contain the kinds of wording that we have addressed. We nevertheless believe that our findings should concern supporters of EBP and encourage them to contemplate taking steps that would influence authors, reviewers, and editors to become vigilant in avoiding wording that could be misconstrued or selectively exploited to imply more empirical support for

the effectiveness of evaluated interventions than is warranted or that authors intend to imply.

APPENDIX
ARTICLES SELECTED FOR THIS STUDY

References marked with an asterisk indicate studies cited in both the PsycINFO sample and the social work research articles sample.

Armour, M. P., & Schwab, J. (2005). Reintegrating children into the system of substitute care: Evaluation of the Exceptional Care Pilot Project. *Research on Social Work Practice, 15,* 404-417.

Ashford, J., & Faith, R. (2004). Testing models of justice and trust: A study of mediation in child dependency disputes. *Social Work Research, 28*(1), 18-27.

Auslander, W., Haire-Joshu, D., Houston, C., Williams, J. H., & Krebill, H. (2000). The short-term impact of a health promotion program for low-income African American women. *Research on Social Work Practice, 10,* 78-97.

Badger, L. W., & MacNeil, G. (2002). Standardized clients in the classroom: A novel instructional technique for social work educators. *Research on Social Work Practice, 12,* 364-374.

Barrett, M., & Wolfer, T. (2001). Reducing anxiety through a structured writing intervention: A single-system evaluation. *Families in Society, 82*(4), 355-362.

Black, B., Weisz, A., Coats, S., & Patterson, D. (2000). Evaluating a psychoeducational sexual assault prevention program incorporating theatrical presentation, peer education, and social work. *Research on Social Work Practice, 10,* 589-606.

Bland, R., & Harrison, C. (2000). Developing and evaluating a psychoeducation program for caregivers of bipolar affective disorder patients: Report of a pilot project. *Research on Social Work Practice, 10,* 209-228.

Bowen, E., Gilchrist, E., & Beech, A. (2005). An examination of the impact of community-based rehabilitation on the offending behaviour of male domestic violence offenders and the characteristics associated with recidivism. *Legal and Criminological Psychology, 10*(2), 189-209.

Bradshaw, W., & Roseborough, D. (2004). Evaluating the effectiveness of cognitive-behavioral treatment of residual symptoms and impairment in schizophrenia. *Research on Social Work Practice, 14,* 112-120.

Bride, B. (2001). Single-gender treatment of substance abuse: Effect on treatment retention and completion. *Social Work Research, 25*(4), 223.

Briggs, H. E., Leary, J. D., Briggs, A. C., Cox, W. H., & Shibano, M. (2005). Group treatment of separated parent and child interaction. *Research on Social Work Practice, 15,* 452-461.

Brooks, F., Nackerud, L., & Risler, E. (2001). Evaluation of a job-finding club for TANF recipients: Psychosocial impacts. *Research on Social Work Practice, 11,* 79-92.

Brooks, F., Zugazaga, C., Wolk, J., & Adams, M. (2005). Resident perceptions of housing, neighborhood, and economic conditions after relocation from public housing undergoing HOPE VI redevelopment. *Research on Social Work Practice, 15,* 481-490.

Brophy, G. (2000). Social work treatment of sleep disturbance in a 5-year-old boy: A single-case evaluation. *Research on Social Work Practice, 10,* 749-760.

*Buttell, F. (2001). Moral development among court-ordered batterers: Evaluating the impact of treatment. *Research on Social Work Practice, 11*(1), 93-107.

*Buttell, F. (2002). Levels of moral reasoning among female domestic violence offenders: Evaluating the impact of treatment. *Research on Social Work Practice, 12*(3), 349-363.

Buttell, F. (2003). Exploring the relevance of moral development as a treatment issue in batterer intervention. *Social Work Research, 27*(4), 232-241.

*Buttell, F. P., & Pike, C. K. (2003). Investigating the differential effectiveness of a batterer treatment program on outcomes for African American and Caucasian batterers. *Research on Social Work Practice, 13*, 675-692.

Carney, M. M., & Buttell, F. (2003). Reducing juvenile recidivism: Evaluating the wraparound services model. *Research on Social Work Practice, 13*, 551-568.

*Carney, M., & Buttell, F. (2004a). A multidimensional evaluation of a treatment program for female batterers: A pilot study. *Research on Social Work Practice, 14*(4), 249-258.

Carney, M., & Buttell, F. (2004b). Psychological and demographic predictors of treatment attrition among women assaulters. *Journal of Offender Rehabilitation, 38*(4), 7-25.

Cauble, E., & Thurston, L. P. (2000). Effects of interactive multimedia training on knowledge, attitudes, and self-efficacy of social work students. *Research on Social Work Practice, 10*, 428-437.

Chan, C. C., Lui, W. W. S., Wan, D. L. Y., & Yau, S. S. W. Evaluating service recipient outcomes in psychiatric residential services in Hong Kong. *Research on Social Work Practice, 12*, 570-581.

Chan, C. L. W., Chan, Y., & Lou, V. W. Q. (2002). Evaluating an empowerment group for divorced Chinese women in Hong Kong. *Research on Social Work Practice, 12*, 558-569.

Chan, K., Yeung, K., Chu, C., Tsang, K., & Leung, Y. (2002). An evaluative study on the effectiveness of a parent-child parallel group model. *Research on Social Work Practice, 12*, 546-557.

Cheung, C. & Man-hung Ngan, R. (2005). Improving older adults' functional ability through service use in a home care program in Hong Kong. *Research on Social Work Practice, 15*, 154-164.

Classen, C., Koopman, C., Nevill-Manning, K., & Spiegel, D. (2001). A preliminary report comparing trauma-focused and present-focused group therapy against a wait-listed condition among childhood sexual abuse survivors with PTSD. *Journal of Aggression, Maltreatment & Trauma, 4*(2), 265-288.

Constantino, J. N., Hashemi, N., & Solis, E. (2001). Supplementation of urban home visitation with a series of group meetings for parents and infants: Results of a "real-world" randomized, controlled trial. *Child Abuse & Neglect, 25*(12), 1571-1581.

Constantino, R., Kim, Y., & Crane, P. (2005). Effects of a social support intervention on health outcomes in residents of a domestic violence shelter: A pilot study. *Issues in Mental Health Nursing, 26*(6), 575-590.

Cooper, B., & Picton, C. (2000). The long-term effects of relocation on people with an intellectual disability: Quality of life, behavior, and environment. *Research on Social Work Practice, 10*, 195-208.

Coulter, S. (2004). Working with a child exposed to community and domestic violence in Northern Ireland: An illustrated case example. *Child Care in Practice, 10*(2), 193-203.

Cummings, S. M. (2003). The efficacy of an integrated group treatment program for depressed assisted living residents. *Research on Social Work Practice, 13*, 608-621.

De la Rosa, I. A., Perry, J., Dalton, L. E., & Johnson, V. (2005). Strengthening families with first-born children: Exploratory story of the outcomes of a home visiting intervention. *Research on Social Work Practice, 15*, 323-338.

Delva, J., Allgood, J., Morrell, R., & McNeece, C. A. (2002). A statewide follow-up study of alcohol and illegal drug use treatment. *Research on Social Work Practice, 12*, 642-652.

Dennis, M., & Stevens, S. (2003). Maltreatment issues and outcomes of adolescents enrolled in substance abuse treatment. *Child Maltreatment: Journal of the American Professional Society on the Abuse of Children, 8*(1), 3-6.

DePanfilis, D., & Dubowitz, H. (2005). Family connections: A program for preventing child neglect. *Child Maltreatment: Journal of the American Professional Society on the Abuse of Children, 10*(2), 108-123.

DiNitto, D. M., Webb, D. K., & Rubin, A. (2002). The effectiveness of an integrated treatment approach for clients with dual diagnoses. *Research on Social Work Practice, 12*, 621-641.

Dodge, K., & Potocky-Tripodi, M. (2001). The effectiveness of three inpatient intervention strategies for chemically dependent women. *Research on Social Work Practice, 11*, 24-39.

Dyches, H., Biegel, D. E., Johnsen, J. A., Guo, S., & Oh Min, M. (2002). The impact of mobile crisis services on the use of community-based mental health services. *Research on Social Work Practice, 12*, 731-751.

Easton, C., Swan, S., & Sinha, R. (2000). Motivation to change substance use among offenders of domestic violence. *Journal of Substance Abuse Treatment, 19*(1), 1-5.

Eckenrode, J., Ganzel, B., & Henderson, C. R. (2000). Preventing child abuse and neglect with a program of nurse home visitation: The limiting effects of domestic violence. *JAMA: Journal of the American Medical Association, 284*(11), 1385-1391.

Edmond, T., Sloan, L., & McCarty, D. (2004). Sexual abuse survivors' perceptions of the effectiveness of EMDR and eclectic therapy. *Research on Social Work Practice, 14*, 259-272.

Fantuzzo, J., Manz, P., Atkins, M., & Meyers, R. (2005). Peer-mediated treatment of socially withdrawn maltreated preschool children: Cultivating natural community resources. *Journal of Clinical Child and Adolescent Psychology, 34*(2), 320-325.

Farber, M. L. Z., & Maharaj, R. (2005). Empowering high-risk families of children with disabilities. *Research on Social Work Practice, 15*, 501-515.

Faul, A. C., McMurtry, S. L., & Hudson, W. W. (2001). Can empirical clinical practice techniques improve social work outcomes? *Research on Social Work Practice, 11*, 277-299.

Faux, T. L., & Black-Hughes, C. A. (2000). Comparison of using the Internet versus lectures to teach social work history. *Research on Social Work Practice, 10*, 454-466.

Festinger, T., & Pratt, R. (2002). Speeding adoptions: An evalutation of the effects of judicial continuity. *Social Work Research, 26*(4), 217.

Finn, J., Kerman, B., & LeCornec, J. (2005). Reducing the digital divide for children in foster care: First-year evaluation of the building skills-building futures program. *Research on Social Work Practice, 15*, 470-480.

Franklin, C., Biever, J., Moore, K., Clemons, D., & Scamardo, M. (2001). The effectiveness of solution-focused therapy with children in a school setting. *Research on Social Work Practice, 11*, 411-434.

Fraser, M. W., Day, S. H., Galinsky, M. J., Hodges, V. G., & Smokowski, P. R. (2004). Conduct problems and peer rejection in childhood: A randomized trial of the making choices and strong families programs. *Research on Social Work Practice, 14*, 313-324.

Fricker-Elhai, A., Ruggiero, K., & Smith, D. (2005). Parent-child interaction therapy with two maltreated siblings in foster care. *Clinical Case Studies, 4*(1), 13-39.

Fu Keung Wong, D., Yu Kit Sun, S., Tse, J., & Wong, F. (2002). Evaluating the outcomes of a cognitive-behavioral group intervention model for persons at risk of developing mental health problems in Hong Kong: A pretest-posttest study. *Research on Social Work Practice, 12,* 534-545.

Gerdtz, J. (2000). Evaluating behavioral treatment of disruptive classroom behaviors of an adolescent with autism. *Research on Social Work Practice, 10,* 98-110.

Gershater-Molko, R., Lutzker, J., & Wesch, D. (2002). Using recidivism data to evaluate project safecare: Teaching bonding, safety, and health care skills to parents. *Child Maltreatment: Journal of the American Professional Society on the Abuse of Children, 7*(3), 277-285.

Gondolf, E. (2000). A 30-month follow-up of court-referred batterers in four cities. *International Journal of Offender Therapy and Comparative Criminology, 44*(1), 111-128.

Gordon, J., & Moriarty, L. (2003). The effects of domestic violence batterer treatment on domestic violence recidivism: The Chesterfield County experience. *Criminal Justice and Behavior, 30*(1), 118-134.

Gordon-Garofalo, V. L., & Rubin, A. (2004). Evaluation of a psychoeducational group for seronegative partners and spouses of persons with HIV/AIDS. *Research on Social Work Practice, 14,* 14-26.

Gregory, C., & Erez, E. (2002). The effects of batterer intervention programs: The battered women's perspectives. *Violence Against Women, 8,* 206-232.

Grote, N. K., Bledsoe, S. E., Swartz, H. A., & Frank, E. (2004). Feasibility of providing culturally relevant, brief interpersonal psychotherapy for antenatal depression in an obstetrics clinic: A pilot study. *Research on Social Work Practice, 14,* 397-407.

Hall, J. A., Dineen, J. P., Schlesinger, D. J., & Stanton, R. (2000). Advanced group treatment for developmentally disabled adults with social skill deficits. *Research on Social Work Practice, 10,* 301-326.

Hamberger, L., Guse, C., Boerger, J., Minsky, D., Pape, D., & Folsom, C. (2004). Evaluation of a health care provider training program to identify and help partner violence victims. *Journal of Family Violence, 19*(1), 1-11.

Harder, J. (2005). Prevention of child abuse and neglect: An evaluation of a home visitation parent aide program using recidivism data. *Research on Social Work Practice, 15,* 246-256.

Harris, M., & Franklin, C. (2003). Effects of a cognitive-behavioral, school-based, group intervention with Mexican American pregnant and parenting adolescents. *Social Work Research, 27*(2), 71.

Hetling, A., & Born, C. E. (2005). Examining the impact of the family violence option on women's efforts to leave welfare. *Research on Social Work Practice, 15,* 143-153.

Hollister, C. D., & McGee, G. (2000). Delivering substance abuse and child welfare content through interactive television. *Research on Social Work Practice, 10,* 417-427.

Howard, A., Riger, S., Campbell, R., & Wasco, S. (2003). Counseling services for battered women: A comparison of outcomes for physical and sexual assault survivors. *Journal of Interpersonal Violence, 18*(7), 717-734.

Huebner, C. (2002). Evaluation of a clinic-based parent education program to reduce the risk of infant and toddler maltreatment. *Public Health Nursing, 19*(5), 377-389.

Huebner, C., Dunlop, M., & Case, A. (2004). Containing violence: A case study illustration of Bion's container-contained model as applied to mother-infant intervention. *Clinical Social Work Journal, 32*(2), 141-157.

Hughes, J., & Gottlieb, L. (2004). The effects of the Webster-Stratton parenting program on maltreating families: Fostering strengths. *Child Abuse & Neglect, 28*(10), 1081-1097.

Jenson, J. M., & Potter, C. C. (2003). The effects of cross-system collaboration on mental health and substance abuse problems

of detained youth. *Research on Social Work Practice, 13,* 588-607.

Johnson, K., & Wagner, D. (2005). Evaluation of Michigan's foster care case management system. *Research on Social Work Practice, 15,* 372-380.

Jones, L. P., Harris, R., & Finnegan, D. (2002). School attendance demonstration project: An evaluation of a program to motivate public assistance teens to attend and complete school in an urban school district. *Research on Social Work Practice, 12,* 222-237.

Jones, L. P., & Okamura, A. (2000). Reprofessionalizing child welfare services: An evaluation of a Title IVE training program. *Research on Social Work Practice, 10,* 607-621.

Kirk, R., & Griffith, D. (2004). Intensive family preservation services: Demonstrating placement prevention using event history analysis. *Social Work Research, 28*(1), 5-16.

Kolko, D., Baumann, B., & Caldwell, N. (2003). Child abuse victims' involvement in community agency treatment: Service correlates, short-term outcomes, and relationship to reabuse. *Child Maltreatment: Journal of the American Professional Society on the Abuse of Children, 8*(4), 273-287.

Kuhn, D. R., & Mendes De Leon, C. F. (2001). Evaluating an educational intervention with relatives of persons in the early stages of Alzheimer's disease. *Research on Social Work Practice, 11,* 531-548.

Layer, S. D., Roberts, C., Wild, K., & Walters, J. (2004). Postabortion grief: Evaluating the possible efficacy of a spiritual group intervention. *Research on Social Work Practice, 14,* 344-350.

Lee, M., Uken, A., & Sebold, J. (2004). Accountability for change: Solution-focused treatment with domestic violence offenders. *Families in Society, 85*(4), 463-476.

Lehman, C. M., Liang, S., & O'Dell, K. (2005). Impact of flexible funds on placement and permanency outcomes for children in child welfare. *Research on Social Work Practice, 15,* 381-388.

Lewandowski, C. A., & Pierce, L. (2002). Assessing the effect of family-centered out-of-home care on reunification outcomes. *Research on Social Work Practice, 12,* 509-621.

Lewandowski, C., & Pierce, L. (2004). Does family-centered out-of-home care work? Comparison of a family-centered approach and traditional care. *Social Work Research, 28*(3), 143-151.

Lewis, J. R., Boyle, D. P., Lewis, L. S., & Evans, M. (2000). Reducing AIDS and substance abuse risk factors among homeless, HIV-infected, drug-using persons. *Research on Social Work Practice, 10,* 15-33.

Lund, C., & Greene, B. (2003). Developing a capacity for self-preservation and emergency management among battered families. *Journal of Family Violence, 18*(4), 181-192.

Marshall, T., & Solomon, P. (2004). Confidentiality intervention: Effects on provider-consumer-family collaboration. *Research on Social Work Practice, 14,* 3-13.

Martsch, M. D. (2005). A comparison of two group interventions for adolescent aggression: High process versus low process. *Research on Social Work Practice, 15,* 8-18.

McFall, J. P., & Freddolino, P. P. (2000). The impact of distance education programs on community agencies. *Research on Social Work Practice, 10,* 438-453.

McNeece, C. A., & Arnold, E. M. (2002). Program closure: The impact on participants in a program for female prostitutes. *Research on Social Work Practice, 12,* 159-175.

Mitchell, C. G. (2001). Patient satisfaction with manualized versus standard interventions in a managed care context. *Research on Social Work Practice, 11,* 473-484.

Nash, J. K., Fraser, M. W., Galinsky, M. J., & Kupper, L. L. (2003). Early development and pilot testing of a problem-solving skills-training program for children. *Research on Social Work Practice, 13,* 432-450.

Newsome, W. S. (2004). Solution-focused brief therapy groupwork with at-risk junior high school students: Enhancing the bottom line. *Research on Social Work Practice, 14*, 336-343.

Nugent, W. R., Umbriet, M. S., Wiinamaki, L., & Paddock, J. (2001). Participation in victim-offender mediation and reoffense: successful replications? *Research on Social Work Practice, 11*, 5-23.

Ogle, R., & Baer, J. (2003). Addressing the service linkage problem: Increasing substance abuse treatment engagement using personalized feedback interventions in heavy-using female domestic violence shelter residents. *Journal of Interpersonal Violence, 18*(11), 1311-1324.

O'Reilly, D., & Dillenburger, K. (2000). The development of a high-intensity parent training program for the treatment of moderate to severe child conduct problems. *Research on Social Work Practice, 10*, 761-788.

Osofsky, J., Rovaris, M., Hammer, J., Dickson, A., Freeman, N., & Aucoin, K. (2004). Working with police to help children exposed to violence. *Journal of Community Psychology, 32*(5), 593-606.

Ozawa, M., & Hong, B. (2003). The effects of EITC and children's allowances on the economic well-being of children. *Social Work Research, 27*(3), 163-178.

Pacifici, C., Delaney, R., White, L., Cummings, K., & Nelson, C. (2005). Foster parent college: Interactive multimedia training for foster parents. *Social Work Research, 29*(4), 243-251.

Patterson, G. T. (2004). Evaluating the effects of child abuse training on the attitudes, knowledge, and skills of police recruits. *Research on Social Work Practice, 14*, 273-280.

Petracchi, H. E., & Patchner, M. E. (2001). A comparison of live instruction and interactive televised teaching: A 2-year assessment of teaching an MSW research methods course. *Research on Social Work Practice, 11*, 108-117.

Pomeroy, E. C., Green, D. L., & Laninghamm L. V. (2002). Couples who care: The effectiveness of a psychoeducational group intervention for HIV serodiscordant couples. *Research on Social Work Practice, 12*, 238-252.

Pomeroy, E., Kiam, R., & Green, D. (2000). Reducing depression, anxiety, and trauma of male inmates: An HIV/AIDS psychoeducational group intervention. *Social Work Research, 24*(3), 156.

Rashid, S. (2004). Evaluating a transitional living program for homeless, former foster care youth. *Research on Social Work Practice, 14*, 240-248.

Rice, A. H. (2001). Evaluating brief structured group treatment of depression. *Research on Social Work Practice, 11*, 53-78.

Rittner, B., & Dozier, C. (2000). Effects of court-ordered substance abuse treatment in child protective services cases. *Social Work, 45*(2), 131-140.

Ronen, T. (2005). Students' evidence-based practice intervention for children with oppositional defiant disorder. *Research on Social Work Practice, 15*, 165-179.

Ronen, T., & Rosenbaum, M. (2001). Helping children to help themselves: A case study of enuresis and nail biting. *Research on Social Work Practice, 11*, 338-356.

Rubin, A., & Babbie, E. R. (2005). *Research methods for social work* (5th ed.). Belmont, CA: Brooks/Cole—Thomson Learning.

Rubin, A., Bischofshausen, S., Conroy-Moore, K., Dennis, B., Hastie, M., Melnick, L., et al. (2001). The effectiveness of EMDR in a child guidance center. *Research on Social Work Practice, 11*, 435-457.

Ryan, J. P., Davis, R. K., & Yang, H. (2001). Reintegration services and the likelihood of adult imprisonment: A longitudinal study of adjudicated delinquents. *Research on Social Work Practice, 11*, 321-337.

Saxe, G., Ellis, B., Fogler, J., Hansen, S., & Sorkin, B. (2005). Comprehensive care for traumatized children. *Psychiatric Annals, 35*(5), 443-448.

Scaletti, R. (2005). Regaining childhood: A case study. *Australian Occupational Therapy Journal, 52*(1), 82-89.

Schilling, R. F., El-Bassel, N., Blansfield Finch, J., Roman, R. J., & Hanson, M. (2002). Motivational interviewing to encourage self-help participation following alcohol detoxification. *Research on Social Work Practice, 12*, 711-730.

Schoech, D. (2000). Teaching over the Internet: Results of one doctoral course. *Research on Social Work Practice, 10*, 467-486.

Schwartz, J., & Waldo, M. (2003). Reducing gender role conflict among men attending partner abuse prevention groups. *Journal for Specialists in Group Work, 28*(4), 355-369.

Shin, S. (2004). Effects of culturally relevant psychoeducation for Korean American families of persons with chronic mental illness. *Research on Social Work Practice, 14*, 231-239.

Slonim-Nevo, V. (2001). The effect of HIV/AIDS prevention intervention for Israeli adolescents in residential centers: Results at 12-month follow-up. *Social Work Research, 25*(2), 71.

Smagner, J. P., & Sullivan, M. H. (2005). Investigating the effectiveness of behavioral parent training with involuntary clients in child welfare settings. *Research on Social Work Practice, 15*, 431-439.

Sowers, K. M., Ellis, R. A., Washington, T. A., & Currant, M. (2002). Optimizing treatment effects for substance-abusing women with children: An evaluation of the Susan B. Anthony Center. *Research on Social Work Practice, 12*, 143-158.

Spinazzola, J., Ford, J. D., & Zucker, M. (2005). Survey evaluates complex trauma exposure, outcome, and intervention among children and adolescents. *Psychiatric Annals, 35*(5), 433-439.

Sprang, G. (2001). The use of eye movement desensitization and reprocessing (EMDR) in the treatment of traumatic stress and complicated mourning: Psychological and behavioral outcomes. *Research on Social Work Practice, 11*, 300-320.

Stevens-Simon, C., Nelligan, D., & Kelly, L. (2001). Adolescents at risk for mistreating their childen. Part II: A home- and clinic-based prevention program. *Child Abuse & Neglect, 25*(6), 753-769.

Stith, S., Rosen, K., McCollum, E., & Thomsen, C. (2004). Treating intimate partner violence within intact couple relationships: Outcomes of multi-couple versus individual couple therapy. *Journal of Marital & Family Therapy, 30*(3), 305-318.

Stocks, J. T., & Freddolino, P. P. (2000). Enhancing computer-mediated teaching through interactivity: The second iteration of a World Wide Web-based graduate social work course. *Research on Social Work Practice, 10*, 505-518.

Sudermann, M., Marshall, L., & Loosely, S. (2000). Evaluation of the London (Ontario) community group treatment programme for children who have witnessed woman abuse. *Journal of Aggression, Maltreatment & Trauma, 3*(1), 127-146.

Sullivan, M., Egan, M., & Gooch, M. (2004). Conjoint interventions for adult victims and children of domestic violence: A program evaluation. *Research on Social Work Practice, 14*, 163-170.

Sundell, K., & Vinnerljung, B. (2004). Outcomes of family group conferencing in Sweden a 3-year follow-up. *Child Abuse & Neglect, 28*(3), 267-287.

Taban, N., & Lutzker, J. (2001). Consumer evaluation of an ecobehavioral program for prevention and intervention of child maltreatment. *Journal of Family Violence, 16*(3), 323-330.

Testa, M. (2002). Subsidized guardianship: Testing an idea whose time has finally come. *Social Work Research, 26*(3), 145.

Thevos, A. K., Thomas, S. E., & Randall, C. L. (2001). Social support in alcohol dependence and social phobia: Treatment comparisons. *Research on Social Work Practice, 11*, 458-472.

Thompson, S. J., Pollio, D. E., Constantine, J., Reid, D., & Nebbitt, V. (2002). Short-term outcomes for youth receiving runaway and homeless shelter services. *Research on Social Work Practice, 12*, 589-603.

Timmer, S., Urquiza, A., Zebell, N., & McGrath, J. (2005). Parent-child interaction therapy: Application to maltreating parent-child dyads. *Child Abuse & Neglect, 29*(7), 825-842.

Tutty, L. M. (2000). What children learn from sexual abuse prevention programs: Difficult concepts and developmental issues. *Research on Social Work Practice, 10*, 275-300.

Tutty, L. M., Bidgood, B. A., Rothery, M. A., & Bidgood, P. (2001). An evaluation of men's batterer treatment groups. *Research on Social Work Practice, 11*, 645-670.

Valentine, P. V., & Smith, T. E. (2001). Evaluating traumatic incident reduction therapy with female inmates: A randomized controlled clinical trial. *Research on Social Work Practice, 11*, 40-52.

Viggiani, P. A., Reid, W. J., & Bailey-Dempsey, C. (2002). Social worker-teacher collaboration in the classroom: Help for elementary students at risk of failure. *Research on Social Work Practice, 12*, 604-620.

Walton, E. (2001). Combining abuse and neglect investigations with intensive family preservation services: An innovative approach to protecting children. *Research on Social Work Practice, 11*, 627-644.

Weisz, A., & Black, B. (2001). Evaluating a sexual assault and dating violence prevention program for urban youths. *Social Work Research, 25*(2), 89.

Weisz, V., & Thai, N. (2003). The Court-Appointed Special Advocate (CASA) Program: Bringing information to child abuse & neglect cases. *Child Maltreatment: Journal of the American Professional Society on the Abuse of Children, 8*(3), 204-210.

Wernet, S. P., Olliges, R. H., Delicath, T. A. (2000). Postcourse evaluations of WebCT (Web course tools) classes by social work students. *Research on Social Work Practice, 10*, 487-504.

Wolf, D. B., & Abell, N. (2003). Examining the effects of meditation techniques on psychosocial functioning. *Research on Social Work Practice, 13*, 27-42.

REFERENCES

American Psychological Association. (2006). *PsycINFO coverage list*. Retrieved April 23, 2006, from http://www.apa.org/psycinfo/about/covlist.pdf

Austin, D. M. (1999). A report on progress in the development of research resources in social work. *Research on Social Work Practice, 9*, 673-707.

Casselman, B. (1972). On the practitioner's orientation toward research. *Smith College Studies in Social Work, 42*, 211-233.

Chwalisz, K. (2003). Evidence-based practice: A framework for twenty-first-century scientific-practitioner training. *The Counseling Psychologist, 31*, 497-528.

Gibbs, L., & Gambrill, E. (2002). Evidence-based practice: Counterarguments to objections. *Research on Social Work Practice, 12*, 452-476.

Glisson, C. (1995). The state of art of social work research: Implications for mental health. *Research on Social Work Practice, 5*, 205-222.

Gordon-Garofalo, V. L., & Rubin, A. (2004). Evaluation of a psychoeducational group for seronegative partners and spouses of

persons with HIV/AIDS. *Research on Social Work Practice, 14*, 14-26.

Jenson, J. M. (2005). Connecting science to intervention: Advances, challenges, and the promise of evidence-based practice. *Social Work Research, 29*, 131-135.

Kirk, S. A., & Fischer, J. (1976). Do social workers understand research? *Journal of Education for Social Work, 12*, 63-67.

Kirk, S. A., & Reid, W. J. (2002). *Science and social work practice*. New York: Columbia University Press.

Messer, S. B. (2006). What qualifies as evidence in effective practice? Patient values and preferences. In J. C. Norcross, L. E. Beutler, & R. F. Levant (Eds.), *Evidence-based practices in mental health: Debate and dialogue on the fundamental questions* (pp. 31-40). Washington, DC: American Psychological Association.

Mullen, E. J., & Streiner, D. L. (2004). The evidence for and against evidence-based practice. *Brief Treatment and Crisis Intervention, 4*, 111-121.

Norcross, J. C., Beutler, L. E., & Levant, R. F. (2005). *Evidence-based practices in mental health*. Washington, DC: American Psychological Association.

Reed, G. M. (2006). What qualifies as evidence of effective practice? Clinical expertise. In J. C. Norcross, L. E. Beutler, & R. F. Levant (Eds.), *Evidence-based practices in mental health: Debate and dialogue on the fundamental questions* (pp. 13-23). Washington, DC: American Psychological Association.

Rosen, A. (2003). Evidence-based social work practice: Challenges and promise. *Social Work Research, 27*, 197-208.

Rosen, A., Proctor, E. K., Marrow-Howell, N., & Staudt, M. (1995). Rationales for practice decisions: Variations in knowledge use by decision task and social work service. *Research on Social Work Practice, 5*, 501-523.

Rosenblatt, A. (1968). The practitioner's use and evaluation of research. *Social Work, 13*, 53-59.

Rubin, A., & Parrish, D. (2007). Views of evidence-based practice among faculty in MSW programs: A national survey. *Research on Social Work Practice, 17*, 110-122.

Sackett, D. L., Straus, S. E., Richardson, W. S., Rosenberg, W., & Haynes, R. B. (2000). *Evidence-based medicine: How to practice and teach EBP* (2nd ed.). New York: Churchill-Livingstone.

Shlonsky, A., & Gibbs, L. (2004). Will the real evidence-based practice please stand up? Teaching the process of evidence-based practice to the helping professions. *Brief Treatment and Crisis Intervention, 4*(2), 137-153.

Task Force on Social Work Research. (1991). *Building social work knowledge for effective services and policies: A plan for research development*. Washington, DC: Institute for the Advancement of Social Work Research.

Thyer, B. (2004). What is evidence-based practice? *Brief Treatment and Crisis Intervention, 4*, 167-176.

Westen, D. I. (2006). Patients and treatments in clinical trials are not adequately representative of clinical practice. In J. C. Norcross, L. E. Beutler, & R. F. Levant (Eds.), *Evidence-based practices in mental health: Debate and dialogue on the fundamental questions* (pp. 161-171). Washington, DC: American Psychological Association.

Zlotnik, J. L., & Galambos, C. (2004). Evidence-based practices in health care: Social work possibilities. *Health and Social Work, 29*, 259-261.

[24]

Fraudulent misrepresentation and eating disorder

Patricia E. O'Hagan

Director of Eating Disorder Resource Centre of British Columbia, St. Paul's Hospital, 1081 Burrard Street, Vancouver, British Columbia, Canada V6Z 1Y6

1. A recent case of service misrepresentation?

In a precedent setting civil decision issued on April 16, 2003, the Hon. Judge J. Gedye found the defendant service provider liable for fraudulent misrepresentation with respect to services in what was "... advertised as a residential eating disorder therapy centre".[1]

Ms. Ness filed a Notice of Claim against Ms. Cunningham, doing business as Lynn Creek Lodge. Ms. Ness submitted to the court an invoice that referred to a "treatment program: 1 month: August 20-Sept. 19, 2001".[2] There was a fee of $5000.00 plus $350.00 for GST for a total of $5350.00, which the plaintiff paid on August 20, 2001.[3] Ms. Ness had found a reference to the Lynn Creek Lodge on the Internet in the summer of 2000. She contacted Ms. Cunningham by phone and had several discussions that resulted in Ms. Ness' decision to participate in the program. Ms. Ness and her mother drove from their home in the interior of BC, to see the centre in North Vancouver. Her mother was skeptical; she did not like the look of the place, but Ms. Ness insisted it was her choice. She chose to stay despite her mother's concerns.[4]

The fees of $5000.00 covering the "primary program" and were to include "room and board, meals and meal support. (Includes shopping, cooking and nutritious snacks. Meals cooked in our kitchen with a focus on organic ingredients and holistic nutrition)". There was no evidence submitted showing provision of nutritious food, no evidence of gardening, nor any form of meal support.[5] Ms. Ness stated that not a single qualified therapist was made available or involved with her during her stay. Ms. Cunningham did not provide proof of any

---

E-mail address: pohagan@providencehealth.bc.ca (P.E. O'Hagan).

[1] *Kim Ness vs. Clare Cunningham dba Lynn Creek Lodge.* (2003) File No: 02-13927, North Vancouver Registry, Provincial Court of British Columbia.

[2] Idem, at 3.

[3] Idem.

[4] Idem, at 4.

[5] Idem, at 5-6.

714   *P.E. O'Hagan / International Journal of Law and Psychiatry 26 (2003) 713–717*

credentials for any therapists. This was despite the description of the program as including an extensive list of therapies.[6]

The misrepresentation of services was based on the material fact that "there was no evidence of "psychologists, art therapists, traditional Chinese medicine doctors" who might have been qualified to work in "psychotherapy resolving underlying issues of disordered eating including group therapy, private counselling and eating disorder education".[7] The Court stated:

> This misstatement was factual, and, I find it was made dishonestly or recklessly, knowing it was false and made with the intention of inducing the plaintiff to enrol in the programme.[8]

And further:

> The seriousness of the situation is relieved only because Ms. Ness apparently did not have a life-threatening eating disorder.[9]

In addition, there were two retreats totaling 14 days that were cancelled without any rescheduling. Ms. Ness attempted to speak with Ms. Cunningham regarding the continually changing schedule and lack of appointments but was only able to speak with Ms. Cunningham at the end of the program.[10] Ms. Ness stated that any benefit gained from her time at Lynn Creek Lodge was because of the rest time spent away from family demands, not from any treatment as advertised.[11] The court awarded damages in the amount of $3754.00 and costs, the amount the plaintiff claimed.[12]

2. The Claude–Pierre case

Another case involving claims of questionable treatment for eating disorders is recounted in a recently published book, *Anorexia's Fallen Angel: The Untold Story of Peggy Claude–Pierre and the Controversial Montreux Clinic*, by McLintock (2002). The book sets out a chronology of events from 1988 through August 2000 about the residential treatment program offered at the Montreux Clinic in Victoria, B.C. The book provides insight into the many disturbing stories of parents, families, friends, and individuals attempting to find treatment and services for eating disorders.

The Montreux case did not involve allegations of fraudulent misrepresentation, but rather an issue of licensing regulations for a residential eating disorder program. The cost to clients

---

[6] Idem, at 6.
[7] Idem, at 12.
[8] Idem.
[9] Idem.
[10] Idem, at 9, 10, 12.
[11] Idem, at 10.
[12] Idem, at 13.

P.E. O'Hagan / International Journal of Law and Psychiatry 26 (2003) 713–717 715

ranged from $500.00 (2002:19) rising to $925 (US) per day (2002:89) for program fees to cover a 24-hour-a-day residential program. The program was ultimately the subject of a ruling by Dr. Richard Stanwick, the Medical Officer of Health for December 1999. Dr. Stanwick found that Montreux had put the health and safety of some of its patient's at risk and must surrender its residential license by January 31, 2000 (2002:278).

The B.C. Director of Licensing, Kersteen Johnston allowed Montreux to remain open pending a hearing of its appeal of Dr. Stanwick's decision. Things then took a surprising turn. Johnston declined to hold a hearing on the appeal, but rather insisted that an informal resolution by agreement was possible, one, which would allow Montreux to remain open. When such a resolution was not achieved, she nonetheless allowed the clinic to remain open (2002:267–268).

Not content to accept this new ruling by Johnston, particularly in light of Dr. Stanwick's findings, Steven Eng, head of the licensing branch for the Capital Health Region and Guy McDonald, lawyer for Licensing branch, Capital Health Region, applied to the B.C Supreme Court, asking it to reverse Johnson's decision. The hearing in the Supreme Court was set for 6:00 p.m. on 25 August 2000 (2002:269).

But in another surprising twist, on the eve of the court hearing, Claude–Pierre turned in her residential licence to Johnston, promising not to run a residential program in Victoria any longer (2002:269). However, the surrender of the licence does not mean what one might expect, the termination of the operation offering any services. As stated by McLintock,

> [t]he law requires an operating licence only for establishments providing their services on a residential basis. Those who want to run a day program or outpatient-counselling program require no licence from the government, no matter how ill-physically or mentally-their clients may be. Unlike residential facilities, such programs have no requirements for the qualifications of either the operators or the staff they hire (2002:273).

Anyone can label himself or herself a counsellor without any training, and offer services to those who are vulnerable and looking for help. As McLintock tells us, the Montreux staff had no specialized training in eating disorders. Some of the staff that were "counseling" patients included family members and past patients who had been previously ill with eating disorders but without any formal training.

> Staff were to be chosen not for their academic background or professional training but for their kindness, patience, and empathy (2002:19).

3. Discussion

From the findings in the *Ness vs. Cunningham* case of fraudulent misrepresentation, and in the *Montreux* case of failure to meet licensing regulations, it is clear that individuals offering community based services in the prevention and treatment of eating disorders need specific professional training. The cases also highlight the vulnerability of a group which will go to extreme lengths, and whose desperation will lead them to incur high financial costs to find help.

It is important that we point out that both boys and girls are vulnerable to eating disorders. How can we best help parents and those struggling to make an informed decision about services and resources when they believe their child needs help now before it becomes a life-threatening illness as in the first case, or when hospitalization has not been successful for recovery?

Birmingham's (2003) article in this issue offers some valuable advice. In *Clinical Decision Analysis and Anorexia Nervosa*, the author states, "with increasing frequency lawyers are being asked to help with decision-making in cases of anorexia nervosa" (2003:XX). The author then set out the statistical method of decision analysis,

> . . .to assist health professionals to make difficult treatment decisions. It can be used to help the legal profession to understand the risks and benefits of each treatment option without the need for the attorneys to have detailed medical knowledge (2003:XX).

Decision analysis is a method of making an informed decision in the clinical setting where anorexia nervosa involves a professional team approach, including family, friends, and the individual.

In a clinical setting specializing in the treatment of eating disorders and where the patient is an adult, the choice of treatments is usually negotiated with hospital team members, the involved parent(s) and the individual being treated. However, when someone is not in a life-threatening situation and being treated in a community setting, the decision making process for treatment is often a trial and error approach. For example, the claimant, Ms Ness was motivated to regain good health and chose to get help at Lynn Creek Lodge. However, her mother did not agree with her decision to participate in that particular program.

It is important to emphasize that once an eating disorder has become a primary strategy for coping in a young girl or boy's life, obtaining help from professionals trained in the specific illness is critical. Without these services and resources, family, friends, and those struggling will be at the mercy of those who are not trained and as a result may do more harm even up to the point of causing sudden death. They may also fall prey to those who have money rather than health as their motivation for offering services.

The clinical decision analysis advanced by the authors in the above-cited article may offer promise for the non-clinical setting as well. Those struggling with eating disorders in their community could benefit by having access to a method of decision-making that would allow for an informed choice. To make the best choice and prevent the progression of the illness would require available and cost effective services along with trained professionals.

Regardless of the severity or stage of an eating disorder, individuals, families, and professionals struggle with the decisions of when to intervene, how to intervene, and, what services will successfully help the patient or client regain their health. The best practice of course is the prevention of the illness through education using the 'do no harm' model.

P.E. O'Hagan / International Journal of Law and Psychiatry 26 (2003) 713–717 717

Over the past five to ten years, eating disorders and disordered eating have gained considerable media attention, several popular books have been written, there are academic specialized journals on the topic, and many videos are available which have resulted in growing public awareness. At the same time, disordered eating behaviours and attitudes are occurring at younger ages for both genders. There are more people offering a range of treatment methods and prevention strategies. From a treatment point of view, the best practice is a team approach with trained qualified staff. Without such provisions of services in place, providers run the risk of legal action, and more importantly, may jeopardize the health and life of the client.

4. Conclusion

Until these two cases, it appears that Canadian court decisions on eating disorders had focused on the problem in the context of motor vehicle accident damage assessments, custody/access disputes, and sexual abuse charges. A search of the eating disorder issues in the major Canadian legal database, *Quicklaw*, in May 2003, produced 88 such Canadian Superior Court cases from 1876 to the present.

It is clear that the two cases cited in this article represent a significant and valuable expansion of case law dealing with eating disorders to include issues related to the health and safety of clients and the availability and qualifications in the provision of services. Caveat emptor is currently the standard by which clients are to judge the quality of community based for profit services. This appears to be a cruel standard for those struggling with a life threatening illness. Perhaps the best we can do is to set overriding principles for guidelines in the delivery of services.

References

McLintock, B. (2002). *The Untold Story of Peggy Claude-Pierre and the Controversial Montreux Clinic*. Toronto, Canada: Harper Collins Publishers.

Birmingham, C. (2003). Clinical decision analysis and anorexia nervosa. *International Journal of Law and Psychiatry, 26*(4), XX.

[25]

SCIENCE AND ETHICS IN CONDUCTING, ANALYZING, AND REPORTING PSYCHOLOGICAL RESEARCH

By Robert Rosenthal

The relationship between scientific quality and ethical quality is considered for three aspects of the research process: conduct of the research, data analysis, and reporting of results. In the area of conducting research, issues discussed involve design, recruitment, causism, scientific quality, and costs and utilities. The discussion of data analysis considers data dropping, data exploitation, and meta-analysis. Issues regarding reporting of results include misrepresentation of findings, misrepresentation of credit, and failure to report results as a result of self-censoring or external censoring.

The purpose of this article is to discuss a number of scientific and ethical issues relevant to conducting, analyzing, and reporting psychological research. A central theme is that ethics and scientific quality are very closely interrelated. Everything else being equal, research that is of higher scientific quality is likely to be more ethically defensible. The lower the quality of the research, the less justified we are ethically to waste research participants' time, funding agencies' money, and journals' space. The higher the quality of the research, the better invested have been the time of the research participants, the funds of the granting agency, the space of the journals, and, not least, the general investment that society has made in supporting science and its practitioners.

CONDUCTING PSYCHOLOGICAL RESEARCH

Let us turn first to considerations of research design, procedures employed in a study, and the recruitment of human participants. In evaluating the ethical employment of our participants, we can distinguish issues of safety from more subtle issues of research ethics. Obviously, research that is unsafe for participants is ethically questionable. However, I propose that perfectly safe research in which no participant will be put at risk may also

Address correspondence to Robert Rosenthal, Department of Psychology, Harvard University, 33 Kirkland St., Cambridge, MA 02138.

be ethically questionable because of the shortcomings of the design.

Issues of Design

Imagine that a research proposal that comes before an institutional review board proposes the hypothesis that private schools improve children's intellectual functioning more than public schools do. Children from randomly selected private and public schools are to be tested extensively, and the research hypothesis is to be tested by comparing scores earned by students from private versus public schools. The safety of the children to be tested is certainly not an issue, yet it can be argued that this research raises ethical issues because of the inadequacy of its design. The goal of the research is to learn about the causal impact on performance of private versus public schooling, but the design of the research does not permit reasonable causal inference because of the absence of randomization or even some reasonable attempt to consider plausible rival hypotheses (Cook & Campbell, 1979).

How does the poor quality of the design raise ethical objections to the proposed research? Because students', teachers', and administrators' time will be taken from potentially more beneficial educational experiences. Because the poor quality of the design is likely to lead to unwarranted and inaccurate conclusions that may be damaging to the society that directly or indirectly pays for the research. In addition, allocating time and money to this poor-quality science will serve to keep those finite resources of time and money from better quality science in a world that is undeniably zero-sum.

It should be noted that had the research question addressed been appropriate to the research design, the ethical issues would have been less acute. If the investigators had set out only to learn whether there were performance differences between students in private versus public schools, their design would have been perfectly appropriate to their question.

Science and Ethics

Issues of Recruitment

The American Psychological Association's (APA) Committee for the Protection of Human Participants in Research and its new incarnation, the Committee on Standards in Research, and such pioneer scholars of the topic as Herbert Kelman have thoughtfully considered a variety of ethical issues in the selection and recruitment of human participants (APA, 1982; Blanck, Bellack, Rosnow, Rotheram-Borus, & Schooler, 1992; Grisso et al., 1991; Kelman, 1968). Only a few comments need be made here.

On the basis of several reviews of the literature, my friend and colleague Ralph Rosnow and I have proposed a number of procedures designed to reduce volunteer bias and therefore increase the generality of our research results (Rosenthal & Rosnow, 1975, 1991; Rosnow & Rosenthal, 1993). Employment of these procedures has led us to think of our human participants as another "granting agency"—which, we believe, they are, since they must decide whether to grant us their time, attention, and cooperation. Part of our treating them as such is to give them information about the long-term benefits of the research. In giving prospective participants this information, we have a special obligation to avoid hyperclaiming.

Hyperclaiming

Hyperclaiming is telling our prospective participants, our granting agencies, our colleagues, our administrators, and ourselves that our research is likely to achieve goals it is, in fact, unlikely to achieve. Presumably our granting agencies, our colleagues, and our administrators are able to evaluate our claims and hyperclaims fairly well. However, our prospective participants are not; therefore, we should tell them what our research can actually accomplish rather than that it will yield the cure for panic disorder, depression, schizophrenia, or cancer.

Causism

Closely related to hyperclaiming is the phenomenon of causism. Causism refers to the tendency to imply a causal relationship where none has been established (i.e., where the data do not support it).

Causism: Characteristics and Consequences

Characteristics of causism include (a) the absence of an appropriate evidential base; (b) the presence of language implying cause (e.g., "the effect of," "the impact of," "the consequence of," "as a result of") where the appropriate language would have been "was related to," "was predictable from," or "could be inferred from"; and (c) self-serving benefits to the causist. Causism is self-serving because it makes the causist's result appear more important or fundamental than it really is.

If a perpetrator of causism is unaware of the causism, its presence simply reflects poor scientific training. If the perpetrator is aware of the causism, it reflects blatantly unethical misrepresentation and deception.

Whereas well-trained colleagues can readily differentiate causist language from inferentially more accurate language, potential research participants or policymakers ordinarily cannot. When a description of a proposed research study is couched in causal language, that description represents an unfair recruitment device that is at best inaccurate, when it is employed out of ignorance, and at worst dishonest, when it is employed as hype to increase the participation rates of potential participants. As a member of an institutional review board, I regret that I have seen such use made of causist language in proposals brought before us.

Bad Science Makes for Bad Ethics

Causism is only one example of bad science. Poor quality of research design, poor quality of data analysis, and poor quality of reporting of the research all lessen the ethical justification of any type of research project. I believe this judgment applies not only when deception, discomfort, or embarrassment of participants is involved, but for even the most benign research experience for participants. If because of the poor quality of the science no good can come of a research study, how are we to justify the use of participants' time, attention, and effort and the money, space, supplies, and other resources that have been expended on the research project? When we add to the "no good can come of it" argument the inescapable zero-sum nature of time, attention, effort, money, space, supplies, and other resources, it becomes difficult to justify poor-quality research on any ethical basis. For this reason, I believe that institutional review boards must consider the technical scientific competence of the investigators whose proposals they are asked to evaluate. Yes, that will increase the work required of board members and change boards' compositions somewhat to include a certain degree of methodological expertise. No, it will not always be easy to come to a decision about the scientific competence of an investigator and of a particular proposal, but then it is not always easy to come to a decision about the more directly ethical aspects of a proposal either.

Poor quality of research makes for poor quality of education as well. Especially when participation is quasi-coercive, the use of participants is usually justified in part by the fact that they will benefit educationally. But if participants are required to participate in poor-quality research, they are likely to acquire only misconceptions

PSYCHOLOGICAL SCIENCE

Robert Rosenthal

about the nature of science and of psychology. When participants' scores on personality scales are correlated with their scores on standardized tests or course grades, and they are told that "this research is designed to learn the impact of personality on cognitive functioning," they have been poorly served educationally as part of having been misled scientifically.

Costs and Utilities

Payoffs for doing research

When individual investigators or institutional review boards are confronted with a questionable research proposal, they ordinarily employ a cost-utility analysis in which the costs of doing a study, including possible negative effects on participants, time, money, supplies, effort, and other resources, are evaluated simultaneously against such utilities as benefits to participants, to other people at other times, to science, to the world, or at least to the investigator. The potential benefits of higher quality studies and studies addressing more important topics are greater than the potential benefits of lower quality studies and studies addressing less important topics. Rosnow and I have often diagrammed this type of cost-utility analysis as a two-dimensional plane in which costs are one dimension and utilities the other (Rosenthal & Rosnow, 1984, 1991; Rosnow, 1990). Any study with high utility and low cost should be carried out forthwith. Any study with low utility and high cost should not be carried out. Studies in which costs equal utilities are very difficult to decide about.

Payoffs for failing to do research

However, Rosnow and I have become convinced that this cost-utility model is insufficient because it fails to consider the costs (and utilities) of *not* conducting a particular study (Rosenthal & Rosnow, 1984, 1991; Rosnow, 1990; Rosnow & Rosenthal, 1993).

The failure to conduct a study that could be conducted is as much an act to be evaluated on ethical grounds as is conducting a study. The oncology group that may have a good chance of finding a cancer preventive but feels the work is dull and a distraction from their real interest is making a decision that is to be evaluated on ethical grounds as surely as the decision of a researcher to investigate tumors with a procedure that carries a certain risk. The behavioral researcher whose study may have a good chance of reducing violence or racism or sexism, but who refuses to do the study simply because it involves deception, has not solved an ethical problem but only traded in one for another. The issues are, in principle, the same for the most basic as for the most applied research. In practice, however, it is more difficult to make even rough estimates of the probability of finding the cancer cure or the racism reducer for the more basic as compared with the more applied research.

This idea of lost opportunities has been applied with great eloquence by John Kaplan (1988), of the Stanford University Law School. The context of his remarks was the use of animals in research and the efforts of "animal rights" activists to chip away "at our ability to afford animal research. . . . [I]t is impossible to know the costs of experiments not done or research not undertaken. Who speaks for the sick, for those in pain, and for the future?" (p. 839).

In the examples considered so far, the costs of failing to conduct the research have accrued to future generations or to present generations not including the research participants themselves. But sometimes there are incidental benefits to research participants that are so important that they must be considered in the calculus of the good, as in the following example:

I was asked once to testify to an institutional review board (not my own) about the implications of my research for the ethics of a proposed project on karyotyping. The study was designed to test young children for the presence of the XYY chromosome, which had been hypothesized to be associated with criminal behavior. The youngsters would be followed up until adulthood so that the correlation between chromosome type and criminal behavior could be determined. I was asked to talk about my research on interpersonal expectancy effects because it was feared that if the research were not done double-blind, the parents' or researchers' expectations for increased criminal behavior by the XYY males might become a self-fulfilling prophecy (Rosenthal, 1966; Rosenthal & Jacobson, 1968, 1992). A double-blind design should have solved that problem, but the board decided not to permit the research anyway.

The enormous costs to the participants themselves of the study's not being done were not considered. What were those costs? The costs were the loss of 20 years of free, high-quality pediatric care to children whose parents could never have afforded any high-quality pediatric care. Was it an ethically defensible decision to deprive scores or hundreds of children of medical care they would otherwise not have received in order to avoid having a double-blind design that had very little potential for actually harming the participants? At the very least, these costs of failing to do the research should have received full discussion. They did not.

DATA ANALYSIS AS AN ETHICAL ARENA

Data Dropping

Ethical issues in the analysis of data range from the very obvious to the very subtle. Probably the most ob-

PSYCHOLOGICAL SCIENCE

Science and Ethics

vious and most serious transgression is the analysis of data that never existed (i.e., that were fabricated). Perhaps more frequent is the dropping of data that contradict the data analyst's theory, prediction, or commitment.

Outlier rejection

There is a venerable tradition in data analysis of dealing with outliers, or extreme scores, a tradition going back over 200 years (Barnett & Lewis, 1978). Both technical and ethical issues are involved. The technical issues have to do with the best ways of dealing with outliers without reference to the implications for the tenability of the data analyst's theory. The ethical issues have to do with the relationship between the data analyst's theory and the choice of method for dealing with outliers. For example, there is some evidence to suggest that outliers are more likely to be rejected if they are bad for the data analyst's theory but treated less harshly if they are good for the data analyst's theory (Rosenthal, 1978; Rosenthal & Rubin, 1971). At the very least, when outliers are rejected, that fact should be reported. In addition, it would be useful to report in a footnote the results that would have been obtained had the outliers not been rejected.

Subject selection

A different type of data dropping is subject selection in which a subset of the data is not included in the analysis. In this case, too, there are technical issues and ethical issues. There may be good technical reasons for setting aside a subset of the data—for example, because the subset's sample size is especially small or because dropping the subset would make the data more comparable to some other research. However, there are also ethical issues, as when just those subsets are dropped that do not support the data analyst's theory. When a subset is dropped, we should be informed of that fact and what the results were for that subset. Similar considerations apply when the results for one or more variables are not reported.

Exploitation Is Beautiful

That data dropping has ethical implications is fairly obvious. An issue that has more subtle ethical implications is exploitation. Exploiting research participants, students, postdoctoral fellows, staff, and colleagues is of course reprehensible. But there is a kind of exploitation to be cherished: the exploitation of data.

Many of us have been taught that it is technically improper and perhaps even immoral to analyze and reanalyze our data in many ways (i.e., to snoop around in the data). We were taught to test the prediction with one particular preplanned test and take a result significant at the .05 level as our reward for a life well-lived. Should the

result not be significant at the .05 level, we were taught, we should bite our lips bravely, take our medicine, and definitely not look further at our data. Such a further look might turn up results significant at the .05 level, results to which we were not entitled. All this makes for a lovely morality play, and it reminds us of Robert Frost's poem about losing forever the road not taken, but it makes for bad science and for bad ethics.

It makes for bad science because while snooping does affect p values, it is likely to turn up something new, interesting, and important (Tukey, 1977). It makes for bad ethics because data are expensive in terms of time, effort, money, and other resources and because the antisnooping dogma is wasteful of time, effort, money, and other resources. If the research was worth doing, the data are worth a thorough analysis, being held up to the light in many different ways so that our research participants, our funding agencies, our science, and society will all get their time and their money's worth.

Before leaving this topic, I should repeat that snooping in the data can indeed affect the p value obtained, depending on how the snooping is done. But statistical adjustments, for example, Bonferroni adjustments (Estes, 1991; Howell, 1992; Rosenthal & Rubin, 1984), can be helpful here. Most important, replications will be needed—whether the data were snooped or not!

Meta-Analysis as an Ethical Imperative

Meta-analysis is a set of concepts and procedures employed to summarize quantitatively any domain of research (Glass, McGaw, & Smith, 1981; Rosenthal, 1991). We know from both statistical and empirical research that, compared with traditional reviews of the literature, meta-analytic procedures are more accurate, comprehensive, systematic, and statistically powerful (Cooper & Rosenthal, 1980; Hedges & Olkin, 1985; Mosteller & Bush, 1954). Meta-analytic procedures use more of the information in the data, thereby yielding (a) more accurate estimates of the overall magnitude of the effect or relationship being investigated, (b) more accurate estimates of the overall level of significance of the entire research domain, and (c) more useful information about the variables moderating the magnitude of the effect or relationship being investigated.

Retroactive increase of utilities

Meta-analysis allows us to learn more from our data and therefore has a unique ability to increase retroactively the benefits of the studies being summarized. The costs of time, attention, and effort of the human participants employed in the individual studies entering into the meta-analysis are all more justified when their data enter into a meta-analysis. That is because the meta-analysis

PSYCHOLOGICAL SCIENCE

Robert Rosenthal

increases the utility of all the individual studies being summarized. Other costs of individual studies—costs of funding, supplies, space, investigator time and effort, and other resources—are similarly more justified because the utility of individual studies is so increased by the borrowed strength obtained when information from more studies is combined in a sophisticated way.

The failure to employ meta-analytic procedures when they could be used thus has ethical implications because the opportunity to increase the benefits of past individual studies has been forgone. In addition, when public funds or other resources are employed by scientists to prepare reviews of literatures, it is fair to ask whether those resources are being used wisely or ethically. Now that we know how to summarize literatures meta-analytically, it seems hardly justified to review a quantitative literature in the pre-meta-analytic, prequantitative manner. Money that funds a traditional review is not available to fund a meta-analytic review.

It should be noted that a meta-analytic review is a good deal more than simply an overall estimate of the size of the basic effect. In particular, meta-analytic reviews try to explain the inevitable variation in the size of the effect obtained in different studies.

Finally, it no longer seems acceptable to fund research studies that claim to contribute to the resolution of controversy (e.g., does Treatment A work?) unless the investigator has already conducted a meta-analysis to determine whether there really is a controversy. A new experiment to learn whether psychotherapy works in general is manifestly not worth doing given the meta-analytic results of Glass (1976) and his colleagues (Smith, Glass, & Miller, 1980). Until their meta-analytic work resolved the issue, the question of whether psychotherapy worked in general was indeed controversial. It is controversial no longer.

Pseudocontroversies

Meta-analysis resolves controversies primarily because it eliminates two common problems in the evaluation of replications. The first problem is the belief that when one study obtains a significant effect and a replication does not, we have a failure to replicate. That belief often turns out to be unfounded. A failure to replicate is properly measured by the magnitude of difference between the effect sizes of the two studies. The second problem is the belief that if there is a real effect in a situation, each study of that situation will show a significant effect. Actually, if the effect is quite substantial, say, $r = .24$, and each study employs a sample size of, say, 64, the power level is .50 (Cohen, 1962, 1988; Rosenthal, 1994; Sedlmeier & Gigerenzer, 1989). Given this situation, which is typical in psychology, there is only one chance in four that two investigations will both

get results significant at the .05 level. If three studies were carried out, there would be only one chance in eight that all three studies would yield significant effects, even though we know the effect in nature is both real and important in magnitude.

Significance testing

Meta-analytic procedures and the meta-analytic worldview increase the utility of the individual study by their implications for how and whether we do significance testing. Good meta-analytic practice shows little interest in whether the results of an individual study were significant or not at any particular critical level. Rather than recording for a study whether it reached such a level, say, $p = .05$, two-tailed, meta-analysts record the actual level of significance obtained. This is usually done not by recording the p value but by recording the standard normal deviate that corresponds to the p value. Thus, a result significant at the .05 level, one-tailed, in the predicted direction is recorded as $Z = +1.645$. If it had been significant at the .05 level, one-tailed, but in the wrong or unpredicted direction, it would be recorded as $Z = -1.645$ (i.e., with a minus sign to indicate that the result is in the unpredicted direction). Signed normal deviates are an informative characteristic of the result of a study presented in continuous rather than in dichotomous form. Their use (a) increases the information value of a study, which (b) increases the utility of the study and, therefore, (c) changes the cost-utility ratio and, hence, the ethical value of the study.

Small effects are not small

Another way in which meta-analysis increases research utility and, therefore, the ethical justification of research studies is by providing accurate estimates of effect sizes, effect sizes that can be of major importance even when they are so small as to have $r^2 = .00$. Especially when we have well-estimated effect sizes, it is valuable to assess their practical importance. The r^2 method of effect size estimation does a poor job of this because an r^2 of .00 can be associated with a treatment method that reduces death rates by as much as 7 per 100 lives lost (Rosenthal & Rubin, 1982). Once we are aware that effect size rs of .05, .10, and .20 (with r^2s of .00, .01, and .04, respectively) may be associated with benefits equivalent to saving 5, 10, or 20 lives per 100 people, we can more accurately weigh the costs and utilities of undertaking any particular study.

REPORTING PSYCHOLOGICAL RESEARCH

Misrepresentation of Findings

Mother nature makes it hard enough to learn her secrets, without the additional difficulty of being misled by

PSYCHOLOGICAL SCIENCE

Science and Ethics

the report of findings that were not found or by inferences that are unfounded. Although all misrepresentations of findings are damaging to the progress of our science, some are more obviously unethical than others.

Intentional misrepresentation

The most blatant intentional misrepresentation is the reporting of data that never were (Broad & Wade, 1982). That behavior, if detected, ends (or ought to end) the scientific career of the perpetrator. A somewhat more subtle form of intentional misrepresentation occurs when investigators knowingly allocate to experimental or control conditions those participants whose responses are more likely to support the investigators' hypothesis. Another potential form of intentional misrepresentation occurs when investigators record the participants' responses without being blind to the participants' treatment condition, or when research assistants record the participants' responses knowing both the research hypothesis and the participants' treatment condition. Of course, if the research specifically notes the failure to run blind, there is no misrepresentation, but the design is unwise if it could have been avoided.

Unintentional misrepresentation

Various errors in the process of data collection can lead to unintentional misrepresentation. Recording errors, computational errors, and data analytic errors can all lead to inaccurate results that are inadvertent misrepresentations (Broad & Wade, 1982; Rosenthal, 1966). We would not normally even think of them as constituting ethical issues except for the fact that errors in the data decrease the utility of the research and thereby move the cost-utility ratio (which is used to justify the research on ethical grounds) in the unfavorable direction.

Some cases of misrepresentation (usually unintentional) are more subtle. The use of causist language, discussed earlier, is one example. Even more subtle is the case of questionable generalizability.

Questionable generalizability

Suppose we want to compare the rapport-creating ability of female and male psychotherapists, as defined by their patients' ratings. We have available three female and three male therapists, to each of whom 10 patients were assigned at random. An analysis of variance yields three sources of variance: sex of therapist ($df = 1$), therapists nested within sex ($df = 4$), and patients nested within therapists ($df = 54$). A common way to analyze such data would be to divide the *MS* sex by *MS* patients to get an *F* test. In such a case, we have treated therapists as fixed effects. When, in our report of the research, we describe our results of, say, $F(1, 54) = 7.13, p = .01$, we have done a study that is generalizable only to other pa-

tients treated by these six therapists, but not to any other therapists (Estes, 1991; Snedecor & Cochran, 1989).

Misrepresentation of Credit

I have been discussing misrepresentation of findings, or the issue of "what was really found?" In the present section, the focus is on the issue of "who really found it?"

Problems of authorship

Because so many papers in psychology, and the sciences generally, are multiauthored, it seems inevitable that there will be difficult problems of allocation of authorship credit. Who becomes a coauthor and who becomes a footnote? Among the coauthors, who is assigned first, last, or any other serial position in the listing? Such questions have been discussed in depth, and very general guidelines have been offered (APA, 1981, 1987; see also Costa & Gatz, 1992), but it seems that we could profit from further empirical studies in which authors, editors, referees, students, practitioners, and professors were asked to allocate authorship credit to people performing various functions in a scholarly enterprise.

Problems of priority

Problems of authorship are usually problems existing within research groups. Problems of priority are usually problems existing between research groups. A current example of a priority problem is the evaluation of the degree to which Robert C. Gallo and his colleagues are guilty of "intellectual appropriation" of a French research group's virus that was used to develop a blood test for HIV, the virus that is believed to cause AIDS (Palca, 1992). Priority problems also occur in psychology, where the question is likely to be not who first produced a virus but rather who first produced a particular idea.

Failing to Report or Publish

Sometimes the ethical question is not about the accuracy of what was reported or how credit should be allocated for what was reported, but rather about what was *not* reported and why it was not reported. The two major forms of failure to report, or censoring, are self-censoring and external censoring.

Self-censoring

Some self-censoring is admirable. When a study has been really badly done, it may be a service to the science and to society to simply start over. Some self-censoring is done for admirable motives but seems wasteful of information. For example, some researchers feel they should not cite their own (or other people's) unpublished data

PSYCHOLOGICAL SCIENCE

Robert Rosenthal

because the data have not gone through peer review. I would argue that such data should indeed be cited and employed in meta-analytic computations as long as the data were well collected.

There are also less admirable reasons for self-censoring. Failing to report data that contradict one's earlier research, or one's theory or one's values, is poor science and poor ethics. One can always find or invent reasons why a study that came out unfavorably should not be reported: The subjects were just starting the course; the subjects were about to have an exam; the subjects had just had an exam; the subjects were just finishing the course; and so on. A good general policy—good for science and for its integrity—is to report all results shedding light on the original hypothesis or providing data that might be of use to other investigators.

There is no denying that some results are more thrilling than others. If our new treatment procedure prevents or cures mental illness or physical illness, that fact may be worth more journal space or space in more prestigious journals than the result that our new treatment procedure does no good whatever. But that less thrilling finding should also be reported and made retrievable by other researchers who may need to know that finding.

External censoring

Both the progress and the slowing of progress in science depend on external censoring. It seems likely that sciences would be more chaotic than they are were it not for the censorship exercised by peers: by editors, by reviewers, and by program committees. All these gatekeepers help to keep the really bad science from clogging the pipelines of mainstream journals.

There are two major bases for external censorship. The first is evaluation of the methodology employed in a research study. I strongly favor such external censorship. If the study is truly terrible, it probably should not be reported.

The second major basis for external censorship is evaluation of the results. In my 35 years in psychology, I have often seen or heard it said of a study that "those results aren't possible" or "those results make no sense." Often when I have looked at such studies, I have agreed that the results are indeed implausible. However, that is a poor basis on which to censor the results. Censoring or suppressing results we do not like or do not believe to have high prior probability is bad science and bad ethics (Rosenthal, 1975, 1994).

CONCLUSION

The purpose of this article has been to discuss some scientific and ethical issues in conducting, analyzing, and reporting psychological research. A central theme has

been that the ethical quality of our research is not independent of the scientific quality of our research. Detailing some of the specifics of this general theme has, I hope, served two functions. First, I hope it has comforted the afflicted by showing how we can simultaneously improve the quality of our science and the quality of our ethics. Second, and finally, I hope it has afflicted the comfortable by reminding us that in the matter of improving our science and our ethics, there are miles to go before we sleep.

Acknowledgments—This article is based on an address invited by the Board of Scientific Affairs of the American Psychological Association (APA) and presented at the annual meeting of APA, Washington, D.C., August 15, 1992. Preparation of this paper was supported in part by the Spencer Foundation; the content is solely the responsibility of the author. I thank Elizabeth Baldwin, Peter Blanck, and Ralph Rosnow for their encouragement and support.

REFERENCES

American Psychological Association. (1981). Ethical principles of psychologists. *American Psychologist, 36,* 633–638.
American Psychological Association. (1982). *Ethical principles in the conduct of research with human participants.* Washington, DC: Author.
American Psychological Association. (1987). *Casebook on ethical principles of psychologists.* Washington, DC: Author.
Barnett, V., & Lewis, T. (1978). *Outliers in statistical data.* New York: Wiley.
Blanck, P.D., Bellack, A.S., Rosnow, R.L., Rotheram-Borus, M.J., & Schooler, N.R. (1992). Scientific rewards and conflicts of ethical choices in human subjects research. *American Psychologist, 47,* 959–965.
Broad, W., & Wade, N. (1982). *Betrayers of the truth.* New York: Simon and Schuster.
Cohen, J. (1962). The statistical power of abnormal-social psychological research: A review. *Journal of Abnormal and Social Psychology, 65,* 145–153.
Cohen, J. (1988). *Statistical power analysis for the behavioral sciences* (2nd ed.). Hillsdale, NJ: Erlbaum.
Cook, T.D., & Campbell, D.T. (1979). *Quasi-experimentation: Design and analysis issues for field settings.* Chicago: Rand McNally.
Cooper, H.M., & Rosenthal, R. (1980). Statistical versus traditional procedures for summarizing research findings. *Psychological Bulletin, 87,* 442–449.
Costa, M.M., & Gatz, M. (1992). Determination of authorship credit in published dissertations. *Psychological Science, 3,* 354–357.
Estes, W.K. (1991). *Statistical models in behavioral research.* Hillsdale, NJ: Erlbaum.
Glass, G.V. (1976). Primary, secondary, and meta-analysis of research. *Educational Researcher, 5,* 3–8.
Glass, G.V. McGaw, B., & Smith, M.L. (1981). *Meta-analysis in social research.* Beverly Hills, CA: Sage.
Grisso, T., Baldwin, E., Blanck, P.D., Rotheram-Borus, M.J., Schooler, N.R., & Thompson, T. (1991). Standards in research: APA's mechanism for monitoring the challenges. *American Psychologist, 46,* 758–766.
Hedges, L.V., & Olkin, I. (1985). *Statistical methods for meta-analysis.* New York: Academic Press.
Howell, D.C. (1992). *Statistical methods for psychology* (3rd ed.). Boston: PWS-Kent.
Kaplan, J. (1988). The use of animals in research. *Science, 242,* 839–840.
Kelman, H.C. (1968). *A time to speak: On human values and social research.* San Francisco: Jossey-Bass.
Mosteller, F., & Bush, R.R. (1954). Selected quantitative techniques. In G. Lindzey (Ed.), *Handbook of social psychology: Vol. 1. Theory and method* (pp. 289–334). Cambridge, MA: Addison-Wesley.
Palca, J. (1992). "Verdicts" are in on the Gallo probe. *Science, 256,* 735–738.
Rosenthal, R. (1966). *Experimenter effects in behavioral research.* New York: Appleton-Century-Crofts.
Rosenthal, R. (1975). On balanced presentation of controversy. *American Psychologist, 30,* 937–938.
Rosenthal, R. (1978). How often are our numbers wrong? *American Psychologist, 33,* 1005–1008.

PSYCHOLOGICAL SCIENCE

Science and Ethics

Rosenthal, R. (1991). *Meta-analytic procedures for social research* (rev. ed.). Newbury Park, CA: Sage.

Rosenthal, R. (1994). On being one's own case study: Experimenter effects in behavioral research—30 years later. In W.R. Shadish & S. Fuller (Eds.), *The social psychology of science* (pp. 214–229). New York: Guilford Press.

Rosenthal, R., & Jacobson, L. (1968). *Pygmalion in the classroom*. New York: Holt, Rinehart & Winston.

Rosenthal, R., & Jacobson, L. (1992). *Pygmalion in the classroom* (expanded ed.). New York: Irvington.

Rosenthal, R., & Rosnow, R.L. (1975). *The volunteer subject*. New York: Wiley.

Rosenthal, R., & Rosnow, R.L. (1984). Applying Hamlet's question to the ethical conduct of research: A conceptual addendum. *American Psychologist, 39,* 561–563.

Rosenthal, R., & Rosnow, R.L. (1991). *Essentials of behavioral research: Methods and data analysis* (2nd ed.). New York: McGraw-Hill.

Rosenthal, R., & Rubin, D.B. (1971). Pygmalion reaffirmed. In J.D. Elashoff & R.E. Snow, *Pygmalion reconsidered* (pp. 139–155). Worthington, OH: C.A. Jones.

Rosenthal, R., & Rubin, D.B. (1982). A simple, general purpose display of magnitude of experimental effect. *Journal of Educational Psychology, 74,* 166–169.

Rosenthal, R., & Rubin, D.B. (1984). Multiple contrasts and ordered Bonferroni procedures. *Journal of Educational Psychology, 76,* 1028–1034.

Rosnow, R.L. (1990). Teaching research ethics through role-play and discussion. *Teaching of Psychology, 17,* 179–181.

Rosnow, R.L., & Rosenthal, R. (1993). *Beginning behavioral research: A conceptual primer.* New York: Macmillan.

Sedlmeier, P., & Gigerenzer, G. (1989). Do studies of statistical power have an effect on the power of studies? *Psychological Bulletin, 105,* 309–316.

Smith, M.L., Glass, G.V. & Miller, T.I. (1980). *The benefits of psychotherapy.* Baltimore: Johns Hopkins University Press.

Snedecor, G.W., & Cochran, W.G. (1989). *Statistical methods* (8th ed.). Ames: Iowa State University Press.

Tukey, J.W. (1977). *Exploratory data analysis.* Reading, MA: Addison-Wesley.

[26]

"Sanctified Snake Oil": Ideology, Junk Science, and Social Work Practice

by Susan Kiss Sarnoff

Abstract

This article explores the pervasiveness of the form of junk science known as advocacy statistics, and its danger to the practice of social work. Using domestic violence statistics as exemplars, the article documents how misinterpretation and refusal to believe data that does not conform to ideology can lead to inaccurate assessments, faulty treatment recommendations, and misallocation of resources. Such practice, which clearly violates the NASW Code of Ethics, reflects poorly on the profession and, most significantly, makes it impossible to understand the true nature of the problem.

CHRISTOPHER WREN OBSERVED THAT, "Politicians are said to use statistics the way drunks use lampposts: for support rather than illumination." Recognizing this, "advocacy statistics" have been a staple of groups vying for government attention — and resources — for as long as government has provided such resources. "Advocacy statistics" consist of spurious "data" that support preconceived ideas rather than offering empirical evidence of the accuracy (or inaccuracy) of those ideas.

This article will explore domestic violence advocacy statistics in a framework that this author has developed and defined as "sanctified snake oil." "Snake oil" refers to any purported solution to a social problem which is unscientific, has not been adequately tested, is incompletely or inadequately defined, is used inappropriately, or stands in the way of a superior alternative. Snake oil becomes "sanctified" when it is funded, mandated, or otherwise endorsed or accepted by a government entity. This suggests that it is effective, even though government requires no proof of effectiveness when it funds or mandates services; nor does it require proof of effectiveness of the orientations or methods of expert witnesses used to determine the guilt of criminal defendants, the removal of children from their parents, and a host of other critical decisions that profoundly affect people's lives and are core roles of social work practitioners. It is facilitated

when media reiterate advocacy statistics and use them to frame public perceptions. The "sanctification" process explains how unwary or uninformed social workers may come to believe that "advocacy statistics" are accurate, by basing their determinations on ideologically-driven, unproven theories, cursory readings or media accounts of research, or any factors other than appropriate evaluation of properly documented research.

Compton and Galaway (1999) observe that it is the mark of a professional to be able to convert knowledge into services uniquely designed for each client. Reid (1995) further clarifies that social work research skills require the abilities to evaluate one's own practice and the effectiveness of other systems that impact on clients and to understand and evaluate the research literature. The *Code of Ethics* dictates that social workers understand, keep abreast, of and even contribute to the knowledge base (NASW 1996b); and this fact was reiterated in the 1996 update of the code, which placed additional emphasis on social worker competence (Reamer, 1998).

Advocacy statistics have the best chance of being accepted when little comparative research exists about what they purport to measure, so domestic violence has been an ideal target for advocacy statisticians. Examples related to domestic violence will be used in this article for this reason, but more importantly because social work's long-standing concern with families, children, women, and victims of violence dictate that social workers have an accurate understanding of all aspects of domestic violence.

The article will define "snake oil" and discuss how it is sanctified, using the paradigms presented in the table. It will then explore fallacies inherent in "sanctified snake oil" and explain how its use has distorted perceptions of domestic violence and prevented social workers from developing more effective responses to this serious problem.

The Snake Oil and Sanctification Paradigms

Issue framing. Best (1990) noted that "ownership" of a problem occurs when a particular construction of a problem gains wide acceptance, when ideologues succeed in becoming the authority on the problem, and when control of social policy regarding the problem rests in their hands. Problems can be framed as either positional

---

Figure 1. *Sanctified Snake Oil*

THE SNAKE OIL PARADIGM

1. Frame the subject so that it cannot be opposed.
2. Once the issue is defined, stretch the concept as broadly as possible in order to:
   a.) Increase the size of the "target" group;
   b.) Make the problem appear to be universal;
   c.) Make the problem appear to be of crisis proportions.
3. Consider anyone who resists identification with the target group to be "in denial," in order to:
   a.) Define all "sufferers" as in need of "treatment;"
   b.) Make treatment seem more effective because many of the treated will not suffer from the problem or will have a mild, easily treatable degree of the problem, and non-improvement can be blamed on denial.
4. Identify "poster children" who "suffer" from the problem but are appealing to the public (e.g., completely innocent and in no way responsible for their circumstances).
5. Use anecdotal evidence (preferably about "poster children") and single, dramatic cases to publicize the problem.
6. Use biased or "cooked" data — if forced to present any statistical proof of the problem.
7. Confuse goals and processes.
8. Confuse satisfaction with effectiveness.
9. Ignore unintended consequences and never admit that they might emanate from the "solution."
10. If criticized for any of the above, attack the opponents instead of their positions.

THE SANCTIFICATION PARADIGM

MEDIA
1. Write "human interest" stories on single, extreme cases, suggesting that they are "typical" of the problem.
2. Publish statistics without consulting source data or confirming accuracy.
3. Oversimplify complex issues and policies.
4. Publish the results of research studies without discussing the methodology of the research (e.g., samples, controls).
5. "Bury" corrections and retractions in back pages and small print.

GOVERNMENT
1. Accept "expertise" at face value.
2. Fund training which presents ideology or "junk" science as fact.
3. Mandate treatment and fund services because of the importance of their goals, without regard to their effectiveness.
4. Provide third-party payments for services so consumers don't care (and often don't know) how much they use.
5. Once services designed to meet a goal are funded, continue funding more of the same rather than insisting on continual evaluation, improvement and innovation. Never consider alternative means of attaining the same goal.

FAMILIES IN SOCIETY · *Volume 80, Number 4*

issues, which may be contested, or as valence issues, which are perceived as incontestable. Beckett (1996) observed that prior to 1985, child sexual abuse was widely perceived as a valence issue. But after 1985, as more people became aware that children's testimony was sometimes being coerced by parents in custody disputes or therapists who did not recognize that their methods constituted "coaching," child sexual abuse became a positional issue, about which many opinions could be reached. Another way to frame issues is *condensationally*, that is, at an abstract and ambiguous level prone to projected emotions and personal associations; or *referentially*, in a specific or concrete way focusing on objective elements and limiting the emotion they can invoke (Bennett, 1980; Edelman, 1977). Ideologues frame their positions condensationally, allowing no alternative views of their issues. Thus, for example, child advocates often assert that all reports of child abuse must be believed, regardless of how implausible they might be or whether innocent people might be harmed in the process.

Concept stretching. Defining every woman who has ever had a shouting match with a loved one as a "victim of domestic violence" enables ideologues to claim huge numbers of afflicted. This also makes their issue seem to be of crisis proportions, and even allows ideologues to claim "universalization" of the problem — that everyone suffers from it to some degree. This exaggeration not only justifies attention to the problem, but justifies higher funding than if the problem were defined more realistically. But the most significant advantage to concept stretching is this: if all those whom ideologues define as suffering from a problem is included in the "target group" for services, because some of those people fit the definition only in the minds of ideologues, some sufferers will later be evaluated as cured (or recovered) —only because they didn't manifest the problem in the first place.

Lanning (1996) noted that concept stretching is used by both sides of the ideological battle. He observed that the child sexual abuse "witch hunt," is characterized by

> . . . the tendency to exaggerate child sexual abuse, to emphasize believing the children, and to criticize the criminal justice system only for the lack of investigation or for acquittals. When child sexual abuse is alleged, they assume it has happened and try to prove it. [In contrast,] the backlash is characterized by a tendency to minimize child sexual abuse, to emphasize false allegations, and to criticize the criminal justice system only for aggressive investigation or for

convictions. When child sexual abuse is alleged, they assume it has not happened and try to disprove it. Each side conveniently fails to define its terminology, or inconsistently uses the terms it does not define. When volume is needed, a child is anyone under eighteen years old. When impact is needed, a child is under twelve years old.

Lanning's description explains how concept-stretching can create the perceptual distortion commonly resulting from advocacy statistics.

Denial. Summit (1992, 1983) theorized Child Abuse Accommodation Syndrome, which conjectured that many victims deny victimization to protect their abuser. Proponents took his speculation to the illogical extreme of claiming that denial of sexual abuse by children should be considered a symptom that supports a finding of abuse. "Among social workers and therapists attached to investigations . . . the word *denial.* . . . [had a] new meaning, one lifted from the lexicon of therapy. . . . [Therefore] the father who denied the charges was especially despicable. . . . As a federal publication [stated] . . . the girl making the accusations must be believed if she is to 'overcome feelings of powerlessness' and 'shake off the effects of sustained manipulation'" (Nathan & Snedeker, 1995). But denial, too, has purposes beyond the obvious. Not only does denial allow ideologues to overcount sufferers (as well as to count sufferers who do not self-identify with the problem) denial enables service providers to argue that, because so many people they define as sufferers fail to seek help, those people should be coerced into treatment.

Poster children. The stars of what Best (1990) defines as "atrocity tales," are "usually selected for [their] extreme nature, but are meant to typify the issue for the public"; they then become the referents for discussions of the "problem in general," such as when stranger abductions are used as referents for all missing children. What ideologues never state, but hope will be assumed, is that poster children and anecdotes and the "atrocity tales" told about them will be assumed to be typical examples, rather than examples hand-picked because their extreme characteristics and tear-jerking "stars" tug at heart strings. Poster children also suggest one of the dirty secrets of ideologues: that they privately despise those they represent, who, unlike poster children, never quite fit their theories or reflect the "innocent victimhood" they want to project onto their causes (Ellis, 1998).

Unintended consequences. All policies have unintended consequences; "sanctified snake oil," however, obfuscates or attributes them to causes other than the policies from which they emanate. For instance, "One study concluded that . . . [restraining] orders have a protective effect for women who were not severely victimized in the first place. If so, peddling them to women in real danger is like selling cancer patients a drug that cures the common cold. . . . Meanwhile, the new laws can make it easy for domestic violence charges to be used as a weapon — a tactic openly advocated by two women who toured the country in the late '80s giving women-only seminars on 'playing to win' in a divorce" (Young, 1999). Similarly, "Douglas Besharov points out that whereas in 1975 about one-third of child abuse cases were dismissed for lack of evidence, today about two-thirds are dismissed . . . between 1979 and 1983, for example, reported cases of child abuse increased almost 50%. But over the same period, the number of substantiated cases actually declined. In other words, the 22,000 increase of reported cases yielded no net increase of real cases" (Krauthammer 1993). Moreover, the cost of investigating all of these reports drained resources that could have been used to investigate serious cases more thoroughly. Costin, Karger, and Stoesz (1996) observed that, "Each year about 50,000 children with severe injuries go unreported . . . 25% to 50% of children who die of abuse or neglect were previously reported to child welfare authorities. . . . Child abuse . . . public policy is inadequate, programs are uncoordinated, and funding is insufficient. The consequences of these factors are predictable: poor morale among child welfare workers, growing legions of angry parents whose children are mistakenly removed from their homes, and children who fail to receive essential care."

The detection of child abuse itself has had unintended consequences, due, "to the fact that Child Protective Services (CPS), state agencies established by federal law, receive a federal bounty for breaking apart families and putting children in foster care" (San Diego Grand Jury, 1994). And results of wrongful prosecutions have included civil litigation against communities and professionals, including social workers (Sarnoff, 1998; NASW 1996b), and limitations to the immunity of mandated reporters. Sadly, it seems that only threats of lawsuits mitigate against the wholesale focus on "case finding" encouraged by these federal funds.

Vilification of opponents. One of the most unfortunate effects of the triumph of ideological rhetoric over logical analysis is that challenges to faulty methodology are often met with personal attacks against those who dare to make the challenges. This does lessen their frequency, but also suggests that there is no reasoned re-

sponse to be made. McNeely, Cook, and Torres (1999) document that McNeely himself, as well as Suzanne Steinmetz and Erin Pizzey, have received attacks against their professionalism and livelihoods as well as their lives for results of research which, while methodologically sound, ran counter to the beliefs of domestic violence orthodoxy.

> ## The "sanctification" process explains how unwary or uninformed social workers may come to believe that "advocacy statistics" are accurate.

Media sanctification. The media play a role second only to government in "sanctifying" snake oil. "Whatever his sanctified line, the true believer is wholly convinced he or she is acting in the very best interests of both the proximate and ultimate truth. And if he is on a newspaper, it is his responsibility to see to it that the readers are told what to think; that they are not distracted by ambivalences and ambiguities; and that no language can be used that could possibly offend any group whose side the paper should be on" (Hentoff, 1992).

These problems are often attributed to bias. While they may reflect bias in some instances, they can as easily reflect superficiality, shabby research (Klaidman & Beauchamp, 1987), or the "triumph of motivated public relations" (Berman, 1998) — and they may not even be intentional (Samuelson, 1995). Oversimplification — to fit a "sound byte" or to discuss a complex policy decision within the confines of a five-hundred-word column, further distorts the public's perception of social issues. Sadly, "TV has been quick to air the scare stories based on junk science and slow to report the hard science that refutes them" (Accuracy in Media, 1997).

Distortion is at its most extreme when media report on statistical studies and scientific research. A cursory reading of almost any popular media report on research, by any but a handful of editors who display a modicum of scientific knowledge, demonstrates that most reporters and commentators are woefully ignorant about the mathematics and politics of research. Most will copy statistics from press releases without confirming their accuracy or seeking alternative interpretations of findings. Pitifully, few understand research methodology well enough to describe it, no less to recognize methodological errors or

FAMILIES IN SOCIETY · *Volume 80, Number 4*

omissions, such as lack of control groups, insufficient sample sizes, or nonrandom samples that nullify results.

For instance, one reason the Wenatchee child sexual abuse witch hunt continued for as long as it did was that, "most journalists just didn't do their job. They blindly reported assertions of people in authority. . . . As one man . . . said, 'The watchdogs turned out to be lapdogs' (Grant, 1997). A rare exception occurred when, "*The Los Angeles Times* published a detailed analysis of the media's coverage of the [McMartin] case, including its own reporting. [It noted that] more than most big stories, McMartin at times exposed basic flaws in the way contemporary news organizations function. Pack journalism. Laziness. Superficiality. Cozy relationships with prosecutors. . . . In the early months of the case in particular, reporters and editors often abandoned two of their most cherished and widely trumpeted traditions — fairness and skepticism. As most reporters now sheepishly admit — and as the record clearly shows — the media frequently plunged into hysteria, sensationalism and what one editor calls 'a lynch mob syndrome'" (Victor, 1993).

Government sanctification. Nathan and Snedeker (1995) reported that social worker Kee MacFarlane presented herself to the Los Angeles District Attorneys' Office as an "expert" in child abuse and offered to "interview" the children who had attended the McMartin PreSchool after allegations of sexual abuse by an employee of that school were reported. However, MacFarlane's experience was not in interviewing children for court testimony (a role traditionally, and legally, assigned to the criminal justice system in any case), nor in determining whether children had been abused — MacFarlane's experience had been treating children who had already been determined to be abused. That is to say, MacFarlane had no experience with children who had not been abused and simplistically believed that any child brought to her had been. Her methods of questioning the children were later determined to have coerced them to lie (after all had initially denied being abused at the preschool).

But none of these facts prevented MacFarlane's agency from receiving both federal and (California) state funds to interview more McMartin children — and to train others in her methods of interviewing children. (Most funders know little about the topic they are funding, and especially in government, this is seen as avoiding conflicts of interest. Instead, funders seek grantees who will reliably spend their grant funds as they promise, because failure to do so carries the greatest sanctions for bureaucrats.) "The budget for the National Center for Child Abuse and Neglect (NCCAN) is an . . . example of

the ritual-abuse panic's coattail effect on funding. In 1983, the agency had only $1.8 million to spend on all types of abuse research and demonstration projects (of that, only $237,000 went to sex-abuse studies). Following the McMartin scandal the next year, NCCAN's budget more than quadrupled, and included $146,000 to Kee MacFarlane to interview and examine more McMartin children. In addition, Childrens' Institute International (CII), MacFarlane's agency, received $350,000 in 1985 from California funds, making the institute that state's first publicly funded training center for child-abuse diagnosis and treatment" (Nathan & Snedeker, 1995).

Why Does the Public Support Snake Oil?

It is preposterous to believe that any issue alone could be the cause of all human difficulties and even more preposterous to think that a single solution could correct a problem in any case. But it is also seductive to believe that finding a single solution could make "all right with the world." American populism favors majority opinion over those of experts — even when the majority remains ignorant of relevant facts. Few Americans understand how to access data, or its sources, and because so much information in this country is presented with a biased slant, many despair of discerning truth and choose sides as if they were selecting ice cream flavors, by preference rather than research. To make matters worse, although we look to science to "fix" many of these problems, Americans have a general disdain for scientific proof and empiricism. Perhaps this stems from the fact that Americans have less knowledge of science and math than their contemporaries in other first-world countries.

The Ideological Nature of Practice

Why Professionals Support Sanctified Snake Oil

Funds allocated to domestic violence "services," which many members of the public assume to be shelter or assistance to help women become self-sufficient, are often used to "educate" people not directly involved with domestic violence, using pseudostatistics that distort their perceptions of the problem (Young, 1999). So pride in being recognized as expert, even inaccurately, as well as the income generated as a result may affect some professionals' ability to perceive the accuracy (or absence) of research.

In addition, a "1988 nationwide survey of over one hundred shelters found that about half stressed feminist activism over assisting battered women" (Gremillion, 1996).

This is also exemplified by the debate within the battered women's movement over disclosing the location of shelters. Proponents feel that visible shelters make the public more aware of domestic violence, make it easier for women to reach shelters, help shelters raise funds and reduce the stigma of battering. Yet such publicity has endangered battered women and shelter workers (Belluck, 1997)

Young (1999) observed that,

Since the late 1970s, the government, no less the media, has treated battered women's advocates as the experts on domestic violence. Advocacy groups have received hundreds of millions in federal and state funding . . . [and] in many states, advocacy groups conduct officially sponsored training seminars for police, prosecutors, and judges. The materials used in these seminars are rife with pseudostatistics meant to show that male violence against women is epidemic. . . . Activists play a prominent role in many courts in their capacity as advisors to the victims and liaisons between them and court personnel — sometimes wielding, Massachusetts lawyer and state legislator James Fagan claims, "more influence and authority than the district attorneys. . . . In many jurisdictions, women who make a domestic violence call are routinely referred for counseling to battered women's groups. Some police departments have also established programs under which volunteers from these organizations accompany officers to the scene of domestic disturbances."

Among these pseudostatistics, the Goldberg and Tomlanovich (1984) study was purported to demonstrate that 22% of emergency room visits by women were for injuries sustained by domestic violence. On its face, this statistic is ludicrous to anyone who is aware of the incidence of injury, especially as a result of automobile crashes, or to anyone who has simply spent time in an emergency room. In fact, the study never made that claim — it asked women in emergency rooms if they had ever experienced domestic violence, and 22% responded that they had. In spite of the facts, the misperceived results of the study were spread with extreme speed and little caution by domestic violence and victim advocates, by journalists happy to regurgitate the advocates' press releases rather than investigate the facts for themselves, and by others who should have known better or at least been more cautious. When a study by McLeer and Anwar

(1989) was similarly misconstrued, this time to reflect a 30% rate of domestic violence injuries, advocates immediately increased their figure.

The government was then forced to fund a large-scale study to determine the accuracy of these figures — because clearly, if they were determined to be accurate, virtually all injury prevention funds should be directed to so large a cause of injury. Rand (1997), however, found that fewer than 2% of women in emergency rooms were there for injuries sustained by domestic violence. Amazingly, advocates were not embarrassed at this failure to have their "facts" so definitively disproved — they simply argued that women are reticent to admit abuse to researchers insensitive in their questioning and summarily disregarded the larger study. As a result, the Violence Against Women Act (VAWA) mandated yet another study. This one was to be jointly conducted by the National Institute of Justice and the Centers for Disease Control and Prevention. Tjaden and Thoennes (1998), who conducted that study, found even lower numbers than did Rand and the study has not been released, only a report presenting the data with a positive spin that fails to con the educated reader has been released.

The proposal for VAWA II goes even farther, "view[ing] as authoritative on matters of domestic violence and child custody and visitation" an American Psychological Association (1996) report titled *Violence in the Family*, which, unlike the attempts to misinform by misrepresenting statistics, includes not a single reference, citation or other allusion, to any specific study. (This is particularly ironic in light of the fact that social scientists almost universally use the APA format to document references.)

Research to determine the effectiveness of various interventions with battered women is also frowned upon — only research that reflects the ideology of advocates is considered acceptable by them.

Research limited only to . . . self-identified at-risk populations would not be tolerated in other areas of scholarly inquiry. Such studies unfortunately present one-sided views of a very complex issue. Research on batterers is narrowly focused and rarely presents a comparison with normal males. This apparently relates to the prevailing view that there are no "normal males" as much as it does to poor design. This research assumes that battering is a fundamental aspect of maleness rather than a pathology which is potentially amenable to correction. Much research, however, clearly shows that there is an increased

incidence in substance abuse and certain person-
ality disorders among batterers. By disallowing
pathology or addictive behaviors to be partly re-
sponsible, some advocacy researchers are able to
declare that maleness itself is the pathology

(Gremillion, 1996). Ironically, no lesser feminist than the
founder of the shelter movement in England, Erin Pizzey
(1982) has spoken out against the distorted ideology that
assumes that women never contribute to domestic violence – an assumption that she fears has endangered the
children left with violent mothers.

> *The National Institute of Justice and the Bureau*
> *of Justice Statistics (1996) reported of domestic*
> *violence that, "there was a wide variation in*
> *how each state defines these offenses, deter-*
> *mines what is counted, and measures or reports*
> *incidents. . . Since some states have adopted*
> *family violence as opposed to domestic violence*
> *statutes, their statistics may include child vic-*
> *tims along with adults . . . some state statutes*
> *apply regardless of the gender of the victims and*
> *the offenders, while others are not as inclusive*
> *of all possible relationships and living situa-*
> *tions. . . . It also becomes a measurement issue*
> *because thresholds along this continuum must*
> *be established to determine whether and how*
> *any given event or action is counted. These de-*
> *cisions have obvious implications for resulting*
> *statistical figures and observations.*

One way that advocacy statistics circumvent these
cautions is to have them disseminated in public hearings.
The resulting "reports" summarize only those parts of
the testimony that ideologues want reflected, and is then
circulated widely (usually at no charge), without verify-
ing its content. For example, the New York City Commission on the Status of Women (1996) produced a summary of hearings on domestic violence that incorporated
many of the debunked facts and statistics discussed earlier. In fact, it was subtitled "Listening with the Third
Ear," to suggest that the discrepancies among the statistics reflected not distortions, but lack of sensitivity on the
part of some researchers. In the summary, reports of the
proportion of women treated for domestic violence
ranged from 25% to 60% of all those seen in emergency
rooms. The only exception to these numbers in the report
was a statement that New York City's Lincoln Hospital
had seen fewer than 1% of domestic violence in its emer-

gency room the previous year. But this statement was explained away by claiming that domestic violence victims
under report. One person who testified used the inflated
statistics to "determine" the cost of domestic violence to
New York City employees, hospitals, criminal justice
agencies, and homeless services.

Lanning (1996) observed that, "Abused children
need more people addressing their needs from the professional perspective and fewer from the personal and
political perspectives. This raises the complex and difficult question of whether individuals with strong political
or personal agendas can even be professionals. While
many can rise above their direct or indirect victimization
and their individual or practical needs, some are deluding
themselves in claiming to have done so."

Despite the fact that the NASW *Code of Ethics*
(1996b) requires that social workers "keep current with
emerging knowledge . . . and fully use . . . research evidence in their professional practice," NASW itself has
been slow to reflect emerging knowledge in its policy
statements, such as that on recovered memories (NASW,
1996a). As a result, many social workers take seminars
that present these inaccuracies as fact in order to earn the
CEUs necessary for license renewal.

Theory, Practice Wisdom, and "Proof"

It has been noted that, "Scientific clinical research
has little or no impact on the practitioner" (Stricker,
1992). If practitioners ignore research, how then do they
develop the ideas on which they base their practice? Most
base them on theories, either self-developed or developed
by others (such as "experts" like Sigmund Freud). Often,
these practitioners actually believe that their work is scientific, erroneously equating theory and even so-called expertise with science. Theory, and its even weaker ancestor,
"practice wisdom," are steps on the path toward the creation of science. Unfortunately, however, many more theoretical paths lead to dead ends than lead to science.

Practice wisdom consists of ideas that practitioners
develop during the course of their work with clients. It
incorporates clues about causes and effects of experiences and behaviors and methods that help people overcome problems. Over time, practitioners are likely to see
numerous clients who share at least some characteristics
or experiences, which lead them to draw conclusions
about particular characteristics or experiences and their
effects. However, practitioners tend to minimize the extent to which geographical conditions (who lives nearby)
and practitioners' own characteristics and contacts affect

the particular clients who choose to use their services. Therefore, they may attribute too much to similarities among clients or assume that their caseloads are typical of those of their colleagues. Sometimes, too, practitioners have ideological (or even pathological) reasons to want clients to reflect particular characteristics and project them onto clients who do not possess them.

Practice wisdom, then, is far from foolproof — it is most effective when, as implied, practitioners are particularly wise, which also implies that they have extensive, broad experience. Practice wisdom is particularly useful when several seasoned practitioners compare notes, for example, to urge their professional societies to address emerging needs or to bring focus on new, growing, or changing problems.

A theory . . . is an educated guess positing that one thing has an effect on something else, which can then be tested and confirmed or unconfirmed.

When practitioners consider altering their practice in response to observations gained through practice wisdom, their next step, after identifying the problem, which is the real contribution of practice wisdom, should be to develop it into a scientifically testable theory. A theory is, then, more than just an idea or problem identification. It is an educated guess positing that one thing has an effect on something else, which can then be tested and confirmed or unconfirmed.

Sometimes, if the need for a service appears urgent but science offers no means of meeting the need, practitioners will base treatment ideas on theory or near-research, that is, on either untested ideas posited to be effective or on research findings about similar but not identical groups. Both methods are justifiable if, indeed, there are no better, proven methods available and if such practice is regarded as experimental, and clients are informed of that fact.

Some clinicians, however, reject these concerns — and professional ethics. Consider the following: "As early as May, 1994, [R. Christopher] Barden [founder and president of the National Association for Consumer

Protection in Mental Health Practices] stated, 'No state or federal funds should be used for any therapy that has not been shown safe and effective.' Language such as this threatens the very field of psychotherapy. The terms *safe* and *effective* and *scientific*, as defined by Barden, do not include the knowledge base that therapists have obtained from clinical observation. Following this logic, proposals such as Barden's put experimental psychologists and laboratory scientists in a watchdog role over therapists" (Quirk & DePrince, 1996).

Experimental psychologists and laboratory scientists are not "watchdogs." Instead, they can be likened to filters through whom responsible, ethical practitioners subject their practice wisdom and theories to reality test their clinical observations — which hardly constitute a knowledge base. Practitioners who fail to do so are clearly in denial about the possibility that their untested methods could be ineffective or even harmful to their patients. And these very practitioners are among those whom promote the pathological nature of denial, as well as the other elements of snake oil.

For example, anatomically correct dolls have not been found to be an effective means of determining whether a child has been sexually abused (Ceci & Bruck, 1995; Gardner, 1991). Yet the Department of Justice currently distributes, in its series of "Portable Guides to Investigating Child Abuse", a booklet titled, *Interviewing Child Witnesses and Victims of Sexual Abuse*, which describes the use of anatomically correct dolls as investigatory tools. The author of this section of the booklet, Kathleen Faller, was recently charged with malpractice for using coercive methods of interviewing children. Faller was not held liable, but even her attorney's comments suggested that it was not methodological competence, but lack of malice, that led to the verdict (Kresnak, 1997). And the Council on Scientific Affairs of the American Medical Association (1985) ruled that refreshing memories with hypnosis, "can involve confabulations and pseudomemories and . . . appear to be less accurate than nonhypnotic recall."

Coercive methodologies are now recognized as the cause of the allegations that created the "ritual satanic abuse" scares of the previous decade. Therapists who believed that children had to be "encouraged" to admit abuse refused to believe denials and rewarded admissions, no matter how implausible. Failing to see that their inducements were causing the childrens' statements, investigators elicited increasingly bizarre stories — about satanic rituals, and involving huge and ever-increasing numbers of offenders. Often investigation ceased only after a child named a social worker or judge as part of the satanic group (Nathan & Snedeker, 1995). This was no doubt caused by these investigators' limited knowledge of the techniques used to obtain the childrens' reports or their ineffectiveness. But it was also caused by the fact that some radical feminist therapists wanted the public to consider child sexual abuse "epidemic," while some fundamentalist Christian therapists, who were also drawn to this "field," wanted to perpetuate the fear of Satan. It was also perpetuated by local "innovations," which discouraged detection of these poor techniques. In Edenton, North Carolina, parents were told that their child victims were eligible for compensation only if they were treated by a handful of doctors and therapists in that city, "that were working on this particular case" (Ceci & Bruck, 1995). In San Diego, the same few "approved" therapists "detected" crimes, "treated" their effects, and approved their payment through state funds (San Diego Grand Jury, 1997). Both methods encourage false reports to pad billings and also risk evidence contamination, as therapists work with multiple victims of the same case. It is allowed to continue, however, due to government support and lack of media skepticism and therefore lack of public awareness. In fact, the *Washington Post* (1997) editorialized that, "Children all too often suffer terribly at the hand of perverse and brutal adults . . . children must be protected not only from predators but from counselors of questionable credentials."

State of New Jersey vs. JQ (1996) quoted Suzanne M. Sgroi (1982), "Validation of child sexual abuse depends upon recognizing behavioral indicators, the capacity to perform investigative interviewing, the ability to do credibility assessment, recognizing physical indicators, and the capacity to perform comprehensive medical examinations. Behavioral indicators of child sexual abuse may be helpful but are rarely conclusive." Even more important, the existence of these indicators, even when they do reflect abuse, offer no clue to the identity of the abuser.

Sometimes these poorly-trained "investigators" simply believed reports of abuse without evidence. For example, the report of the investigation into Breezy Point Day School noted that, "It appears that both the caseworker and the attending psychologist based their conclusions in part, upon an entirely false premise — that the child . . . had undergone a medical examination which revealed evidence of some trauma to the vagina. To the contrary, the medical examination by the family pediatrician disclosed no such evidence and was entirely contrary to this initial report by the mother" (Rubinstein, 1990). In other cases, such as that in Jordon, Minnesota, evidence of actual abuse was "lost" In the morass of incompetent investigations that identified so many offenders and victims that the truth was eventually undeterminable (Wexler, 1995).

Some of the workers believed these cases because they believed that children never lie about abuse (and did not comprehend that many of these children were only believed when they finally did lie). Other professionals believed that statistics proved that few cases are false. However, this was often a misapprehension. For instance, in regard to a study by Jones and MacGraw (1987) of 576 Denver cases, that found "53% indicated, 23% unfounded, 24% insufficient information, 6% malicious, 17% wrong but not malicious," (Ceci & Brock, 1995). "Some commentators have concluded that only a small proportion of reports (around 6%) are false. However, this is a misunderstanding of the data because the percentage of false reports is the entire 23%; 6% are deliberate lies, but the other 17% are just as baseless as the lies, even though they may be honest mistakes. And they can do just as much harm." These findings correspond with those of two other major studies, Thoennes and Tjaden (1990) who studied 9,000 families in custody disputes and found that 50% were likely cases, 17% were uncertain, and 33% were unlikely; and Faller (1991) who found 35% of cases to be false. But Faller rejected her finding out-of-hand because it was too high (Ceci & Bruck, 1995).

Expert witnesses. As more and more child abuse cases move from family court to criminal court, prosecutors seek to bolster the testimony of child protection workers not only with testimony about professionally developed syndromes, but with the testimony of "experts" who would interview children and claim that their evaluative abilities prove the childrens' abuse. However, many so-called experts lack credentials, present unreliable theories as facts, and intentionally confuse or misrepresent issues and evidence (Schmitt, 1997; Sherman, 1997; Huber, 1991). "Fewer than one hundred of the nation's 3,688 colleges and universities may be considered research universities, and more than half of higher education R&D expenditures are concentrated in forty institutions. Yet 441 institutions offer Ph.D. degrees, and faculty members increasingly define their work as research" (Straus, 1997).

"Experts . . . are not required to cite scientific evidence — a vague reference to their own experience or unpublished research will often do — and they are virtually certain to try to buttress the claims of the lawyers who hired them, not matter how farfetched . . . Judges are supposed to screen out testimony that is not reliable and relevant . . . but judges are not trained to evaluate scientific testimony" (Angell, 1998). One reason that this can occur is that, "no factual record is kept of how often [experts] are proved wrong by later events" (Sowell, 1997).

Mental health practitioners are largely ineffective in making determinations about human behavior — and least effective in making predictions about future behavior — regardless of the evidence of past activities. What little the mental health industry can offer in the sense of "statistical likelihood" is also prone to identify innocent people as criminals and criminals as either innocent or not guilty (Dawes, 1994), and is usually due to some bogus "abuse excuse" (Dershowitz, 1994). Fake experts also tend to use tools, such as Rorschach and other projective tests, which have never proven predictive (Hagen, 1997; Dawes, 1994).

"The problem is not that children are making false child abuse accusations, but that faulty evaluators are in some cases leading to misdiagnoses" (Schetky, 1989). No mental health technology enables a practitioner to predict future behavior, but "experts" testify everyday to the likelihood that a particular person "will kill again" or "has been rehabilitated" or "has been abused" — and courts act on these spurious claims; yet many clinicians who lack research training as well as skills testify based on their own clinical experiences, which tend to be extremely narrow at best (Hagen, 1997). The government perpetuates this by funding "training" programs that present unproven theories, disproven theories, and pure ideology as fact.

A related problem with expert testimony is that many courts accept treating therapists as experts in cases involving their own clients. But therapy is based on relationship, so any therapist who has treated an individual for enough time to testify should be assumed to be too biased to act as an expert in that patient's case (not to mention the fact that few treating therapists have the skills or training required of true court experts). Evaluation, which is not based on relationship, is not subject to these compromises.

Some expert witnesses do not simply testify to bogus science but are outright frauds. In the Breezy Point Day School case, for instance, James Stillwell presented himself as an expert on ritual child abuse, and, "as the founder and president of the National Agency Against the Organized Exploitation of Children, Inc. Stillwell claimed that his agency ". . . had wide-ranging experience in 'looking for' and uncovering 'satanic stuff;' that [it] employ[ed] in excess of three hundred people . . . [and] that he [had] worked with federal and county authorities," including the FBI. "An investigation into [his]

background . . . disclose[d] no such affiliations." It did find, however, that Stillwell had "no formal training or education beyond receiving his high school graduate equivalency diploma;" and that he was actually the only employee of his "organization," which operated out of a post office box (Rubinstein, 1990).

Recognizing The Fallacies Inherent in Sanctified Snake Oil

Flawed Reasoning

Data only have meaning for those who can and are willing to understand them. This requires first having at least a rudimentary understanding of research and statistics. Then it requires applying that understanding to each new set of information with which one is presented. In many cases, even people with knowledge of statistics fail to question research that they choose to believe, due to wishful thinking. Self-fulfilling prophesies results from two other forms of flawed reasoning: hermeneutic reasoning, in which interpretation depends on premises held by the interpreter (satanic abuse exists because I believe in Satan); and representative thinking, or making a judgement on the basis of the degree to which characteristics match a stereotype.

Investment effect suggests that the more time and other resources people devote to believing something, the less willing they will be to change their beliefs. This offers a clue to why many professionals find it impossible to disabuse themselves of notions that have been disproved, but which have formed the core of their research, teaching or practice. "Expectancy effect . . . dictates that exposure to a mixed body of evidence ma[kes] both sides even *more* convinced of the fundamental soundness of their original beliefs, in part because they were more critical of research that refuted their beliefs than of research that supported them" (Paulos, 1988).

In its first stage, mental standstill fixes the principles and boundaries governing a political problem. In the second stage, when dissonances and failing function begin to appear, the initial principles rigidify. This is the period when, if wisdom were operative, reexamination and rethinking and a change of course are possible, but they are rare as rubies in a backyard. Rigidifying leads to increase of investment and the need to protect egos; policy founded upon error multiplies, never retreats. The greater the invest-

ment and the more unacceptable is disengagement. In the third stage, pursuit of failure en-
larges the damages. (Tuchman, 1984)

"People's preferences influence not only the kind of
information that they consider, but also the amount they
examine [and] what we believe is heavily influenced by
what we think others believe. We favor or oppose . . .
various . . . 'lifestyle' practices in part because of what we
think other people think, or do, about these matters. [Re-
search demonstrates] . . . that peoples' own beliefs, values, and habits . . . bias their estimates of how widely
such views and habits are shared with others . . . people
have been shown to be particularly likely to exaggerate
the amount of perceived social support for their beliefs
when they have an emotional investment in the belief
. . . we are selectively exposed to information that tends
to support our beliefs . . . we are also exposed to a biased
sample of people and their opinions" (Gilovich, 1991).

Huber (1991) coined the phrase *junk science*, which
he defined as "a hodgepodge of biased data, spurious inference, and logical legerdemain, patched together by researchers whose enthusiasm for discovery and diagnosis
far outstrip their skill. . . . It is a catalog of every con-
ceivable kind of error: data dredging, wishful thinking,
truculent dogmatism, and, now and again, outright
fraud." One reason that junk science often goes unde-
tected is that attorneys and other biased consumers of research reject experts who disagree with their contentions
and suppress research which conflicts with their agendas
(Sherman, 1997; Crosson, 1994).

Separating Science From Snake Oil

Ellis (1997) observed that, "Academic analysis follows where the argument leads, but activism wants only
support for a predetermined direction. Academic researchers are intrigued by the structure of arguments,
whereas activists only want to win them." Huber (1991)
also observed that, "All real science questions contain
what Karl Popper calls 'stopping rules.' Statements of scientific fact are statements that could be systematically
shown to be false (if they are false) after some finite, circumscribed inquiry. Questions that are forever open,
questions that can be answered only one way or not at all,
are the domain of philosophy and religion, not science."

Conclusion

It is unfortunate that advocacy statistics distort pub-

lic perceptions of the magnitude and contours of all forms
of domestic violence. But it is singularly dangerous when
they distort the perceptions of professional social workers. Social work clinicians who rely on these inaccurate
perceptions may have exaggerated expectations of finding
domestic violence in the histories of their clients and may
even disbelieve any client who denies having been abused.
When abuse does exist, such social workers may have a
distorted sense of its effects on client functioning. They
may even perceive clients only through the prism of domestic violence, rather than as individuals with many
unique and diverse strengths who are affected by myriad
social forces. Such workers may also fail to make differential diagnoses and treatment plans for minor and serious abuse and ignore or minimize violence committed by
women clients, endangering their children and partners.
Social workers who practice at the macro-level may design services that fail to differentially target the needs of
victims of domestic violence of all types, and may consequently fail to allocate resources appropriately.

The most recent revision of the *Code of Ethics*
(NASW 1996b) strengthened and expanded the emphasis
on competent treatment informed by effective research.
The *Code of Ethics* also reiterated the dictate that social
workers hone their skills in research evaluation, keep
current with emerging knowledge in the field, and subject
their practice to the rigors of evaluation, which they then
feed back to the knowledge base through publication.
However, the sanctified snake oil of advocacy statistics
make it difficult for even conscientious social workers to
separate accurate research from junk science. This is particularly true when inaccurate or incomplete information
is presented at professional conferences, in government
publications and from government-sponsored service
providers. Yet social workers must learn the difference,
and the profession must make doing so a priority, because failure to do so can lead to loss of licensure, which
affects the public's perceptions of social workers in general, not just of the incompetent few.

Finally, social workers and the profession must do
more than reactively correct misperceptions based on
junk science. They must encourage accurate research and
publication into the areas plagued by advocacy statistics,
because only then will social workers be able to increase
their understanding of the many seemingly intractable
problems of society, such as domestic violence, and create the climate for developing and implementing meaningful solutions to them.

References

Accuracy in Media. (1997). The scandal of news censorship on TV. *AIM Report.* Washington, DC: Author.

American Psychological Association. (1996).*Violence in the family.* Washington, DC: Author.

Angell, M. (1998). Trial by science. *New York Times,* December 9.

Beckett, K. (1996). Culture and the politics of signification: The case of child sexual abuse. *Social Problems, 43*(1), 57-76.

Belluck, P. (1997). Shelters for women disclosing their locations, in spite of risk. *New York Times.* August 10.

Bennett, L. (1980). *Public opinion in American politics.* New York: Harcourt Brace Jovanovich.

Best, J. (1990). *Threatened children.* Chicago, IL: University of Chicago Press.

Ceci, S. J., & Bruck, M. (1995). *Jeopardy in the courtroom: A scientific analysis of children's testimony.* Hyattsville, MD: American Psychological Association.

Compton, B. R., & Galaway, B. (1999). *Social work processes.* Sixth edition. Pacific Grove, CA: Brooks/Cole.

Costin, L. B., Karger, H. J., & Stoesz, D. (1996). *The politics of child abuse in America.* New York: Oxford University Press.

Council on Scientific Affairs. (1985). Scientific status of refreshing recollection by the use of hypnosis. *Journal of the American Medical Association,* April 5.

Crosson, C. (1994). *Tainted truth.* New York: Touchstone Books.

Dawes, R. M. (1994). *House of cards: Psychology and pychotherapy built on myth.* New York: Free Press.

Dershowitz, A. M. (1994). *The abuse excuse.* New York: Little, Brown & Co.

Edelman, M. (1977). *Political language: Words that succeed and politics that fail.* New York: Academic Press.

Editorial. (1997).*Washington Post,* May 24.

Ellis, J. M. (1997). *Literature lost.* New Haven, CT: Yale University Press.

Ellis, R. J. (1998). *The dark side of the left.* Topeka, KS: University of Kansas Press.

Faller, K. (1991). Possible explanations for child sexual abuse allegations in divorce. *American Journal of Orthopsychiatry, 61,* 86-91.

Gardner, R. A. (1991). *Sex abuse hysteria: Salem witch trials revisited.* Cresskill, NJ: Creative Therapeutics.

Gilovich, T. (1991). *How we know what isn't so.* New York: The Free Press.

Goldberg, W., & Tomlanovich, M. (1984). Domestic violence victims in the emergency department. *Journal of the American Medical Association,* June 22-9, 32, 59-64.

Grant, T. (1997). *Wenatchee and the media's reflexive acceptance of hysteria.* Paper prepared at "A Day of Contrition Revisited: Contemporary Hysteria Condemns the Innocent." A Conference Organized by the Justice Committee. Salem, MA: January 14.

Gremillion, D. H. (1996). Domestic violence as a professional commitment. In R. Simon, (Ed.), *From data to public policy* (pp. 53-59). New York: Women's Freedom Network and University Press of America, Inc.

Hagen, M. A. (1997). *Whores of the court.* New York: ReganBooks.

Hentoff, N. (1992). *Free speech for me — but not for thee.* New York: Harper Perennial.

Huber, P. (1991). *Galileo's revenge.* New York: Basic Books.

Jones, D., & MacGraw, J. M. (1987). Reliable and fictitious accounts of sexual abuse in children. *Journal of Interpersonal Violence, 2.*

Klaidman, S., & Beauchamp, T. L. (1987). *The virtuous journalist.* New York: Oxford University Press.

Krauthammer, C. (1983). Defining deviancy up. *New Republic,* November 22.

Kresnak, J. (1997). U-M cleared in child evaluation. Father loses lawsuit over abuse inquiry. *Detroit Free Press,* November 26.

Lanning, K. (1996). The 'witch hunt,' the 'backlash,' and professionalism. *The APSAC Advisor, 9*(4).

McLeer, S. V., & R. Anwar, R. (1989). A study of battered women presenting in an emergency room. *American Journal of Public Health,* January, 65-6.

McNeely, R. L., Cook, P. W., & Torres, J. B. (1999). Is domestic violence a human issue? *Journal of Human Behavior in the Social Environment,* Fall.

National Association of Social Workers National Council on the Practice of Clinical Social Work. (1996a). *Evaluation and treatment of adults with the possibility of recovered memories of child sexual abuse.* Washington, DC: Author.

National Association of Social Workers Delegate Assembly. (1996b). *Code of ethics of the National Association of Social Workers.* Washington, DC: Author.

National Institute of Justice and the Bureau of Justice Statistics. (1996). *Domestic and sexual violence data collection.* Washington, DC: Author.

New York City Commission on the Status of Women. (1996). *Report of the Committee on Domestic Violence.* New York: Office of the Mayor, January 1996.

Paulos, J. A. (1988). *Innumeracy: Mathematical illiteracy and its consequences.* New York: Hill and Wang.

Pizzey, E. (1982). *Prone to violence.* England: Hamlyn Publishing.

Quirk, S. A., & DePrince, A. P. (1996). Childhood trauma: Politics and legislative concerns for therapists. In S. Contratto & M. Janice Gutfreund (Eds.), *A feminist clinician's guide to the memory debate.* New York: Haworth Press, Inc..

Rand, M. R., & Strom, K. (1997). *Violence-related injuries treated in hospital emergency departments.* Washington, DC: U.S. Department of Justice.

Reamer, F. (1988). The evolution of social work ethics. *Social Work,* November, 488-500.

Reid, W. J. (1995). Research overview. *Encyclopedia of social work, 3.* Eighteenth edition. Washington, DC: National Association of Social Workers.

Rubenstein, A. M. (1990). *Report: investigation into Breezy Point Day School.* Doylestown, PA: Office of the District Attorney.

Samuelson, R. (1995). *The good life and its discontents.* New York: Random House.

San Diego County Grand Jury. (1994). *Analysis of child molestation issues. Report No. 7.* June 1. San Diego , CA: Author.

Sand Diego County Grand Jury. *Final Report 1996-1997.* June 27. San Diego, CA: Author.

Sarnoff, S. K. (1999). A case study in advocacy research.*Women's Freedom Network Newsletter,* May-June.

Sarnoff, S. K. (1998). Assessing the costs of false allegations of child abuse: A prescriptive. *Issues in Child Abuse Allegations,* Summer/Fall, 108-115.

Schetky, D. (1989). Resolved: Child sexual abuse is overdiagnosed: Affirmative. *Journal of the American Academy of Child and Adolescent Psychiatry, 28*(5).

Schmitt, R. B. (1997). Who is an expert? In some courtrooms, the answer is "nobody." *Wall Street Journal,* June 17, A1 and A8.

FAMILIES IN SOCIETY · *Volume 80, Number 4*

Sgroi, S. (Ed.) (1982). *Handbook of clinical intervention in child sexual abuse.* Lexington, MA: Lexington Books.

Sherman, L. W. (1997). *Preventing crime: What works, what doesn't, what's promising.* Washington, DC: U.S. Department of Justice

Sowell, T. (1997). Victims of the 'helping professions.' *New York Post,* December 27.

Snedeker, N., Snedeker, D., & Snedeker M. (1995). *Satan's silence.* New York: Basic Books. *State of NJ vs. JQ (1993) 130 NJ 554, 617 A. 2nd 1196.*

Straus, J. C. (1997). College costs too much, fails kids. *USA Today,* July 17.

Stricker, G. (1992). The relationship of research to clinical practice. *American Psychologist, 47,* 543-49.

Summit, R. (1992). Abuse of the child abuse accommodation syndrome. *Journal of Child Sexual Abuse, 1*(4).

Summit, R. (1983). The child abuse accommodation syndrome. *Child Abuse and Neglect, 7*(2).

Tjaden, P., & Thoennes, N. (1998). *Prevalence, incidence, and consequences of violence against women: Findings from the National Violence Against Women Survey.* Washington, DC: U.S. Department of Justice, November.

Thoennes, N., & Tjaden, P. The extent, nature and validity of sexual abuse allegations in custody/visitation disputes. *Child Abuse and Neglect, 14,* 151-63.

Tuchman, B. (1984). *The march of folly.* Boston: G. K. Hall and Co.

Victor, J. S. (1993). *Satanic panic.* Chicago, IL: Open Court Press.

Wexler, R. (1995). *Wounded innocents.* New York: Prometheus Books.

Young, C. (1999). *Ceasefire: Beyond the gender wars.* New York: Free Press.

Susan Kiss Sarnoff is assistant professor, *Ohio University, Department of Social Work, Athens, OH, 45701-2979.*

Manuscript accepted: May 6, 1999

[27]

ADDENDUM 2
SOME PRINCIPLES FOR
A NEW PROFESSIONAL ETHICS
BASED ON XENOPHANES' THEORY OF TRUTH

Karl R. Popper

I should like to put forward some principles for a new professional ethics, which for a long time I have felt is badly needed, principles based on

THE UNKNOWN XENOPHANES

Xenophanes' theory of truth and connected with his moralism and intellectual honesty.

For this purpose I shall first characterize the old professional ethics, and perhaps caricature it a little, in order to compare and contrast it later with the new professional ethics that I propose. Should this new ethics turn out to be a better guide for human conduct than the traditional ethics of the intellectual professions – the ethics of scientists, physicians, lawyers, engineers, architects, and also civil servants, and most importantly, the ethics of politicians – then I may be allowed to claim that new things can be learnt even in the field of ethics.

Both the *old* and the *new* professional ethics are based, admittedly, upon the ideas of truth, of rationality, and of intellectual responsibility. But the old ethics was based upon the ideas of personal knowledge and of the possibility of reaching certainty; and therefore upon the idea of *authority*. The new ethics, by contrast, is based upon the ideas of objective knowledge and of uncertain knowledge. This means a fundamental change in thinking, and with it a change in the *role* played by the ideas of truth, of rationality, and of intellectual honesty and responsibility.

The old ideal was to *possess* both truth and certainty and, whenever possible, to *guarantee* truth by means of a proof. This ideal, which to this day is widely accepted, corresponds to the personal ideal of the sage – not, of course, to the Socratic ideal of wisdom, but rather to the Platonic ideal of the initiated seer: of the Platonic philosopher who is, at the same time, a royal ruler, an authority.

The old imperative for the intellectual was: 'Be an authority! Know everything (at least in your chosen field of expertise)!' Once you are recognized as an authority, your authority will be protected by your colleagues; and you must, of course, reciprocate by protecting their authority.

The old ethics here described leaves no room for mistakes. Mistakes are not allowed; and therefore the confession of mistakes is not allowed. I do not need to stress that this old professional ethics is intolerant. Moreover, it has always been intellectually dishonest: it leads especially in medicine and politics to the covering up of mistakes for the sake of authority ('closing ranks').

I suggest, therefore, that a *new* professional ethics, fit not only for scientists, be based upon the following twelve principles.

1   Our objective conjectural knowledge continues to exceed more and more what *one* person can master. *Therefore there are no authorities.* This holds true even within the various medical specialities.

2   *It is impossible to avoid all mistakes,* or even all those mistakes that are, in themselves, avoidable. Mistakes are continually being made by *all* scientists. The old idea that mistakes can be avoided and that one is

therefore in duty bound to avoid them must be revised: it is itself a mistake.

3   *It still remains our duty to do everything we can to avoid mistakes.* But it is precisely in order to avoid them that we must be aware of the difficulty in avoiding them, and of the fact that nobody succeeds in avoiding them all; not even the most creative scientists who are guided by intuition succeed. Although we can do nothing without it, intuition is more often wrong than right.

4   *Mistakes may be hidden in our best-corroborated theories*, and it is the specific task of the scientist to search for such mistakes. Finding that a well-corroborated theory or a much-used practical technique is mistaken may be a discovery of the greatest importance.

5   *We must therefore change our attitude to our mistakes.* It is *here* that our practical ethical reform must begin. For the attitude of the old professional ethics leads us to cover up our mistakes, keep them secret, and to forget all about them as soon as possible.

6   The new basic principle is that in order to avoid making more mistakes than we need make *we must learn from the mistakes we do make*. To cover up mistakes, therefore, is the greatest intellectual sin.

7   *We must, therefore, be constantly on the lookout for mistakes*, especially our own mistakes. When we find them we must remember them; and we must scrutinize them from all aspects, in order to understand better what went wrong.

8   A *self-critical attitude*, frankness, and openness towards oneself become, therefore, part of everyone's duty.

9   Since we must learn from our mistakes, *we must also learn to accept*, indeed accept with thanks, *their being pointed out to us by others*. When we draw other people's attention to their mistakes, we should always remember that we ourselves have made similar mistakes. And we should remember that the greatest scientists have made great mistakes. This is certainly not meant to imply that our mistakes are, generally, forgivable: we must never let our attention slacken. But it is humanly impossible to avoid making mistakes, and when we draw the attention of others to their mistakes, we might help them by pointing this out too.

10   We must be clear in our minds that *we need other people to discover and correct some of our mistakes (as they need us)*; especially people who have grown up with different ideas, in a different cultural atmosphere. This too leads to toleration.

11   We must learn that self-criticism is the best criticism; but that *criticism by others is a necessity*. It is nearly as good as self-criticism.

12   *Rational (or objective) criticism must always be specific*: it must give specific reasons why specific statements, specific hypotheses appear to be false, or specific arguments invalid. It must be guided by the idea of getting

THE UNKNOWN XENOPHANES

nearer to objective truth. In this sense it must be impersonal, but also sympathetic.

I ask the reader to consider what I am proposing here as suggestions. They are meant to point out that, in the field of ethics too, one can put forward suggestions which may be discussed and improved by critical discussion, as Xenophanes and his successors, it seems, were among the first to discover.

The more or less universal acceptance of the conjectural character of science has meant a fundamental change in the attitude of scientists towards refutations of mistaken theories, even of their own. A similar change in attitude to human fallibility has not yet taken place in politics and within our different institutions. If I dream of a democratic utopia, it will be one in which a parliamentary candidate can hope to attract votes by the boast that he discovered during the last year 31 serious mistakes made by himself and managed to correct thirteen of them; while his rival discovered only 27, even though he admitted correcting thirteen of his own mistakes. I need not say that this will be a Utopia *of toleration*.

Editorial note

Owing to its fairytale origin, which will not be related here, no part of this volume got into 'the Popper Archive', so from that point of view *The World of Parmenides* may be considered Sir Karl Popper's last philosophical publication on which he worked to the end of his life. Essay 2 on Xenophanes, which is the only essay among those printed here that Sir Karl left unfinished, has been completed from numerous handwritten drafts and other documents, kindly made available by Mr and Mrs Raymond Mew, Sir Karl's literary executors, according to two main lists of contents found among the papers of Sir Karl's *Nachlass*: (X_1) three structurally similar lists with various keywords added over a period of time, and (X_2) one list entirely different from the others.

The X_1-lists comprise seven sections and carry a number of keywords (here written in brackets): (I) 'Xenophanes as a Co-founder of the Greek Enlightenment' (a teacher who wanted to teach so as to become unnecessary!); (II) 'Notes on the Life of Xenophanes' (Colophon, Miletus, Anaximander; refugee); (III) 'The Misunderstood Cosmology' (fields of force in which disturbances cause vibrations that spread like waves); (IV) 'Relation to Parmenides' (*demas* versus *melea* or *melos* – *melea* hardly occurs in Xenophanes? Cartesian Rationalism, sphere); (V) 'Enlightened Theology' (the Logic of Supreme Power, the Ethics of Supreme Power; the Critique of Anthropomorphism is fundamental, see Mansfeld I, p. 16, Back to Anaximander! das Zitat); (VI) 'Moralism: the Defence of Civilization Against the Gods' (the dramatists; Die Existenz der Welt und der Menschenwelt

THE WORLD OF PARMENIDES

beruht auf Gerechtigkeit: Gott, der Mächtige, muss gerecht sein); (VII)
'Logic and Epistemology'. (Between Sections VI and VII a reference to E.
R. Dodds, *The Greeks and the Irrational*, 1951, is noted.)

The X_2-list of contents also sketches out seven sections, but with
different titles, and it gives other keywords and carries the heading 'On
the Greatness of Xenophanes': (1) 'Anti-Anthropomorphism, Theology';
(2) 'The Summary of Theology, B34, Truth versus Certainty' (Monotheism
– as good, or better, than the Christian or Jewish one. The Old Testament
God is an envious god: you must not have other gods besides me!); (3)
'Two Popular Senses of Scepticism' (both deriving from 'no criterium of
truth'); (4) 'Two Kinds of Objects of Knowledge: Laws and Stable Environment – the *Momentary* Dangers and Gain-Situations'; (5) 'Xenophanes
the First and Best of Greek Epistemologists' (he said 'no criterion of truth,
but, if we go on searching, then our conjectural knowledge may become
better'. This is the only sound epistemology); (6) 'B27 and Empedocles'
Misinterpretation, confirmed by Aristotle'. (All B27 is correct: the Sun is a
big gas ball); (7) '"The Spherical God"' (Three possibilities: (i) The god is
spherical according to Aristotle: the unmoved mover; (ii) Xenophanes got
it from Parmenides; (iii) Xenophanes' god is not spherical. We cannot
know, but I would opt for the third (1), the first (2), the second (3)).

Destiny allowed Sir Karl to cover only a part of the topics indicated in
these lists of contents and, for some of them, only in a very first approx-
imation. This has invariably affected both the order of presentation and the
contents of the present sections of the Xenophanes essay. No doubt, had
this essay been completed by Sir Karl himself the shape of it would have
been different; however, the main topics and arguments have been saved
and reproduced according to his views on Xenophanes – although with an
emphasis and detail less characteristic than he would have given it had he
been allowed to write out as a whole his original reconstruction of
Xenophanes' contribution to science and philosophy.

In the present version of Essay 2, *Section 1*, which originally introduced
the essay, describes Xenophanes as a founder of the Greek Enlightenment.
The Preamble that now precedes Section 1 comes from a separate, handwritten note. The first part of *Section 2* on Xenophanes' early life has been
carried over from a larger manuscript beginning with the words 'Xenophanes had a hard life', while the second part of this section stems from a
typescript entitled 'Three Notes on Xenophanes'; the model of Xenophanes' Earth and the text to notes 11 and 12 as well as the text to
note 18 have been copied from an inscription made by Sir Karl in June
1984 on the flyleaf and p.[I] of his master copy of *Die beiden Grundprobleme
der Erkenntnistheorie*, Tübingen, 1979. The main text of *Section 3* on Xenophanes' misunderstood cosmology also comes from 'Three Notes on
Xenophanes'. *Section 4* about Xenophanes' theology has been compiled
from one manuscript joined with several shorter manuscripts and comments

THE UNKNOWN XENOPHANES

noted in separate handwritten documents. The same holds for *Section 5* on Xenophanes' theory of knowledge, where the first part (including the paragraphs to which notes 24 and 25 refer) has been adapted from two manuscripts, while the last part draws on some pages of a paper entitled 'Toleration and Intellectual Responsibility', published in K. R. Popper, *In Search of a Better World*, London, 1992, where Xenophanes' theory of truth is outlined; the four paragraphs on Kepler come from a footnote which Sir Karl prepared in 1990 for a revised version of the latter paper when he still wanted it included as an essay in the present collection. The main text of *Section 6* on Xenophanes' moralism comes from the paper on toleration, while the last four paragraphs of this section have been pieced together from scattered remarks, some of which were noted directly on the lists of contents. The main text of *Section 7* comes from shorter manuscripts in German and English; the hypothesis about Xenophanes as a precursor of Herodotus has been carried over from the manuscript starting 'Xenophanes had a hard life'. *Addendum 1* comes from 'Three Notes on Xenophanes' and *Addendum 2* has been adapted from the paper on toleration. (Wording in square brackets has been inserted to connect manuscript fragments not originally combined by Sir Karl himself. Notes indicated or planned by the author have been tentatively written out by the editor and similarly bracketed. The titles of Sections 2–7, not in brackets, have been adapted from the preliminary lists of contents to announce the main themes of the appropriate sections. Ed.)

Part VIII
Ethical Issues Regarding Professional Education and Schools of Social Work

[28]

Believing and doing: values in social work education

Helen Harris Perlman

A value has small worth if it can not be transmuted from idea or conviction into some form, quality, or direction of behavior

Helen Harris Perlman, D. Litt., is Samuel Deutsch distinguished service professor emeritus, School of Social Service Administration, University of Chicago, Chicago, Illinois.

Ages ago I entered the first grade, a teacher's dream of an open vessel thirsty for knowledge and, yes, for values to be poured into it. Every morning the gong rang at nine and some twenty of us rose up and put our right hands upon the general area of our hearts and pledged allegiance to our flag and to the country for which it stood. By about the fourth grade and some 796 pledges later I had begun to wonder about my flag and the country for which it (and we) stood. Why did we say that same thing every day, and then abruptly flop into our seats and turn to doing our sums and tables? What was it for, I wondered; what did it have to do with the other things we did? And, because I could not fathom its use or its meaning in relation to anything else we did, it became for me, and probably for my fellow pupils, a kind of nonsense chant like those we used when we jumped rope or bounced ball. Perhaps it had the unifying value of a group ritual, but little more, because it was largely mouth-talk even though it emerged from touchingly pious-looking faces.

I suppose mouth-talk from pious faces is common among us all even as adults when we talk about values in the blue—in their remoteness from action in specific situations, when we "pledge allegiance" to those values that are so abstract and so lofty that no one would gainsay them. Peace, equality, freedom, and justice, all are pure gold values, and everyone treasures them. The dignity and worth of every human being, the right to self-determination, the reciprocity between man and his society and between rights and responsibilities—these are values reiterated in social work—but they are not exclusive to social work. They are espoused by every politician from far left to far right; they are popular slogans inscribed in our national documents and upon our national monuments. They are so high level as to be safe and impregnable. They are also so general and abstract that they may be subject to radically different interpretations. No one would be against them. What is subject to argument, to opposition, or given to violence, is how they should be operationalized, by what instruments and means they may best be achieved. As soon as any one of us is pushed to move from belief to doing, from abstract to concrete, from the ultimate to the proximate values, then the conflicts and the differences and the varied interpretations of their meaning begin.

Values that guide behavior

I am, then, about to make a flat-footed value judgment. It is that a value has small worth except as it is moved, or is moveable, from believing into doing, from verbal affirmation into action. A value—defined here as a cherished belief, an emotionally invested preference or desideratum—has small worth if it can not be transmuted from idea or conviction into some form, quality, or direction of behavior. The power of a value lies in its governance and guidance for action. If values are to serve as action guides, they must be "drawn down to earth." They must be "operationalized," changed into instruments that fashion and direct our doing.

It is usual to speak of this level of values as "lower," but there is nothing disparaging in that term. They are "lower" in the sense that they are grounded in the hard realities of time and place and person-in-situation. Their pure gold may have to be alloyed with some baser metals, to be sure, but that is toward fashioning them into firm and strong instruments available for every-day use.

It is these operating, instrumental values, those that guide and govern what we do in our daily living, to which I will attend, relinquishing with reluctance the headier pleasures of the pure and the absolute. Our question is: How, in education for a profession—social work in this instance—can values be taught and incorporated and applied so that they serve not as defensive shibboleths, but as guides to professional action in its daily, commonplace forms?

It is necessary as a prologue that we recognize and understand that the very existence of social work in the special forms it has taken in this country is the expression of some ultimate values. We did not make ourselves up. We were, and are, created by our society that says "we hold these human welfare values to be essential." Social work then, is our society's invention of an instrument, publicly and privately forged and supported, by which its averred goals for human welfare may be actualized. What social work *has* invented are the ways and means, the strategies, the modes of *action* by which these values may be realized. Social work's specialness, then, is at the level of proximate instrumental values. Our specialness lies in the particular knowledges, skills, and resources that we have developed or organized by which the

over-arching values may be drawn upon, reached for, and actualized. What is better, rather than worse, for this family or person whose worth and dignity we affirm? How, faced by internal and external constrictions, may this person yet be helped to become self-determining? What means and resources must be found, created, or made available in order that people may be readied to give care and be responsible to their families or community? These are some of our practical questions in pursuit of our cherished ultimate values.

We begin with the recognition that students come to professional education for the practice of social work already deeply imbued with values. They are value-carriers, whether they know it or not, even those who have recently encountered and espoused the "value" called "neutrality" and "scientific disinterest." Like every one of us, the social work student is often quite unconscious of the values that silently and powerfully guide his internal and external behaviors. The "still small voice" of our long-ago incorporated consciences, and the more accessible and articulated pushes and pulls of our ego- and social-ideals have all been taken in through our pores, so to speak. They have been absorbed from the inputs of influential parents, friends, teachers, books, and other media, taken in and made our "own" because they have had emotional power and meaningfulness at times of our emotional impressionability, or vulnerability, or openness.

When a value, belief, or commitment becomes part of us, we tend to take it for granted. It is "natural" or "normal"; we are scarcely aware of how it affects how we see and feel things, how we judge them, and how our actions are shaped by those perceptions and assessments. Then, at some moment, we are brought up short by an uncomfortable awareness of a grinding of the gears, a blockage between a cherished belief and a situation that challenges its purity or its practicability. It is this sudden awareness and questioning of long-held values of self and of the social work profession, that the student of social work experiences acutely, both in the classroom

Believing and doing: values in social work education

and in his agency field practice.

It is a discomfort which in moderation is much to be desired. It is necessary to the modifications of thought, feeling, and action that constitute the connections between believing and doing; the passage from seeking knowledge because it holds interest or is self-enhancing, to seeking it in order to be of use to others. To these ends the teacher in social work education, whether of social work's helping processes or of its problem-areas, whether concentrating upon the individual or the society, whether in the classroom or in the social agency, must, in alliance with the student, grapple with the ends and means of social work values.

"Divine discontent"—the teacher as model

One of the most valuable attributes of any teacher is that he should remain somewhat uncomfortable, and paradoxically, that he should be comfortable with his discomfort. I speak of the discomfort that is the product not of personal anxiety or malaise, nor of some sense of personal inadequacy, but the product of intellectual and emotional grappling with the facts of disparity, discrepancy, and distance between what is known and what is yet to be understood,—between what we value and the demands of situational realities. It is the condition the poet calls "divine discontent," divine, I suppose, in that it serves not to yield merely to griping and grumbling or despair and resignation, but rather in that it acts as a constant spur toward searching for what is better rather than worse, toward discovering the lesser of evils or the greater of goods.

So equipped, the teacher begins with one necessary condition for influencing another: that of being a "model." Among other attributes and behaviors it involves a constant searching for congruence between believing and doing, for identifying those proximate values that are in the direction of ultimate ones as well as those that violate them; it includes honest recognition of the relativism of many values and the frequent conflicts among them; it

demonstrates tolerance and humility in the face of the imperfections of human beings, including that of being a social worker.

Such "modeling" is easier said than done. It is probably easier in the protected ambience of a classroom than in the hurly-burly of practice when what is done must often be done quickly—and thought about afterwards, often in the dark of sleepless hours. But the honest facing up to not knowing and the uncertainties and conflicts about values as they are carried into action, whether at the level of personal help or political strategy, that shared recognition of the gap between "ought" and "can," "should" and "shall," forms a strong emotional bond between teacher and student. And, as has been said, beliefs, attitudes, and ideals are best incorporated when such a bond is alive. So grappling with values is central to the emotional and thought changes that professional preparation involves.

The "modeling" of honesty, of awareness of gaps between the ideal and the real, of the consistent effort to reconcile them when that is possible, and to face inherent conflict when it is not, to recognize incongruences among themselves and between them and actions that seem imperative at a given time and place, ought to characterize teaching in every part of the social work curriculum.

One of the instrumental values that social work education claims and cherishes is that professional education should be an integrating experience, that the student should consistently be challenged and helped to see the parts in relation to the whole and the connections between ends and means. This goal is valuable because the subject matters of social work are diverse and complex, and among the surest ways of binding us together, of, for example, directly helping the community organizer and the caseworker see and feel their kinship, are our commonly held, though differently striven for, values. It follows that all good teaching, whether in class or field, requires that every abstract notion or idea that is held to be a guide or precept for action must be examined for its implications for what is to be done. And, conversely, that every decision about what and how to do must be scrutinized in the light of the values to which we claim allegiance. The questions are simple ones: What good is this? For whom? What is problematic about it? Why is this more or less desirable than that? What consequences are likely to be the outcome of this position or action? The questions are simple: the answers are not. But the grappling with ambiguities, conflicts, and irreconcilables, the exercise of thought and responsible choice and decision is the essence of professional education. In these efforts the teacher must take active responsibility.

Selecting professional values

How do teacher and student decide and choose among values? What makes us believe something is good, desirable, better for people's well-being? What makes us move in the direction the belief points to? We make a value judgment. I know this is anathema to many so-called social scientists who aim for scientific purity and total neutrality in their researches. There is probably not a class or field teacher of social work who has not had the student who, on hearing that the teacher believes one thing rather than another, will say, indulgently or indignantly as the case may be, "But *that* is a value judgment!" As if to say, "But you are violating a sacred scientific tenet!" (I have thus far been able to control my impulse to say, "And so are you!" Because *he* is valuing too, except his value is total neutrality and mine is a commitment in a given direction.) Whether even the purest of sciences can ever be "disinterested" is open to at least a quizzical eyebrow. But in a profession one must stand for something; one professes to certain desiderata and standards; therefore one is charged with the responsibility to analyze, to assess, and to make judgments. No doctor hesitates to make a value judgment when he encounters a disease; no lawyer desists from making a value judgment when he encounters crime or lesser conflicts; no teacher can avoid making value judgments as he examines his school

program and the individual students who grapple with it. And, no social worker committed to enabling human beings to carry their work and love tasks in personally satisfying and socially acceptable ways, can avoid the continuous facing up to the judging of what seems, at this time and place, to be better or worse, desirable or noxious to individual, group, or community well-being.

Clearly, there must be some safeguards to such judgments so that they are not simply the product of personal passions or subjective preferences. That is where teachers in both classroom and field practice agency have vital educating roles beyond that of encouraging free inquiry.

There are three sources which the teacher draws upon for the clarification, as far as possible, and objective consideration of values and their implications for action. One is the body of empirically established knowledge; another is the body of experiential knowledge; and the third is that of such theory as seeks to explain and to order observed phenomena.

Within the biological and behavioral sciences there is a rapidly growing corpus of research which supports, or in many instances changes, social work's conceptions of what is good or better or necessary for human well-being. Our working value judgments may then be based upon established facts. Perhaps it goes without saying that the teacher needs to know and impart, or at least point the way to, those facts.

A number of research experiments show, for example, that the capacity to love, to respond affectionately, and later to "socialize" with others stems from early body contacts and emotionally gratifying communications between a mothering person and the infant. A number of other researches reveal that moderate quantities of sensory and muscular stimuli from a nurturant environment—talk, play interchanges, and playthings—arouse and exercise many perceptive and responsive capacities in young children. The implications in these simple but important findings are that a caseworker sees mother-child closeness as "valuable," and that

Believing and doing: values in social work education

value is placed upon creating gratifying responsive transactions between a baby and the people and objects in his environment. What the caseworker then does, arranges for, counsels, and suggests is shaped by this firm knowledge. And how a community worker or organizer draws his blueprint for a child-care facility for instance, will be in consonance with these values derived from research.

The second foundation undergirding social work's instrumental values is that of its vast store of experiential knowledge. Here again the teacher is responsible both to transmit and to guide and involve the learner in becoming familiar with it. Over years of repeated experience with certain forms of human difficulties and social problems, social work has accumulated (though, unfortunately, has not always articulated and systematized) a deep and wide knowledge of the interchanges between the individual psyche and the social conditions within which it develops. No professional group, for instance, has had as much experience as has social work with money—or lack of money, or having to ask for "unearned" money as have social workers. None has experienced as many people from foreign countries and cultures trying to gain a new foothold in a strange and complex land. None has known as many children suffering neglect or actual abuse. From these and like experiences we have developed a number of instrumental values which point the way to our professional behaviors. We argue adequacy of money grants and housing arrangements not just on the lofty basis of our valuing equality of opportunity. We argue it further on the basis of our valuing man's initiative and social responsibility, a value that emanates from our experience that chronic deprivation tends to result in apathy and alienation. Further, we have repeatedly experienced, for example, that a child removed from his parents, vicious or inadequate though they may be, still yearns for them and carries some idealized image of them in his mind and heart. So the social worker values the child's own family as his best environment until the situation proves untenable. Thus, our initial effort in child welfare work is to influence and change conditions within the child's own family. When that effort fails, as it often may, the value of the child's feeling connected with his blood-tie family creates the delicate balance between the caseworker's commitment to affirm and protect the child's need for roots at the same time as he may have to be moved to grow in new soil.

Connected with the value-creating and value-shaping knowledge of research and experience is a third foundation stone. It is theory—the attempt to explain psychological and social phenomena, the propositions put forward by thinkers, whether in social work or elsewhere to identify some commonalities or principles, or to make some order out of their often variegated first-hand observations. Such proposals offer temporary guides to what appear to be the formulation or re-thinking of instrumental values. That the teacher in class or field must provide the means by which such explanatory theory and its implications for believing and doing become part of the student's professional equipment is obvious. What is not always equally obvious is that such teachers must also alert the student (perhaps himself too, now and then) to the fact that this is indeed a body of theory, useful toward systematizing thinking and in illuminating understanding, but subject to further inquiry and meticulous observation.

The propositions of theory say "perhaps," "it is possible," "for the nonce it seems" that this explanation holds directions for what we do and what we should value. The problem in these tentative propositions occurs when we do not recognize that they express probability or possibility. Rather, out of some need for certainty or because of their own subjective inclinations we grab onto them as "the truth." The whole course of the use and abuse of Freudian theory, for example, might have been different if people had not so passionately leaped to aver that the idea of the oedipal complex is "absolutely true" or "absolutely false," is a sacred idea or an insane one. So would a whole set of instrumental values that evolved from that complex proposition—values, say, about the nuclear family versus communal group living, or about what is desirable in sex education of children. Perhaps it is in this area especially that the teacher himself must remain rigorously self-aware, that his predilections for this or that theoretical construct or fragment not thrust him into over-valuing its "truth" or power. In this most uncertain of all worlds, there is nothing for it but to say, to ourselves and to those we teach, "as of now," "at this time," "it is proposed," and "it seems to be the case" that this, rather than that, will produce the better, rather than the less good, consequences.

Some inherent conflicts

The reality is that even those values that have arisen out of rigorous research findings have often been turned topsy-turvy by some contradictory and equally rigorous research. Each day's newspaper carries the report of some new findings in the most precise of physical sciences that prove that what was thought to be "good" or "essential" for health last year has now been shown to be malignant; from the less precise but respectable behavioral sciences, that certain educational modes guaranteed to prepare a child for college turn out to be destructive to his creativity; that what was held to be a potent environmental influence has now been established as secondary to genetic endowment. We must face the fact, therefore, that knowledge itself is far from immutable. It changes, and with it the instrumental values that are its derivatives.

Yet another fact of reality requires that we keep flexible and continuously at work in assessing, weighing, making choices, and tolerating uncertainties. It is a fact that the further one moves down from absolute values, the closer one comes to specific persons and specific conditions, the more do values become relativistic. That is, the more do they require that the judgment of what is or is not desirable must take a number of variables into consideration.

(Even at the level of absolute or ultimate values there are such questions to be faced. For example, in a given society or for a given person, is justice or compassion the higher value?) Certainly, as one moves toward the earthy levels of everday life there occurs a loss of purity, an increase of relativism, and often an emergence of conflict between and among values themselves.

As examples of such conflicts: We hold human life to be precious and we exult in this century's advances in saving children whose physical-neurological conditions, were they unattended by medical science, would result in early death. And at the other end of the life span, we value the extension of life in the aged. And yet, and yet. We grow aware that many of those "saved" children become a life-long misery to their parents and to themselves; that extended old age may become mere vegetation, burdensome to the senile person himself, to his children, and to the community that can not build fast enough or well enough the means to house and care for him.

These are value conflicts for all of us, perhaps particularly for the medical profession. But in social work too, such examples abound of clashes between values. Whose well-being do we hold to be of greater value: the psychotic patient or the people whose lives he may affect? Do we put him away into a hospital to rehabilitate him or to protect those he may harm? When he is judged to be ready for discharge, and he is my client, I become his advocate. I become passionately concerned that his achieved, if frangible, state of mental balance should be maintained, and that his family should readmit him to its bosom, that employers should open jobs to him. When I am his family's caseworker, however, I become their advocate, I resist his return to them because his "cure" is precarious, because the group welfare is of greater import than the single individual's, because they may need protection from him. And so on, in all our thinking about the individual and the group, about parental versus children's rights, indeed about almost any social problem, because value

Believing and doing: values in social work education

conflicts inhere in most of them. (One is tempted to echo the comment attributed to H.L. Mencken to the effect that there is no social problem for which there can not be found a solution that is simple, neat, and wrong.)

Instrumenting values

The recognition of the relativity of instrumental values does not at all mean that "anything goes." Nor does it allow us to shrug off a conflict with a cynical "that's the way it is." If indeed we "profess" to striving for the greater well-being of the many people whose lives we touch, it requires that we struggle to clarify our means in relation to our avowed ends, our beliefs in relation to our behaviors. It requires that we be able and willing to mentally juggle a number of considerations at one time and to make responsible and often admittedly imperfect choices among them. Those choices are responsible when they are made in the light of what is currently known or held to be true, and in awareness of what valued end is being reached for. To develop this responsible behavior the social work teacher must help his student exactly as the student must learn to help his client: to face, to taste and to chew, to consider, weigh, and choose those adaptations between self and conditions, between what is wished for and the demands of reality, that are the essence of living. Perhaps the mark of maturity, whether in a professional person or in any one else, is the recognition that in an imperfect world the most cherished values themselves must contain imperfection, and that decisions and choices of action must take into account both what is most to be desired and the specific limitations and possibilities of this time, this place, and this person.

It is both a delicate and difficult job. Students of social work come to us afire with idealism, and it is important that we do not douse that fire but, rather, use it to forge the instruments that are to be its product. Most of the values with which the student comes are at high levels of ultimacy. Some of them are unrealistic outgrowths of myths that have been circulated

in the recent culture of the young. Many have been passed around and espoused during college bull sessions, accompanied by a sense of superiority over the benighted state of the rest of the world. Few have been tested in the blood and sweat of living them out or helping others to do so.

"I believe," says the student, "in the individual's right to self-actualization." Good! So does social work. It values human worth and human potential. That is why we work at putting together opportunities and processes by which self-realization may be exercised. Now, "self-actualization" (or "self-realization" or "self-determination") means in real life, that is, what exactly? Does it, do you feel, mean "rugged individualism?" Does it allow for stepping on someone else? In a particular case, for instance, does it encourage a husband and father to abandon his wife and two babies because they seem to be in his way? They *are* in his way, true. Whose self-actualization are we concerned with? And, further, do you believe any responsibilities accompany a person's rights? Like what? What ways do you see of coping with the life-long struggle between a person's rights and his obligations? Are any compromises possible? or necessary?

What is illustrated here is clear. It is, first, the teacher's affirmation of an ultimate value which everyone treasures, to which our hearts leap up. But then there follows the forcing of thought, the exercise of discriminative judgment about the actual operation and instrumentation of that value—its explicit meaning as it is carried into action, the limitations and complications in it as soon as the individual is seen as joined with others, whether in marrage or parenthood or any other form of social contract, its sometime conflict with other cherished values, and so forth.

Such questions and conflicts in our value systems must not be glossed over. They require thought that weighs and balances, and that includes openness to compromise. Compromise is hard for the young, but it is an ever-present necessity of life if beliefs are to be translated into action. One may need to compromise with the time it takes or the detours that must be traveled to go from where one is to the goal one reaches for, and certainly often with accepting some less than ideal solution.

"Going to college is a middle-class value," says the student (whose own college education has conveniently supplied him with that concept). "And I don't want to impose my middle-class values on my client." His client is an intelligent, black adolescent, the only son of a mother whose hopes have been shattered by his recent drop-out from high school.

"That's good!" says the social work teacher. "I mean about your not wanting to impose your values on another person. Because that would run counter to a basic value in social work—the individual's right to make his own decisions. One day soon we must talk about that ideal and its meaning. Whether, for instance, self-determination includes acting on impulse or whether it means making a considered, knowledgeable choice. And we will need to talk also about whether there is a difference between imposing on and influencing people. But first let's look at this business of middle-class values. What are they, anyhow? Are they bad because they are middle-class? Does the economically lower-class person necessarily subscribe to a different set of values about everything? Does that class value ignorance? Or failure? Do the poor want to stay poor, or do they hope to move up in the world? Taking your young client as an example—what does he value for himself? Do you know about that?"

What is briefly illustrated here is again the several-fold approach to the examination of values both in definitional terms and in operational outcomes. What has been called to the student's attention is that the unexamined value is not worth holding. And, that beyond saying what a value means, by definition and generically, it must be scrutinized for its probable consequences as it is translated into action. Further, it can not be assumed that so-called "class values" or "culture values" are carried in the same degree or kind by every individual within a given group. In-

deed, true valuing of a person requires that *his* particular values, *his* desired ends, should be drawn out and considered if along with respect for the person we value his self-awareness and self-direction.

Involving students in clarifying their own values

Several years ago I developed a course on "Utopias and Human Welfare." My original objective was to help students to see that they are part of a long and often radiant tradition of reaching for a more perfect society, of the fashioning of social blueprints for the betterment of human existence. To both my own and the students' surprise, a second objective rose to predominance: the need to identify, face, examine, question, reevaluate, and restructure a whole complex of values that they, and I too, unthinkingly, had carried, believed in, and now found ourselves confronted with.

The students start with a zealous commitment to the idea of a society that offers the greatest good to the greatest number. So they support such legislation and regulation as will insure this value. Then they go first to live in Plato's Republic, later, in its modern counterpart, B.F. Skinner's *Walden Two*. Suddenly they are acutely uncomfortable with the infringements upon their own taken for granted individual rights. They are passionately attached to the notion and their experience of individual freedom. Then they become suddenly aware of the actual narrow boundaries which curtail their self determination in their everyday lives. Now they argue and tussle with questions such as where *laissez-faire* should end and social constraints begin; with the relation between freedom and control; with the questions of the conditions that must underpin freedom.

Again, they are firmly for "excellence." What other value could one hold for one's chosen leaders? Yet (reluctantly recognized) this desire implies elitism. On the other hand, does egalitarianism tend to

Believing and doing: values in social work education

have a down-grading effect, at the risk of valuing mediocrity?

Some warmly approve of communal living arrangements; yet few are personally ready to give up the pleasures and pains of the nuclear family. "Happiness" is unanimously valued. But what is it? What does it mean, exactly? There is considerable "unhappiness" about the shallowness of all human feeling induced in Aldous Huxley's *Brave New World*, where the avoidance of pain is a governing value. So questions fly about, asking whether "happiness" as a constant state of being is possible, whether creativity requires some soil of discomfort, whether our culture's valuing of "happiness," undefined and unexamined, has not created a great deal of personal unhappiness.

And so we go—shaken up by our recurrent awareness of the paradoxes and conflicts in our own value system, rocked by the embarrassed laughter at the recognition of the jumble of often incompatible values we have carried, and with the earnest struggle by each of us to find some workable adaptations between ideal and real.

What I illustrate by these few examples is the need for all of us to put our guiding and often unrecognized values under the scrutiny of their implications for action; our need to recognize how two or more high-level values may, at the point of being translated into action, be in sharp conflict; the fact that values infuse not only those segments of social work education that deal with the understanding of and direct service to individuals and small groups, but also those subject matters dealing with large-scale organizations, with policies and planning. The need for conscious awareness of the values that influence our doing applies at every level of social work. Not only may subjective and unanalyzed values motivate the case- and group-worker, but community planners, researchers, indeed, all of us are pushed and pulled by often unseen value assumptions and commitments. Only as we continuously raise these assumptions and commitments to full consciousness can we take possession of them.

Otherwise we, and consequently our practice, are possessed by them.

Thus the identifying and examining of action-guiding values ought to be part of every learning experience offered in social work education. This belief is a personal "value-judgment" and I admit it, cheerfully. It is a judgment based on an educational value stated earlier: that preparation for a profession should be an integrating experience, to enable the learner to see parts in connection to the whole, the ideal in relation to the possible, the cherished belief in its effect upon action, the "truth" and its consequences. Such questioning, probing, assessing, and exercise of judgment, such conscious decision-making dialogue between what I believe and what I do, must go on both within and between teacher and learner until it becomes an engrained mode of thought for each of them. It is the distinguishing mark of a professional helper that he not only is knowledgeable, that he not only is skillful, but that he is constantly striving for a "fit" between what he believes in and what he tries to make happen. Further, it is our values that bind us together, those which we all stretch to achieve even as we share together the uncertainties, the conflicts, the ifs, ands, or buts of the instruments and processes by which to grasp at them.

Cynicism and technology— traps for the unwary

In today's world, and certainly in that of social work, we desperately need that dogged search for a sense of congruence and connectedness between what we believe and what we do. Under the present day's shifting and splintering of values there lies a two-forked temptation in every profession to escape looking at its dilemmas. One is the escape into easy cynicism and the other is the escape into techniques or technology.

"A cynic," according to Oscar Wilde (himself a skeptic, not a cynic), "is a man who knows the price of everything and the value of nothing." One ponders on how a cynic is made. It seems to me that he was once an idealist whose illusions have been shattered. He was a person who once believed beyond belief, who admitted only of absolutes, whose values were such overblown bubbles that they could only burst in their contact with the dirt and crosswinds of reality. "All or nothing," he said in effect. "What is not all good is no good at all". So, protecting against his inevitable sense of defeat he turns to contempt, and abandons all consideration of values. He does what he does for want of something better. He seeks a professional degree only as a kind of "union card". He knows the price of everything and the value of nothing.

In the past few years there has been a marked rise in cost-accounting activities in many social agencies. That is as it must be. We should be held accountable. We should ask and be asked what it costs to do what we do and also how effectively we do what we do. But in the scramble to justify dollars and cents and to show results, one is aware that an overarching, pertinent value question should be asked and answered. That is "Why do you do what you do?" "What is its assumed or provable good?" "What is its value?"

A second tempting by-path in the search for certainty and security in our disordered world is toward technology worship, that of the hope and faith that certain techniques, or tricks-of-the-trade, will provide the panaceas, and will turn the screw of personal or social miseries and malaise. Chiefly, technology asks "Does it work?" Its proponents tend to assume that "If it works, it is good." They do not always ask, "Good for whom?" or "Toward what end?" or "Relative to what other possible alternatives?" Thus, there often ensues the experience of finding that some technically perfected machine or method that "works"

turns out to be noxious, "bad for people" in unanticipated ways, creating or carrying new problems in its wake.

Social work is not free of this push into technology—the search, sometimes frantic, sometimes funny or troubling, for some foolproof technique that "works," some way of helping people faster, more easily, more dramatically. In the one-tracked quest of "how to do it," the "why," the values, may be lost to sight. There may, for example, be many needful people who do not fit into the mode of a given technique, so they may be cast off; there may be quick cures of small symptoms with calculated or naive ignoring of the malaise or malady they express; there may be manipulation of people in ways that undermine human rights; there may be schemes for social reform that carry within them, unnoticed, seeds of social destruction. And the professional person himself may become, in Max Weber's phrase, a "specialist without spirit."

Every profession has its cynics and those who hold technique to be both their most valued instrument and goal. But no profession survives or thrives because of them. We survive as a profession when we represent and carry into action our culture's valued beliefs and commitments. We thrive as a profession when we can forge and demonstrate the ways by which those desired and desirable goals may be approached, reached for, and occasionally even grasped and actualized. To this ongoing task of giving life to the ideals of social work education we must continuously translate believing into doing, must continuously search out the integrations between what we profess and how we act. This task is the essential condition for a profession's wholeness, and, certainly, it is a condition for the mental and emotional wholesomeness of its practitioners.

[29]

THE RELATIONSHIP BETWEEN SCHOOLS OF SOCIAL WORK, SOCIAL RESEARCH AND SOCIAL POLICY

Richard M. Titmuss*

ONE of the odd paradoxes of international conferences of this kind is their custom of expecting the impossible from speakers and from those who have, perforce, to listen to them. We are expected to address our thoughts to immensely broad subjects which virtually defy definition in one language and culture let alone fifty; and to explore topics which will have meaning in societies preoccupied, at one end of the spectrum of wealth and poverty, with how to make self-consciousness bearable in human relations and, at the other end, with how to alleviate mass famine and disease. In short, we are expected to generalise about the human condition on a world scale; a task more appropriate, I would have thought, for religious leaders, theologians and politicians than for social workers or for people like myself described, recently and somewhat aptly by one of my Israeli social work friends, as 'faculty errand boys.'

The heart of the paradox lies in the fact that in our daily lives in Schools of Social Work we rarely if ever venture out into such academically hazardous waters. We do not discuss social research, social policy and the role of Schools of Social Work in abstract, universal terms. When we discuss such subjects at all — which I suggest is very seldom — we do so in concrete, specific frameworks. We talk about people's feelings and facial responses in the casework relationship but always in the context of particular clients or groups of clients. When we discuss social policy we do so in terms of particular, defined, problems; the need for cash aid to assist migrant workers to return to their homes; the need for better provision for abandoned children and so forth. When we discuss research — which is to-day like science an important word only to be uttered in tones of hushed and devout reverence — we have in mind specific, small and tangible projects.

What I am saying is that in our daily round of activities with students, colleagues, clients and agencies we tend to restrict ourselves to the immediate, the intimate, the precise and the manageable. And
" .... last year's words belong to last year's language. And next year's words await another voice".

We behave like Ibsen once did when he turned to village politics for some of the reasons that lead some people to turn to social work; because social action can be more psychologically comforting, and because here is something in the human condition small enough in scale to comprehend and to believe in. And it was also Ibsen, some of you will remember, who made one of his characters say that he did not read much because he found reading "irrelevant." Social workers like doctors can similarly find reading irrelevant confronted, as they generally are, by the urgencies of human misery, and the limitless bounds for exploring interpersonal relations.

Why, then, do we choose such all-embracing global topics (as the one I am now approaching with obvious hesitation) when we come together at international gatherings of this kind? And here I should add that social workers are not peculiar in this respect; psychiatrists, lawyers and sociologists are also addicted to surveying the cosmos.

I suppose one immediate and obvious answer is that it makes a change; that commodity, we are told, is good for the middle classes in all societies; it is a mark of professional and academic progress; and an example to set for the poorer classes who are so reluctant to move out of their accustomed habits and ways of life. We must get on, and we are helped to do so if others lag behind. But there is another and more understandable reason. If the purpose of such conferences as this is to exchange experiences, to broaden horizons, and to discuss uncommon as well as common problems, then we need to avoid a choice of subject which will encourage participants to indulge in competitive national 'success stories'. I must therefore apply the hint to myself and leave on one side an account of the role of my colleagues at the London School of Economics in the areas of social work, social research and social policy.

As I have now reminded you, the subject was chosen for me. I may be permitted, therefore, to examine first the assumptions which it appears to contain.

Much the most important is the assumption that there should be such a relationship: that Schools of Social Work *should* engage in research, and that through the medium of research findings and in other ways the Schools *should* influence the social policies of

* Mr. Richard M. Titmuss is Professor at the London School of Economics and Political Science.

their own countries, governmental and private. In effect, the implication is that it is a mark of a 'good' School — an index or criterion of standards — for research to be part of its functions, and for such research to be so formulated that it may or will contribute to the shaping of policy.

Now these assumptions, implicit in the subject I have been asked to discuss, should not be accepted uncritically. Nor does it follow that Schools of Social Work can only influence policies by prosecuting research. Historically, they have contributed to the shaping of policy in many countries through a variety of methods, formal and informal: by having representatives on committees of inquiry; by bringing pressure to bear on officials and politicians; by using the press and other channels of communication; and by gently persuading important people, sympathetic to the goals of social work, to talk to other important people. The Charity Organization Societies in England and in the United States had certainly developed this delicate art to a high standard in the nineteenth century. The historical evidence that is now available shows that in England the Charity Organisation Society exercised a profound influence on poor law policies eight years ago; much more powerful, though it was conducted in private and without the aid of research, than the efforts of most Schools of Social Work in the world to-day. But I remain doubtful whether the views expressed in this relationship between important people represented the opinion of those who carried the heat and burden of social work in practice. It is much more likely that policy and administration were influenced by those who were not practitioners: that what they had to say embodied the value judgments of the upper-classes occupying honorific positions at the apex of social work institutions.

The times have changed, and while these processes no doubt continue in many societies it has come to be recognised that they are no longer sufficient nor wholly satisfactory. Both those who are concerned with the making of policy and those who are concerned with its application in practice increasingly require that social policy should be more rationally based on ascertained and tested fact. In other words, it has come to be believed that social policies are more likely to be effective in practice if they are grounded in a basis of fact about reality. This belief has in part been fostered by the great achievements of scientific research in the physical world. It is only natural that workers in the field of social studies should wish to catch a little of the prestige that descends on those who engage in research.

To return, however, to the main point of my discussion. If, to proceed further, we may accept for the purposes in hand the basic assumptions underlying this choice of subject, I want now to examine the nature of the case for undertaking research. I do not wish at this stage to restrict the argument to instrumental research; that is, to research which is wholly directed to influencing policy. Research, as one particular form of intellectual activity in Schools of Social Work and other institutions concerned with the social situation, can have a number of functions and play a variety of roles. Influencing the policies of governments and private agencies is only one.

Why then in general is social research undertaken? In part it depends, of course, on what we want to study; on what we are curious to find out; on what theories we want to develop; on what expectations are placed on us by society at large. But aside from these considerations, there are at least four major groups of motives or reasons for prosecuting social research. These I will call — in no order of relative significance — the *Professional Status Case*, the *Social Policy Case*, the *Ethical Case*, and the *Education Case*. Of course they all overlap and get mixed up in reality, but I chose to classify them in this way because one can only discuss one thing at a time.

The Professional Status Case

In the hierarchy of social values which contribute to the prestige of a profession that particular activity which we call 'research' stands very high. If, moreover, it can be described as 'pure' rather than 'applied' research the professional groups concerned can almost claim to have entered the ranks of the immortals. At least they have been suitably attired. They have been purified in the waters of 'value-free' science; they are unconcerned with the relevance of their studies to this horrid and mundane world; they have published while others have perished in an inferno of uncertain status, vocational teaching and 'doing-good'.

Satirical and exaggerated though this may be, I am sure that many teachers in Schools of Social Work will appreciate the point. During the last twenty years or so, economists, sociologists, psychologists and other social scientists have understandably desired to emulate the scientists and research workers inhabiting the world of physical and biological phenomena. While this has undoubtedly set higher standards of relative objectivity for the social sciences and has advanced knowledge in many respects the consequences have not all been admirable.

Research and publication have been elevated to the detriment of teaching; research has been seen solely as a means of individual self-advancement sometimes at the expense of defenceless groups who have unethically been made the subject of investigation; methodology has been made compulsorily 'respectable' for all to the point of boredom for the many; the most incurious and unimaginative souls have been led to think that a questionnaire, a random sample of delinquents, and a computer could entirely compensate for the lack of an idea and, finally, policy-makers have been persuaded to postpone action until research has been undertaken, Ph. D's acquired and the professional reputation of the participants has been suitably enhanced.

Society can be asked to pay a heavy price for scientism induced or begotten by professionalism. Bernard Shaw once said that "professions are conspiracies against the laity"; scientism can be too. We know that in the field of medicine there has been a proliferation of trials of new drugs in the sacred name of science and professional advancement without adequate ethical safeguards for patients. For the same reasons, we know that psychologists and sociologists have asked children questions about their parents which no social worker, worthy of the name, could possibly condone. There is, in short, a danger that concern for the value and uniqueness of the individual human being may be diminished if the scientific outlook spreads to embrace more and more of human affairs; it is after all in the nature of science to be chiefly preoccupied with groups, trends, laws and generalisations. And it is a characteristic of the less gifted and less perceptive research worker to cordon himself off in a tiny area of specialised study. As most of us realize at some time in our lives, it is great comfort to acquire "one small allotment in the vastness of the knowable" [1] where one feels a little more at home and in peace; a little more professionally secure.

Research workers retire to cultivate their ten square inches of social phenomena for much the same reasons as caseworkers continually reexamine their feelings about dominant mothers and passive fathers, and doctors retreat behind the scientific barricades of the hospital. They are all looking for security and neutrality to protect and perfect their professional souls in an increasingly complex and changing world.

These may well be dangerous and unjust thoughts; in voicing them I would not wish you to think that I am opposed to the advance of science and rationality in human affairs. On the contrary, I believe that we need more research and more study, theoretical and applied, in the field of the social sciences. Only in such ways, and always seeing research as a servant and not as a master, will man be able to obtain some better control over his environment and acquire more freedom to develop his talents and his personality. As Vivekanda has said "There is no good work that has not a touch of evil in it. . . . We should engage in such works which bring the largest amount of good and the smallest measure of evil" [2] Social research should not be excepted from the application of this principle.

Having warned you of what should be avoided in the 'why' and the 'how' of research, I want now to examine the case for more research related to social policy.

The Social Policy Case

The essence of the 'social' case for more research in the field of policy is that it may enlarge human freedoms. This is true insofar as the findings and application of research substitute fact for assertion; reality for myth; tolerance for prejudice. Social diagnosis is needed as well as individual therapy: the two should go hand-in-hand in Schools of Social Work. To pursue the latter, while neglecting the former is to fall into the error, however unconsciously, of seeing the function of diagnostic casework as (and I quote from Miss Gordon Hamilton's work) "adaptation to reality". [3] Two assumptions underly this conception of the caseworker's function which has appeared in a substantial number of textbooks. The first is that reality is something which the caseworker knows but the client does not; the second is that if adaptation is genuinely to take place reality must genuinely be accepted by the caseworker.

The ultimate logic of this is to make the caseworker a prisoner of the collective *status quo;* consequently, she will have little or nothing to contribute to the shaping of social policy. She will not in fact desire to do so. This is another way of saying, what Professor Lipset, the sociologist, said recently in his book *Political Man,* that we in the West have reached the end of the political dialogue. The caseworker and the sociologist thus both deny in their different ways that reality like love (in Thomas Hardy's words) "is never stationary".

The inescapable fact, regardless of whether we like

(1) Combrich E. H., *The Tradition of General Knowledge*, L.S.E., 1962 p. 15.
(2) *Thus Spoke Vivekanda*, (Madras, Shri Ramakrishna Math, 1955), p. 35.
(3) Hamilton G., *Principles and Techniques in Social Case Work*, (Ed., C. Kasius), 1950, p. 89.

the world as it is to-day, is that we are all living in a period of startlingly rapid change. In the past, economic and social changes were effected only at the price of immense hardship. The amount and rate of change under way to-day, and affecting all countries in varying degrees, may in some areas be less crudely evident in strictly economic terms but the consequences as a whole may be no less profound — though more subtly expressed — in generating social frustration and psychological stress. In other respects, economic and industrial changes dominate the problems of societies in transition. In all countries, the question of "how we live together in society" is made more insistent by the widespread and pervasive effects of technological change. Yet little is known about how all these factors of change are affecting levels of poverty and need, patterns of family living, and community relations. Change, however induced, cannot take place without people being hurt. In consequence, new and different social needs are continually arising, many of which are (or should be) the direct concern of social workers and social welfare programs.

To identify and meet these needs and to minimise and prevent the hardships caused by change, social policy should be better informed. More and better data about the human condition, constructive and critical, should be at the disposal of policy-makers and administrators. Their particular myths — about poverty and unmet need, about racial prejudice, about social injustice — require to be attacked by community diagnosis. Research can be one weapon — though as I have said by no means the only one — in the challenge to be more intelligent and rational in the process of shaping and applying social welfare measures. Nor is the argument for research in these fields wholly an instrumental one; the findings of such research can be of general educational value in advancing our knowledge of human behaviour in situations of change.

Should Schools of Social Work contribute to this process of community diagnosis and, by so doing, help to educate society in the need for action? For me, there is only one answer to this question. The alternative could mean, in the ultimate analysis, accepting the position that there is little truth in the claim of social work to be more in touch than any other profession with the poor and the unable, and that all it can offer is individual therapy in the context of a social reality wholly determined by others.

The Ethical Case

Ethical problems of confidentiality and the legal rights of clients as citizens continually confront the

social worker as they do members of other professions. The day-to-day administration of social policy as well as the detailed formulation of policy itself also involves basic ethical issues. Let me give you one example, illustrating the ethical components of policy, which will, I hope, underline the need for research by Schools of Social Work. Although this particular example is drawn from experience in the United States, there is little doubt that it could be paralleled in most countries in the world which have established some system of public assistance however rudimentary.

In many American States, and in the District of Columbia, it is common practice for authorities to make unannounced inspections of the homes of persons receiving public assistance. Often such searches are made without warrants and in the middle of the night. The purpose of the inspections is to check on recipients' eligibility for assistance. Eligibility, under state and local law (in the United States and many other countries), may be determined by various aspects of a family's circumstances, including the presence or absence of an adult man capable of supporting the family. The demand for entry may carry with it the threat, express or implied, that refusal to admit will lead to discontinuance of public assistance. And many of those on public assistance are unable for reasons of poverty, ignorance or fear to protect their own rights as citizens.

Mr. Charles Reich, Assistant Professor of Law at Yale University, published last year a study of 'Midnight Welfare Searches'.[4] He came to the conclusion that these invasions of privacy, as commonly practised, represented "a flagrant violation of the fourth and fourteenth amendments of the Federal Constitution". "A not uncommon psychology", commented Mr. Reich, "leads those who dispense welfare to feel it only just that the beneficiaries give up something in return. To some public officials, opening one's home to inspection evidently seems a reasonable condition to impose on those whose homes are supported by a public agency. In many other ways, subtle and obvious, the recipients of public bounty are made to pay a similar price. They may be asked to observe standards of morality not imposed on the rest of the community".

Social self-criticism is an essential part of the democratic process, and it is a tribute to Mr. Reich that this study in a neglected area of social policy should have been made. In how many other countries, one is led to ask, would not similar studies be justified to-day?

This question is of special concern to Schools of Social Work because of their responsibilities for teach-

(4) Reich C. A., *Yale Law Journal*, Vol. 72, No. 7, p. 1347, 1963.

ing and for providing the leadership that is expected of them in relation to professional standards. It raises in particular, however, two basic ethical issues. The first is: should recipients of welfare be discriminated against in respect of certain fundamental rights and have different standards of morality imposed on them? And the second is: should social workers take part, directly or indirectly, willingly or unwillingly, in such practices as those described by Mr. Reich?

In recent years, Mrs. Audrey Harvey in England and Mr. Keith-Lucas and Mr. Alvin Schorr in the United States have examined different aspects of these basic issues.[5] The latter, in a paper published in 1962, offered evidence that casework practice had been moving toward more coercive behaviour, thus contradicting one of the central commitments of social work; namely, free advice for clients and the enlargement of self-determination.

Many social workers in the United States and other countries are aware of the public and private pressures which may drive them into situations of moral conflict. The National Association of Social Workers in the United States has protested vigorously about the violation of the civil rights of welfare recipients and has condemned the unethical implications of "midnight raids."[6] Social workers in Washington have published a report on the functioning of the public welfare system and have drawn attention to the punitive aspects of various regulations.[7] In London, groups of social workers have been formed specifically to study the ethical and practical implications of restrictions and restraints in social welfare programmes.

These are illustrations of the role of research and inquiry in areas of basic concern to social work. To explore such questions fully would take me far outside my terms of reference. In any event, this would be difficult because when one examines the literature for a number of countries it is surprising to find how few studies have been made. My purpose in raising them in this general way, however, was to point the need for research, and to suggest that here at least was an area of social policy of vital concern to Schools of Social Work because of its ethical implications for professional standards, as well as its social and psychological implications for those at the receiving end of welfare.

The Educational Case

Finally, I turn to the fourth of my reasons for sup-

posing that Schools of Social Work should engage in research in the social policy area. By now, I have probably already said enough to substantiate the arguments for research on educational grounds. However, there are one or two further points which I may add by way of conclusion.

Education, as distinct from propaganda, is about freedom; it increases awareness of possible choices. To enable clients better to exercise choice is an integral part of the functions of social work and here, it may be said, the social worker as an individual enacts an educational role which is sanctioned as such by society. Furthermore, I would submit that social work as an institution (like medicine and the law) has a broad educational role in relation to public opinion at large to diagnose, explain and inform.

Historically, individual social workers in many countries have contributed to educating the community about the need for social action; that is to say for collective policies, public and voluntary, to change environments and situations and to provide for unmet needs. They have identified and described particular and general problems of poverty, ignorance, neglect, deprivation and injustice. They have done so not primarily for professional reasons but because of a compassionate concern for the welfare of others, and because of their own inner needs to continue to live with a sense of helplessness; it was therefore necessary to call attention — to be articulate about — the greater helplessness of others.

Today, this problem of community education is more complex. Social work, like other 'service' occupations, has become more organised and professionalized and thus subject to codes of neutrality. Moreover, many more social workers today are employees of large organisations or agencies, public and private, and subject, as employees, to regulations enjoining political neutrality. These codes or expectations required by professional and employing bodies call for supposedly objective attitudes which demand (as Professor Everett Hughes has pointed out in another context) "an apparent neutrality toward those very problems where neutrality makes one appear a potential ally of the enemy."[8] We may interpret the "enemy" in this case as those who support the prevailing system of values in society and their attendant social provisions and policies.

(5) Harvey A., *Casualties of the Welfare State*, 1960; Keith-Lucas A., *Decisions About People in Need*, 1957; Schorr A. L., *Social Work*, Vol. 7, No. 1, pp. 60-5, 1962. See also Mencher S., *Social Work*, Vol. 8, No. 3, p. 59, 1963, and Keith-Lucas A., *Social Work*, Vol. 8, No. 3, p. 66, 1963.
(6) *Midnight Raids*, A Statement by the National Association of Social Workers Inc., New York, 1964.
(7) *The Public Welfare Crisis in the Nation's Capital*, Metropolitan Washington Chapter, National Association of Social Workers, 1963.
(8) Hughes Everett C., "The Academic Mind: Two Views", *American Sociological Review*, Vol. 24, No. 4, 1959.

To these new problems of community diagnosis and education I must add another. Theoretical and methodological advances in the social sciences in recent decades have meant that the analysis and description of social problems can no longer be conducted by social workers in isolation and with the relatively cruder tools of the past. It is not enough for social workers to talk to social workers; to be effective in this broad educational role they now need allies. In the past, these allies were sought in the higher reaches of the class and power structure; today, they have also to be found in the social sciences.

All these reasons, I suggest, support the case for Schools of Social Work to engage in research and to devote some of their studies to problems of social policy; its formation, application and revision. The trend towards professionalization combined with changes in the contractual relations between social workers and their employers has in particular placed — almost unwillingly — new and heavy responsibilities on Schools of Social Work. As yet, these have been little recognised. But Schools of Social Work are not alone in this respect. More division of labour within professional groupings; more emphasis on technical skills and expertise; more 'bigness' in the organisation and distribution of personal service; more explicit codes of neutrality; all these factors are affecting the professions in general, and medicine and social work in particular. They are making it harder for the individual practitioner and his or her professional association or trade union to play a critical, protesting and educational role in society. Thus, some part of this role now devolves — if it devolves anywhere — on teaching institutions. In short, and for our purposes, on Schools of Social Work.

Professor Dorothy Emmet in England has wisely said that the description and definition of a profession "has a moral element built into it".[9] To this I would add that if Schools of Social Work are not to be limited to training in techniques they also must now have a functional moral element built into them.

(9) Emmet D. L., "The Notion of a Professional Code," *Crucible*, Oct. 1962, p. 104.

[30]

An Innovative Approach to Educating Medical Students about Pharmaceutical Promotion

Michael S. Wilkes, MD, PhD, and Jerome R. Hoffman, MA, MD

ABSTRACT

Prescription drugs comprise approximately 9% of the total cost of health care in the United States. The manner in which doctors obtain information about new and changing pharmaceuticals obviously has the potential to have a profound impact on health care costs, pharmaceutical companies' profits, and the quality of health care. Patterns learned in medical school undoubtedly influence physicians' future behaviors. The authors describe an educational program, in which university pharmacists portrayed pharmaceutical company representatives to model a promotional presentation, that they designed to generate critical thinking among third-year medical students regarding the influence of pharmaceutical representatives on the prescribing practices of physicians. The authors also provide information suggesting that the program increased the uncertainty many students felt about the accuracy and ethics of standard drug "detailing." *Acad. Med.* 2001;76:1271–1277.

Prescription drugs comprise approximately 9% of the total cost of health care in the United States, but physicians who are responsible for such prescribing are frequently unaware of both the costs and the consequences,[1] and in many cases the prescriptions that are written lack adequate medical indications. Over 85% of today's prescription drugs have been introduced into clinical practice in the past 30 years: A 55-year-old physician who graduated in the mid-1960s learned about only a small minority of the medicines in current use during his or her formal training. In the year 2000 alone, the Food and Drug Administration (FDA) approved 98 new drug products. How doctors obtain the information about new and changing pharmaceuticals that will inform their choices when prescribing obviously has the potential to have a profound impact on health care costs and pharmaceutical companies' profits.

There are a variety of ways for physicians to attempt to stay current with new medicines, including reading publications in peer-reviewed and non–peer-reviewed journals and newsletters and participating in continuing education courses. Some of these courses are funded by part of the enormous amount of money that the pharmaceutical industry spends on promotions to physicians.[2] The industry also supports "detailing" activities, publications, and research projects, and the distinction between promotion and education is frequently unclear.[3–7] Proprietary advertising frequently fails to conform to the FDA's guidelines regarding fairness and accuracy.[7,8] There is, however, substantial evidence that promotional money is well spent, from the point of the view of the companies, because it greatly influences physicians' behaviors.[9] Even young physicians in residency training programs appear to accept a great deal of such material uncritically.[10]

As directors of a medical school curriculum designed to focus on aspects of (among other things) health care economics, medical ethics, clinical pharmacology, and evidence-based medicine, we have been interested in fostering critical thinking among students. We are also keenly interested in teaching students how to access and evaluate information in the medical literature as it becomes available. Because we are aware that students and house officers interact regularly with pharmaceutical representatives, we created an educational program for students that we hoped would educate them about some elements of drug marketing, and help them to evaluate the choices they will have in dealing with proprietary interests in the future. In conjunction with this program we devised a pre- and

Dr. **Wilkes** is professor of medicine and vice dean for education, University of California, Davis, School of Medicine, and former senior chair of UCLA's Doctoring Curriculum. Dr. **Hoffman** is director of the Doctoring Program and professor of emergency medicine at the University of California, Los Angeles, UCLA School of Medicine.

Correspondence should be addressed to Dr. Wilkes, UC Davis School of Medicine, 1 Shields Avenue, MS-1C, Davis, CA 95616; e-mail: ⟨mwilkes@ucdavis.edu⟩. Reprints are not available.

post-program questionnaire to evaluate its impact on students' attitudes about the accuracy and ethics of standard drug detailing.

EDUCATIONAL INTERVENTION

UCLA's Doctoring Program

The University of California, Los Angeles, UCLA School of Medicine's (UCLA's) Doctoring Program[11] is a vertically and horizontally integrated longitudinal curriculum that runs through all four years of medical school. In their third year of the program, small groups of seven to eight students and two faculty tutors meet every other week to evaluate standardized cases, with a goal of promoting skills, attitudes, and knowledge in a variety of areas not traditionally addressed in the clinical portion of medical school. Key topic areas are ethics, health care economics, health services, preventive medicine, clinical pharmacology, clinical decision making, behavioral medicine, and communication skills.

All of the small-group faculty participate in a full-day training session at the beginning of the academic year and attend a one-hour faculty development session prior to the beginning of each day's three-hour group exercise. This ongoing faculty development ensures standardization and continuity in the presentation of the central educational issues of each session.

Pharmaceutical Promotion Exercise

The educational exercise was designed as a component of the Doctoring Program to address the impact of pharmaceutical manufacturers on physicians' behavior. The session was scheduled toward the very end of the academic year (June), and students were not given any advance notice of the content of the exercise. The course's faculty was informed about the program through the

regular distribution of a faculty tutor guide describing the exercise in detail two weeks before the small-group session occurred. Faculty members were asked not to reveal anything about the nature of the exercise to students prior to its completion. On the day of the educational intervention small-group faculty attended a one-hour training session co-taught by the university pharmacists and one of the course directors who created the exercise. The faculty development session stressed the overall objectives of the exercise:

1. To understand the reasons for detailing pharmaceuticals to the medical profession
2. To understand potential advantages and disadvantages of pharmaceutical–medical professional interactions
3. To understand the impact of pharmaceutical promotion on health care costs
4. To discuss possible reasons in support of and against accepting gifts intended to influence prescribing behaviors
5. To understand the accuracy and honesty of information that is conveyed to physicians by pharmaceutical company detailers

The exercise itself consisted of a presentation by UCLA full-time pharmacists playing the role of a pharmaceutical representative before each of the small groups. Each pharmacist gave the eight students and two faculty members in each group (18 groups total, meeting on four separate mornings) a 20-minute talk on the virtues of a non-sedating antihistamine. The students were unaware that these "drug reps" were actually UCLA pharmacists.

The students were told at the outset of the session that the Doctoring Program's directors had decided that, because students would be exposed to pharmaceutical representatives on a regular basis throughout their careers, one such encounter should be presented

in the Doctoring Program. They were further told that the drug reps, all of whom represented the same pharmaceutical company, would have an opportunity to make a brief presentation to the group on behalf of a very popular and aggressively marketed medication, and would then be willing to answer questions, both about the product itself and about their presentation. The drug reps brought handouts, supportive educational and promotional materials (including items such as pens and writing tablets), and a snack of bagels and cream cheese (actually provided by the Doctoring Program) to the meeting.

The five pharmacists who portrayed the drug reps were UCLA Pharmacy and Therapeutics Committee members, drug information specialists, and ambulatory and inpatient clinical pharmacists, including one individual who had previously worked as a pharmaceutical representative. The pharmacists had all previously attended two training sessions run by the course directors and pharmacy director in which institutional policies and procedures and FDA guidelines regarding pharmaceutical representatives were reviewed. The participating pharmacists had had extensive personal experience meeting with pharmaceutical representatives in the course of their duties. The pharmacists selected the medication to be detailed in the intervention (a non-sedating antihistamine) because it was one that was actively being promoted. Further, the pharmacists had seen the current marketing approaches that had been used by the pharmaceutical representatives promoting the drug. These pharmacists' experiences were collated and reviewed for conformity with overall industry tactics and standards. A presentation script was developed, with the help of the UCLA Director of Pharmaceutical Services, to allow the pharmacists to make standardized presentations to the students. The pharmacists used actual materials that had previously been given to the university's pharmacy by the manufacturer of the drug being "detailed." The pharmacists practiced the presentations individually and together to assure that the standardized goals were accomplished and that the presentations, while deliberately designed to accent the benefits associated with the drug being promoted, sounded believable, and did not contain any outright untruths. In addition, the presentations were scripted so that each contained the following elements:

1. Anecdotal references to use by physicians at other university hospitals
2. Somewhat exaggerated (favorable) claims about toxicity and side effects
3. Claims of effectiveness citing information based on doses different from those used in common practice
4. No mention of adverse effects
5. Assertions about relative efficacy without supporting documentation
6. No information about costs
7. Reference to "their" product by its trade name, but to all products of potential competitors by generic name only

After the "drug rep" finished the prepared talk, the students were encouraged to ask questions. If the following questions were not asked by students, faculty were instructed to ask how much the drug cost relative to competitors, what the side effects of the drug were compared with other drugs, and whether there had been any trials comparing the drug head-to-head with competitively marketed agents (other second-generation antihistamines). Once all questions were answered (in a standardized, reproducible manner, as well as could be anticipated) the drug reps were thanked and left the room. Students were then led through an exercise intended to critique the presentation, and specifically to address whether:

• the presentation had been balanced,
• the presentation had been accurate,

• the presenter had adequately backed up his or her claims,
• the presenter had discussed economic implications of use of the drug,
• the presenter had fairly compared the promoted drug with alternatives,
• this had been a useful educational experience, and
• the student would be more or less likely to use the drug in question after hearing the presentation.

Following this 20-minute discussion the drug rep was invited back into the classroom and reintroduced to the students as a university pharmacist and drug information consultant. The hospital pharmacists were asked to explain how their presentations reflected actual marketing strategies, as well as to point out any distortions or omissions they had made during their initial presentation.

The pharmacists talked with the students about the training and background of pharmaceutical detailers, and the process of common marketing approaches, including the use of claims and comparisons, gifts, and sponsored talks. In addition, the students explored how and why manufacturers manipulate information to benefit sales of their products. The group discussed what impact promotional activity has on health care, the impact of detailing on the costs of drugs to consumers, and possible reasons and rationales physicians give for accepting or refusing to accept gifts from manufacturers. As the last part of the exercise, the students were shown how to access unbiased, evidence-based drug information using the university hospitals' computer system. This completed the educational intervention.

Pre–Post-intervention Survey

Before the small-group sessions began, the students completed a self-administered, anonymous questionnaire containing 26 items dealing with the interface between the pharmaceutical manufacturers and the medical profession. The questionnaire had previously been pilot tested on a group of fourth-year medical students to assure that the questions were understandable and to measure the time needed to complete the instrument. The third-year students were asked to provide their opinions to help assess the relationship between pharmaceutical manufacturers and trainees. Specific instructions to the students read:

> Recent UCLA Department policies have limited contact between pharmaceutical detailers and trainees. This policy has led to a debate in some sectors. The pharmaceutical industry contends that their activities provide an educational service to students, residents, and faculty. Others feel such practices are simply marketing strategies with no educational value. We have decided to allow representatives of several companies to come here to make a presentation to you about one of their drugs. The *only other stipulation* was that we be allowed to critique their talk.
>
> Before we ask them to come in this morning, we would like to ask you a few questions about how you feel about the services they provide. Take five minutes and complete the anonymous survey.

We also administered a post-intervention survey (completed as part of a larger mandatory year-end medical school curriculum-assessment exercise). This survey took place 12 weeks after the educational session and involved a post-intervention self-administered questionnaire, which examined the same attitudes included in the pre-intervention survey.

IMPACT OF THE INTERVENTION

Full data from the questionnaires were available for 120 students (12% of the students did not complete both questionnaires, because of illness, away rotations, or vacation). Group demographics and data about the types and degrees of contact between the students and pharmaceutical marketing representatives are shown in Table 1. During the third year of medical school every member of the third-year class had received at least one gift from a pharmaceutical company, and more than a third had been given a dinner at a restaurant and free drug samples. There was no apparent difference in students' acceptance of such gifts based on gender or ethnicity.

Attitudes toward Interactions with Pharmaceutical Manufacturers

Students' attitudes toward drug company sponsorship of research, drug company–physician interactions (detailing), and drug advertisements as educational tools changed after their participation in the educational program (see Table 2). In each case, these changes were mostly reflected by increases in the numbers of students who had initially been confident that the issue in question was not problematic, but who then had become uncertain about this. For example, responses to the post-intervention questionnaire showed that, while a few more students disagreed with the statement that "drug company sponsored research is indispensable," many more were unsure whether this was true. The same effect was found regarding their views about whether material presented at drug company-sponsored seminars is "unbiased," whether "such drug company-sponsored research is as likely to reach negative conclusions about the company's drugs as is research from an alternative sponsor," whether "when drug companies give physicians pens, calendars, or other non-educational materials, this biases the subsequent behavior of those physicians," and whether product information presented in drug advertisements serves an educational purpose.

The majority of students did not feel that it was unethical for physicians to interact with pharmaceutical company representatives, and this attitude was not dramatically affected by the intervention. However, more students were "uncertain" about every one of the issues addressed on the questionnaire after the intervention (see Tables 2 and 3). Very few students perceived an ethical conflict between providing the best possible care to patients and accepting small trinkets from a pharmaceutical company, and only a third found a problem with accepting free meals at a restaurant.

Attitudes toward Future Behaviors

After the educational exercise, even fewer students (25%, compared with 35% initially) felt they were sufficiently "skilled" to be able to critically assess claims made by pharmaceutical advertisements and promotions. Once again, this change primarily reflected an increase in the number of students who now felt "uncertain" in this area.

Similarly, after the educational intervention, the number of students who stated they would want to have drug company representatives available to them during their residency decreased from 86% to 61%. This was not because more students felt clearly opposed to such an arrangement (only 8% at both of the assessments), but because of a concomitant increase in the number of students who felt uncertain about the desirability of such an arrangement (6% to 31%). The same pattern was evident with regard to their expectations about meeting with detailers after completion of residency training.

About one third of our students felt that voluntary guidelines would be an effective method of assuring that drug company promotional and educational activities are accurate and fairly balanced. More than three fourths felt that the FDA should aggressively punish drug companies that violate established rules regarding balance and accuracy.

Table 1

Characteristics of 120 Third-year Medical Students Participating in an Intervention on Pharmaceutical Promotion	
Characteristic	
Mean age	26 years
Men	57%
Race or ethnicity	
African American	14%
White	42%
Latino American	9%
Asian American	35%
Received a gift at some time during medical school	
Small personal items (e.g., pen or mug)	95%
Book or other learning tool	68%
Medical tool (stethoscope, EKG caliper, etc.)	31%
Dinner at a restuarant	35%
Piece of clothing with drug or company name on it (hat, umbrella, tee shirt, etc.)	17%
Free drug samples	43%
Other	5%

Table 2

Third-year Medical Students' Pre- and Post-intervention Responses to Statements Concerning Pharmaceutical Companies' Interactions with Physicians

Statement	Pre-test		Post-test	
	% Agree (Mean)	% Uncertain	% Uncertain	% Agree (Mean)
When drug companies sponsor physicians to go to seminars at resort locations this biases the subsequent behavior of those physicians (e.g., they prescribe more of the company's product).	18 (3.49)	18	33	46* (2.77)
When drug companies give physicians textbooks or other educational materials, this influences their subsequent behavior.	18 (3.44)	16	31	32 (3.92)
When drug companies give physicians pens, calendars, or other non-educational materials, this biases the subsequent behavior of those physicians.	13 (3.53)	12	29	20* (3.82)
Drug company promotions are less likely to be about unique drugs than about drugs that are essentially similar to drugs made by other companies.	31 (2.90)	43	49	41 (2.74)
Drug company gifts to physicians do not significantly increase health care costs to patients.	26 (3.11)	36	48	13 (3.28)
Product information presented in a drug advertisement provides you with educational material about the drug.	49 (2.75)	28	41	43† (2.73)
Once they have finished their formal training, have no alternative but to rely on drug company detailing to learn about new drugs.	6 (3.8)	9	19	8 (3.65)

*$p < .05$; †$p < .01$.

Table 3

Third-year Medical Students' Pre- and Post-intervention Responses to Statements Concerning Beliefs about the Ethics of Pharmaceutical–Medical Community Interactions

Statement	Pre-test		Post-test	
	% Agree (Mean)	% Uncertain	% Uncertain	% Agree (Mean)
It is unethical for academic researchers to be funded by drug companies to do research.	12 (3.41)	35	31	12 (3.45)
It is unethical for academic experts to take money from drug companies for giving lectures on topic of their own choosing.	11 (3.56)	43	57	12 (3.43)
It is unethical for academic experts to take money from drug companies for giving lectures at company sponsored seminars.	12 (3.53)	23	37	13 (3.37)
It is unethical for physicians to accept drug company funding to attend seminars at resort locations.	26 (3.30)	18	32	33* (3.02)
It is unethical for physicians to accept free textbooks or other educational materials from drug companies.	18 (3.40)	13	22	27 (3.88)
It is unethical for physicians to accept free pens, calendars, or other non-educational materials from drug companies.	3 (3.83)	11	26	4 (3.67)
It is less ethical for fully trained physicians in practice to accept gifts from drug companies than it is for house officers or students (who are typically making far smaller salaries and who are not charging for their services).	8 (3.84)	15	17	14 (3.42)

*$p < .05$.

DISCUSSION

Physicians prescribe pharmaceuticals throughout their professional lives, but because new drugs are being approved and marketed so quickly, it is likely that most current medical students will ultimately prescribe a great many medicines about which they had received no training in medical school or residency. The pharmaceutical industry spends enormous amounts of money promoting its products to physicians, and pharmaceutical promotions are indeed one of the primary sources of information many physicians rely upon in making drug choices, as well as in "learning about" unfamiliar medications.

There is evidence, however, that promotional material may not always be balanced, accurate, or fair, such that uncritical acceptance of claims made by a proprietary interest can lead to widespread prescribing patterns that are hard to justify on the basis of the medical literature.[7,8] Habits learned in medical school may affect behaviors throughout physicians' careers, so we designed this exercise to try to encourage students to think critically when presented with promotional material from pharmaceutical companies. We designed this innovative educational exercise to challenge some non-critical beliefs already established in the minds of many third-year students and to lead them to question the reliability of promotional presentations.

We chose to perform the exercise, rather than merely presenting information from the literature reflecting concerns about pharmaceutical promotions, because we felt the latter approach would probably be met with skepticism. Many physicians respond with disbelief, or even hostility, when it is suggested that their judgments can be influenced or distorted by "gifts" and favors from industry. It is our experience that many students, likewise, feel patronized, or offended, when "lectured to" about ethical issues such as those raised by physicians' interactions with pharmaceutical representatives (particularly when these interactions come with financial inducements attached). Although we did feel some discomfort about having hospital pharmacists pretend to be actual company representatives, we ultimately felt that this was not a major concern because students would learn the true nature of the exercise before leaving the session. Furthermore, we felt the stimulation associated with this "live" presentation would give us the opportunity to make an impression upon students and facilitate serious discussion of complex issues.

We made every effort to assure that the exercise itself was fair by asking the UCLA Department of Pharmacy to design a presentation that honestly reflected standard industry presentations. The pharmacists who participated had all had extensive experience with drug representatives and company promotions, and all had studied this issue extensively during their own training at UCLA. Presentations contained no demonstrably false statement about the drug being promoted, but included the types of emphases and suggestions that are commonly used to make a product seem most desirable. The participating pharmacists did bring a small amount of food for the students, but the level of "inducements" was very low for a promotional presentation. The pharmacists' discussions of their presentation, once the students were aware of the true nature of the exercise, stressed the subtle ways that positive attributes can be emphasized and less positive ones can be avoided or sidestepped. The presentations never suggested that promotions include lies or unethical behavior on the part of representatives.

The pre- and post-intervention results, while far from definitive, do suggest that the students' attitudes were affected by this exercise. Furthermore, the primary impact does seem to have been that the students became more uncertain about the issues raised, rather than that they adopted frankly negative beliefs or feelings. Regardless of whether the questions dealt with the accuracy of companies' promotions and presentations, the quality of sponsored research, the nature of the interaction between physicians and company representatives, or students' individual behaviors in the future, a majority of the students apparently had no concern or ethical doubt prior to the exercise, whereas a greater number of such students expressed uncertainty about the same matters three months later.

We have no idea to what extent these probable changes in attitude are durable, or whether (even in the short term) they would actually be associated with changes in behaviors. We do not believe our duty as educators, though, is to influence our students to adopt particular positions at the expense of others. Rather, our duty is to raise questions and concerns in the minds of students, and teach them to think critically—including about aspects of the "medical culture" into which they have been so forcefully introduced. We believe that this exercise, which raises issues medical students will have to confront throughout their careers, was successful in stimulating that process.

The authors are extremely grateful for the assistance of the Department of Pharmaceutical Services at UCLA and particularly for the guidance and support of UCLA Pharmaceutical Director Diane Zelba, PharmD.

REFERENCES

1. Caudill TS, Johnson MS, Rich EC, McKinney WP. Physicians, pharmaceutical sales representatives, and the cost of prescribing. Arch Fam Med. 1996;5:201–6.
2. Wolfe SM. Why do American drug companies spend more than $12 billion a year pushing drugs? Is it education or promotion? Characteristics of materials distributed by drug companies: four points of view. J. Gen Intern Med. 1996;11:637–9.
3. Wahlbeck K, Cheine M, Esssali MA. Clozapine vs. typical neuroleptic medication for schizophrenia. In: Cochrane Collaboration.

Cochrane Library. Issue 4. Oxford Update Software, 1998.

4. Cho MK, Bero LA. The quality of studies published in symposium proceedings. Ann Intern Med. 1996;124:485–9.

5. Lexchin J. Interactions between physicians and the pharmaceutical industry: what does the literature say? Can Med Assoc J. 1993; 149:1401–6

6. Orlowski JP, Wateska L. The effects of pharmaceutical firm enticements on physician prescribing patterns: there's no such thing as a free lunch. Chest. 1992;102:270–5.

7. Stryer D, Bero LA. Characteristics of materials distributed by drug companies: an evaluation of appropriateness. J Gen Intern Med. 1996; 11:575–83.

8. Wilkes MS, Doblin BH, Shapiro MF. Pharmaceutical advertisements in leading medical journals: experts' assessments. Ann Intern Med. 1992;116:912–9.

9. Chren MM, Landesfeld CS. Physicians' behavior and their interactions with drug companies. JAMA. 1994;271:684–9.

10. Ziegler MG, Lew P, Singer BC. The accuracy of drug information from pharmaceutical sales representatives. JAMA. 1995;273:1296–8.

11. Wilkes M, Slavin S, Usatine R. Doctoring: a longitudinal generalist curriculum. Acad Med. 1994;69:191–3.

Part IX
The Obligation to Attend to
Harming in the Name of Helping

[31]

Reification of Psychiatric Diagnoses as Defamatory: Implications for Ethical Clinical Practice

Sonja Grover, PhD, CPsych

Lakehead University
Thunder Bay, Ontario, Canada

While the mental health professional generally has beneficent motives and an honest belief in the DSM diagnoses assigned to clients, such diagnoses may yet be defamatory when communicated to third parties. Mental health diagnoses invariably lower the individual's reputation in the eyes of the community. At the same time, DSM diagnoses are but one out of a myriad of possible interpretive frameworks. DSM descriptors for the client's distress thus cannot be said to capture the essence of the client's personhood. When a diagnosis is published as if it captured a definitive truth about an individual psychiatric client, it is, in that important regard, inaccurate. That is, such a communication meets the criterion for a reckless disregard for the truth or an honest belief but without reasonable basis insofar as it is considered to be anything more than a working hypothesis. Hence, in certain cases, DSM labeling may constitute defamation.

Keywords: DSM diagnostic categories, defamation, ethics, clinical practice, mental disorder

Why write an article on whether DSM-IV diagnostic categories (American Psychiatric Association, 1995) might be comprised of terms that are defamatory when communicated beyond the client-therapist context? The answer is that the question of whether the DSM-IV or any subsequent version is potentially defamatory is not a quaint academic intellectual teaser, but rather a fundamental human rights issue. That psychiatric diagnosis is damaging to one's reputation in the community is not generally disputed despite protestations from the progressively minded in some quarters to the contrary: "One could argue that any person who is 'freeze-framed' . . . with an identity as a mental patient finds that identity ultimately damaging" (R.W. Manderscheid, 1993, cited in Susko, 1994, p. 94).

Reputation is a vital aspect of personal identity and psychological integrity and one aspect of the human right referred to as "security of the person." When one's reputation is assailed there is generally some level of psychological distress. Birchwood, Mason, and colleagues (1993) found that perceived stigmatization was a significant predictor of depression in persons diagnosed at some point with mental illness. If the assault on one's good name is profound enough there may even ensue a loss of self-esteem and some confusion about self-identity. Further, the loss of reputation can severely impact one's ability to exercise one's liberty rights. This is to say that the diagnosis when published will in all likelihood damage the reputation and interfere with the range and quality of life choices available to the individual so labeled. For instance, should an individual be regarded as untrustworthy and manipulative as a function of their "borderline personality" diagnosis, this may affect employment prospects. If the individual is viewed as volatile and unpredictable given the diagnosis of "anti-social personality disorder," this is likely to affect the potential for successful interpersonal relationships with those who have made such pre-judgments based on the diagnosis. The label of "schizophrenic" (even if qualified by the phrase "in remission") may lead to inferences about a potential for future cognitive disin-tegration and associated lack of mental competence for those who come to know the di-agnostic information. This may in turn influence such matters as the individual's bid for political or other responsible office and so on.

CONFIDENTIALITY AND QUALIFIED PRIVILEGE

It should be understood that the issue in this paper is not one of breach of confidentiali-ty. Rather, the concern is with the potential defamatory nature of DSM diagnoses even when there is consent for communication of the diagnosis to particular others.[1] However, note that the consent may not be truly informed in that the full implications of having the diagnosis and of having it communicated to others may not be adequately understood by the client at the time he or she proffers their consent. Consider in this regard that there is evidence that internalizing the medicalization of one's DSM-defined "mental health problem/disorder" is a strong predictor for depression (White, Bebbington, Pear-son, Johnson & Ellis, 2000). Further, it has been found that those who accept explana-tions of their experience as one of having experienced a "psychotic episode" are also more prone to depression than those who resist integrating the experience in this way (Jackson et al., 1998). One is safe to assume that the client had acceded to the DSM la-bel, to the extent they did, in the hopes that the entire process would alleviate psycho-logical distress. Thus, significant depression as a function of receiving the DSM diagnosis may suggest, at least for some voluntary clients, a lack of full informed consent in subject-ing themselves to the diagnostic process and in agreeing to have the diagnosis communi-cated to certain third parties. (This is aside from the issue of whether the consent to treatment and communication of the diagnosis to others was genuinely voluntary. This is difficult to discern given the societal pressure to cooperate in all respects in the hopes of conforming one's behavior and reports of personal experience to the norm).

The client may even have provided consent for the sharing of diagnostic information prior to knowing what diagnosis, if any, would ultimately be communicated. The client may, in some instances, only come to learn the diagnosis at the same time or after the di-agnosis is communicated to others, such as a referring physician (as when the client has been referred for psychiatric evaluation as part of the process relating to a personal injury suit which involves a claim for emotional distress). In another example, the client may provide consent for the results of a psychiatric interview to be communicated to an em-ployer as part of the process of substantiating an application for worker's compensation in regard, for instance, to job-related stress. In the latter case, the client may not always ful-ly appreciate the long-term implications (i.e., should the psychiatrist communicate an unexpected diagnosis such as "malingering") (Guriel & Fremouw, 2003). Second, the communication of the diagnosis may be in terms of a definitive statement regarding the essence of the individual, an alleged summary descriptive term, if you will, for the nature of the individual's very personhood. Both of the aforementioned situations meet the criterion for a communication which is not privileged. Although the occasion may be covered by qualified privilege, as when a psychiatrist communicates the diagnosis to the referring family physician, the words written or spoken may yet not be protected. This by virtue of the fact, as mentioned, that there is an absence of truly informed consent authorizing the communication and/or the psychiatric diagnosis constitutes a defamatory statement. It may be defamatory as it reflects a reckless disregard for the truth or a (clinical) belief/presumption without reasonable basis given its reification of both the symptom descriptions and the diagnosis itself without adequate scientific evidence (i.e., there is no consensus on any biological marker and/or the eligibility criteria and/or the disorder as a separable disease or disorder entity).

The fallaciousness of reifying DSM diagnostic categories is evidenced, for instance, by the fact that the validity of various long-established DSM categories such as schizophrenia has been attacked in part due to the non-specific nature of many of the attributed symptoms (Gallagher, Gernez, & Baker, 1991). The scientific status of other "conditions" such as "post-traumatic stress disorder" (PTSD) has also been held suspect since there is no certain way to distinguish between the alleged genuine disorder and simple malingering of symptoms. Malingering is a possibility given the subjective nature of the eligibility criteria for disorders such as PTSD, which rely heavily on client self-reports of symptoms. Other diagnoses such as "attention deficit disorder" have been considered by some researchers and clinicians as suspect since there is no biologic marker for the disorder, and no commonly accepted assessment method focusing on symptoms that are not simply continuous with those seen in the non-clinical population (LeFever, Arcona, & Antonuccio, 2003). In addition, the validity of DSM categories in general has been challenged on the basis that often the categories cannot be reliably measured and therefore their validity also cannot be assessed (reliability here referring to mental health workers independently reaching the same conclusions regarding diagnosis when using the same DSM eligibility criteria and the same assessment tools [Kirk, 1994]). Due to such evidence as the foregoing, it is therefore not reasonable to hold DSM categories to be relatively accurate and definitive statements about the nature of the person so diagnosed.

LOSING THE SELF TO THE DSM

As a consequence of the DSM diagnosis, is the client, in effect, loses the freedom to redefine him or herself in future. For instance, once a schizophrenic, in practice, always regarded as a schizophrenic (even if "in remission"); once an alcoholic, always considered an alcoholic, but now perhaps a "recovering" alcoholic, and so on. The psychiatric diagnosis thus comes to allegedly reflect something core and always latent in the individual. This notion of continuing risk is sometimes expressed in terms of genetic predisposition to mental disorder even though, as Jacobs (1994) points out, most genetic or biologic disorders do not in fact require a social-environmental contributor in order to become manifest (i.e., the late onset disorders such as Huntington's disease have no identifiable social contributor or trigger). Psychiatric labels impose on the "psychiatrically disordered" individual a self which derives from the story created by the DSM diagnosis. Further, the mental health community is not satisfied until the individual internalizes, to the extent possible, that DSM–defined self (as, for example, schizophrenic). Where the DSM diagnosis is internalized by the client, it is taken to be a sign of at least partial "recovery" and a reason for cautious optimism about the longer-term prognosis. The latter in part since the client, having acceded to and identified with the assigned DSM diagnosis, will likely also more readily accept the alleged efficacy of particular therapist-preferred treatment modalities, thus ensuring better compliance. The problem is that there is no convincing evidence that DSM categories are anything but one possible interpretive framework among many. Thus the self which is imposed via the DSM story may in fact be fictional and in important ways non-reflective of the lived experience of the subject so named: "The self of narrative identity is the I that tells stories about itself, exists in those stories, and conceives its identity in terms of those stories" (Phillips, 2004, p. 314).

Yet, the mentally ill individual often comes to embrace the DSM diagnosis, given the pressure to do so and since the DSM diagnosis provides a unifying framework for interpreting the varied and often confusing experiences which the individual considered "mentally ill" may be undergoing. The fact that providing such a unifying story may be emotionally and intellectually satisfying to those who are doing the labeling of such disturbing phenomena as psychosis (and perhaps also to the client) does not, however, in itself establish that the diagnosis is veridical. Indeed, it may be that the disordered individual is, through their symptomatology, telling their own story. In doing so they may be engaged in constructing a new identity (self), one that others (or even they) may not always apprehend but a story that captures their lived experience more adequately than does the DSM diagnosis. In practice, society regards: "narrative identity . . . as a mark of what it is to be a person or a self" (Phillips, p. 326). Hence, the DSM narrative too defines the individual's personhood. The question then becomes just how accurate and useful that DSM story is.

DSM categorization has important psychological effects in that "the way in which individuals label their experiences has been associated with perceived quality of life" (Lobban, Barrowclough, & Jones, 2003, p. 178). To the extent that the DSM label robs the individual of his or her *self-constructed* self and de-contextualizes the experience, psychological damage may ensue. This damage is then additional to any previous distress caused by the symptoms associated with the mental disorder. Thus, for instance, individuals have been found to be more likely to suffer post-psychotic depression when they attribute their psychotic symptoms to something "internal to the self" as opposed to contextual factors (Birchwood, Iqbal, Chadwick, & Trower, 2000a, 2000b). This focus on an internal locus for the cause is more likely when a DSM conceptual framework is relied upon to make sense of symptoms given the underlying medical model. Biologic explanations of psychiatric symptoms may relieve stress in the short-term for some by relieving personal responsibility for the "illness." However, such explanations may cause considerable distress in the longer term due to their engendering a sense of lack of internal control and a separate but unwelcome identity as someone constitutionally different from the non-clinical population (McGorry & McConville, 1999).

The individual loses not only the freedom to redefine their essence apart from the diagnosis but also the freedom to assign their own meanings to their personal distress and experiences. Rather, these experiences are translated into symptoms devoid of personal meaning and these symptoms into diagnostic categories emanating at the root from some biologic cause over which the client has no control. The choice is to internalize the language of the therapist in assigning any meaning to the experience of "mental illness" or to resist and be left with no one with whom to share any sort of social reality at all:

> Modern . . . medicine does not typically pay attention to *patient's interpretations* of their symptoms and illnesses. . . . With naming comes a transfer of ownership of the person's mind and body to the professional. If someone's brain is diseased, that individual ceases

to be viewed as a responsible owner of his or her mind/body. (Susko, 1994, p. 93, some emphasis added)

In essence, DSM tells its own stories. From the DSM perspective, the client's stories and meanings are but a reflection of illness rather than meaningful to any degree and generally not viewed as a potential vehicle for moving toward self-efficacy.

DSM AS AN INTERPRETIVE VERSUS OBJECTIVE, EMPIRICAL DIAGNOSTIC SYSTEM

The DSM-IV diagnostic categories and any future revisions are better viewed as inter-pretive frameworks rather than objective descriptive or scientifically confirmed explanatory conceptual systems. As one author has put it: "The caseness approach [re-ferring to DSM categorization] engenders *a certain* story and meaning, but it is essen-tially the same story for everyone who is so labeled: 'I have a mental illness caused by a chemical imbalance in my brain . . .'" (Susko, 1994, p. 96, portion in square brackets added for clarity). The point here is not to diminish the possibility of important bio-logical contributors to various behaviors and processes that we might label mental ill-ness or to deny the suffering that is often associated with such states. Rather, what is being highlighted is the tenuous nature of a DSM diagnosis when it is held to capture who this person is or has become. In this regard, consider that even if one were to un-derstand fully the biological contributors to a manifestation of mental illness, one would not necessarily comprehend the personal meaning of the particular form and content of symptoms, nor how they relate to and reflect the individual's history and current concerns (compare Georgaca, 2004) The DSM-IV as currently employed cre-ates the implicit pretense, however, that one can categorize not just "symptoms" but the people who express them. The DSM categories serve to equate the person with the symptoms. For instance, one does not simply *have* schizophrenia; one *is* a schizophrenic; one does not just have obsessive-compulsive disorder; one *is* an obsessive-compulsive. This trend is more pronounced for the "mental illnesses" than for most any other dis-orders recognized as importantly biologically based even when there are psychiatric cor-relates or effects associated with the disorder.

The DSM categories define who one *is* and not just what one *has* in the way of symp-tom expression or disease entity be the latter regarded as a mental or physical phenome-na or both. Yet, it has been shown that even persons with significant psychotic symptoms—to use the DSM conceptual framework—can often be trained how to modify or reduce their psychiatric symptoms by altering their beliefs about them (Tarrier, Har-wood, Yusopoff, Beckett, & Baker, 1990). Since the expression of many of the mental "disease" categories listed in the DSM can, at times, be altered as a function of the client and the therapist's beliefs about the "condition," there is not necessarily any static truth embedded in the DSM categories. Thus, in communicating a DSM diagnosis, the psychi-atrist or other mental health worker errs if the presumption is that the diagnosis captures something fundamental about the core of the client's personhood. In respect of certain DSM categories, such as sociopathy, it is even widely but incorrectly assumed among many in the field that something about moral character and not just personality or cogni-tive style is being conveyed. The contention here is, in contrast, that there exists no professional or scientific expertise sufficient to define, categorize, or describe the com-plexities of another's *personhood*.

Even when the client is psychotic, the DSM does not capture the unchanging essence of that human being. There is in such a case a personhood present as opposed to a vacuum into which the psychiatrist can properly inject his or her own version of the individual's being by attributing to the client the persona defined by a particular DSM diagnosis. Thus it is that cognitive behavior therapy has some efficacy in that psychotics can be assisted in altering belief systems that underlie delusions and such so as to develop a new world view and construct their old or a new persona (i.e., Chadwick & Birchwood, 1994; Freeman et al., 1998; Lewis et al., 2000; Wykes, Parr, & Landau, 1999). These cognitive behavior therapy approaches have been referred to as "normalizing." This in that they are premised on a notion of a dimensional definition of mental illness where symptoms and complexes of symptoms are viewed as on a continuum existing in both the clinical and non-clinical population, rather than as indices of who has or does not have a disorder (Johns & J. Van Os, 2001, p. 1137). (Distinguishing features between the two groups may thus be in terms of frequency and severity of symptoms or instead ability to cope with the symptoms, or combinations of such factors or the like.)

Note also that recovery seems to be facilitated when persons who have experienced what is generally referred to as a psychotic episode "split off" the experience rather than integrate it into the self (McGlashan, Levy & Carpenter, 1975). In the latter case, it is as if the individual has come to cope by adopting the view that psychiatric symptoms can occur also in the general non-clinical population but do not define the self. There is also evidence of the potential ability to control to a degree those psychiatric symptoms, even psychotic symptoms, by altering beliefs about the symptoms, their cause, meaning, and controllability. These findings challenge the utility of a view of the severely mentally disordered as manifesting some sort of disease entity that can be treated but symptomatically leaving essentially unaltered the underlying constitutional difference which predisposes the individual to mental illness given the right circumstances.

ON THE VERACITY OF DSM CATEGORIES

The veridical quality of the DSM as a means of differentiating "us" from "them" has been undermined given the presence of psychotic traits and symptoms in non-clinical populations. Not only is there a notable prevalence rate of psychotic symptoms such as auditory hallucinations occurring in the non-clinical population at some point in their lives even when not under stress[2] (the rate varying depending on the measure used), but there is also an association between various reported psychotic symptoms within individuals in non-clinical groups (Johns & J. Van Os, 2001). Thus mental health symptoms are viewed by some experts in the field as on a continuum with normal experience rather than as indices of a disease entity with symptom clusters that can be categorically defined as in the DSM:

> . . . dimensional definitions of symptoms can be less stigmatizing than categorical distinctions, as they imply that patients with a diagnosis of schizophrenia [for example] are not distinctly different from non-patients. In contrast, the categorical view of schizophrenia as a qualitatively different disease experience facilitates the frequently observed process of equating the person with his or her illness. (Johns & J. Van Os, 2001, p. 1137)

Thus there is disagreement in the medical and psychological literature about whether "mental illness" (a) represents: a state quite different from that experienced by segments of the non-clinical population or (b) reflects symptoms occurring in the non-clinical population as well but exacerbated due to inadequate coping that may be compounded also by inadequate social support (Jacobs, 1994). DSM diagnosis communicated to a third party is then not covered by the justification defense (truth defense) to the degree that it conveys a notion of some understood highly distinctive disease process of mind and/or body that sets the individual apart in some very fundamental way from the non-clinical population. In fact there is controversy about whether severe mental disorder is biologically based, a function of a combination of biologic and social factors, or (iii) solely the consequence of "imposed suffering" to which such individuals have been exposed for "substantive periods of their formative years" (Jacobs, 1994, p. 17) (the latter perhaps creating psychopharmacological effects within the body such that cause and effect are no longer distinguishable). Regardless of one's theoretical orientation, what is clear is that many mental health experts espouse substantively different conceptions of mental illness. The reality of various DSM categories and the system as a whole is thus highly contentious, as reflected in the following quotes:

> . . . the recognition of disorder is a social and interactional issue both in the sense that the judgment of disorder is based on social criteria and in the sense that diagnosis is an interpersonal process with its own inherent social order. (Georgaca, 2004, p. 87, commenting on the work of Palmer, 2000)

> Others argue that diagnosis is not a process of identification or recognition of disorder, but rather a process of active construction of disorder and of transforming the person to a mental patient. (Georgaca, 2004, p. 87)

> We have argued . . . that research on psychotic speech maintains the concept of thought disorder by ignoring the role of the listener, rater and researcher in the assessment of the intelligibility of speech. (Georgaca, 2004, p. 88)

The DSM diagnosis therefore, depending on one's perspective as a mental health theoretician/practitioner, may be grounded to differing degrees, if at all, on the existence of therapist-interpreted actual symptom clusters relating to particular disordered mental processes and/or diseases. "Mental illness" is thus variously considered biologically based with markers yet to be discovered or as a social construction influenced by the sociocultural context in which the symptoms and the diagnostic classificatory scheme emerged (or something in between) (Georgaca, 2004). For a concrete example of mental illness as a social construction, consider the ongoing debate on whether Asperger's syndrome (a diagnostic category included in the DSM-IV) represents a separate diagnostic category or subcategory or in fact does not exist at all (these individuals being rather high-functioning autistics that cannot be differentiated in terms of substantively different eligibility criteria than those used to screen for autism) (Dickerson Mayes, Calhoun, & Crites, 2001). Communication of the diagnosis to persons other than the client—even when covered by qualified privilege—cannot then be defended via "justification" (the truth defense). This is due to the wide range of perspectives among mental health professionals on the uniqueness and even very existence of the condition or symptoms referred to by the diagnosis. Who and how one is labeled may have less to do with an accurate scientifically-based description of any unique mental characteristics of the individual than with: (a) who is at highest risk of such labeling having become caught up in the mental health system and (b) who is at highest risk of having their "symptoms" viewed as maladaptive. This once more is not to deny that mental illness may involve suffering but how much of that suffering is maladaptive and/or due to the experience itself and how much is due to society's reaction to it is unclear.

The interpretive nature of the DSM categorization scheme is constantly underplayed or, on occasion, even ignored in much of the mainstream literature. Instead, there is "an empiricist account when describing diagnosis as a process of objectively identifying symptoms independently of the clinician's characteristics and orientation" (Georgaca, 2004, p. 88). In the present context, this is an essential point in that it explains why the notion of a psychiatric diagnosis assigned by a mental health worker is generally not held to be defamatory. Such diagnoses are inappropriately regarded as objective and non-interpretive. As these diagnoses are made in good faith, the contention has been in almost every instance that they are ipso facto non-defamatory even when communicated to third parties and even if unanticipated damage to the client's reputation results. The argument here has been, however, that to the extent that the diagnosis refers to some presumed fundamental truth about the client's "self" or "person" (something more than but a theoretical description of interpreted behaviors) then the words spoken or written are defamatory and unprotected. That is, the communication demonstrates a reckless disregard for the truth or a belief without reasonable basis that cannot be saved by qualified privilege and which causes in many instances deep personal injury. That personal injury arises since the diagnosis may be perceived by self and others as a kind of social declaration that the individual has lost the self to some degree or perhaps even completely. Such a perceived "loss of autonomy" and "entrapment in the illness" has been associated with a greater likelihood of feelings of humiliation and depression for individuals diagnosed with psychiatric illness (Birchwood, Iqbal, et al., 2000a, 2000b; Birchwood, Mason, et al., 1993).

CONCLUSION

We have considered the possibility that DSM diagnosis may simply be a tool in a tautological process in which the "diagnosis . . . frames which symptoms are noted and reinforced" (Susko, 1994, p.92) and serves to reify the diagnostic category. As a result, the psychiatrist or other mental health worker is often misled into a feeling of confidence regarding the diagnosis given that it is they themselves who have imbued it with such meaning. That meaning derives from the fact that the therapist "discovers" in the client's complex of *therapist-interpreted* behaviors a set of "symptoms" that are weighted so as to confirm the diagnosis (compare Barrett, 1998). This is much as it is for the reader of personal astrological chart predictions. The reader finds meaning in their astrological personality profile as a consequence of they themselves creating the artificial links between the complex happenings of their personal lives on the one hand and the rather non-specific descriptions and predictions in the astrological reading. To avoid this pitfall, mental health workers must come to regard DSM categories and eligibility criteria as but "working hypotheses" (whether viewed in terms of categories or the dimensional perspective emphasizing symptoms as occurring along a continuum such that there is no dichotomy between clinical and non-clinical groups in terms of the presence or absence of such symptoms in either group). These psychiatric diagnoses are to be assessed then in terms of what good they do for the client in terms of increasing their self-efficacy and *joie de vie* and revised when they do more harm than good. With that cautious approach DSM categories or a dimensional analysis may be a possible tool for considering certain theoretical perspectives in working with a client rather than defamatory labels that *assign* an individual a static and damaging persona.

Too often mental health clients have been denied the right to be protected from exacerbations of their mental anguish through psychiatric diagnoses which: (a) reduce their complex and dynamic selves to a static reified DSM category and (b) lead to inferences about some profound deficit in the cognitive, affective, and/or moral domain, the origin of which is held to be for the most part internal rather that a function of the dynamic sociocultural context or interplay between the biological and contextual factors. The end result then is a defamatory labeling which negates the individual's autonomous self apart from that self as conceptualized through the lens of the DSM. Justice demands that communication of DSM categorical diagnoses as reified mental disease entities that accurately describe or explain the self of the individual so labeled should result in legal liability for the mental health professional publishing the diagnosis. Afterall, justice is a basic human need, as Taylor explains (2003), which every person is entitled to have met. The psychiatric patient must then not be precluded from using the defamation law to restore his or her dignity, sense of self, and good standing in the community when the circumstances warrant. Hopefully, the language used in conveying interpretations using the DSM will be tentative, as it should be if clinical practice is to meet a higher ethical standard in this regard.

NOTES

1. There are a myriad of ways in which DSM diagnoses are communicated to parties other than the client with or without the client's informed consent. For example, such diagnoses may become public when the individual is involuntarily committed and the information is communicated to family members who are caretakers or to other physicians as a result of a routine consultative process. Where the client is hospitalized or under court order it may be communicated to the various attorneys and other court officials without the client's consent. Schoolchildren may have such diagnoses in their school records to which open access is granted to various school personnel with the records following the child after a school transfer, thus spreading the DSM label to an ever-wider circle. Thus the child—the actual client—has not provided consent. It can be argued that the legal guardian cannot be presumed in every such case to have provided genuine proxy consent "on behalf" of the child. This is the case since the child might not have provided such consent had they been competent and understood the potential negative implications of having the diagnosis made public.

2. For example, the non-clinical individual may be a new anxious mother who clearly hears her baby cry for her mother though the infant has in fact not made a sound, or an adult mourning the loss of a loved one who hears the deceased's voice while being aroused from a nap.

REFERENCES

American Psychiatric Association. (1994). *Diagnostic and statistical manual of mental disorders* (4th ed.). Washington, DC: Author.

Barrett, R. J. (1998). Clinical writings and the documentary construction of schizophrenia. *Culture, Medicine and Psychiatry, 12*, 265-299.

Birchwood, M., Iqbal, Z., Chadwick, P., & Trower, P. (2000a). Cognitive approach to depression and suicidal thinking in psychosis: I. Ontogeny of post-psychotic depression. *British Journal of Psychiatry, 177*, 516-521.

Birchwood, M., Iqbal, Z., Chadwick, P., & Trower, P. (2000b). Cognitive approach to depression and suicidal thinking in psychosis: II. Testing the validity of a social ranking model. *British Journal of Psychiatry, 177*, 522-528.

Birchwood, M., Mason, R., MacMillan, F., et al. (1993). Depression, demoralization, and control over psychotic illness: A comparison of depressed and non-depressed patients with chronic psychosis. *Psychological Medicine, 23*, 387-395.

Chadwick, P., & Birchwood, M. (1994). The omnipotence of voice: A cognitive approach to auditory hallucinations. *British Journal of Psychiatry, 164*, 190-201.

Dickerson Mayes, S., Calhoun, S. L., & Crites, D. L., (2001). Does DSM-IV Asperger's disorder exist? *Journal of Abnormal Child Psychology, 29*, 263-271.

Freeman, D., Garety, P., Fowler, D., Kuipers, E., Dunn, G., Bebbington, P., et al. (1998). The London-East Anglia randomized control trial of cognitive-behavior therapy for psychosis IV: Self-esteem and persecutory delusions. *British Journal of Clinical Psychology, 37*, 415-430.

Gallagher, A. G., Gernez, T., & Baker, L. J. V. (1991). Beliefs of psychologists about schizophrenia and their role in its treatment. *Irish Journal of Psychology, 12*, 393-405.

Georgaca, E. (2004). Talk and the nature of delusions: Defending sociocultural perspectives on mental illness. *Philosophy, Psychiatry, and Psychology, 11*, 87-94.

Guriel, J., & Fremouw, W. (2003). Assessing malingered post-traumatic stress disorder: A critical review. *Clinical Psychology Review, 23*, 881-904.

Jackson, H. J., McGorry, P. D., Edwards, J., Hulbert, C., Henry, L. Francey, S., et al. (1998). Cognitively-oriented psychotherapy for early psychosis (COPE): Preliminary results. *British Journal of Psychiatry, 172*(Suppl. 33), 92-99.

Jacobs, D. H. (1994). Environmental-failure-oppression is the only cause of psychopathology. *The Journal of Mind and Behavior, 15*, 1-19.

Johns, L. C., & J. Van O's (2001). The continuity of psychotic experiences in the general population. *Clinical Psychology Review, 21*, 1125-1141.

Kirk, S. A. (1994). The myth of the reliability of DSM. *The Journal of Mind and Behavior, 15*, 71-86.

LeFever, G. B., Arcona, A. P., & Antonuccio, D. O. (2003). ADHD among American schoolchildren. *The Scientific Review of Mental Health Practice, 2*(1). Retrieved April 13, 2004, from http://www.srmhp.org

Lewis, S. W., Tarrier, N., Haddock, G., Bentall, R., Kinderman, P., & Kingdon, D. (2000). A multi-centered randomized controlled trial of cognitive-behavior therapy in first- and second-episode schizophrenia: The Socrates trial. *Schizophrenia Research, 36* (1-3), 329.

Lobban, F., Barrowclough, C., & Jones, S. (2003). A review of the role of illness models in severe mental illness. *Clinical Psychology Review, 23*, 171-196.

McGorry, P. D., & McConville, S. B. (1999). Insight in psychosis: An elusive target. *Comprehensive Psychiatry, 40*, 131-142.

McGlashan, T. H., Levy, S. T., & Carpenter, W. T. (1975). Integration and sealing over: Clinically distinct recovery styles from schizophrenia. *Archives of General Psychiatry, 32*, 1269-1272.

Palmer, D. (2000). Identifying delusional discourse: Issues of rationality, reality and power. *Sociology of Health and Illness, 22*, 661-678.

Phillips, J. (2004). Psychopathology and the narrative self. *Philosophy, Psychiatry, and Psychology, 10*, 313-328.

Susko, M. A. (1994). Caseness and narrative: Contrasting approaches to people who are psychiatrically labeled. *The Journal of Mind and Behavior, 15*, 87-112.

Tarrier, N., Harwood, S., Yusopoff, L., Beckett, R., & Baker, A. (1990). Coping Strategy Enhancement (CSE): A method of treating residual schizophrenic symptoms. *Behavioral Psychotherapy, 18*, 283-293.

Taylor, A. J. W. (2003). Justice as a basic human need. *New Ideas in Psychology, 21*, 209-219.

White, R., Bebbington, P., Pearson, J., Johnson, S., & Ellis, D. (2000). The social context of insight in schizophrenia. *Social Psychiatry and Psychiatric Epidemiology, 35*, 500-507.

Wykes, T., Parr, A. M., & Landau, S. (1999). Group treatment of auditory hallucinations: Exploratory study of effectiveness. *British Journal of Psychiatry, 175*, 180-185.

Offprints. Requests for offprints should be directed to Sonja Grover, PhD, CPsych, Lakehead University, 955 Oliver Road, Thunder Bay, Ontario, P7B 5E1, Canada. E-mail: sonja.grover@lakeheadu.ca

[32]

This review highlights the importance of recognizing the possibility for doing harm when intentions are good. It describes several examples showing that well-planned and adequately executed programs provide no guarantee for safety or efficacy. The author concludes with recommendations for scientifically credible evaluations to promote progress in the field of crime prevention.

Keywords: interventions; treatment; crime prevention; random assignment; evaluations; harm

Cures That Harm: Unanticipated Outcomes of Crime Prevention Programs

By
JOAN McCORD

The *New York Times* published an article on Thursday, 4 April 2002 announcing that "a trade group representing British pharmaceutical companies publicly reprimanded Pfizer for promoting several medicines for unapproved uses and marketing another drug before it received government approval" (p. C5). The reprimand was justified because the drugs had not been appropriately tested for safety. Pfizer risked causing harm. No such reprimand could possibly occur in the fields of social intervention.

Researchers, practitioners, and policy makers have begun to understand that evidence is required to identify effective programs to reduce crime. Yet they typically couple the desire for evidence with an inappropriately nar-

Joan McCord, a professor of criminal justice at Temple University, earned a Ph.D. in sociology from Stanford University. Her research has focused on social environments that are conducive to various types of crimes and on the impacts of a variety of kinds of social interventions designed to reduce crime. She has coauthored or edited eleven books and authored more than one hundred articles in the field of criminology. For her contributions to research, she has received the Durkheim Prize from the International Society of Criminology and the Sutherland Award from the American Society of Criminology. Recently, the Society for Research on Adolescence awarded its Social Policy Best Journal Article Award for one of her coauthored articles.

NOTE: The author thanks David Weisburd and Anthony Petrosino for their helpful comments on an earlier draft of this article.

row focus. They ask, Does the program work or not? This question is too narrow because it fails to recognize that some treatments cause harm. Intervention programs may, for example, increase crime or the use of drugs. They may decrease the punitive impact of sanctions available to the criminal justice system. They may, perhaps, result in reductions in the ability to cope with life—or even in premature death. Unless social programs are evaluated for potential harm as well as benefit, safety as well as efficacy, the choice of which social programs to use will remain a dangerous guess.

No public reservoir of data permits evaluating whether a given type of program meets even minimum requirements to provide benefits and avoid harm either to recipients of the social programs or to the communities from which they come. Yet social harm is costly to the public, perhaps even more costly than physical harm.

Reluctance to recognize that good intentions can result in harm can be found in biased investigating and reporting. Many investigators fail to ask whether an intervention has had adverse effects, and many research summaries lack systematic reporting of such effects (Sherman et al. 1997).

What has been called a publication bias appears when analyses show that a higher proportion of studies that reinforce popular opinions than those that do not get into peer-reviewed journals (Dickersin and Min 1994; Easterbrook et al. 1991; Scherer, Dickersin, and Langenberg 1994). In summarizing the results of studies evaluating publication bias, Colin Begg (1994) reported that "most studies of the issue have consistently demonstrated that positive (statistically significant) studies are more likely to be published" (p. 401).

One reason for what appears to be a code of silence about adverse effects is fear that all social programs will be tainted by the ones that are harmful. That fear, perhaps justified in some quarters, would be like blocking publication of potentially damaging effects of Celebrex, thalidamide, or estrogen because the publication could slow experimental work in disease prevention. Social programs deserve to be treated as serious attempts at intervention, with possibly toxic effects, so that a science of intervention can prosper.

What follows is a discussion of some social programs that have been carefully evaluated using experimental designs with random assignment to a treatment and a comparison group. They have been found to have harmful effects, and for this reason, they are important experiments. Knowledge that well-designed, carefully implemented social programs can produce unwanted results should set a solid foundation for insisting that all social programs should be coupled with evaluations that have scientific credibility.

The Cambridge-Somerville Youth Study

The Cambridge-Somerville Youth Study was a carefully designed, adequately funded, and well-executed intervention program. Furthermore, a scientifically credible research design played a central role in its construction.

Richard Clark Cabot funded, designed, and, until his death, directed the Cambridge-Somerville Youth Study. As a professor of clinical medicine and social ethics at Harvard, Cabot had made a mark in medicine by showing how to differentiate typhoid fever from malaria. His etiological study of heart disease was widely recognized as an important contribution to the field. He had introduced social services to Massachusetts General Hospital and had been president of the National Conference on Social Work. Not surprisingly, in turning to the problem of crime, Cabot insisted on using a scientific approach, one that aimed to alleviate the probable causes of crime but also one that would permit adequate tests of the results of intervention.

Social programs deserve to be treated as serious attempts at intervention, with possibly toxic effects, so that a science of intervention can prosper.

Cabot's beliefs about the causes of crime derived in part from the work of William Healy and Augusta Bronner, prominent researchers who codirected the Judge Baker Foundation (later known as the Judge Baker Guidance Centre) in Boston. Healy and Bronner reviewed four thousand delinquent cases, half from Chicago and half from Boston. Having discovered that less than 10 percent of the delinquents in their study had come from good homes, Healy and Bronner (1926) concluded that "where to place a large measure of responsibility, where to direct a strong attack in treatment and for prevention of delinquency stands out with striking clearness" (p. 129).

Cabot hypothesized that even rebellious youth from ghastly families "may conceivably be steered away from a delinquent career and toward useful citizenship if a devoted individual outside his own family gives him consistent emotional support, friendship, and timely guidance" (Allport 1951, vi). The Cambridge-Somerville Youth Study would test this hypothesis.

The study began with a matched case design. Staff hired by the youth study solicited names of boys younger than ten who were living in the congested urban environments of Cambridge and Somerville, Massachusetts. To avoid stigmatizing the program, scout leaders as well as the police contributed to the pool of names.

Laboriously, the staff gathered information about the boys, their families, and the neighborhoods of their homes. Each boy was matched to another of similar age, social background, somatotype, and temperament. A toss of a coin determined which member of each matched pair would be placed into the treatment group and which into the control group.

When a match was identified and the coin had been tossed, a counselor visited the home of the treatment boy. These caseworkers visited the homes as frequently as weekly, when that seemed necessary, but the average frequency was twice a month. Treatment lasted an average of five and one-half years.

The logic of the study required being convinced that the treatment and control groups would have turned out similarly but for the introduction of treatment. Therefore, the groups were compared after a reduction of caseloads due to war-time gas restrictions had taken place in 1942. After the reduction, 253 matched pairs of boys remained in the program. No biases were discovered in the comparisons.

No reliable differences were discovered in comparisons of age, intelligence, whether referral to the youth study had been as "difficult" or "average," or the delinquency prediction scores assigned by the selection committee on the basis of the boys' family histories and home environments. No reliable differences appeared in comparisons regarding the boys' physical health as rated by the doctor after a medical examination, in mental health, in social adjustment, in acceptance of authority, or in social aggressiveness as reflected by teachers' descriptions of the boys. Nor were reliable differences found in ratings of adequacy of the home, disruption of the home, delinquency in the home, adequacy of discipline, standard of living, occupational status of the father, social status level of the elementary school attended by the boy (a measure based on the occupational levels of fathers whose children attended the school), or quality of the neighborhood in which the boys resided. Thus, the randomization within matched pairs had succeeded in producing two groups of boys who were substantially similar prior to the beginning of the treatment program.

During the period of treatment, counselors (most of whom had professional degrees in social work) provided friendly guidance to the boys, counseled parents, assisted the families in a variety of ways, and referred the boys to specialists when that seemed advisable. Boys in the treatment group were tutored, taken to a variety of sports events, and encouraged to participate in the woodwork shop provided by the youth study. Counselors encouraged the boys to join community youth groups and helped them get jobs. Many were sent to summer camps to take them away from the heat of the city.

Counselors were not permitted to accompany the boys to court. Nor were they permitted to include boys from the control group for any of their activities. Of course, boys in the control group received whatever services were provided by other organizations.

When the program terminated in 1945, more than half the treatment boys had been tutored in academic subjects, more than one hundred received medical or psychiatric attention, almost half had been sent to summer camps, and most of the boys had participated with their counselors in such activities as swimming, visits to local athletic competitions, and woodwork in the project's shop. The boys and their parents called on the social workers for help with such problems as illness and unemployment. They talked with their counselors about their hopes and ambitions as well as about their fears and defeats.

Although a discouraging number of boys in the treatment group were known to have broken the law, at the close of treatment, many boys identified as maladjusted when they entered the program had made fairly good adjustments. Had improvement from prediction been accepted as the measure of success, the program might have been judged effective.

To determine whether the improved adjustment should be attributed to treatment, interviewers tracked down 148 boys who had been in the control group. The interviewers gathered information from the boys, their families, and their school principals. Dr. Helen Witmer was brought into the program to help in its evaluation. She classified each boy among the 148 pairs in terms of adjustment. Disconcertingly, the results indicated that almost equal numbers of the control and the treatment group did better than had been anticipated at the beginning of the project. (See Powers and Witmer 1951 for a more complete description of the program and its early evaluation.)

Additional disappointment came in 1948 from the Massachusetts Department of Probation. Court records showed that a slightly larger number of boys in the treatment group had been in court, 96 versus 92, and they had been charged with a slightly larger number of offenses, 264 versus 218.

Gordon Allport, president of the Board of Directors for the Ella Lyman Cabot Foundation, called for patience. He believed that the program might have prepared the boys to benefit from experience. If so, treatment effects might appear as the youth matured.

Between 1975 and 1981, when the boys were reaching middle age, my research assistants and I retraced the 253 matched pairs who had remained in the program after the cut in 1942. We located 98 percent of them. Questionnaires sent to men from the treatment group asked how, if at all, the program had helped them. Two-thirds of the respondents claimed that the program was helpful, with most of these men amplifying their judgments by specifying ways in which the project or the counselors had improved their lives. These testimonials included claims that the program had helped the men become law-abiding citizens, that it had helped to provide a better understanding of people, and that it had provided evidence that there were "people around who care." Many mentioned that the program had kept them "off the streets," that they were helped by having someone with whom they could talk, and that the counselors had affected their values. Some noted that the program had put them on the right track. Others mentioned the friendships encouraged or the talents acquired. With these subjective endorsements in hand, we sought objective evidence of the program's effects.

We tracked court records both in Massachusetts and in the states to which the men had migrated. We tracked mental hospital records and records from facilities for treatment of alcoholism. We obtained death records to confirm deaths when this was reported, and we searched death records for men who had not been found.

Comparisons between the treatment and control groups showed that for the majority of pairs ($n = 150$), treatment had no measured effect on the objective outcomes. Nevertheless, for the 103 pairs who had different outcomes, those who had been in the treatment program were more likely to have been convicted for crimes indexed by the Federal Bureau of Investigation as serious street crimes. Those who had been in the treatment program had died an average of five years younger. And those who had been in the treatment program were more likely to have received a medical diagnosis as alcoholic, schizophrenic, or manic depressive (McCord 1978, 1981, 1992).

In 1945, counselors had identified thirty-eight boys as having received the most benefit from the program. Among this select group, twenty-two appeared neither better nor worse than their matches in the control group. Four of the men turned out better than their matches, but twelve turned out worse. Thus, even among those whom the staff believed it had helped most, the objective evidence failed to show that the program had been beneficial.

One might argue that these results had nothing to do with the treatment program. Two comparisons suggest that this argument is wrong.

The first is that adverse treatment effects increased with increased intensity and duration of treatment. That is, the treatment program appeared to reflect a dose response. Boys whose counselors more frequently visited them and those in the treatment program the longest were most likely to fare badly as compared with their matched mates in the control group.

The second is that adverse effects occurred only among boys whose families had cooperated with the program. Families were divided into those who presented problems of cooperation and those who did not. Counselors had dictated reports about each of their interactions with the boys or the families, so most of the case records included several hundred pages. Cases were considered to have shown problems of cooperation if the counselor reported such difficulties or if the case record was exceptionally short (fewer than twenty-five pages), indicating little interaction.

Among the pairs in which the treatment family was uncooperative, the control and treatment boys were equally likely to turn out badly. Among the pairs in which the treatment family was cooperative, however, there were twenty-seven pairs in which the treatment boys turned out better but fifty-two pairs in which the treatment boys turned out worse. These comparisons strongly suggest that the treatment itself had been harmful.

To evaluate effects of the various treatment approaches, I computed an adverse odds ratio by dividing the number of pairs in which the treatment boy did worse than his match by the number of pairs in which the treatment boy did better than his match for each of the major emphases of the treatment program. Adverse odds ratios less than 1 indicate benefits of the treatment program. Conversely, ratios greater than 1 indicate harmful effects of the treatment program.

The odds ratio for bad outcomes for an emphasis on encouraging the boy to participate in community youth groups such as Boy Scouts and YMCA was 1.75 (35:20). That for an emphasis on providing academic help was 1.91 (42:22). The odds ratio for an emphasis on personal problems was 3.5 (28:8). And that for an emphasis on family problems was 3.75 (30:8). No emphasis seemed to have produced benefits from treatment.

Treatment in the Cambridge-Somerville Youth Study had specifically included summer camp. The camps selected for placement were not designed for troublesome kids. They catered to a general population, one for which summer camping offered an alternative to city heat and boredom as well as the pleasures of outdoor activities.

Without appropriate equivalent comparisons in which both efficacy and safety are evaluated, we cannot know which treatments ought to be considered beneficial.

In part because I had developed a theory that would predict increased deviance through close association with peers one wanted to impress, I focused on effects of summer camp (Dishion, McCord, and Poulin 1999). The construct theory of motivation suggests that people construct their motives through the way they perceive choices and that these perceptions are influenced by perceived actions of their associates (McCord 1997, 1999, 2000). At summer camp, misbehaving boys would have unsupervised time during which they would be likely to brag about deviance. A bragging effect would be particularly noticeable among those sent to camp more than once. After the first summer, these boys would have known what camp was like and be in a position to estimate the effects of their reported daring (whether or not these reports were factual).

Among the 253 matched pairs assessed for follow-up, 125 of the treatment boys had been sent to summer camp, and 128 were not. The odds ratio for bad outcomes among those not sent to summer camp was 1.12 (28:25), that for the 59 boys sent to summer camp once was 1.33 (16:12), and that for the 66 boys sent to summer camp at least twice was 10.0 (20:2). In short, none of the treatment approaches showed measurable benefits, and some, particularly repeated placement in summer camps, resulted in harm.

I will summarize with the following list:

1. The Cambridge-Somerville Youth Study was carefully planned.
2. It was based on knowledge that poor families in disorganized neighborhoods were at high risk for crime.
3. Counselors had been trained to carry out their roles, and weekly conferences ensured that they were doing so.

4. Counselors integrated services provided by other available agencies with their own.
5. The program included youth with good as well as bad prognoses so that participation was not stigmatizing.
6. The youth study aimed to change many features of the environment, providing the boys with prosocial guidance, social skills, and healthful activities.
7. The program gave medical assistance and tutoring as well as guidance to both parents and youth.
8. Clients, for the most part, were satisfied with the program.
9. The program lasted five and one-half years, covering the period when the boys were between the ages of 10.5 and 16.
10. The program could be scientifically evaluated because its founder insisted that evaluation was central to the advance of social intervention practices.

Had there been no control group, evaluators might have concluded that the program was beneficial because so many of the treatment boys were better adjusted than anticipated. Or because two-thirds reported beneficial effects for themselves, evaluators might have judged that the program was effective. But these judgments would have been contrary to objective evidence that the program resulted in adverse outcomes for many of the participants.

Let me emphasize again the fact that the Cambridge-Somerville Youth Study was effective. The intervention had lasting effects. These effects were not beneficial.[1] The important legacy of the program, however, is its contribution to the science of prevention. Because the design supports scientifically credible conclusions, it showed that social interventions can have long-term effects. The results also serve to remind anyone willing to heed the warning that we do not yet know how to ensure benefits for youth in need of assistance.

Other Counterproductive Programs

The Cambridge-Somerville Youth Study is not alone in showing that sensible ideas and adequate implementation may produce interventions that fail to achieve their beneficial goals. The following sections describe some others.

Court volunteers

Many courts in the United States encourage volunteer counselors to work with delinquents. Few of these receive adequate evaluation. An exception occurred when Martin Gold, who was director of the Program on Children, Youth, and Family Life at the University of Michigan Institute for Social Research, arranged to evaluate Volunteers in Probation. The program had already won community respect.

Police, caseworkers, or judges could assign probationers to the Volunteers in Probation program. Participation required consent from both the juvenile and his or her guardian. The consent form requested participation in a study involving Volunteers in Probation. Random assignment took place after this consent was obtained, with two out of three being assigned to the program and one of three to a control group. Those in the control group received the ordinary services of the court, whereas those in the participation group were assigned to group counseling, individual counseling, and tutoring services provided by the volunteers. Evaluations occurred after six months and again after twelve months.

Both self-reports and official records showed that participation in the program inhibited a decline in criminality. Those assigned to the control group and those who had been assigned to the volunteer program but had not participated in it decreased their rates of crime. Those who participated in the volunteer program, however, increased the number of crimes they reported committing. Their court records, too, showed increases in crime as measured by the number of their police contacts (Berger et al. 1975).

Berger et al. (1975) summarized, "While we found some ways that the volunteer service was delivered that seem superior to other ways, none of these proved superior to providing no volunteer service at all" (p. VIII-2). Surprised and disappointed by the results of their study, Berger et al. cautioned,

> To those who may feel that other such programs, perhaps their own, are so much superior or so different from this program that our findings and recommendations are irrelevant to them, we urge caution. The staff responsible for this program has reasons good enough for them to feel that their program was effective when this study began, and without this study might still have no reason to feel otherwise. If there is anything that such a study as this one demonstrates, it is the danger of relying exclusively on faith in good works in the absence of systematic data. (Pp. VIII-1–VIII-2)

Group interaction training

Several studies have reported deficiencies in the social skills of delinquents. Hoping to reduce delinquency, many schools developed programs designed to increase the social skills of potential delinquents by giving them practice in discussing issues with well-adjusted peers. Typically, adult leaders guide the discussions. The programs have been called Positive Peer Culture, Peer Culture Development, Peer Group Counseling, and Guided Group Interaction. Several of the programs claim to be highly successful. Few have been evaluated using scientifically credible designs.

In 1982-1983, Gary Gottfredson (1987) arranged to have students in public schools of Chicago randomly selected for inclusion in either the treatment or the control group of a Guided Group Interaction program. Positive leaders, negative leaders, troublesome children, and average children were included in the pool. Fifty-one percent of both the treatment group and the control group were male, Caucasians were approximately equally distributed between the groups, and the groups were equivalent in terms of the prestige of parental occupations, prior police contacts, and age. School tardiness, attachment to parents, self-reported delinquency, and waywardness were used as measures of outcome.

Overall, the results for elementary school children showed no effects. For the high school students, however, the Guided Group Interaction program tended to increase misbehavior and delinquency. Gottfredson (1987) summarized the posttreatment comparisons: "the present results lend no support to any claim of benefit of treatment. . . . For the high school students, the effects appear predominantly harmful" (p. 708).

A somewhat different approach toward training young adolescents to have increased social skills has backfired in a program administered by the Oregon Social Learning Center. There, aggressive youngsters were randomly assigned to one of four groups: a teen training group that encouraged self-regulation and socialized behavior, a parental training group that encouraged parents to track their youngsters' behavior and to praise them for positive deeds, both, or one in which tapes and booklets substituted for group interaction. Whereas the parental training group (without peer training) seemed to show benefits, both groups assigned to peer training turned out worse than the no-interaction controls (Dishion and Andrews 1995).

Activities programs

Because of the poverty in which so much delinquency is embedded, many observers have concluded that delinquency might be reduced if alternative recreation were available. The Social Options for Teenagers Like You (S.O.F.T.L.Y.) program in Australia was designed as an activities program to provide healthful recreation to delinquent adolescents. In addition, the program was designed

> to develop socially relevant skills, develop an awareness of options, teach skills to create
> further options, teach decision-making, planning and organizational skills (being at the
> same time aware of the effects of the choice on self and others), and reduce recidivism.
> (Dufty and Richards 1978, ii)

The program consisted in group activities guided by peer group leaders trained by a supervisor to attend to the participating teenagers' interests. Weekly meetings provided support to the leaders.

Normally, groups met twice a week. Attempts were made to include parents in the meetings, a process facilitated by rotating meeting places among participants' homes. During the first weekly meeting, the group planned the activity to be carried out during the second meeting. Peer groups lasted between ten and twelve weeks.

The experimental group included ten peer groups with four to seven participants in each. Although forty-six teenagers were originally selected, only thirty-nine participants took part in both baseline and follow-up evaluation. A control group of teenagers was matched on sex, age, offending history during six months prior to the initial interview, guardianship, race, nationality of parental figures, work involvement of parental figures, and intellectual capacity.

Assessments were carried out for the experimental group just before the groups were formed and again six months later. For the comparison group, assessments were carried out when a match was identified and then six months after this identification.

The evaluation included measures of school and work involvement as well as delinquent activity. Reliable differences were not found for the former.

Court records identified a greater number of offenders among the treatment group during the first three months following completion of the intervention. Both groups decreased their rates of offending, but only the control group showed a significant decrease in the number of offenses committed. Dufty and Richards (1978) concluded that "this means that S.O.F.T.L.Y. as it currently operates has a detrimental effect on the 'delinquently inclined' by increasing recidivism once the intervention ceases" (p. 42). As a consequence of the evaluation, the S.O.F.T.L.Y. program was disbanded.

Scared Straight

Inmates designed a program, popularly known as Scared Straight, on an assumption that delinquency could be prevented by giving wild youngsters a taste of what it would be like to be imprisoned. The project started in Rahway Prison in New Jersey, where its endorsement by judges helped to make a convincing film that popularized the program.

Without scientifically respectable evaluations, Scared Straight projects were adopted in thirty-eight states. Congress held hearings about the program because researchers were skeptical. Miller and Hoelter (1979) found the town from which thirteen of seventeen youngsters in the film had come. They learned that some of the teenagers in the film claimed to have committed crimes to prove they were not scared.

Finally, careful research was carried out, with random assignment to San Quentin's Squires Program or to a control group. Twelve months later, 81 percent of the experimental group and 67 percent of the control group had been arrested (Lewis 1983). Other scientifically credible evaluations, too, have shown that attempts to scare teenagers into better behavior is not a successful enterprise (Petrosino, Turpin-Petrosino, and Buehler 2002).

Summary and Conclusions

I have described five types of programs that seemed promising but had harmful effects. Evidence about two of these—those involving court volunteers and those providing healthful group activities—appear in what has been called the fugitive literature. That is, despite solid research designs, the results have not been published. Evidence about adverse effects from social programs is hard to find in part because of a strong bias against reporting adverse effects of social programs. Authors of studies that fail to produce evidence of beneficial outcomes sometimes do not bother to submit their reports for publication. But also, those who do submit for publication tend to receive delays or rejections attributable to the unpalatable message they convey.

Many people seem to be willing to believe favorable results of inadequate evaluation designs. Some accept testimonials from clients who express their appreciation of a program. Against the claim that these provide valid evidence of effect, it should be noted that each of the programs described above would have been counted as successful by this criterion. Yet the clients would have been better off had they not participated in the programs.

Some argue that without comparison groups, measures taken before and after intervention can be used for valid evaluations. But changes over time occur for a variety of reasons, many of which are not documented. If changes are favorable and are more likely to occur in the absence of a program, the program should not be considered beneficial. The Cambridge-Somerville Youth Study might have been considered beneficial had improvements over prediction been accepted as the measure of outcome.

[E]ach of the harmful programs described above had been considered beneficial prior to its evaluation.

Often, one finds resistance to scientifically credible evaluations on the grounds that one ought not deprive some clients of the benefits given to others. Yet each of the harmful programs described above had been considered beneficial prior to its evaluation. Without appropriate equivalent comparisons in which both efficacy and safety are evaluated, we cannot know which treatments ought to be considered beneficial.

I have read several final reports of intervention programs that describe outcomes that are significantly worse than those in the comparison but include in the executive summary only results favorable to the program, often adding that the size of the sample precludes obtaining significant differences favoring treatment.

When results of the Cambridge-Somerville study were first published (and they were published only on the condition that a critical article would be coupled with its publication), I received threatening phone calls and notes. When I gave talks about these results, in many audiences, people shouted ugly names at me.

Researchers typically fail to consider whether social programs have had adverse effects, looking only for favorable results of treatment. Government agencies sponsor intervention programs with no provision for adequate evaluation. These are problems for the advancement of social well-being.

Yet providers of social services do not have a right to harm their clients. Nor do most providers wish to do so. But the social climate that buries evidence of harm is powerful. That social climate must be changed.

Clearly, social programs can have enduring effects. Although some popular interventions have harmful effects, of course, other intervention programs benefit their clients. Without scientifically credible evaluations, we cannot learn which programs are beneficial and which are harmful.

It is not enough to evaluate a program once. As noted by Weisburd and Taxman (2000), "The strength of experimental designs in specifying treatment impacts for specific populations does not in itself overcome the weaknesses associated with single site research studies" (p. 316).

Even when replications suggest that a particular type of program is effective, we should not assume that the program will work under new conditions. Historical changes, for example, in the definitions of crime or availability of drugs or of employment might alter the outcome of particular interventions. Demographic differences such as age, sex, or ethnicity might affect whether an intervention is effective. Different places, with different practices (e.g., regarding day care, medical coverage, or education), might reflect the influence of unmeasured variables on the relationship between interventions and outcomes. As Peter Grabosky (1996) noted in his review of unintended consequences of crime prevention strategies, "What works in Wollongong might fail on Palm Island" (p. 39).

Canada bears many similarities to the United States. Nevertheless, the Center for Children & Families in the Justice System wisely recognized that programs effective in some environments might not be effective in different environments. It brought the promising multisystemic therapy (Henggeler, Melton, and Smith 1992; Henggeler et al. 1993) from the United States to Ontario, Canada. The Canadian program involved a multisite design with random assignment to treatment and comparison groups. The comparison groups received the usual treatments in each of the four cites involved in the study. Program fidelity was monitored. Survival curves for convictions of 407 youth at six months, 363 at one year, 239 at two years, and 115 at three years give no indication of benefit from the program. Alison Cunningham (2002), director of research and planning for the project wrote, "Because the control group has the same outcomes as the MST [multisystemic therapy] recipients, it is unsafe to conclude that the two American studies are sufficient evidence to justify the wide-spread adoption of MST in Canada" (p. 11).

Social programs can cause crime as well as reduce it. They also can increase illness and reduce the ability of clients to cope with life's challenges. Effects of criminal justice interventions on education, mental health, and job performance deserve attention. A practice that decreases crime but increases alcoholism or mental illness might not be considered a net gain either by the clients or by the community that supported the program.

Potentially harmful effects of drugs have been recognized, and drug companies are required to keep track of reports of problems with the medications they advertise and sell. These can be subject to periodic review. Similar standards might be embraced for social programs. Recognizing that programs can have harmful effects may be critical to acceptance of experimental designs for evaluating social interventions.

Clearly, if social practice is to be improved, continuing evaluation should be an integral part of social interventions. Whenever possible, these evaluations should employ random assignment of similar people to either treatment or comparison groups. Always, the outcome should be measured in ways that do not rely on the typically favorable biases of clients, program providers, and sponsors. The evaluations should, of course, include a check for evidence of adverse effects as well as benefits.

We do not know the dimensions of variation that affect social programs. Careful collection of data to document the process of treatments and their effects should become as essential in the field of criminology as it is in the field of highway or air-line safety.

It would be extremely useful to have not only a data repository that provides systematic reviews of high-quality research, as will the Campbell Collaboration (Farrington and Petrosino 2001), but also one that collects information about particular programs in specific venues. If evaluation becomes an expected part of program administration, and all well-designed programs and their evaluations contribute toward such a data repository, knowledge about the safety and effectiveness of social programs would begin to accumulate, and informed decisions could be made.

Note

1. Discussion of possible causes for these effects can be found in McCord (1978, 1981) and Dishion, McCord, and Poulin (1999).

References

Allport, Gordon. 1951. Foreword. In *An experiment in the prevention of delinquency: The Cambridge-Somerville Youth Study*, edited by E. Powers and H. Witmer. New York: Columbia University Press.

Begg, Colin B. 1994. Publication bias. In *The handbook of research synthesis*, edited by Harris Cooper and Larry V. Hedges. New York: Russell Sage.

Berger, R. J., J. E. Crowley, M. Gold, J. Gray, and M. S. Arnold. 1975. *Experiment in a juvenile court: A study of a program of volunteers working with juvenile probationers*. Ann Arbor: Institute for Social Research, University of Michigan.

Cunningham, Alison. 2002. *One step forward: Lessons learned from a randomized study of multisystemic therapy in Canada*. London, Canada: Centre for Children and Families in the Justice System.

Dickersin, Kay, and Y.-I. Min. 1994. Publication bias: The problem that won't go away. *Annals of the New York Academy of Sciences* 703:135-46.

Dishion, Thomas J., and David W. Andrews. 1995. Preventing escalation in problem behaviors with high-risk young adolescents: Immediate and 1-year outcomes. *Journal of Consulting and Clinical Psychology* 63 (4): 538-48.

Dishion, Thomas J., Joan McCord, and François Poulin. 1999. When interventions harm: Peer groups and problem behavior. *American Psychologist* 54 (9): 1-10.

Dufty, B. J., and W. Richards. 1978. Evaluation of S.O.F.T.L.Y. Unpublished manuscript, Australian Institute of Criminology, Canberra.

Easterbrook, P. J., J. A. Berlin, R. Gopalan, and D. R. Matthews. 1991. Publication bias in clinical research. *Lancet* 337:867-72.

Farrington, David P., and Anthony Petrosino. 2001. The Campbell Collaboration Crime and Justice Group. *Annals of the American Academy of Political and Social Science* 578:35-49.

Gottfredson, Gary D. 1987. Peer group interventions to reduce the risk of delinquent behavior: A selective review and a new evaluation. *Criminology* 25 (3): 671-714.

Grabosky, Peter N. 1996. Unintended consequences of crime prevention. *Crime Prevention Studies* 5:25-56.

Healy, William, and Augusta F. Bronner. 1926. *Delinquents and criminals: Their making and unmaking.* New York: Macmillan.

Henggeler, Scott W., Gary B. Melton, and Linda A. Smith. 1992. Family preservation using multisystemic therapy: An effective alternative to incarcerating serious juvenile offenders. *Journal of Consulting & Clinical Psychology* 60:953-61.

Henggeler, Scott W., Gary B. Melton, Linda A. Smith, Sonja K. Schoenwald, and J. H. Hanley. 1993. Family preservation using multisystemic therapy: Longterm follow-up to a clinical trial with serious juvenile offenders. *Journal of Child & Family Studies* 2:283-93.

Lewis, Roy V. 1983. Scared Straight—California style. *Criminal Justice and Behavior* 10 (2): 284-89.

McCord, Joan. 1978. A thirty-year follow-up of treatment effects. *American Psychologist* 33 (3): 284-89.

———. 1981. Consideration of some effects of a counseling program. In *New directions in the rehabilitation of criminal offenders*, edited by Susan E. Martin, Lee B. Sechrest, and Robin Redner. Washington, DC: National Academy of Sciences.

———. 1992. The Cambridge-Somerville Study: A pioneering longitudinal-experimental study of delinquency prevention. In *Preventing antisocial behavior: Interventions from birth through adolescence*, edited by Joan McCord and Richard E. Tremblay. New York: Guilford.

———. 1997. He did it because he wanted to . . . In *Motivation & delinquency*. Vol. 44 of *Nebraska symposium on motivation*, edited by D. Wayne Osgood. Lincoln: University of Nebraska Press.

———. 1999. Understanding childhood and subsequent crime. *Aggressive Behavior* 25:241-53.

———. 2000. A theory of motivation and the life course. In *Social dynamics of crime and control: New theories for a world in transition*, edited by Susanne Karstedt and Kai-D Bussmann. Portland, OR: Hart.

Miller, Jerome G., and Herbert H. Hoelter. 1979. *Prepared testimony: Oversight on Scared Straight.* Washington, DC: Government Printing Office.

The New York Times. 2002. 4 April, p. C5.

Petrosino, Anthony, Carolyn Turpin-Petrosino, and John Buehler. 2002. *The effects of Scared Straight and other juvenile awareness programs on delinquency.* Issue 3 of *Cochrane library.* Oxford, UK: Update Software.

Powers, Edwin, and Helen Witmer. 1951. *An experiment in the prevention of delinquency: The Cambridge-Somerville Youth Study.* New York: Columbia University Press.

Scherer, Roberta W., Kay Dickersin, and Patricia Langenberg. 1994. Full publication of results initially presented in abstracts: A meta-analysis. *Journal of the American Medical Association* 272:158-62.

Sherman, Lawrence W., Denise C. Gottfredson, Doris L. MacKenzie, John E. Eck, Peter Reuter, and Shawn D. Bushway. 1997. *Preventing crime: What works, what doesn't, what's promising.* Washington DC: U.S. Department of Justice, National Institute of Justice.

Weisburd, David, and Faye S. Taxman. 2000. Developing a multicenter randomized trial in criminology: The case of HIDTA. *Journal of Quantitative Criminology* 16:315-40.

[33]

Confidentiality in a Preventive Child Welfare System

Eileen Munro

Emerging child welfare policies promoting preventive and early intervention services present a challenge to professional ethics, raising questions about how to balance respect for service users with concern for social justice. This article explains how the UK policy involves shifting the balance of power away from families towards state and professional decision making. The policy is predicated on sharing information between professionals to inform risk and need assessment and so poses a problem for the ethic of confidentiality in a helping relationship. This article examines the arguments for information sharing and questions whether the predicted benefits for children outweigh the cost of eroding family privacy and changing the nature of professional relationships with service users.

Keywords Child Welfare; Child Protection; Risk Assessment; Information and Communications Technology; Preventive Services; Confidentiality

Introduction

At first sight, a policy of prevention and early intervention in child welfare looks beguilingly altruistic. It has many persuasive attractions: it could reduce the amount of distress or harm experienced by the child; problems may be easier to tackle while they are still at a low level; if effective, the policy might reduce the cost to society of responding later to severely problematic older children and adults.

Prevention and early intervention services also seem more appealing than the current state of child welfare systems in many developed countries. They have become dominated by reactive services for serious problems, especially problems of child abuse and neglect (Audit Commission 1994; Department of Health 1995; Waldfogel 1998). Many find this frustrating and irrational: so often, the families presenting with severe and complex abuse problems were clearly showing low-level signs of difficulty for years beforehand but had been unable to obtain services because the threshold for access had become so high. Practi-

Eileen Munro is a Reader in Social Policy. Correspondence to: Eileen Munro, London School of Economics, Houghton Street, London, WC2A 2AE, UK; E-mail: e.munro@lse.ac.uk

tioners now faced with intransigent difficulties wish that help had been offered earlier to prevent the situation deteriorating. Not only would the problems have been easier to solve but also the children would have endured less adversity and harm.

But such a change in policy raises a set of questions about the power balance involved in implementing it. Who needs preventive help and what type of help do they need? Who decides what is in the child's best interests? Should help be available universally or targeted on specific groups? Should it be available on a voluntary basis for those families who want to take up a service or should the need for a service be determined by professional assessment followed by encouraging, or even coercing, the family to accept the service?

These are the questions that the UK government has faced as it has drawn up ambitious plans to tackle problems of social exclusion, criminality, and child abuse in England.[1] The conclusions it has reached have led to policies that, when fully implemented over the next two years, will change the relationship between the family and the state and the relationships between the family and professionals in the helping professions. In its concern to tackle the social injustice experienced by children born into disadvantage, the government is placing a greater onus on the professional network to take responsibility for children's outcomes and for judging needs. The policy therefore includes an emphasis on sharing information between professionals to monitor children's development and improve risk and need assessment. This article will explain why information sharing has taken such a prominent role in the new policy and discuss the implications for professional practice and, in particular, for the professional ethic of confidentiality that has been so fundamental to practice in the caring professions.

The New Children's Policy in England

The new approach to children's policy, embodied in the Green Paper *Every Child Matters: Change for Children* (The Treasury 2003) (hereinafter referred to as ECM), aims to develop preventive and supportive services for all children. In the Introduction to the Green Paper, the prime minister begins by saying that it is being published as the government's response to the inquiry into the death of Victoria Climbie, who suffered severe abuse at the hands of her carers before being murdered by them (Laming 2003). The goal of the ECM policy, however, is far more ambitious than just reducing the incidence of abuse and neglect. In its broadest formulation, it is to help all children fulfil their potential. UK Prime Minister Tony Blair sums up the political aim in his introduction to the Green Paper:

---

1. This article refers to the UK government making children's policy specifically for England, not for the United Kingdom. Responsibility for children's services in the other three countries of the United Kingdom is devolved to the Northern Ireland Assembly, the Scottish Assembly, and, partially, to the National Assembly for Wales.

> This country is still one where life chances are unequal. This damages not only those children born into disadvantages, but our society as a whole. We all stand to share the benefits of an economy and society with less educational failure, higher skills, less crime, and better health. We all share a duty to do everything we can to ensure every child has the chance to fulfil their potential. (The Treasury 2003, p. 6)

A key element of the new policy is to move from a reactive service for a few to a preventive service for the many:

> We need to shift away from associating parent support with crisis interventions to a more consistent offer of parenting support throughout a child and young person's life. We will work towards a mix of universal and targeted parenting approaches, including advice and information, home visiting and parenting classes. (The Treasury 2003, para. 3.6)

Within this all-embracing agenda, however, certain groups are identified as key priorities: the policy: "aims to reduce the numbers of children who experience educational failure, engage in offending or anti-social behaviour, suffer from ill health, or become teenage parents" (The Treasury 2003, p. 5). The social exclusion action plan (HM Government 2006a) gives more detail of the priority groups and the reasons for selecting them. A "cycle of disadvantage" is identified in which "deprivation in one generation is likely to pass down to the next. For example, the daughter of a teenage mother is twice as likely as the daughter of an older mother to become pregnant in her teen years" (HM Government 2006a, para.1.4). The aim of the action plan is to "mitigate the lifelong effects of social exclusion and prevent them being passed down to future generations" (HM Government 2006a, para. 1.5). The size of the problem is estimated as "about 2.5% of every generation seem to be stuck in a life-time of disadvantage" (Blair 2006b).

Historically, concerns about problem families have been fired by a mixture of concern for the injustice experienced by the underprivileged and concern for the negative impact of their problematic behaviour on society (Parton 2006). This combination is apparent in the current policy. There is a condemnation of the social injustice of being born to a position in society where children lack the same opportunities as their more privileged peers. But there is also a strong concern that these children may become a problem for society: they may become criminals or make little economic contribution. A new term has been coined to describe the problems they present: high-cost/high-harm adult outcomes (Feinstein & Sabates 2006, p. 1).

Who Needs Help?

Deciding who needs help is a complex problem. The first issue to address is whether the answer should be based on a rights or a needs approach.

44   MUNRO

Since the United Kingdom has ratified the UN Convention on the Rights of the Child, it has committed itself to respecting the rights of children. This Convention has an impressive international endorsement. It has been ratified by all countries in the world except the United States and Somalia, which have indicated their intention to ratify by taking the initial step of signing it. In listing children's rights, the Convention provides a checklist of their needs (e.g. for family life, healthcare, education, protection from abuse, etc.). The Convention, however, has limited practical value in that it is phrased in such general terms that further definition is required to apply it to specific contexts. This, in fact, was essential as a means of reaching some area of agreement between the diverse range of cultures in the world.

In practice, the UK government has not drawn on the Convention framework in its policy, preferring instead to take a needs approach. In parliamentary debates on the Children Bill, it was made clear by the Minister for Children that a rights approach was not the basis for its policy when rejecting amendments from the House of Lords that anchored the legislation in the rights framework (Hansard debates for 13 September 2004). This has the significant effect of changing the basis for receiving a service from being a right to being assessed by someone else as having a need, and allows the government to set its own priorities about which needs to tackle. Instead of using the Convention on the Rights of the Child, the government has chosen to define needs in relation to five overall targets or preferred outcomes: be healthy, stay safe, enjoy and achieve, make a positive contribution, and achieve economic well-being. Even when the meaning of these targets is expanded by the set of performance indicators (DfES 2004), there is, as with the Convention, further work needed to apply them in particular instances.

Who should do this further work? Should need be defined by family members themselves, in accordance with their values and beliefs, and their judgements about what is in a particular child's best interests? Should it be defined by experts, in the light of their specialist knowledge of child development? Or should it be defined by the government, the paymaster of the helping services, taking account also of what is in the best interests of the country?

In practice, definitions of need tend to result from some combination of all three points of view, with no one voice being supreme. However, the balance of power between them becomes significant when we move on to the next question of how to identify children in need of help. The three main strategies mentioned in government documents echo these three points of view. They are:

(1) family members themselves seeking help;
(2) professionals in contact with the family judging that the child is developing, or is at risk of developing, problematic behaviour and making a referral to the appropriate service;

(3) screening all families for the presence of risk factors, identifying a sub-group as "high risk" for outcomes of major political concern, and then targeting services on them.

Service Provision (1): Families Seeking Help

The option of families identifying a need and seeking help is a familiar one and it accords well with a liberal society such as England where parents have, traditionally, been given the primary responsibility for their children's upbring-ing. Their responsibility has involved not only duties, such as ensuring children receive an education, but also powers, such as deciding what religion they should be taught, or what medical care they should receive. This option accords well with the political rhetoric about the autonomy of the family, the expertise of the parents in knowing what is in their child's best interests, and the state's reluctance to intervene.

The rights of parents are set out in the Children Act 1989, section 3(1). The primary role of the family is endorsed by the UN Convention on the Rights of the Child. Article 5 sets out parents' powers and duties that states should respect:

> The responsibilities, rights and duties of parents or, where applicable, the members of the extended family or community as provided for by local custom, legal guardians or other persons legally responsible for the child, to provide, in a manner consistent with the evolving capacities of the child, appropriate direction and guidance in the exercise by the child of the rights recognized in the present Convention.

It is important not to overstate the autonomy of the family. Parents are subject to extensive rules and forceful guidance on the proper way to bring up their children (King & Piper 1995, p. 2).

The option of families seeking help does not imply a passive role for the helping professions or for the state. Services may advertise their availability and seek to advise families on how to recognize when help might be useful. The health visiting service is a good example of a well-known support service that is available universally but taken up on a voluntary basis. Professionals who are already in contact with the family may identify additional need and suggest seeking help. At the level of the state, public health education seeks to inform families of healthier options (e.g. of what is a nutritious diet and how to minimize the risk of obesity).

From families' point of view, the main problem they have experienced is that, in practice, there are inadequate services available so that families with low-level problems are often turned away without receiving the help they seek. Increasing resources would alleviate this problem but governments are, under-standably, concerned about keeping control of public spending and, if services were more readily available, it is difficult to predict what the level of unmet need might be. In addition, families who currently find the help and support they need from informal sources might start using public services instead, fuelling the level of demand even further. Economic factors place a restriction on how much the state can respond to families' requests for help.

When the family is the key decision maker, it is easier to implement the professional ethics about respecting users, supporting their right to control their lives, and respecting diversity. However, leaving authority with the family does lead to concerns about social justice. What about the families who do not seek help despite their children having unmet needs? What duty does the state have to protect children from inadequate care? How strenuous should official efforts be to ensure all children have the opportunity to fulfil their potential, even when their parents do not share the state's concerns or beliefs about what is in the child's best interests?

Historically, the state has intervened forcibly in English family life very little so that the threshold for invading the private family space has been set relatively high at the level of significant harm. When the inadequate care amounts to serious child abuse or neglect then coercive measures may be taken and the professional ethic of confidentiality will be breached to ensure accurate assessment of the risks to the child.

The key relevant aspect of abuse and neglect is that abusive and neglectful parents often go to great lengths to conceal their actions; we are essentially trying to expose a crime. In these circumstances, it would be unrealistic to rely on parents giving consent to the sharing of information that would incriminate them. The importance of sharing information has been demonstrated repeatedly in inquiries into child deaths. For the United Kingdom, the landmark illustration of this was the case of Maria Colwell whose death in 1973 led to a major public inquiry into child protection services (DHSS 1974). The inquiry revealed how a number of agencies had had partial pictures of Maria's life which, taken independently, produced only moderate concern in practitioners but, once put together, showed that she was suffering extreme abuse and neglect for many months before her death. As a result of cases like this, it has become well established that a family's right to privacy is limited when there are child protection concerns. This principle is recognized, in law, in the Human Rights Act 1998 and the Data Protection Act 1998 and, in professional practice, by the ethical guidance on confidentiality (e.g. General Medical Council 2004, para. 29).

With other child welfare concerns, parents are not generally trying to hide their problems in such nefarious ways but they may have any of a number of reasons for not wanting to engage with formal services. Some may prefer to handle the problems on their own or by relying on support from families and communities. Some may feel it is a waste of time to ask for help because they know how limited resources are or they had a bad experience in previous contact with the service. To some degree, parents' willingness to accept help depends on how it is made available. It can be argued that there would be a greater take up of services on a voluntary basis if they were offered in a more accessible and user-friendly way, drawing on the research findings on service users' views (e.g. Quinton 2004).

However, there is one further group of parents who refuse to engage with services: those who do not use services but who are living in circumstances that the government deems to make them socially excluded. They are described as groups "that have generally failed to fulfil their potential and accept the opportunities that most of us take for granted" (HM Government 2006a, para. 1.16). This group seems to be a particular concern to the government, which sees them as being too unreliable and untrustworthy to be left in charge of decision making about their children. It is this group that leads to political rhetoric with an authoritarian ring: "there is not going to be a solution unless we are sufficiently hard-headed to say that from a very early age we need a system of intervention" (Blair 2006a); "social inclusion means tough policies" (Armstrong 2006).

The group is referred to as "hard to reach" but there is an ambiguity in the meaning of this phrase. It does not appear to mean hard to find since one of the complicating factors in helping them is considered to be the number of agencies involved with them (HM Government 2006a, para. 1.21). Blair uses the phrase "hard to reach" to refer both to those who are hard to engage in a helping relationship and those who are hard to help effectively (Blair 2006b). If they are already in contact with several agencies and so engaged in some form of relationship, it is unclear how much professional lack of resources or skill contributes to the failure to help them effectively.

Concern about this group of "hard to reach families" seems to be a major factor in inspiring the emphasis on information sharing as central to the ECM policy because, like abusive parents, they are less likely to co-operate and agree with professional judgements about their children.

Service Provision (2 and 3): Professional Need Assessment and Screening

In developing preventive services, one decision to make is between primary and secondary prevention (Farrington 2006). Primary prevention involves offering a service to all families. This can be at a national level, such as the English health visiting service, or in specified areas—the early SureStart schemes were located in areas of deprivation but were then available universally to all who lived there. In a secondary prevention policy, screening and risk assessments are carried out to identify "high-risk" families and then services are targeted on them.

With the ECM policy for England the government has decided to opt primarily for secondary prevention, targeting services on those deemed most at risk. Consequently, monitoring and assessing parental factors as well as children's development becomes a central concern. The concept of children "at risk" has now been extended from its familiar meaning of children at risk of abuse to include a number of other outcomes that the government wishes to change, in particular children at risk of social exclusion and at risk of anti-social and delinquent behaviour.

48   MUNRO

The government draws on research about children's development and outcomes to conclude that it is possible to assess risk accurately: "There is now a
wealth of empirical data to analyse. The purport of it is clear. You can detect and
predict the children and families likely to go wrong" (Blair 2006b). The two main
sets of research that they consult are studies on crime and anti-social behaviour
(summarized by Farrington 2006) and on the prediction of which children will be
high cost/high harm in adult life (summarized by Feinstein & Sabates 2006). The
literature on predicting child abuse and neglect is not mentioned in policy
discussions of social exclusion.

The importance of monitoring and the dominance of professional judgement
and decision making over the families' own views are illustrated in the central
importance ascribed to inter-professional sharing of information:

> A positive commitment to information sharing between professionals and
> agencies, taking full advantage of the opportunities set out under statute, is
> the only way to ensure that all children and young people are provided with the
> most appropriate support as and when they need it. (The Treasury 2003, p. 2)

And

> Good information sharing is the key to successful collaborative working and early
> intervention to help children and young people at risk of poor outcomes. (DfES
> 2005b, p. 1)

To improve information sharing, the government committed itself to removing
the legal and technical barriers:

> the Government will remove the legislative barriers to better information
> sharing, and the technical barriers to electronic information sharing through
> developing a single unique identity number, and common data standards on the
> recording of information. (The Treasury 2003, p. 8)

The groundwork for removing the legal obstacles to sharing information has been
set out in the Children Act 2004. Section 10 of the Act places a duty on each
children's services authority to make arrangements to "promote cooperation"
between itself and relevant partner agencies to improve the well-being of
children in its area in relation to: physical and mental health, and emotional
well-being; protection from harm and neglect; education, training and recreation; the contribution made by them to society; and social and economic well-
being. Section 12 requires children's services authorities to establish information
sharing and assessment databases covering ALL children living in the area served
by the authority. The government intends these databases to be tools to assist a
wide range of practitioners in achieving the five outcomes for all children and
young people identified in the legislation. The databases are not intended to be
focused narrowly on child protection or child abuse, but aim to improve the
sharing of information between professionals in order to improve the well-being
of all children.

The technical obstacles to sharing information are tackled by two key strategies: providing standardized forms for recording data about families for use by all professional groups, and developing an ICT system so that data are recorded electronically in a way that is readily accessible to the various agencies and practitioners involved with families (Anderson *et al*. 2006).

The key data collection systems will be:

- The information sharing index (IS index). This will contain basic details of all children in England, including all professionals in contact with them and their contact details. Professionals will enter an "indication" (formerly called a "flag of concern") to show that they have important information to share, have made an assessment, or are taking action. The index will contain no sensitive case information, such as the child being on the child protection register.
- The Common Assessment Framework (CAF). This is a "nationally standardized approach to conducting an assessment of the needs of a child or young person and deciding how those needs should be met" (downloaded from < www.everychildmatters.gov.uk > 21 February 2006). It should be completed by any professional when they consider that a child has additional needs that require the involvement of more than one service. The idea is to save time by undertaking one assessment that can be used thereafter by any other agency offering a service to the child. It includes a wide-ranging set of data covering every aspect of a child's health and development, including details about the parents and siblings.
- The Integrated Children's System (ICS). This is an electronic case management system for children's social services that will include the case records of all children known to social workers. The ICS contains a set of 27 forms, nine for each of three categories: children in need, children in need of protection, and children looked after.

In addition, there are databases in health, education and criminal justice but the extent to which they will be linked is not yet clear.

Evaluating a Screening Programme

The purpose of collecting and sharing so much information about families is to permit screening for high-risk families. The strategy of screening populations for problems is well-established in medicine, though rarer in relation to social problems. It may involve identifying those with early signs of a disease and offering treatment (e.g. cervical cancer screening) or those who have the risk factors that make them at higher than average risk of developing a disease and therefore merit monitoring for signs of emerging disease or being given advice on how to reduce the risk factors (e.g. screening for high blood pressure).

50   MUNRO

While there is an obvious attraction to the idea that we are able to predict, intervene, and so prevent serious social problems, the introduction of a screening programme for a social problem needs to be measured against the same scientific criteria as screening for medical problems, such as screening for cervical cancer. There are three key criteria against which to judge a screening programme: predictive accuracy, treatability, and the level of damaging effects.

Predictability: does the screening process result in risk assessments with an acceptably high rate of accuracy? In predicting risk of child abuse and neglect, existing risk instruments lead to an unacceptably high level of false positives (families inaccurately deemed to be high risk) and a high level of false negatives (dangerous families wrongly judged safe) (Munro 2004; Peters & Barlow 2003). With respect to predicting criminality and social exclusion, the reports are mixed:

> Any notion that better screening can enable policy makers to identify young children destined to join the 5 per cent of offenders responsible for 50–60 per cent of crime is fanciful. Even if there were no ethical objections to putting "potential delinquent" labels round the necks of young children, there would continue to be statistical barriers. Research into the continuity of anti-social behaviour shows substantial flows out of—as well as in to—the pool of children who develop chronic conduct problems. This demonstrates the dangers of assuming that anti-social five-year-olds are the criminals or drug abusers of tomorrow. (Sutton *et al.* 2005, p. 5)

Farrington (2006), whose review of the criminology literature is cited by the government, concludes that predictive accuracy is insufficient and comes down in favour of primary rather than secondary prevention (i.e. *not* trying to screen and target high-risk families).

Feinstein and Sabates (2006), however, come to the opposite conclusion in respect to the literature on high-risk/high-harm families. The discrepancy is partly explained by the fact that Farrington is looking at predicting serious criminality, which is relatively rare, whereas Feinstein and Sabates consider a wide range of poor adult outcomes that are more common. Their optimistic judgement on predictability is also qualified. They warn that:

> Children move in and out of risk in terms of their own development and their levels of contextual risk. Therefore, it is important that the policy mechanisms allocating interventions and support to children and families are flexible and able to track and monitor levels of risk, not always intervening at the first sign of risk but equally able to provide early interventions that may reduce the need for more substantive and costly later interventions. This requires a considerable degree of local practitioner skill. (Feinstein & Sabates 2006, p. 35)

Ultimately, judgements about "acceptable" levels of accuracy come down to a moral judgement: how many innocent children is it acceptable to wrongly label "a future menace to society" (Blair 2006a) in order to catch a high number of accurate predictions?

Treatability: can the condition predicted by screening be usefully treated? Can we confidently say that we know how to tackle effectively the diverse range of factors predictive of poor adult outcomes? It is impossible to give a simple answer to such a complex question. There are undoubtedly some grounds for optimism in judging our ability to offer effective help that improves children's outcomes, but success, while significant, is modest. In a review of interventions for reducing criminality, for example, McLaren (2000) offers the remarkably wide estimate of between a 5 and 50 per cent success rate. To judge whether these were worth providing, we would also need to know the cost per child treated and to consider how else that money might have been spent.

The level of damaging effects: this applies to both the screening process itself and to the subsequent interventions used to alter the condition. The proposed screening system for England requires a major change in the balance of power between families and professionals and its repercussions are as yet unknown. If midwives take on the task prescribed by the prime minister of judging "which parents will be dysfunctional and which children will grow up to be a menace to society" (Blair 2006a), it might have a harmful effect on parents' willingness to confide in them.

The impact of professionals being able to offer less confidentiality is also potentially serious. Since the preventive policy is premised on the free flow of information between practitioners in order to identify and track children at risk of some problem, it is perhaps inevitable that government guidance mentions confidentiality and privacy only in a negative light. They are repeatedly referred to as "obstacles" to the efficient functioning of the integrated management system being developed for children's services. However, privacy and confidentiality are rights and therefore not to be disregarded lightly. Moreover, they have practical value: there is a substantial body of research that shows that people value a confidential helping relationship and will withhold information if they are not sure that it will be treated in confidence (Wattam 1999; Hallett *et al.* 2003). Recent studies of children's views of the new information-sharing proposals have produced a consistent message from children that, while they appreciate the need to breach confidentiality sometimes when there is a risk of significant harm, breaching it for other problems will deter young people from asking adults for help and advice (CRAE 2006; Hilton & Mills 2006).

We also need to consider whether the interventions provided have any harmful effects. The government rightly stresses the need to evaluate the new services (HM Government 2006a) but evaluative studies need to look for harm as well as success and they need to be conducted rigorously to maximize the reliability of the findings. Rutter (2006) is highly critical of the government's standard of evaluation of SureStart schemes, arguing that political considerations led them to ignore advisers and create an initiative that was impossible to evaluate because that could "carry the danger of showing that a key policy was a mistake". It would have been feasible and highly desirable to have conducted a random controlled trial which would have led to a more reliable judgement about whether large sums of public money were being put to the best use.

Overall, the case for a screening programme is not compellingly made. It carries uncertain benefits and certain losses in that it erodes people's privacy and right to confidentiality. Neither primary nor secondary policies have been tested adequately at this stage but there is a case for trying the less intrusive option first and seeing what progress can be made on a voluntary basis—finding out whether adequate resources can be provided and testing the effectiveness of the interventions offered.

Consent

The negative consequences of sharing information about families might be lessened if it were done only with families' consent. Government guidance endorses obtaining consent as necessary in some cases and good practice in others (HM Government 2006b). However, this respect for the user's choice is diluted by the clear assertion, within the guidance, that giving consent is essential for providing effective help and so it is presented as the rational thing to do:

> Sharing information is vital for early intervention to ensure that children and young people with additional needs get the services they require. It is also essential to protect children and young people from suffering harm from abuse or neglect and to prevent them from offending. (DfES 2006, p. 1)

The belief that giving consent is the sensible thing to do is also illustrated by the requirement that practitioners need to "understand how to present genuine choices to young people and how to obtain consent to sharing information" (DfES 2005a, p. 8).

This biased view of the rationality of giving consent colours the way that consent may be sought and carries with it the implication that anyone who withholds consent is in some way questionable. Indeed, in one illustrative vignette, it is suggested that it is acceptable to seek consent from a parent with the warning that if it is withheld it will be interpreted as grounds for suspecting the parent of being abusive or neglectful (DfES 2005b).

To be legally valid, consent needs to be free and informed, which the Information Commissioner clarifies as:

> Consent should always be freely given, thus any document prepared by the data controller to obtain consent should not contain any coercive element, and lack of consent should not generally cause any detriment to the individual, particularly in respect of any statutory rights that individual has. (Information Commissioner, pers. comm. 2006)

Evidence from trials of the databases gives cause for concern about the way in which the issue of obtaining consent is being handled. In trials of the CAF, it was found that professionals did not seek the necessary consent from the family in 20 per cent of cases (Brandon *et al.* 2006). There is anecdotal evidence from other pilots that consent is being required as a condition for receiving a service.

For professionals used to offering a confidential service, current developments present problems: Besides its therapeutic value, confidentiality is an important ethical principle in showing respect for individuals, supporting their right to control their lives, and respecting diversity. However, professionals will need to reach a clear understanding of when and with whom they may be required to share information so that their clients know the limits of confidentiality before giving them sensitive and personal information. In order to obtain informed consent they will also need to understand the way in which shared information will be used and may be accessed by other agencies.

Conclusion

The UK policy on prevention in child welfare includes a praiseworthy commitment to tackling the social injustice experienced by those children born into adverse circumstances that restrict their opportunities for achieving their potential in life. However, by opting for secondary instead of primary prevention it rests on a number of risky assumptions: that professionals can accurately predict which children will be problematic, that they can intervene effectively, using coercion if necessary, to change the course of children's development, and that there will be adequate resources to meet the needs identified through screening. It fails to consider what harm may be caused by the process of surveillance of families and by labelling children as future problems.

Rejecting the rights approach to defining children's needs that is embodied in the UN Convention on the Rights of the Child, the government has opted for its own set of targets and performance indicators. These can be criticized for placing too much value on the needs of society (for well-educated, healthy, law-abiding citizens) compared with the needs of the individual child. This imbalance is evidenced in the failure in policy documents to discuss children with special needs—those with physical disabilities and learning difficulties—whose need for support is immense but who are low risk for being high-cost/high-harm adults. Recent research has shown that most local authorities are ignoring disabled children in their children and young people's plans (EDCM 2006).

In policy debates, there seems to be an assumption that there is some objective measure of what is in a child's best interests and some objective standards of good parenting applicable in all social circumstances. The possibility of rational disagreement between a parent and a professional on what is in the child's best interests at a particular point in their lives is not addressed. As a French critic has commented, such an assumption of objectivity is unfounded and conceals the power struggle involved in reaching decisions about what is in a child's best interests:

54   MUNRO

> Which social classes, which sub-cultures, which professions or institutions, or
> which combination of these are going effectively to insert their social, moral and
> psychological values into the process of determining the child's best interests?
> (Stender 1979)

This failure to recognize the potential for conflict illustrates what is possibly the
most serious problem with the UK policy. "Power corrupts" is a well-known
truism but there is no acknowledgement of the possible danger of increasing
state power over families. There is no recognition of the fact that liberal
societies have placed a high value on privacy and confidentiality precisely
because they present an obstacle to the state. While the state sees this in
a negative light, the individual values it as a protection of their freedom. The
professional ethic of confidentiality is seen by the government as an *obstructive*
barrier to be removed in implementing their monitoring and assessment
programme but this should remind us that the ethical principle is playing its
rightful part as a *protective* barrier, defending the individual against excessive
intrusion by the state.

References

Anderson, R., Brown, I., Clayton, R., Dowty, T., Korff, D. & Munro, E. (2006) *Children's Databases—Safety and Privacy*, Information Commissioner's Office, Wilmslow, Cheshire.

Armstrong, H. (2006) 'Social Inclusion means Tough Policies'. *The Observer*, 5th September, 2006. <http://observer.guardian.co.uk/comment/story/0..1865337. html>. Accessed 6 September 2006.

Audit Commission (1994) *Seen but not Heard: Co-ordinating Community Child Health and Social Services for Children in Need*, HMSO, London.

Blair, A. (2006a) BBC News interview, 30 August 2006, available at: <www.bbc.co.uk>. Accessed 15 September 2006.

———. (2006b) "Our Nation's Future—Social Exclusion", speech to Joseph Rowntree Foundation, York, 5 September 2006, available at: <www.pm.gov.uk/output/ Page10037.asp>.

Brandon, M., Howe, A., Dagley, V., Salter, C., Warren, C. & Black, J. (2006) *Evaluating the Common Assessment Framework and Lead Professional Guidance and Implementation in 2005–6*, Research Report RR740, DfES, London.

Children's Rights Alliance for England (CRAE) (2006) *Children and Young People Talk about Information Sharing*, CRAE, London.

Department for Education and Skills (DfES) (2004) *Guidance on the Children and Young People's Plan*, DfES, London.

———. (2005a) *The Common Core of Knowledge and Skills for the Childcare Workforce*, DfES, London.

———. (2005b) *Cross Government Guidance—Sharing Information about Children and Young People—Consultation*, DfES, London.

———. (2006) "Fact Sheet: Information Sharing Practice", downloaded from <www.ecm. gov.uk/informationsharing> (2 February 2006).

Department of Health (1995) *Child Protection: Messages from Research*, HMSO, London.

Department of Health and Social Security (DHSS) (1974) *Report of the Committee of Inquiry into the Care and Supervision Provided in Relation to Maria Colwell*, HMSO, London.

Every Disabled Child Matters (ECDM) (2006) *Off the Radar: How Local Authority Plans Fail Disabled Children*, available at: < www.edcm.org.uk> . Accessed 15 September 2006.

Farrington, D. (2006) "Childhood Risk Factors and Risk-focused Prevention", available at: < www.pm.gov.uk/output/Page10035.asp> . Accessed 15 September 2006.

Feinstein, L. & Sabates, R. (2006) *Predicting Adult Life Outcomes from Earlier Signals: Identifying those at Risk*, Report for the PMSU, available at: < www.pm.gov.uk/output/Page10033.asp> . Accessed 15 September 2006.

General Medical Council (2004) *Confidentiality: Protecting and Providing Information*, GMC, London.

Hallett, C., Murray, C. & Punch, S. (2003) "Young People and Welfare: Negotiating Pathways", in *Hearing the Voices of Children: Social Policy for a New Century*, eds C. Hallett & A. Prout, RoutledgeFalmer, London.

Hilton, Z. & Mills, C. (2006) *"I Think it's about Trust": The Views of Young People on Information Sharing*, Office of the Children's Commissioner, London.

HM Government (2006a) *Reaching Out: An Action Plan on Social Exclusion*, Cabinet Office, London.

————. (2006b) *Information Sharing: Practitioners' Guide*, DfES, London.

King, M. & Piper, C. (1995) *How the Law Thinks about Children*, Arena, Aldershot.

Laming, H. (2003) *The Victoria Climbie Inquiry: Report of an Inquiry by Lord Laming*, The Stationery Office, London.

McLaren, K. (2000) *Tough is not Enough—Getting Smart about Youth Crime*, Ministry of Youth Affairs, Wellington, New Zealand.

Munro, E. (2004) "A Simpler Way to Understand the Results of Risk Assessment Instruments", *Children and Youth Services Review*, Vol. 26, no. 9, pp. 877–87.

Parton, N. (2006) *Safeguarding Childhood: Early Intervention and Surveillance in a Late Modern Society*, Palgrave Macmillan, Basingstoke.

Peters, R. & Barlow, J. (2003) "Systematic Review of Instruments Designed to Predict Child Maltreatment during the Antenatal and Postnatal Periods", *Child Abuse Review*, Vol. 12, pp. 416–39.

Quinton, D. (2004) *Supporting Parents: Messages from Research*, DfES, London.

Rutter, M. (2006) "Is Sure Start an Effective Preventive Intervention?", *Child and Adolescent Mental Health*, Vol. 11, no. 3, pp. 135–41.

Stender, F. (1979) "Les confits entre parents pour la garde des enfants: quel rôle jouent les professionels?", *Revue Internationale de l'enfant*, 41 (June) (quoted in King & Piper 1995, p. 2).

Sutton, C., Uttting, D. & Farrington, D. (2005) *Support from the Start: Working with Young Children and their Families to Reduce the Risks of Crime and Anti-social Behaviour*, Home Office Research Brief RB524, March 2005, Home Office, London.

The Treasury (2003) *Every Child Matters: Change for Children*, The Stationery Office, London.

Waldfogel, J. (1998) *The Future of Child Protection*, Harvard University Press, Cambridge, MA.

Wattam, C. (1999) "Confidentiality and the Social Organisation of Telling", in *Child Sexual Abuse: Responding to the Experiences of Children*, eds N. Parton & C. Wattam, Wiley, Chichester.

[34]

How to Win Friends and Not Influence Clients:
Popular but Problematic Ideas
that Impair Treatment Decisions

William O'Donohue & Jeff Szymanski, Northern Illinois University

Although the role of science in human affairs has been debated within the general culture (e.g., Snow, 1961) and within the philosophy of science (e.g., Feyerabend, 1978) there is substantial agreement in the mental health professions and particularly within behavioral clinical psychology that the results of scientific research are useful or even essential for informing clinical practice (McFall, 1991). Despite wide agreement with this general conception, research indicates that there are numerous problems with clinicians actually using research in their clinical decisions (Cohen, Sargent, & Sechrest, 1985; Morrow-Bradley & Elliott, 1986; O'Donohue, Curtis, & Fisher, 1985). In fact, one study failed to find evidence of any systematic decision processes regarding what assessment and treatment methods to use in their cases (O'Donohue, Fisher, Plaud & Curtis, 1990). Thus, there is apparently an interesting conflict: Clinicians generally agree that science is important for clinical decision making but in practice it is not frequently used. The question becomes, why is this the case? Below we will explore several ideas that in our experience have a surprising popularity which we think contribute to this problem and which we believe are all incorrect.

1. Due to various factors existing research is not relevant to my real world concerns.

This may be a reference to an external validity problem: extent research investigates dissimilar subsets of some critical design facets: e.g., a different kind of client in a somewhat different situation, or a different subtype of this problem, or with a somewhat dissimilar type of therapist. The truth of this claim needs to be carefully investigated. It should not simply be globally asserted as sometimes it can be plainly false. In many cases research exists that is at least partially similar to the clinician's situation. When this is not the case the research should not be judged irrelevant in an *a priori* fashion. Rather, the external validity of this research (generalizability; Cone, 1988) should be regarded as an open, empirical question that therapists can address by conducting their own research (e.g., case study, single subject design, etc) and in doing so, add important information regarding the external validity of a finding to the literature.

Second, another response to this claim is: Then on what body of knowledge are you providing your expert services? Claim 1 is often asserted as if there is some alternative body of relevant knowledge, although this repository of allegedly accurate information is seldom explicitly described. Science has been associated with a historically unprecedented growth of knowledge and has no equally credentialed rivals for the empirical questions associated with psychotherapy. Thus the three most reasonable courses of action would be to: 1) test an extrapolation from existing research; 2) to not treat; 3) or to test a novel hypothesis. Thus, this claim seems to be at least partly based on a fallacy of a mythical alternative.

Finally, questions need to be put to the individual who makes this claim: Do your informed consent procedures clearly inform the client (as well as any third party reimbursers) that research is irrelevant to what you are prescribing? Do these also accurately characterize the body of information that you are relying on for your services, including a faithful description of the weaknesses of this? Do you accurately characterize the full range of alternatives, including attempting the best extrapolation from the most relevant existing scientific literature?

Replacement belief: The relevance of research lies on a continuum. Sometimes it is directly relevant; sometimes much less so. In the later cases, practitioners need to construe this as an open, empirical question about generalizability and conduct a relevant study to test extrapolations or novel hypotheses.

2. Attempting to use research is a waste of time because there usually are conflicting results.

Although there continues to be some conflicting results in the literature, there are also some robust and consistent results. For example, exposure based techniques have consistently been shown to be effective with the various Anxiety Disorders (Foa, Olasov Rothbaum, & Kozak, 1989); cognitive therapy with depression (Barber & DeRubeis, 1989; Clark & Beck, 1989); and behavioral marital therapy for relationship distress (Wood & Jacobson, 1985) just to name a few. In addition, a greater degree of clarity has been introduced into the literature by attempting to identify what conditions are necessary in order for a particular intervention to be effective. For example, although systematic desensitization has generally been shown to be effective when working with persons suffering from simple phobias, it will not be helpful if the individual has difficulty using imagery, if he or she has a number of fears, or if he or she is high in arousability (Masters, Burish, Hollon, & Rimm, 1987).

This also points to the importance of doing thorough assessments. That is, if certain interventions are found to be effective only if certain conditions exist, then it would be important to assess for those conditions. An example is provided by Foa et al. (1989). They pointed out that exposure and response prevention is effective for the majority of persons with obsessive-compulsive disorder (i.e., ritualizers), but not for a particular subset of them (i.e., ruminators). Finally, even if some degree of ambiguity remains in the literature about what would be the optimal intervention to use for a particular case, the current research can still be used as a guideline to narrow down the various choices into a smaller subset of possible interventions.

Replacement belief: Research can point to consistently effective interventions for some disorders, and where this consistency does not exist in the literature guidelines are available to assist in constructing a subset of possible interventions that has the best evidential record.

3. Research indicates that all therapies are equally effective, so it doesn't matter what techniques I use.

Although initially associated with the Dodo verdict (Stiles, Shapiro, & Elliott, 1986), and given the inherent problems with this methodology (Brown, 1987), some of the most persuasive evidence against Claim 3 comes from meta-analytic studies which *have* demonstrated differences between the various therapeutic approaches. For example, Smith and Glass's (1977) meta-analysis of treatment outcome found the average effect size for systematic desensitization to be .91, with rational emotive therapy and behavior modification at .77

and .76, respectively. Whereas Eclectic therapy and Gestalt therapy evidenced the smallest effect sizes, .48 and .26 respectively. In addition, two re-analyses of Smith and Glass's data found that behavior therapy was significantly superior to psychodynamic therapy (Andrews & Harvey, 1981; Searles, 1985). Finally, Shapiro (1985) found overall effect sizes for cognitive behavioral therapies was between .39 and .68 standard deviations larger than for dynamic and humanistic therapies.

In addition to the findings from meta-analytic studies, some researchers have also found that although the use of different interventions have shown no differential effectiveness at post-test, there are differences in relapse rates. For example, differences have been found in relapse rates for those treated with cognitive therapy versus antidepressant medication for depression (Barber & DeRubeis, 1989).

Finally, research using the dismantling paradigm (Kazdin, 1980) has made initial attempts at identifying what conditions or "ingredients" increase or decrease the effectiveness of various interventions. That is, which components of a treatment package account for the most positive change? Does adding or subtracting a component from a treatment package increase effectiveness or not? Should a behavioral intervention be used in addition to the use of drugs or cognitive therapy? Although this procedure has not been widely used, several studies have shown that adding or subtracting different components of the treatment package does result in differential effectiveness (e.g., Jacobson, 1984; Kazdin & Mascitelli, 1982; Kornblith, Rehm, O'Hara, & Lamparski, 1983; Mattick, Peters, & Clarke, 1989; Nezu & Perri, 1989).

Replacement belief: Meta-analytic studies have shown differences between the various types of therapy, others have found differences in relapse rates, dismantling studies have demonstrated that adding or subtracting different components of an intervention result in differential effectiveness; and many treatments have no evidence regarding their effectiveness, thus there are different bodies of evidence for the efficacy of various treatments. Therefore, it is important to accurately analyze the research record to identify which intervention would be the most effective to use for a particular individual since they are not all equivalent.

4. Research is something that academics do but that I cannot do.

There has been a substantial amount of exegesis on the meaning of the hyphen in the scientist-practitioner model of clinical psychology and clinical training. Claim 4 takes the hyphen as indicating more or less exclusive choice point—the hyphen as an "or". One wonders to what degree some of the current problems are the result of this syntactical ambiguity. McFall (1991) has recently argued that all clinical psychologists should constantly practice as clinical scientists. In his view clinical psychologists in all roles and situations are constantly confronted with empirical questions and as such ought to use the specialized research skills that comprise the best epistemological procedure to help solve these problems. He states that others can do therapy cheaper (and perhaps with as much effectiveness, especially given the research on the efficacy of paraprofessionals and lay people). He suggests that research skills are what distinguishes clinical psychologists from other mental health professionals.

Somewhat more radically, Krasner and Ullmann (1965) have argued that therapy is research and research is therapy. This is not merely a piece of catchy rhetoric but rather it captures a profound insight. The most general point is that the epistemic conditions for successful therapy are equivalent to the epistemic conditions for sound research. That is, the clinician in the course of therapy must ask, "What factors actually influence the state of affairs that the client wants to change?" To answer this question the clinician must, after establishing a stable baseline, manipulate hypothesized factors (independent variables) while measuring the effects on the outcome variable (dependent variable). And of course to adequately and clearly answer the question other conditions need to be met: psychometrically adequate measures must be used, only one variable manipulated at a time, and control conditions that rule out relevant alternative hypotheses such as placebo effects. In short, when we as clinicians are attempting to ameliorate some state of affairs we are inevitably involved with causal hypothesis testing and in order to help the client (help cause change) we must conduct research/therapy. Thus research is not optional but rather an essential element of the problem solving situation presented in the clinic.

Moreover because of the inevitable generalizability question (over such facets as time, therapist, client, etc.) clinical practice cannot simply be data-based but must also be data-generating. There is no assurance that past regularities will hold for different facet elements: this must be continually tested for at a minimum, time is always changing.

Replacement belief: The problem situation in clinical practice necessarily calls for the clinician to conduct research with each of his or her clients.

5. My "clinical judgment" and "intuition" can be more useful than research results.

Assertions such as this led researchers like Meehl and the Chapmans to investigate how accurate "clinical judgment" really is. First, Meehl (1956) found that clinicians' judgments are generally inferior to actuarial judgments. Upon further investigation, it appeared as though this superiority was due to the fact that clinicians tend to underutilize base rate information, which is very similar to the findings of Kahneman and Tversky (1973). Secondly, Chapman and Chapman (1967) demonstrated our vulnerability to confirmatory strategies. That is, clinicians tend to find relationships between variables based on their prior expectations of what relationships they expect should exist rather than what relationships actually exist. In addition, Oskamp (1965) has shown that giving judges more information increases their confidence in their decision even though the accuracy of their decision does not increase.

Experimental methods, on the other hand, have mechanisms set in place to minimize these various errors in judgment. For example, the use of counterbalancing, randomization of subjects, blind experimenters, replication, and statistics all help to minimize the effects of confirmatory strategies while maximizing our predictive power and our ability to accurately assess covariation.

Replacement belief: Although clinicians may believe that their "clinical judgment" appears to be accurate, it is subject to a variety of errors that research results are less susceptible to. Consequently, it is important to supplant intuitive beliefs with conclusions based upon experimental findings.

6. Consuming research is a fairly hard, expensive time-consuming activity.

Certainly properly consuming research takes some time and effort. However, the real question is whether the benefits outweigh these costs. Again, one must also consider what the alternative is: Is there a method which involves ignoring research that has a superior cost/benefit ratio?

Moreover, research has become increasingly easy to consume: 1) Some publishers (Allyn & Bacon, Springer) have published series of excellent data-based practitioner-oriented guidebooks; 2) The primary psychological literature is more easily accessible using CD ROM technology; 3) Journals such as *Psychology Review* (and *the Behavior Therapist*) have attempted to provide informative reviews of clinically relevant literature; 4) Granting agencies have become increasingly concerned about dissemination issues and now require explicit description of dissemination activities in grant applications; 5) Researchers can be contacted for their therapy protocols; and 6) Larger mental health organizations can take advantage of their economies of scale and form research teams whose function it is to write treatment review/manuals that are data-based and data-generating (O'Donohue & Dyer, in press).

Replacement belief: Consuming research is not that expensive anymore and it is a cost-beneficial action for me and my clients.

7. Ignoring research does not harm my clients or me.

Not harming clients would involve providing them the most-cost effective therapy and assessment methods relevant to their problem. Anything other than this harms them by unnecessarily prolonging their problem, creating more sequelae and associated effects of the problem, as well as wasting their time, energy and money. In more extreme cases in which an ineffective or iatrogenic therapy or invalid assessment measure is given it can cause them to become disenchanted with therapy and stop all efforts at improvement. (One wonders how many informal learned helplessness protocols are being enacted in therapy rooms across the nation.)

Poorly informed practice harms the practitioner also in several ways. First, it can cause insidious harm to the professional's reputation when clients do not get better. Second, as practice is somewhat exposed to competitive market forces, the demand for the services becomes appropriately vulnerable to more effective therapy. Third, there is insidious harm to the profession (and therefore indirectly to the individual practitioner) when outside evaluators (3rd party reimbursers, national health care reformers) form the view that the cost-benefit analysis does not suggest much third party reimbursement for mental health services.

Replacement belief: Ignoring re-

search does harm to my clients, myself, and my profession.

8. Clinicians who make poor treatment decisions should be tolerated and condoned.

If the previous point is correct then the question becomes, How should clinicians be treated who are unnecessarily harming clients and the profession by their neglect of the relevant research literature? Tolerance and condoning does not appear to be the optimal response as it tends to preserve an undesirable *status quo.*

In fact tolerance—although often a good thing—has in our view been inordinately stressed in this field. An all too common view is that therapists should be open-minded and accept all points of view. But what is often given short shrift is the fact that this directly conflicts with a critical, scientific point of view which asserts that a proposition is accepted as a direct function of its evidential credentials. Although morally it is important to avoid *ad hominem* attacks and to ensure one respects the person; it may be equally as importantly morally to fairly criticize claims so that these can improve or be replaced by more accurate assertions.

To paraphrase a useful heuristic once given by Paul Meehl, the question of an appropriate intellectual response may be, "How would I respond to the clinician's assertions if I knew that these assertions were involved in the treatment of one of my loved ones?" We also have an intellectual responsibility to our clients and our colleagues. In fact we would go so far as to say that the field has been harmed by the "tolerance" of the behavior and assertions of individuals who practice psychotherapy in a way that is not optimally consistent with the research literature.

Alternative belief: Poor therapy decisions should be criticized and those making these should be educated regarding more accurate beliefs and decision making. Appropriate escalation should be conducted with individuals who persist in making poor treatment decisions on the grounds of ethical concerns regarding client welfare.

Conclusion

9. I am usually or often correct, and I can point to treatment successes as confirmations of this.

Part of the reason for ignoring the research literature may be that clinicians believe that they are doing sufficiently well without paying attention to it. However without systematically designed data-generating therapy they really have no basis for believing this. On what basis can they call the treatment outcome a "success"? How do they know that with no therapy or placebo or an alternative therapy the client would not be better off? There may be little else behind this belief than confirmation bias, placebo effects, and clients who want to please their therapists by "faking good".

Alternative belief: Feedback from clinical cases is ambiguous and therefore controlled observations are needed before I can tell if I'm correct.

Conculsion

The applied sciences differ in their degree of success and efficacy. Engineering in applying the basic physical sciences has amassed an impressive array of successes from air conditioning to moon landings. In the 20th century the medical sciences, applying the basic biological sciences, have also had a tremendous impact upon ameliorating suffering and prolonging life. However, would these disciplines have had the same success if their practitioners displayed the kind of beliefs regarding research use that we have argued are popular among mental health professionals?

To be sure, applied psychology is hampered partly by the relative lack of success of the basic behavioral sciences. However, we suggest that an additional contributor to the relative inefficacy of applied psychology are the beliefs which support a lack of appreciation and a neglect of what information research has revealed. We suggest that until these beliefs are directly challenged and modified what is known from research will be unnecessarily underutilized in a manner which causes damage to our clients, ourselves and our profession.

References

Andrews, G., & Harvey, R. (1981). Does psychotherapy benefit neurotic patients? A re-analysis of the Smith, Glass, and Miller data. *Archives of General Psychiatry, 38,* 1203–1208.

Barber, J. P., & DeRubeis, R. J. (1989). On second thought: Where the action is in cognitive therapy for depression. *Cognitive Therapy and Research, 13,* 441–457.

Brown, J. (1987). A review of meta-analyses conducted on psychotherapy outcome research. *Clinical Psychology Review, 7,* 1–23.

Chapman, L. J., & Chapman, J. P. (1967). Genesis of popular but erroneous psychodiagnostic observations. *Journal of Abnormal Psychology, 72,* 193–204.

Clark, D. A., & Beck, A. T. (1989). Cognitive theory and therapy of anxiety and depression. In P. C. Kendall and D. Watson (Eds.), *Anxiety and depression: Distinctive and overlapping features,* (pp. 379–411). New York: Academic Press, Inc.

Cohen, L. H., Sargent, M. M., & Sechrest, L. B. (1985). Use of psychotherapy research by professional psychologists. *American Psychologist, 41,* 198–206.

Cone, J. D. (1988). Psychometric considerations and the multiple models of behavioral assessment. In A. Bellack & M. Hersen (Eds.) *Behavioral assessment.* (p. 42–66). New York: Pergamon.

Feyerabend, P. (1978). *Science in a free society.* London: NLB.

Foa, E. B., Olasov Rothbaum, B., & Kozak, M. J. (1989). Behavioral treatments for anxiety and depression. In P. C. Kendall and D. Watson (Eds.), *Anxiety and depression: Distinctive and overlapping features,* (pp. 413–454). New York: Academic Press, Inc.

Jacobson, N. S. (1984). A component analysis of behavioral marital therapy: The relative effectiveness of behavior exchange and communication/problem-solving training. *Journal of Consulting and Clinical Psychology, 52,* 295–305.

Kahneman, D., & Tversky, A. (1973). On the psychology of prediction. *Psychological Review, 81,* 237–251

Kazdin, A. E., & Mascitelli, S. (1982). Covert and overt rehearsal and homework practice in developing assertiveness. *Journal of Consulting and Clinical Psychology, 50,* 250–258.

Kornblith, S. J., Rehm, L. P., O'Hara, M. W., & Lamparski, D. M. (1983). The contribution of self-reinforcement training and behavioral assignments to the efficacy of self-control therapy for depression. *Cognitive Therapy and Research, 7,* 499–528.

Krasner, L., & Ullmann, L. P. (1965) *Research in behavior modification.* New York: Holt, Rinehart & Winston.

Masters, J. C., Burish, T. G., Hollon, S. D., & Rimm, D. C. (1987). *Behavior therapy:*

Techniques and empirical findings, (3rd ed.). New York: Harcourt Brace Jovanovich.

Mattick, R. P., Peters, L., & Clarke, J. C. (1989). Exposure and cognitive restructuring for social phobia: A controlled study. *Behavior Therapy, 20,* 3–23.

McFall, R. M. (1991). Manifesto for a science of clinical psychology. *The Clinical Psychologist, 44,* 75–88.

Meehl, P. E. (1956). Wanted—a good cookbook. *American Psychologist, 11,* 263–272.

Morrow-Bradley, C., & Elliot, R. (1986). Utilization of psychotherapy research by practicing psychotherapists. *American Psychologist, 41,* 188–197.

Nezu, A. M., & Perri, M. G. (1989). Social problem-solving therapy for unipolar depression: An initial dismantling investigation. *Journal of Consulting and Clinical Psychology, 57,* 408–413.

O'Donohue, W., Curtis, S. D., & Fisher, J. E. (1985). Use of research in the practice of community mental health: A case study. *Professional Psychology: Research and Practice, 16,* 710–718.

O'Donohue, W., Fisher, J. E., Plaud, J. J., & Curtis, S. D. (1990). Treatment decisions: Their nature and their justification. *Psychotherapy, 27,* 421–427.

Oskamp, S. (1965). Overconfidence in case-study judgments. *Journal of Consulting Psychology, 29,* 261–265.

Searles, J. S. (1985). A methodological and empirical critique of psychotherapy outcome meta-analysis. *Behaviour Research and Therapy, 23,* 453–463.

Shapiro, D. A. (1985). Recent applications of meta-analysis in clinical research. *Clinical Psychology Review, 5,* 13–34.

Smith, M. L., & Glass, G. V. (1977). Meta-analysis of psychotherapy outcome studies. *American Psychologist, 32,* 752–760.

Snow, C. P. (1961). *The two cultures and the scientific revolution.* Cambridge: Cambridge University Press.

Stiles, W. B., Shapiro, D. A., & Elliott, R. (1986). "Are all psychotherapies equivalent?" *American Psychologist, 41,* 165–180.

Wood, L. F., & Jacobson, N. S. (1985). Marital distress. In D. H. Barlow (Ed.), *Clinical handbook of psychological disorders: A step-by-step treatment manual,* (pp. 344–416). New York: The Guilford Press.

Correspondence regarding this manuscript should be sent to William O'Donohue, Ph.D., Dept. of Psychology, Northern Illinois University, Dekalb, IL 60115.

Part X
The Ethics of Technology

[35]

Screening for Depression:
Preventive Medicine or Telemarketing?

D. Cohen and K. Hoeller

In this editorial, the authors critically examine a recent recommendation by the United States Preventive Services Task Force that all adults visiting primary care practitioners be routinely "screened" for depression. Drug industry funding for depression screening campaigns, popular but unproven assertions that depression is a "biochemical disorder," and the banality of antidepressant prescribing are seen to motivate the proposal. The full report cited by the Task Force omits information on the lack of effectiveness of antidepressants compared to placebo and recognizes that the potential harms of screening have not been studied.

After rejecting the idea in 1996, the United States Preventive Services Task Force (USPSTF), a panel convened by the United States Public Health Service and made up of 15 experts in public health, recommended in May 2002 that primary care physicians and nurses routinely screen their patients for depression and immediately initiate treatment if patients screen positively. The screening test consists of asking two questions to patients who consult their physician or health care provider for any reason whatsoever: "Over the past two weeks, have you felt down, depressed, or hopeless? Have you felt little interest or pleasure in doing things?"

Although the recommendation is couched in the language of a scientific advance in preventive medicine, in our view it exhibits the basic characteristics of a telemarketing effort. It is unsolicited, disturbing to one's peace of mind, and probably sells something one neither needs nor can afford to buy.

The idea that sadness, discouragement, and sometimes self-harm have physical causes and solutions is both ancient and widespread. However, we believe that more critical judgment is needed when medical experts ponder submitting virtually the entire adult population to a "screening test" for depression. This idea began in the early 1990s with a depression screening week every October on many of the nation's college campuses as well as other media and "informational" events for the general public underwritten by the companies who make and sell antidepressant drugs (see, for example, www.depression-screening.org, a website sponsored by the National Mental Health Association but made possible by a grant from Eli Lilly and Company). These companies also funded studies to evaluate the "effectiveness" of these campaigns. Over the last decade, several publications reported on the numbers of individuals who presented themselves or were "out-reached" during the campaigns, who met brief DSM criteria for depression, who were referred for psychiatric treatment, and so on.

Results from these studies, as well as from studies on the effectiveness of the drug and psychotherapeutic treatment of depression, are found in a substantial report (Pignone et al., 2002) that offers the evidentiary basis for the recommendation by the USPSTF.

However, nowhere in this recommendation might one surmise that the medical science of diagnosing and treating depression is far from exact. The USPSTF did not have to address this issue, as it and millions of Americans seem to have become convinced by drug company propaganda that depression is caused by a chemical imbalance in their brains, requiring lifelong drug treatment. The fact remains: no conclusive scientific evidence supports this belief. And of course, no physical test can confirm a diagnosis of depression (or any other mental illness).

If an individual screens positively, the USPSTF recommends that an interview for a formal diagnosis of depressive disorder should be pursued by the clinician. Given the training and experience of most physicians today, the context of primary care medicine, and the extraordinary banality with which antidepressants have been dispensed over the last decade, it is likely that the outcome for most patients will be a drug treatment costing patients nearly $200 a week. To pursue this drug treatment for several months or years—with its inevitable retinue of drug withdrawals, "relapses," switches, and dose increases and decreases—only two or three annual self-reports of gloom will suffice, even to scientifically minded physicians and tight-fisted insurance companies.

How did we get here? Prozac irrevocably changed unhappiness into "depression," the planet's second costliest and deadliest preventable disease. For 15 years, the pharmaceutical industry carpet-bombed professionals and the public with the idea that depression is a dangerous metabolic disturbance like diabetes, and that available drugs are effective and prophylactic. Gradually, this idea is bound to lose its appeal as the dark side of antidepressants emerges in the public light. Yet, as the miracle veneer wears off Prozac-like antidepressants, new initiatives to maintain or expand markets must follow. This explains why well-known drugs whose patents expire are marketed under new brand names for "new" conditions (e.g., Prozac into Sarafem for pre-menstrual dysphoric disorder) and why a previously untreated age group (children) transforms overnight into the group with the fastest-growing rate of psychotropic drug treatment (e.g., a 166% increase, to 3.76 million, in the number of prescriptions to youth in the United States for antidepressants from 1996 to 2000) (Mina, 2002). It also explains the often announced "discovery" that most people who might report depressive symptoms are untreated (that is, not taking prescribed proprietary drugs) and the ensuing recommendation that they should, therefore, receive treatment as a public health measure.

Can people be so unaware of their existential turmoil that doctors need to ferret it out on a mass scale? We think the idea absurd. We also think that most people know that solving their emotional problems lies not in crudely altering brain chemistry but in taking positive actions, learning new skills, and creating more favorable circumstances. What reasons do people have to believe that family practice doctors, who have no time to talk to patients anymore, and who themselves have succumbed to psychiatric propaganda, will do anything more than say, "Take Prozac weekly and don't call me in the morning?"

Peter Breggin (1994) in *Talking Back to Prozac*, Roger Greenberg and Seymour Fisher (1997) in *From Placebo to Panacea*, Elliott Valenstein (1998) in *Blaming the Brain*, Charles Medawar (1997) in "The Antidepressant Web," David Healy (1999) in *The Antidepressant Era*, Joseph Glenmullen (2000) in *Prozac Backlash*, and Terry Lynch (2001) in *Beyond Prozac*—among other authors—have marshalled, from widely varying perspectives, compelling arguments to show that recent simplistic ideas about "depression" have little scientific basis; they mostly reflect deep social and cultural transformations, especially about embracing "cosmetic psychopharmacology." These ideas have led millions to be exposed to the risks of prolonged use of, and withdrawal from, psychoactive drugs. However, the critical analysis of the key clinical trials—specifically, those produced by drug manufacturers for the sole purpose of obtaining FDA approval for their products and therefore resolutely biased to produce positive results for these products—shows antidepressants to have *at best a very small* advantage over placebos (Kirsch, Moore, Scoboria, & Nicholls, 2002). The Kirsch et al. meta-analysis of the efficacy data (consisting of 47 randomized placebo-controlled studies) submitted to the FDA for the six most widely prescribed antidepressants approved between 1987 and 1999 is not cited in the Pignone and colleagues report. It was published three months after the report was concluded. Here are its main findings:

> Approximately 80% of the response to medication was duplicated in placebo control groups, and the mean difference between drug and placebo was approximately 2 points on the 17-item (50-point) and 21-item (62-point) Hamilton Depression Scale. Improvement at the highest doses of medication was not different from improvement at the lowest doses. (Kirsch et al., 2002)

Contrast Kirsch and colleagues' observation of virtual clinical equivalence between antidepressants and placebo to the USPSTF (2002) summary of antidepressant treatment effectiveness:

> Antidepressant medications for major depression, including tricyclic antidepressants (TCAs) and selective serotonin reuptake inhibitors (SSRIs), are clearly more effective than placebo.

A vast screening effort will enable drug companies, who already entertain extremely privileged relationships with physicians, to know even more precisely who and where future customers are. Cases have already been reported of people, including youths, receiving unsolicited Prozac in the mail. These cases illustrate the simple fact that physicians and pharmacies (offered ever-more attractive financial incentives to refer individuals for or maintain them on drug treatment), can be expected to confuse telemarketing with medicine.

The billions of dollars that pharmaceutical companies spend each year convincing doctors and the public to opt for drugs will be even more efficiently targeted and joined to private and public systems of depression treatment and follow-up. Can there be any doubt about the outcome? We predict that more populations and indications for drug treatments will be discovered. How all this will actually translate into positive health and well-being outcomes for individuals or populations will, of course, remain to be determined.

So will any potential *harm* ensuing from screening and treatment. This critical issue is addressed in a mere 83 words in the entire Pignone and colleagues (2002) report:

> The potential harms of screening include false-positive screening results, the adverse effects of treatment, the adverse effects and costs of treatment for patients who are incorrectly identified as being depressed, and the potential adverse effects of labeling.
> The trade-offs between benefits and harms are an important component of the decision to screen or not to screen for depression. *We currently have insufficient information about the harms of screening (false positives and labeling) to create a balance sheet to inform the decision to screen.* (emphasis added)

Plainly stated, the available evidence does not allow one to suggest that benefits of screening and treating will outweigh harms. The USPSTF acknowledged this lack of data: "None of the research reviewed provided useful, empirical data regarding these potential [harms]." Nonetheless, its recommendation statement still managed to include the following statement: "The USPSTF concluded the benefits of screening are likely to outweigh any potential harms."

Finally, we have known that the doctor-patient relationship is no longer a refuge of confidentiality and autonomy. The medical panel's recommendation reminds us again that a once private encounter, as Thomas Szasz laments in *Pharmacracy* (2001), has moved squarely into the realm of public health and "harm prevention." Indeed, if detecting, treating, and preventing depression is so easy, and if depression causes injury, then clinicians must detect depression, and they can be held responsible for their patients' misbehavior. Is every doctor who will fail to screen for depression a potential defendant in a malpractice suit? And, as one commentator (Richman, 2002) has asked, is every patient who refuses to undergo treatment following a positive screen and a diagnosis a potential candidate for involuntary treatment?

In our view, the recommendation of the USPSTF deserves vastly more critical analysis as an example of money, pseudo-science, and professional acquiescence converging to create "mental health policy."

REFERENCES

Breggin, P. R., & Breggin, G. R. (1994). *Talking back to Prozac: What doctors aren't telling you about today's most controversial drug*. New York: St. Martin's Press.

Glenmullen, J. P. (2000). *Prozac backlash: Overcoming the dangers of Prozac, Zoloft, Paxil, and other antidepressants with safe effective alternatives*. New York: Simon and Schuster.

Greenberg, R. P., & Fisher, S. (1997). Mood-mending medicines: Probing drug, psychotherapy, and placebo solutions. In S. Fisher & R. P. Greenberg (Eds.), *From placebo to panacea: Putting psychiatric drugs to the test* (pp. 115-171). New York: John Wiley & Sons.

Healy, D. (1997). *The antidepressant era*. Cambridge, MA: Harvard University Press.

Kirsch, I., Moore, T. J., Scoboria, A., & Nicholls, S. N. (2002). The emperor's new drugs: An analysis of antidepressant medication data submitted to the U.S. Food and Drug Administration. *Prevention and Treatment, 5*(23). Available at http://journals.apa.org/prevention

Lynch, T. (2001). *Beyond Prozac: Healing mental suffering without drugs*. Dublin, Ireland: Marino Books.

Medawar, P. (1997). The antidepressant web: Marketing depression and making medicines work. *International Journal of Risk and Safety in Medicine, 10*, 75-126.

Mina, V. B. (2002, June 23). Psychiatric drug use soars among children. *Sacramento Bee*. Available at http://www.sacbee.com/content/news/story/3316700p-4344829c.html

Pignone, M., Gaynes, B. N., Rushton, J. L., Mulrow, C. D., Orleans, C. T., Whitener B. L., Mills, C., & Lohr, K. N. (2002, May). *Screening for depression* (Systematic Evidence Review No. 6.) Prepared by the Research Triangle Institute, University of North Carolina Evidence-based Practice Center under Contract No. 290-97-0011 (AHRQ Publication No. 02-S002). Rockville, MD: Agency for Healthcare Research and Quality. Available: http:// www.ahrq.gov/clinic/uspstfix.htm

Richman, S. (2002, August). The newest medical threat. *Jefferson Review*. Available at http://www.fff.org/comment/com0208d.asp

Szasz, T. (2001). *Pharmacracy: Medicine and politics in America*. Westport, CT: Praeger.

U.S. Preventive Services Task Force. (2002, May). *Screening for depression: Recommendations and rationale*. Rockville, MD: Agency for Healthcare Research and Quality. Available: http://www.ahrq.gov/clinic/3rduspstf/depression/depressrr.htm

Valenstein, E. S. (1998). *Blaming the brain: The truth about drugs and mental health*. New York: The Free Press.

[36]

Viagra: Medical Technology Constructing Aging Masculinity

GREGORY GROSS

The College of St. Rose

ROBERT BLUNDO

University of North Carolina at Wilmington

Medicalization and commodification of the body through technology in the form of Viagra and other erectile dysfunction drugs is reinforcing the cultural expectations that ageing men are required to age well to maintain youthful masculinity. Ageing well is explored as it relates the construction of masculinity, sexuality and ageing men's bodies.

Key words: *aging, masculinity, men, bodies, sexuality, cultural expectations*

Old age is full of death and full of life. It is a tolerable achievement and it is a disaster. It transcends desire and it taunts it. It is long enough and far from long enough.   Ronald Blythe, 1979, p. 29

[The male organ has been a seen as many things over the course of history], both noble and coarse. The penis was an icon of creativity; it was the link between the human and the sacred, an agent of bodily and spiritual ecstasy that hinted of communion with the eternal. Yet it was also a weapon against women, children, and weaker men. It was a force of nature, revered for its potency, yet just as amoral. It tied man to the cosmic energy that covered the fields each year with new herds and corps—and just as often destroyed them. The organ's "animal" urgency didn't trouble the ancients. Didn't the gods combine the human and savage in their own amours? All these complexities and contradictions, the very unpredictability of life itself, were embodied by one body part above all in antiquity—the penis.
                                                      David Friedman (2001)

Introduction

The demand that little boys give up their dependency for a masculinity based on dominance and performance continues to have many consequences for the aging man. Boys start the process of discounting nature and human connections and in the end their own humanity and sense of dignity in the face of aging and dependency. The construction of masculinity within the dominant American culture is based on independence and competition and central to this masculine construct is youthful energy and physicality. Masculinity requires not only success in the competitive world of work but sexual dominance and prowess for men to maintain their "youthful" masculine identity. Aging men are faced with not only the inevitable fact of aging but with the social constructs of what that means to them or should mean to them from a society that is oriented toward youth. The paradox for men is that even though "ageism" has been attacked and challenged, in reality it still exists and is deeply engrained in our youth oriented society. In its place has come the "aging well" or positive ageing agenda whereby society still derides those who do not "age well." Men are now faced with aging that must have the air of youthfulness and vitality, and this includes sexual performance.

Viagra and the newer erectile dysfunction drugs are a part of this increasing expectation that has very quickly become a cultural phenomenon spread across the mass media. Viagra has entered into the mainstream of conversations and is a part of American culture. This paper explores the medicalization and commodification of men's sexual functioning and its impact on aging men and their sense of masculinity.

A Culture of Aging Well

As in most life matters today, the meaning of what it is to "age" has been turned over to the professional, in this instance the geriatric social worker, urologist, gerontologists, geriatric medical specialists, and economic interests. Over the past century "old age was removed from its ambiguous place in life's spiritual journey, rationalized, and redefined as a scientific problem" (Cole, 1992, p. xx.). Medicalization and commodification now provide the "scientific" management of aging. The concern produced is not only with understanding and controlling the aging process, but expectations that one must "age well" as if "aging" was merely a disembodied process that can be managed and kept at bay. The consequence of this scientific enterprise has been to find out how to treat illness and diseases that afflict the person as he ages and it has extended the life expectancy and produced better health for many. This rational approach has paralleled the critique of "ageism" which proclaims that chronological age does not determine the quality of one's life. The assumption is that older people *should* be physically healthy and sexually active.

Both men and women are now presented with a culture that does not see growing old as a natural process, as part of the human condition, but a "problem" to overcome. There is a demand that men and women remain vibrant, healthy and functioning. When men or women show vulnerabilities or signs of aging, our social and personal constructs produce a level of contempt and hostility toward this physical and mental decline. In particular, contempt and hostility are directed at the physical consequence of aging in women (Susan Sontag, 1979). For men, the outer appearance of graying hair and lines can bring a "look of distinction" for a brief while. Men's aging vulnerability is most often focused on his sexual performance, his penis. Weak or nonexistent erections are a "secret" fear for most men as they age. The new culture of "Aging Well" for men means that an aging penis should still perform well. Within the past several years since the advent of Viagra and Senator Dole promoting erectile dysfunction as acceptable for prime time television, an enormous cultural shift is taking place that supports and promotes this cultural and personal expectation that all penises, regardless of age, should maintain a youthful performance standard.

Viagra Goes Mainstream Culture

Viagra and its rivals have entered the global narrative. Viagra shows up nearly everywhere. An EBSCO search on 5/15/04 turned-up no fewer that 751 items. For example, journals such as *Psychology of Women Quarterly, Science Now, Archives of Andrology, Women and Therapy, Sexual Relationship and Therapy,* and *Urologic*

Nursing. Surprising, though, are the large number and range of items in the popular press. *Time* and *Newsweek* did extensive coverage of Viagra, but then again so did *Outdoor Life, Advertising Age, Economist, Forbes, The Wall Street Journal, Business Week, Esquire, Good Housekeeping, Money, Popular Science, Brandweek, NEA Today, Chemical and Engineering News, People, Mediaweek, Consumers' Research Magazine, Discover, Asia Week, Civilization, Kiplinger's Personal Finance Magazine* and others. This explosive proliferation of media coverage heightens public awareness of Viagra and more important, gives Viagra a public blessing for discourse about the product and use of the product. A brief examination of the rhetoric of Viagra reveals ambivalence. The messages are mixed. Along with sober sounding titles, such as "Intracavernous Injections for Erectile Dysfunction . . . for Sildenafil Citrate" (*International Journal of Impotency Research*, 2002) or "Drug Aimed to Rival Viagra Posts Positive Clinical Trials" (*Wall Street Journal*, 12/10/02) are titles reflective of the underlying social significance of male erections through double entendre. Examples include "Hard times with Viagra" (*Advocates*, 4/29/03), "A Potent Breakthrough" (*Time*, 3/31, 03), "New Drug Keeps Sufferers Up All Night" (*Student BMJ*, 3/03), "No More Heavy Breathing" (*Outside*, 3/03), "Hard Facts" (*Men's Health*, 6/02), "Hot Products (*BRW*, 10/31,02), "Bigger is Better When it Comes to the G Spot" (*New Scientist*, 7/6/02), and "Bill and Maureen Would Like Their Sex Life Back" (*Choice*, 3/00). These titles with their "wink-wink, nudge-nudge" lighten up the subject of Viagra and impotence while at the same time noting that to use Viagra is still within the realm of ridicule and shame. Viagra has now entered the discourse on masculinity. The social construction of masculinity is now incorporating this public discourse into the cultural definitions of how men should perform sexually as aging men. Masculinity as a performance of expectations is reinforcing the dominant metaphor of masculinity, man as machine (Friedman, 2001; Gergen, 2001; Murphy, 2001,).

Social Construction, Language and Masculinity

Social constructionist theory suggests that through discourse and within a culture, people come to understand and know themselves. This is a continuous creative process through language and its many forms of expression. Language and discourse shape how we understand both ourselves and others in an ongoing interactional process (Lakoff and Johnson, 1980; Berger and Luckman, 1966; Shotter, 1993). Most important is the fundamentally metaphorical nature of language and conversation (Lakoff and Johnson, 1980). Connecting images of unrelated objects or ideas give a dynamic meaning beyond the physicality of a thing or object. George Lakoff and Mark Johnson (1980) believe that our metaphorical conceptual system of ideas and thoughts are not just thoughts but constructs that "also govern our everyday functioning, down to the most mundane detail" (page 3). Our cultural conventions expressed as metaphor tell us more than we understand one thing in terms of another. When Lorenzo Anello, the father in Robert De Niro's film, *A Bronx Tale* (Gatien, 1993), tells his son that he should be careful on this date because "sometimes the little head tells the big head what to do," Lorenzo has just introduced a very complex cultural construct about a man's penis as well as about the meaning of masculinity. Masculinity and the penis are inseparable. The notion that the penis has a mind of its own is a metonymy for the man, and in this case, can be the man's master. In this instance, the penis is removed from the body and given a separate life of its own. The penis takes on a certain independent instrumentality. That is, *it*, the disembodied penis, can do something and make something happen. In turn, having a mind of its own, it is seen as both a companion and an adversary. Given this metaphorical construction, men are left with both a lack of responsibility and a loss of control (Murphy, 2001). Yet, paradoxically, they understand the penis to be under their control and the penis [usually given a name by the man or sexual partner] is assumed to respond to the man's will and in many ways represents the man's prowess. Significantly, the penis becomes a much regarded part of a man's body over the man's lifetime and remains a central construct for aging men's masculinity.

The language constructs for what it means to be a man encompasses many metaphorical meanings. Man as machine (penis as machine, as a tool) is the most dominate metaphor in use. Peter Murphy (2001) describes this metaphor as conveying the construction of a "cold, disembodied, efficacious piece of equip-ment"(p.17). He goes further to note that "true masculinity as a finely tuned, well-oiled, unemotional, hard, and cost-effective apparatus deeply informs the way we conceive of manhood" (Murphy, 2001, p.17). This leads to considering their sexual rela-tionships as instrumental. That is, the penis as a fine working ma-chine that rises to the occasion and performs "as a wrought-iron machine part ready to be turned on at the flick of a switch" (Mur-phy, 2001, p. 22). To not perform in this way means a breakdown, a defective machine, a failure and questions the masculinity of a man. Yet, medical science and the pharmaceutical industry have given men a way out. Medicalization has transformed the penis into a physiological hydraulic system out of man's control. There in lies the excuse, it's not a failure of masculinity or manhood but a break down in the mechanical system (Bordo, 1998; Tiefer, 1994). Now men can be free to find biochemical repairs that restore the performance level required for manhood.

Men's Response to the Aging Body/Machine

Mary Gergen (2001) offers some clues to how to begin to understand men's response to their aging bodies. She noted that in contradistinction to women, who see their bodies as "inter-nalized, secret, and potentially polluted," men view their own bodies "especially their sexual aspects, . . . [as] externalized" for not only are the male genitals outside, external to the body, so too are men's experience of and meaning of those organs as body parts in the sphere of identity and the sphere of the social. Gergen (2001) notes, for example, that men view their bodies as machines that serve them in outer-directed means or arenas. Men's autobiographies, by way of illustration, unfold around career issues, with the body either independent of their career or a tool at his disposal for advancing that career. Often men do not mention this body at all except as a servant to the man-master who directs that body to the furtherance of non-bodily aims. In fact, typically men see their bodies as a taken-for-granted asset, like a heartbeat, to be confronted only at or near the point of its failure and then generally confronted via anxiety and denial.

While the body stands central in identity formation for a woman, the body should remain above and beyond concern for a real man (Gergen, 2001, pp. 73–79).

Gergen (2001) asserts that with aging and disability such constructions of the body-self play out in three primary scripts. The first carries a self-congratulatory theme ("I'm not is such bad shape for a fifty year old"); the second the begrudging theme ("My mind's as sharp as ever but I'm going to pot fast"); the broken defenses theme ("Life has played a dirty trick on me. I'm gonna die") (pp. 83–84). Any of these three scripts can inform the sexual self-narrative, especially in the middle to later years when men may begin to notice changes in over all physical abilities and, in particular, genital functioning. All three share in common a focus on performance, a reaction to their slowing of a well-oiled machine and as a challenge to this finely constructed sense of masculinity.

Aging men continue their pattern of relating to the physicality of self, a valuing of the body for what *it does* rather than for what *it is*. Therefore, it is the elements of stamina, strength, energy, sex drive and activity that is the central focus and "taken for granted" assumption of men's identity (Franzoi and Chang, 2000, pp. 185–188). Aging men, for example, can become alarmed at a reduction of the force of urination, viewing this reduced force as troubling in and of itself as a form of functional deteriorization and also as a precursor to the big one—impotence and, alas, death.

Since Eden the body has been constructed as part of nature that houses the self. "Once thought to be the locus of the soul, then the centre of dark, perverse needs, the body has become fully available to be 'worked upon' by the influences of high modernity" (Giddens, 1991, p. 218). The body as "object" and "mechanical" drives the contemporary self-view perhaps more than any other trait in our age of commodification and medical-ization. Whether framed in terms of self-care, esteem building, or narcissism, no previous generation before today's middle aged has spent as much time and money on reflection on the body-self, or its machine/self, its job-done self. Complicating that evolving complexity is technology that no longer simply helps the body but now *creates* the body and changes the body self as well as the body culture. Dyens (2001) notes "From . . . the pierced teenagers of our cities, from concentration camp prisoners to victims of nuclear radiation, the twentieth century will be remembered as the body century, a century where the living body was blurred, molded, and transformed by technology and culture (p. 3).

Francis Fukuyama (2002) finds that discoveries in genetics, cosmetic pharmacology, and neuropharmacology along with our ability to decode and even alter DNA, and the rise of the use of psychotropic drugs have fostered three social trends: 1) the medicalization of almost everything, 2) th marketization of this medicalization, and 3) the expansion of the therapeutic realm to a variety of kinds of conditions (p.53).

Medicalization requires that a human situation be dichotomized into representing a "healthy" state or the opposite an "unhealthy state." Tiefer (1994) describes the process as a "gradual social transformation whereby medicine, with its distinctive ways of thinking, models, metaphors, and institutions, comes to exercise authority over areas of life not previously considered medical" (p. 365). The penis and its functioning has been in the process of medicalization for two decades now and with Viagra and other similar drugs has become a medical problem to be addressed through medical procedures.

Man's Closest Companion and Biochemistry

Prior to 1983, urologist had been waging an unsuccessful struggle with psychiatry for control of the field of male sexual functioning. Freud's ideas of psychogenic causes of male sexual problems had dominated up until a meeting of the American Urologist Association in Las Vegas when medical technology caught up. Dr. Giles Brindley, a British urologist, presented a paper on a new non-surgical method of "treating" impotence (Friedman, 2001). On the stage, he demonstrated his new findings by injecting his own penis as part of the presentation and paraded his pharmaceutically induced erection down the aisle for the urologists to see for themselves. That stroll down the aisle "gave birth to the newest idea of the penis: a totally medicalized organ stripped of its psychic significance and mystery and transformed into a tiny network of blood vessels, neurotransmitters,

and smooth-muscle tissue knowable only to a credentialed scientist . . . In this singular moment, human sexuality, the healing
profession, and man's relationship with his penis underwent a
huge transformation" (Friedman, 2001, p.255). It was now within
the purview of the medical expert to set the standards of size
and performance against which all penises would be measured
(Friedman, 2001). Not only a medical standard but inherent in the
standard is the cultural expectation for men's penises to "perform
like power tools with only one switch-on and off" (Bordo, 1998,
p. 90).

Viagra goes beyond prosthesis in that Viagra is not an add-
on to the body. Yet it is more than a mere drug. Viagra changes
penile functioning and in the end sexual functioning. The machine is improved from the inside, not merely lubricated as one
might improve an engine on the inside. On the inside something
happens to the machine to make it perform better than it had
before. Although a physician plays a role in its use, the user of
Viagra encounters this improvement not in the doctor's office
and not just in the bed but also in the consumer realm as a
commodity in the market place. "Defining and experiencing the
body in a consumer world is less a matter of anatomical precision
and unambiguous uniqueness and more a matter of . . . the site
of style in postmodern culture" (Lyon, 1999, p. 81). Malleable
and subject to all manner of alteration and enhancement, the
body has become plastic and can substitute as the "real me,"
one's true self (p. 81). Thus, the use of Viagra may affect identity as well as relationships in a way not associated with other
common drugs. Aspirin may free the headache but Viagra can
awaken dormant longing. The relational history of the person
or couple can appear to reverse course, bringing new expectations, demands for performance and pleasure. Polkinghorn (1988)
warns that the personal life narrative runs the risk in old age of
being little more than an epilogue. "Life is not over but the story
is" (p. 106). Viagra thus offers a promise—or at least a shot—
for a restoried life. The penis gets promoted because today the
body is so well promotable. The body, as well as pleasure, has
become a key resource for commercial exploitation in a market
place that valorizes desire and its purchase (Lyon, 1999, pp. 84–
85). "Life organized around consumption . . . must do without

norms: it is guided by seduction, ever rising desires and volatile wishes-no longer by normative regulation' (Bauman, 2000, p. 76). Men's sexuality has become "deprivatized" and has become a commercial entity, a commodity to be packaged and a demand created. This commodification has become a media entity, a series of social constructed signs or images that define and redefine the pill, the penis, their use, and in doing so, has consequences for aging men's sense of masculinity. In short, Viagra has also become a media event—topic of the talk show, artifice of the ad, and juice of the joke—and by extension, so has men's sexual performance.

Conclusion

This social discourse around Viagra and erectile dysfunction is shaping how ageing men understand themselves as men and as sexual men. The expectation continues for ageing men to think of themselves as sexual performers, reinforcing the notion of themselves as machines capable through repair to perform forever.

The "romantic" version and construction of "aging well" *misrepresents* many of the realities of aging for men (Fleming, 1999; McCallum, 1997). The reality is that with all of the increasing medicalization and medical technology aging and death are still inevitable. Growing older does come with its physical consequences even though longevity has increased for most men in our society. Things do go wrong and there is an accumulation of degeneration that cannot be stopped. In many cases men with heart conditions and blood pressure problems are strongly advised not to take these drugs. Using a somewhat distant analogy from a study of aging and dancers, Wainwright and Turner (2003), suggest that "ageing ballet dancers trying to dance the classical roles of their youth is an example of the futility of ignoring the resistance of reality-the reality that the body is ageing physiologically as well as culturally in a context that bounds its decline tightly" (p. 284).

The cultural discourse on ageing as expressed in mass media presents "good" ageing, where bodies are youthful and usually engaged in some activity or sport (Featherstone and Wernick, 1995; Tulle-Winston, 2000). These same images are used in the erectile dysfunction ads for Viagra , Levitra and Cialis, where couples are shown vibrant and youthful, who are seemingly able to experience a non-ageing sexual life. Significantly, given the cultural expectation of aging well, "individuals are taught that they have a responsibility to attain perfection" Faircloth, 2003,p. 19). Ageing men are expected to remain youthful when in fact the reality is that they are not young and are facing the inevitable decline that is central to human existence.

Thomas Cole (1993) reminds us that "growing old and dying, like being born and growing up, will remain part of the cycle of organic life, part of coming into being and passing away that make up the history of the universe" (p. xxv). It is Thomas Cole's (1993) contention that we are at the end of a century where by technology has "undermined [our] ability to understand and accept the intractable vicissitudes of later life" (p. xxv). Viagra has contributed to men's lifelong stance as independent and competitive machines that have struggled against dependency and "weaknesses" through out life to maintain a "masculine" stance within society. Men have been engaged in a lifelong attempt to disconnect from the body as anything other than a vehicle to obtain successes and with the caveat that it isn't supposed to break down. When it does, it needs to be repaired and put back on the road again. There does come a point where repairs will not get it back on the road and therein lies the frightful fate ageing men have been running from nearly all there lives. No amount of technology will prevent the inevitable cycle of organic life. The issue is how ageing men will live out this final episode. Will it be the frantic search for youth in an attempt to push away dependency and forgo connection? Thomas Cole (1993) believes that:

> American culture . . . has responded to the anxieties of growing old with a psychologically primitive strategy of splitting images of a "good" old age of health and virtue, self-reliance, and salvation from a "bad" old age of sickness, sin, dependency, premature death and damnation. Rooted in the drive for unlimited individual accumulation of health and wealth, this dualism has hindered our culture's ability to sustain morally compelling social practices and existential vital ideals of ageing. (P. 230)

The realities of a life of *doing masculinity* has left older men with few connections and meanings beyond success and competition. In some ways Viagra and medicalization are demanding that this continue on. The question is to what purpose. Is sexual intercourse or the expectation of sexual performance the answer to aging men's growing frailties? Once again, Thomas Coles (1993) provokes us to consider aging out side of medicalization and commodification:

> Ageing, like illness and death, reveals the most fundamental conflict of the human condition: the tension between infinite ambitions, dreams, and desires on the one hand, and vulnerable, limited, decaying physical existence on the other—the tragic and eradicable conflict between spirit and body. (p. 239).

Medicalization and commodification have "blinded" aging men in the midst of a technological culture to consider "revaluing" the journey of life.

References

Bauman, Z. (2000). *Liquid Modernity*. Malden, MA: Polity Press.

Berger, P.L., & Luckman, T. (1966). *The social construction of reality*. New York: Anchor Books.

Bordo, S. (1998). Pills and power tools. *Men and masculinities*, 1, July, 87–90.

Blythe, R.(1979). *The view in winter*. New York: Harcourt Brace Jovanovich.

Cole, T.R. (1992). *The journey of life: A cultural history of aging in America*. New York: Cambridge University Press.

Gatien, P. (Producer), & De Niro, R. (Director). (1993). *A Bronx Tale* [Motion Picture]. United States: Savoy Pictures.

Giddens, A. (1991). *Modernity and self identity: Self and society in the late modern age*. Cambridge, UK: Polity.

Dychtwald, K (1999). *Age power*. New York: Jeremy P. Tarcher/Putnam

Dyens, O. (2001). *Metal and flesh–the evolution of man: Technology takes over*. Cambridge, MA: MIT Press.

Faircloth, C. A. (2003). *Introduction*. In C. A. Faircloth (Ed.), *Aging bodies Images and everyday experience (pp. 1–28)*. Walnut Creek, CA: Altamira Press.

Featherstone, M. & Warnick, A.(Eds.).(1995). *Images of ageing: Cultural representations of later life*. London: Routladge.

Fleming, A.A. (1999). Older men in contemporary discourses on ageing: absent bodies and invisible lives. *Nursing Inquiry*, 6, 3–8.

Franzoi, S., & Chang, Z. (2000). The socio cultural dynamics of the physical self: How does gender shape body seteem? In J. Holstein and G. Miller (Eds.), *Perspectives on social problems* (pp.179–201). Stamford, CT: JAI Press.

Friedman, D. M. (2001). *A mind of its own*. New York: Penguin Books

Fukuyama, F. (2002). *Our posthuman future*. New York: Farrar, Straus, and Giroux.

Giddens, A. (1991). *Modernity and self identity: Self and society in late modern age*. Cambridge, UK.: Polity

Lakhoff, G., & Johnson, M. (1980). *Metaphors we live by*. Chicago: The University of Chicago Press

Lyon, D. (1999). *Postmodernity*. Minneapolis, MN: University of Minneapolis Press.

McCallum, J. (1997). Health and ageing: the last phase of the epidemiological transition. In A. Borowski, S. Encel, & E. Ozanne (eds.), *Ageing and social policy in Australia*.(pp. 54–73). Melbourne, Vic: Cambridge University Press.

Murphy, P. F. (2001). *Studs, tools, and the family jewels*. Madison, WI: The University of Wisconsin Press.

Polkinghorn, D. E. (1988). *Narrative knowing and the human sciences*. Albany, NY: State University of New York Press.

Sheehy, G. (1999). *Understanding men's passages: Discovering the new map of men's lives*. New York: Ballantine.

Shotter, J. (1993). *Conversational realities*. Thousand Oaks, CA: Sage Publications.

Sontag, S. (1979). "The double standard of aging." In J. W. Williams (Ed.), *Psychology of women: Selected readings*. New York: Norton.

Tangenberg, K. and Kemp, S. (2002). *Embodied practice: Claiming the body's experience, agency, and knowledge for social work*. Social work, 47 (1), 9–18.

Tiefer, L. (1994). The medicalization of impotence: normalizing phallocentrism. *Gender and Society*, 8, 3, 363–377.

Tulle-Winton, E. (2000). Old bodies: In P. Hancock et al. (Eds.), *The body, culture and society: An introduction*. Buckingham, UK: Open University Press.

Wainwright, S. P., & Turner, B.S. (2003). Ageing and the dancing body. In C. A. Faircloth (Ed.), *Aging bodies: images and everyday experience* (pp. 259–292). Walnut Creek, CA: Altamira Press.

[37]

Did I Make the Grade? Ethical Issues in Psychological Screening of Children for Adoptive Placement

Sonja Grover

Lakehead University
Thunder Bay, Canada

This article suggests that psychological evaluations as a "screen for normalcy" with a view to adoption are a breach of the child's right to psychological integrity and privacy under international human rights law. A foreseeable outcome of such psychological screens, especially for the older foster child who has experienced multiple placements, is an unreliable mental health diagnosis. Normal, albeit maladaptive, potentially modifiable coping strategies arising in the context of family disruption come after the psychological screen to be labeled as an indicator of mental health disorder. This, in turn, may inappropriately interfere with the child's adoption prospects. It is suggested that psychological screens for normalcy of preadoptive children represent a misuse both of psychology and psychiatry for they are motivated more by the needs and interests of social institutions involved in the adoption process rather than by those of the child.

The United States Department of Health and Human Services (2003) reported that in September 2001 there were 542,000 children in the foster care system in that country while it is estimated that 805,000 children were in foster care for some period in that year. Given such numbers, the foster care system is sorely lacking in resources in terms of social work staff and available foster care placement, among other things (Hochman, Hochman, & Miller, 2003). Due to changes in federal mandates and views about adoption, there are many older children now available for adoption in the system who urgently need to be placed (Kirby & Hardesty, 1998). In 2003, there were 126, 000 children in the U.S. foster care system waiting to be adopted, 64% of whom had been in the system for more than 2 years (Hochman et al., 2003). Child Welfare is thus under considerable pressure to place these large numbers of children, some of whom are hard to place due to older age or exceptionality. At least 17% of children in foster care in the United States in 2000 (an estimated 91, 828 children) had been in the child welfare system for 5 or more years (Perez, O'Neil, & Gesiriech, 2003). The longer children stay in the foster care system, the higher the risk that they will have had multiple foster placements and thus also suffer the insecurities that are associated with such an experience. For instance, the U. S. Department of Health and Human Services (2003) reported that in 2002 of those children who had been in care less than 12 months, 81% had had two or fewer placements, while that number dropped to only 39% for children who had been in the system for 4 or more years.

Children who remain in the foster care system until they are no longer of an age to be covered by protective services generally have poor outcomes. One study found that 37% of the latter group leaving foster care in 1995 had not completed high school, 12% had been homeless at least once since their discharge from foster care, and 18% had been incarcerated at some point since their discharge (Courtney, Piliavan, & Grogan-Kaylor, 1995). In 2003, 7% of the children in foster care aged out of the system without having a permanent family, and 2% were runaways (Hochman et al., 2003). Considering all of the aforementioned statistics, it is perhaps not surprising that Child Welfare would respond to demands from prospective long-term foster parents or adoptive parents for a form of "quality assurance" regarding preadoptive children in foster care. Part of that quality assurance comes in the form of offering prospective parents a psychological assessment of the child even where there is no clinical indication that the child has a mental health disorder. Sometimes such assessments are also court ordered for the purpose of sorting out placement issues and screening for psychiatric disorder in the child. This, even though the child may be coping as well or even better than can reasonably be expected given the traumatic family disruptions and other stressors he or she may have experienced such as multiple placements. Such preadoptive psychological evaluation for the purpose of ruling out mental heath disorder was lauded in a paper by Kirby and Hardesty (1998), an American Psychological Association-selected article made freely available in full text due to its importance. Kirby and Hardesty (1998) explained that:

> Psychological assessment may be sought by agencies, courts, or potential adoptive parents . . . to address the so-called normalcy of the OPC [older pre-adoptive child] . . . The individuals requesting this service may be unclear regarding the questions a psychological evaluation may address and the recommendations it could provide. (portion in brackets added for clarity, p. 429)

The abbreviation OPC used in the above article refers to an older preadoptive child, which term the authors took to mean "the child who first becomes available for adoption at 15 months or over but who is likely to range from 2 to 12 years of age" (Kirby & Hardesty, 1998, p. 429). The issue of screening preadoptive children in foster care for "normalcy" apparently has not stirred any debate either in academic or psychology practice communities since the inception of psychological evaluation for this purpose. The objective here is to stimulate just such a discussion of the ethical issues raised by this practice. The ethical issues center in large part around the question of whose needs are in fact being served by such psychological screening for normalcy of the child in foster care at the point at which a long-term placement decision is to be made. Kirby and Hardesty (1998), while recognizing the importance of acting in the child's best interest, did not appear to view the preadoptive child as the client:

> Who is the client? The assessor is typically hired by, and works for, the child welfare system or the state, either as an outside evaluator or by order of the court. (p. 444)

The implication in the Kirby and Hardesty (1998) paper is then that the client varies depending on who has hired the psychologist to do the assessment.

The objectives in the current article are to point out that: (a) the child in care is always the client regardless of who has hired the psychologist to do the assessment; (b) there are important ethical issues concerning the use of psychological evaluations that are driven by pressure from various consumer groups

(Child Welfare, the courts, private adoption agencies, prospective long-term foster parents or adoptive parents, and others) rather than the needs of the actual client (the child in an insecure foster care placement); and (c) psychologists have a duty to act as advocate for the child in foster care.

WHAT'S WRONG WITH PSYCHOLOGICAL SCREENING FOR "NORMALCY" OF THE OLDER PREADOPTIVE CHILD AT THE REQUEST OF PROSPECTIVE PARENTS, THE COURTS, OR OTHER INTERESTED PARTIES?

The use of psychological assessment as a routine screen for normalcy places the preadoptive child at considerable risk of receiving a highly unreliable and unjustified mental health label which may interfere with placement:

> Children diagnosed . . . will reside longer in pre-adoptive status and are less likely to receive an adoptive placement than other children who may be perceived as "normal." This situation is particularly true if the psychologist does not discuss within the report a) the current functioning of the child with the disability and b) the possibility of or degree to which there may be deterioration or remediation of the disability or condition. (Kirby & Hardesty, 1998, p. 444).

Thus, children's prospects for adoption or long-term stable foster placement may be preempted via an uncalled for psychological assessment. That is, an assessment instigated not due to various clinical indicators related to the child's current functioning, but rather due to the wishes and interests of third parties. The manner in which issues are framed in the psychological report as well as its comprehensiveness—both of which are within the discretion of the individual psychologist—may also affect the child's placement prospects. Psychologists conducting such assessments routinely make long-range forecasts regarding the potential ability of the child to adjust well in the placement despite the fact that such predictions are largely nonempirically based:

> the research demonstrating what variables are associated with successful adoptive placement are sparse. . . . More research on older pre-adoptive and adoptive children is sorely needed, particularly research that emphasizes adjustment issues. . . . (Kirby and Hardesty, 1998, p. 445)

The child may thus be blocked from an adoptive placement due to the results of such screening psychological evaluations even where no emotional problems are apparent to justify the evaluation in the first instance. Further, the child cannot be presumed to have delegated proxy consent to Child Welfare for the assessment as from a child-centered point of view, the potential outcomes of such a psychological screening may be considered as quite adverse to the child's best interests. Thus, one cannot contend that had the child the competence to give consent, he or she would have done so. At the same time, the clinical history in terms of the child's actual functioning, framed without reference to mental health diagnoses, may not have jeopardized a placement.

The psychologist's report, as Kirby and Hardesty (1998) point out, will also likely be determinative in regard to whether the child has access to other parties with whom the child has bonded, such as former foster families or members of the child's biological family, parents, or even siblings. Such testing is thus very "high stakes":

> The outcome of the assessment will massively affect the lives of the participants. . . . For instance if the OPC is found to have a social, emotional, or behavioral problem, potential families may decide against placement. . . . Caution is needed because negative findings severely limit potential placement. (Kirby & Hardesty, 1998, p. 443)

Kirby and Hardesty (1998) urge caution in conducting such preadoptive psychological screens considering the likely impact of the results upon the long-term well-being of children currently in foster care. However, just how such caution is to be exercised is unclear given the lack of national standards applied by any oversight body regarding such assessments. Further, as the aforementioned authors themselves point out, for example: "Measures of social and emotional functioning exhibit lower reliability; some measures commonly in use offer no evidence for reliable and valid interpretation" (Kirby & Hardesty, 1998, p. 435). This is particularly disturbing given that children in foster care are likely to suffer considerable emotional distress due to their unstable living arrangements and separation from family. Correct in-context interpretation of any expected and common emotional symptoms of the child in foster care requires excellent clinical skill and not necessarily a full-blown psychological screen. The latter runs the risk of inappropriate mental health labeling of the child in foster care sometimes using instruments of questionable relevance and/or reliability and validity. Kirby and Hardesty (1998) in opposition to this view recommend as a screen for normalcy of the preadoptive child administering a full battery of psychological instruments directed to cognitive assessment (including nonabbreviated intelligence tests), socio-emotional tests including tests of maturation, neuropsychological tests as a matter of routine. This on the presumption that such difficulties are not uncommon in this population, and in addition to gathering the complete history from diverse sources including former and current teachers, physicians, foster parents, and the like. Note also that a profound issue of privacy arises in this context:

> When an agency or court seeks evaluation of a child, the resulting report and recommendations usually become part of the court record and are available to all interested parties. . . . (Kirby & Hardesty, 1998, p. 433)

The latter, this author would argue, results in a gross violation of the child's privacy rights. This is particularly so as the evaluation is being used as a screen for normalcy rather than due to existing clinical indicators necessitating further investigation for treatment planning. Consider in this regard the American Psychiatric Association position statement on Identification of Abuse and Misuse of Psychiatry:

> Since confidentiality is critical to patient care, psychiatrists must be sure the information and/or records they provide are sensitive to the mental health interests of the persons and/or populations with whom they are working. It is important to release the least amount of information possible to accomplish the desired function (Principle 7). (American Psychiatric Association, 1998)

Clearly in the case of preadoptive children in foster care, the results of psychological screens for normalcy and any stigmatizing mental heath diagnoses associated with the evaluation are indiscriminately available in the court record for any number of persons with a claim to make. This may in the long term be quite detrimental to the child's best interest and mental well-being.

In sum, then, psychologists have the power to affect a child's chance at placement in an adoptive family by: (a) performing screening psychological assessments of normal children coping with personal tragedy, which assessments may lead to unreliable mental health diagnoses given the child's unsettled situation; and (b) making long-range predictions without empirical basis about the child's potential for adequate adjustment in a prospective adoptive home. Note further that various psychologists use different psychological and other clinical assessment tools. Each of these psychological instruments have particular validity and reliability issues and are associated with varying levels of false-positive rates regarding mental health disorder. Such assessment for mental health problems and long-term adjustment prospects is notoriously unreliable given: (a) the often fluid nature of the child's emotional and situational status, and (b) the lack of validity of the instruments with regard to such a predictive purpose. The reliability of such assessments will also be influenced by the age of the child such that the results are likely to be less reliable the younger the child (recall that the older preadoptive child in this context refers to children as young as 15 months and from preschool to age 12).

Despite such concerns Kirby and Hardesty (1998) argue for the continued practice of psychological screening of children for suitability regarding adoptive placement even when the children exhibit no obvious signs of emotional or other disorder that would normally spur a full psychological evaluation:

> Until more is known about OPC's (older pre-adoptive children), assessment and treatment of this population will remain in the hands of talented, dedicated, but research-deprived practitioners. (Kirby & Hardesty, 1998, p. 445, portion in brackets added for clarity)

It is here contended, in contrast, that psychological evaluation of the preadoptive child is justified only where such is clinically indicated. Such intervention is not legitimate in this view where the prime objective is to meet the quality assurance demands of prospective adoptive parents or to resolve the ethical dilemma of the courts in deciding appropriate placement. Rather, interviews with the child and the prospective family along with detailed histories are more relevant and do not place the child at automatic risk of a mental health diagnosis. It is to be noted that access to adequate monitoring and periodic psychological assessment where there are clinical indicators as well as continuity of care in mental health treatment of children in foster care in the United States is notoriously lacking (as is sufficient attention to the children's other health care needs) (Horwitz, Owens, & Simms, 2000, Simms, Dubowitz, & Szilagyi, 2000). In fact, it has been reported that more often than not, any existing psychological or emotional problems worsen the longer the child is in foster care (Simms, Dubowitz, & Szilagyi, 2000). Improper diagnosis and inadequate follow-up are no doubt important contributors in this regard among other factors. Thus, it is not at all certain that most children diagnosed with a mental health problem as part of the preadoptive screening process and who are not placed do in fact receive any follow-up treatment even supposing such were indicated. The foster children diagnosed with a mental health disorder as part of the psychological screening for normalcy in preparation for possible adoption are thus more likely than not to be among the majority who simply languish in the foster care system without receiving any intervention at all or sporadic ineffectual mental health care. The child is thus left with compounded problems having been stamped below "grade A," making them less marketable as potential adoptees and receiving, in spite of this fact, less than adequate support within the system.[1]

CONFLICT OF INTEREST ISSUES

It should be acknowledged that psychologists performing psychological screening of children for placement purposes where there are no obvious clinical indicators are in a potential conflict of interest position. Should most foster children psychologically screened for "normalcy" with a view to placement be found to be "normal," the testing would be viewed as having no significant discriminatory power. This, in turn, would likely ultimately severely curtail the demand for such in-depth and relatively costly psychological screening. Hence, there is an appearance at least of a potential for bias in the interpretations made of the psychological evaluation results, whether or not such a bias in fact exists.

THE PSYCHOLOGIST AS ADVOCATE FOR
THE PREADOPTIVE CHILD IN FOSTER CARE

Kirby and Hardesty (1998) caution psychologists not to become advocates for the preadoptive child they are assessing and state the following:

> It is tempting in these cases to view oneself as the advocate for the child. However, the assessor must avoid "selling" the child (e.g. interpreting the results in an overly favorable rather than realistic manner). (p. 444)

Recall in this regard that preadoptive psychological assessments especially for children with no obvious clinical signs have no established empirical validity in terms of their efficacy in predicting adjustment to the adoptive home. It is unclear, therefore, what would constitute an unrealistic interpretation of the results in regard to the issue at hand, that is, the child's suitability for placement in terms of the likelihood of a good adjustment. This author would argue also that it is in fact the job of the psychologist to be an advocate for the child (Grover, 2002a, in press). To interpret the child's functioning in a hopeful manner, especially where there are no obvious significant clinical indicators prior to psychological assessment, seems quite reasonable. Yet, the child in foster care it seems is caught in a no-win situation. Such children are being subjected to psychological assessment with the risk of being assigned a serious mental health label often simply due to their family circumstance and history. For instance, the child who shows distrust or otherwise has altered his social interactions to be more hypervigilant or else demonstrates more neediness in that regard is at risk of being labeled as suffering from "reactive attachment disorder. The differential diagnosis is made in large part with reference to the child's troubled past in terms of the child having experienced inadequate care or even abuse and neglect" (World Health Organization, 1992). Likewise, multiple placements can serve as a rationale for a mental health assessment and diagnosis of the child as implied by the following statement by Kirby and Hardesty (1998): "Multiple placements may signal that the child experiences complicated attachment issues or conduct problems" (p. 434). That is, the child's mental health may be questioned without determining the adequacy of the screening of foster or adoptive parents by Child Welfare and whether inadequate screening was a factor in the multiple placements. Further, multiple placements may have resulted due to the lack of available long-term placement spaces. Child Welfare agencies are unlikely to be forthcoming about flaws in the system that necessitated multiple placements due to no cause attributable to the child. A child with a history of multiple placement may thus be especially at risk of receiving a highly suspect and damaging mental health diagnosis that would not have been applied but for the preadoptive psychological screen.

Behaviors that might have been viewed as part of a normal adjustment process can come through "psychological assessment" to be viewed as pathological. For instance, why should a child who has been in multiple foster placements and denied access to their biological family not be angry and lacking in trust? Why should a child who has had multiple social workers due to the high rate of turnover in the system not feel depressed and betrayed?[2] Such a response is not a sign of a mental health disorder but a sign of a child in foreseeable high distress (Grover, 2002b). Such distress will be evident from the information gathered by the social worker from the foster parents and in speaking to the child. The question should then become whether the prospective parents are prepared to provide the support for the child to make a healthy transition to the new long-term setting or not. To accept or not accept such a child is the prerogative of the prospective parents. However, it is not within the legitimate purview of the Child Welfare system, the courts, or the prospective parents to cause the child to be unjustifiably assigned a psychiatric diagnosis because they are having difficulty coping with extraordinary stressors. Many of the responses that result in psychiatric labels for the preadoptive child are better understood as realistic coping mechanisms for dealing with the highly stressful and abnormal situation represented by foster care and especially multiple placements. Consider, for instance, the reflections of Shalita who attended six schools due to multiple shifts in foster placement and remarked: "I completely disconnected myself from people because I had to" (Hochman et al., 2003).

CONCLUSION

The right to a family—be it adoptive or biological—and the right to access the biological family or be a continuing member of the biological family unless the child's best interests are otherwise served are stipulated in: (a) the "UN Convention on the Rights of the Child" (United Nations, 1989) and the "UN Declaration on Social and Legal Principles relating to the Protection and Welfare of Children with Special Reference to Foster Placement and Adoption Nationally and Internationally" (United Nations, 1986), among other human rights instruments. These are then fundamental human rights that ought not be tampered with by preadoptive evaluation aimed at: (a) detecting mental health problems where there are no preexisting clinical indicators or (b) making long-range predictions regarding potential for good adjustment, which are in fact unreliable. There is much that needs fixing in the American foster care system if the best interests of children are to be better served:

> If the system worked as intended—if foster care were truly a temporary shelter until children could return home or be adopted—much of the stigma of long, uncertain years in foster care would be relieved. That would require say the voices from the inside, a fresh look—and greater attention to—prevention, reunification, and adoption, as well as to meeting the needs of children in foster care. (Hochman et al., 2003, p. 22)

Preadoptive psychological assessment of older foster children as a screen placing the child at risk of a psychiatric label is not likely to facilitate these children's successful transition to reunification with the biological family or adoptive placement. It is time that preadoptive children and others in the foster care system be liberated from the high risk of mental health labeling simply by virtue of their being in the system. It is well recognized that the extraordinary situational factors that such children have experienced in their families and through multiple foster care placements and often lengthy stay in foster care create high emotional distress. However, the child's normal situation-specific coping strategies, even though perhaps nonadaptive, must not be pathologized. Yet, this is likely to occur as a result of preadoptive psychological evaluations designed to screen for "normalcy." Such maladaptive coping may often be rectified through a supportive placement in an adoptive home or other long-term placement. Psychologists must take care not to be a prime instrument blocking the child's placement in a secure and loving environment due to unreliable and devastating mental health labeling. Preadoptive psychological screens for normalcy with possible DSM-IV diagnosis as an outcome to meet the needs of the prospective adoptive parent or to solve the court's placement decision dilemma are here considered then both a misuse of psychiatric knowledge and ill-advised psychological practice. In this regard, it is valuable for psychologists as well as others addressing the mental health needs of children in foster care to take to heart the wisdom of Articles 2 and 6 of the American Psychiatric Association (1998) position statement on the abuse and misuse of psychiatry:

> It is the psychiatrists' primary responsibility to use their clinical skills and knowledge for the benefit of their patients. External social, political, management and economic forces should not be the primary consideration (Article 2).
>
> It is the psychiatrists' responsibility when working in the context of an organization or social or political environment to advocate for the mental health needs of the community or population in which he/she is working (Article 6).

What should be clear from the foregoing discussion is that psychological screening for normalcy of the older preadoptive child in foster care is not consistent with the best interests of the child but rather serves the interests of external parties. Such a practice should properly be abandoned by mental health practitioners.

NOTES

1. Specialized assessment and referral services, including mental health services provided to the child by health and allied health practitioners experienced in working with foster children, produce good outcomes where such a service is part of an ongoing monitoring process to support the child and includes attention to the child's educational needs (Horwitz, Owens, & Simms, 2000).

2. Case worker turnover in the Child Welfare system in the United States is very high, with an estimated 20% of public caseworkers and 40% of private caseworkers leaving the system each year (Hochman, Hochman, & Miller, 2003, p. 19).

REFERENCES

American Psychiatric Association. (1998). *Position statement of the APA on identification of abuse and misuse of psychiatry*. Retrieved March 1, 2004, from http://www.psych.org

Courtney, M., Piliavan, I., & Grogan-Kaylor, A. (1995). *The Wisconsin study of youth aging out of out-of-home care: A portrait of children about to leave care*. Madison: University of Wisconsin.

Grover, S. C. (in press). Advocating for children's rights as an aspect of professionalism: The role of frontline workers and children's rights commissions. *Child and Youth Care Forum*.

Grover, S. C. (2002a). Psychologist as child advocate: Ethical and legal issues in the clinical context. *University of Cincinnati Law Review, 71*, 43-70.

Grover, S. C. (2002b). Conduct disordered behavior as an adaptive response to stress. *Ethical Human Sciences and Services: An International Journal of Critical Inquiry, 4*, 1-6.

Hochman, G., Hochman, A., & Miller, J. (2003). *Foster care: Voices from the inside*. Report commissioned by The Pew Commission on Children in Foster Care. Retrieved March 1, 2004, from http://pewfostercare.org/research

Horwitz, S. M., Owens, P., & Simms, M. D. (2000). Specialized assessments for children in foster care. *Pediatrics, 106*, 59-66.

Kirby, K. M., & Hardesty, P. H. (1998). Evaluating older pre-adoptive foster children. *Professional Psychology: Research and Practice, 29*, 428-436.

Perez, A., O'Neil, K., & Gesiriech, S. (2003). *Demographics of children in foster care in 2000*. Report prepared for The Pew Commission on Children in Foster Care. Retrieved March 1, 2004, from http://pewfostercare.org/research

Simms, M. D., Dubowitz, H., & Szilagyi, M. A. (2000). Health care needs of children in the foster care system, *Pediatrics, 106*, 909-918.

United Nations. (1989). *Convention on the Rights of the Child: Adopted by the U.N. General Assembly, November 20, 1989, and entering into force September 2, 1990*. Retrieved March 1, 2004, from http://www.unesco.org

United Nations. (1986). *Declaration on Social and Legal Principles relating to the protection and welfare of children with special reference to foster placement and adoption nationally and internationally: Adopted by the U.N. General Assembly resolution 41/85*. Retrieved March 1, 2004, from http://www. unhchr.ch

U.S. Department of Health and Human Services, Administration for Children and Families, Administration on Children, Youth and Families, Children's Bureau. (2003). *Preliminary estimates of children in foster care FY 2001, 2002*. Retrieved March 1, 2004, from http://www.acf.hhs.gov/programs/cb/publications/afcars/report8.htm

World Health Organization. (1992). *ICD-10 classification of mental and behavioral disorders*. Retrieved March 1, 2004, from http://www. mental-health-matters.com

Offprints. Requests for offprints should be directed to Sonja Grover, PhD, CPsych, Faculty of Education, Lakehead University, 955 Oliver Road, Thunder Bay, ON, Canada P7B 5E1. E-mail: sonja.grover@lakeheadu.ca

[38]

'Problematics of Government', (Post) Modernity and Social Work

NIGEL PARTON

Nigel Parton is Professor in Child Care Studies at the University of Keele and author of *Governing the Family: Child Care, Child Protection and the State* (Macmillan, 1991).

SUMMARY

This paper attempts to locate contemporary developments and tensions in social work within current debates in social theory concerning the problematics of government and (post) modernity. It argues that modern social work emerged in a period of 'welfarism' which has now passed and that as a consequence social work has not simply been restructured in the era of neo-liberalism but is exposed as an activity particularly concerned with *managing* family life via the exercising of moral judgements and negotiating responsibilities. As a consequence the essential ambiguities of social work are more self evident than previously, and rather than constituting problems to be overcome, articulate the central elements of what it is to do social work. The article concludes by, tentatively, outlining the implications of such an analysis and how it may help us to understand what is going on and how we might proceed.

It is generally agreed that we are living through an important period of change in social work—in its priorities, organization and day-to-day practices—and that its rationale and social location are shifting in fundamental ways. My aim in this paper is to stand back a little from the detail of the flux and the associated intensity and confusions that many of us are experiencing at this time and try to analyse what is going on in the context of wider social changes and current debates in social theory. The paper attempts to articulate and take further certain concepts and ideas which informed a previous more empirical and detailed study of child protection and child care (Parton, 1991).

Essentially I will be arguing that the emergence and legitimation of *modern* social work from the late nineteenth century onwards was interrelated with and dependent upon the increasing attempts within *modern*

Correspondence to Nigel Parton, Professor in Child Care Studies, The University of Keele, Keele, Staffordshire ST5 5BG.

society to refine *modern* systems of social regulation whereby increasingly complex personal troubles and public issues could be responded to and were thereby constituted. Following Donzelot (1980) I will argue that *modern* social work provided a set of practices and knowledges whereby individuals who presented problems could be integrated into society according to the techniques of moralization, normalization and tutelage, and that the space occupied by social work, the 'social', emerged at a midway point between individual initiative and the potentially all-encompassing state. The origins of *modern* social work lie in the ways in which the population could be rendered thinkable and a target for political action. It was a particular element of a new type of 'biopolitics' (Foucault, 1979) which came to characterize the organization of *modern* society. Biopolitics links the individual and family with a range of collective authorities in the state. This opened up individuals to the focused and continuous gaze of the authorities, with the aim of enlisting their willing, self-disciplined involvement in political rule (Rose, 1990; Stenson, 1993). Michel Foucault and post-Foucauldian analyses of governmentality prove very productive in helping to understand and deconstruct the nature of social work in *modern* society.

Further, however, I will argue that it may no longer be appropriate to focus on the nature and emergence of *modern* social work to understand our contemporary experiences. Increasingly it seems that we have embarked on a new era which many social theorists now refer to as *post-modern*. If so, in order to understand contemporary social work and how it may be changing it is crucial to analyse the nature of the post-modern and how this differs from what went before. Ironically, while Foucault may be regarded (Boyne and Rattansi, 1990) as making a significant contribution to post-modern social thought, the primary object of his analysis was the modern world. Thus while I will be drawing, particularly in the earlier parts of the paper, on Foucauldian analysis, it will be one of my central conclusions that the nature of contemporary social work is changing in ways which are taking us into quite new areas. These cannot simply be seen as an extension of the practices which characterized the nature of social work in its *modern* emergence. However, the identification of what constitutes the essential elements and priorities of contemporary social work in this post-modern era can only be tentative. While it is unlikely that social work is being/will be transformed in ways which are unrecognizable, it is the argument of this paper that it is important that we address these issues and thereby clarify the nature of the task(s) for both those doing social work and those on the receiving end. Essentially the paper is concerned with trying to identify and articulate the realities of contemporary social work and what can be realistically claimed on its behalf and expected of it.

While a number of previous projects (particularly Rojek *et al.*, 1988, and McBeath and Webb, 1991) have grappled with the implications of recent theorizing about post-modernity for social work, and drawn upon such theorizing as a basis for developing a new conceptual base for practice, this paper is more modest. Its primary purpose is concerned with describing and outlining the situation that social work finds itself in. It is primarily descriptive and in the process tries to analyse where we are rather than being concerned with what should be done and how post-modern perspectives might inform this. Until such issues are clarified it seems inappropriate to make suggestions as to how we *should* proceed. However if the analysis and descriptions do speak to the experiences of social workers and help us understand where we are that in itself may put us in a better position to influence what goes on around us and identify a set of issues which require our attention.

THE 'PROBLEMATICS OF GOVERNMENT'

There can be little doubt that over the last twenty years, virtually from the moment of its *modern* emergence, state social work has been subject to considerable political and public criticism, and that this has both reflected and informed the changes currently being experienced within social work. No longer is social work a private professional activity between practitioners and clients; it is carried out under the sometimes partial, sometimes full, scrutiny of the wider society. To understand the changing nature of social work thus requires an understanding of the changing nature of political power and the state. A number of writers have recently attempted to relocate and develop the analysis of the state in terms of the 'problematics of government' (Burchell *et al.*, 1991; Miller and Rose, 1990; Parton, 1991; Rose, 1990; Rose and Miller, 1992), and argue that analyses that assume that the exercise of political power should begin with an analysis of the 'sovereign state' are mis-placed. These more recent approaches attempt to develop, refine and apply Foucault's concept of 'governmentality'.

Foucault argued that the idea of governmentality has increasingly dominated politics since the eighteenth century. Governmentality refers to the 'ensemble formed by the institutions, procedures, analyses and reflections, the calculations and tactics, that allow the exercise of this specific albeit complex form of power' (Foucault, 1979, p. 20), and it is the regulation of the population which has proved its unending con-

cern. Such an approach does not reduce the exercise of political power
to the actions of the reified sovereign state, but draws attention to the
range of mechanisms whereby different groups and forms of knowledge
regulate, and thereby construct and constitute, the lives of individuals,
families and the community. This conception of political power is hence
both wider and more complex than analyses which reduce politics to
the activities, priorities and decisions of the state. Similarly such a conception does not attempt to reify the state as necessarily functional,
autonomous or monolithic, or as wholly concerned with social control
(Cohen and Scull, 1983).

The concept of governmentality both broadens and redirects the analysis of political power. It recognizes that the exercise of power takes
place via an ever shifting set of alliances between political and nonpolitical authorities. Professionals and other 'experts' are crucial to its
operation, but they also have their own interests and priorities which
means that day-to-day policy and practice are neither unified, integrated
or easily predictable. Similarly social regulation, while discursively constrained, is not simply imposed from above in the form of direct constraint or imposition but via encouraging and supporting individuals to
exercise their own freedoms and choices, thereby allowing government
'at a distance'. As Rose and Miller (1992) have outlined:

Power is not so much a matter of imposing constraints on citizens as of 'making
up' citizens capable of bearing a kind of regulated freedom. Personal autonomy
is not the antithesis of political power, but a key term in its exercise, the more
so because most individuals are not merely the subjects of power but play a
part in its operation (p. 174).

According to Rose and Miller, government is best understood as a
domain of cognition, calculation, experimentation and evaluation. This
domain is inextricably linked to the activities of experts and their fields
of knowledge in which human conduct is analysed, rendered calculable,
and administered. These activities are carried out through various, often
competing, 'local tactics of education, persuasion, inducement, management, incitement, motivation and encouragement' (p. 175).

The concept of governmentality implies that the very existence of a
field of concerns we call 'policy' should itself be treated as in need of
explanation. It highlights the diversity of powers and knowledges which
are entailed in rendering fields of practice knowable and amenable to
intervention (Foucault, 1986). Policy should be analysed in two ways.
First, policy should be located in discussions about the proper ends and
means of government. These discussions articulate the shifting political
rationalities and justifications for what should be done, by whom, at
what cost, for/to whom, and with what overall conception of the 'good

society', and of the desirable directions and methods of social change. But secondly, policy should also be analysed in terms of the technologies of government, whereby the particular technical devices of writing, listing, numbering, computing, etc. render an issue as a knowable, calculable, and administrable object. If issues or areas of concern are to be transformed into new areas of government, the information must be available—statistics, reports and so on—for a domain to become susceptible to evaluation, calculation and intervention. Similarly, for intervention to take place certain techniques or 'technologies' are required which provide the particular mechanisms through which the object of concern can be modified and normalized. Such technologies may appear quite mundane and refer to the:

techniques of notation, computation and calculation; procedures of examination and assessment; the invention of devices such as surveys and presentational forms such as tables; the standardisation of systems for training and the inculcation of habits; the inauguration of professional specialisms and vocabularies; building designs and architectural forms—the list is heterogeneous and is, in principle, unlimited (Miller and Rose, 1990, p. 8).

This analysis of govermentality takes as central the discursive field within which concerns, needs and problems are defined, delineated and given priority, and the way they are responded to. It is concerned with the analysis of discourses and their changing character. By referring to discourses this approach gives weight to the linguistically constituted character of reality. This does not mean that discourses are 'mere words'. Discourses are structures of knowledge, claims and practices through which we understand, explain and decide things. In constituting agents they also define obligations and determine the distribution of responsibilities and authorities for different categories of persons such as parents, children, social workers, doctors, lawyers and so on. They are impersonal forms, existing independently of any of these persons as 'individuals' (Foucault, 1977b; 1978). They are frameworks or grids of social organization that make some social actions possible whilst precluding others. A discourse is best understood as a system of possibility for knowledge and for agency (Philp, 1985; Woolgar, 1986). It is a system of possibility that allows us to produce statements which can be either true or false.

Both the nature of and the priorities for social work have undergone important changes in recent years. How has this come about, and what are the essential elements of contemporary policy and practice? An analysis of discourse will not only outline the significance of changes in language in social work but will also provide insights into the nature of contemporary policy and practice itself. What forms of policy and prac-

14   NIGEL PARTON

tice have emerged in social work and what types of knowledge inform this? An analysis of the changes in social work discourse will outline how the sphere of operations for social work has been circumscribed and prioritized, and how in the process new possibilities for social workers and those on the receiving end have opened up. In attempting such an analysis we need to identify the shifting 'conditions of possibility' for social work and the nature of the 'space' which it occupies, and how this might be changing. This space is both theoretical and practical. It is the space which provides the rules for the formation of statements and the changing rules and priorities of day-to-day practice. Similarly it is through this space that the nature of social work is related to the changing rationalities and technologies of government.

SOCIAL WORK AND THE EMERGENCE OF 'THE SOCIAL'

One of Foucault's central objectives was to provide a critique of the way modern societies regulate and discipline their populations by sanctioning the knowledge-claims and practices of the new human sciences — particularly medicine, psychiatry, psychology and criminology — which provided the opportunity for the emergence of the 'psy' complex (see also Ingleby, 1985, and Rose, 1985). He argued that these new disciplines legitimated new knowledge claims and forms of social regulation which subverted the classical order of political rule based on sovereignty and right. They instituted a regime of power exercised through disciplinary mechanisms and the stipulation of norms for human behaviour. The normal family, the healthy child, the perfect wife and the proper man both inform ideas about ourselves and are reproduced and legitimated through the practices of the 'psy' complex. According to Foucault, from the eighteenth century onwards, these new knowledges increasingly colonized the old powers to such an extent that the more traditional forms of law and judicial rights were transformed. No longer were the crucial decisions taken in the courtroom according to the criteria of judicial rights, but in the hospital, the clinic or the welfare office, according to the criteria of 'normalization'. Even when decisions were taken in the courtroom, these were increasingly colonized by the 'psy' complex according to these same criteria (Foucault, 1977a).

Normalizing disciplinary mechanisms which attempt to subject the individual to training require a knowledge of the whole person in their social context, and depend on medico-social expertise and judgements for their operation. They depend on direct supervision and surveillance, and they emphasize the need to effect change in character, attitudes and behaviour in an individualized way. They are concerned with underlying causes and needs and attempt to contribute to the improvement of those being served as well as to social defence. Because the 'psy' professions have the exclusive insight into the problems and the knowledge and techniques required, they are allowed wide discretion to diagnose and treat, and thereby normalize.

Foucault identifies three processes involved in discipline: hierarchical surveillance; normalizing judgement; and the examination. Hierarchical surveillance provides a non-reciprocal monitoring gaze in which the bearers of power are able to create individual knowledge about human bodies over a continuous basis (Foucault, 1977a, pp. 170–6). Normalizing judgement involves a continuous discretionary evaluation of conduct in the context of floating standards between positive and negative poles, which allows the application of detailed impositions and privileges (Foucault 1977a, pp. 177–83). According to Foucault the examination:

combines the techniques of an observing hierarchy and those of normalising judgement. It is a normalising gaze, a surveillance that makes it possible to qualify, to classify and to punish. It establishes over individuals a visibility through which one differentiates them and judges them (Foucault 1977a, p. 184).

Such a disciplinary mode of power embodies many of the activities of the 'dividing practices' whose central concern is constructing, modifying and operationalizing classificatory systems and of which medicine and social work are seen as prime examples.

From the early nineteenth century the primary elements of the 'disciplinary' society emerged, and surveillance, classification, examination, ordering and coding techniques of power began to pervade through the social body. No longer was it appropriate to see power as repressive, since knowledge validated power and turned it to productive ends, opening up new practices and possibilities. The new forms of knowledge such as medicine, psychiatry and social work (or philanthropy as it was constituted then) were directly related to the exercise of power and helped create new objects of concern, investigation and intervention and thus accumulated new bodies of information (Miller 1987).

A number of writers (Cohen, 1985; Garland, 1985; Rose, 1985) have argued that the central elements of the changing forms of social regulation originally identified by Foucault grew in significance during the late nineteenth century and throughout the twentieth century. While the old institutions—such as the prison—have remained, new community-based initiatives have developed, thus expanding the system of non-custodial social regulation and taking in new and more diverse areas of social life, while intensifying the intensity of the old ones. The visibility, own-

16   NIGEL PARTON

ership and identity of the systems of social regulation have become increasingly vague as the boundaries between them, and between them and the community, become blurred. The family, the school and the community itself are absorbed into and permeated by the newly developing and increasingly pervasive mechanism of social regulation. Such changes are legitimated by the inevitable failures of the old mechanisms to fulfil their objectives, and the system becomes self-perpetuating. With more and more areas of expertise brought in, with their different knowledges, priorities and interests, the system becomes ever more complex, making integration and mutual understanding more difficult. As a consequence the systems of classifications, to allocate cases and demarcate areas of responsibility, become ever more sophisticated and central.

The emergence of philanthropy and subsequently social work during this period has provided a particular set of policies and practices which have both refined and complicated discipline together with the modern rationalities and technologies of government. More particularly it has provided a particular dimension of and contribution to what Jacques Donzelot (1980) has referred to as the 'social'. The emergence of the 'social' and social work in particular is associated with the transformations that took place from the mid-nineteenth century onwards around an increasing grid of intersecting and interrelated concerns and anxieties about the family and the community more generally. The 'social' discourse developed as a hybrid in the space identified between the private and the public spheres. It produced and was reproduced by new relations between the law, administration, medicine, the school, and the family. Central to its emergence was the incorporation of a range of philanthropists into the judicial process in respect of children and young people, and the emergence of psychiatry as a specialism which informed not only judicial decisions but the practice of the successors to the philanthropists–social workers. The subsequent growth and establishment of social work and its increasing centrality to the state in Britain, culminating in the Seebohm reforms in the late 1960s and early 1970s, was driven by a variety of anxieties associated with the care of and neglect and cruelty to children, and the potential threat young people might pose in terms of their actual or potential delinquent/criminal behaviour or other forms of anti-social behaviour in later life.

The emergence of the 'social' and the practices of social workers, who were its primary technologists, was a positive solution to a major problem posed for the liberal state (Hirst, 1981). Namely, how can the state establish the health, development and, hence, rights of individual family members who are weak and dependent, particularly children, while promoting the family as the 'natural' sphere for caring for those individuals, and thus not intervening in all families, which would destroy the autonomy of the private sphere? Philanthropy, and subsequently social work, developed at a midway point between individual initiative and the all-encompassing state. It provided a compromise between the liberal vision of unhindered private philanthropy and the socialist vision of the all-pervasive and all-encompassing state which would take responsibility for everyone's needs and hence undermine the responsibility and role of the family.

Issues in relation to the child exemplify these difficulties: for children to develop their full health and sensibilities, they could not be left to the vagaries of the market and the autonomous patriarchal family (Dingwall and Eekelaar, 1988). The emergence of the 'social' was seen as the most appropriate way for the state to maintain its legitimacy while protecting individual children. For the liberal state:

> the unresolved problem is how child rearing can be made into a matter of public concern and its qualities monitored without destroying the ideal of the family as a counterweight to state power, a domain of voluntary, self-regulating actions (Dingwall, Eekelaar and Murray, 1983, pp. 214–15).

Originally, with the emergence of modern industrial society, this activity was carried out by voluntary philanthropic organizations, and Donzelot (1980) argues that two techniques were of significance in their relationship with families particularly on behalf of children—what he calls 'moralisation' and 'normalisation'. 'Moralisation' involves the use of financial and material assistance which was used as leverage to encourage poor families to overcome their moral failure. It was used primarily for the deserving poor who could demonstrate that their problems arose for reasons beyond their control. 'Normalisation' applied to attempts to spread specific norms of living via education, legislation or health, and involved a response to complaints, invariably from women about men, and hence provided a means of entry into the home. In return for this guidance, and moral and minimal material support, philanthropic workers were given an insight into what was happening inside the home and leverage to bring about changes in behaviour and lifestyle. Clearly, however, there were problems if individuals did not co-operate or did not approach the worker in the first place, so that children and other weak and dependent family members were left to unbridled parental devices.

In the late nineteenth and early twentieth centuries such philanthropic activities were increasingly absorbed into the formal institutions of the state. This process continued through to the early 1970s with the introduction of local authority social service departments as the 'fifth social service' (Townsend, 1970). While moralisation and normalisation were to be the primary forms of contact, this was increasingly framed in legislation which would also give the possibility for coercive intervention. 'Tutelage', as Donzelot calls it, based on the notion of preventive intervention, would combine a number of elements, though coercive intervention would be used for the exceptional circumstances where the techniques or moralisation and normalisation had failed.

During much of the twentieth century the growth and formalization of modern social work and its absorption by the state was based on attempts to develop new strategies of preventive penology on behalf of young people who were identified as actual or potential threats. It was concerns about the growth of crime and delinquency and the apparent failures of the more traditional judicial and community forms of social regulation that provided the central rationale for the growth of social work (Hall, 1976; Cooper, 1983; Harris and Webb, 1987).

However, the space occupied by social work was complex. It both interrelated with and was dependent on a number of other more established discourses, particularly law, health/hygiene, psychiatry and education. While the space which it occupies between the public and the private is a crucial one, a variety of discourses impinge on and interpenetrate it. It is for this reason that social work is potentially such a contested area and one subject to diverse and sometimes competing rationales and definitions. Thus, while it is important that social work has a diffuse mandate so that it can be interpreted and operated in a variety of ways, this leaves it in an ambiguous position. Perhaps most crucially, this ambiguity arises from its sphere of operation itself: between civil society, with its allegiances to individuals and families, and the state, in the guise of the court and its 'statutory' responsibilities. Social work is an essentially ambiguous, uncertain and contested arena.

This ambiguity captures the central, if sometimes submerged, element of social work as it emerged from the late-nineteenth century onwards. Social work essentially occupies the space between the respectable and the deviant or dangerous classes, and between those with access to political and speaking rights and those who are excluded (Philp, 1979). It fulfils an essentially mediating role between those who are actually or potentially excluded and the mainstream of society. In the process, it mediates not only between the excluded and state agencies, but crucially between other diverse state agencies and discourses, together with a wide range of private, voluntary and other philanthropic agencies, and the diverse overlapping discourses which inform and construct them.

The goal of much social work is to go beyond the 'dividing practices'—the normal and deviant—implied by discipline, to the processes which were of central concern to Foucault in his later work. whereby human beings turn themselves into subjects (Foucault, 1979). Social work alludes 'to *the underlying character, the hidden depths, the essential good, the authentic and the unalienated*' (Philp, 1979, p. 99).

In doing so, the social worker produces a picture of the individual client as a subject which is not immediately visible to the doctor, the courts or the social security officer, but which exists as s/he 'really' or potentially 'is'. The concern with discipline shifts towards that of regulation. If discipline is modelled on the gaze and based on the examination, the normalizing judgement and hierarchical observation, regulation operates through interioration, the confession and talking whereby individuals both take on and express themselves as subjects. While discipline produces knowledge by constituting individuals as objects of scientific discourse, regulation provides knowledge of subjects in their subjectivity. Whereas the former relies on experts drawing on more traditional, objectivized, positivistic science, the latter relies on experts who draw upon interpretive knowledge and use themselves and their insights and understanding of relationships as their primary technologies of practice.

SOCIAL WORK AND THE SPREAD OF 'WELFARISM'

While the sphere of government is wide-ranging and complex and social work strategies form only a small element within it, none the less, they are a crucial part of the process which draws individuals and families into the sphere of government. This is done not essentially through repression 'but through the promotion of subjectivity, through investments in individual lives, and the forging of alignments between the personal projects of citizens and the images of social order' (Miller and Rose, 1988, p. 172). Social work provides an important, but ambiguous, strategy to enable 'government at a distance', or indirect methods of social regulation, to take place. It is important if the liberal ideal of maintaining autonomous free individuals who are at the same time governed is to be realized.

For social work to operate quietly and in an uncontested way it requires a supportive social mandate together with an internal professional confidence and coherence. The latter, particularly in the period following the Second World War, was provided primarily by a body of knowledge borrowed from neo-Freudianism and ego-psychology, while the professional aspirations veered towards medicine and psychiatry. Similarly, the growth of social work from the late nineteenth century onwards ran in parallel with and was interrelated with the development of social interventions associated with the establishment of the welfare state in the post-war period—what Rose and Miller refer to as 'welfarism'. For Rose and Miller (1992) the growth of 'welfarism' is best understood not simply in terms of the growth of the interventionist state but as a particular form of government through which a variety of political forces 'seek to secure social and economic objectives by linking up a plethora of networks with aspirations to know, programme and transform the social field' (p. 192).

The key innovations of 'welfarism' lay in the attempts to link the fiscal, calculative and bureaucratic capacities of the apparatus of the state to the government of social life. As a political rationality 'welfarism' was structured by the wish to encourage national growth and well-being through the promotion of *social* responsibility and the mutuality of *social* risk, and is premissed on notions of *social* solidarity (Donzelot, 1988). Both the rationality and central technologies of 'welfarism' were given particular articulation via the twin and closely interrelated approaches developed around the work of John Maynard Keynes and William Beveridge. The emergence of 'welfarism' rested on twin pillars—one Keynesian and the other Beveridgian.

The Keynesian element stood for an increase in government in terms of attempts to manage economic demand in a market economy through judicious intervention, for example, by increased public expenditure during a recession, especially with the aim of maximizing production and maintaining full employment. The great depression of the inter-war years had demonstrated that left to itself the capitalist market economy could not function properly. The economic and social costs of a *laissez-faire* approach led to a drastic fall in production and mass unemployment, and political and social unrest was high. The waste and inefficiency of a market economy could be corrected through moderate forms of intervention. Keynesianism stood for state intervention from the demand side of the economy to ensure a high level of economic activity and full employment. We might say this provided the economic component of 'welfarism'.

Beveridge's notion of insurance (in its widest sense) against the hazards of a market economy, on the other hand, formed the social component. Unlike the Keynesian economic argument, the social argument for 'welfarism' was not new. Since the days of Bismarck in Germany and Lloyd George in Britain, most capitalist countries had developed forms of social protection underwritten and coordinated by the state. What was new in the post-war period was that the principle of state intervention was made explicit, and the institutional framework which would make state responsibility for maintaining minimum standards became a reality. This involved pooling society's resources and

GOVERNMENT, (POST) MODERNITY AND SOCIAL WORK 21

spreading the risks. Social insurance summed up this departure. Universality of population coverage, comprehensiveness of risks covered, adequacy of benefits, and the citizenship notion of state social services (provided as of right to all and not as a form of charity to the few) were the hallmarks of the Beveridge approach.

Social insurance fundamentally transformed the mechanisms that integrated the citizen into the social order. Not only were individuals to be protected from the evils of 'Want, Disease, Idleness, Ignorance and Squalor', but they would be constituted as citizens bound into a system of solidarity and mutual inter-dependence. It was seen as a scientific and statistical method of encouraging passive solidarity amongst its recipients. Everyone would contribute and everyone would benefit, though some more than others. The overall rationale of welfarism was to make the liberal market society more productive, stable and harmonious; and the role of government, while more complex and expansive, would be positive and beneficent.

A number of assumptions can be seen to characterize the development of 'welfarism' in the twenty-five years after the Second World War, and these were taken for granted by a wide range of academics, politicians, administrators and professionals. The institutional framework of universal social services was seen as the best way of maximizing welfare in modern society, and it was assumed that the state worked for the whole society and was the best way of progressing this. The social services were instituted for benevolent purposes meeting 'social needs', compensating socially caused 'diswelfares', and promoting 'social justice'. Their underlying functions were ameliorative, integrative and redistributive. Social progress would continue to be achieved through the agency of state and professional intervention. Increased public expenditure, the cumulative extension of statutory welfare provision and the proliferation of government regulations, backed by expert administration, represented the main guarantors of equity and efficiency. Social scientific knowledge was given a pre-eminence in ordering the rationality of the emerging professions who were seen as having a major contribution to developing individual and social welfare.

Not surprisingly during this period social work and welfarism more generally were imbued with a degree of optimism which believed that measured and significant improvements could be made in the lives of individuals and families via judicious professional interventions. In the context of the institutional framework of the other universal state welfare services, while social work was constituted as a residual service, it was based on a positive and optimistic view of those it was working with and what could be achieved. The modern development of social work continued to be located in the space between the respectable and the dangerous classes, but the latter had been reconstituted. Not only, in the context of full employment, rapid growth and universal services, did they no longer constitute a 'class', but they were no longer dangerous. A major assumption of welfarism is that, apart from a very small number, because the depraved are essentially deprived or misguided, everyone is treatable or can be rehabilitated. Social problems were located in a few families and could be treated. There was a consensus that social work was a positive development in the context of the development of 'welfarism'.

This consensus had a number of dimensions. It was assumed that the interests of the social worker, and hence of the state, were similar to, if not the same as, those of the people they were trying to help. It was essentially a benign, but paternalistic, relationship. Interventions in the family were not conceived as a potential source of antagonism between social workers and individual family members. It was assumed not only that many problems had their genesis within the family, but that their resolution resided there as well. When it was felt that a family required modification this would be primarily on the basis of the normalizing techniques of counselling, help and advice. Because the social worker was working on behalf of a beneficent state, if an individual did come into state care this was assumed to be necessarily in their interests. Social work, whether in a field, day-care or residential context, was a positive experience for all concerned.

The optimism which infected the attitudes and claims of social workers in this post-war period was reflected in the confidence of the state and the wider society in their ability to effect change through their therapeutic and counselling skills. Interventions which had therapeutic intentions necessarily had therapeutic outcomes, and it was social workers who had the essential knowledge required and thereby knew what was best for all concerned. Social work was allowed a degree of independence and discretion to carry out its work. In the process the essential ambiguities, tensions and uncertainties which lay at the core of its operation remained submerged.

SOCIAL WORK IN THE NEO-LIBERAL ERA

Perhaps one of the great ironies is that at the point at which modern social work emerged to play an important part in the welfarist project 'welfarism' itself was experiencing considerable strains in both its political rationality and technological utility. Before modern social work could establish its sphere of operations 'welfarism' itself was seen as in crisis. In this crisis the rationale and activities of social work were

GOVERNMENT, (POST) MODERNITY AND SOCIAL WORK   23

particularly vulnerable to criticism and reconstruction as it could be seen to personify all that was problematic in welfarism.

The problems encompassed both the economic and social spheres from the mid-1960s onwards. In the economic sphere they included: a slow-down in economic growth (particularly in Britain compared to its western competitors); increased difficulties in controlling inflation; a gradual increase in unemployment which became rapid in the 1970s; and a growth in proportional terms of the public sector in comparison to the private productive sectors of society. In the social sphere they included: the rediscovery of poverty and significant areas of continued and growing social deprivation; the growth of violence in terms of crime, trade union militancy and social indiscipline generally; a decline in individual responsibility and attachments to the traditional nuclear family; and a failure of the various 'social sciences' and the various modern experts who operated them to contribute to social well-being.

The possibility of supplanting welfarism by a new rationality of government was provided by approaches informed by neo-liberalism and the new right (Levitas, 1986; Gamble, 1988) and which were increasingly dominant from the mid-1970s onwards. The central element of both the critique and recommendations for change was that both the political rationalities and technologies of government pursued by 'welfarism' were themselves central to the problems and thus required fundamental change. Neo-liberalism required a fundamental break with 'welfarism' in terms of its moralities, explanations, vocabularies and technologies, and thus indicated the need for a new form of government and new discursive practices.

For neo-liberalism and the new right, the problems in the economic and social spheres were clearly interrelated. Two factors were seen to lie at the core of the problems, and the growth and activities of modern social work were implicated in both. First, the state was seen as a burden on the wealth creating/productive sectors of society. Social services, as with any state activity, generated high taxes, increased budget deficits, acted as a disincentive to work, and encouraged an overloaded class of unproductive workers. In the process government was subject to overload resulting from higher expectations and the increased demands placed upon it from all quarters, including the claims of the bureaucracies and experts who had grown under its auspices. Dependency was institutionalized across the social body. Secondly, and very much related, the operation of 'welfarism' in the hands of the new experts, of which social work was perhaps *the* prime example, encouraged soft, permissive attitudes to deviance, fecklessness and the actual and potentially violent—the traditional dangerous classes. Permissiveness did not simply drain resources, but undermined responsibility and eroded the

24   NIGEL PARTON

family which was seen, along with the market, as central to the successful operation of social well-being and order.

Perhaps the key demonstration of the inadequacies of modern social
work was that there was growing evidence during the 1970s that it
simply did not work. A number of pieces of research showed that social
work and rehabilitative interventions of various sorts and in relation to
a wide range of needs and problems did not produce the outcomes that
their supporters claimed (Allen, 1981; Croft, 1978; Gaylin *et al.*, 1978;
Fischer, 1978). More crucially however, the evidence from a series of
child abuse tragedies seemed to demonstrate that social workers had
failed in their professional responsibilities and statutory duties. The
enquiries into the tragedies (DHSS, 1982; DoH, 1991) showed that such
failures were not simply a consequence of individual professional error
and incompetence but pointed to fundamental problems built into the
attitudes, priorities, organization and training of social workers (Parton,
1985; 1991). Recent scandals and public enquiries into the treating of
children and young people whilst *in* public care have taken this evidence
of the failures of modern social work to new levels of intensity (Social
Services Inspectorate, 1991; Staffordshire County Council, 1991).

As a result the recent assault on modern social work can be seen
as a specific case of the neo-liberal critique that has dominated
government in recent years: antagonism towards public expenditure
on state welfare; an increasing emphasis on individual self-help and
family support; an extension of commodification of social relations;
and the general collapse of the consensus underpinning 'welfarism'.
Neo-liberalism stresses the importance of individual responsibility,
choice and freedom; it supports the disciplines of the market against
interference of the state, urging reductions in taxation and public
expenditure; and while stressing the need for a reduced state, requires
a strong state to establish certain modes of family life and social
discipline. The strategy consists of a coherent fusion of the economic
and the social. It has its roots in an individualized conception of
social relations whereby the market is the key institution for the
economic sphere, while the family is the key institution for the social
sphere. It does not constitute an abdication of state responsibility
but rather a reformulation of what· those responsibilities might be.
New service boundaries and forms of resource allocation and an
increased emphasis on assessment, together with the means to regulate and review, are increasingly key elements for social work.

More particularly for social service departments, three paramount
responsibilities have been identified which have framed all the changes
over recent years: to take a comprehensive strategic view of all sources
of care available in an area; to recognize that the direct provision of

services is only part of a local pattern; and that a major part of their function is in promoting and supporting the fullest possible participation of other and different sources of care.

At the same time, however, the emphasis on social responsibility and social risk is recast. For neo-liberalism the political subject is less a social citizen with powers and obligations deriving from membership of a collective body, than an individual whose citizenship is active. It is an individualized conception of citizenship where the emphasis is upon personal fulfilment and individual and family *responsibility*. In the process the social work role to assess 'risk' and allocate scarce resources in an individualized way, particularly with the dangerous, isolated and neglected, becomes not just its central activity but central to the operation of welfare services more generally. The technologies of assessment are central to the operation of the 1989 Children Act, the 1990 NHS and Community Care Act, and the 1991 Criminal Justice Act.

These neo-liberal programmes have also been consonant with a range of other critiques of 'welfarism' that have emerged in recent years from a variety of civil libertarians, academics, feminists, socialists, ethnic minorities and other community and interest groups, none of whom would identify themselves with the new right or neo-liberalism.

What has emerged is a reinterpretation of government which, while heavily influenced by and riven through with neo-liberal principles, has much wider appeal and support. This emerging arena is often referred to as 'welfare pluralism' (Johnson, 1987) and has a number of features. First, an emphasis on plural provision whereby a greater proportion of social care is provided by voluntary agencies, private organizations and community initiatives. State provision should be minimal and reserved for areas where no-one else is providing. Second, decentralization and a community orientation of the statutory services themselves. The predominant mode of provision should be community-oriented, implying flatter organizational structures and a different interpretation of professionalism—recognizing that the consumer or user knows best and that informal sources of care should be reinforced and not supplanted wherever possible. Third, the introduction of contractual rather than hierarchical accountability, whereby relationships within and between welfare organizations should be specific and formal and services should be contracted out to voluntary and private agencies wherever possible. Similarly, at the consumer/professional interface the nature of the relationship and the focus of the work should be formally spelt out in a contract which can be subject to regular monitoring and review. Finally, in emphasizing the need for greater monitoring and inspection, the participation of consumers should be central to decision-making and future plans.

26   NIGEL PARTON

In the process, the role and practices of managers become crucial. It is managers, as opposed to the professionals, who are seen as the powerful actors in this new network. Managers become the new mediators between the expert knowledge(s), individual and community needs, and the allocation of scarce resources—in effect harmonizing overall objectives and day-to-day practice. More specifically, notions of management frame and supplant the central activities of the professionals themselves and the forms of knowledge they draw upon. No longer are social workers constructed as therapists or caseworkers, but as care or case managers coordinating and operationalizing care packages, where their knowledge of resources and networks is crucial and where, again, notions of monitoring and review are central.

The apparent failure of the social sciences to produce the knowledge and techniques in wide areas of social life whereby problems and needs could be reduced or ameliorated has resulted in an emphasis on improving multi-agency and multi-disciplinary work. As a consequence, an increasing emphasis in policy and practice has been put upon refining systems, producing procedures and guidance and overhauling intra- and inter-organizational structures.

The central skills and activities are concerned with assessment, planning, care management, negotiating, coordinating, using information technology, and operating the law and procedures. Not surprisingly more and more time is spent on administration; in meetings; on writing reports; and on liaison—rather than on direct work with clients or, as they are now constructed, users and consumers. I am not suggesting that these are new activities and skills for social work, simply that they now constitute *the* central activities of what it is to be a social worker. In effect social workers are constituted as managers of family life for certain sections of the population.

The increased emphasis on management, evaluation, monitoring, and constraining professionals to write things down, is itself a form of government of them, and more crucially, of those with whom they are working. It forces them to think about what they are doing and hence makes them more accountable against certain norms. In the process, power flows to the centre or agent who determines the professionals' inscriptions, accumulates them, analyses them in their aggregate form, and can compare and evaluate the activities of others who are entries in the chart. An increasing emphasis is placed on the production of mission statements, objectives, outcomes, statistics, community care plans, and annual reviews. The management of information itself becomes the central rationale for policy and practice, from those in central government to professionals on the front line.

THE EMERGENCE OF (POST) MODERNITY

How far can these changes be explained by: the changing role of the state; the emergence of neo-liberalism and the new right; Thatcherism; and the effects of research or academic critiques? While these and other factors undoubtedly play a part, they are not either singularly or in combination sufficient to explain the changes or to provide an account of the current state of social work.

Recent debates and analyses in social theory about whether and how far modern western societies have entered a new period—what is referred to as post-modernity—are productive in this respect. While there is considerable discussion about how far post-modernity consti-tutes a distinct break with modernity or how far it constitutes a 'period of high modernity', there is some agreement as to what constitute the essential contours and elements of the phenomenon under discussion (Giddens, 1990; Smart, 1991; Rosenau, 1992).

Notions of post-modernity have essentially developed from immanent critiques of modernity. Modernity, as a summary term, refers to the cluster of social, economic and political systems which emerged in the West around the eighteenth century and became increasingly pervasive through the nineteenth and twentieth centuries. Modernity involved the recognition that human order is neither natural nor God-given but essentially vulnerable and contingent but can, by the development and application of science, be subject to human control. Contingency was discovered together with the recognition that things could be regular, repeatable and predictable, and hence ordered. According to Bauman, the vision of politicians joined with the practices of professionals and scientists in a common strategy to improve the world. The vision was of a hierarchical harmony reflected in the uncontested and uncontestable pronouncements of reason. According to Bauman (1992, p. xiv) 'the modern, obsessively legislating, defining, structuring, segregating, class-ifying, recording and universalising state reflected the splendour of uni-versal and absolute standards of truth'.

During the twentieth century profound changes have occurred in developed societies, which have undermined such visions. Post-modernity refers to a social condition which is not simply a phase beyond modernity. Rather it is modernity coming to terms with itself together with the characteristic features of modern organization and thought, which were present more or less from the beginning but whose implica-tions have only become apparent in recent years. In effect the seeds of post-modernity have been evident throughout the modern period. What has happened is that these have only now become evident for what they are.

28   NIGEL PARTON

Post-modernity is characterized by a *fragmentation* of modernity into forms of institutional pluralism, marked by variety, contingency, relativism and ambivalence—all of which modernity sought to overcome. The post-modern condition is the condition of modernity emancipated from false consciousness, unrealistic aspirations and unrealizable objectives.

The distinguishing features of modernity were the understanding of history as having a definite and progressive direction; the attempt to develop universal categories of experience, representation and explanation; the idea that reason can provide a basis for all activities; and the belief that the nation state could coordinate and advance such developments for the whole society and thereby constitute the nature of society itself. The guiding principle of modernity was the search to establish reliable foundations for generalizable knowledge, policy and practice. This very principle, however, has eventually come to subvert the project it was aimed to realize. The aim of substituting proof for the unexamined bases of tradition, dogma and religion has eventually turned out to be self-destructive. 'Welfarism' was, in hindsight, a particular condition of modernity in an advanced form. But the aims, principles and practices which it embodied carried the seeds of its own destruction. The discovery that knowledge has no foundations, that empirical findings are simply assertions, and that there is no ultimate proof or truth, is existentially and socially very unsettling. Ironically such discoveries are the end result of the development of progress itself.

For those who continue to think in modern terms the emergence of such paradoxes presents problems which need to be overcome or resolved. But for a number of post-modernists, such as Bauman, they are distinctive features of the new social order. Post-modernity is simply 'modernity come to its senses'. One consequence of the undermining of universal science, knowledge and truth, is that all views, interests and arguments are potentially valid—it relocates politics as central to everyday life. More particularly, the ambitions and responsibility of the state are reduced and policy shifts away from the state or is actively shed on its own initiative. It dissipates and splits into a plethora of localized and partial policies pursued by local or partial interests. Under the post-modern condition, grievances which in the past would have cumulated into a collective political process and been addressed to the state, stay diffused and stimulate further autonomy.

However, not all politics in the era of post-modernity are unambiguously post-modern. In the modern era the politics of inequality and redistribution was the central focus of political conflict. With the advent of post-modernity, while displaced from its central focus, it remains a central feature. In fact not only are inequalities not alleviated, they proliferate. However, the politics of inequality is increasingly expressed

GOVERNMENT, (POST) MODERNITY AND SOCIAL WORK 29

in terms of attempts to establish individual and social rights for diverse categories of the population rather than the explicit redistribution of property, wealth and income. The most conspicuous social division under post-modern conditions is one between seduction and repression: between 'the choice and lack of choice, between the capacity of self-constitution and the denial of such capacity, between autonomously conceived self-definitions and imposed categorizations experienced as constraining and incapacitating' (Bauman, 1992, p. 198).

The redistributive aims of the resulting struggle are mediated by the resistance against repression of human agency. According to Bauman, in its post-modern form, conflicts bare their true nature—that of the drive toward freeing human agency—which in modern times tended to be hidden behind ostensibly redistributive battles. Seduction becomes the paramount tool of integration and is made possible once the market succeeds in making consumers dependent upon it. Market-dependency is guaranteed and self-perpetuating once men and women, now consumers, cannot proceed with the business of life without tuning themselves to the logic of the market. In contrast, repression is reserved as the paramount tool of regulation for the growing numbers on the margins of society who cannot be absorbed into market dependency. Social work is thus exposed in its central mediating role between those who are actually or potentially excluded and the mainstream of society and still, more crucially, between the post-modern social processes of seduction and repression and those of modernity, whose essential skills and technologies of practice are based on notions of assessment, monitoring and managing individuals and situations. No longer are the discursive practices, as in the modern era, so evidently derived from those associated with the 'psy' complex, where knowledge seemed to have a basis in certain social and psychological truths concerning the individual.

CONCLUSIONS

In this paper I have drawn on recent analyses concerning the 'problematics of government' and post-modernity to provide a preliminary account of the current state of social work and how it might be changing. More particularly I have argued that the emergence of *modern* social work as a discourse was characterized by a fragile discursive practice, fragile in part because of being constrained and interpenetrated by more traditional discourses. Foucauldian and post-Foucauldian analyses, while productive in understanding this process, are only partially helpful in explaining more recent developments. What such analyses have done, however, in helping to undermine the modern welfarist project,

30   NIGEL PARTON

has been to contribute to current debates about whether we are entering a new era—the post-modern—characterized by pluralism, variety, contingency and relativism, where beliefs in rational science, knowledges, truth and the universal state are undermined.

It is not surprising, therefore, that social work is now experienced as being particularly complex and subject to tremendous tensions, ambiguities and fragmentation. Increasingly it feels as if social work does not have a core theoretical knowledge base, and that there is a hole at the centre of the enterprise. In this situation a new discourse has emerged concerning management, monitoring, evaluation and assessment which claims to provide the mechanisms for holding things together and which in the process seems to be central in constituting the nature of contemporary social work itself. Such an analysis certainly appears bleak in its implications. If, however, it provides a realistic appraisal of where we are it may provide a basis from which to intervene. Certainly the potential for more localized interventions and changes is opened up. Similarly we need to recognize that notions of localized power and politics should be much more central in conceptualizing what social work is and what it is to do social work. In recognizing that traditional notions of professionalism, experts and truths are changing and subject to flux and fragmentation, the possibilities for us to take hold, in a self conscious way, of what we do and the way we do it should not be dismissed.

REFERENCES

Allen, F. A. (1981) *The Decline of the Rehabilitative Ideal: Penal Policy and Social Purpose*, London, Yale University Press.

Bauman, Z. (1992) *Intimations of Post-modernity*, London, Routledge.

Boyne, R. and Rattansi, A (eds) (1990) *Post-modernism and Society*, London, Macmillan.

Burchall, G., Gordan, C. and Miller, P. (1991) *The Foucault Effect: Studies in Governmentality*, London, Harvester-Wheatsheaf.

Cohen, S. (1985) *Visions of Social Control. Crime, Punishment and Classification*, Cambridge, Polity Press.

Cohen, S. and Scull, A. (eds) (1983) *Social Control and the State: Historical and Comparative Essays*, Oxford, Basil Blackwell.

Cooper, J. (1983) *The Creation of the British Personal Social Services 1962-74*, London, Heinemann.

Croft, J. (1978) *Research in Criminal Justice* (Home Office Research Study, No. 44), London, HMSO.

DHSS (1982) *Child Abuse: A Study of Inquiry Reports 1973-1981*, London, HMSO.

DoH (1991) *Child Abuse: A Study of Inquiry Reports 1980-1989*, London, HMSO.

Dingwall, R. and Eekelaar, J. (1988) 'Families and the state: an historical perspective on the public regulation of private conduct', *Law and Policy*, 10, 4, pp. 341-61.

Dingwall, R., Eekelaar, J. and Murray, T. (1983) *The Protection of Children: State Intervention and Family Life*, Oxford, Basil Blackwell.

Donzelot, J. (1980) *The Policing of Families: Welfare Versus the State*, London, Hutchinson.

GOVERNMENT, (POST) MODERNITY AND SOCIAL WORK 31

Donzelot, J. (1988) 'The promotion of the social', *Economy and Society*, 17, 3, pp. 395–427.

Fischer, J. (1978) 'Does anything work', *Journal of Social Science Research*, 1, pp. 215–43.

Foucault, M. (1977a) *Discipline and Punish*, London, Allen Lane.

Foucault, M. (1977b) *The Archaeology of Knowledge*, London, Tavistock.

Foucault, M. (1978) 'Politics and the study of discourse', *Ideology and Consciousness*, Spring, No. 3, pp. 7–26.

Foucault, M. (1979) *The History of Sexuality, Vol. 1: An Introduction*, London, Allen Lane/Penguin Press.

Foucault, M. (1986) 'Space, knowledge and power', in Rabinow, P. (ed.) *The Foucault Reader*, Harmondsworth, Penguin.

Gamble, A. (1988) *The Free Economy and the Strong State: The Politics of Thatcherism*, London, Macmillan.

Garland, D. (1985) *Punishment and Welfare: A History of Penal Strategies*, Aldershot, Gower.

Gaylin, W., Glasser, I., Marcus, S. and Rothman, D. (1978) *Doing Good: The Limits of Benevolence*, New York, Pantheon Books.

Giddens, A. (1990) *The Consequences of Modernity*, Cambridge, Polity Press.

Hall, P. (1976) *Reforming the Welfare: The Politics of Change in the Personal Social Services*, London, Heinemann.

Harris, R. J. and Webb, D. (1987) *Welfare, Power and Juvenile Justice: The Social Control of Delinquent Youth*, London, Tavistock.

Harvey, D. (1990) *The Condition of Postmodernity*, Oxford, Blackwell.

Ingleby, D. (1985) 'Professionals as socialisers: the "Psy Complex" ', in Scully, A. and Spitzer, S. (eds) *Research in Law, Deviance and Social Control 7*, New York, Jai Press.

Johnson, N. (1987) *The Welfare State in Transition: The Theory and Practice of Welfare Pluralism*, London, Wheatsheaf.

Levitas, R. (ed.) (1986) *The Ideology of the New Right*, Cambridge, Polity Press.

McBeath, G. B. and Webb, S. A. (1991) 'Social work, modernity and post-modernity', *Sociological Review*, 39, 4, pp. 745–62.

Miller, P. (1987) *Domination and Power*, London, Routledge.

Miller, P. and Rose, N. (1988) 'The Tavistock programme: the government of subjectivity and social life', *Sociology*, 22, 2, pp. 171–92.

Miller, P. and Rose, N. (1990) 'Governing economic life', *Economy and Society*, 19, 1, pp. 1–31.

Parton, N. (1985) *The Politics of Child Abuse*, London, Macmillan.

Parton, N. (1991) *Governing the Family: Child Care, Child Protection and the State*, London, Macmillan.

Philp, M. (1979) 'Notes on the form of knowledge in social work', *Sociological Review*, 27, 1, pp. 83–111.

Philp, M. (1985) 'Michel Foucault', in Skinner, O. (ed.) *The Return of Grand Theory in Human Sciences*, Cambridge, Cambridge University Press.

Rojek, C., Peacock, G. and Collins, S. (1988) *Social Work and Received Ideas*, London, Routledge.

Rose, N. (1985) *The Psychological Complex: Psychology, Politics and Society in England, 1869–1939*, London, Routledge and Kegan Paul.

Rose, N. (1990) *Governing the Soul: The Shaping of the Private Self*, London, Routledge.

Rose, N. and Miller, P. (1992) 'Political power beyond the State: Problematics of government', *British Journal of Sociology*, 43, 24, pp. 173–205.

Rosenau, P. M. (1992) *Postmodernism and the Social Sciences: Insights, Inroads and Intrusions*, New York, Princeton University Press.

Smart, B. (1991) *Modern Conditions, Post Modern Controversies*, London, Routledge.

Social Services Inspectorate (1991) *Children in the Public Care: A Review of Residential Child Care*, London, HMSO.

Staffordshire County Council (1991) *The Pindown Experience and the Protection of Children: the Report of the Staffordshire Child Care Inquiry*, Staffordshire County Council.

32   NIGEL PARTON

Stenson, K. (1993) 'Social work discourse and the social work interview', *Economy and Society*, 22, 1, pp. 42–76.
Townsend, P. (ed.) (1970) *The Fifth Social Service: A Critical Analysis of the Seebohm Proposals*, London, The Fabian Society.
Woolgar, S. (1986) 'On the alleged distinction between discourse and praxis', *Social Studies of Science*, 16, pp. 309–17.

ACKNOWLEDGEMENTS

I would like to thank Bill Jordan, Judith Milner, Chris Parton and Mark Philp, together with the two anonymous *British Journal of Social Work* assessors, for their help and critical comment on an earlier version of this paper.

Part XI
Promising Directions for the Future

[39]

Ethical Decisionmaking

M. Leever, G. DeCiani, E. Mulaney and H. Hasslinger

Child welfare professionals make decisions on behalf of the state that affect the lives of children and families. Considering all the interests at stake, how do professionals know that their actions are ethical? In making sound decisions, professionals should not rely solely on personal values or intuition, but should incorporate the standards of the profession and current knowledge about the problem with which they are dealing, consult superiors and colleagues, and think critically about the decisions that they must make. When the decision involves an ethical dilemma, professionals should use a model for ethical decisionmaking. The importance of taking these steps in making professional decisions flows from the role of the child welfare professional. As stated in the Illinois *Code of Ethics for Child Welfare Professionals*:

> The child welfare professional is a person who functions in a societally sanctioned decisionmaking capacity for neglected and/or abused children and their families. When individuals accept the role of child welfare professional and the delegated authority inherent in that role, they publicly acknowledge having the professional responsibilities which accompany that authority. Society and agency clients, therefore, have legitimate expectations about the nature of professional intervention as it occurs in one-on-one professional/client interactions, in the management and administration of those providing intervention, and in policy decisionmaking.

To assist child welfare professionals in understanding the nature of ethical decisionmaking, this chapter provides an overview of professional ethics and values and outlines a model for ethical decisionmaking to assist in managing ethical dilemmas. A starting point for ethical decisionmaking is a code of ethics that articulates the values of the profession and sets the guidelines and boundaries of conduct for all within the profession. The Illinois *Code of Ethics for Child Welfare Professionals* and similar codes of ethics for child welfare and other professions describe core values and provide ethical guidance for the profession.

VALUES AND THE FIDUCIARY RELATIONSHIP

There are two concepts that provide a framework for ethical decisionmaking and ethical conduct in providing child welfare services: *values* that underlie ethical child welfare practice and the *fiduciary relationship* that exists between the child welfare professional and the client.

A value is a desirable quality, condition, or practice. When an ethical decision is required, critical thinking is needed about the underlying values and how they should be applied. Values can be described in a variety of ways. Values, for example, may be intrinsic or instrumental. A value is said to be intrinsic if it is desired for its own sake and not for the sake of something further. Examples of intrinsic values are life, security, health, freedom, and self-determination. A value is said to be instrumental if it is desirable as a means to either another instrumental value or an intrinsic value. Wealth, for example, may be considered an instrumental value because it normally is desired as a means to freedom and security. Values also may differ as to whether they are based on principles or standards of right behavior. Values, for example, such as honesty, confidentiality or fairness are expressed as principles or standards of right behavior whereas other values, such as wealth or power, reflect desires that individuals may have as part of a satisfying life, but which do not necessarily relate directly to ethical behavior.

The foundation of the child welfare profession centers around the intrinsic values of protecting children and preserving families. From this foundation, additional values have been identified for respectful intervention with families. As identified in the Illinois *Code of Ethics for Child Welfare Professionals* and generally agreed upon by child welfare professionals, the core child welfare values are:

- Protection of children
- Preservation of families
- Respect for families
- Respect for persons
- Client self-determination
- Individualized intervention
- Competence
- Loyalty
- Diligence
- Honesty
- Promise-keeping
- Confidentiality

In addition to these core child welfare values, agencies with religious affiliations may have certain specific religious principles that affect their child welfare practice.

A fiduciary relationship is a relationship that exists between a professional and a client that is dependent on the client's trust in the professional. As is typically the case in professional-client relationships, the relationship between a child welfare professional and the client is inherently unbalanced because the professional possesses far greater power than the client. Whether the client is voluntary or nonvoluntary, the client must be able to trust that child welfare professionals will use their specialized knowledge and skills in ways that are consistent with professional values. Specifically, clients must be able to trust that child welfare professionals will exercise their authority in the best interest of the child. When child welfare professionals betray the trust that is integral to fiduciary relationships, their unethical conduct affects both clients and the public as a whole.

ETHICAL DECISIONMAKING

In many situations that arise for child welfare professionals, two or more professional values will apply, making it difficult to determine the right course of action. Child welfare professionals must be able to make sound ethical decisions in complicated situations, recognizing that the consequences may not be fully predictable. Ethical decisionmaking is the process of evaluating ethically relevant considerations in choosing a course of action. It is systematic and impartial, having little to do with personal preferences, beliefs, or feelings, and it requires questioning initial feelings, intuitions and biases to discover sound reasons for acting in one way rather than another. Ethical decisionmaking is a skill that can be practiced and improved. This chapter provides a model for ethical decisionmaking that professionals can use to strengthen their skills in this area.

It is important to note that some situations requiring ethical decisionmaking may require a review of relevant literature and research. In addition, when a situation has significant ethical implications for the client, consultation with supervisors and colleagues may be necessary to determine the most appropriate course of action. When situations arise in which a supervisor is uncertain regarding the right course of action, she should seek consultation with the ethics board of the agency or another resource.

An eight-step decisionmaking model may be used to make ethical decisions in complex child welfare matters. To illustrate the use of this model, summarized in Table 1-1, the following case example will be used:

> Maria is the caseworker for Joseph, age 13. Joseph's mother abandoned him when he was seven. Her parental rights were terminated. When he was younger, Joseph often made idealized statements about his mother and expressed longing for her return. In the past three years, Joseph has ceased asking about his mother and now enjoys a good relationship with

Table 1-1. Model for Making Ethical Decisions

(1) State the problem.

(2) **Check the facts.** Does the evidence support the alleged facts? Have all needed facts been gathered? Which facts are irrelevant? Have the relevant research and literature been identified?

(3) Develop a list of alternative courses of action.

(4) Discern what is ethically at stake in relation to each of the alternatives:

a)   The relevant ethical principles.

b)   The likely harms and benefits to the parties involved.

c)   Relevant laws.

d)   Relevant agency policies.

e)   Relevant rights and the responsibilities that correspond with those rights.

(5) Test alternatives.

Ethical standards test: Does one option fit better with the relevant ethical principles, agency policies, and laws than other alternatives?

Outcomes test: Does one option promise more benefit or less harm than other alternatives?

(6) **Make a decision.** Prioritize based on which option is consistent with the most important values and choose the alternative that maintains the most important values.

(7) Check the conclusions.

Publicity test: Would the decision stand if it were to be published in the newspaper?

Goosey-Gander Test: Would the decision stand if the decisionmaker were adversely affected by it? (Is what is good for the goose, good for the gander?)

Colleague Test: What would colleagues say about the problem and the selected option? Would colleagues raise any problem with the selected option?

Professional Test: What might the profession's governing body or ethics committee say about the option? Would their response be sound?

Organizational Test: What would the agency's ethics officer or legal counsel say about the selected option? Would that response be sound?

(8) Plan for prevention of the problem in the future.

What would make it less likely that such a decision must be made again? Are there steps that could be taken at the professional level to avoid the problem in the future? Are there steps that could be taken at the organizational level to avoid the problem in the future?

(Ozar & Sokol 1994; Davis 1997; Gambrill & Gibbs 2002)

his current foster parents, who are in the process of adopting him. Maria was recently informed of the death of Joseph's birthmother and struggles with the decision of whether or not to tell Joseph.

Step 1: State the problem.

The first step in ethical decisionmaking is to state the problem clearly. The key to defining an ethical problem is to identify two or more ethically important considerations that are in conflict. When the problem is specified in this manner, initial ethical worries may prove unwarranted, or the ethical problem may be quite different from what it initially appeared to be. In the case example, the problem might be stated as the competing values of Maria's obligation to be truthful with Joseph (and/or Joseph's right to know of his mother's death) and Maria's responsibility to refrain from harming Joseph.

Step 2: Check the facts.

Ethical decisionmaking requires that the child welfare professional work with facts and not with unwarranted assumptions or suppositions. Facts must be determined and verified to ensure that the correct values are prioritized and that important relevant values are not overlooked. When the child welfare professional confirms the facts of a case, she can clarify any unwarranted assumptions that may have been made, identify any additional information that is needed, and identify and set aside irrelevant information. In the case example, if Joseph's mother's death were a rumor that Maria heard from someone in the neighborhood where he formerly lived, she should not consider telling Joseph until she verifies that the death occurred.

Checking the facts should clarify the following: Joseph's mother has died; Joseph does not know that his mother has died; Joseph has a good relationship with his foster parents; and information about Joseph's mother caused him pain in the past.

Step 3: Develop a list of alternative courses of action.

The next step is to develop a list of all possible courses of action. For example, in the case study, Maria could:
- Not tell Joseph.
- Tell Joseph plainly.
- Decide to tell Joseph only if he asks.
- Not tell Joseph even if he asks.
- Inform Joseph's foster parents and have them tell Joseph.

There may be additional options which Maria will add as she proceeds with the decisionmaking process.

Step 4: Identify what is ethically at stake in each alternative.

Making good ethical decisions requires the ability to recognize what is ethically at stake in any given situation. As assessment of what is ethically at stake requires an understanding of:

- The professional's own personal values

- Relevant ethical principles of the profession

- Current information in the field

- Relevant laws, regulations, and agency policies

- Relevant rights and corresponding responsibilities and the individuals who have these rights and responsibilities

- Current data and research in the field that further inform the above

In the case example, Maria should consult the code of ethics for her agency and any laws, rules, or agency policies bearing on such disclosures to children in care. She should be aware of how her own personal ethical code may affect her view of the situation and not let it override professional values. She may find, as is the case in the Illinois *Code of Ethics for Child Welfare Professionals*, that those professional values include honesty and the duty to minimize harm to a client. Applying these values, she may wonder whether she would be dishonest if she were to choose not to inform Joseph about his mother's death. She may also wonder whether telling him or not telling him will cause him unwarranted emotional harm, both in the short term and in the long term. She will realize that she faces a possible conflict between the two values of honesty and minimizing harm. With regard to rights and responsibilities, she may intuitively feel that Joseph has a right to know about his mother, but she may not be sure whether her corresponding responsibility is to proactively inform him or just truthfully answer if he asks. She must also sort out her responsibilities toward the foster parents. For example, she may have an ethical responsibility to be honest and cooperative with them but a legal responsibility to retain decisionmaking authority in the case.

Finally, Maria should consult current research to learn whether any studies have addressed the emotional impact of revelations of a parent's death on a child of Joseph's age and experience. There might also be research on the opposite side of this question:

Can long-term emotional harm result from a child's later realization that important facts about his identity were concealed from him? Using knowledge in this way is called evidence-based practice, "the conscientious, explicit, and judicious use of current best evidence in making decisions about the care of individuals" (Sactrett, Richardson, & Haynes, 1997).

Step 5: Test alternatives.

There are two general approaches to testing alternatives through a process of ethical decisionmaking: the ethical standards test and the outcomes test. The ethical standards test holds that certain actions are inherently ethical or unethical, and the outcomes test holds that actions are ethical or unethical depending on whether they result in beneficial or harmful outcomes to those involved. Professionals may have a preference for one test over another but should use both tests when making ethical decisions.

The Ethical Standards Test

The ethical standards test evaluates ethical rightness by appealing to a set of ethical standards and values. This approach (called "deontological" by ethicists) holds that certain actions are inherently unethical because they treat persons as objects; violate agreements or promises; or are irrational in some way. When faced with an ethical decision, the child welfare professional should first consult an ethical code or other ethical resource in order to choose the course of action that best conforms with the relevant ethical standards. This method of ethical decisionmaking is relatively straightforward: the child welfare professional selects the course of action that best fits with articulated ethical standards.

Some ethical standards, such as avoiding conflicts of interest, are made explicit in professional codes. Other ethical standards, such as "do not lie," may be both codified as ethical standards for a profession and exist as unwritten social standards. In either case, ethical standards express values.

The ethical standards approach commonly refers to rights. A right is an entitlement that creates corresponding responsibility for others, to act in a certain way or to refrain from interfering with the individual who holds the right. Recognition of rights increases the likelihood that individuals treat one another in an acceptable way. Rights may be classified in a number of ways:

> **Positive or Negative.** A right is positive if it requires others to take affirmative action in a certain way or to meet a certain need. For example, a child has a positive right to a safe and secure environment.

Parents, the child's caregiver, or the state must exert effort to ensure the child's safety and security. A right is negative if it requires that others refrain from interfering. For example, a parent's right to raise his or her child as he or she sees fit requires that others not interfere.

Universal or Particular. Everyone is entitled to a universal right. An example is the right of each person to food or shelter. A right is particular if it only applies to certain individuals in specific situations. A particular right is a client's right to confidentiality in a professional relationship.

Absolute or Qualified. A right is absolute if it cannot be taken away or overridden, such as a child's right to be protected from abuse. A right is qualified if the right can be overridden. Parents have the right to care for their children as they see fit only to the extent that they protect their children from harm.

To reason effectively with regard to rights, it is important to identify a right as positive or negative, universal or particular, and absolute or qualified. For example, a parent has a right to raise her own child, but her right is qualified and may be overridden by the child's absolute right to be raised in a safe environment. When a conflict develops between the parent's right to parent and the child's right to safety, the absolute right will prevail over the qualified right. The nature and extent of any responsibility will depend on the nature of the right to which it corresponds. A positive right generates the responsibility to take proactive steps in response to that right, whereas a negative right is associated with the responsibility to refrain from interfering.

Applying the ethical standards test to the case example, the following might take place:

> Maria consults the agency's code of ethics. When she finds that it requires honesty with clients, she believes that Joseph has a right to know, which implies that she would have a responsibility to tell him of his mother's death. She concludes that it would be unethical to withhold such information from Joseph. She is aware that Joseph may possibly experience emotional distress, but nevertheless, she tells him of his mother's death.

Many child welfare professionals would make the same decision as Maria. It is important, however, to consider the limitations of this test:

First, when using this approach, it may be difficult to resolve conflicts among standards. In the case example, Maria has both the responsibility to be honest with Joseph and also not to harm him. She may believe, based on her second responsibility, that informing Joseph of his mother's death would harm him. Which ethical standard—honesty or the duty not to harm—is more important?

Second, it may be difficult to apply general ethical standards to specific situations. Codes of ethics, by nature, are general. Any attempt to anticipate a myriad of specific ethical dilemmas would lead to several thick volumes of text, and even in such a case, the exact situation that must be addressed may not be covered. Consequently, a set of ethical standards may not be as helpful as a professional would hope in giving clear guidance on day-to-day situations.

Third, framing ethical issues in terms of rights is only a starting point. To have a right to act in a certain way means only that it is permissible to act that way. The question remains whether one may ethically do so. For example, an adoptive parent may have a right to prohibit any contact between his adopted child and the child's birthparents. Nevertheless, depending on the circumstances, the child's best interest may mean that birthparents be allowed to participate in the child's life, and allowing contact may be ethically advisable.

Fourth, merely stating that a right exists does nothing to clarify the extent of an individual's responsibility. Further, stating the existence of a right is not helpful in identifying who, in particular, has the responsibility. Determining that Joseph has a right to know, for example, does not clarify who would have the responsibility to tell him about his mother's death.

Fifth, the reference to rights can obscure what, in reality, is ethically at stake in a situation because individuals often claim rights without a clear basis for their claim. A foster parent, for example, may claim the right to prohibit visits between a child and the child's biological parent because of concerns about the impact of visits on the child. When they are not carefully considered, claims to rights may get in the way of clear ethical discussion.

The Outcomes Test

A second test in ethical decisionmaking is the outcomes test. Although this test acknowledges the usefulness of the ethical standards test, the outcomes test evaluates ethical rightness on the level of benefit that an action produces as opposed to other alternatives. Under this approach, an ethical action is that action, among all available alternatives, that produces the most favorable balance of benefit over harm to all those involved. Benefit primarily refers to the promotion of such intrinsic values as physical and emotional health, security, fulfillment, and freedom. Harm refers to the diminution of those values. When applying the outcomes test, both short-term and long-term consequences must be considered. For example, misleading a client may provide certain short-term benefits to the client, but in the long run, it may harm the client in significant ways as well as undermine the professional relationship.

The decisionmaking process involved in the outcomes test consists of developing alternative courses of action and selecting the one that maximizes benefit and minimizes harm for all of the involved individuals both in the short and long term. The outcomes test necessarily requires prioritization of alternative courses of action based on outcomes. Prioritization of options takes into account three main factors: the degree of potential harm and benefit, the likelihood that harm and/or benefit will occur, and the number of persons affected.

If Maria used the outcomes test to reach her decision, the following might occur:

> Maria considers the consequences of informing Joseph of his mother's death. She predicts that it would cause him emotional distress, and given his traumatic experience with abandonment, she believes that the news may cause him to act out. Because he is now doing very well in his preadoptive home and not talking about his mother, she believes that he may benefit from not knowing. Maria feels that the potential harm outweighs any benefits of informing Joseph. She decides not to tell him unless he asks about his mother.

Although Maria decided not to tell Joseph because she thought that doing so would likely cause more harm than benefit, others might disagree. Another person might balance the harm and benefit differently, concluding that withholding the information, in the long run, may result in more harm than benefit. It is important to note that different ethical tests do not automatically lead to different conclusions and that the ethical standards and outcomes tests will often suggest the same course of action. Use of both approaches together, however, is key to making effective, organized ethical decisions.

Like the ethical standards test, the outcomes test has limitations. First, outcomes may be difficult to predict. Maria, for example, assumes that Joseph would be upset and act impulsively if he discovered his mother has died, but his reaction may be quite different.

Second, the focus of the outcomes approach may not give sufficient attention to other significant ethical considerations. For instance, the outcomes approach conceivably could be used to justify lying to maximize benefit or minimize harm. Maria, for example, might decide to mislead Joseph about his mother even if he asks to minimize the possibility of emotional distress.

Third, the outcomes approach might cause the child welfare professional to overlook relational duties. When there is a personal or professional relationship, certain obligations arise to the other party that do not exist as to others. A child welfare professional, for example, has special obligations to her client that she does not have to non-clients. Acting in accordance with these responsibilities may or may not maximize benefit in a given situation, but, nevertheless, will be ethically required. In the case study, for example, Joseph's foster parents might urge Maria not to inform him of his mother's death. Maria might reason, on the basis of their wishes, that withholding the information would maximize benefit for Joseph and his foster parents (or minimize harm to them). Nonetheless, because Maria's primary responsibility is to Joseph, she must base her decision on her duties to Joseph and not upon the desires of his foster parents.

Fourth, the outcomes approach has historically been criticized for promoting the benefit of the majority while marginalizing the minority. In situations in which one cannot maximize benefit for everyone, an outcomes approach may recommend maximizing benefit for as many people as possible. As a consequence, individuals who are not among the majority will not enjoy the benefit. Questions about fairness or justice are raised when decisions yield such outcomes.

Because of the limitations of both approaches, it is best to integrate both into the ethical reasoning and decisionmaking process. The approaches reflect two levels of ethical reasoning, with the first level appealing to ethical standards. In the many cases in which standards conflict or are too general to be helpful, it becomes important to consider the possible outcomes of different courses of action. In such situations, the course of action that promises the most favorable balance of benefit over harm (both short-term and long-term) is usually, though not always, the better alternative.

Step 6: Make a choice.

Once the ethical standards test and the outcomes test have been conducted, a choice must be made. In many instances, conflicts will occur between important values and it will not be possible to pursue an alternative that preserves all of the relevant values. Prioritizing alternatives involves prioritizing ethical standards and outcomes.

Prioritizing ethical standards and outcomes is the most difficult part of the decisionmaking process. The following are guidelines for this process:

1. Ethical standards and outcomes that prevent basic harms (such as death, serious physical injury, or lack of food or shelter) should be a first consideration in prioritizing ethical concerns (Reamer, 1990). As an example, the removal of children from their parents' custody is justified when there is a risk of physical harm to

them because the prevention of serious harm overrides the parents' right to keep their children in their home.

It sometimes happens that allowing a client to exercise her individual freedom (self-determination) could harm others. As an example, the value of confidentiality may be overridden when maintaining confidentiality would place at risk the life or physical well-being of others. If a parent reveals to a counselor that she abuses her children, the counselor must report this even though it was shared in confidence. The duty to report is even stronger because of the counselor's commitment to abide by ethical standards of his or her profession. In such cases, professionals forfeit the right to act in ways that may be permissible for others. Mental health and child welfare professionals, for example, are obligated to report any suspected instances of child abuse or neglect, whereas members of the general public are encouraged but are not ethically required to do so. Another example of professional conduct that would be ethically justifiable based on the prevention of basic harms is in the domestic violence arena. A professional might deny knowing the whereabouts of a woman fleeing domestic violence if he is confronted by her abuser. A lie may be ethically acceptable because it protects the life or physical well-being of another.

2. Although it is generally true that a risk of basic harm should take priority over all other ethical considerations, a risk of basic harm may be overridden by an individual's right to freedom (or self-determination) when the harm threatened is only to himself (Reamer, 1990). A 15-year-old, for example, may decide that he does not want to be adopted and may refuse an opportunity to meet a prospective adoptive family. Although others may feel that adoption is in his best interests, he has the right to self-determination (as discussed more fully in Chapter 3).

It is important to note that in some cases, a self-determined decision that brings harm to the individual herself may also harm those who depend on her. For example, a mother may decide to remain in an abusive situation and her children may suffer emotional harm when they witness the ongoing abuse.

How should Maria make her choice about telling Joseph? She needs to weigh the importance and practical consequences of the two ethical principles at stake here: honesty and minimizing harm. If there were little harm that could be predicted from telling Joseph, honesty would be the best course. Predicting harm to Joseph may be complicated, however. How prepared is Joseph to process this information? What would be the emotional impact on him both now and into the future from telling or not telling him? How important is it to his sense of personal identity to know about his birthmother? Could the adoption process be derailed if he were told? To determine these things, Maria should pay close attention to Joseph's behaviors and statements. She should consult with his foster parents and therapist, if any, and look back through his case file for clues to how he might react. She should check research in the field to see if there are relevant studies about the psychological reactions of abused children to the death of a birthparent, or on the necessity of emotional ties to the birthfamily as an element of personal identity. Finally, she should weigh all the benefits of telling that she has identified against the predicted negative consequences in Joseph's case and choose the weightier side of the scale. As should be apparent, the right option will be heavily dependent on the specific facts in Joseph's case.

Step 7: Check conclusions.

Once Maria has reached a tentative conclusion, she should discuss it with her supervisor before executing her decision. By nature, ethical dilemmas tend to be complex and require educated judgment calls. A caseworker should always think through the problem with a supervisor unless it is impossible because of time constraints. If her agency has an ethics committee, the professional could also ask the committee's advice.

The professional might also consider what others would say; how she herself would react if she were among those negatively affected by the decision; or how other colleagues would respond. If these reactions would be negative, it is important to isolate the reasons. Is there something that has been missed or ignored in the analysis? These methods of checking conclusions, however, are not as important as the professional's reasoning through the ethical standards or outcomes test. Although the reactions of others can assist in identifying errors in reasoning, it is also important to recognize that colleagues will not always support a professional's decision. At the same time, the ethical decisionmaking process should not be used in isolation, but in conjunction with colleagues, particularly supervisors.

Because Joseph's mother has already passed away, Maria can take some time to make her decision and check her conclusions. She can consult with her supervisor, ethics committee, and other professionals about her ethical reasoning process. If the situation were more of an emergency (for example, if Joseph's mother were dying and requested to see him), Maria might only have time to consult with her supervisor. Since there are rarely answers in ethics that do not involve unavoidable harms, the more consultation Maria seeks, the more comfortable she should feel that her solution maximizes benefits and minimizes harms to Joseph.

Step 8: Avoid similar dilemmas in the future.

After the professional has made and checked her decision, the next step is to ask if this situation could have been avoided, and if so, how. Future dilemmas can sometimes be avoided through a careful assessment of the level of support received from supervisors and colleagues in the decisionmaking process. Thought should be given regarding others who should be consulted if a similar dilemma arises in the future. Finally, consideration should be given to whether the ethical problem was caused by organizational factors. Would a rule or policy change have prevented the problem? If so, what can be done to change organizational factors that contributed to the situation?

Could Maria's dilemma have been avoided or minimized? Are there contributing factors that could be addressed so that similar problems do not occur in the future? Some ethical dilemmas are inevitable, and this may be one of them. If, for example, Maria knew in advance that Joseph's mother was terminally ill, she might have had more time to think through the problem or broaden her options. Perhaps giving Joseph a chance to say goodbye to his mother or asking her to leave some memento which could be given to Joseph would produce a better outcome for the child. In general, the death of a birthparent of a child in foster care is not an unusual occurrence; Maria's agency might consider providing caseworkers with an outline of the right questions to ask and options to consider in such a situation.

SUMMARY

Child welfare professionals should be familiar with and turn to the existing codes of ethics when making decisions that have ethical consequences. As an example, the Illinois *Code of Ethics for Child Welfare Professionals* articulates the values of the profession and principles necessary for working within fiduciary relationships. Codes of ethics, however, do not offer pat solutions for every ethical dilemma that can occur in child welfare, and professionals may have to make difficult choices that require sacrificing one ethical value to maintain another. Child welfare professionals should consider ethical decisionmaking a necessary skill they can always improve. Ethical decisionmaking should not be done in isolation but in collaboration with supervisors, administrators, and ethics boards. The eight steps of the decisionmaking model outlined in Table 1-1 can assist with most ethical dilemmas.

CASE STUDIES FOR CHAPTER 1

Case Study 1-1. Lindy, a child welfare caseworker, makes quick decisions about his clients based on his first impression of them. Most of his clients, according to Lindy, are "immoral" because they have had children out of wedlock, are living "in sin," or are addicted to drugs. He feels that because of their "corrupting" influence on children, these parents do not deserve to have their children returned to them. What effect will Lindy's attitudes likely have on his casework?

Case Study 1-2. Tasha, a client whose children are currently in foster care, loves her children. On several occasions, she has been come very close to having them returned home. On each of the three occasions when her children were about to be returned home, however, she has done something to "sabotage" their return. Her caseworker has begun to wonder if Tasha wants her children returned to her. Is there a third option that her caseworker can offer other than returning her children to her or terminating parental rights?

Case Study 1-3. For the first time, Jennifer is working with a client, Sue, who is said to have a mental illness. Jennifer intuitively thinks that there may be special considerations that apply to her work with Sue. What issues should she anticipate? What resources should she use? Should she consult with others?

Case Study 1-4. Jared, a foster care caseworker, cannot decide if he should recommend a change in the permanency goal for Shari (a 13-year old) from adoption to independence. What are the likely benefits and harms he must consider?

Case Study 1-5. Delera likes her client Patty very much. Because Patty knows that Delera drives past her home when she leaves work, Patty asks Delera for a ride. Delera's first reaction is to take Patty home because she knows that this help will make it easier for Patty to get to her night job on time. Delera then remembers that her coworkers never drive their clients home. What should Delera do?

Case Study 1-6. Clark decides not to recommend to the court that Debbie's children return home because Debbie did not attend mandated parenting classes. The court, however, continues the case after determining that Debbie could not have attended parenting classes because she did not have transportation and could not arrange child care for the two children at home with her. What should Clark be thinking about for future cases?

References

Davis, M. (1997). Developing and using cases to teach practical ethics. *Teaching Philosophy, 20,* 374–375.

Gambrill, E., & Gibbs, L. (2002). Making practical decisions: Is what's good for the goose good for the gander? *Research on Social Work Practice, 4*(1), 31–46.

Ozar, D., & Sokol, D. (1994). *Dental ethics at Chairside: Professional principles and practical applications.* St. Louis: Mosby-Year Book, Inc.

Reamer, F. G. (1990). *Ethical dilemmas in social service* (2nd ed.). New York: Columbia University Press.

Sactrett, D. L., Richardson, W. S., Rosenberg, W., & Haynes, R. B. (1997). *Evidence-based medicine: How to practice and teach EBM.* New York: Churchill-Livingston.

[40]

The Impact of the UK Human Rights Act 1998 on Decision Making in Adult Social Care in England and Wales

Ann McDonald

This paper explores the impact of the Human Rights Act 1998 on decision making in adult social care in England and Wales. It focuses on a review of the Act by the government in June 2006 and subsequent new guidance on implementation addressed to policy makers, managers and practitioners. The meaning of "rights" in contemporary legal and social theory is considered and the potential of human rights law to improve the experiences of service users is evaluated in the light of recent research findings and proposed policy changes.

Keywords   Human Rights; Adult Social Care; Decision Making

This paper explores the extent to which systems for organizing and delivering social care services are able to support human rights in a modern context. The impact of the UK Human Rights Act 1998 has recently been under review by the government, and new guidance (Department for Constitutional Affairs (DCA) 2006a, b, c) has been produced for managers and decision makers in all public services. Human rights have also been researched from a practice and service-user perspective: Ellis (2004) has described the "poor fit" between human rights and the policy and operational context of social care; Zarb (2006) has gone further, and has argued that the very system by which support is currently organized and delivered can actually put people's human rights at risk. Human rights are a contested area for legal theorists in respect both of the source of their authority and the extent to which rights can be said to exist independently of their application. The context of neo-liberal (Clarke & Newman 1997) and managerialist agendas (Hugman 1991; Harris 2003) affects both agency practice and practitioner attitudes to human rights. The focus throughout is on the rights guaranteed by the European Convention on Human Rights as incorporated into domestic law by the Human Rights Act 1998, and their interpretation by decision

Ann McDonald is a Senior Lecturer in Social Work in the School of Social Work and Psychosocial Sciences at the University of East Anglia, UK. Correspondence to: Ann McDonald, School of Social Work and Psychosocial Sciences, University of East Anglia, Norwich, NR4 7TJ, UK; E-mail: ann.mcdonald@uea.ac.uk makers and by the courts in one specific social care context, namely the provision of community care services for adults. Though the Human Rights Act 1998 is a piece of UK legislation, the systems for delivering social care services that are referred to in this article are those of England and Wales.

Rights in Legal Theory

An examination of human rights law requires a consideration of conflicting theories about the nature of legal rights, which raise questions either explicitly or implicitly about the extent to which rights are the product of their social or decision-making context. Major divisions within legal philosophy exist historically, and in contemporary discourses, between adherents to natural law theories, to positivist theories and to realist and critical theories of law (McLeod 2003). Natural law theories of human rights locate their source and their authority either in religion or in a humanistic discourse of the inalienable rights of human beings; human rights thus exist prior to and independently of government, and are subject merely to interpretation by officials acting in a judicial capacity (Fuller 1969). Consequently, international conventions and national laws may ultimately be seen as invalid in so far as they breach or misinterpret natural law rights (Finnis 1980). The difficulties in quantifying the content of such natural laws led Jeremy Bentham, originally writing in 1780, to describe the theory of natural law as "nonsense on stilts"; he and other legal positivists saw the authority of law as deriving from the utilitarian collective good to which individual interests might necessarily be subordinated (Bentham 1982).

The focus on the positivist hierarchical creation of law was most clearly expressed by H. L. A. Hart (Hart 1994) as the "command" theory of law; law as a union of primary and secondary rules where primary rules of conduct laid down by a legislature or deriving from common law were reinforced by sanctions for their breach. The normative qualities of rules in guiding action by individual legal subjects was taken to operate within a clear separation of powers, whereby the judiciary were neutral interpreters of the will of the legislature as put into effect through executive decision making (Summers 1971). However, challenges to the assumed predictability of laws within such a system had already been made by commentators who saw that the requirements of the law were directed not so much at individuals as at the officials who operated the legal system (Llewellyn 1960). The actions of administrators and of judges were thus constitutive of rights rather than simply responses to claims. This "realist" view of law accepted that the context within which decisions were made and the opinions of the decision maker would influence the outcome of particular cases. Analysis of such decisions would lay bare the power issues inherent within the decision-making process. This focus on law as a rationalization of an unequal struggle for power between different interest groups, including the state, was subsequently extended by critical theorists (Hutchinson & Monahan 1984) to explore the way in which law could perpetuate injustice and inequalities in society (McLeod 2003).

Two issues thus emerge: disputes about the extent to which the concept of human rights can exist outside of a legislative framework; and the extent to which rights are created rather than interpreted by decision makers within a legal system (MacCormick 1974).

For Dworkin (1977), talk of rights in general, and rights against the state in particular, was an indication that a society was divided and appeals to a common goal were not being heeded. Rights, then, were to be seen as "at least a basis for demanding a compromise" (Dworkin 1977, p. 267). But Dworkin also raises a critical dichotomy within the rights discourse about the idea of equality. In a contemporary context, this dichotomy is particularly relevant to the difference between an approach to rights based on political notions of non-discrimination, most often expressed within equal opportunities legislation, and demands for social and economic rights to a fair distribution of resources by socially marginalized groups. Dworkin (1977, p. 184) expresses this as the difference between a right to treatment as an equal, a right to be treated with the same respect as anyone else, and a right to equal treatment, a right to an equal distribution of an opportunity or resource. The question then becomes whether a rights agenda will merely ameliorate the worst examples of unequal treatment in a procedural sense by decision makers working to a largely unaltered legislative mandate, or whether a focus on human rights can act as a catalyst for social change at an institutional level, within which social workers and other decision makers as well as lawyers have a vital advocacy and constitutive role.

The European Convention on Human Rights

Ife (2001) distinguishes between "first-", "second-" and "third"-generation rights, within international documents describing human rights. First-generation rights are civil and political rights seen in democratic societies; second-generation rights are economic, social and cultural rights; and third-generation rights are collective rather than individual rights which look to the securing of environmental protection and peaceful co-existence. The emphasis within the European Convention on first-generation civil and political rights reflects its historical roots within post-war Europe as an intended bulwark against future totalitarian regimes (Wadham & Mountfield 2006). The scope, value content and legal form taken by the European Convention on Human Rights thus reflects existing power relationships in the countries that it represents, as do other international conventions on human rights (Woodiwiss 2005). The European Convention on Human Rights is a modest document in many ways: its focus is on civil and political rights within existing hierarchical systems rather than economic and social rights; and it has nothing at all to say about collective rights to the enjoyment of natural resources or community-generated goods. Its universalism is also limited; states are allowed a "margin of appreciation" in the interpretation of the Convention in acknowledgement of different political and cultural traditions within Europe. The doctrine of proportionality in assessing interference with Convention rights which operates on the national plane also places a heavy reliance on the integrity of formal decision makers in arbitrating between different interest groups. In terms of the potency of the rights that the Convention guarantees, only a minority of rights are absolute; others are limited or qualified rights giving further restrictions upon their application. Article 5, for example, on freedom from detention contains within it exceptions relating to police powers and powers of compulsory detention relating to mental disorder. Article 8, on respect for private and family life, is qualified in so far as any interference must be prescribed by law, pursue a legitimate aim and be limited to the extent necessary in a democratic society. Article 14 also, far from being a total prohibition on discrimination, merely outlaws discrimination in the exercise of any other substantive Convention right.

So, in terms of the historical antecedents of our current rights agenda, Singh (1997) sees the European Convention on Human Rights simply as embodying a regional political consensus within a given historic period on key civil and political issues, without any necessary reference to a "higher" source of validity derived from natural law. The preponderance of qualified rights in the Convention itself points to a utilitarian concept of rights. Gearty (2004) similarly rejects any analysis of the Human Rights Act 1998 in terms of its compatibility with the rights of human beings in any natural law sense, locating its philosophical and political importance within discourses about the "rights of the citizen", and, more fundamentally, within the traditional English common law principles of respect for civil liberties, the principle of legality, and respect for human dignity.

The Human Rights Act 1998

The intended purpose of the Human Rights Act 1998 was to "Bring Rights Home" (Steyn 2000, p. 549) to enable individuals in the United Kingdom to bring human rights-based claims in local venues and national courts, instead of having exclusively to bring actions against the state before the European Court of Human Rights in Strasbourg (DCA 2006a). There was also a desire to embed respect for human rights into the fabric of public services and decision making and in this way to influence the relationship between the individual and the state. Introducing new remedies for breaches of human rights was designed to hold authorities to account for their actions and to enable appropriate compensation to be given to individuals (Wadham & Mountfield 2006). The Human Rights Act 1998 contains a number of important restrictions, however: the Act in its direct or "vertical" effect applies only to public authorities and not to private bodies; individuals seeking to challenge breaches of rights must have "victim" status; and the power of the courts to deal with breach of rights in primary legislation is limited to the making of declarations of incompatibility, rather than a power to strike down Acts of the legislature.

So, the function of the Human Rights Act 1998 is to set down minimum standards of legally acceptable behaviour by the state, but in a context fashioned by contemporary notions of the limits of state responsibility for individual citizens' well-being. Context will thus be of critical importance (McLeod 2003) and will involve considerations of the nature of modern-day citizenship, of the proper role of the state and of the operation of issues of responsibility, risk and control. It is not surprising, then, that it was these issues which prompted a review of the Human Rights Act itself very recently in the United Kingdom.

The review of the Human Rights Act in June 2006 was undertaken in response to criticisms within the government and in the popular press that the existence of the Act was a barrier to protecting citizens against harm. Two particular legal decisions had led to this concern: the decision that hijackers of an international passenger plane could not be returned to their country of origin where they were at risk of torture; and the discharge from detention by the parole board of a convicted sex offender who went on to re-offend (DCA 2006b). In terms of the separation of powers, the review could be seen as a response by the executive to the authority of the judicial arm of the state. At the end of this process, the Human Rights Act 1998 emerged with a clean bill of health, but also with an agenda to "relaunch" the Act targeted at both managers and practitioners in public authorities, including those in the health and social care fields.

The Department for Constitutional Affairs has subsequently produced three new documents: *Making Sense of Human Rights* (DCA 2006a), for frontline staff and junior managers; *Human Rights: Human Lives* (DCA 2006b), for junior and middle managers and a third new edition of its *Guide to the Human Rights Act 1998* (DCA 2006c), for middle managers and local strategists. The questions are: into what sort of health and social care world is the Human Rights Act 1998 being relaunched for re-interpretation, and to what extent will the context of its operation support or limit the enjoyment of human rights, however conceptualized, by users of those services?

The Social Policy Context in the United Kingdom

The social policy context within health and social care is broadly again a utilitarian view of service provision focusing on quantifiable outcomes for individuals receiving support to remain in the community. For adult social care, this is reflected in rationing devices that strive for geographical equity by setting national frameworks but that crystallize eligibility in terms of the location of individuals within a risk/need matrix. Unsurprisingly, given the social and professional focus on risk analysis and risk management, protecting the public (the trigger for the Human Rights Act 1998 review in 2006) has a high premium attached to it under such a system. Though championed by the independent living movement, and expressed in official statements of intent such as the White Paper on *Health and Social Care* (Department of Health 2006), Kantian notions of individual choice, control, freedom and independence are likely to be respected only if they also meet utilitarian requirements of keeping populations safe or economically active. The notion of "rights" that such policies support is likely, therefore, to be focused on equal opportunities to compete for scarce resources, rather than absolute entitlements to subjectively defined levels of service or income. Hence, the link between pursuing employability and maintenance on welfare benefits, only for long enough to enable return to work (or a basic survival level in the case of those who are past retirement age) to be achieved. The expectation that individual effort will be forthcoming, and that it is the way (the only way?) to achieve rewards reflects a neo-liberal view of the world that emphasizes individual responsibility for finding work, for supporting a family, and for saving for old age.

In terms of "citizenship", which for lawyers such as Gearty (2004) links the state and individual rights, it appears that some citizens are less able than others to influence government action and to acquire or retain social capital. Charting the development of theories of citizenship since the introduction of the welfare state, Lister (2004) has described the way in which those who are marginalized by society (the old, the sick) are excluded from full participation and hence the inability to influence policy in the political sphere. Further disadvantage will be apparent on the basis of ethnicity, race, class and gender (Lister 2003). Contemporary notions of social citizenship are thus based not on an equitable distribution of society's goods but on strict eligibility criteria applying to rationed and means-tested services. When applied to a rights agenda, this interpretation of citizenship aligns with a differentiated neo-liberal view of rights (C. McDonald 2006), where "rights" are seen as interpretation by powerful groups of concessions that they will make, rather than legitimate claims to minimum standards of treatment by individuals and groups as part of their social contract with the state. In this context, appeal to European standards of anti-discriminatory practice will not transcend national interests So, in Dworkin's terms, there may be a right to be treated equally as a competitor for scarce resources rather than a right to equal treatment as an older person or a person with needs for support. This correlation between contemporary notions of citizenship and critiques of rights makes it unlikely that the introduction of the Human Rights Act will significantly on its own affect the experiences of socially disadvantaged groups.

The Legislative Context of Community Care

There is a significant dynamic at work between the introduction of the Human Rights Act in 1998 and the modernizing agenda of health and social care throughout the United Kingdom, with which it is contemporaneous. Notions of consumerism (Schwer 2001) and the commodification of care (Harris 2003) which developed from the community care reforms of the early 1990s in the United

Kingdom (A. McDonald 2006) have led to the development of markets and partnerships within a mixed economy of service provision. As might be expected, "rights" in this context have developed with a strong emphasis on procedural propriety rather than substantive entitlement. And the notion of holding agencies to account for their actions has had to grapple with the independent status of a multiplicity of service providers. Some of the leading developments in human rights law have dealt with challenges to these agendas. Furthermore, the Human Rights Act 1998 when applied to a community care context has had to respond to an existing legislative framework in England and Wales which emphasizes the (limited) duty upon statutory bodies, such as local authorities and healthcare bodies to provide services, rather than the claims of service users to independence, choice, rights and dignity (Woolhead *et al.* 2004). Even from a positivist viewpoint, the content of most welfare law is deficient (Clements 2004). Though the Human Rights Act 1998 provides an overarching structure for the interpretation of legal rules, primary legislation is unlikely to contain within it explicit guarantees of rights to care or to support. New primary legislation would have had the normative effect of embedding entitlements to minimum levels of service, instead of relying on secondary interpretation open to influence either by resource constraints or official perceptions of need, in order to assure respect for human rights. The fact that pre-existing primary legislation has not been changed, and cannot be changed by the simple operation of the Human Rights Act, is a considerable weakness within the legal regime for community care in England and Wales.

In the context of current community care law, the relationship between rights and duties is fundamental to an understanding of the law (Clements 2004; McDonald & Taylor 2006). Though there is a duty to assess the need for community care services (in Section 47 of the National Health Service and Community Care Act 1990), the statutes that govern service provision are a tangled web of duties and powers; some services are compulsory once a particular threshold of need is met (accommodation under the National Assistance Act 1948 is a good example here of a duty), but some services—e.g. laundry and meals on wheels—are a mere power. Using Hohfeld's (2001) analysis, it can be seen that rights and duties are relational in the sense that every claim to a right must provoke or be based on a correlative duty (in our case on the part of a public authority) to respect that right either by their action or (if it involves a freedom from compulsory intervention) by their inaction. When there is a positive duty to provide services, a right to receive such services is well established, albeit at a level of need set to match resource constraints; when there is merely a power to provide services, the recipient of those services is entirely dependent upon the judgement and resources of the decision maker—a largely utilitarian response. Superimposing the idea of human rights upon this legal framework raises interesting issues of the extent to which Human Rights Act arguments can and will affect both the assessment process and the amount or quality of resources that are provided.

Critical issues arise in a range of social care contexts. For example, a human rights perspective on disability not only highlights the importance of independent living as a means of ensuring that disabled people can exercise their rights but may also be used to assess social care practice generally, in relation to the promotion of respect, equality, personal autonomy, social inclusion and participation (Parker 2004). In relation to mental health services, human rights issues arise concerning restrictions on freedom of movement, confidentiality, consent to treatment, privacy, security and gender dignity (Mental Health Act Commission 2006). Public services also play an important role in acknowledging carers' human rights in respect of their health and safety and their right to family life, often involving a crucial balancing of choices between the carer's own health and that of the person they support (Carers UK 2006). Such "balancing" of rights goes to the heart of the European Convention's emphasis on proportionality and the duty of the state to put in place a legal framework to balance different or competing rights against each other and against the interests of the wider community (Carers UK 2006). Thus the campaigns by the disability movement for citizenship rights, the identification of mental health service user needs and the examples provided by the carers' movement provide an important framework for the examination of Human Rights Act arguments generally in a social care context.

Making Decisions

The operationalization of legal rules at first-level managerial and practitioner level is also subject to a changing organizational context. The context here is managerialism (Clarke & Newman 1997) which seeks to routinize decision making by focusing on the transactional rather than the human impact of decision making. This administrative aspect of decision making is critical to some of the fundamental theories about how law operates in society. So Lipsky, in his (1980) study of street-level bureaucrats, mirrored the views of the American realist movement in considering that the requirements of the law were not directed at individuals but at the officials who operate the system of allocating resources and dealing with disputes; it is they who decide, for example, whether a person has suffered significant harm so as to be in need of protection, or whether standards in residential care are adequate. As enforcers of the law they are to all intents and purposes creators of legal rights and responsibilities for the individuals whose cases they adjudicate. To a large extent the Department for Constitutional Affairs' guidance recognizes this by the careful provision of decision-making guides for frontline managers and workers, inviting them to identify the situations in which they will need to balance interference with the Convention rights against the public interest. The inference is that frontline workers are made aware of these guides, either through keeping up to date by being given management guidance or training or by further individual study of professional issues.

This emphasis on frontline decision makers' creativity constitutes them as a source for good, if they make appropriate decisions; as a source of repression if they are seen to be unduly restrictive in their interpretation of situations; and as the locus of blame when things go wrong. Yet the current employment context for social workers is seen as inhibiting both creativity and reflexive practice. Fook (2000), for example, describes how current managerialist approaches to welfare both inhibit individual practitioners from using their discretion in positive ways and also push responsibility down the organization when policies are ineffective or inefficient at the operational level.

Application of the Human Rights Act

Though litigation may be a rare event in the life of an agency, the bodies ultimately responsible for the interpretation and implementation of the Human Rights Act are the courts. In common law jurisdictions, such as the United Kingdom, the law develops piecemeal as test cases are brought and judgments given that create precedent. In a sense, judges are also officials within the legal system subject to similar policy and administrative pressures to those felt by legal personnel at lower levels. The difference is that they are at the apex of this system; they may even be the system. As Oliver Wendell Holmes, Justice of the American Supreme Court, famously argued: "The prophecies of what the courts will do in fact and nothing more pretentious are what I mean by the law" (Holmes 1881, p. 173). In looking at the interpretation of human rights, the willingness of the judiciary to scrutinize policy and practice decisions is important for confidence in the robustness of its check on the legislature and executive. Particular decisions are also illustrative of the current orientation of the courts towards issues of resource allocation, choice, dignity and protection. Have the courts on the whole supported individuals against the state? In the words of Dworkin (1977), have rights been used as "trumps" against contentious policies or have the courts tended to endorse official interpretations of the limits of state responsibility?

The evidence is mixed, with the courts more likely to see the Human Rights Act as being relevant to their decision when traditional issues of civil liberties rather than requests for resources are under consideration. Hence the issues that triggered the 2006 review were those that posed challenges to immigration and penal practice, not those in which eligibility for state-funded health and social care had been an issue.

With respect to the latter, generally the courts have followed a traditional stance in not intervening when difficult decisions of resource provision have to be made. In line with general principles of administrative law, the courts have scrutinized such decisions for procedural correctness rather than substantive support for Convention rights.

R (Dudley and Whitbread and Others) v. *East Sussex County Council* [2003] EWHC 1093 (Admin) is an example; this was an application for judicial review of the decision of East Sussex County Council to close a long-term residential home for older people in order to use the site for intermediate care which would attract grant funding. Kay J. concluded that any breach of the (qualified) Article 8, respect for home and family life, was justified by the high demand for care in the context of restricted budgets and cheaper provision in the private sector. The consultation process had been fair, and individual care assessments had shown that basic needs could still be met. In utilitarian terms, then, individual interests were to be subordinated to economic interests within the public sphere, where value for money was the overriding concern.

The most significant limitation, however, on the use of the Human Rights Act 1998 to challenge care home closures is the decision in the Court of Appeal in *R (Heather, Ward and Callin)* v. *The Leonard Cheshire Foundation and the Attorney General* [2002] All ER 936. Here the Leonard Cheshire Foundation, a voluntary-sector body, wished to close a residential unit and distribute its resources elsewhere. The court decided that the provision of residential care by an independent-sector provider of this sort was not a "public function" within the meaning of Section 6(3) of the Human Rights Act 1998 and therefore not subject to the Act. The decision stands as a judicial endorsement of neo-liberal approaches to welfare and a major obstacle to equality of standards throughout a mixed economy of care. It places reliance upon the commissioning body's ability to enforce contract specifications in order to protect vulnerable service users. This might be acceptable if "best value" regimes did not have to focus on balancing consumer satisfaction against economic and political imperatives (Humphrey 2003), but because the majority of residential care is now provided by the independent sector, the judgment has the effect of leaving service users without a direct remedy for poor care provision; in effect, without rights in the Hohfeldian sense of having duties owed directly to them.

The Scope of the Act

The *Guide to the Human Rights Act 1998* (DCA 2006c) provides further examples of complex situations needing interpretation in the light of the Convention; so it is said that Article 2 may impose on hospitals and medical staff a duty to take positive steps to promote life, and a duty upon the state to safeguard the public from dangers presented by the state itself or by other individuals. This extends to the care of prisoners, those compulsorily detained under the Mental Health Act, and victims of domestic violence. Article 3 requires the state properly to investigate and to respond to allegations of abuse and to provide proper monitoring of vulnerable individuals. The extent to which the European Convention proactively supports the enjoyment of dignity and choice is less clear, since in English law there has been in primary legislation no uncontested standard of minimum entitlement to health and care services. Though Article 8 may be engaged when individuals in the community are at risk of losing their home or family, quantifying in positive terms the obligation upon the state to support family life raises fundamental questions as to the proper role of the state and the extent to which the European Convention has changed the boundaries of this role. The cases here are worthy of discussion in terms of the potential for organizational deficiencies and administrative rule making to subvert individual rights; but in these cases the courts have been more willing to apply a "realist" view and to find breaches of rights where a duty to provide care has been acknowledged but not fulfilled because of delay or incompetence.

Bernard v. *Enfield Borough Council* [2002] HLR 46 was the first case in which there was a successful application for damages under the Human Rights Act 1998 in a community care context. Mrs Bernard, a disabled mother of six children, was given accommodation by the local authority in which she was unable to use her electric wheelchair, to attend to her personal care needs, or properly participate with her husband in family life. An assessment under Section 47 of the National Health Service and Community Care Act 1990 found a need for a suitably adapted property, but there was a delay of 20 months in making one available. Though no breach of Article 3 was found, it was held that Article 8 established a positive obligation upon the local authority which it had breached not only in respect of Mrs Bernard but also in respect of her husband. Judicial criticism of the failure of the local authority to co-ordinate and respond to professional assessments under both the community care legislation and the Housing Acts is a positive encouragement for agencies to co-operate in finding solutions, rather than to retreat behind their own administrative boundaries.

When the issue under scrutiny is the provision of residential care or compulsory detention, the compromises inherent in balancing rights against risks, as in, for example, the locking of doors and the delivery of medication, are inherently vulnerable to challenges based on individual notions of privacy and personal liberty. In residential settings, inadequate stimulation, social isolation and poor healthcare have more commonly been conceptualized as a quality issue, rather than a rights issue (National Care Standards Commission 2004). But there is evidence that rights-based arguments may be used successfully to challenge clear deficiencies in administrative decision making. Respect for individual dignity is central to Article 3, and even temporary interference with that right may constitute a breach. The European Court of Human Rights recognized this in *Price* v. *UK* (*The Times*, 13 August 2001), where the detention overnight in a police cell of a disabled woman was held to breach Article 3, not because of the detention per se, which was justified, but because no proper arrangements were made for her to attend to her personal care, or to sleep other than in a wheelchair. So, the Department for Constitutional Affairs, in its *Guide to the Human Rights Act 1998* (DCA 2006c, para. 3.22), sees breaches of Article 3, in particular, as being dependent upon:

- The nature, seriousness and duration of the treatment;
- How it affects the person mentally and physically;
- How old the person is;

- Whether they are male or female; and
- Their state of health.

It is also acknowledged that severe discrimination based on race might constitute degrading treatment "and this might extend to other forms of acute discrimination" (DCA 2006c, para. 3.25). So, breaches of Article 3, whether or not intentional, may be premised upon institutional practices experienced by vulnerable individuals as degrading or inhumane.

Public authorities may formalize their practice in order to anticipate litigation claims, thus placing a premium upon adherence to policy and process over individual discretion. Paradoxically, such administrative rule making may in itself lead to Human Rights Act 1998 challenges. Though the Human Rights Act enables compromises to be reached between individual and collective interests through the devices of "proportionality" and "justification", the act of balancing must be specific to the issues raised by every particular case. In administrative law terms, the agency must not fetter its discretion by routinizing decision making into blanket policies. So in *R (A and B) v. East Sussex County Council (no. 1)* [2003] EWHC 167, the Court of Appeal was critical of the local authority for applying a blanket "no handling" policy without taking into account the particular needs and wishes of two disabled young women and their families. Clearly, in assessments of this sort, attention to subjective issues of dignity and psychological needs should be balanced against physical needs, and will involve a negotiation between the service-users' wishes and the safety of care providers and informal carers. The case amply illustrates the complexities inherent in applying human rights issues to decision making but also the potential for using legal remedies to challenge the routinization of care.

Organizational Responses

So, what is good administrative practice? A key question is the extent to which public authorities are able and willing in the current political climate to develop a human rights agenda proactively. Official guidance assumes a positive stance. The Department for Constitutional Affairs (2006c) *Guide to the Human Rights Act 1998* aims for a shared understanding of human rights issues; more confidence in key state bodies; encouragement of more openness and participation; and greater unity and fairness achieved through shared basic values in policy making and individual decision making. (To some extent this assumes that individuals are aware or made aware of their human rights in order to participate; see below.) The positive use of human rights in the development of policy and decision-making processes seeks to counteract a view of human rights as the province chiefly of lawyers and as a basis for litigation. Key words used are "protection", "respect" and "dignity" when speaking directly to those responsible for delivering public services, since:

> All public authorities in the U.K. have an obligation to respect the Convention rights. That means that you must understand those rights and take them into account in your day-to-day work. That is the case whether you are delivering a service directly to the public or devising new policies or procedures. (DCA 2006a, p. 14)

If awareness of human rights issues is to act as a catalyst for cultural change within organizations, a values-based approach needs to be underpinned by an analytical framework for decision making to facilitate both a top-down and a bottom-up approach. The recent guidance to practitioners from the Department for Constitutional Affairs (DCA 2006b, p. 51) focuses on this analytical approach by providing a decision-tree to establish which rights under the European Convention may be engaged; whether those rights are absolute, limited or conditional; and whether interference with those rights is in accordance with the law, necessary in a democratic society, and proportionate. The positive benefit of such an approach is that complex issues are identified, facts are scrupulously described and interference with rights is properly evaluated so that any action is justified and documented. In this way, the treatment of vulnerable individuals and/or groups is placed under the spotlight, multiple sources of discrimination can be aggregated, and disproportionate interventions can be challenged. Conflicts between public authorities and individuals and groups can be made manifest. A human rights approach is thus made more searching than a consumerist approach that surveys only satisfaction with the quality of service that is actually provided rather than the choices that were discarded in selecting those services. But unless organizations (as represented by their policies and their employees at all levels) engage proactively with potential service users to define the meaning of support for life, non-degrading treatment, respect for family life and for religion, it will continue to be the voices of administrators and of lawyers that are heard. Returning to the citizenship debate, involving citizens in policy formation is a prerequisite for embedding acceptable interpretations of human rights within organizations.

Changing Cultures

Thus far in this argument, the potential for systems and individuals to change in response to human rights arguments has been welcomed, albeit with concerns about the robustness of such changes in the context of weak primary legislation and the rationing of resources along consumerist lines. However, fundamental difficulties remain, and have been highlighted in recent research into the impact of the Human Rights Act. The British Institute of Human Rights (Watson 2002), in a survey of the impact of the Act on vulnerable groups, including older people and people with disabilities, found that service users and clients had very little understanding of the idea that they had rights at all, let alone rights that were protected by the Human Rights Act; some suggested that the awareness shown by service providers was not much better. Evidence to the Health Select Committee inquiry into Elder Abuse from the National Care Standards Commission (NCSC 2004) found that the majority of complaints alleging poor practice or neglect could in effect be seen as constituting abuse or maltreatment under Article 3, although only 1 in 10 complainants made a specific allegation of this. Age Concern (2002) in its *Human Rights Act Position Paper* also emphasizes the importance of positive obligations upon public organizations to protect rights as well as to be responsive to maltreatment and lack of care. A recent survey by Carers UK, mapping existing research and carers' experiences against the Human Rights Act, similarly concluded that owing to inadequate consideration of carers' needs, and inadequate resources, "the Human Rights Act has not yet been of value to carers and their lives" (Carers UK 2006, p. 14).

Ultimately, the success of the Human Rights Act 1998 will depend upon the extent to which it has changed the culture of decision making to one based on respect for rights (Age Concern 2002). This has far-reaching implications not only for the quality but also for the design of services. The evidence prior to 2006 of public authorities' willingness to engage with a human rights agenda does not support optimism. Of 175 public bodies surveyed by the Audit Commission in 2003, only one council had made general information on the Human Rights Act 1998 available to the public. Though it might be expected that agencies were fearful of complaints, more worryingly:

> most failed to see the benefits of using human rights as a vehicle for service improvement by making the principles of dignity and respect central to their policy agenda, which would place service users at the heart of what they do. (Audit Commission 2003, para. 20)

Arguably, a failure properly to place service users at the heart of planning on human rights issues is attributable to pre-existing trends in the organization of services along managerialist lines that will be difficult to retrieve. Changes in the way that services are conceptualized and delivered in themselves have had an insidious and destructive impact on the standing of disadvantaged individuals as citizens of liberal democracies (C. McDonald 2006). If human rights arguments are to be used not just to rescue small numbers of individuals who have suffered obvious maltreatment, respect for rights needs to be built into agency policy and the practice of individual decision makers in respect of all stages in the provision of community care services.

The Response of Individual Decision Makers

As Cranston (1985) makes clear, whether legal rights become accomplished social facts depends upon a number of factors: people being aware of their rights; officials recognizing that they are under a duty to give effect to those rights; and the existence of remedies for breach of those rights. What, then, is the evidence that practitioners generally are able and willing to take a rights-based stance? The recent Social Care Institute for Excellence review (Braye & Preston-Shoot

2005) on teaching and assessing social work law, concludes from consultations undertaken with service users that:

> there is a clear invitation from service users for practitioners to work alongside them to ensure that law is used positively to uphold people's rights. Rights and citizenship are key principles to be observed when applying the law. (Braye & Preston-Shoot 2005, p. xiv)

This assumes, of course, that there is concordance between social workers and service users in acknowledging issues of rights and citizenship. Other research shows that this may not be the case. Both Morris (1994) and Priestley (2000) found that there were differences of perception between social workers and organizations of disabled people, with social workers emphasizing official definitions of need and disabled people speaking the language of claim rights. Rummery (2002) also found that social workers appeared to have accepted rather than challenged structural and organizational limitations on a rights-based approach to assessment and service delivery, treating access to assessment as a privilege rather than a right, and limiting participation in problem definition. More recently, Ellis (2004) found that frontline social care staff did not have an understanding of the rights contained in the Human Rights Act 1998 and many viewed social rights as conditional and dependent upon the fulfilment of obligations by service users. The vacuum created by the absence of human rights knowledge is seen by Ellis as enabling defensive practice to take place and allowing managerial, utilitarian agendas of citizenship to inform practice. In such a climate, challenges to structural inequalities do not happen and oppressive practice is perpetuated. It is not possible for legal rights to flourish if their potential beneficiaries are seen as unworthy and excluded because, as is argued, no one who does not have freedoms socially is granted them legally (MacKinnon 1989).

Though the values and attitudes of the individual decision maker will be critical for the enforcement of legal duties, the potency of structural issues and the orientation of the organization will inform those attitudes. Merely teaching managers and/or decision makers about the law, which is the focus of the Department for Constitutional Affairs guidance, will not therefore be sufficient in itself. On the other hand, an approach to training that combines visible senior management commitment with focus groups of participants from different levels within the organization has proved effective in making a human rights framework a real and recognized part of regular activity across the organization (Mental Health Act Commission 2006). The focus thus shifts positively to securing rights rather than simply restraining breaches of the Act; and to developing proactively a rights agenda to make a real difference to organizational practice rather than relying on vulnerable individuals and groups to harness their resources to take legal action.

Future Changes

Making possible an active human rights agenda requires change at a structural, organizational and individual practitioner level (Gearty 2004). It will not be possible to meet the aspirations of the White Paper on *Health and Social Care* (Department of Health 2006) to show individuals respect and to give them choice without redesigning services and the legal framework within which they are delivered to reflect the expressed needs of service users and to guarantee delivery. This is probably achieved more securely with changes to primary legislation that are more clearly designed to incorporate a strong value base. Involving service users in the design of such legislation and in agency policy is crucial; as Woolhead *et al.* (2004) make clear, having a presence in the community that is protected requires a more proactive stance on human rights than simply protection from harm or the monitoring of minimum standards of living.

On the international plane, the first new human rights instrument of the twenty-first century has been the UN Convention on Protecting the Rights of Persons with Disabilities (2006). This new instrument focuses specifically on the citizenship of disabled people and, following a process of consultation with representatives of disabled people worldwide, contains provisions that are sensitive to the needs of different ethnic groups and of women. However, it is also acknowledged that the implementation of such a Convention will require a strategy that positively transforms expectations of disabled people at a societal level and that goes beyond a "negative compliance" based as it historically has been on the avoidance of discrimination rather than the promotion of inclusion and participation (Massie 2006).

The creation in 2007, in Great Britain, of a Commission for Equality and Human Rights may act as a catalyst by bringing together new combinations of issues. The Commission will be able to take a proactive stance in promoting and explaining human rights law as well as taking up cases on its own account. The Commission will incorporate the work of the existing Commissions for Racial Equality and Disability Rights and the Equal Opportunities Commission, and will thus be able to tackle discrimination on multiple levels. It may become less possible to see human rights as something in which only activists or lawyers are engaged, if human rights become part of the governance of social care. Then it will become everyone's responsibility to identify, to acknowledge and to respond to human rights. Crucially, the success of the Commission will depend upon the extent to which it is able to move on from the institutionalization of low expectations, low status and disadvantage (Massie 2006).

Conclusion

Major legal changes have been made possible at an international and national level in support of human rights. At an institutional level, the new Department

92   McDONALD

for Constitutional Affairs Guidance is designed to reinvigorate organizational awareness of human rights; but unless processes of assessment and service delivery are sensitized, in their operation, to human rights issues, a dichotomy will remain between "law in books" and "law in action". This sensitization needs to happen at practitioner level also, so that there is less discrepancy between the ideals of social work and what social workers do in practice (Ellis 2004). Again, this is dependent upon the context in which social work takes place; when societies prioritize risk aversion, when competition for scarce resources is institutionalized, and when the focus is shifting from the social rights of marginal people to their social responsibilities, it will remain difficult to promote a human rights agenda. Change at structural, organizational and individual level is thus needed effectively to fulfil the mission of bringing rights home.

References

Age Concern (2002) *Human Rights Act Policy Position Paper*, Age Concern, London.
Audit Commission (2003) *Human Rights: Improving Public Service Delivery*, Audit Commission, London.
Bentham, J. (1982) *An Introduction to the Principles of Morals and Legislation*, Methuen, London.
Braye, S. & Preston-Shoot, M. with Cull, L.-A., Johns, R. & Roche, J. (2005) *Teaching, Learning and Assessment of Law in Social Work Education*, Social Care Institute for Excellence, London.
Carers UK (2006) *Whose Rights are they Anyway? Carers and the Human Rights Act*, Carers UK, London.
Clarke, I. & Newman, J. (1997) *The Managerial State: Power, Politics and Ideology in the Remaking of Social Welfare*, Sage, London.
Clements, L. (2004) *Community Care and the Law*, 3rd edn, Legal Action Group, London.
Cranston, R. (1985) *Legal Foundations of the Welfare State*, Weidenfeld & Nicolson, London.
Department for Constitutional Affairs (DCA) (2006a) *Making Sense of Human Rights: A Short Introduction*, DCA, London.
——. (2006b) *Human Rights: Human Lives. A Handbook for Public Authorities*, DCA, London.
——. (2006c) *A Guide to the Human Rights Act 1998*, 3rd edn, DCA, London.
Department of Health (2006) *Our Health, Our Care, Our Say: A New Direction for Community Services*, Department of Health, London.
Dworkin, R. (1977) *Taking Rights Seriously*, Duckworth, London.
Ellis, K. (2004) "Promoting Rights or Avoiding Litigation? The Introduction of the Human Rights Act 1998 into Adult Social Care in England", *European Journal of Social Work*, Vol. 7, no. 3, pp. 321–40.
Finnis, J. (1980) *Natural Law and Natural Rights*, Clarendon Press, Oxford.
Fook, J. (2000) *Social Work: Critical Theory and Practice*, Sage, London.
Fuller, L. (1969) *The Morality of Law*, Yale University Press, New Haven.
Gearty, C. (2004) *Principles of Human Rights Adjudication*, Oxford University Press, Oxford.
Harris, J. (2003) *The Social Work Business*, Routledge, London.
Hart, H. L. A. (1994) *The Concept of Law*, 2nd edn, Oxford University Press, Oxford.

Hohfeld, W. (2001) *Fundamental Legal Conceptions as Applied in Judicial Reasoning*, Ashgate, London.

Holmes, O. W. (1881) *The Common Law*, Macmillan, London.

Hugman, R. (1991) *Power in Caring Professions*, Macmillan, Basingstoke.

Humphrey, J. (2003) "New Labour and the Regulatory Reform of Social Care", *Critical Social Policy*, Vol. 23, no. 1, pp. 5–24.

Hutchinson, A. & Monahan, P. (1984) "Law, Politics and Critical Legal Scholars: The Unfolding Drama of American Legal Thought", *Stanford Law Review*, Vol. 36, pp. 199–244.

Ife, J. (2001) *Human Rights and Social Work: Towards Rights-based Practice*, Cambridge University Press, Cambridge.

Lipsky, M. (1980) *Street-level Bureaucracy: Dilemmas of the Individual in Public Services*, Sage, New York.

Lister, R. (2003) *Citizenship: Feminist Perspectives*, 2nd edn, Palgrave, Basingstoke.

——. (2004) *Poverty*, Polity Press, Cambridge.

Llewellyn, K. (1960) *The Common Law Tradition: Deciding Appeals*, Little, Brown, Boston.

MacCormick, N. (1974) "Law as an Institutional Fact", *Law Quarterly Review*, Vol. 90, pp. 102–29.

MacKinnon, C. (1989) *Towards a Feminist Theory of the State*, Harvard University Press, Cambridge, MA.

Massie, B. (2006) "Finding the Wormhole: Achieving Equal Citizenship for Disabled People", 4th Annual Disability Lecture, St. John's College, Cambridge, 9 May, available at: http://www.disabilitydebate.org/news/press_releases/finding_the_wormhole_ach ievin.aspx (accessed 3 January 2007).

McDonald, A. (2006) *Understanding Community Care: A Guide for Social Workers*, 2nd edn, Palgrave, Basingstoke.

McDonald, A. & Taylor, M. (2006) *Older People and the Law*, Policy Press, Bristol.

McDonald, C. (2006) *Challenging Social Work: The Institutional Context of Practice*, Palgrave, Basingstoke.

McLeod, I. (2003) *Legal Theory*, 2nd edn, Palgrave, Basingstoke.

Mental Health Act Commission (2006) *Making it Real: A Human Rights Case Study*, Mental Health Act Commission, London.

Morris, J. (1994) "Community Care or Independent Living?", *Critical Social Policy*, Vol. 40, pp. 25–45.

National Care Standards Commission (NCSC) (2004) *Evidence to the Health Select Committee Inquiry into Elder Abuse*, available at: < www.publications.uk/pa/cm200304/cmselect/cmhealth/111/1101.htm > (accessed 16 January 2007).

Parker, C. (2004) *Independent Living and the Human Rights Act 1998*, Disability Rights Commission, Social Care Institute for Excellence and National Centre for Independent Living, London.

Priestley, M. (2000) "Adults Only: Disability, Social Policy and the Life Course", *Journal of Social Policy*, Vol. 29, no. 3, pp. 421–39.

Rummery, K. (2002) *Disability, Citizenship and Community Care: A Case for Welfare Rights?*, Ashgate, Aldershot.

Schwer, B. (2001) "Human Rights and Social Services", in *The Law and Social Work: Contemporary Issues for Practice*, eds L. A. Cull & J. Roche, pp. 73–80, Palgrave, Basingstoke.

Singh, R. (1997) *The Future of Human Rights in the United Kingdom: Essays on Law and Practice*, Hart, Oxford.

Steyn, Lord (2000) "The New Legal Landscape", *European Human Rights Review*, Vol. 6, pp. 549–54.

Summers, R. (1971) "The Technique Element in Law", *California Law Review*, Vol. 591, pp. 733–68.

Wadham, J. & Mountfield, H. (2006) *Blackstone's Guide to the Human Rights Act 1998*, 4th edn, Oxford University Press, Oxford.

Watson, J. (2002) *Something for Everyone: The Impact of the Human Rights Act and the Need for a Human Rights Commission*, British Institute for Human Rights, London.

Woodiwiss, A. (2005) *Human Rights*, Routledge, Abingdon.

Woolhead, K., Calnan, M., Dieppe, P. & Tadd, W. (2004) "Dignity in Older Age: What do Older People in the United Kingdom Think?", *Age and Ageing*, Vol. 33, pp. 165–70.

Zarb, G. (2006) "From Paupers to Citizens: Independent Living and Human Rights", paper presented at the "Human Rights: Transferring Services?" Social Care Institute for Excellence and Disability Rights Commission conference, London, 27 March 2006, available at: http://www.scie.org.uk/news/event/humanrights06/index.asp (accessed 23 April 2006).

[41]

Towards Embracing Clinical Uncertainty

Lessons from Social Work, Optometry and Medicine

MARLEE M. SPAFFORD, CATHERINE F. SCHRYER,
SANDRA L. CAMPBELL AND LORELEI LINGARD
*University of Waterloo, Canada, University of Waterloo, Canada, University of Waterloo,
Canada and University of Toronto, Canada*

Abstract

- *Summary*: The oral transmission and transformation of client information in an apprenticeship setting provides a rich environment in which to observe students and their expert supervisors managing uncertainty. In this Canadian-based study, we examined the communicative features of 12 social work supervisions involving social work students and their supervisors and enriched our observations with subsequent interviews of the participants.
- *Findings*: Social work students viewed the acknowledgement and examination of uncertainty as a touchstone of competent social work. This observation contrasted with our past study of medical and optometry students who focused on personal deficit and a distrust of acknowledging uncertainty. Our observations and interviews revealed a *unique professional signature* to the *novice rhetoric of uncertainty* (seeking guidance, deflecting criticism, owning limits, showing competence) that suggests differing professional identities and contextual settings.
- *Applications*: An attitudinal shift toward accepting and trusting uncertainty in medicine and optometry may facilitate an enriched educational environment for students and a more open dialogue with patients about uncertainty. The *unique professional signatures* of this rhetoric offer insights into how professional identity shapes attitudes and behaviors toward uncertainty and suggest a source of tension within interdisciplinary healthcare teams.

Keywords case presentation   optometry and medicine   professional identity   social work   supervision   uncertainty

Journal of Social Work 7(2)

Study Excerpts from Three Novices

Social work student:

> I'd go to [my supervisor] if I wasn't sure and I would say, '[Supervisor's name], you gotta give me feedback because I'm not sure if I'm on the right track or I'm not on the right track.' (S6)

Optometry student:

> Sometimes [optometry students] are afraid to ask questions because they don't want to be looked at as being stupid. (S5)

Medical student:

> I think to point out things that you don't know is sort of shooting yourself in the back. (S5)

Introduction

The above excerpts were uttered by professional students we interviewed during our Canadian-based, multi-disciplinary study of novice case presentations. The social work student expresses a comfort with acknowledging uncertainty in the presence of an instructor. This novice comfort with uncertainty forms a clear departure from the attitudes expressed by medical and optometry students. In earlier phases of our study, optometry and medical students demonstrated a *novice rhetoric of uncertainty* during their case presentations that was focused on personal deficits in skill and knowledge and was something that these students preferred to hide, if possible (Lingard et al., 2003a; Spafford et al., 2006).

Increasingly, the role that uncertainty plays in health- and social care is being acknowledged and examined (Fox, 1957, 1980, 2000; Atkinson, 1984; Katz, 1984; Geller et al., 1990; Mishel, 1990; Brashers, 2001; Timmermans and Angell, 2001; Healy, 2003; Lingard et al., 2003a; De Graves and Aranda, 2005). As field knowledge boundaries and provider/client relationships shift and transform, it becomes more critical that providers know what they know, know what they don't know, and know what to do across these differing landscapes. This evolution of how researchers conceptualize uncertainty has encouraged us to investigate the lessons that different professions can provide about this core attitude in healthcare.

Our research seeks to understand the discourse of uncertainty among professions who work to improve the well-being of others, albeit from potentially different vantage points. Our view of health resonates with that of the World Health Organization and numerous national organizations (e.g. the Canada Association of Social Workers) who have defined health as 'the state of complete physical, mental, emotional, spiritual and social well-being, not merely the absence of disease or infirmity' (Canadian Association of Social Workers, 2006). In this paper, we investigate the differences in managing uncertainty across professions that address aspects of health and welfare – social work,[1] optometry and medicine – and we reflect upon what these differences say about professional socialization and identity formation. In our view, a profession's rhetoric of uncertainty reflects its professional identity and shapes the care provided.

Uncertainty

Attitudes toward uncertainty are central and potentially problematic in communication practices. Uncertainty exists when 'details of situations are ambiguous, complex, unpredictable, or probabilistic; when information is unavailable or inconsistent; and when people feel insecure in their own state of knowledge or the state of knowledge in general' (Brashers, 2001: 478). For example, healthcare providers and their patients often encounter complexity and ambiguity in decisions about both diagnoses and treatment options (Mishel, 1990). The attitude that practitioners develop toward uncertainty is important because it can shape how they approach critical tasks such as clinical decision making. Timmermans and Angell (2001) found in their study of medical residents that a dislike of clinical uncertainty led to a tendency to seek quick answers in the literature and a dogmatic clinical approach.

While Fox (1957, 1980, 2000) portrays medicine as becoming increasingly constrained by a clinical uncertainty that is born from the limitations of 'individual knowledge', the limitations of 'knowledge in the field', and the challenge of distinguishing the two limitations, others (e.g. Light, 1970; Atkinson, 1984; Katz, 1984; Geller et al., 1990) have uncovered medicine's tendency to train for certainty and in some cases over-certainty. The concept of training for certainty resonates with the views of others (e.g. Babrow and Kline, 2000; Brashers, 2001) who argue that an 'ideology of uncertainty reduction' pervades medicine (Brashers, 2001: 487). Brashers points out that uncertainty in healthcare typically yields a negative emotional response (e.g. anxiety, fear) yet its presence can also produce positive (e.g. hope, optimism) and neutral (e.g. indifference) emotional responses. The growing emphasis on the communication of health risk information and the vigilant surveillance of people's health with improved screening methods is intended to reduce uncertainty about the likelihood of disease and death yet it has produced a society divided into the 'chronically ill and worried well' (Brashers, 2001: 487). For Brashers and others (e.g. Berger, 1995) the emphasis on uncertainty is misplaced; rather than trying to reduce uncertainty, we should be learning how to manage the effects of uncertainty. Brashers summarizes four strategies for managing uncertainty: 1) seek or avoid information, 2) adapt to chronic uncertainty, 3) provide social support, and 4) manage the management of uncertainty. Unexamined in the literature is our contention that professional socialization and identity help to shape the attitude and approach taken toward uncertainty.

Journal of Social Work 7(2)

Professional Socialization and Identity Formation

Structurationists, such as Giddens (1984, 1993) and Bourdieu (Bourdieu and Wacquant, 1992) offer us a mechanism for gaining insights into core professional attitudes such as certainty and uncertainty. For these theorists, attitudes and behaviors are outcomes of a complex dynamic which occurs between individuals and their community. Structurationists help us to recognize that agents (e.g. social workers) and social structures (e.g. the social work profession) interact in a dialectical relationship that yields sets of social practices (e.g. supervision[2]). The duality of agents and social structures leads to social practices that both shape and constrain their users (Giddens, 1984). As novices move through their professional training programs, they learn to deploy profession-specific formats of these social practices. This process, laden with both explicit and tacit values, has a powerful socializing effect on students who must learn to successfully intervene in their profession's social world while surviving the process of being evaluated (Schryer et al., 2003).

A consideration of a profession's historical roots is germane to understanding its unique culture of professional socialization, its communication practices, and its identity formation. For example, one of the professions we have studied in Canada is optometry[3] – its roots are located in the field of opticianry. While all opticians initially restricted the scope of their work to making optical instruments (e.g. spectacles), some began to offer sight testing.[4] By the end of the 19th century, this division was reflected by two different names: dispensing opticians, for those who made and fit spectacles; and optometrists, for those who provided sight testing. Since optometry's break from the field of opticianry, its sights have been firmly set on the field of medicine. Initially a drugless profession, optometry has sought to expand its scope of practice into the arena of medicine (e.g. instilling diagnostic pharmaceutical agents, prescribing therapeutic pharmaceutical agents, performing laser surgery). Today's optometrist is described as 'an independent primary healthcare provider who specializes in the examination, diagnosis, treatment, management and prevention of disease and disorders of the visual system, the eye and associated structures as well as the diagnosis of ocular manifestations of systemic conditions' (Canadian Association of Optometrists, 2005). Optometrists entering practice in Canada today have typically completed at least three years of university sciences before entering a four-year optometry degree program that includes clinical apprenticeship placements. Despite significant training advances, each attempt by optometry to increase its scope of practice has been met with resistance from medicine – an opponent that predates it by almost 5000 years, outnumbers it by a ratio of 14:1 and outweighs it significantly in political capital. Understandable tensions emerge at the borders of these fields (for example, see Eger, 1968; Kelly, 1976; Begun and Lippincott, 1980; Croes, 1996; Stevens et al., 2000) and contribute to the transformation of social practices within and between these professions.

Spafford et al.: Towards Embracing Clinical Uncertainty

More recently, we have begun studying social work in Canada, a profession which began as a response to the social crises precipitated by the 'industrial revolution' in Western Europe and North America. During the 18th and 19th centuries, social problems such as poverty, overcrowding, poor housing, poor health (e.g. addiction, disease), prostitution and child neglect became concentrated in urban centers and attributed to the working classes (Social Work, 2005). Social work developed as a philanthropic activity working at the borders of more formal statutory initiatives that targeted education, working conditions, sanitation, prisons, and policing. With time, social work became an increasingly professional activity carried out by the state or by sectors working on its behalf. Today, social workers address determinants of health among individuals, families and communities, with some specializing in fields of practice such as child welfare, family services, corrections, gerontology or addictions (Social Work, 2005).

Social work practice is influenced by numerous factors, including: 1) the degree of government intervention in social welfare policies, legislation, and services, 2) the power-dependency relationship between social programs and government, 3) the collective conscience of its society, 4) the profession's credibility in the face of government-mandated cutbacks to social programs, and 5) the relationship between research and practice within the profession (Gibelman, 1999, Aronson and Sammon, 2000; Graham and Al-Krenawi, 2000; Edwards et al., 2006). Depending on the country, these tensions play out differently for the profession of social work (e.g. Aronson and Sammon, 2000; Graham and Al-Krenawi, 2000; Manthorpe et al., 2005; Edwards et al., 2006).

Professional socialization and identity formation is salient to every profession, and for social workers, who routinely collaborate with professionals outside their field, their socialization process has been strongly shaped by their contested role within the context of health as well as the overlap and conflict of their role with other professions (Clark, 1997). For example, stark contrasts have been noted by those who have examined the socialization of both physicians and social workers in healthcare settings (e.g. Mizrahi and Abramson, 1985; Qualls and Czirr, 1988). Social workers are trained to address social, personal and behavioral dimensions of health and relationships while traditional medicine, with its reductionist and scientific foci, has often discounted these elements and relegated familial and social issues toward the periphery of patient care (Mizrahi and Abramson, 1985; Clark, 1997). Even the mindset of assessment is widely disparate as social workers are trained to 'rule in' dimensions of a person's situation (e.g. psychosocial and economic factors) while physicians have traditionally been taught to 'rule out' information (e.g. social history)[5] that has been deemed extraneous (Qualls and Czirr, 1988).

The research on interdisciplinary healthcare teams reveals problematic attitudes that can interfere with client care and reveal disparate professional identities. The sources of interdisciplinary team conflict include 'differing professional and personal perspectives, role competition and turf issues,

159

differing interprofessional perceptions of roles, variations in professional social-ization processes, physician dominance of teams and decision-making, and the perception that physicians do not value collaboration with other groups' (Leipzig et al., 2002: 1142). The root of these team conflicts begins early as there is no clear focus on interdisciplinary teamwork in the training and education of health professionals, who complete much of their training housed in their separate professional schools. Leipzig et al.'s study (2002) of medical residents, social work and practice nursing students revealed two core beliefs among medical residents that differed from social work and practice nursing students: 1) the primary purpose of the interdisciplinary healthcare team was to assist physicians in achieving treatment goals for patients, and 2) physicians should be able to override team decisions. The assumption of professional autocracy and superiority by medicine over what it deems 'allied professions' is not new. For example, after reviewing both medical and social work education early in the 20th century, Flexner concluded that, unlike medicine, social work was not a profession because social workers were required 'to be mediators between various agencies, rather than professional agents themselves' and the scope of social work lacked 'definite and specific ends' (in Phillips, 2000: 215). The impact of Flexner's declarations almost a century ago cannot be understated as his views are still a source of interest and comment within both professions (e.g. Austin, 2001; Bonner, 2002; Dornan, 2005). While physicians have largely main-tained Flexner's view that social work's mediator role is inconsistent with substantive professional agency, social workers regard their mediation function – between players in a system, between elements in a system, and between systems themselves – as a clear demonstration of their professional agency.

Demographically, medicine, optometry, and social work in North America are predominantly White professions (around 63–65%) (US Department of Labor, 2001; Spafford et al., 2002). While social work has remained largely a women's profession (around 78%), there has been a relative feminization in the past 30 years of historically male professions such as optometry (54%) and medicine (43%) (US Department of Labor, 2001; Spafford et al., 2002). When considering professional border skirmishes, two demographic features are particularly telling: optometry is the far smaller profession in North America (28,000 optometrists versus 391,000 physicians and 493,000 social workers) and the social work profession is estimated to be growing at a rate of 30% through 2010 (US Department of Labor, 2001; Statistics Canada, 2003; National Associ-ation of Social Workers, 2005). Social work's extraordinary growth rate situates it at the nexus of two competing forces: escalating demands for social services and declining governmental funding for these services.

The professional identities of physicians, optometrists and social workers are each shaped and constrained by their historical underpinnings, scope of practice, interdisciplinary temperaments, contested professional spaces, and state support.

Case Presentations

The communication of patient or client information between professionals is a common yet complex practice. During the course of a provider–client relationship, information about the client must be collected, constructed, transported and presented to suit varying audiences. In professions such as medicine, optometry and dentistry, this communication tool is called the *case presentation*. In hospitals, medical students routinely must 'present a patient case' to an attending or senior physician. This medical case presentation may occur in the hospital corridor, near a nursing station or, less often, by a patient's bedside. Genre theorists have noted that symbolic tools, such as the case presentation, shape their users as the users shape the tool (Schryer, 1994). Interestingly, these discourses can shape and reproduce these communities in tacit or unexpected ways (Pare, 1993; Segal, 1993; Lingard and Haber, 1999). As we have previously noted (Lingard et al., 2003a), case presentation participants use this discourse not only to communicate patient facts but to induce changes in the listener's attitudes or actions regarding the production and protection of scientific objectivity (Arluke, 1977; Hunter, 1991), professional socialization (Anspach, 1988; Atkinson, 1988; Pomerantz et al., 1995; Lingard and Haber, 1999) and regulatory reinforcement within the professional community (Cicourel, 1986).

Lave and Wenger (1991) describe how apprenticeship discourses, like the novice case presentation, allow the student to participate legitimately, albeit peripherally, in the professional community as they are guided through the motions of diagnosis and persuasive argument without the associated responsibilities. The novice case presentation is a unique subset of case presentations because it serves both patient care and educational activities (Schryer et al., 2003; Lingard et al., 2003b). This duality is supported by theorists like Russell (1997) who agree that discourses such as the case presentation can serve various and sometimes competing activities.

The tool for orally communicating client information in social work differs from the medical case presentation model that has been described thus far. Early in the development of the social work field, charitable organizations which were the first to employ social workers encouraged more experienced social workers to 'supervise' the caseload of less experienced workers. The purpose of 'supervision' extends beyond that of communicating client information to include overlapping elements of education, administration and support (Hawkins and Shohet, 1989; Brashears, 1995). The focus of and support for social work supervision has varied over the field's history (Rabinowitz, 1987; Tsui, 1997), but despite these debates supervision still retains a strong presence in the training of social workers (Kadushin, 1992; Shulman, 1993; Bruce and Austin, 2000). During apprenticeship supervisions, social work students have the opportunity to reflect upon the content and process of both the student–client sessions and the supervision itself. Page and Wosket (1994) note that the social work 'trainee supervision' and 'practitioner supervision' differ in a number of important ways. For example, they found that students are more likely to focus on issues of technique while established practitioners are more likely to focus on analyzing relationship dynamics. In fact, a growing literature is grappling with the complexities of the social work supervision dynamic (e.g. Brashears, 1995; Tsui, 1997; Tsui and Ho, 1997; Csiernik, 2001; Bailey, 2004; Miller et al., 2005; Sherer and Peleg-Oren, 2005).

Case presentation and supervision provide opportunities to study the professional's ability to manage both uncertainty and certainty. By observing novices in case presentations and supervision, we gain opportunities to learn about the socializing power of this discursive tool. As we have previously noted, 'healthcare students must learn to manage uncertainty amid the tensions that emerge between clinical omniscience and the "truth for now" realities of the knowledge explosion in healthcare' (Spafford et al., 2006: 81). In our earlier studies of novice case presentations (Lingard et al., 2003a; Spafford et al., 2006), we found that both medical students and optometry students demonstrate a *novice rhetoric of uncertainty* that focuses on responding to their personal deficits in knowledge and skill. Their focus differs from the *professional rhetoric of uncertainty* displayed by clinical instructors who focus on managing uncertainty by means such as assessing the relevance and reliability of clinical data (Lingard et al., 2003a).

In our previous work (Lingard et al., 2003a; Spafford et al., 2006), we identified that a *novice rhetoric of uncertainty* contains four potential behaviors: '*seeking guidance*', '*deflecting criticism*', '*owning limits*', and '*proving competence*'. We have observed clinical novices '*seeking guidance*' from their supervisors regarding facts, analysis and permission, and '*deflecting criticism*' as a pre-emptive step to ward off anticipated criticism or as a self-defensive response to received criticism. In addition, we have noted instances of clinical novices '*owning limits*' of their knowledge or skill and '*proving competence*' through the display of knowledge during the case presentation. We have also noticed that not all four aspects of the *novice rhetoric of uncertainty* will be displayed in each professional group.

While we found optometry and medical students both displayed instances of '*seeking guidance*' and '*deflecting criticism*', only optometry students displayed instances of '*owning limits*' and only medical students displayed instances of '*proving competence*'. We found that the differences in novice rhetoric were shaped, in part, by a divergence in professional identity – in that medicine was prone to assuming an attitude of 'moral authority' while optometry was prone to deferring to a 'higher authority' (Spafford et al., 2006: 89). We also noted that the tendency of students to engage in instances of '*owning limits*' or '*proving competence*' was a function of the opportunity to rehearse their case presentation. Unlike optometry students, who were assigned to an out-patient optometry clinic where case presentations began moments after assessing the patient, medical students often had an opportunity to rehearse their case presentation when assigned to in-patient hospital wards. '*Owning limits*' was a more natural outcome of presenting 'on the fly' (optometry students), while *'proving competence'* was a more likely behavior of rehearsing or show-casing the case presentation before a resident (medical students). These instances of novice rhetoric reveal a duality of logic behind what healthcare students include in case presentations, as some material holds relevance for patient care while other material holds relevance for advertising novice membership as student apprentices (Lingard et al., 2003a).

Like other practitioner attitudes, uncertainty is reflected in and reproduced by the practitioner's practice. Much of the work on uncertainty to date has centered on medicine but we have wondered how other professionals, with their different professional identities and socializations and their different health perspectives, experience, portray and communicate uncertainty. Our interest in professional identity formation led us to study the novice case presentation in different professions that work to improve the well-being of others. The differences we noted in a *novice rhetoric of uncertainty* between optometry and medical students made us wonder how social work students regard uncertainty.

The following study examines the communicative features of certainty and uncertainty in novice social work supervision and considers how these features contribute to the development of professional identity in social work students. We also reflect on how these features compare with our earlier studies of case presentations delivered by medical and optometry students and consider the different contextual and cultural features that produce these unique discursive trajectories. Through our examination of uncertainty discourse in different fields, we believe that professions can learn lessons from each other about the management of uncertainty.

Methods

Participants

This study of social work student supervisions is part of a larger multi-disciplinary, multi-institutional research program that has been investigating the role of case presentations in the socialization of professionals. Our research program has involved 29 professional students and 25 apprenticeship instructors in social work, optometry and medicine. We recorded oral novice presentations and the teaching exchanges that accompanied them as well as interviews of both students and their instructors.[6] Descriptions of the methodologies employed in the medical and optometry case studies have been published (e.g. Schryer et al., 2003, 2005; Lingard et al., 2003a, 2003b; Spafford et al., 2004)

In the social work case study, participants were students registered in a Master of Social Work (MSW) degree program at a Canadian university and MSW-trained social workers, employed in either a hospital or a social service setting.[7] As part of the MSW degree, students complete two practicum placements in social agencies where they receive practice education and supervision.

A typical placement involves three or four days per week of on-site activity for four months.

Subsequent to receiving institutional ethical approval, participant recruitment was initiated, in the form of information meetings and individual information letters. Between the Spring of 2002 and the Spring of 2003, eight MSW students and eight social workers consented to participate in the study.

Field Observation Data Collection

Twelve oral supervisions and the teaching exchanges related to them were audio-recorded.[8] Six observations occurred in broad-based counseling centers with individual, group and community services. Three of the observations occurred at hospitals, two occurred in a correction-based facility and one occurred in a facility focused on children's services. Eight MSW students (six women, two men) and eight social workers (six women, two men) participated in the field observations. Repeat observations were purposefully distributed across the sample to track development of some students over time. There were no other people present during the supervision sessions. All observations were transcribed and rendered anonymous.

Interview Data Collection

All 16 participants from the field observations were interviewed. The 45-minute interview script reflected trends and issues arising from the observational data. Each participant was asked open-ended questions about the nature and purpose of supervision in the practicum placement. All interviews were transcribed and rendered anonymous.

Data Analysis

All observations and interviews were included in the data analysis. Qualitative analysis methods were employed that have been described elsewhere (Lingard et al., 2003a, 2003b; Schryer et al., 2003; Spafford et al., 2004, 2006). Consistent with a grounded theory method (Strauss and Corbin, 1998), the 184 pages of observation transcripts were individually read by four researchers for emergent trends in supervision strategies. During ongoing discussions, a coding structure was articulated from examining, applying, refining and confirming these trends across the data. Within each strategy, common instances were clustered into themes and sub-themes once a pattern of occurrence across the data set was observed. Instances that applied to more than one theme were noted under each relevant theme. This iterative analysis process occurred during approximately 60 hours of group discussions with the four researchers and a research assistant. Codes were tested, expanded, contracted or deleted after application to the 186 pages of interview transcript data. The research assistant applied the coding structures to the complete data sets using QSR NVivo qualitative data analysis software (Kelle et al., 1995). Difficulties or emerging patterns arising from this analysis were reported back to the research team for further analysis and revision.

Data analysis revealed five major themes: 1) Student Strategies, 2) Professional Strategies, 3) Teaching Strategies, 4) Identity Formation, and 5) Case Presentation and Record Keeping Strategies (Lingard et al. 2003a, 2003b; Schryer et al., 2003; Spafford et al., 2004, 2006). This paper reports on the instances in the transcripts that we coded as student strategies as they pertained to uncertainty.

Results and Discussion

Attitudes Toward Uncertainty

The social work students in our study embraced uncertainty as a normal and expected part of their work and they saw the management of uncertainty as a central role for supervision. These attitudes marked a significant departure from those expressed by medical students (Lingard et al., 2003a) and optometry students (Spafford et al., 2006) who viewed uncertainty with trepidation and something to be avoided in case presentations, if possible.

As the opening interview excerpt of this paper and the following interview excerpts indicate, social work students looked to their supervision sessions as opportunities to openly address with their supervisors their uncertainty:

> *S3*: Supervision is more for when I'm stuck. Like I think I did the okay thing but I want to double check.

> *S5*: [Supervision is for] kind of just deciding what you need to talk about. So if there's a particular situation that you don't know how to deal with.

Social work students described supervision as a rich source of 'feedback', 'a sounding board for brainstorming', and an opportunity 'to get you to think . . . in a different way'. This positive attitude toward owning uncertainty and learning to manage it radically departs from the attitudes displayed by medical and optometry students, who worried that admitting uncertainty in a case presentation reflects a personal deficit and triggers a negative evaluation (Lingard et al., 2003a; Spafford et al., 2006). The duality of patient care and student education seen in medical and optometry case presentations constrained both the novice and the expert discourse.

Social work students were encouraged to identify and address their areas of uncertainty. These interview excerpts with two of the social work supervisors reflect this attitude:

> *I4*: If I had a student saying, 'You know, I still don't know what to do with this client' . . . I wouldn't right away assume that, you know, the student had done something incorrect or had left something out. I'd want to look at the process.

> *I5*: The format that I usually use is asking them to bring forward any cases first that they're, um, perplexed by and would like more input on or something that they've had a personal reaction to.

The social work supervisors accepted that there would be uncertainty and consciously tried to create an environment in which students could safely explore and manage their uncertainty. In the novice social work supervision, an admission of uncertainty did not raise a flag of concern or signal a personal deficit. One supervisor (I4) spoke of the parallels between the student–supervisor relationship and the student–client relationship, indicating that in both relationships it was important to 'try to create an atmosphere of safety and build trust'.

Behaviors Toward Uncertainty

Social work students, unlike optometry and medical students, viewed uncertainty as a normal element of their apprenticeships and supervisions as important opportunities to learn how to manage this uncertainty. We wondered how the more positive attitude toward uncertainty of social work students would translate into their behaviors toward uncertainty. We found that the social work students in our study demonstrated a greater range of strategies toward managing uncertainty than their optometry and medical counterparts.

In our examination of novice behaviors toward uncertainty, we have identified four potential student strategies that comprise the *novice rhetoric of uncertainty*: '*seeking guidance*', '*deflecting criticism*', '*owning limits*', and '*showing competence*'. Only social work students displayed all four of these strategies. In all three professions we have studied (social work, medicine and optometry), students display *seeking guidance* and *deflecting criticism* strategies (Lingard et al., 2003a; Spafford et al., 2006). Independent of a novice's core attitude toward uncertainty, seeking guidance is an efficient learning strategy and deflecting criticism is a natural outcome of being a student. The three types of professional students can be differentiated by whether they display *owning limits* and/or *showing competence* and we believe these differences reflect their differing professional identities.

i. **Seeking guidance** A useful and efficient learning strategy is to *seek guidance* from accessible experts. In keeping with this strategy, social work students in our study routinely asked their supervisors for guidance regarding factual information or process. A typical factual inquiry occurred during one of S1's supervisions, 'Would [post partum blues] happen even though she's on the Paxil?' Another student wondered what the protocol was for establishing where the client could live:

> *S3*: What if she decides she doesn't want to go to a nursing home but wants [names organization] or she wants to go live with [names person]? Does she have a choice over that?

Spafford et al.: Towards Embracing Clinical Uncertainty

In these instances, the social work students addressed gaps in knowledge about facts or protocol. More often, social work students sought guidance regarding management options or challenges. One social work student wanted advice regarding her approach with a client who had displayed suicidal ideations:

> *S5*: I think that ... I'm handling it appropriately but part of it is – I hear other people at school, when they're doing case presentations and stuff, talk about clients who are suicidal ... who they ended up having hospitalized or whatever. And I don't think I need to do that here but I just want to sort of run this scenario by you and make sure that I'm doing what I need to be doing.

In high stakes assessments, where the wrong assessment could lead to significant client harm or death (e.g. in this case where the client has suicidal ideations), the social work students felt a need to solicit specific feedback from their supervisors regarding risk assessment and management as it related to the accuracy of the client assessment. Social work students also sought guidance when they struggled with a component of the student–client relationship:

> *S2*: You know what I mean? It's hard to get closure on that. Like ... the stuff that I'm telling him is sinking in but yet he still has all this [other] stuff. Like how do you close a case like that?

In this instance, S2 sought help from her supervisor when she neared the end of her practicum and needed to end her relationship with the client, yet it was obvious there were numerous unaddressed issues.

It is important to note that in these instances when social work students sought guidance from their supervisors, the supervisors did not typically offer a set answer but rather one or more ways to examine the issue. For example, one supervisor described the student–client relationship and the parallel supervisor–student relationship:

> *I2*: Social workers don't tell people what to do ... We want to more or less help somebody do their own thinking and develop their own skills and pursue their own goals and sort of get a sense of empowerment through that. So it's one thing for me to say that that's what a therapist does, but then I have to model that, you know, in the relationship with the students. So instead of saying well you really shouldn't have done this – you really should have done that, it's more of a Socratic questioning process.

Social work students concurred with this view of social work and supervision:

> *S2*: That's such a big social work thing – is not to tell you what to do but [to] get you to think about it a different way and that's the biggest thing a supervisor does.

The social work student strategy of *seeking guidance* was also displayed by medical students (Lingard et al., 2003a) and optometry students (Spafford et al., 2006). The difference lies in the attitude behind this strategy, with social

work students viewing the acknowledgement and examination of uncertainty
as a touchstone of competent social work, and optometry and medical students
exhibiting a distrust of acknowledging uncertainty in front of their instructors
who were expected to evaluate them negatively for displaying uncertainty
(Lingard et al., 2003a; Spafford et al., 2006). Despite these differing perspectives, each type of novice student sought guidance from their instructors.

ii. **Deflecting criticism** *Deflecting criticism* is a natural consequence of being a
student. This student strategy can exist in either a *pre-emptive* form in which
students make statements in an attempt to ward off anticipated or feared
critique or a *self-defensive* form in which students attempt to defend their
position against explicit criticism from their instructors. Social work students
demonstrated both forms of *deflecting criticism*. For example, in response to an
instructor (I4) saying, 'It just seems to me you get drawn into these debates with
this [client]. I don't know if that's where you want to be', the student displayed
a self-defensive form of deflecting criticism:

> *S4*: No I don't. It's just like – what are you supposed to do? Just sort of say, 'Well we
> can't. Let's not discuss that.' It's sort of a fine line between looking like ... you
> don't care about what he's saying and trying to sort of help him to look at it from
> a different angle. I just thought that [my approach] might be more helpful than
> sort of saying, 'Well, I'm not going to argue with you on this ... we're not really
> here to do that.'

Most often, social work students engaged in anticipatory strategies to ward
off potential criticism about not making progress with a client. For example, one
student said:

> *S7*: Yeah, I feel like there's just so much work that needs to be done, you know?
> (laughs) Um, I guess ... that part is overwhelming to me and it's hard to really get
> him focused on something to stick with for the session. Sometimes, it's been like
> two sessions [and] he'll be like – I'm still saying, 'Well let's work on boundaries',
> you know, kind of a thing. And he's like, well, he's got another story to tell.

By deflecting responsibility onto the client (who was hard to 'focus'), the
student attempted to ward off anticipated but undelivered criticism from his
instructor about the lack of progress in the sessions. These social work students
most often attributed responsibility to their clients for insufficient contact and
lowered adherence. The act of deflecting responsibility onto others is a strategy
we have also observed in optometry students who, rather than attributing
responsibility onto their patients, attribute responsibility for their knowledge
and skills onto other instructors in absentia (Spafford et al., 2006). In both cases,
the strategy attempts to refocus the criticism away from the student.

iii. **Owning limits** The social work students routinely displayed *owning limits*
during supervision. They owned limits about their knowledge and more
commonly about their strategies of assessment and management. An example

of owning knowledge limits was displayed during a discussion with a supervisor, who guided the student through some conceptual terminology:

> *S3*: So the first [issue] is translate negotiate. And I was thinking about that one and I have a hard time conceptualizing that one – it's just individual one on one . . .

More commonly, social work students owned their limits regarding how to proceed in the assessment and management of their clients. Sometimes, these declarations were a general 'I don't know how to proceed', as in these two examples:

> *S1*: So I don't know where I'm going to go with her. I'm going to see the follow up. She's also aware that, if she wanted to continue, I'd be available for that.

> *S7*: I guess I get overwhelmed by his [presentation] because he's a big talker and . . . he's quite open and honest and so that works well but he's very . . . all over the place with his thoughts and it's really hard to keep him focused on one area.

Social work students routinely advised their supervisors when they were unsure of how to proceed. By owning their limits, the discussions tended to proceed onto alternate or additional strategies they could try to implement in future sessions with their clients.

Social work students also routinely displayed *owning limits* couched within a revelation about their clients or themselves as seen in these two excerpts:

> *S2*: The parents are from Argentina – [client name] was born right after they got to Canada. So I never knew this. For some reason I've never got into – or the cultural discussion never happened. And we hypothesized that that's what turned her mother into an alcoholic – she never drank back then.

> *S8*: I said [to another social work student], 'I got my lumps the hard way too but I learned.' And I said, 'You have to detach otherwise you're going to burn out and you're going to get emotionally involved and then you start making crazy decisions like this intervention.'

Social work students were encouraged to reflect on the sessions with their clients and this experience enabled them to examine the boundaries of their skills and knowledge without shame and demonstrate what they had learned from the experience.

We have found that *owning limits* is a student strategy displayed by both social work students and optometry students (Spafford et al., 2006) but not medical students (Lingard et al., 2003a). We link the inter-professional divergence in this aspect of their *novice rhetoric of uncertainty* to professional identity and contextual features of the discourse.

Medical students are routinely reminded of medicine's superiority to other professions such as social work and optometry in terms of its longevity, scope of practice and prestige (Becker et al., 1961; Sinclair, 1997) and social work and optometry students quickly learn of their profession's sub-ordinate places with respect to medicine (Begun and Lippincott, 1980; Phillips, 2000; Stevens et al.,

2000). We believe *owning limits* is a more likely behavior in those who must learn to defer to a higher authority (Spafford et al., 2006). While social work occurs both inside and outside the bio-medically oriented health sector, those social workers who work within its borders routinely encounter medicine's presumption of superiority (e.g. Leipzig et al., 2002).

As noted earlier, opportunities to prepare for these types of communication practices through rehearsal occur for medical students (but not optometry or social work students) and these opportunities may make owning limits less contextually feasible for medical students.

iv. Showing competence The social work students displayed *showing competence* during supervision although this strategy was the least frequent strategy in their *novice rhetoric of uncertainty*. Social work students demonstrated to their supervisors what they had learned from resources including the literature and other social workers, as in the following two examples:

> *S2*: So I wanted to go over some of the cool things I learned from [another social worker]. I wanted to just quickly read some of these to you.

> *S4*: Like I think when you grow up in a certain experience – because everyone is both shaped by their experience and creates their own experience – so there is a dualism there. That's what the current developmental research suggests.

Some social work students displayed *showing competence* by providing a big picture perspective of their role in social work, as this student did:

> *S8*: Yeah . . . and I've learned. When I first started, I was like . . . 'I want a big role and go the extra mile' but then, it's like – you know what – 'I can't!' You can't and you can't personalize it otherwise you cry at every pitfall. You become too involved and then it becomes about you instead of the client. You just can't do that.

Showcasing competence by displaying a reflective and global view of their role as social workers is unique to these novices. The more reflective discourse of these social work students is consistent with their field and consistent with a developing professional identity that focuses on relationships and their boundaries. While we have found that medical students also displayed instances of showing competence, they did so through the display of more factual information rather than personal reflection (Lingard et al., 2003a). We view *showing competence* as a logical student strategy in two situations: when students are imbued with a sense of *moral authority* or a sense of *safety*. The former situation is apparent among medical students, who quickly learn to locate their superior place in the healthcare hierarchy (Spafford et al., 2006), while we see evidence of the latter situation with social work students, who viewed supervision as a safe place to try on ideas, to exchange ideas, and to solicit and receive constructive feedback. These excerpts from two of the social work students and one of the social workers display this orientation of safety:

S2: The social work thing is forming relationships and . . . you form a relationship with your supervisor this way . . . you get to trust that person. You get to know them a lot better . . . [then] I think . . . the more honest you can be with them about what you're learning – what your problems are.

S3: If you didn't get comfortable with your supervisor or you didn't have that kind of relationship, you could be missing out on part of that experience . . . You could miss out on lots of things because you may not feel comfortable discussing, uh, things that you need to be discussing.

I4: [Supervision is] a parallel to the therapeutic process. When you have your first meeting, one of the responsibilities for the therapist is trying to explain what their view is, what the process looks like, clarify roles, expectations, set goals . . . provide reassurance when it's needed. Try to – right from the start – try to create an atmosphere of safety and build trust.

For students to display *showing competence*, they must feel either safe to share and err as in the case of social work or entitled to display authority as in the case of medical students. We also suspect that the rehearsal opportunities for medical students facilitate their display of the *showing competence* discourse.

Implications

Health professions can learn lessons from each other about their respective attitudes toward and approaches to uncertainty. An 'ideology of uncertainty reduction' (Brashers, 2001) is evident in our interviews of both optometry and medical students. Their distrust of announcing their uncertainty during case presentations motivates them to side-step uncertainty, if possible. Students we have studied in medicine and optometry learn to address uncertainty across a discursive landscape that is shaped by the overlapping activities of patient care and student education and the competing perspectives of clinical omniscience versus 'truth for now' knowledge. By contrast, social work students in this study are socialized to embrace uncertainty as a natural element of professional work and development. As a result, they view the acknowledgement and examination of uncertainty as a touchstone of competence rather than a personal deficit meriting punishment. Interestingly, this observation held across the different social work settings we encountered – individual-based and community-based settings. It is interesting to note that social work has had to face uncertainty in terms of its disputed borders, its varied training approaches, and its future in the light of increasing demands amid decreasing fiscal support (Aronson and Sammon, 2000). An attitudinal shift toward accepting and trusting uncertainty in medicine and optometry might facilitate an enriched educational environment for novices and a more open dialogue with patients about issues of uncertainty.

While we note attitudes towards uncertainty in our study differentiate students in social work from those in optometry and medicine, we have observed that there is a *unique professional signature* to the *novice rhetoric of uncertainty* displayed by these three types of professional students. These findings help to deepen our understanding of the *novice rhetoric of uncertainty* (Lingard et al., 2003a; Spafford et al., 2006). Of the four types of student strategies we observed during case presentations and supervisions (*'seeking guidance'*, *'deflecting criticism'*, *'owning limits'*, and *'showing competence'*), optometry students did not display instances of *showing competence* and medical students did not display instances of *owning limits*. These differences in professional stance – already apparent in novices – demonstrate the power of professional identity formation.

Our findings help to build on earlier work (e.g. Schryer, 1994; Lingard and Haber, 1999; Lingard et al., 2003a; Spafford et al., 2006) that reveals how symbolic tools like the case presentation shape the agents (in this case, students) and they in turn shape the tool. We have also exposed, in part, the disconnect that can occur between attitudes and behaviors and the resulting tensions that emerge when the activities of practice and student education compete. The novice case presentation is further revealed as a site of intense socialization where many of the attitudes and behaviors toward uncertainty displayed by novices are not explicitly taught and yet powerful tacit messages routinely emerge (Lingard et al., 2003a; Spafford et al., 2006). Our Canadian-based interdisciplinary study of novice case presentations has involved 29 professional students and 25 apprenticeship instructors in social work, optometry and medicine. Further research in other contexts will refine and elaborate our findings towards a generalizable theory of uncertainty and professional identity.

Our work linking the *novice rhetoric of uncertainty* to professional identity has implications for interdisciplinary team work which highlights the challenges encountered by diverse team members (e.g. social workers in the healthcare field and physicians). The *unique professional signature* of the *novice rhetoric of uncertainty* may point toward a source of tension within interdisciplinary healthcare teams. In situations where team members adopt different positions regarding the acknowledgement and management of uncertainty, the motivation for and the direction of care may be at odds. In such circumstances, the accompanying rhetoric may only uncover the presence of tension rather than its source, leaving patient care paying the price of inter-professional acrimony. Our findings are particularly relevant in light of the burgeoning interest in interprofessional education – an educational innovation in the last decade in which two or more professions learn with and from one another to facilitate subsequent collaboration in practice (Clark, 1997; Graham and Barter, 1999; Carlisle et al., 2004; D'Eon, 2004; McNair, 2005; O'Neill and Wyness, 2005). This emerging idea transcends the historical silo approach to professional education in which each type of profession educates its students away from the influence and 'interference' of other professions. O'Neill and Wyness (2005) invoke

Spafford et al.: Towards Embracing Clinical Uncertainty

Clark's sense of professional socialization (1997) when they describe inter-professional education 'as a process of "dual socialization" . . . that involves the development of identity as a member of a profession as well as an inter-professional team' (p. 433). There are indications in the literature that a move toward interprofessional education might allow professional students to discover shared values, deepen their understanding of other professional roles, learn new strategies from other professional perspectives, and develop collaborative practice skills (e.g. O'Neill and Wyness, 2005). The rhetoric of students in medicine, optometry and social work that we observed offers insights into how professional identity shapes attitudes and behaviors toward uncertainty. Through this portal, professionals can better envisage professional practice that can move closer towards embracing uncertainty.

Acknowledgements
This research was funded by a grant from the Social Sciences and Humanities Research Council of Canada (#410-00-1147). The optometry data were collected by Tracy Mitchell-Ashley and Catherine Schryer. Lara Varpio applied the research group coding structures using QSR NVivo qualitative data analysis software.

Notes
1. We recognize that the scope of social work is such that there are social workers who do not identify themselves as healthcare providers, yet our view of health – as more than an absence of disease and infirmity – has yielded our perspective that social workers do address critical elements of health.
2. Supervision is an oral discourse of social work in which client information is discussed within the overlapping contexts of educational, administrative and therapeutic agendas (for example, see Hawkins and Shohet, 1989). In using the term supervision in this paper, we do not wish to invoke a medical model of clinical supervision but rather a 'work-based supervision' posture more in keeping with social work (Bailey, 2004).
3. The Greek roots of the word optometry are *optikos* (seeing) and *metron* (to measure). Optometry emerged as a profession that measured eyes and vision.
4. Sight testing involves measuring certain aspects of the eye in order to determine a spectacle lens prescription.
5. The patient-centered care movement in medicine is shifting the field's traditional tendency to ignore social issues.
6. Throughout the course of this multi-disciplinary study, we observed 16 medical case presentations, involving 10 medical students and 9 pediatricians, 31 optometry case presentations, involving 8 optometry students and 6 optometrists, and 12 social work supervisions, involving 8 social work students and 8 social workers. We also interviewed 11 medical students, 10 pediatricians, 4 optometry students, 4 optometrists, 8 social work students and 8 social workers (40 of the 54 participants were in both the observation and interview groups).
7. In Canada, social workers complete a minimum four-year baccalaureate degree (BSW) in social work at a university accredited by the Canadian Association of Schools of Social Work. Many also complete a master's degree (MSW), and some – destined more for academic or policy analysis-oriented careers – complete a doctoral

degree (PhD) in social work (Canadian Association of Social Workers, 2006).

8. The participants, rather than a research assistant, operated the audio-recorder during the social work supervisions (this differed from our observations of medical and optometry student case presentations). We discovered during initial observation attempts that the social work participants were inclined to make attempts to engage the research assistant during the supervision, thus shifting the focus of the observation. Before a recorded supervision, we instructed participants on the operation of the audio-recorder.

References

Anspach, R. (1988) 'Notes on the Sociology of Medical Discourse: The Language of Case Presentation', *Journal of Health and Social Behavior* 29(4): 357–75.

Arluke, A. (1977) 'Social Control Rituals in Medicine: The Case of Death Rounds', in R. Dingwall, C. Heath, M. Reid and M. Stacey (eds) *Health Care and Health Knowledge*, pp. 108–25. London: Croom Helm.

Aronson, J. and Sammon, S. (2000) 'Practice Amid Social Service Cuts and Restructuring', *Canadian Social Work Review* 17(2): 167–87.

Atkinson, P. (1984) 'Training for Certainty', *Social Science and Medicine* 19(9): 949–56.

Atkinson, P. (1988) 'Discourse, Descriptions and Diagnosis', in M. Lock and D. Gordon (eds) *Biomedicine Examined*, pp. 57–97. Dordrecht: Kluwer.

Austin, D. (2001) 'Special Issue: Flexner Revisited: Guest Editor's Foreword', *Research on Social Work Practice* 11(2): 147–51.

Babrow, A.S. and Kline, K.N. (2000) 'From "Reducing" to "Managing" Uncertainty: Reconceptualizing the Central Challenge in Breast Self-exams', *Social Science and Medicine* 51(12): 1805–16.

Bailey, D.I. (2004). 'The Contribution of Work-based Supervision to Interprofessional Learning on a Masters Programme in Community Mental Health', *Active Learning in Higher Education* 5(3): 263–78.

Becker, H., Greer, B., Hughes, E. and Strauss, A. (1961) *Boys in White: Student Culture in Medical School*. Chicago: University of Chicago Press.

Begun, J.W. and Lippincott, R.C. (1980) 'The Politics of Professional Control: The Case of Optometry', in J.A. Roth (ed.) *Professional Control of Health Services and Challenges to Such Control*. Greenwich, CT: JAI Press.

Berger, C.R. (1995) 'Inscrutable Goals, Uncertain Plans, and the Production of Communicative Action', in C.R. Berger and H.M. Burgoon (eds) *Communication and Social Influence Processes*, pp. 1–28. East Lansing: Michigan State University Press.

Bonner, T.N. (2002) *Iconoclast: Abraham Flexner and a Life in Learning*. Baltimore, MD: Johns Hopkins University Press.

Bourdieu, P. and Wacquant, L. (1992) *An Invitation to Reflexive Sociology*. Chicago, IL: University of Chicago Press.

Brashears, F. (1995) 'Supervision as Social Work Practice: A Reconceptualization', *Social Work* 40(5): 692–9.

Brashers, D.E. (2001) 'Communication and Uncertainty Management', *Journal of Communication* 51(3): 477–97.

Bruce, E.J. and Austin, M.J. (2000) 'Social Work Supervision: Assessing the Past and Mapping the Future', *The Clinical Supervisor* 19(2): 85–107.

Spafford et al.: Towards Embracing Clinical Uncertainty

Canadian Association of Optometrists (2005) 'What is an Optometrist?', URL (consulted May 2005): http://www.opto.ca

Canadian Association of Social Workers (2006) 'CASW Presents the Social Work Profession', URL (consulted January 2006): http://www.casw-acts.ca

Carlisle, C., Cooper, H. and Watkins, C. (2004) '"Do None of You Talk to Each Other?": The Challenges Facing the Implementation of Interprofessional Education', *Medical Teacher* 26(4): 545–52.

Cicourel, A.V. (1986) 'The Production of Objective Knowledge: Common Sense Reasoning in Medical Decision Making', in G. Bohme and N. Stehrif (eds) *The Knowledge Society: The Growing Impact of Scientific Knowledge on Social Relations*, pp. 87–122. Dordrecht: D Reidel.

Clark, P.G. (1997) 'Values in Health Care Professional Socialization: Implications for Geriatric Education in Interdisciplinary Teamwork', *The Gerontologist* 37(4): 441–51.

Croes, K. (1996) 'Despite a Likely Nasty Battle, ODs may End Up Doing PRK', *Primary Care Optometry News* 1(1): 5.

Csiernik, R. (2001) 'The Practice of Field Work: What Social Work Students Actually Do in the Field', *Canadian Social Work* 3–5(2): 9–20.

De Graves, S. and Aranda, S. (2005) 'When a Child Cannot be Cured: Reflections of Health Professionals', *European Journal of Cancer Care* 14(2): 132–40.

D'Eon, M. (2004) 'A Blueprint for Interprofessional Learning', *Medical Teacher* 26(7): 604–9.

Dornan, T. (2005) 'Osler, Flexner, Apprenticeship and the "New Medical Education"', *Journal of the Royal Society of Medicine* 98(3): 91–5.

Edwards, R.L., Shera, W., Reid, P.N. and York, R. (2006) 'Social Work Practice and Education in the US and Canada', *Social Work Education* 25(1): 28–38.

Eger, M. (1968) 'A New Threat to Optometric Law', *Journal of the American Optometric Association* 39(1): 27–8.

Fox, R. (1957) 'Training for Uncertainty', in R.K. Merton, G. Reader and P.L. Kendall (eds) *The Student Physician*, pp. 207–41. Cambridge, MA: Harvard University Press.

Fox, R. (1980) 'The Evolution of Medical Uncertainty', *Milbank Memorial Fund Quarterly* 58(1): 1–49.

Fox, R.C. (2000) 'Medical Uncertainty Revisited', in G.L. Albrecht, R. Fitzpatrick and S.C. Scrimshaw (eds) *The Handbook of Social Studies in Health and Medicine*, pp. 409–25. London: Sage.

Geller, G., Faden, R.R. and Levine, D.M. (1990) 'Tolerance for Ambiguity among Medical Students: Implications for their Selection, Training and Practice', *Social Science and Medicine* 31(5): 619–24.

Gibelman, M. (1999) 'The Search for Identity: Defining Social Work – Past, Present, Future', *Social Work* 44(4): 298–310.

Giddens, A. (1984) *The Constitution of Society: Outline of the Theory of Structuration*. Berkeley, CA: University of California Press.

Giddens, A. (1993) 'Problems of Action and Structure', in P. Cassel (ed.) *The Giddens Reader*, pp. 88–175. Stanford: Stanford University Press.

Graham, J.R. and Al-Krenawi, A. (2000) 'Contested Terrain: Two Competing Views of Social Work at the University of Toronto, 1914–1945', *Canadian Social Work Review* 17(2): 245–60.

Graham, J.R. and Barter, K. (1999) 'Collaboration: A Social Work Practice Method', *Families in Society: The Journal of Contemporary Human Services* 80(1): 6–13.

Journal of Social Work 7(2)

Hawkins, P. and Shohet, R. (1989) *Supervision in the Helping Professions. An Individual, Group and Organizational Approach*. Milton Keynes: Open University Press.

Healy, T.C. (2003) 'Ethical Decision Making: Pressure and Uncertainty as Complicating Factors', *Health and Social Work* 28(4): 293–301.

Hunter, K.M. (1991) *Doctors' Stories: The Narrative Structure of Medical Knowledge*. Princeton, NJ: Princeton University Press.

Kadushin, A. (1992) *Supervision in Social Work*, 3rd edn. New York: Columbia University Press.

Katz, J. (1984) *The Silent World of Doctor and Patient*. New York: Free Press.

Kelle, U., Prein, G. and Bird, K. (1995) *Computer-aided Qualitative Data Analysis: Theory, Methods, and Practice*. Thousand Oaks, CA: Sage.

Kelly, C. (1976) 'The Mouse that Roars – or Squeaks?', *The Optical Journal and Review of Optometry* 113(5): 33–5.

Lave, J. and Wenger, E. (1991) *Situated Learning: Legitimate Peripheral Participation*. Cambridge: Cambridge University Press.

Leipzig, R.M., Hyer, K., Wallenstein, S., Vezina, M.L., Fairchild, S., Cassel, C.K. and Howe, J.L. (2002) 'Attitudes Toward Working on Interdisciplinary Healthcare Teams: A Comparison by Discipline', *Journal of the American Geriatrics Society* 50(6): 1141–8.

Light, D. (1970) 'Uncertainty and Control in Professional Training', *Journal of Health and Social Behavior* 20(4): 310–22.

Lingard, L. and Haber, R.J. (1999) 'Teaching and Learning Communication in Medicine: A Rhetorical Approach', *Academic Medicine* 74(5): 507–10.

Lingard, L., Garwood, K., Schryer, C.F. and Spafford, M.M. (2003a) 'A Certain Art of Uncertainty: Case Presentation and the Development of Professional Identity', *Social Science and Medicine* 56(3): 603–16.

Lingard, L., Schryer, C., Garwood, K. and Spafford, M. (2003b) '"Talking the Talk": School and Workplace Genre Tension in Clerkship Case Presentations'. *Medical Education* 37(7): 612–20.

McNair, R.P. (2005) 'The Case for Educating Health Care Students in Professionalism as the Core Content of Interprofessional Education'. *Medical Education* 39(5): 456–64.

Manthorpe, J., Hussein, S. and Moriarty, J. (2005) 'The Evolution of Social Work Education in England: A Critical Review of its Connections and Commonalities with Nurse Education', *Nurse Education Today* 25(5): 369–76.

Miller, J., Corcoran, J., Kovaves, P.J., Rosenblum, A. and Wright, L. (2005) 'Special Edition: Field Education in Social Work Field Education: Student and Field Instructor Perceptions of the Learning Process', *Journal of Social Work Education* 41(1): 131–45.

Mishel, M.H. (1990) 'Reconceptualization of the Uncertainty in Illness Theory', *Image: Journal of Nursing Scholarship* 22(4): 256–62.

Mizrahi, T. and Abramson, J. (1985) 'Sources of Strain Between Physicians and Social Workers: Implications for Social Workers in Health Care Settings', *Social Work in Health Care* 10(3): 33–51.

National Association of Social Workers (2005) General Fact Sheets, URL (consulted March 2005): http://www.naswdc.org

O'Neill, B.J. and Wyness, A. (2005) 'Student Voices on an Interprofessional Course'. *Medical Teacher* 27(4): 433–8.

Spafford et al.: Towards Embracing Clinical Uncertainty

Page, S. and Wosket, V. (1994). *Supervising the Counselor: A Cyclical Model*. London: Routledge.

Paré, A. (1993) 'Discourse Regulations and the Production of Knowledge', in R. Spilka (ed.) *Writing in the Workplace: New Research Perspectives*, pp. 111–23. Carbondale, IL: Southern Illinois University Press.

Phillips, D.G. (2000) CSWJ Forum: 'Is Clinical Social Work a Profession? Preliminary Considerations', *Clinical Social Work Journal* 28(2): 213–25.

Pomerantz, A., Ende, J. and Erickson, F. (1995) *Precepting Conversations in a General Medical Clinic. The Talk of the Clinic: Explorations in the Analysis of Medical and Therapeutic Discourse*. Hillsdale, NJ: Lawrence Erlbaum Associates.

Qualls, S.H. and Czirr, R. (1988) 'Geriatric Health Teams: Classifying Models of Professional and Team Functioning', *The Gerontologist* 28(3), 372–6.

Rabinowitz, J. (1987) 'Why Ongoing Supervision in Social Casework: An Historical Analysis', *The Clinical Supervisor* 5(3): 79–90.

Russell, D.R. (1997) 'Rethinking Genre in School and Society: An Activity Theory Analysis', *Written Communication* 14(4): 504–54.

Schryer, C.F. (1994) 'The Lab Versus the Clinic: Competing Sites of Genre', in A. Freedman and P. Medway (eds) *Genre and the New Rhetoric*, pp. 105–24. London: Taylor and Francis.

Schryer, C.F., Lingard, L., Spafford, M. and Garwood, K. (2003) 'Structure and Agency in Medical Case Presentations', in C. Bazerman and D. Russell (eds) *Writing Selves/Writing Society: Perspectives on Writing*, pp. 62–96. Fort Collins, CO: The WAC Clearinghouse and Mind, Culture, and Activity.

Schryer, C.F., Lingard, L. and Spafford, M.M. (2005) 'Techne or Artful Science and the Genre of Case Presentations in Healthcare Settings', *Communication Monographs* 72(2): 234–60.

Segal, J.Z. (1993) 'Strategies of Influence in Medical Authorship', *Social Science and Medicine* 37(4): 521–30.

Sherer, M. and Peleg-Oren, N. (2005) 'Special Edition: Field Education in Social Work Differences of Teachers', Field Instructors', and Students' Views on Job Analysis of Social Work Students', *Journal of Social Work Education* 41(2): 315–28.

Shulman, I. (1993) *Interactional Supervision*. Washington, DC: NASW Press.

Sinclair, S. (1997) *Making Doctors: An Institutional Apprenticeship*. Oxford: Berg.

Social Work, The University of Edinburgh (2005) 'Social Work History', URL (consulted March 2005): http://www.socialwork.ed.ac.uk

Spafford, M.M., Lingard, L., Schryer, C.F. and Hrynchak, P.K. (2004) 'Tensions in the Field: Teaching Standards of Practice in Optometry Case Presentations', *Optometry and Vision Science* 81(10): 800–6.

Spafford, M.M., Schryer, C.F., Lingard, L. and Hrynchak, P.K. (2006) 'What Healthcare Students Do with What They Don't Know: The Socializing Power of "Uncertainty" in the Case Presentation', *Communication and Medicine* 3(1): 81–92.

Spafford, M.M., Sharma, N., Nygaard, V.L. and Kahlou, C. (2002). 'Diversity within the Profession: Part 1: Trends and Challenges', *Optometric Education*, 27(4): 114–21.

Statistics Canada (2003) Occupation – *2001 National Occupational Classification for Statistics (720), Class of Worker (6) and Sex (3) for Labour Force 15 Years and Over, for Canada, Provinces, Territories, Census Metropolitan Areas and Census Agglomerations, 2001 Census*, URL (consulted March 2005): http://www.statcan.ca (links: Census; Topic-based tabulations; 11 February 2003 release date).

Journal of Social Work 7(2)

Stevens, F., van der Horst, F., Nijhuis, F. and Bours, S. (2000) 'The Division of Labour in Vision Care: Professional Competence in a System of Professions', *Sociology of Health and Illness* 22(4): 431–52.

Strauss, A.L., and Corbin, J. (1998) *Basics of Qualitative Research: Techniques and Procedures for Developing Grounded Theory*, 2nd edn. Thousand Oaks, CA: Sage.

Timmermans, S. and Angell, A. (2001) 'Evidence-based Medicine, Clinical Uncertainty, and Learning to Doctor', *Journal of Health and Social Behavior* 42(4): 342–59.

Tsui, M. and Ho, W. (1997). 'In Search of a Comprehensive Model of Social Work Supervision', *The Clinical Supervisor* 16(2): 181–205.

Tsui, M.S. (1997) 'The Roots of Social Work Supervision: An Historical Review', *The Clinical Supervisor* 15: 191–8.

US Department of Labor: Bureau of Labor Statistics (2001) *2001 National Occupational Employment and Wage Estimates*, URL (consulted March 2005): http://www.bls.gov (links: Occupations; Employment; About 2001 National, State and Metropolitan Area Occupational Employment and Wage Estimates; 2001 National, State and Metropolitan Area Occupational Employment and Wage Estimates; Healthcare Practitioners and Technical Occupations).

MARLEE M. SPAFFORD is an optometrist, an associate professor in the School of Optometry at the University of Waterloo, and a Fellow of the American Academy of Optometry. Her research program investigates aspects of healthcare professional education, communication, socialization and equity. Address: School of Optometry, University of Waterloo, Waterloo, Ontario, Canada N2L 3G1. [email: mspaffor@uwaterloo.ca]

CATHERINE F. SCHRYER is a rhetorician and an associate professor in the Department of English Language and Literature at the University of Waterloo. Her research interests involve investigating genres or text types in specific social contexts, combining textual analysis with qualitative data gathering techniques.

SANDRA L. CAMPBELL is a social worker and an assistant professor in Renison College's School of Social Work at the University of Waterloo. Her research interests involve organizational power, decision making as it relates to elders, and the development of social work educational strategies.

LORELEI LINGARD is a rhetorician, an associate professor in the Departments of Paediatrics and Health Policy, Management, and Evaluation, and an educational scientist in the University of Toronto's Wilson Centre for Research in Education. Her research program explores team communication patterns as they impact on novice socialization and patient safety.

Name Index